PETER KARSTEN is Professor of
History and Sociology at the University
of Pittsburgh.

Between Law and Custom

When British authorities established "settler" colonies in North America and the Antipodes (New Zealand, Australia, South Africa, Fiji) from the early seventeenth to the late nineteenth centuries, they introduced Law through parliamentary statutes and Colonial Office oversight, and they dispatched governors and judges to the colonies. These jurists set aside some aspects of English Common Law to meet the special conditions of the settler societies, but the "Responsible Governments" that were eventually created in the colonies and (when that lawful engine failed to suffice) the British immigrants themselves set aside even more of the English law, exercising "informal law" – popular norms – in its place. The settler-champions of their newfound property rights fought the Crown's efforts to stem their attacks upon the customary rights of the native inhabitants. (Ironically, this was the very same fight many of them and their ancestors had fought in the seventeenth and eighteenth centuries in the British Isles against the extinguishing of their ancient customary rights there.)

Law and popular norms clashed over a range of issues, including ready access to land, the property rights of aboriginal people, the taking of property for public purposes, master-servant relationships, and crown/corporate liability for negligent maintenance and operation of roads, bridges, and railways. Drawing on extensive archival and library sources in England, the United States, Canada, Australia, and New Zealand, Karsten explores these collisions and arrives at a number of conclusions that will surprise.

Peter Karsten is Professor of History and Sociology at the University of Pittsburgh.

Between Law and Custom

*"High" and "Low" Legal Cultures in
the Lands of the British Diaspora –
The United States, Canada, Australia,
and New Zealand, 1600–1900*

Peter Karsten

University of Pittsburgh

CAMBRIDGE
UNIVERSITY PRESS

PUBLISHED BY THE PRESS SYNDICATE OF THE UNIVERSITY OF CAMBRIDGE
The Pitt Building, Trumpington Street, Cambridge, United Kingdom

CAMBRIDGE UNIVERSITY PRESS
The Edinburgh Building, Cambridge CB2 2RU, UK
40 West 20th Street, New York, NY 10011-4211, USA
477 Williamstown Road, Port Melbourne, VIC 3207, Australia
Ruiz de Alarcón 13, 28014 Madrid, Spain
Dock House, The Waterfront, Cape Town 8001, South Africa

http://www.cambridge.org

First published 2002

Printed in the United Kingdom at the University Press, Cambridge

Typeface ITC New Baskerville 10/12 pt.   *System* LaTeX 2$_\varepsilon$ [TB]

A catalog record for this book is available from the British Library.

Library of Congress Cataloging in Publication Data
Karsten, Peter.
Between law and custom : "high and low legal cultures" in the lands of the
British diaspora – the United States, Canada, Australia,
and New Zealand, 1600–1900 / Peter Karsten.
p.   cm.
Includes bibliographical references and index.
ISBN 0-521-79283-5 (hbk.)
1. Common law – History.   2. Common law – Reception – History.
3. Customary law – History.   I. Title.
K588 K37   2001
340.5'7 – dc21   2001025809

ISBN 0 521 79283 5 hardback

An earlier version of the Animal Trespasses section of Chapter 4
appeared in *Law & Society Review* 32 (1998): 63–92.

For

Professor Bruce Kercher of Macquarie Law School,
"a one-man version of the Selden Society,"* with gratitude for
his pioneering efforts in revealing to us all, free of charge,
The Law as determined by British Diaspora jurists in cases
decided by the New South Wales Supreme Court in its first
several decades of existence (www.law.mq.edu.au/scnsw)

And for

The administrators and staff of the Alexander Turnbull
Library, Wellington, New Zealand, deft and helpful collectors
and keepers of the records of past popular norms and the
images that sometimes illustrate them

* Professor Ian Hollaway's apt phrase.

We have continued, as you, to cite the decisions of Mansfield and Eldon and their successors. The divergences have been so slight, compared with the whole body, that like the mountains of the moon, they are lost to the distant eye.
– David Dudley Field, "Address to Dalhousie University Law School Convocation, Halifax, Nova Scotia, 1885," 19 *American Law Review* (1885), 617

You could scarce believe what legal intricacies are familiar here, in this early stage of settlement. Though it is a new country, settlers retain all their old manners, habits, prejudices, and notions of a sturdy, free, commercial, litigious people.
– Barrister–Settler George Moore, JP, to his brother, Jan. 1, 1833, from Western Australia

Our colonists are becoming fonder of law every day.
– George Moore, diary entry, March 15, 1832

Civil law is an admirable institution any where except on a frontier situated in the center of an Indian Country...
– J. F. Hamtramck, Commanding Officer, Ft. Knox, to Secretary of War Henry Knox, March 21, 1792, noted in Francis Prucha, *American Indian Policy*, 69

The power of the law is unavoidably feeble when compared with the predominant inclinations of any large body of the people. In [South Australia] unpopular regulations, unless supported by a force... overwhelming, must become little more than a dead letter.
– Colonial Office Undersecretary James Stephen, in a draft reply to the South Australia Commissioners, Oct. 27, 1836

... [T]he uncontrollable force of the natural laws of society to which even Governments must bend have prevented the efficient protection of the [Six Nations'] Indian Reserves....
– Investigative committee report of the legislature of Upper Canada, 1847

True equality before the law in a society of greatly unequal men is impossible: a truth which is kept decently buried beneath a monument of legislation, judicial ingenuity and cant.
– Douglas Hay in "Poaching and the Game Laws on Cannock Chase," in *Albion's Fatal Tree*, Hay et al. eds. (1977), 189

Jacko [a hired hand in Queensland] probably knew nothing of law or justice in the abstract, but he greatly valued law when exercised against those he hated.
– Anthony Trollope, *Harry Heathcote of Gangoil* (1873)

What is common in community is not shared values or common understanding so much as the fact that members of a community are engaged in the same argument..., in which alternative strategies, misunderstandings, conflicting goals and values are threshed out.
– David Sabean, *Power in the Blood* (1984), 29

Men stuck to their bargains and negotiated their disputes.... A man would have been excluded if he had shown himself to be unneighborly.... The Common law on these matters was clear and well enforced: A man was obliged to put his neighbor's need ahead of his own and everyone did.... No one ever declined.... The social penalty would have been too severe.
– John Kenneth Galbraith, describing life in his family's Ontario community in the nineteenth and early twentieth century, in *The Scotch*

Laws are sand; customs are rock.
– Mark Twain

Contents

x   Contents

Contents

List of Illustrations

List of Tables

Introduction

Colonists have always carried their own Laws with them, observing these formal rules in the new settings to which they have migrated. How could they fail to do so? Laws pervade one's culture, and, as the Roman poet Horace observed, "they change their skies but not their minds, who sail across the seas." But many colonists, in time, come to reject certain of these Laws as being out of sync with their perceived needs. "The true problem" worthy of analysis, anthropologist Bronislav Malinowski maintained, is "not to study how human life submits to rules – it simply does not; the real problem is how the rules become adapted to life"[1] – that is, how do people alter rules that others would have them live by when those rules no longer appear to be compatible with new conditions or surroundings? Horace's words apply well to much of the behavior of the British Diaspora of the seventeenth, eighteenth, and nineteenth centuries – to those who left the British Isles to settle North America and the Antipodes. But so do those of Malinowski. The tension between these two descriptions of how people regulated their affairs and property is the central subject matter of this book.

In the course of my writing this, American law enforcement officers completed a successful siege of a group of white supremacists holed up in a farmhouse in Jordan, Montana. Calling themselves "the Freemen," these Bible-quoting foes of all forms of existing government had armed themselves, threatened neighbors, claimed federal range land, bilked banks, refused to pay taxes, filed false liens against the homes of local judges, and created their own government complete with what they call "Common Law Courts." The Freemen resemble their fellow travelers (the Aryan Nations, the Posse Comitatus, The Order, the Covenant, the Sword and Arm of the Lord, and the various "Militias"), in that they claim the right to supplant such existing legal authority as they do not accept with a self-crafted "common law" of their own. Active throughout much of the Midwest, Great Plains, Rocky Mountains, and

---

[1] Bronislav Malinowski, *Crime and Custom in Savage Society* (1926), 127.

1

the Northwest, these anarchic organizations appear to many as a new and frightening blight on the rural landscape.

They are frightening enough, and their firepower, communications capabilities, and capacity for fraud, terrorism, and mayhem is new in scale and scope. But in another sense they are at least a little familiar. After all, we are all a *bit* defiant now and then when it comes to certain rules of law. We jaywalk, double-park, xerox sheet music, and download songs from Napster without paying royalties; we walk dogs in places where they aren't allowed, and some of us in the States interpret I.R.S. rules rather liberally come April. Most of these traits hardly constitute major threats to public order or fiscal well-being (something that the "Militias" collectively may be said to pose); moreover, while these more modest defiant traits are not "lawful," they represent for many "the norm," and in that sense they may be said to be popular or "common law" rules, created in a less overt but ultimately more effective fashion than any of the Freemen's "Common-Law Courts."

In any event, groups like these, resisting authority or defying legal rules, may be detected in one form or another in the history of every major British colonial settlement. Resistance to authority and defiance of legal rules are recurrent themes in the history of the Diaspora who left Britain for North America or the Antipodes in the seventeenth, eighteenth, and nineteenth centuries, be that resistance organized, as was that of the Sons of Liberty, the various claim associations of the frontier communities, or the group of lawyers in Upper Canada who destroyed the printing press of a Liberal editor in the 1830s; be it essentially unorganized but communally accepted, as was that of the typical squatter or moonshiner; or be it merely tolerated, as was the Megantic Outlaw among Scots in Lower Canada, Ned Kelly among many ordinary folk in Victoria, Te Kooti among many Maori, and George Magoon among Downeasterners in late nineteenth century Maine.

Free-born Britons and their North American and Australasian Diaspora were generally quite law-abiding folk, proud of their homelands, and thus choosing to name their New World hamlets after their Old World ones. Their Old World laws went with them, but they took their customs and the "rights as Englishmen" too. Long before the appearance of the Freemen, disaffected Britons, Americans, Canadians, Aussies, and Kiwis created their own "common law" when they found themselves at loggerheads with British statutes and Common-Law rules of property or contract that seemed inconsistent with their conditions or climate. The Colonial Office, Parliament, and the Law Lords of Privy Council in London sought to regulate, indeed at times to control, the ways that British Diaspora immigrants to North America and the Antipodes acquired land, interacted with indigenous people, and administered their affairs. For example, Parliament legislated on the treatment of slaves in the British colonies from 1815 to 1833 and then abolished slavery altogether.

In the first stage of settlement, the British Crown's governors, judges, magistrates, and legislative councils issued proclamations, created ordinances, and rendered judicial decisions in each colony, and this Law was but rarely out of step with that of the Mother Country. For example, in 1828 the government of the Crown Colony of the Cape of Good Hope created Ordinance 50, declaring all free people to be equal before the Law irrespective of race, as, indeed, they were in England (but had not been until that date in that formerly Dutch colony). At this stage of development we might say that "the Center" or "the Core" set the legal standards for its "Periphery." But, even at this first stage, the ways that ordinary folk actually *behaved* could be quite different from, sometimes at odds with, the formal Law.

A second stage of legal development occurred when the colonial Diaspora leaders effectively persuaded Parliament to grant them the constitutional power to make Law for themselves, to be administered by officials responsible to their elected assemblies (hence styled the era of "Responsible Government"). First accomplished by rebellion and force in "the thirteen colonies" that became the United States, this process of wresting the Law-making authority from Crown and Parliament came quite nonviolently in the other Diaspora lands, largely in the second and third quarters of the nineteenth century. Thereafter, while the newly empowered Diaspora legislatures engaged in a good deal of copy-cat adoption of statutes created by the Parliament at Westminster, they also struck out on their own; the "Periphery" increasingly found its own legislative voice.

The Law[2] as expounded in courts is the forum where ordinary people generally face off against one another (and sometimes against the State) if they are going to do so. I wanted to know how well or poorly certain statutes, Colonial Office instructions, and English Common-Law rules were applied in the lands of the British Diaspora[3] by both British- and native-born governors and jurists. What were the norms and rules

---

[2] In order to accent or draw attention to the contrasts or differences between "formal" and "informal" law – that is, statutes and common-law rules, on the one hand, and popular norms, on the other – I will always capitalize the former (the Law/ Common Law).

[3] I recognize, of course, that the seventeenth, eighteenth, and nineteenth century newcomers to North America and the Antipodes included other Europeans and Africans, but, for most of these years immigrants from the British Isles predominated and English Law prevailed (except in the mixed-origins legal world of Lower Canada/Quebec, Louisiana, and South Africa). Hence, as a convenient "short-hand," I will refer to the Canadian, United

that ordinary people employed to resolve property and contract disputes, and what happened when these two legal cultures collided?

When popularly generated norms prevail for long enough periods of time, they often come to be viewed by jurists as constituting "customary law" and thereby are granted the status of "Law." I do *not* limit my inquiry to such rules as came to be accepted as customary law by jurists. In the first place, the rules that people of British origin lived by from day-to-day were of notoriously recent vintage, quite unlike "customs" that had prevailed for centuries. In the second place, while the judicial branch of the early-modern English State did come to embrace some popular customs as "customary law," it also rejected others. The views of the first few generations of legal anthropologists and historians, that "the law" simply grew out of and absorbed "customs" as "civilization advanced,"[4] has proven to be quite inadequate. The tension between developing States and popular customs and norms in the sixteenth, seventeenth, and eighteenth centuries was often violent and irreconcilable. And, in the third place, whether these informal norms were accepted or not as Law by jurists, their *practice* at any moment by ordinary folk in one or another of these Diaspora settlements has been sufficient cause for me to report them. When farmers, dairymen, grazers, sea captains, and manufacturers came to understandings with ploughmen, shepherds, domestics, sailors, and artisans that ignored some aspects of the Common Law governing labor contracts; when buyers and sellers adjusted terms oblivious to the Law of Sales; when neighbors resolved fencing disputes and animal trespasses without recourse to ordinances or courts, they thereby supplanted the formal rules of the statutory and Common Law and, in a sense, created their own "common law."

There is another facet to this story of tension between the formal Law brought with the British Diaspora jurists and governors and the customary law of ordinary people: The British Diaspora settlers were not the only people inhabiting North America and the Antipodes whose popular norms were, at times, in conflict with the English Common Law of the courts created there. The Aboriginal people of those lands possessed customs of their own, created over the centuries, regarding right to land, water, fish, and game. They had norms regarding the exchange of goods and services which also differed in some regard from the rules employed by the Diaspora settlers and their courts. This book,

States, Australian, and New Zealand colonies/states/dominions throughout as "the lands of the British Diaspora."

[4] James C. Carter, *Law: Its Origins, Growth and Function* (1907); Henry Maine, *Ancient Law* (1861); Paul Bohannan, *Justice and Judgement Among the Tiv* (1957). For a critique of this perspective see Stanley Diamond, "The Rule of Law versus the Order of Custom," 38 *Social Research* 42 (1971). And see Simon Roberts, *Order and Dispute* (N.Y., 1979), Chapter 11.

then, tells the story of conflict between the Law, the popular norms of Diaspora settlers, and the customary law of the Aboriginal peoples of North America and the Antipodes, a comparative tale of past human behavior, of power, and culture.

WHAT I ASK ABOUT FORMAL LAW

Let me begin by offering two cases to illustrate some of the questions I am asking about the formal Law. One day in 1873 a man by the name of Ray, in navigating a sidewalk in Petrolia in Upper Canada (Ontario), tripped first on a trap-door hinge and then on a warped sidewalk plank. Injured, he sued the township, but was "nonsuited" by the trial court judge – that is, the judge held that, as a matter of Law, the township was not liable to Mr. Ray. Ray's appeal to the Upper Canada Court of Common Pleas from this decision was rejected. In his opinion, Chief Justice Hagarty clearly signaled that lower courts were expected to be unfriendly to suits aimed at establishing the liability of municipal corporations for accidents like this one, accidents their modest municipal resources were incapable of preventing:[5]

> The warping of a plank, the starting of a nail, the upheaval of the ground from the action of frost, constantly form inequalities [in the levels of sidewalks].... Unless we declare it to be the duty of a village corporation – when they try to improve the streets, in a place not many years taken from the forest, by laying down wooden sidewalks – to insure every passer-by against every un-evenness or inequality in the levels, we can hardly hold these defendants liable.

One who focused solely on Chief Justice Hagarty's language and rea-soning might conclude that he and his colleagues applied Common-Law rules "instrumentally" – that is, with a socioeconomic purpose, in this case one friendly to municipal corporations. But were one to shift one's attention to a decision handed down only two years after *Ray*, by the counterpart and equal of Hagarty's Court of Common Pleas, Upper Canada's Court of Queen's Bench, one might conclude that Queen's Bench jurists had been cut from different cloth entirely. A man named Castor had been injured in the town of Uxbridge in April 1875 when a sulky he had hired hit a telegraph pole that had been left in the road. He had also been nonsuited by the trial judge. He

---

[5] *Ray v. Corp. of Petrolia*, 24 UCCP 73 at 77 (1874). Compare with Hagarty, C. J., in *Boyle & wife v. Corp. of Town of Dundas*, 25 UCCP 420 at 429 (1875): Issues in this case are of "most vital interest to Canadian municipalities.... We can-not but see that attempts are often made to fasten on them a most onerous burden of responsibility, sometimes wholly disproportioned to their means and resources."

appealed to Queen's Bench where Chief Justice Harrison reviewed English, Canadian, and especially United States authorities to hold that townships put on notice of obstructions left in the road could be deemed liable to those who struck and were injured by them. Harrison observed that "we cannot do better than follow the reasoning of the American Judges" on this issue, and, more particularly, he said that this course was the appropriate one to follow in order to induce townships to exercise care in the maintenance and supervision of the highways, sidewalks, and bridges under their care:[6]

> Any other course would, I fear, be destructive of the efficiency
> of our roads and would be opposed to what I take to be the real
> intention of the Legislature, which is, to have the roads reasonably
> fit for travel.

Here Chief Justice Harrison's quite deliberate interpretation of the relevant statute had the "instrumental" effect of *increasing* the liability of Ontario's municipal corporations. What is one to make of this apparent contrast in styles of these two superior courts, exercising, as they did, identical powers and jurisdictions? Did appellate court jurists use such "instrumental" rationales often? When they did, were they more likely to produce procorporate or proplaintiff results? How often did they borrow rationales from what they called "American" courts, the several state (and one federal) supreme courts in the United States? As courts of a British colonial province, were they not strictly bound by English precedent?

I have asked these questions of the courts of Upper Canada as well as those of the courts of six other Canadian provinces, the Supreme Court of the Dominion of Canada, the regional New Zealand supreme courts and its Court of Appeals, and the supreme courts of New South Wales, Victoria, Queensland, South Australia, Tasmania, and Western Australia.[7] Several of these high courts addressed the same issues with

---

[6] *Castor v. Corp. of Town of Uxbridge,* 39 UCQB 113 at 124 (1876). Mr. Castor lost his appeal, however, on the other issue, his driver's contributory negligence.

[7] I have also given some attention to both the Law and popular norms in Ireland, Wales, South Africa, and Fiji, and I have included Lower Canada (Quebec), which was, by the end of the nineteenth century an explicitly Civil (French)-Law jurisdiction. But I have not chosen to include the decisions of British colonial courts in nineteenth century India in this particular comparative analysis because they draw much more heavily upon systems of law (both Muslim and Hindu) other than that of England than did the courts of Lower Canada/Quebec, and because that conquered British dominion was not populated by a significant percentage of British emigrants who expected (except from the handful of urban East India Company courts) "the Common-Law rights of Englishmen," as many did for some time in Lower

regard to injuries incurred on publicly maintained walks, roads, and bridges as had those of Upper Canada, and some of these also appeared to reason "instrumentally" in fixing the limits of corporate

Canada/Quebec. I also devote less attention (outside of Chapter 1) to Fiji and South Africa. The former never endured more than about 2,000 British Diaspora (largely planters) among its 140,000 native population (albeit it was a British governor who began the process of introducing tens of thousands of Indian laborers to Fiji in the late nineteenth century). Moreover, Fiji did not experience *wholesale* the imposition of British Law.

British settlement in South Africa, while more substantial than in India, still numbered, as late as 1895, less than 200,000 out of a European population of 520,000 (largely Dutch/Boers), in a colony that included nearly another 3,500,000 native Africans. Indeed, by 1904 British Diaspora appear to have outnumbered the Boers in only one of the colony's four provinces (Natal), where no more than 97,00 Boers and Britons shared the land with hundreds of thousands of Bantus, Zulus, and Basutos. Moreover, South African Law contains substantial elements of European Civil Law because of its Dutch antecedence. (A. F. Hattersley, *The British Settlement of Natal* (1951), 99; W. Basil Warsfold, *South Africa* (1895), 1–2, 21, 27, 241; John Eddy and Deryck Schrender, eds., *The Rise of Colonial Nationalism: Australia, New Zealand, Canada and South Africa. 1880–1914* (Sydney, 1988), 211; Ellison Kahn, "The Role of Doctrine and Judicial Decisions in South African Law," in *The Role of Judicial Decisions and Doctrine in Civil Law and Mixed Jurisdictions*, ed. Joseph Dainow (Baton Rouge, 1974), 224, 233.

My look at India, Nigeria, Malayia, Jamaica and other such British "plantation, trade and tribute" possessions tomorrow. My tale of "settlement" Diaspora lands, today.

On Quebec, see Vince Masciotra, "Quebec Legal Historiography, 1760–1900," 32 *McGill Law Journal* 712 (1987); Evelyn Kolish, "The Impact of the Change in Legal Metropolis on the Development of Lower Canada's Legal System," 3 *Canadian Journal of Law and Society* 1 (1988); Murray Greenwood, "Lower Canada (Quebec): Transformation of Civil Law, from Higher Morality to Autonomous Will, 1774–1866," 23 *Manitoba Law Journal* 192 (1996); David Howes, "From Polyjurality to Monojurality: The Transformation of Quebec Law, 1875–1929," 32 McGill *Law Journal* 523 (1987); and Howes, "Dialogical Jurisprudence," in *Canadian Perspectives on Law and Society*, ed. W. W. Pue and B. Wright (Ottawa, 1988); on India, see Eric Stokes, *The Peasant and the Raj: Studies in Agrarian Society and Peasant Rebellion in Colonial India* (Cambridge, 1978); Ranajit Guta, *A Rule of Property for Bengal* (Paris, 1963); M. P. Jain, "Custom as a Source of Law in India," 3 *Jaipur Law Journal* 96 (1963); and Bernard Cohn, "Law and the Colonial State in India," in *History and Power in the Study of Law*, ed. June Starr and Jane Collier (Ithaca, 1989), 131ff. (on confusing ancient Indian customary law with contemporary rules). See also Sir Kenneth Roberts-Wray, *Commonwealth and Colonial Law* (London, 1960), and T. O. Elias, *British Colonial Law: A Comparative Study of the Interaction between English and Local Laws in British Dependencies* (London, 1962).

liability.[8] All of them wrestled with the question of how much use they might make of American decisions. But others simply cited what they believed to be the appropriate English precedent and noted that they were bound to follow such precedent.

Canadian, Australian, and New Zealand jurists (hereafter referred to as CANZ jurists) did not formally have available to them an option chosen by some high courts of the United States – that of creating a "principled exception" to the English rule. All of the North American and Antipode colonies had "received" all of the Mother Country's Common Law, as well as all such parliamentary statutes as had been created prior to the date of the creation of their own Responsible Governments.[9] But, unlike their American counterparts, these jurists of British colonies, provinces, and dominions were not empowered to make new Common Law for themselves. Their decisions were subject to review by Britain's Privy Council in the event that the decision of the relevant colonial high court had concerned a damage award greater than a (relatively high) statutory threshold, or had raised an important issue of statutory interpretation.[10] This hindered CANZ jurists then from simply distancing their "judge-made" legal rules from those of the "Mother Country" in the ways that American state supreme courts sometimes did, but it did not totally prevent some from finding other ways around unappealing English precedents.

How common was it for Canadian, Australian, and New Zealand jurists to dismiss American precedents with unfeigned contempt?[11] How common, on the contrary, were decisions that drew "on the

---

[8] See, for example, *Rayan v. Mayor, etc. of Malmsbury*, 1 VR(L) 23 (1870); *Badenhop v. Mayor, etc. of Sandhurst*, 1W., W., & a'B. (Victoria) 136 (1864); *Featherston Rd. Bd. v. Tate*, 1 GLR (NZSC) 38 (1898); *Kinnealy v. City of St. John*, 30 New Br. R 46 (1890); *Rohan v. Muncip. of St. Peters*, 8 SRNSW 64 (1908); *Geldert v. Muinicip. of Picton*, 23 Nov. Sc. R 483 (1891) (Weatherbe, J., diss.); *Patterson v. Corp. of City of Victoria*, 5 Br. Col. R. 628 (1897); *Taylor v. City of Winnipeg*, 12 Manit. R. 479 (1898).

[9] See, for example, R. Else-Mitchell, "The Foundation of New South Wales and the Inheritance of the Common Law," 49 *Journal of the Royal Australian Historical Society* 1 (1963); J. E. Cote, "The Reception of English Law," 15 *Alberta Law Review* 29 (1977); and Christopher English, "Newfoundland's Early Laws," 23 *Manitoba Law Journal* 65 at 71 (1996); Alex Castles, "The Reception and Status of English Law in Australia," 2 *Adelaide Law Review* (1963).

[10] For most of the critical years that this book addresses, the damages threshold was £500. Privy Council cases were not available in published reports until 1829 (except with regard to high seas prizes (1809)). William Holdsworth, *The Named Reporters*, in *Anglo-American Legal History Series: Contemporary Law Pamphlets*, ed. Allison Reppy (N.Y. 1943), Series 1, No. 8, p. 12.

[11] As did Darley, C. J., in *Patterson v. Borough of Woollahra*, 16 LR (NSW) 228 (1895).

combined authority of both" English and American opinions as if they were of equal weight?[12] The question is worth asking because American jurists in these years were rewriting some Common-Law rules in intriguing ways. How many of these jurists believed, with Justice Burton, of the Supreme Court of New South Wales in 1841, that the more English rules, principles, and customs were "introduced in to this Colony in the administration of justice, the better it would be for its inhabitants"?[13] We know that while Justice Lutwyche, of Queensland's Supreme Court believed he would "always" be "guided" by the decisions of English and Scottish courts, he also believed that he and his colleagues "ought to extend a similar comity to the Supreme Courts of the Australasia colonies, whenever it can be shown that the law which they are called upon to administer is the same as that which is in force here."[14] How common was it for CANZ jurists to extend such recognition and respect? How many, on the contrary, were as willing as Justice Meredith, or Justice Innes, to speak harshly on occasion of a particular English rule?[15] How many others found ways to elude such a rule by pleading the exceptionality of "local conditions,"[16] by distinguishing the facts of the case before them from the offending English precedent,[17] or by simply obfuscating?

The conventional wisdom is that nineteenth century American jurists altered the Common-Law rules they had "received" from English courts in ways that favored corporate defendants, economic efficiency, "market liberalism," or economic growth.[18] I have recently argued, to the contrary, that when nineteenth century American courts did occasionally alter "received" Common-Law rules, they generally did so out

[12] Wilkins, J., in *Lovatte v. Salter & Twining*, 3 Nov. Sc. R 387 at 399 (1858).

[13] *The Australian*, Apr. 8, 1841, p. 2, quoted in J. M. Bennett, *A History of the Supreme Court of New South Wales* (Sydney, 1974), 35.

[14] In *MacDonald v. Tully*, 1 *Queensland Law Journal* 26 at 29(1879).

[15] Meredith, J., in *Cornell v. Town of Prescott*, 20 Ont. C. of A. 49 at 54 (1892); Innes, J., in *Sanderson v. Smith*, 3 LRNSW 31 (1882). Cf. Hagarty, C. J. O., in *Matthews v. Hamilton Powder Co.*, 14 Ont. C. of A. 261 at 265 (1887).

[16] See, for example, Proudfoot, J., in *Church v. Fuller*, 3 Ont. (QB) 417 at 420 (1883); or Galt, J., in *Drake v. Wigle*, 24 UCCP 405 at 409 (1874).

[17] See, for example, the utterly opposite ways that Taschereau, J., and Gwynne, J., interpreted the facts in *Price v. Roy*, 29 Can. S.C. 494 (1899), the one to aid the plaintiff, the other to turn her away. See also the diary entries of Denniston, J., in J. G. Denniston, *A New Zealand Judge* (Wellington, 1939), 124–27.

[18] See, for example, Morton Horwitz, *The Transformation of American Law, 1780–1860* (Cambridge, Mass., 1977); Richard Posner, *An Economic Analysis of Law* (Boston, 1972); Christopher Tomlins, *Law, Labor, and Ideology in the Early American Republic* (N.Y., 1993); Lawrence Friedman, *A History of American Law* (2nd ed., N.Y., 1985).

of a humane sense of compassion for individual plaintiffs who came
before them at a considerable disadvantage in the litigation balance-
of-power.[19] (I will note these innovations, where relevant, throughout
this book.) I believe most American jurists in the nineteenth century
were more generous to poorer, weaker, and younger plaintiffs than
had previously been allowed, and I attribute this to the evangelical

[19] Thus a substantial number of American jurisdictions moved away from older
English proemployer rules regarding breaches of labor contracts to more
equity-based rules allowing a worker who quit before his contract was completed to recover the value of his labor (*quantum meruit*). Similarly, many
American jurisdictions, especially in the West and South, tended to hold
to the seventeenth century English rule that allowed a third-party beneficiary of a contract the right to sue for damages or specific enforcement,
while British and New England courts of the nineteenth century united to
reject such a litigant that right. Where variations appeared in this regard,
American courts tended to be more willing to permit *gift* beneficiaries (spin-
ster daughters, widows, orphans) to sue than *creditor* beneficiaries. In matters of tort law, many of the same American jurisdictions came to reject
the New York, Massachusetts, and English rule that allowed a defendant,
charged with injuring a child through negligence, to raise the child's contributory negligence as a bar. By the 1860s and 1870s most American high
courts had decided that a small child could not be deemed to have sufficient
capacity to assess the risks in order to be viewed as behaving in a negligent
manner. Furthermore, most of these courts also decided (contrary to the
rule in England, New York, Massachusetts, and a handful of other largely
eastern states) that any negligence of the child's parent, in permitting the
child to venture into a dangerous setting, could not be imputed to the
child as contributory negligence. Similarly, most jurisdictions (again, distinctly southern, mid-western, and western) came to reject an English rule
that prevented a child, injured on another's negligently managed property,
from suing for damages if the child was trespassing. An increasingly child-
centered culture that valued youthful play and outdoor activity appears to
have produced a "legal fiction": These children, led to wander by "childish
instincts," had been "tempted" into danger by "attractive nuisances" such
as railroad turntables and other unguarded, whirling machinery; hence the
child was no trespasser, but had been "invited" to the danger, and the owner
of the machinery was liable if the dangerous object had been negligently
maintained. In the 1840s and 1850s American juries began awarding substantially larger damage awards than they had previously granted, that is,
as soon as railroads began to injure passenger in derailments or collisions,
or to hit "strangers" at railway crossings, and I found that these awards
were larger, proportionately, than those of the 1980s. Moreover, appellate
courts approved most of these awards to passengers and strangers (despite
the contributory negligence rule) and within a generation found enough
exceptions to the fellow-servant and assumption of risk rules to uphold similarly large awards to a significant percentage of litigant railroad workers
who would have simply been nonsuited by English judges. A "deep pocket"
theory of tort compensation was clearly dominant in American jurisdictions

religious movements of the antebellum years and to "humanitarianism," a quasi-religious force that vied with doctrinal legal reasoning in nineteenth century America, as well as to democratic impulses and the electing of jurists, more evident in the western, southern and midwestern jurisdictions than in at least two of the eastern-seaboard states. This "humane" judicial propensity in civil Common-Law suits can be compared to and is associated with the emergence of the "best interest of the child" doctrine in custody and adoption law, the antislavery movement, and the campaigns against flogging, cruelty to animals, and capital punishment.[20]

These movements were also powerful in England, resulting in statutes such as those abolishing slavery in the West Indies and regulating Polenesian Island labor contracting for Fiji and Australia, but they

by 1850, and it can be detected simultaneously in the rise of contingency fee arrangements between lawyers and tort plaintiffs (another American innovation), in the rise of medical malpractice cases, and in the expanding of municipal liability (for defective roads, sidewalks, public utilities, and bridges). Peter Karsten, "'Bottomed on Justice': A Reappraisal of Critical Legal Studies Scholarship Concerning Breaches of Labor Contracts by Quitting or Firing in Britain and the U.S., 1630–1880," 34 *American Journal of Legal History* 213 (1990); Karsten, "The 'Discovery' of Law by English and American Jurists of the 17th, 18th, and 19th Centuries: Third Party Beneficiary Contracts as a Test Case," 9 *Law and History Review* 327, (1991; Karsten, "Explaining the Fight over the Attractive Nuisance Rule: A Kinder, Gentler Instrumentalism in the 'Age of Formalism,'" *10 Law and History Review* 45, (1992); Karsten, *"Heart" versus "Head": Judge-Made Law in Nineteenth Century America* (Chapel Hill, 1997), chs. 3, 5, 8, and 9.

20 On these topics see, generally, Hermann Kantorowitz, *The Spirit of British Policy* (N.Y., 1932), Chapter 3; Frank Klingberg, *The Anti-Slavery Movement in England* (Yale Univ. Press, 1926), chs. 2 and 3; and Crane Brinton, "Humanitarianism," in *Encyclopedia of the Social Sciences* (N.Y., 1937). More specifically, see Macello Maetro, *Voltaire and Beccaria as Reformers of Criminal Law* (1942); Harold Langley, *Social Reform in the U.S. Navy, 1798–1862* (Urbana, 1967); Seymour Drescher, *Econocide: British Slavery in the Era of Abolition* (Pittsburgh, 1984); Drescher, *Capitalism and Antislavery: British Mobilization in Comparative Perspectives* (N.Y., 1987); James Turner, *Reckoning of the Beast: Animals, Pain, and Humanity in the Victorian Mind* (Johns Hopkins U. Press: Baltimore, 1980), 79–83; William L. Brown, *An Essay on Sensibility: A Poem in Six Parts* (2nd ed, London, 1791); John H. Langbein, *Torture and the Law of Proof: Europe and England in the Ancient Regime* (Chicago, 1977); Peter Karsten, *Law, Soldiers, and Combat* (Westport, Ct., 1978), 21–22; Geoffrey Best, *Humanity in Warfare* (N.Y., 1980); Louis Maser, *Rites of Execution: Capital Punishment and the Transformation of American Culture, 1776–1865* (N.Y., 1989); Alice Felt Tyler, *Freedom's Ferment* (1944); and Michael Grossberg, *Governing the Hearth: Law and the Family in Nineteenth Century America* (Univ. of North Carolina Press, 1985), Ch. 7.

had little effect on the rules and doctrines of England's Common-Law courts.[21] This book explores the extent of the independent effect of humanitarian and "democratic" impulses in Canada, Australia, and New Zealand on both the legislative and the Common Law of those Diaspora jurisdictions.

One case, well-known to legal historians and tort specialists, that especially intrigued me at first was *Victorian Ry Commissioners v. Coultas* (H. of L., 1888). In 1886 the Supreme Court of Victoria affirmed a jury award of £342 to a woman frightened in a near collision at a railroad crossing. The "nervous shock" she thereupon experienced had caused her to become ill later. On appeal, however, the Law Lords of Privy Council in London reversed this decision: Such suits, in the absence of any evidence of actual physical injury ("touching") accompanying the fright-producing incident, would create a "wide field opened for imaginary claims."[22]

An Australian court that had sought to create an exception to the "touching" requirement in personal injury torts had thus been reprimanded by the Mother of All Common Law.[23] But beginning in 1889, the year after the Privy Council's judgement had appeared, certain American state courts more independent of the Privy Council than was Victoria's, abandoned the "touching" requirement: Where near collisions due to negligence produced fright which then led to "violent convulsions" or miscarriages, "common sense," "reason," and "analogies of the law" became grounds for American jurists to allow damages for such injuries. Justice William Rumsey of New York's Supreme Court noted in this regard that while Privy Council had not allowed recovery of damages for this sort of injury, he and his colleagues were free to disagree with those august Law Lords: "The weight to be given to any decided case as an authority depends not alone upon the rank of the court, but upon solidity of the reasons upon which the decision is founded, and the perspicuity and precision with which those reasons

[21] A few exceptions: By the 1830s English courts had adopted the "best interest of the child doctrine" in custody cases; though even this rested upon statutory authority. Later in the century her courts adopted the "last clear chance" and *res ipsa loquitur* rules in negligence cases. See *Davies v. Mann*, 10 M&W 546, 152 ER 588 (EX. 1842); *Byrne v. Boadle*, 2 H&C 722 (1863). Cf. *Heaven v. Pender*, 11 QBD 506 (1883) (a negligent tort defendant liable for injuries suffered by plaintiff despite lack of privity with plaintiff).

[22] *Victorian RR Commissioners v. Coultas*, 13 App. Cas. 222 at 226 (H. of L., 1888).

[23] But see *Daly v. Commissioners of Railways*, 8 Western Australia Law Reports 125 (1906), where the court distinguished between the *Coultas* ruling and the facts in *Daly*.

are expressed."[24] Most of the pro-plaintiff judicial innovations within the Common Law in the nineteenth century appear to have been initiated by American courts; but in this case, it had been an Australian court that had led the way.

Now let me make clear: I was not simply searching for innovations, or attempting to document the source of such innovations in the fashion of a history of ideas. Given what we know of British Colonial and Dominion courts prior to the present generation, I would have been very surprised to find much willingness to challenge directly British precedent in Canada, Australia, or New Zealand, at least after the first few decades of what Bruce Kercher has styled "frontier law."[25] What I was looking for was evidence of how these CANZ jurists faced problems in property, contract, and tort similar to those that had perplexed American jurists as these regions opened to settlement, experienced modernization, and witnessed the creation of new enterprises and entities, new farms, ranches, factories, cities, streetcars, macadamized roads, insurance companies, steamships, and railroads. I wondered whether some of these Westminster-bound jurists in one or more colonies might display traits, attitudes, or propensities comparable to one or another of the perspectives that American legal historians have identified in the opinions of nineteenth century American jurists. How often did one or another of these perspectives ever inform the judgements of any CANZ jurists? I knew that by 1837 *English* jurists were treating American opinions as being merely "of interest" rather than in any way authoritative, and I suspected that CANZ jurists would have eventually felt compelled to follow that lead, but how completely?[26] I was thus interested to see whether CANZ jurists, faced with problems generated by such enterprises and entities, made use of the non-English ways that certain American jurisdictions had faced them. But, in the absence of evidence that they actually knew of the actions of their American peers, I was content simply to learn how they faced their

---

[24] *Purcell v. St. Paul City Ry*, 48 Minn. 34, 50 NW 1034 at 1035 (1892); *Illinois Central RR v. Latimer*, 128 Ill. 163, 21 NE 7 (1889); *Hill v. Kimball*, 76 Tex. 210, 13 SW 59 (1890); *Missouri Pacific v. Kaiser*, 82 Tex. 144, 18 SW 305 (1891); *Sloane v. Southern California RR*, 111 Cal. 668, 44 Pac. 320 (1896); *Yoakum v. Kroeger*, (Tex. Civ. App.), 27 5W 952 at 954 (1894); *Mack v. South Bound RR*, 52 S.C. 323, 29 SE 905 (1898); and *Mitchell v. Rochester Ry*, 4 Misc. Rpts. 575, 25 NY Sup. 744 at 749 (1893) (for Justice Rumsey's views).

[25] Kercher, *An Unruly Child: A History of Law in Australia* (Sydney, 1995).

[26] See Patteson, J., in *Beverley v. Lincoln Gas Light & Coke Co.*, 6 Ad. & E. 829 at 837, 112 ER 318 at 321 (Q.B., 1837); James, L. J., in *North British & Mercantile Ins. Co. v. London, Liverpool, & Globe Ins. Co.*, 44 L.J. Ch. 537 at 538 (1877); Lord Halsbury in *In re Mo. SS Co.*, 42 Ch. D. 321 at 330 (1889).

own problems, given the constraints of their colonial or Dominion status.[27]

These questions are, by their nature, those of the field of Comparative intellectual history: Why did "great minds" (or in this case great, and a number of not-as-great jurists) favor one view of what "the Law" is, or should in the case before them be, over another? Comprehending the values, or even the views, of nineteenth century CANZ jurists has not been an easy task. Bruce Kercher recently noted that "nineteenth century Australian Common Law is largely unknown to legal historians," and, as Paul Finn has said of Australian jurists in these years, "biographical detail is spare," and "one is left, for the most part, with merely the law reports" as "testimonies of attitude." These, he believes, "can be inexact if not misleading in many instances."[28] I have tried to support my judgements with biographical or other evidence of the positions jurists held, but Finn is right; sometimes one must simply make careful use of opinions which were themselves carefully crafted. All I can promise is that after several years of utilizing this sort of evidence, I believe that I have developed an "ear" for the moments when the author's personal views can indeed be heard in his *dicta*.

WHAT I ASK ABOUT INFORMAL "LAW"

Knowing how CANZ jurists dealt with English (and American) precedents, and with Canadian and Australasian "circumstances and conditions," is interesting; but at *least* as interesting is the question of how important The Law actually *was* in the lands of the British Diaspora. To answer *that* question, one first has to know what The Law *was, not* just to legislatures and high court jurists, but to trial judges, attorneys, arbitration panels, magistrates, juries, and others in Britain, the United States, Canada, Australia, and New Zealand. How often were statutes and high court rules avoided, evaded, or ignored? Secondly, at a more basic level, one has to know what the "informal laws" (that is the customs and popular norms of conduct) were that ordinary folk in Britain

---

[27] It is also possible to compare certain legislative solutions to specific problems faced in America, Canada, and the Antipodes, and I will note these when appropriate, but my primary concerns herein are jurists, juries, and "popular" law. For a comparative analysis of legislative solutions in Canada, South Africa, and the Antipode colonies, and their impact on the mother country, see Jeremy Finn, "Reverses in the Flow: English Adoption of Law from the Empire," paper presented at the Australia & New Zealand Law and History Conference, Melbourne, July, 1998.

[28] Kercher, *An Unruly Child: A History of Australian Law* (Sydney, 1996), 137; Paul D. Finn, *Law and Government in Colonial Australia* (Melbourne, 1987), 165.

and her Diaspora lands actually observed in conducting such everyday (but important) affairs as the resolution of land-title, boundary, lease-hold, sales, labor-contract, trespass, or injury disputes. In short, quite apart from high court *haute culture*, what were the "low" legal cultures like in the lands of the British Diaspora during the three centuries before World War I?

Drawing upon the insights and findings of anthropologists, sociologists, and social historians, we know first that lower courts do not always follow religiously the rules and norms set down for them by supreme court jurists,[29] and, second, that many potential legal disputes do not reach the entry-level stage of a lawsuit, let alone the full-fledged status of courtroom litigation. Resolution of disputes often occur at the unofficial level of the insurance adjustor, or at a more private, interpersonal level governed by expected neighborly norms. Sometimes these norms appear to have been shaped by forces largely indifferent to the rules enunciated with care by high-court jurists, and at times they appear to have been quite contrary to them.[30]

Aware of these modern-day observations, I wanted to know something of both the private, interpersonal "law" of individuals and the more public legal culture of magistrates and juries in the British Diaspora lands that would serve as a complement and counterpart to what I sought to know about the high court jurists of these jurisdictions.

A few examples, drawn from the domain of property law: Despite the niceties of the Law with regard to real property, squatters abounded in the British Diaspora lands of North America and the Antipodes. Those entitled to be styled "Proprietors," by virtue of their possession of some document granting them lawful title to land, could find their forests laid waste in ways every bit as bold as any yeoman with blackened face did to a forest or its keeper in early or mid-eighteenth century England. Thus John Henry, the agent of the Penn family in Morris County, New Jersey, complained in 1747 that the local Justice of the Peace, Jonathan Whitaker, refused to prosecute those who had cut and hauled timber on Penn land to Whitaker's sawmill even though their names appeared on the logs because there was "no such thing in nature as to wrong the Devilish Proprietors," or so he reported Whitaker to have said.[31]

---

[29] See, for example, Walter Murphy, "Lower Court Checks on Supreme Court Authority," 53 *American Political Science Review* 1017 (1959).

[30] See, for example, Robert Ellickson, *Order Without Law: How Neighbors Settle Disputes* (Cambridge, 1991).

[31] E. P. Thompson, *Whigs and Hunters: The Black Act,* 136; Henry, quoted in Brendan McConville, "Those Daring Disturbers of the Public Peace: Agrarian Unrest and the Struggle for Political Legitimacy in New Jersey, 1701–1783," Ph.D. thesis, Brown Univ., 1992, p. 177.

Other "daring disturbers of the public peace" claimed to hold possessory rights derived from previous squatters, via purchase from indigenous people, or in more radical fashion (sometimes citing John
Locke) by virtue of their having mixed their labor with the land, instead
of from the Crown or one who had acquired title from the Crown. In
North America squatters sometimes tested the limits and capabilities of
the Common-Law rules, as when those on land granted to Proprietor
Josiah Little, near Bakerstown, Maine, told him in 1787 they hoped to
acquire title to the land from Massachusetts authorities without purchasing it from Little, but that "if we cannot git it any other way [we]
will [buy it] of you."[32] Were the proprietor to seek to evict such a squatter, he might find a "common law" at work in the "twelve good men,
tried and true" who heard the case. Thus, proprietor Thomas Talbot
of western Ontario complained to that colony's attorney-general in
1827 that George Bateman, who had unlawfully "purchased" a lot on
Talbot's estate from a settler who had failed to fulfill Talbot's conditions, was "able to make the stupid jury believe that the land was
his."[33] Meanwhile, "down under," those who "squatted" on the land
were the great graziers, who eventually secured vast leaseholds for
a few farthings an acre, and then openly threatened farmers who
sought to "select" land on these vast leaseholds under new statutory
provisions.[34] Similarly, the LAW of slavery was widely resisted, both by
slaves themselves and, eventually, by their sympathizers, the Abolition-
ists, as well. Moreover, though the Law of fencing and animal trespass
was clearly spelled out in colonial statutes and municipal ordinances,
people tended to ignore such laws and make arrangements more convenient in these matters (and still do, as Robert Ellickson has recently
found in Shasta County, California).[35] Of course even these "common law" popular norms could be violated, as when Rebecca Nurse
"fell a railing" at Benjamin Holton in Salem Village, Massachusetts,
in 1689, and told her son "to go and get a gun and kill our piggs
and let non of them to go out of the field" because "our pigs got
into her field, tho our pigs were sufficiently yoked and their fence was
down in several places."[36] This sort of trespass could lead to similar

---

[32] Alan Taylor, *Liberty Men and Great Proprietors: The Revolutionary Settlement in
the Maine Frontier, 1760–1820* (Chapel Hill, 1990), 236.

[33] Fred C. Hamil, *Lake Erie Baron: The Story of Colonel Thomas Talbot* (Toronto,
1955), 56–87.

[34] Stephen H. Roberts, *The Squatting Age in Australia, 1835–1847* (Melbourne,
1935), 169.

[35] Ellickson, *Order without Law: How Neighbors Settle Disputes* (Cambridge, 1991).
For more on this subject see Chapter 4.

[36] Steven Nissenbaum and Paul Boyer, eds., *The Salem Village Witchcraft Papers*
(3 vols., N.Y., 1977), II, 600.

tension in the other lands of the British Diaspora (as we will see in Chapter 4).

How often and under what circumstances did popular norms conflict with the Common or statutory Law? When it did, how did that conflict play out? When did the Law win? When was it simply ignored or supplanted by "common law"? The mere identification of such conflict is one thing, but I also ask (if I do not always fully answer, to my satisfaction) what the difference was – that is, *why* did the Law win certain conflicts, the "common law" of popular norms, others?

A MAP OF THE TERRITORY

This book concerns tensions between the Law and popular norms regarding three central human domains: Land (Property Law), Agreements (Contract Law), and Accidents (Tort Law).[37] Issues within each of these three arenas are addressed in a "high" and "low" legal culture mode. The first chapter explores both the Law and "customs" with regard to property, including the customary property rights of Aboriginal people; the second explores the same conflict over landlord–tenant relations; the third, over questions of title to land; the fourth, over encroachment on one's title, such as "takings," trespasses, and easements. A fifth chapter compares "high" and "low" legal cultures with regard to sales agreements, third-party beneficiary contracts, and contingency-fee contracts; the sixth does the same with regard to labor, construction, and service contracts.[38] A seventh chapter considers the formal Law of negligence (accident law); an eighth explores the "real" law of accidents – that is, the arenas of settlements, trial courts, and jury awards. A concluding chapter adds some data on other legal issues not falling clearly into one of the three issues addressed more

---

[37] I can't address every issue in a single book covering three centuries and plenty of territory; hence I have omitted from consideration the domains of family law, constitutional law, and criminal law (except as these have coincidentally overlapped at times one or another aspect of a topic being addressed).

[38] While I refer from time to time to slavery, I have not included this involuntary life-long labor "contract" in the scope of this study. Much has been written on this subject, and much of that work is of high quality; I did not feel I was likely to be able to add enough to that story to warrant the additional time and space. For those seeking to know more of the "high" and "low" legal cultures of slavery in the lands of the British Diaspora, I suggest Thomas Morris, *Southern Slavery and the Law* (Chapel Hill, 1996); Eugene Genovese, *Roll, Jordan, Roll: The World the Slaves Made* (N.Y., 1974); Herbert Aptheker, *American Negro Slave Revolts* (N.Y., 1963); and Michael Craton, *Testing the Chains: Resistance to Slavery in the West Indies* (Ithaca, 1982).

systematically, and seeks to clarify what we may have learned from all of this.

I don't insist that this comparative analysis of certain issues involving land, agreements, and accidents in the lands of the British Diaspora is *the* story of the "high" and "low" legal cultures there and the tensions sometimes evident between them; much more work (including more attention to criminal and family law, municipal ordinances, attorneys, legislatures, indeed the general subject of popular norms themselves) would be required before one could make that sort of claim. But I *do* believe that I have limned the basic contours of these cultures. Of course readers like you constitute the common-law court that will ultimately decide this, and I will have no appeal from that decision to any Privy Council.

ACKNOWLEDGMENTS

I am grateful to the New Zealand–United States (Fulbright) Educational Foundation for providing me a Senior Research Fellowship at the Alexander Turnbull Library, Wellington, New Zealand in 1992. I also want to acknowledge the support of the Dean of the Faculty of Arts and Sciences at the University of Pittsburgh and the Director of the University's Center for International Studies for providing research assistance over the past few years for visits to Chicago, Australia, England, and Canada. One does not always need major research grants to conduct useful work, which is fortunate since such grants are fast becoming unattainable for most scholars. But my university appreciates the role that small travel-to-research grants can play in our pressing back of the Frontiers of Knowledge.

The entire staff at the Turnbull and at the nearby National Archives of New Zealand, Heather Tonnes of Victoria University's Law Library, and Mr. Leon Warniski, Head Reference Archivist at the Archives of Ontario, were most accommodating and helpful. I appreciated both their help and their real enthusiasm for what I was up to. Good archivists are the scholar's most valuable allies. I had many.

Good colleagues are great research comrades-in-arms. I am grateful to Professor Bruce Kercher at Macquarie University Law School for his hospitality and assistance provided during my trips to Australia the same year, for his rich collection of data on hundreds of cases heard by the Supreme Court of New South Wales from 1824 through the 1830s (an on-going project, available to all at www.law.mq.edu.au/scnsw), and for the useful dialogue on the issues addressed in this book we have had over the past few years. Bernie Hibbitts, Erik Zissu, Bob Hayden, Stuart Anderson, Daniel Ernst, and John McLaren have read portions of this book or have responded with collegiality to questions: I have appreciated this, and may regret that I did not take more of their suggestions (or that I took too many).

While I have dug prodigiously in libraries and archives for many months for material relevant to this undertaking at Kew Gardens, Chicago, Toronto, Ottawa, Montreal, Wellington, Christchurch, Melbourne, Sydney, and Brisbane, I readily allow that as much as 33 percent of my evidence (largely appearing in Part I) is "derivative" – that is, drawn from the published works of other scholars. The late Herman Kahn defined "intellectuals" as "those who get virtually all of their ideas and information second-hand." The broad, comparative character of this book meant that I could not help but benefit from a number of well-researched, focused studies. I refer to these and their authors throughout, but I want to single out here some of those to whom I am particularly indebted: Jane Neeson, Peter King, Jane Samson, David Swinfen, W. P. Morrell, Paul Knaplund, and Rande Kostal (on Britain); Richard White, Charles Brooks, Wilma Dunaway, James Merrell, John Mack Faragher, Donald Pisani, Stephen Aron, Alan Taylor, Brendan McConville (on the United States); Robert Foster, Bruce Kercher, Rob McQueen, Henry Reynolds (on Australia); Brian Young, R. W. B. Risk, Sidney Harring, Hamar Foster, Sean Cadigan (on the Canadas); David V. Williams, Bryan Gilling, Ann Parsonson, Richard Hill, Allan Ward, Ian Wards (on New Zealand); Peter France (on Fiji); John S. Galbraith and William M. MacMillan (on South Africa); and Jeremey Finn (on comparative legislation).

PART ONE

Land

1

Law versus Customs

"No land is occupied which is not stolen."
– Mark Twain

Between 1575 and 1825, successive English Parliaments responded to calls from "improvement"-minded aristocrats and gentry with legislation that arranged for the purchase and extinguishing of customary rights held by cottagers, cottiers, crofters, and yeomen tenant–farmers in one village, fen, and forest after another. Pasturing of animals on "the commons," hunting game and mining coal in forest, fishing in rivers and fens, and gleaning grain in harvested fields, gathering reeds, sand and firewood from "the waste" would cease as commonly held fields, fens, and forests were privatized and enclosed.

Many of the parties to this process, "the Enclosure Movement," both beneficiaries and losers, migrated to "the Colonies" carved out by the British Crown in North America and the Antipodes. Some of the same struggles between those who championed the Law and private property and those who sought to preserve or restore some of those beleaguered customs played out in the fields, forests, rivers, and mines of those colonies. But these struggles were relatively insignificant ones compared to the replay of what had transpired in the British Isles, now featuring a new cast of characters: On one side were pitted the Diaspora newcomers, both the former winners *and* losers of the enclosure wars, who championed a notion of property rights that privileged the "improvers" of the soil and protected their individual, exclusive use of land and water with Law; on the other, the native inhabitants of North America and the Antipodes, who defined property rights differently, as shared or multiple-uses to the game, tubers, berries, minerals, and the like, based on custom and family. *This* struggle seemed to have ended by 1900 with the Diaspora settlers in firm control of most resources (though in the past generation the Original People/First Nations have found receptive ears and voices in the high courts of the United States, Canada, Australia, New Zealand, and South Africa, and the struggle has thus moved to arbitration panels, tribunals, and legislative committees).

COMMONERS, CUSTOMARY PROPERTY RIGHTS, AND THE
LAW IN THE BRITISH ISLES

Ireland

As the English strengthened their grip on Ireland in the late sixteenth
and early seventeenth centuries they found it to their advantage in administering their Gaelic and Anglo-Norman subjects to replace their
marchland counciliar courts (based on the medieval law of conquest)
with Common-Law courts. Hans Pawlisch tells the story well. Such
Gaelic legal customs as tanistry[1] and partible inheritance created problems for those arriving with Letters Patent to run their newly acquired
"plantations." Gaelic rules of tenure and inheritance were relatively
foreign to Common-Law rules, and as such Sir John Davies and his
fellow jurists found it useful to abrogate those Gaelic rules that confounded the plans of the "planters," requiring those holding tenure
under Gaelic rules of law to surrender them and have their titles re-
granted by the English Crown. This soon set into motion a second
measure, the requirement that all Irish heirs "sue livery" (pay feudal
fees associated with the English law of "wardship" to the Crown's Court
of Wards and Liveries).[2] We will say more of the clash between Irish
customs and English Common Law in the next chapter, where we consider landlord–tenant relations, but for now suffice it to say that the
Crown cut deeply into the customary laws of the Irish in the early
seventeenth century, just as it would those of the Scottish, English,
and Welsh in ensuing years, and as it ultimately would those of the
aboriginal people of North America and the Antipodes as well.

England, Scotland, and Wales

Many of those who emigrated to North America and the Antipodes
in the seventeenth, eighteenth, and early nineteenth centuries had
enjoyed certain customary legal privileges in the British Isles, and

[1] Think of it as a practice of the leading members of a Gaelic clan naming
someone to the office of tanist, or chiefly-successor, in the lifetime of one
clan chief, with rights and privileges regarding the disposition of significant
amounts of clan lands.

[2] Hans Pawlisch, *Sir John Davies and the Conquest of Ireland* (Cambridge, 1985),
12, 47–48, 50, 81. Cf. Kenneth Nicholls, "Some Documents on Irish Law
and Custom in the 16th Century," 26 *An. Hibernia* 103–30 (1970); Hugh
Kearney, "The Ct of Wards & Liveries in Ireland, 1622–1641," 57 *Proceedings of the Royal Irish Academy* (1955); David Konig, "Colonization and the
Common Law in Ireland and Virginia, 1569–1634," in *The Transformation
of Early American History*, ed. James Henretta, et al. (N.Y., 1991), 70–92; and
D. Sutherland, "Conquest and Law," 15 *Studia Gratiana* 35 (1972).

many had witnessed or been the actual victims of efforts to extinguish those rights. For centuries, Welsh villagers had enjoyed the customary rights of *cymorth* (rural neighborhood aid) and *tai unnos* (freehold right to whatever a man could build and enclose in a single day and night); English and Scottish cottage owners had enjoyed access to commonly owned meadows, fens, heath, stream-beds, sea-shores, and quarries; rights to pasture cows, sheep, fowl, or hogs ("levancy" and "couchancy"); to gather firewood, sand, stone, rushes, herbs, mushrooms, nuts, flowers, birds, crabapples, and berries ("turbary," "botes," and "estover"); or to glean grain after the harvest. Those living in or adjacent to the great forests had enjoyed the rights to gather fallen timber, or the right to create a personally dug mine pit. And many claimed the "right" to hunt game in the forest preserves, regardless of such legal "rights" to that game asserted at Law by the Lawful owners.

A number of these customary property rights had been recognized by the Common-Law courts over the years, and some were still being recognized in the nineteenth century.[3] But others had fallen victims of the Enclosure Movement in the seventeenth, eighteenth, and early nineteenth centuries. In those years, landowners acquired special legislative measures enabling them to enclose as their own property certain commonly held meadows and other "waste" land, and to drain fens that had previously been held in common by cottagers of those communities. In the first century and a half of this enclosure movement, those whose centuries-old rights were being seized, demanded and often secured from Parliament, "full and proper compensation" for their financial losses, but in the second half of the eighteenth century this enclosure movement entered a final, uglier phase. The "commoners" or "cottagers" who now lost their privileges may have at times been undercompensated for their losses by the 500 commissioners employed for that purpose. And the movement was substantial; between 1750 and 1815, for example, some two-thirds of all agricultural land in Northamptonshire was converted by parliamentary fiat from open, commonly held fields to enclosed, private property.[4]

---

3 See, for example, *Jones v. Williams*, 107 ER 916 (1837) (regarding the right to taking wood in a forest), and J. M. Lightwood, *A Treatise on Possession of Land* (1894), 12 ("acts of slight importance, such as the gathering of sea-weed, the taking of shell-fish, and the planting of stakes for fishing nets, are often conclusive in claims founded on the alleged possession of foreshore [sea-shore]").

4 The best account of the phenomenon in the years relevant to this book is J. M. Neeson, *Commoners: Common Right, Enclosure, and Social Change in England, 1700–1820* (Cambridge, 1993). See also Roger Manning, *Village Revolts: Social Protest and Popular Disturbances in England, 1509–1640* (Oxford, 1988), 84–87, 280–81; T. M. Martin, "The Cost of Parliamentary

British peasants who relied on common land for nutrients, fuel, pasture, grazing, and a host of other household needs were adversely affected by the Enclosure Movement. Called "crofters" in Scotland, "commoners" or "cottagers" in England, they had for centuries shared the seasonal efforts of maintaining and utilizing the commons with their more affluent, propertied farmer-neighbors. They had exchanged produce and finished-goods with them, had participated in the manorial and Borough-English courts that administered the by-laws and customary rules of the commons, and had processed with their minister and fellow villagers of all stations around the parish boundaries each year in the ceremony of Rogation, praising God for the fruits of the earth and offering an "Amen" as the minister read the curse from Deuteronomy, 27:17, against "he who removeth his neighbor's land-mark."[5]

There were from time to time a number of disputes over how many cattle or sheep cottager A or farmer B was allowed to graize on the common land (issues of "levancy" and "couchancy"), how much wood could be taken from the waste (an issue involving the rights of "turbary," "botes," and "estover"), how many rights attended a cottage at sale, or how much of a fine might ensue from the hayward's report of a downed fence. But these and other such issues were generally susceptible to resolution at arbitration, in the local court (with the sanction of the Court of Chancery), *or* in the court of self-help. Thus, in the village of Harold, Bedfordshire, cottages simply turned their cows into the ripening wheat of one who had cultivated the right-of-way of a pasture. In J. M. Neeson's words, "if going to law in the eighteenth century required a long purse, breaking by-laws required a thick skin, and more." Keep in mind that the Common Law permitted private relief against one who had committed a nuisance. The cottagers in Harold probably believed that their action was quite lawful, while Robert and Thomas Broxon of Runcorn surely knew that their assault on the keeper of the Park at Halton (for his confiscating the bags of acorns they had been gathering there) was unlawful.[6]

Enclosure in Warwickshire," 9 *Birmingham University Historical Journal* 144 (1964); and M. E. Turner, "The Cost of Parliamentary Enclosure in Buckinghamshire," 21 *Agricultural Historical Review* 35 (1973).

[5] J. M. Neeson, *Commoners: Common Right, Enclosure, and Social Change in England, 1750–1820* (Cambridge, 1993), 12, 100, 183, 320, 324.

[6] Neeson, *Commoners*, 117; T. C. Curtis, "Quarter Session Appearances and their Background: A 17th Century Regional Study," in *Crime in England, 1550–1800*, ed. J. S. Cockburn (Princeton, 1977), 136; *Delabeere v. Beddingfield*, 2 Vern. 103, 23 ER 676(1689). See also C. Searle, "Custom, Class

One of the more interesting of these battles has been described by E. P. Thompson: In both the seventeenth and eighteenth centuries the English monarchy sought to enclose Richmond Park, immediately south of London proper. When Charles I walled several parishes out, "the murmur and noise of the people was too near London not to be the common discourse," as Lord Clarendon observed. Parishioners pulled down parts of the park's new deer wall; the Crown put them back up. In 1755 one man, John Lewis, finally sued the gatekeeper for obstructing an ancient footway. Lewis won a jury trial, and when he found that the ladders the judge had ordered to be provided those who sought to use the footway had rungs set too far apart for children and "old men," he returned to court and was told by the judge, Sir Michael Foster, "I desire, Mr Lewis, that you would see [the ladders] so constructed that not only *children and old men*, but OLD WOMEN too, may get up."[7]

The enclosure of the commons by special acts of Parliament changed these customs forever. Commoners were rarely able to mount effective resistance in Parliament, and sometimes reacted to the loss of their rights with violence – burning the fence posts and rails, destroying the gates and locks, and pulling down the trees and summerhouses of the enclosers. These angry outbursts did not avert the enclosures, however. Magistrates and county officials sometimes dispatched dragoons. The fence posts and rails went back up. By the early nineteenth century, as many Britons considered migration to North America or the Antipodes, many peasants were being made landless.[8]

Common-Law English jurists had protected the customary rights of leaseholders against unscrupulous landlords in the sixteenth centuries with the action of ejectment, albeit by 1607 the Court of Common Pleas had limited rights of pasturage on the commons to those who possessed an interest of some kind in a dwelling in the town. But deferential to Parliament, jurists raised few objections to these enclosure statutes, and, on occasion, a few of these men, impressed by the arguments of the agricultural economists of their day, facilitated the process by

---

Conflict and Agrarian Capitalism: The Cumbrian Customary Economy in the 18th Century," 110 *Past & Present* 121 (1986).

7 Thompson, *Customs in Common* (N.Y., 1991), 111–13. See also Eric Hobsbawm, "Scottish Reformers and Capitalist Agriculture," in *Peasants in History* (Oxford, 1960).

8 John Morrill, *The Revolt in the Provinces, 1630–1660* (London, 1975), 34; David Underdown, *Revel, Riot and Rebellion* (Oxford, 1985), 108; Neeson, *Commoners*, 191–92, 263, 267, 278–79; E. P. Thompson, *Customs in Common*, 98–99; H. Perkins, *The Origins of Modern British Society, 1780–1880* (London, 1969), ch. 10.

altering some Common-Law traditions regarding customary property rules.[9]

David Jones reports popular protests against enclosures in Wales that were "no more than attempts to enforce a kind of natural justice." There the customs of *cymorth* and *tai unnos*, said to be based on ancient Welsh law, led to resistance to various parliamentary-sanctioned enclosures of common land in Snowdonia, Cardiganshire, and Caernarvonshire. Their turbary (peat), grazing, and quarrying rights were at risk, as was their right to such "improvements" as their *tai unnos* measures had produced. When the local gentry-beneficiaries of the enclosures began to act on their new rights, they were met with determined resistance: Mobs assaulted some; their sheep were maimed or killed; their fences and hedges were burned. "We will Levell them" one notice read; "there shall not be any Farms or houses [of enclosers] built on Mynydd Back, but what they shall be pulled down, without any Poor man shall come, then he shall build a House and make a Field, and we will help him," read another. When one or another of their neighbors was jailed for pulling down a fence or obstructing an encloser, a mob might well descend on the jail and release him or her. In September 1812, a clerk described the scene when he and his brother, a commissioner, supervised the surveying of the Pistyll commons: "We had not been there an hour before about forty persons, men and women and children, assembled and after reasoning with the men for some time and telling them the consequences of opposing the Surveyor I think they had made up their minds not to molest them, until a fresh set of women from the neighborhood of Llithfaen came up who immediately abused the men for their supineness and commenced a salute of sods upon the Commissioner and the Surveyor and the old women continued to do so until we came to the boundary of Nevin and Pistill when the action became general and the Commissioner, the Surveyor and myself were obliged to retreat." Ringleaders were, at times, identified and prosecuted, but often pardoned before the expiration of their sentences, "for," as one official put it, "if they come out of Gaol otherwise ... they may probably take it into their heads to pull down the rest of the Inclosures made under the Act of Parliament."[10]

J. M. Neeson also reports that in a few locales some customary commons rights were reasserted: In one instance, in 1830, some forty years

[9] *Smith v. Gateward*, 6 Coke Rpts. f. 59 (C.P., 1607); A. W. B. Simpson, *A History of Land Law* (Oxford, 1986), 107–14, 163–65, 169; Neeson, *loc. cit.*, 19, 46, 262.

[10] David J. V. Jones, *Before Rebecca: Popular Protests in Wales, 1793–1835* (London, 1973), 4, 36, 40, 42–47.

after enclosure, commoners reentered an enclosed fen in Chippenham, Cambridgeshire, to gather fuel for the village poor, and the magistrates refused to entertain complaints against them. In another, inhabitants of Helmdon were reported to have regarded as common property a stone quarry despite its enclosure. Decades of trespasses led the quarry "owner" to fence it with barbed wire and thorns, "as people looked on it as their right and fetched stones without my knowing."[11] Customary property traditions did not vanish with the rap of a parliamentary gavel or the reading of a Westminster opinion. They survived as long as they made social or economic sense, had widespread public support, and could resist or outlast the efforts of local elites to enforce the enclosure.

Peter King and J. M. Neeson tell us of one lingering tradition, the gleaning of grains after the harvest. Gleaning would often provide enough grain, peas, and beans to feed a family from harvesttime to Christmas. And the straw and fieldstalks could be mixed with manure for one's garden or burned to dry malt. Cottagers defended their customary gleaning rights with an intensity that a combination of self-interest and principle usually generates. Mrs. Sarah Orpin, an Essex landowner, took to sending her hired children and her hired hand back after the harvest for the crop residual in the 1770s; in time she received an annonymous threat of "a fire" when "your corn is in the barn." She had "glent up what the pore should have had," and her local keeper-of-the-customs wanted her to know how "shame[ful]" it had been for to "rob the pore" and to appreciate their right to "seek revenge" in self-help.[12] Despite a ruling by Common Pleas in 1788 that the custom of gleaning was not privileged or protected at Common Law, it "survived and prospered none the less" in "most villages with arable fields." Thus, Jane Neeson writes, "in the 1870s in more than fifty Northamptonshire parishes the gleaning bell still rang out to open and close the fields."[13]

---

[11] Neeson, *Commoners*, 76, 183.

[12] The threat was printed in the London Gazette (August 1773), as reported by E. P. Thompson in *Albion's Fatal Tree*, ed. Douglas Hay, et al. (1975), 311.

[13] Peter King, "Gleaners, Farmers, and the Failure of Legal Sanctions in England, 1750–1850," 125 *Past & Present* 116(1989); Jane B. Neeson, "An 18th Century Peasantry," in *Protest and Survival*, ed. John Rule and Robert Malcolmson (London, 1993), 40; Neeson, *Commoners*, 313–14; *Steel v. Houghton*, H. Bl. 5, 4 CP, 126 ER 32(C.P. 1788). Peter King's thick description of this case reveals that General Cornwallis, shortly after his capitulation at Yorktown, decided to enclose common lands within his Tinworth estates. While he was serving as governor in India, his agents and tenants appear to have targeted John Houghton and his wife, local defenders of common rights, with this expensive suit.

But the fact is, that these exceptions to the success of the enclosure movement appeared to be limited to relatively unsubstantial property: wood-scraps for fuel, walkways, harvest leavings, and quarry stones. Arable fields and pastures enclosed and most fens that had been drained, remained so. As E. P. Thompson put it, courts in the late eighteenth century shifted the older emphasis on rights *in* property (such as cottages) to rights *of* property (such as fee simple title). A rhyme of those days had it that "the law locks up the man or woman/Who steals the goose from off the common/But leaves the greater villain loose/Who steals the common from the goose." In the midseventeenth century Thomas Fuller sagely summed up the consequences to "the fenmen," who objected to the loss of their "freedom to catch pike and duck" once the fens were drained in order to fatten the bullocks and sheep of local landlords: "If they be taken in taking that bullock or sheep, the rich men indicteth them for felony; whereas the pike or duck were their own goods, only for the pain of catching them."[14]

Take note now that this practice of compulsorily transforming customary rights into Common-Law property would be repeated with results at least as tragic throughout all of the lands settled by the British Diaspora. But this time it would be the Aborigines who would lose their pike and ducks, their land, streams, and forests.

The Law and popular customs also clashed over the right to hunt game. The forests and forested estates of the aristocracy and some of the wealthier gentry were placed off-limits to all but their owners and tenants as preserves for the pheasant, fox, and deer hunts they relished as well as for the valuable stands of timber and warrens of marketable rabbits. This produced claims of commoners, copyholder yeomen, farmers, the lesser gentry, and some magistrates as well, that customs, sometimes centuries old, had permitted locals to net and snare game birds, hares, and rabbits on this heath or moor, in that forest. This is why Edward Christian would claim in his *Treatise on the Game Laws* (1821) that "every magistrate knows that it is the common defense of a poacher, that it is very hard that he should be punished for taking what he has as good a right to as any other man." And it is why one steward complained to his noble employer "there is no answering for a Common Jury (who must Try the Indictment) as they have in general a Strong Byass upon their Minds in favor of Poachers, being professed Enemies to all Penal Laws that relate to the Game." Witnesses conveniently lost their memories; informers suffered retaliation. But most of the aristocracy and wealthy gentry insisted on

---

[14] Christopher Hill, *From the Reformation to the Industrial Revolution* (London, 1967), 153; E. P. Thompson, *Customs in Common*, 130–40.

enforcement of the Law their class had crafted in Lords and Commons, and *sometimes* they succeeded, securing fines of five pounds and costs-of-court, expenses that could drive a cottager, collier, indeed, many a small farmer, to the wall, and occasionally dispatching poachers to Australia as transported felons (such as the two convicts assigned to Assistant Protector of Aborigines Le Souef at Port Phillip in 1840, both of whom had been convicted of poaching on the estate of Le Souef's cousin!).[15]

The common people saw themselves as the heirs to the mantle of Robin Hood; they read not "the book of parliament," as one M. P. (Member of Parliament) put it in 1829, but, rather, they "read the book of nature," wherein they "saw that the hand of nature made game wild" and thus free to the taker. Joseph Arch, the leader of the National Agricultural Labourer's Union, told a parliamentary committee in 1872 that he believed hares and rabbits to be "the fair property of anybody who [could] take [them]." Anthony Liddell, a Northumberland poacher, found his authority in the Bible, "which he had read with great attention thro' and through." Laws that "appeared to him to clash with the laws laid down" in the Bible "he treated with contempt," and he "maintained that the Fowls of the Air and the Fish of the Sea were free to all men." As such, "Game Laws or Laws to protect the fisheries had no weight with him." Similarly, an Oxfordshire J. P. (Justice of the Peace) reported in March, 1852, that "the peasantry" believed "all the wild things under heaven were free for all." Allan Howkins, a leading student of this phenomenon, tells us that "this belief," that "game was *ferae naturae*," prevailed for centuries as "an underground law," resistant to even the most restrictive parliamentary measure of all, the Game Law of 1831, which limited the killing of game to the *owners* of the land in question. With mere *tenants* now placed in the same category as poaching cottagers, and an expensive hunting license now required, the legal hunting population declined by 1840 to less than one in 400. None the less, a sympathetic police force and a defiant rural poor virtually voided the Law in many parts of England.[16]

---

[15] Manning, *Village Revolts*, chapter 11: "Poaching"; Christian, *A Treatise*, 293, noted in Douglas Hay, "Poaching and the Game Laws on Cannock Chase," in Hay, et al., eds., *Albion's Fatal Tree* (1977), 207; Albert Le Souef, "Personal Recollections of Early Victoria," A2762 (CY233), Mitchell Library, Sydney. And see Hay, 194, 198, 211, 222–34; and *Cooper v. Marshall, Cope v. Marshall*, 1 Burr. 259, 97 ER 303 (K.B., 1757).

[16] Alan Howkins, "Poaching and the Game Laws, 1840–1880," in Sandra Burman and Barbara Harrell-Bond, eds., *The Imposition of Law* (N.Y., 1979), 278, 285.

NEW AND IMPORTED CUSTOMARY LAW IN THE LANDS
OF THE BRITISH DIASPORA

In the lands settled by the British Diaspora there were few *new* customary claims advanced by these settlers of commonly held property rights, both because there were fewer settlements that contained lands held in common and because there was less time for new customs to come into being. (The rule of the Common Law with regard to customs, after all, was that the customary right being claimed had existed "from time out of mind," not the sort of claim made very easily in a relatively new colonial settlement.)

But a *few* customary rights *were* created. We will meet one, born on the Grand Banks, pertaining to the fisherman's rights to a share of the catch, in Chapter 6. Bruce Kercher reports another in New South Wales: Those settling that first Australian colony "held their lands on chains of oral agreements and scraps of paper" (a phenomenon that prevailed as well in several North American colonies in the seventeenth century). The early judge-advocates in New South Wales simply ignored both the Common-Law rules regarding the presence of the Great Seal on such transfers of title, and the proclamations of that colony's governors regarding written titles and proper registration, since "custom was already entrenched" (see Chapter 3). The same may be said of the forms of mortgaging and foreclosure in Western Australia: Attorney George Moore told his brother in Dublin in 1833 of "a short-cut mode of mortgaging land here, which will make it change hands with rapidity." Moore justified rendering land "as transferable as any other property" since "we have nothing to do with the old feudal reasons for making land inalienable." In 1838 he wrote of "an information" he had just filed "in the nature of a bill for foreclosure." "You would have been horrified to see the bill," he teased his brother: "I left out all the charging and confederating and interrogating parts, and did not make use of one word that was not absolutely necessary, so that the whole bill was contained in part of a sheet of paper." When the Land Claims Commissioners in Fiji made their final report in 1882 to Governor Des Voeux, they explained that the difficulties they had faced in resolving the land claims of Diaspora planters (many of whom were from Australia): The evidence of a deed was frequently "merely a sale note of the most irregular and informal character, written on any scrap of paper procurable...."[17]

---

[17] Kercher, *Unruly Child,* 51; Kercher, *Debt, Seduction & Other Disasters: The Birth of Civil Law in Convict New South Wales* (Annandale, NSW, 1996), 126; Moore, *Diary of Ten Years Eventful Life in Western Australia* (1884), 179, 364; W. P. Morrell, *Britain in the Pacific Islands* (Oxford, 1960), 388–89.

Several other customs devolved from the day-by-day doings of Spanish, French, and British traders and settlers in California, the southwest, Louisiana, and the Mississippi and Ohio Valleys. These residents, some with roots well over 100 years deep, had developed tradition-bound claims to water, alluvial soil, salt pans, and fish by the time that the Common Lawyers and their courts arrived in the early and mid-nineteenth century. Their disputes went, routinely, to *alcaldes* and notaries "knowing the temperament and character of each one of the inhabitants of their respective jurisdictions," officials "cognizant of the manners & customs prevailing in the district in regard to fences, animals, & above all, the sale & trading in horses" in order "to settle their differences & pass judgements on their disputes," as one commandant at Natchez wrote of those in his domain. Consequently these Spanish and French residents could burst into outrage and sometimes violence, when those rights were infringed upon, often by the *nouveau arrives* as in Louisiana and St. Louis in the early nineteenth century, California in mid-century, and New Mexico territory in the 1870s.[18] Let one example, drawn from the work of George Dargo, suffice.

Residents of New Orleans claimed and enjoyed the customary right to the alluvial sand and soil along the Batture St. Mary, basing their claim on their understanding of the rule in the Spanish *Partidas*. They claimed as well the right to use the Batture as a wharf. In 1807, recently arrived attorney Edward Livingston successfully represented John Gravier's claim of title to the Batture before the newly created Superior Court (comprised of three Common-Law jurists). Livingston

[18] See Richard White, *The Middle Ground: Indians, Empires and Republics in the Great Lakes, 1650–1815* (Cambridge U. P., 1991), 423 (on appointment of J. M. P. Legras by American authorities as "Judge of the Court" at Vincennes in 1784 to arbitrate disputes); Stuart Banner, "Written Law and Unwritten Norms in Colonial St. Louis," 14 *Law & History Review* 33 at 51, 63 (1996); Banner, "The Political Function of the Commons: Changing Conceptions of Property and Sovereignty in Missouri, 1750–1850," 41 *American Journal of Legal History* 61 at 74–75 (1997) (French residents owning common rights to fenced fields protest actions of Spanish lieutenant governor to grant some to merchants in 1788, and actions of U.S. commandant at St. Charles to survey and grant commonly held fields in 1804); David Langum, *Law and Community on the Mexican-Californian Frontier* (Norman, 1987); Fredrick Nolan, *The Lincoln County War* (Norman, Okla., 1992), 49, 174 (on Mexican residents of New Mexico territory's violent reaction to Anglo settlers' abuse of irrigation ditches on Tularosa Creek in 1873 and to Anglo landowners' halting of the "traditional right to haul salt from the saline lakes" near San Elizario in 1877). For French examples of the same struggle between customary and newer positive law in the nineteenth century see Eugene Weber, *Peasants into Frenchmen: The Modernization of Rural France, 1870–1914* (Stanford, 1976), 57–60.

received one-third of the Batture under a contingency fee arrangement as his reward, but when he sought to "improve" his new property,
his workers were driven away by a crowd of angry locals. The new governor, William Claiborne, sought to defuse the tension by persuading
President Jefferson to order the Batture seized as part of the public domain, and the governor thereupon enjoined Livingston from further
activities there and restored the residents' customary uses. Livingston
sued the federal authorities to regain the use of the property, but
conceded the residents most of their customary uses in the process.
Stuart Banner described French and Spanish residents of pre-1804
St. Louis, not New Orleans, but his verdict seems equally appropriate
to the Batture St. Mary dispute as well: They "understood law as something rising up from the bottom." The "ordinary practices of ordinary
people, worked out over countless human interactions, by their sheer
repetition became rules binding the community." The American officials who took control of these French communities after the Louisiana
Purchase, to the contrary, "understood law as something handed down
from the top."[19]

The Customary Law of Hunters, Fishermen, and Miners in the Lands of the British Diaspora

"They change their skies, but not their minds, who sail across the
sea," and as I have said, this describes the British Diaspora emigrants
to North America and the Antipodes; they brought their customs
in their seachests. Some New England communities recreated such
English customs as that of commonly held pasturage ("the commons")
complete with its customary rules, and these prevailed for some time.[20]
More significantly, miners claimed their customary rights to self-
management in the many goldfields located in nineteenth-century Di-
asporaland; and hunters, fishermen, and women claimed their

---

[19] George Dargo, *Jefferson's Louisiana: Politics and the Clash of Legal Traditions* (Cambridge, Mass., 1975), 76ff; Banner, "Written Law & Unwritten
Norms," 71. See also David Reichard, "The Politics of Village Water Disputes in Northern New Mexico, 1882–1905," 9 *Western Legal History* (1996)
(Pueblo Indians, Hispanic, and British Diaspora settlers contend for irrigation ditch (*acequia*) rights in the territorial court, pitting customary
water-sharing practices devised before *alcalde* courts against the Common-
Law rule of prior appropriation).

[20] See, for example, David Grayson Allen, *In English Ways: The Movement of
Societies and the Transferal of Local Laws and Custom to Massachusetts Bay in the
Seventeenth Century* (1981). The traditional rights of "commoners" slowly
died out; we no longer graze cows on the Green in New Haven, for example.
But in the mid-nineteenth century, a number of cities would create new
park-commons rights (of "strolling"), as in New York's Central Park.

customary rights in the "woods" and "bush," and in the rivers, bays, and coastal waters.

The Customary Rights of Hunters and the Law

Throughout the colonies of North America British Diaspora settlers claimed the right to hunt game in much the same fashion as they had in the British Isles. Some of the royal charters (such as Pennsylvania's) recited the Common-Law right of settlers "to fowl and hunt upon the lands they hold, and all other lands not enclosed, and to fish in all waters of said lands." But many settlers claimed more. One English visitor to the Carolina backcountry in the early eighteenth century marveled in his diary at the "large scope" that "property hath" in the New World: Hunting was "being as freely and peremptorily enjoyed by the meanest planter, as he that is the highest in dignity," and there were "no strict laws" to "bind" the "privileges" of "a poor laborer that is master of his gun" such as to "satisfy the appetite of the rich alone." Another English visitor offered a similar view a century later:

> People go where they like, and, as to wild animals, shoot what they like. There is the Common Law, which forbids *trespass*, and the Statute Law ... of ... trespass *after warning*. [But] nobody that I ever hear of *warns people off*. [21]

Many farmers and other landowners did eventually "post" their land, of course, claiming advantage of the Law. But there is plenty of evidence that the "customary law" of the mass of hunters did not respect such "postings." William Elliott reported in the late 1850s that "the right to hunt wild animals" was "held by the great body of people" as "one of their franchises." They "submit with the worst possible grace!" to "all limitations" on what he called "their code." "Ferae naturae" were "the property of him who can take them – irrespective of any conflicting right in the owner of the soil." Elliott represented the following exchange as a scene he had observed in a Carolina courtroom, where a hunter, sued for trespass, was being cross-examined by the landowner's counsel:

COUNSEL: Would you pursue a deer if he entered your neighbor's inclosure?
WITNESS: Certainly.
COUNSEL: What if his fields were planted, and his cotton growing, or his grain ripe?

---

[21] John Lawson, *The Historie of Carolina* (1714), 29; William Cobbett, *A Year's Residence in the United States* (2nd ed., 1819), 376; quoted in James A. Tober, *Who Owns the Wildlife? The Political Economy of Conservation in Nineteenth-Century America* (1981), 27.

WITNESS: It would make no difference; I should follow my dogs, go where they might!

JUDGE: And pull down your neighbor's fence, and trample on his fields?

WITNESS: I should do it – though I might regret to injure him!

JUDGE: You would commit a trespass; you would be mulcted in damages. There is no law for such an act!

WITNESS: It is hunter's law, however![22]

These were not Elliott's sentiments, mind you; he was one of the new breed of American "gentlemen–sportsmen" who had emerged by the mid-nineteenth century, quite imitative of "the hunt set" of the British Isles. Like other readers of *American Sportsman* and *Forest and Stream,* Elliott represented an elite, conservationist minority, who sought to protect dwindling species of game with statutes. Influenced as Elliott was by the perspective of his British counterparts, he attributed these objectionable popular norms to "the labouring emigrants from England," positing that it was *they,* "who, mixing with the [working] classes of our own white population," had led them to "their deep disgust at the tyranny of the English game laws." Such immigrants were prompted by "the sorest and best remembered of their griefs – transportation, for killing a hare or partridge!"[23] This surely overstated the importance of relatively *recent* English emigrants on popular norms, but it may have captured the essential sentiments of much *earlier* ones. In any event, the people's "code" on the subject was stated by "A Vermonter" who told the readers of *Forest and Stream* in 1876 that it was "better *every* game bird and fish be destroyed" than to permit property owners, "who appear to think they ought to be the only ones who should have the right to hunt and fish," to "post" their land.[24]

It seems clear that juries in such cases were quite reluctant to convict such "trespassers" unless their conduct had been persistent and outrageous, explicitly "market-oriented" or "outsiders." Jurymen in rural Colorado were probably no more discriminating in these matters than those elsewhere. While they acquitted local "poachers," they were "only too glad" to convict a gentleman–sportsman "stranger in the land, or one coming from the city or town," for "coming down and killing 'their' game." Perhaps Wisconsin's district attorneys and justices of the peace were not uncharacteristic either in their ignoring the rulings of the state's supreme court by declaring the state's fish and

---

[22] William Elliott, *Carolina Sports by Land and Water* (1859), 32–33, 285–86, 289–90; quoted in Stuart Marks, *Southern Hunting in Black and White: Nature, History and Ritual in a Carolina Community* (Princeton, 1991), 32.

[23] Elliott, 291–92.

[24] "A Vermonter," 7 *Forest and Stream* (Dec. 14, 1876), 297, quoted in Tober, 121.

game statutes unconstitutional and refusing "to hear the cases brought before them."[25]

Colonial American assemblies concerned about the depletion of game began to pass seasonal limits on the hunting of deer and wildfowl and to restrict the netting of salmon in the early eighteenth century. But these and a host of later statutes were out of sync with the "customary law" of the hunter-majority. Thus, New Hampshire's statute limiting the hunting of deer (passed in 1740) was simply unenforced until the creation of the office of State Game Commissioner in 1878. Settlers in the Valley of the Lower Thames in Ontario "paid little attention" to a conservation-minded statute passed in 1839, prohibiting the killing of game in the spring and summer. Some were thereupon hauled into court, but these individuals paid relatively modest fines that did little to check the practice. When Maine's legislature, inspired by the growing "gentleman–sportsman" tourist trade, passed statutes in the late nineteenth century designed to limit one's seasonal quota of moose and elk, local "Down Easterners" reacted with anger and defiance. One man, George Magoon, acquired lasting fame by killing a game warden who had sought to arrest him.[26] California's modest efforts in the late nineteenth century to protect spawning salmon met resistance from those who sought wildlife for something other than their own dietary sustenance or mere sport: One defendant admitted in court to having illegally netted salmon. The judge thereupon instructed the jury that the evidence warranted a guilty verdict, but the jury "found him not guilty" after little more than "a ten-minute deliberation," or so the California State Board of Fish Commissioners reported in 1892. They added that their officials were then "followed" from "the court-room to the hotel, and from the hotel to the [railroad] station," by "a howling mob of thirty to forty men and boys," all in all "a most insulting demonstration."[27]

Despite the fact that Australia was still made up of colonies subject to British Law, the story appears to have been much the same there – that is, settlers of all social status hunted game with weapons of their choice essentially without interference from the Law. From a cattle station on the Goulburn in the mid-nineteenth century John Cotton wrote an old "billiard-playing" friend of his in London that it was "not

[25] Colorado State Fish & Game Commission Report, 1904/06, cited in Tober, 132; Elliott, 292.

[26] See Edward Ives, *George Magoon and the Down East Game War: History, Folklore, and the Law* (Urbana, 1988) F. C. Hamil, *The Valley of the Lower Thames, 1640 to 1850* (Toronto, 1951), 213, 259.

[27] Biennial Report of the State Board of Fish Commissioners, 1891–92, 18, delightfully reported in James Tober, *Who Owns the Wildlife*, 138n.

necessary to take out a license to carry a gun; one shoulders it at pleasure and hunts without fear of trespassing." Of necessity, Cotton armed his stationhands as well, and he knew they hunted too. In fact, the "master" and the "servant" often hunted side by side.[28]

Mining Customs and the Law

Since the Middle Ages, Cornish tin miners had enjoyed their own Stannary parliament to determine the rights and duties of miners in that corner of the English realm. They had secured the right of entry over the waste land of another for mining purposes, the same right that would be asserted on the public and private lands of North America and the Antipodes. Similarly, the "free miners" of the Forest of Dean had for centuries been governed by their own Mine Law Court and were entitled, upon coming of age, each to his own "gale," or tract of land for a mine pit, as well as to the customary rights of pannage and estover in the Forest.[29] The formal Law with regard to mines in the first major American "gold rush" in California was that of Spanish Civil Law, that the State held the subsurface rights to all mineral wealth. But the U.S. military governor of the recently conquered California territory quickly "abolished all Mexican mining laws and customs." He then "considered selling" twenty to forty-acre plots, or "charging miners a license fee of $100 to $1000 for the privilege of working claims" a month after gold had been discovered (January 1848). But that July he visited the miners' camps, and, despite the fact that he had 660 soldiers available to him, he sagely changed his mind. Deploying troops in the gold-rush region would have been an invitation to them to desert. In any event, he reported that, "upon considering the large extent of the country" and "the character of the people engaged," he was "resolved not to interfere, but to permit all to work freely."[30] Consequently, disputes among the gold-rush "Argonauts" of the late 1840s and early 1850s, were resolved by a kind of on-the-spot court comparable to the marketplace's pie-powder courts – the "miner's meeting"(see Illustration 1). "Anyone who desired could call a meeting," the first historian of American mining, Charles Shinn, wrote in the early 1880s. "A person who thought himself wronged would tell his friends, and they would tell others, till the miners of the region would assemble, if they thought the case sufficient, but, if not, would

---

[28] Maie Casey, *An Australian Story, 1837–1907* (Melbourne, 1960), 81.

[29] Ralph Anstis, *Warren James and the Dean Forest Riots* (1986), 7, 14.

[30] Colonel Richard Mason, quoted in Pisani, 127 (the words in quotation-marks describing Mason's original plans are Pisani's). Cf. Ray August, "Gringos and Mineros: Hispanic Origins of American Mining Law," 9 *Western Legal History* 147 (1996).

Illustration 1.   Samuel T. Gill depicted a dispute over a claim in the
gold diggings fields of southeastern Australia in the early 1850s. In
"The Claim Disputed" one can see miners responding to the call of an
adjacent digger for a meeting to resolve the matter according to the
customary laws of miners. (La Trobe Picture Collection, State Library
of Victoria, 967186.)

ignore the call." Shinn quoted one "old pioneer" as saying "we needed
no law until the lawyers came," and he referred to "camp-custom" and
"honor between men." Shinn's account may have been romanticizing
the mining communities of the American West; there is plenty of evidence that violence was used against Mexican and Chinese miners, for
example. But, more generally, it sounds very much like the descriptions of other mining communities in the Antipodes and Canada in
the same century. (Thus, Anthony Trollope, the novelist, who observed
miners in both the Americas and the Antipodes, concluded that their
system of self-policing worked, both before and after the arrival of
the formal Law. Speaking of the process at the Gympie minefields in
Queensland, Trollope wrote that "the miners do not fight and knock
each other about. . . . They not infrequently go to law. They do not
punch each other's heads."[31])

[31] Trollope, *Australia and New Zealand* (2 vols., London, 1873), I, 82. See also
   Thomas Stone, "The Mounties as Vigilantes: Perceptions of Community
   and the Transformation of Law in the Yukon, 1865–1897," in *Historical*

Bogue Ejecting the Squatters.—See page 6.

Illustration 2.   Charles Nahl's "Bogue Ejecting the Squatters" (from
Old Block's Sketch-Book depicting life in the California gold fields, also
in the early 1850s) suggests that claim infringements of a blatant nature may not have required a miners' meeting. (California Historical
Society, North Baker Research Library, FN-30963)

With miners, one of the central issues was protecting one's "claim"
from "jumpers" when one was away, assaying the month's gold yield
and purchasing supplies. Miners in the California Gold Rush years
were vitally concerned with questions of title, and in the first stages of
activity there was often no local authority to turn to. A notice at the
claim-site might warn that Thomas Hall intended to protect his stake
"by shotgun amendments," or that John Searle would defend his "at
the pint of the sichs shuter [sic] if legally Necessary so taik head and
good warnin" (see Illustration 2). Claims were often overlapping, or
temporarily abandoned, and establishing the time that the parties had
arrived on the scene or filed a claim could prove difficult for easy and
amicable resolution. Who was "jumping" whom?
    Another major problem concerned water. Some California gold-
rush miner "codes" rejected the Common Law's "prior appropriation"
rule, which would have allowed the first on the scene to turn water
from its natural channel for their own ends. Water was to be shared.

Perspectives on Law & Society in Canada, ed. Tina Loo and Lorna McLean
    (Toronto, 1994), 124.

When "miners' meetings" and arbitration efforts failed to curb violators of these "codes," Donald Pisani tells us, miners "dynamited ditches, chopped down wooden diversion dams, and tore down or burned flumes."[32] But once the in-stream days had given way to the hillside-oriented, shovel, pick, and spade pursuit of gold in sinuosities, and then in turn to the hydraulic savaging of the hillside, the formal Law was called upon – by the hydraulic-mining corporations who could not provide sufficient water power for the process without the application of the "prior appropriation" rule. This placed small-scale mine partnerships at a disadvantage. One group of such Argonauts complained in a local newspaper in October, 1853, that the hydraulic-mining companies were tyrants who had "crept into our midst" in "the form of a lamb." "The community" was being "gored into surfdom [sic]" by "a two-horned beast, whose right horn is bread, and the left horn water." And the courts were more enemy than friend in this process, for the small-scale mine operators were being warned by the companies that "we are to be harassed and embarrassed with endless and perplexing law suits, that will cost more than all the claims are worth...."[33]

Most gold fields in British Columbia, the Yukon, Victoria, Queensland, and New Zealand were also without formal Law officers in their first several months. The "law" in this hiatus was provided, as in the American West, by "miners' meetings." These functioned satisfactorily throughout most of the Antipodes, British Columbia, and the Yukon. In Victoria, however, miners were called upon to pay a monthly fee to goldfield commissioners for the right to work a claim in the 1850s (see Illustration 3). After all, the Crown claimed demesne title to all subsurface precious minerals. In the vast goldfields of Victoria, especially at Ballarat in 1854, miners resisted this fee collection, held protest meetings, torched a hotel that had housed licensing officials, publicly burnt their licenses, and circulated "manifestos" condemning "despotism" that were deemed "treasonable" by the authorities. An army regiment was dispatched; it stormed the miners' stockade (see Illustrations 4 and 5). Some thirteen miners were tried for high treason in Melbourne, where the jury acquitted them all. Between 1851 and 1861 the population of Victoria rose by a factor of eight, and most of the new residents were miners. By 1855, the miners had secured the franchise and eight seats on the Legislative Council of Victoria, and this led to the replacement of the monthly fees with a one-time fee for "the right to mine" and an export tax of 2s. 6d. per ounce on the

[32] Pisani, " 'I am Resolved not to Interfere but permit all to work freely': The Gold Rush and American Resource Law," 77 *California History* 123 (1998–99), 136.
[33] Quoted in Pisani, 136.

Illustration 3. California's military governer declined to collect license fees for the privilege of gold mining, but Victoria's chose to do so, dispatching police to verify compliance, as indicated in Samuel T. Gill's "The Licence Inspected," 1851. (La Trobe Picture Collection, State Library of Victoria, H86.7.)

gold, thus shifting most of the financial burden to the more successful diggers. The Law's Goldfield Commissioner's courts were replaced as well, with elected miners' courts.[34]

On New Zealand's South Island the goldfields near Nelson were policed initially by elected committees of twelve miners, but constables

---

[34] J. M. Powell, *The Public Lands of Australia Felix* (Oxford, 1970), 59; C. P. Billot, *The Life and Times of John Pascoe Fawkner* (Melbourne, 1985), 287–95; Kercher, *Unruly Child*, 131–33; John Molony, *Eureka* (Ringwood, 1984), 100.

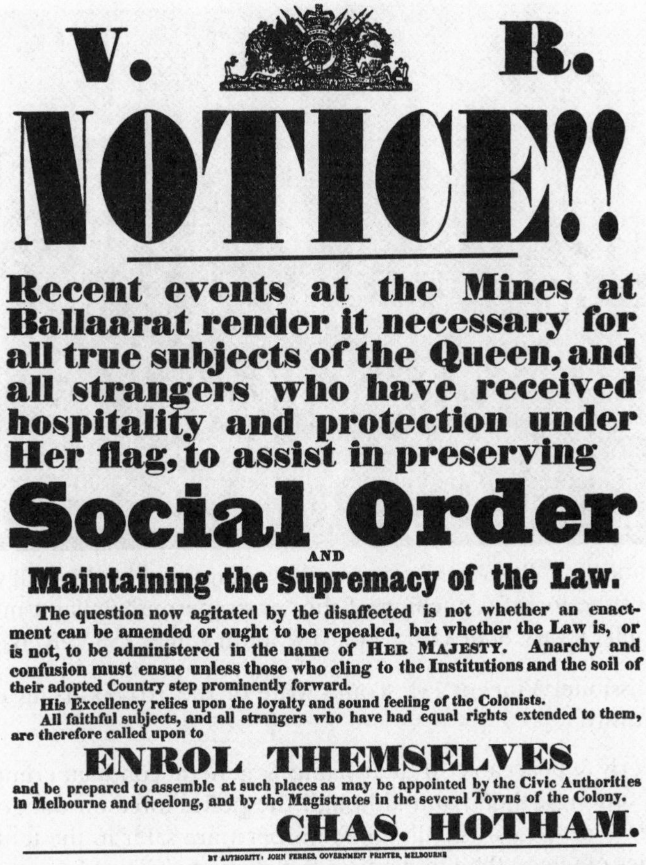

V. R.

NOTICE!!

Recent events at the Mines at Ballaarat render it necessary for all true subjects of the Queen, and all strangers who have received hospitality and protection under Her flag, to assist in preserving

Social Order

AND

Maintaining the Supremacy of the Law.

The question now agitated by the disaffected is not whether an enactment can be amended or ought to be repealed, but whether the Law is, or is not, to be administered in the name of HER MAJESTY. Anarchy and confusion must ensue unless those who cling to the Institutions and the soil of their adopted Country step prominently forward.

His Excellency relies upon the loyalty and sound feeling of the Colonists.

All faithful subjects, and all strangers who have had equal rights extended to them, are therefore called upon to

ENROL THEMSELVES

and be prepared to assemble at such places as may be appointed by the Civic Authorities in Melbourne and Geelong, and by the Magistrates in the several Towns of the Colony.

CHAS. HOTHAM.

BY AUTHORITY: JOHN FERRES, GOVERNMENT PRINTER, MELBOURNE

Illustration 4. The Crown responded to their "illegal" behavior with this call for volunteers to "assist in preserving Social Order and Maintaining the Supremacy of the Law." (La Trobe Picture Collection, State Library of Victoria, H33816.)

were welcomed when they finally appeared. Several years later, in 1861, gold was detected further south in the Otago district and miners again formed their "own police and government" before welcoming constables who agreed to "operate, inter alia, a code of mining" that had been "drawn up by the miners." Victoria's goldfield constables had been detested and were remembered, because they had been the ones to collect the monthly fees, and because they received half of all fines imposed by the assistant goldfield commissioners there for any noncompliance. Otago's officialdom avoided this pitfall from the start, opting for the export-tax alternative. Hence, in 1862, Goldfield

Illustration 5. Push soon came to shove, captured by this Ball water-
color of the forceful quelling of the "obstreperous" Ballarat miners.
(Mitchell Library, State Library of New South Wales, ZSS V2B/Ball/7.)

Commissioner Vincent Pyle could write of the 10,000-strong miner
community:

> Orderly & peaceable in their habits & general conduct, crime is
> rare amongst them, and although the police-force on the gold-
> fields is necessarily small, life & property are safer in the tented
> gullies of Otago than in many of the cities of civilized Europe.[35]

As in Victoria, New Zealand miners could be less "orderly" when
they perceived officialdom interfering with their "right" to find gold
wherever it had been reported. In 1869, gold was discovered in the
Wangapeha region of the South Island; within weeks over 100 men
were digging at Blue Creek. One policeman reported their resistance
to "official efforts to survey the land for farming." "The men," Charles
Broad told Robert Shallcross, the Island's Chief Inspector, "are in an
utter state of rebellion to all authority." An effort to arrest the leaders was forcefully resisted. "They did not care for the consequences,"

---

[35] Richard Hill, *Policing the Colonial Frontier: The Theory and Practice of Coercive
Social and Racial Control in New Zealand, 1767–1867* (2 vols., Wellington,
1986), II, 544, 545, 582–83, 602, 726. See also A. G. Shaw, "Violent Protest in
Australian History," 15 *Historical Studies* No. 60 (1970); and Owen Morgan,
"The Crown's Right to Gold and Silver in New Zealand," 1 *Australian Journal
of Legal History* 51 (1995).

Broad reported; consequently he and his men retreated "down-valley."
Judge Richmond declared the miners to be in a state of insurrection,
as indeed they were. But that was as much as Richmond's Law could
accomplish; the government balked at further use of force and surrendered the ground, declaring the area a goldfield, which by then
it clearly was. (Robert Shallcross, the Chief Inspector, became a silent
partner in one claim himself.)[36]

The American and Antipodal experiences were quickly drawn upon
in British Columbia when gold was discovered on the Fraser River.
American miners at Wild Horse Creek elected a judge, sheriff, and
prosecutor "until the proper authorities arrive." There were only two
revenue collectors and only one magistrate in the region in the first
year of the Fraser River gold-rush, and Cole Harris tells us that "the
miners hardly took them seriously."[37]

But if the Law posed no threat to the Fraser River miners, the Indian
tribes of that region did. Governor Douglas reported that they "threatened to 'make a clean sweep' " of those miners at Hill's Bar in June,
1858, for having taken "large quantities of gold" from "their country." A strong force of native warriors approached Yale in August. This
prompted a group of miners from the States to organize a "militia."
Negotiations produced a survey of the lands that the tribes wanted to
be protected as well as the dispatch of some magistrates to help protect them. Thereafter the tribes accepted the miners, sold them produce and game, and some Indians took jobs in the mine camps.[38] The
Hudson's Bay Company's governor for the region, Sir James Douglas,
tried to mandate mining fees, registration, and regulation from above,
but "could not withstand the hordes of invading miners who imposed
on themselves their own regulations, which, if not legal, were not
demonstrably illegal and were far more practical." So, in 1859 Governor Douglas accepted this arrangement, formalizing it along
Australian and New Zealand lines by proclaiming into existence Gold-
Fields Commissioners overseeing miner courts and Mining Boards, to
be created upon the petition of 100 miners in order to register claims
and allocate water rights.

36 Richard Hill, *The Colonial Frontier Tamed: New Zealand Policing in Transition,
    1867–1886* (Wellington, 1989), 165.
37 Harris, *Resettlement of British Columbia*, 110.
38 Sidney Harring, *White Man's Law*, 188, 195; Fisher, *Contact and Conflict*,
    95–118. For other evidence of Indian-miner tension in Canada see Cole
    Harris, *Resettlement of British Columbia*, 122; and Rhonda Telford, "Aborigi-
    nal Resistance in the Mid-Nineteenth Century: The Anishnabi, Their Allies,
    and the Closing of the Mining Operation at Mica Bay and Michipicoton
    Island," 5 Camp Wanapitei Colloquium (Sept. 27, 1999).

But when Chief Justice Matthew Begbie set aside a jury verdict in
a claims-jumping case that one of these miners' courts had heard in
the Fraser River in 1865, and decided the case on appeal himself, over
500 miners gathered before the Richfield courthouse within a week
to condemn his action, ask for his removal, and petition the legislature of British Columbia for a statute to halt the setting aside of jury
verdicts. The legislature did so in 1867, by limiting all appeals from
miners' court to questions of law. Consequently, as Tina Loo has shown,
Justice Begbie declared that he was unable to hear an appeal from the
magistrate's verdict, inasmuch as the only issue in doubt had been a
factual one – namely, had one duly-licensed mining company and its
men abandoned a mine-site, permitting a second company of miners
to move in, or had they *not* abandoned it? The magistrates who heard
the case decided that the company had not, but they were unable to
get the second company of miners to obey their order to relinquish
the mine. The new governor of British Columbia visited the site in an
effort to secure compliance without violence, and officials managed
to arrest and place on trial seven of the recalcitrants. They were sentenced to terms of three months imprisonment, but six of the seven
refused to go to jail! Thereupon the governor secured a compromise:
two days of incarceration with the doors unlocked in exchange for a
promise that their appeal would indeed be heard, not by Begbie, but by
his nemesis, Joseph Needham, Chief Justice of the Vancouver Island
Supreme Court. The six men thereupon marched off to jail where
they enjoyed "grog," visits from their friends, "songs," and "a derisive
hoot at the officials. . . . " Justice Needham then found against them,
affirming the findings of the magistrates, and the appellant company
of recently liberated miners finally surrendered the mine. The Law
had managed a measured triumph, but largely on terms acceptable to
the trespassers.[39]

Miners' meetings later resolved disputes again in the Yukon in the
1890s (yielding reluctantly to more formal legal authority with the arrival of Royal Canadian Mounties in 1896).[40] But "miners' meetings"
were cumbersome. Just as the first gold-rush "Argonauts" in California

[39] Tina Loo, *Making Law, Order and Authority in British Columbia, 1821–1871*
(Toronto, 1994), 116–21.
[40] David Ricardo Williams, "The Administration of Criminal and Civil Justice
in the Mining Camps and Frontier Communities of British Columbia,"
in *Law & Justice in a New Land: Essays in Western Canadian Legal History*,
ed. Louis Knalfa (Calgary, 1986), 220–22; Thomas Stone, "The Mounties as Vigilantes: Perceptions of Community and the Transformation
of Law in the Yukon, 1885–1897," in *Historical Perspectives on Law &
Society in Canada*, ed. Tina Loo and Lorna McLean (Toronto, 1994),
124.

soon created three-man committees to settle disputes, during the Alaska–Yukon Gold Rush of the 1890s that generation of miners policed their domain in that same fashion. And, once again, this system of self-generated "law" appears to have worked reasonably well. As one who worked at Circle City in 1896 put it, "Here there was no murder, stealing, or dishonesty, and right was right and wrong was wrong as each individual understood it. Here life, property and honor were safe.... "[41]

Customary Fishing Rights and the Law

Establishing title to one's claim or farm was the *sine qua non* for settlers and miners alike; the land they sought was fixed, bounded. Hunters and trappers sought access to unbounded, unsettled land. Fishermen and women might require the rights of a riparian landowner if the catch they sought were spawning salmon, but those trolling coastal waters for cod, shrimp, sardines, or tuna, or pursuing whales throughout the oceans faced fewer such problems: Their "range" was open; their harvest, free (though they might decide to agree to divide up a bay or coastal range).

Early New England fishermen were authorized to "make use of such harbours and grounds" that had not yet been purchased from the Proprietors, and "to take timber and wood at their pleasure." Some purchased small tracts of their own for a cottage, a garden, a small orchard, and a few animals. Competition and frontier orneryness initially checked the creation of peaceful modes of resolving disputes. Companies of fishermen sometimes encroached on one another's cod drying sites, "pulling downe, ruinateinge, and breakeing up" the moorings, stages, and flakes of others', as at Piscataqua, Marblehead, and various harbors in Massachusetts and Maine during the mid- and late seventeenth century. In short, the first few generations of New England fishermen could be "trouble-som people" to the Massachusetts Bay Colony's first governor, John Winthrop. In Newfoundland, as we will see in Chapter 3, it would be the government that would stand in the way of fishermen and their families who sought title to a plot for a potato garden and a house; Newfoundland was seen by mercantilist Britain as a refitting place for the cod fishery, not a homeland. But

---

[41] Charles H. Shinn, *Mining Camps: A Study in American Frontier Government* (New York, 1884), 25–30, 112, 123, 126, 250ff; Arthur T. Walden, *A Dog Puncher on the Yukon* (Boston, 1928), 45, noted in Thomas Stone, "The Mounties as Vigilantes: Perceptions of Community and the Transformation of Law in the Yukon, 1885–1897," in *Historical Perspectives on Law & Society in Canada*, ed. Tina Loo & Lorna McLean (Toronto, 1994), 123. Compare John Phillip Reid, *Law for the Elephant: Property and Social Behavior on The Overland Trail* (San Marino, Calif., 1980).

persistent fishermen finally acquired title to their little farms there none the less.[42]

American whalers developed customary rules regarding the ownership of "fast" and "loose" whales by the late eighteenth century, and both English and U.S. federal-district judges honored these customs.[43] And the Diaspora settlers living along the rivers of colonial British North America where salmon spawned exercised customary riparian rights to fish with weirs, racks, and scoop nets, and were prepared to ignore or to savage politically those legislators who undermined those rights, be they in Rhode Island, Pennsylvania, Massachusetts, or elsewhere.[44] In the waters of the Sacramento River and the San Francisco Bay, Greek and Italian salmon fishermen formally divided the gill-net harvest among some one hundred-odd boats from 1872 on, allocating each no more than forty fish per day in order to maintain both the supply and the fresh-market price. Chinese shrimpers and abalone hunters "arbitrated their own conflicts" and divided their fishing grounds. U.S. Fish Commission researcher David Starr Jordan reported to Congress in 1887 that "everything is governed by laws which the fishermen have made for themselves." The monopolistic character of this division of the spoils-of-the-sea offended Progressive politicians in the fin-de-siecle, who used Law to destroy it. "In the process," Arthur McEvoy observes, they exposed the fish "to the full force of market pressures and ultimately encouraged depletion."[45]

Even more intense tensions developed between Indian communities exercising such customary fishing rights in Nova Scotia, the Great

[42] Gerald Sider, *Culture and Class in Anthropology and History: A Newfoundland Illustration* (Cambridge, 1986), 114; Daniel Vickers, *Farmers and Fishermen: Two Centuries of Work in Essex County, Massachusetts, 1630–1850* (Chapel Hill, 1994), 103, 122.

[43] Elmo Hohman, *The American Whaleman* (1928), 66, 166; Herman Melville, *Moby Dick* (1851), ch. 89 (Penguin ed., 1972, 504–05); *Addison & Sons v. Row*, 3 Paton (Scotland) 339 (1794); *Fennings v. Lord Grenville*, 1 Taunt. 241, 127 ER 825 (C.P., 1808); *Swift v. Gifford*, 23 Fed. Cas. 558 (D. Mass. 1872); Oliver Wendell Holmes, Jr., *The Common Law* (Boston, 1881), 212 (p. 168 in 1963 Little, Brown ed.).

[44] See Gary Kulick, "Dams, Fish and Farmers: [18th century Rhode Island]," in *The Countryside in the Age of Capitalist Transformation*, ed. Jonathan Prude (Chapel Hill, 1985); Carl Bridenbaugh, *Cities in the Wilderness: The First Century of Urban Life in America, 1625–1742* (N.Y., 1964), 382–83 (on rioting against Pennsylvania statute in 1738 banning fish weirs and racks in the Schuylkill); Theodore Steinberg, *Nature Incorporated: Industrialization and the Waters of New England* (Cambridge, Mass., 1991); Harry Watson, " 'The Common Rights of Mankind': Subsistence, Shad, and Commerce in the Early Republican South," 83 *Journal of American History* 13 (1996).

[45] Arthur McEvoy, *The Fisherman's Problem: Ecology and Law in the California Fisheries, 1850–1980* (N.Y., 1986), 95–99.

Lakes, the Oregon Territory, California, Australia, and New Zealand and the efforts of Diaspora governments and fishermen to infringe on those rights.[46] And it is this tension, between the customary property rights of the indigenous people of North America and the Antipodes, and the Law of British Diaspora fishermen, miners, hunters, pastoralists, and farmers, that we turn our attention to next.

THE CENTRAL CONTEST: THE LAW OF ENGLAND AND OF
THE RESPONSIBLE GOVERNMENT OF THE LANDS OF THE
BRITISH DIASPORA CONFRONT CUSTOMARY PROPERTY
RIGHTS OF THE ABORIGINAL INHABITANTS OF NORTH
AMERICA AND THE ANTIPODES

Propitious Beginnings: The Law's Accommodative Epoch

None of the lands settled by the British Diaspora were uninhabited. For tens of thousands of years the "aboriginals" had hunted, fished, and gathered roots and berries, and many had cultivated the soil as well in North America and the Antipodes. Now their lands were sought by the people of an expanding British Empire. How would the Law mediate the conflicting property claims of aboriginal and newcomer? How did the British Diaspora ultimately acquire lawful title to the aboriginal's patrimony?

Whether title to native land was acquired by transfers acceptable to the Crown or by illegal private sale, "quiet enjoyment" of such title was often not possible without the resolution of some basic cultural

---

[46] Responsive to instructions from the Crown, Governor James Douglas crafted some fourteen treaties with tribes on Vancouver Island in the early 1850s, offering guarantees regarding their fisheries, but his successors were not as scrupulous. See Hamar Foster, "The Saanichton Bay Marina Case: Imperial Law, Colonial History & Competing Theories of Aboriginal Title," 23 *Univ. of British Columbia Law Review* 629 (1989). See also Desmond Sweeney, "Fishing, Hunting and Gathering Rights of Aboriginal Peoples in Australia," 16 *Univ. of New South Wales Law Journal* 97 (1993); P. G. McHugh, "Maori Fishing Rights and the North American Indian," 6 *Otago Law Review* 65 (1985); D. E. Sanders, "Indian Hunting and Fishing Rights," 38 *Saskatchewan Law Review* 45–243 (1970); Leslie Upton, *Micmacs and Colonists*; Dianne Newell, *Tangled Webs of History: Indians and the Law in Canada's Pacific Coast Fisheries* (Univ. of Toronto Press, 1993); and Arthur McEvoy, *The Fisherman's Problem: Ecology and Law in the California Fisheries, 1850–1980* (Cambridge Univ. Press, 1986), ch. 1. And look for the ongoing work of Douglas Harris, whose paper, "The Law Runs Through it: Fish Weirs, Sport Fishing, Seine Nets and Lumber Mills on the Cowichan River," describes the conflict over legal norms in the late nineteenth century, between the Cowichan people of Vancouver Island, immigrant fishermen, and the lumber industry.

disputes. In Australia, New Zealand, and Canada, as in the thirteen colonies and the American West, there would be disagreements between the aboriginal peoples and the Diaspora newcomers over rights to wild resources (fish and game in the unfenced "waste" ("woods," "bush")), disputes regarding precisely who had the right to represent all the native inhabitants in the alienation of the land, and often a failure of communication across the Diaspora and native cultures as to what exactly was meant by "ownership."[47]

In the early seventeenth century, English Law had it that all transfers of title to land from natives to colonial settlers was to be administered solely by the Crown, which by virtue of having "discovered" its colonies was their lawful owner of all the land in its "sovereign" capacity. Thus, Crown officials were the only ones sanctioned to acquire title from (that is, to "extinguish" the property rights of) the native inhabitants, and it was the only party from whom Diaspora settlers were to purchase land. Colonial governors made reasonably clear to settlers by proclamation and ordinance that no one was to purchase land from the native inhabitants excepting properly authorized officials of the Crown, and that any such acquisition by one other than an officer of the Crown or one of its duly chartered proprietors would not be recognized as legitimate.[48] This measure was intended to control the rate and pace of settlement and to preclude the fraudulent behavior

---

[47] A few examples at this point: Helen Rountree, *Pocahontas's People: The Powhatan Indians of Virginia through Four Centuries* (Norman, 1991), 128; Henry Reynolds, *Frontier: Aborigines, Settlers and Land* (St. Leonard's, NSW, 1987); Peter Taylor, *Station Life in Australia* (Sydney, 1988), ch. 6; Yasuhide Kawashima, *Puritan Justice and the Indian: White Man's Law in Massachusetts, 1630-1763* (Middletown, CT, 1986); Robert A. Williams, *The American Indian in Western Legal Thought: The Discourses of Conquest* (N.Y. 1990); Wilcomb E. Washburn, *Red Man's Land/White Man's Law: A Study of the Past and Present Status of the American Indian* (N.Y. 1971); and Imre Sutton, *Indian Land Tenure* (1975).

[48] Ian Brownlie, *Treaties and Indigenous Peoples* (Oxford, 1992), 31–35; Y. Kawashima, *Puritan Law and Indians*, 48 (on Massachusetts Bay Act of 1634 and Plymouth Colony ordinance of 1643); Frederika Hackshaw, "Nineteenth Century Notions of Aboriginal Title and their Influence on the Treaty of Waitangi," in *Waitangi*, ed. I. H. Kawharu (Oxford, 1989), 92, 103; Kent McNeil, *Common Law Aboriginal Title* (Oxford, 1989).

E. P. Thompson makes the all too common mistake of assuming that, because New England colonial leaders spoke of their biblical "higher right" to the land, that they also "appropriated" it from the native inhabitants without formal sales to colonial officials and subsequent transfers (*Customs in Common*, 165). This oversimplifies the process, albeit the *consequences* were at times as Thompson implied. See Kawashima, *Puritan Justice and the Indian*, 47–51, 60–61, 67–68.

that some British settlers quickly demonstrated they were capable of in their treating with individual natives for access to land. These rules were applied in New England, Pennsylvania, Nova Scotia, Vancouver Island, Victoria, and New Zealand in the generation of settlement, aided by officials with titles such as "Superintendent of Indian Affairs" or "Chief Protector of Aborigines."[49] Some illustrations follow.

The Thirteen Colonies/United States

In 1652, the Virginia Assembly granted that native tribes "keepe those seates of Land that they now have, And . . . noe person . . . be suffered to Intrech, or plant uppon Such places as the Indians claim, or desire, until full Leave from the Governor, & Councill, or Commissioners of that place," and they set aside fifty acres per warrior. Among the Virginia tribes involved in this measure was the Powhatans who believed that the rights to land that they had sold to the newcomers were akin to a usufructory "use" and that it would revert to them if not enclosed and used in timely fashion.[50] In 1660, Umpanchala, sachem of the Algonquins living in the recently settled Springfield region of the Massachusetts Bay colony, exchanged tribal land for trade debts, reserving the "liberty to hunt deere or other wild creatures and to take fish & to set wigwoms on ye comons & to take wood & trees for us." Several ordinances were created in the Massachusetts Bay colony further to protect natives by preventing the placing of liens against native-owned land for debt and by prohibiting the plying of natives with liquor to induce land transfers, and measures were taken by the governors and general court of that colony to see that these laws were enforced.[51]

Similarly, the Board of Trade directed the governor of New York in 1761 to settle no one on land occupied by members of the Iroquois

---

[49] The British Crown was not the only sovereign to appoint such protectors of Indians, to be sure; the Spanish preceded them in this regard, creating Bartolome de las Casas "Protector de los Indios" for the Americas, and later creating courts to hear cases involving Indian property rights (Juzgado de los Indios).

[50] Helen Rountree, *Pocahontas's People: The Powhatan Indians of Virginia through Four Centuries* (Norman, Okla., 1991), 128.

[51] See Stephen Potter, *Commoners, Tribute, and Chiefs: The Development of Algonquian Culture in the Potomac Valley* (Charlottesville, 1993), 195; Kawashima, *Puritan Justice and the Indian*, 60–61, 67–68; Harry Wright, "The Techniques of 17th Century Indian-Land Purchases," 77 *Essex Institute Historical Collections* 185 at 193 (1941); L. J. Priestley, "Communal Native Title and the Common Law: Further Thoughts on the Gove Land Rights Case," 6 *Federal Law Review* 150 (1974) (on the treatment of natives in Virginia and the Treaty of Lancaster with the Iroquois).

Confederation and to remove squatters from their lands. The board was apprised by their man in Iroquois Country, Sir William Johnson, that the tribes comprising the Iroquois Confederation understood the concept of land ownership, contrary to what they might have been told by New York's speculator community as "proclaimed" by the colony's assembly (that they were "unlettered Barbarians who keep no certain Memorials, have very indistinct Notions of private Property, use no land Marks, nor have any Inclosures"). The natives, Sir William wrote, were "perfectly well acquainted" with the "exact original bounds" of their land, which was divided into customary-use "shares to each family." They virtually never "infringe upon one another or invade their neighbours' hunting grounds." Sir William advised Governor Kempe in November, 1765, that "Common-Law" rules were inappropriate in dealing with the Iroquois inasmuch as such rules, "happily devised for *our* use," were made "before the discovery of America," and therefore "in many cases prove a bar" to the Iroquois "getting justice."[52]

Alibamon Mingo, paramount chief of the Choctaw, told a British official in 1765 that he was "not of the opinion that in giving land to the English, we deprive ourselves of the use of it. On the Contrary," he went on to say, "we shall share it with them. . . . Therefore we need not be uneasy that the English Settle upon our Lands as by that means they can more easily Supply our wants."[53]

Pennsylvania Susquehanna natives told David Brainerd in 1744 that their God "commanded them to live by hunting . . . and not to conform to the custom of the white people" with regard to land use. Throughout the eighteenth century, the Penn Proprietors, the Crown, and the United States government all took steps to protect the native tribes in the enjoyment of their customary property rights. Thus, for example, the commanding officer at Fort Pitt burned the dwellings of squatters on the Cheat River, acting on orders of General Thomas Gage, while in South Carolina the Crown's Superintendent of Indian Affairs,

---

[52] *Journal of the Assembly*, 4 Oct. 1764; Johnson to Board of Trade, 30 Oct. 1764, and to Kempe, 6 Nov. 1765, noted in Daniel Hulseboch, "Imperia in Imperio: The Multiple Constitutions of Empire in New York, 1750–1777," 16 *Law & History Review* 319 at 360–62 (1998).

One such customary rule, regarding Navajo matrilinear inheritance, was quite foreign to the Common Law: A Navajo mother buried her child's umbilical cord on the piece of land she wanted the child to inherit. (Gloria Valencia Weber, "Recovering Native Visions in Content of Indian Law," a paper presented at a Conference of the American Society for Legal History, Oct. 23, 1998, in Seattle, Washington.)

[53] Daniel Unser, *Indians, Settlers and Slaves in a Frontier Exchange: The Lower Mississippi Valley before 1783* (Chapel Hill, 1992), 125.

John Stuart, persuaded the colony's Council to void a massive, "improper" lease of Catawba land, deceptively obtained by William Henry Drayton in 1772. "They did not understand that he was [going] to Settle the whole of their Land," a witness to Drayton's parlay with the Catawba headmen explained.[54]

In the Cherokee Nation land occupied by individual Indians was regarded as their private property; unoccupied land (hunting grounds), held in common. Neither were regarded at first as alienable to a non-Cherokee. Hence, for some time in the eighteenth century the Cherokee believed they had the right to hunt and pass freely over such land as the Nation had "sold," that land "sales" were in the nature of life-estate leases – that is, that "land transfers would terminate with the death of the individual purchaser with whom they had negotiated."[55]

In November, 1767, Sir William Johnson negotiated a scandalous "purchase" from Iroquois leaders of much of what now constitutes Kentucky and Tennessee. The Iroquois had not consulted with the Shawnee, the actual inhabitants of the affected Ohio Valley region, let alone their traditional enemies, the Cherokee, who inhabited the ceded region south of the Kanawka River. Lord Hillsborough, the colonial secretary, scolded Johnson for the "improper conditions" in this Treaty of Ft. Stanwix, and managed to remove the Cherokee's domain from its terms.[56] After the War of Independence, the Continental Congress signed the Treaty of Hopewell with the Cherokee people, guaranteeing them their remaining lands and fixing their boundaries. But large numbers of Diaspora squatters harassed the Cherokee and their Creek and Chickasaw neighbors over the next several years, and the new Federal Congress entered into new treaties with these tribes in 1791 and 1796, paying them for some of the land still occupied by squatters, drawing new boundaries, and prohibiting the purchase of Indian land by individuals. In 1797, several thousand squatters were removed from Cherokee land, though most were allowed to return the next year when Congress again purchased those lands from the Cherokee. Some twenty-two years later, several hundred white families were again removed from Cherokee and Chickasaw lands by the United States Army, and in 1817 Major General Andrew Jackson recommended to the Secretary of War the seizure and sale of

54 James Merrell, *Into the American Woods* (Norton, N.Y., 1999), 177; Merrell, *The Indian's New World: Catawbas and Their Neighbors from European Contact through the Era of Removal* (N.Y., 1991), 202.
55 John Phillip Reid, *A Law of Blood: The Primitive Law of the Cherokee Nation* (1970), 132–33, and, generally, ch. 13; Wilma Dunaway, *The First American Frontier: Transition to Capitalism in southern Appalachia, 1700–1860* (Chapel Hill, 1996), 46.
56 McConnell, *A Country Between*, 251–54.

cattle driven illegally onto Cherokee land to graze (though Secretary
George Graham was content to direct him instead simply to drive the
cattle off).

Later, in what is now northwestern Illinois and eastern Iowa
Lieutenant Colonel Zachary Taylor twice removed white miners from
lead mines on Sac and Fox lands.[57] By 1800 many Shawnee and
Delaware Indians had been resettled on the lower Missouri River,
between Sainte Genevieve and Cape Girardeau. Diaspora squatters
began to encroach upon the tribes almost immediately. The first governor of the territory reported to President Jefferson in 1805 that he
was aggressively pursuing Jefferson's instructions to remove all such
squatters. Two years later Shawnee and Delaware tribal leaders urged
Indian agent Louis Lorimer to forward to Washington a petition complaining of "encroachments" that "remain unchecked." Lorimer did
so, and for several years two successive governors (Meriwether Lewis
and William Clark) initiated prosecutions against "Intruders," utilizing
native American deputies to help enforce the removals.[58]

American governors, councils, and jurists were regularly called upon
throughout the seventeenth, eighteenth, and nineteenth centuries to
interpret the language of treaties with Indian tribes, adjudge colonial and state statutes and actions affecting Indian rights, and define
Indian property rights. A few examples: In 1638, the Connecticut
colonists sought legal advice from the governor and general council of the Massachusetts Bay Colony. A sachem of "the Indians of the
River" named Sequin had arranged for a grant of land to the town
of Wethersfield on the condition that he could settle among them.
But "when he came to Wethersfield and set down his wigwam, they
drave him away by force." In retaliation, he "procured" the Pequot
Indians to deliver a retaliatory raid against the townsfolk. What was
the law that should be followed in such an event, the Connecticut
magistrates asked. Governor John Winthrop and his council answered
that "if the cause were thus," Sequin was justified to "right himself
by force or fraud, and that by the law of nations." Moreover, even
though Sequin's measures had done far more damage to them than
they had done to him, "that is not considerable in point of a just war."

---

[57] Francis Prucha, *American Indian Policy in the Formative Years* (Cambridge,
Mass., 1962), 12, 47, 153, 158, 181; Richard White, *The Middle Ground*, 319.
See also the Proclamation of the Continental Congress of Sept. 1, 1788,
ordering intrusions in violation of the Treaty of Hopewell to cease and
directing the Secretary of War to prepare forces to eject the intruders.
Noted in Prucha, 39.

[58] John Mack Faragher, "More Motley than Mackinaw: From Ethnic Mixing
to Ethnic Cleansing on the Frontier of the Lower Missouri, 1783–1833,"
in *Contact Points*, ed. Andrew Cayton and Fredricka Teute (Chapel Hill,
1998), 315–17.

He added that Sequin was also not bound "to seek satisfaction first in a peaceable way." It was "enough that he had complained of it as an injury and breach of covenant." Winthrop's contemporaries more familiar with the conditions of Just War theory would have disagreed with him as to his understating of Augustine's "principle of proportionality" and his failure to appreciate Augustine's requirement that rulers seek peaceful resolution before engaging in war, but that is not the point. Governor Winthrop made a genuine effort to apply the principles of International Law as he understood them to an event that privileged Indians at the expense of his fellow Diaspora newcomers. (And according to Winthrop, Connecticut took his council's advice to heart and entered into a solemn treaty with Sequin to resolve the matter.)[59]

Later, in the 1660s, Connecticut's Court of Assistants itself overturned the decisions of a Dedham town jury to dispossess local Indians in Natick from land claimed by Dedham's English settlers. The Court noted that the English had "encouraged" the Naticks to engage in "improvements" (clearing, fencing, barns) for which they had been given no compensation. This, "added to their native [property] right, w[hi]ch cannot, in strict justice" be treated as being "entirely extinct," warranted judgement in their favor. The English Diaspora in Dedham received a new town of 8,000 acres. Some of these settlers continued to harass the Natick Indians, ripping up their fences, but the Court continued to side with the natives, who by the early eighteenth century had adopted "English inheritence practices" so that "family lines" might "remain intact," a "hybrid system of communal and individual landholding that withstood challenges from land-hungry English neighbors," and a group of Indian "Proprietors" to "manage communal lands corporately."[60]

---

[59] *John Winthrop's Journal, 1630–1649*, ed. James K. Hosmer (2 vols., N.Y., 1908), I, 256–57 (1908), cited in Karen Kupperman, *Settling with the Indians: The Meeting of English and Indian Cultures, 1580–1640* (Totowa, N.J., 1980), 184–85.

[60] Jean O'Brien, *Dispossession by Degrees: Indian Land and Identity in Natick* (New York, 1997), 38–39, 75–80; Peter Hoffer, *Law and Peoples in Colonial America* (2nd ed., Baltimore, 1998), 73.

Robert Grumet argues that Suscaneman, a Matinecock sachem, "often managed" to get "formal colonial recognition of the validity" of the title to or boundaries of Matinecock land by "selling unclearly bounded adjacent tracts to contending colonists," thereby "encouraging land disputes among the Europeans while clouding claimant titles." This may give Suscaneman more agency, or credit for sophistication, than he would have claimed for himself, but to the extent that he did act consciously in this way "by exploiting the litigation process," he certainly benefitted his people. Grumet, "Suscaneman and the Matinecock Lands, 1653–1703," in R. Grumet, ed., *Northeastern Indian Lives, 1632–1812* (Amherst, 1996), 127.

In the early eighteenth century, New York's colonial jurists were asked to decide a lawsuit pitting the Mohegan Indians against Connecticut. In 1659, the Mohegans had agreed to make land available to that colony in the form of a trust fund for the tribe's long-term benefit. In time, they became dissatisfied with the ways that fund was being administered. At one critical stage of this litigation the Crown created a special Commission of Review, comprised of New York's jurists, to apply the Law of Nations to the case. Judge Daniel Horsmanden and his colleagues assumed jurisdiction on the grounds that the Mohegans were "a Separate and Distinct People" with "a Polity of their own. . . . " It was "apparent," Horsmanden wrote, that "the Crown looks upon them not as Subjects." " 'Tis as plain in my Conception, that the Crown looks upon the Indians as having the Property of the Soil of these Countries." Their property rights, however usufructory in nature they might be, were intrinsic, not derived "by his Majesty's Grant of particular Limits of them for a Colony." Consequently "his Subjects" (the Connecticut colonists here) were not to appropriate their land " 'till they have made fair and Honest Purchase of the Natives."

Judge Cadwallader Colden dissented from this view, arguing that the Mohegans could not be regarded as a separate sovereign people, and that, in any event, to hold, as his colleagues had, that they *were*, "in this Country," would be "of Dangerous Consequences."[61] And Colden's views eventually prevailed, echoed by the counsel for Connecticut in its controversy in 1782 with Pennsylvania over property rights to the Wyoming Valley. Arguing before the Confederation's Court of Commissioners, Connecticut's attorney pressed upon them the common legal view that the Crown had not purchased land from any of the native tribes because of any legal duty to do so, but for a more practical reason – to "purchase peace and quiet."[62]

---

[61] Mark Walters, "*Mohegan Indians v. Connecticut* (1705–1773) and the Legal Status of Aboriginal Customary Laws and Government in British North America," 33 *Osgoode Hall Law Journal* 785 at notes 142 & 144 (1995).

[62] L. J. Priestley, "Communal Native Title and the Common Law: Further Thought on the Gove Land Rights Case," 6 *Federal Law Review* 150 at 167 (1974).

Horsmanden's view *were* echoed in a counterpart argument, offered by another Connecticut attorney representing Connecticut settler/trespassers who claimed title of land in colonial New York via a Wappinger Indian chief. See Oscar Handlin & Irving Mark, eds., "Chief Daniel Nimham v. Morris, Robinson & Phillipse – An Indian Land Case in Colonial New York, 1765–1767," 11 *Ethnohistory* 226–27 (1964); Mark & Handlin, "Land Cases in Colonial New York, 1765–67: The King v. Prendergast," 19 *New York Univ. Law Quarterly Rev.* 165–94 (1942).

This position was eventually enshrined in American Law in two landmark decisions of the Supreme Court of the United States, *Johnson v. McIntosh* (1823) and *Worcester v. Georgia* (1832). In his opinions, Chief Justice John Marshall maintained that, via the Law of Discovery, the British Crown and its heir, the United States, held sovereign title to all the land, that the native tribal inhabitants' rights were those of "tenants at will" of the lands they and their ancestors had simply "wandered over" for centuries, and that the U.S. government had the right of "first refusal" to the sale of all Indian tenancy rights – that is, tribes who sold that property right to any but a duly authorized representative of the U.S. government transferred nothing of any real value. Marshall *did* allow, however, in an important aside, that these native tribes were nations (albeit "domestic dependent" ones) that required the formality of treaties regarding that tenancy.[63]

The Canadian Provinces

When the British seized and were awarded the French colony of Arcadia in the early eighteenth century, they removed some French settlers and opened it to British settlement as Nova Scotia in the early eighteen century. In the process, they encroached upon the lands and customary rights of the native Micmacs as well. The Micmacs had coexisted with French traders and missionaries for several generations, and their unease with these new British settlers soon led to warfare. One treaty between a group of Micmac chiefs and the British governor in 1726 promised to leave the Micmacs their traditional hunting and fishing privileges in exchange for recognizing King George as "the Rightful Possessor of the province," but other Micmacs rejected this surrender of sovereignty, and warfare continued. The Crown thereafter sought to ensure the Micmacs with regard to Indian property customs in legal terms that sounded much like the language used by Daniel Horsmanden in colonial New York. A second treaty in 1748 promised the Micmacs "free liberty of Hunting & fishing as

---

[63] *Johnson v. McIntosh*, 21 U.S. 543 (1823); *Worcester v. Georgia*, 6 Peters (U.S.) 515 (1832); Prucha, *American Indian Policy*, 47, 153; Jill Norgren, *The Cherokee Cases: The Confrontation of Law and Politics* (1996); Richard Monikowski, "The Actual State of Things: American Indians, Indian Law, and American Courts between 1800 and 1835," unpub. Ph.D. diss., Univ. of New Mexico, 1997.

Both the Indian-hating Governor of Tennessee, John Sevier, in 1796, and the more sympathetic President John Quincy Adams, in 1828, also described Indian land tenure as "no fee simple" but rather "the lowest kind of tenancy, namely that of tenants at will" (Sevier) or "tenants at discretion" (Adams).

usual," and in 1762, Lieutenant Governor Jonathan Belcher, a contemporary of Judge Horsmanden's, prepared (but did not widely circulate) a proclamation promising "to protect" the Micmacs "in their just Rights & Possessions" to land "reserved or claimed" as well as "a common right to the Sea Coast from Cape Fronsac outwards for fishing without disturbance," and warning Diaspora squatters on Micmac land that they would be dealt with "with the utmost Rigour of the Law."[64]

These promises were sometimes kept, as when Jacob Powell, a magistrate, leased timber-cutting rights from a group of Richibucto Micmacs in 1809 and was rebuked; inasmuch as the lease had not been signed by all members of the band, it was voided.[65] Later, in the mid-1830s, a number of Scottish squatters on Micmac land received eviction notices. They petitioned the legislature for relief, but that body's Indian Committee rebuffed them and "published a notice" to be posted on all Indian reserves, requiring all Diaspora trespassers to remove themselves and their belongings by July 1, 1837. But, as Sidney Harring has shown, neither this step, nor a similar one taken in 1845, effectively checked squatter encroachments on the lands of the Micmac.[66]

In 1763, at the close of the Seven Year's War, the British government issued a proclamation creating trans-Appalachian Indian reserves and threatening squatters on the lands of natives in what is now

---

[64] Leslie F. S. Upton, *Micmacs and Colonists: Indian-White Relations in the Maritimes, 1713–1867* (Vancouver, 1979), 43–44, 59, 88, 95, 150–51.

[65] Indeed, this sensitivity to aboriginal custom can be seen most clearly in a case involving the law of marriage contracts. In 1867, when Justice Monk of Quebec's Superior Court held that, while the French and English took *some* of *their* respective national law with them to the trading posts their people had established in the Northwest, "yet will it be contended that the territorial rights, political organization such as it was, or the laws and usages of Indian tribes, were abrogated – that they ceased to exist when [French and British fur traders] began to trade with the aboriginal occupants? . . . It is beyond controversy that they . . . were not even modified in the slightest degree in regard to the civil rights of the natives." *Connolly v. Woolrich*, 11 Lower Can. Jur. 197 at 204–05 (1867), affirmed on appeal in 17 R. J. R. Quebec 266 (1869) (the case involved the legality in Montreal of the marriage of a Hudsons' Bay officer and a Cree woman); noted in Brian Slattery, *Ancestral Lands, Alien Laws: Judicial Perspectives on Aboriginal Title* (Univ. of Saskatchewan Native Law Centre, 1983), 14–15.

But then Monk found himself in dissent, his view rejected, in 1881, in *Fraser v. Pouliot* (7 QLR 147) where Quebec's Court of Queen's Bench denied the legality of just such a marriage. Harring, *White Man's Law*, 172–73.

[66] Sidney Harring, *White Man's Law*, 179.

Quebec and Ontario.[67] Thereafter, throughout the nineteenth century, the Crown entered into treaties with the Mississaugua, Chippewa, Ottawa, Teuchamitsa, Blackfoot, a number of Pacific-Coast tribes, and the half-native Metis of the Canadian prairie, eventually creating native reserves and trust funds from the sale of ceded land. Needless to say, these treaties varied in their equitable characteristics and eventual effectiveness. For example, Governor Haldimand's grant of the Grand River reserve to Britain's Iroquois allies in 1795 was adjudged by Upper Canada (Ontario)'s Court of King's Bench in 1835 to be without legal significance, in that the deed lacked the Great Seal of the Crown. This rendered the Six Nations Indians at Grand River "mere tenants at will to the Crown," Justice Burns later explained. Moreover, that court's chief justice, Sir John Beverley Robinson, insisted that the Common Law could not "recognize any peculiar law of real property applying to the Indians – the common law is not part savage and part civilized."[68] Upper Canada's Indian Act of 1839 was intended to protect Indian reserves from squatters and timber thieves, but its criminal provisions lacked bite because its terms were rarely enforced by Diaspora officials. And the tribal councils' own law enforcement officers (like the Six Nations' "forest bailiffs," empowered to eject tribal members from land occupied without council authority, or to prevent the taking of wood from a neighbor's land) were insufficient to the task.[69]

In 1863, the native inhabitants of Manitoulin Island in Lake Huron threatened the operators of a Diaspora-owned fishery "on unceded tribal lands." Drawing knives, some fifty Indians "forced the abandonment of the fishery." Ontario's government sent fishery inspector

---

[67] The modern-day province of Ontario was known, prior to 1867, first as Upper Canada, later as Canada West. I will remind the non-Canadian reader throughout by using both its contemporary and its modern names simultaneously.

[68] *Doe ex D. Jackson v. Wilkes*, 4 UCKB (OS) 142 (1835) (a case that Sidney Harring (*White Man's Law*, 67) reads differently); *Doe ex d. Sheldon v. Ramsay*, 9 UCQB 105 at 123 (1852) (for C. J. Robinson's quoted views) and 134 (for the view of J. Burns reflecting on his understanding of the 1835 case).

This is not to say that Robinson's powerful court was unwilling to render decisions of advantage to native peoples, for while Crown officials and legislators in Upper Canada were prepared to grant "a great deal of land to squatters [on Indian land] who had improved it," Robinson's court never sanctioned such grants. Harring, 72.

[69] Harring, 31, 149; John Noon, *Law and Government of the Grand River Iroquois* (1949), 117–18. The Six Nations' Grand Council was not without clout when it came to disputes involving inheritances, costs of improvements, and occupancy rights. Harring, 149.

William Gibbard and thirteen armed police to the scene. After considerable shouting and pushing, the parties agreed that the natives would not be arrested, but would attend a "government hearing" into the matter. But within a few days Gibbard "broke his agreement" by arresting Oswa-ane-mekee, "one of the law-makers" of the Manitoulin Islanders. A vacationing Toronto attorney secured the man's release, and when Gibbard levied new charges, the attorney secured bail for Oswa-ane-mekee. Thereafter, Gibbard was murdered enroute to Collingwood "by parties unknown," and the charges against the Indian lawmaker were dropped.[70] In any event, the governors of Ontario commissioned boards of inquiry in 1840, 1844, and 1856 to address the problems. These recommended "that reserve lands be granted to individual Indians in fee simple," a proposal that Indian tribal councils protested, preferring their own property rules. But legislation flowing from the efforts of these commissions did exempt Indian reserves from property taxes and made it difficult for Diaspora traders to fleece individual Indians out of land for liquor or trading-post debt, and for this the Colonial Office and its men-on-the-scene, such as Governors Sir Francis Bond Head and Sir Charles Bagot, were largely responsible.[71]

Provincial and Dominion officials could, of course, be swayed by the advice of either missionaries or speculators or both, thus crafting treaties that corresponded to the perception these particular Diaspora voices had of the needs, welfare, and customary rights of the native inhabitants.[72] A case in point has been provided by Dianne Newell, regarding the aboriginal people's salmon fisheries of the Pacific Northwest: For several thousands of years tribes in what is now British Columbia had effectively harvested the several species of salmon that

---

[70] Reported by Sidney Harring, *White Man's Law*, 152–53. Cf. Cole Harris, *The Resettlement of British Columbia*, 134 (on the confrontation between Fraser River Indians and government commissioners over the decision to stop natives from fishing due to a landslide caused by construction of the Canadian Northern Railway near Hell's Gate), and Harring, 149 (on the Grand Council of the Six Nation's appeal to the League of Nations in 1921 from an Ontario appellate court decision affirming a fish warden's seizure of a Mohawk woman's net).

[71] Harring, 31, 95.

[72] Tennant, "Aboriginal Rights and the Canadian Legal System," in John McLaren, ed., *Law for the Elephant, Law for the Beaver* (Regina, Sask., 1992), 106–27; Maureen A. Donohue, "Aboriginal Land Rights in Canada: A Historical Perspective on the Fiduciary Relations," 15 *American Indian Law Review* 369 (1991); Douglas Sanders, "The Queen's Promises," in *Law & Justice in a New Land*, ed. Louis Knafla (1986), 103; D. N. Sprague, "Canada's Treaties with Aboriginal Peoples," 23 *Manitoba Law Journal* 341 (1996); Dennis Madill, *British Columbia Indian Treaties in Historical Perspective* (Ottawa, Dept. of Indian & Northern Affairs, 1981).

spawned in the streams and rivers of that coast. In 1874, Dominion officials urged the government of British Columbia to fulfill its obligation
(under Article 13 of the British Columbia Terms of Union Agreement
of 1871) to convey to the Dominion "tracts of land" for the benefit
of these native communities, and noted that "great care should be
taken that the Indians, especially those inhabiting the Coast, should
not be disturbed in their customary fishing grounds, which should be
reserved for them previous to white settlement in the immediate vicinity of such localities." Two years later Governor-General Lord Dufferin
toured British Columbia and concluded that "if an Indian can prove
a prescriptive right of way to a fishing station, or a right of way of any
other kind, that right should no more be ignored than if it was the
case of a white man."[73] British Columbia's Attorney-General George
Walkem, responding both to the Dominion's Indian Affairs office and
the urging of Anglican missionary William Duncan, offered reserves
for each tribe that included "their fishing stations, fur-trading posts
and settlements," but little else. This may have satisfied the Reverend
Duncan, whose mission station at the Tsimshian village of Metlakatla
would include a salmon cannery by 1881, but it meant that natives in
British Columbia were provided with smaller reservations than anywhere else in Canada, amounting to little more than an average of
five hectares per native.[74]

The Antipodes

The first late-eighteenth century British "discoverers" of southeastern
Australia reported the region to be essentially uninhabited, prompting
the *terra nullius* position later adopted by the Crown, but the next several waves of Diaspora migrants discovered otherwise. In New South
Wales, Western Australia, Van Dieman's Land (Tasmania), Victoria,
and South Australia one early visitor or government official after another reported the continent to be populated by tribal people with
quite territorial notions of ownership and clear boundaries, who were
quite prepared to fight with one another or anyone else "concerning
the right of fishing or dwelling in some particular cove." In 1807, the

---

73 Molyneaux St. John, *The Sea of Mountains: An Account of Lord Dufferin's Tour
through British Columbia in 1876* (London, 1877), 223–24; Harring, *White
Man's Law*, 212.

74 Dianne Newell, *Tangled Webs of History: Indians and the Law in Canada's
Pacific Coast Fisheries* (Univ. of Toronto Press, 1993), 56–57. Compare with
Arthur McEvoy, *The Fisherman's Problem: Ecology and Law in the California
Fisheries, 1850–1980* (Cambridge Univ. Press, 1986), ch. 1. And see Douglas
Harris, *Fish, Law and Colonialism: The Legal Capture of Aboriginal Salmon
Fisheries in British Columbia* (University of Toronto Press, 2001).

Governor of New South Wales, P. G. King, allowed to William Bligh (his successor) that he had "ever considered" the aboriginal people to be "the real Proprietors of the Soil." From "King George's Land" (Western Australia) Richard Dale described "each tribe" in 1834 as occupying "a large and determinate tract which is sub-divided into smaller portions as hunting-grounds for individuals, who jealously watch over and instantly retaliate [against] encroachment upon their shares."[75] In 1836, Francis Armstrong added that land in Western Australia was "apportioned to different families" and was "beyond doubt an inheritable property among them, and they boast of having received it from their father's fathers to an unknown period way back." In 1839, George Moore described aboriginal ownership and inheritance rules in Western Australia in precisely these terms. Robert Menli Lyon told Western Australians in 1833 that they had "seized upon a land that is not yours." The lands of the Australian aborigines "have descended to them from their fore-fathers from time immemorial," by which he clearly meant by customary law; thus he added:

> Their title deeds require not the wrangling lawyers to prove them to be correct. They have the seal of Heaven – the sanction of Him who 'divided to the nations their inheritance.'[76]

South Australia's Governor Gawler held that "the natives have ... very distinct and well defined proprietary rights ... they hunt the game upon, catch the fish in and eat the roots of their own districts just as much as the English gentleman kills the deer and sheep upon or the fish in his private park." Another dispatch from Gawler, this time to the Colonial Office, prompted James Stephen to "minute" in 1840 that "these Tribes had Proprietary in the Soil – that is, in particular sections of it which were clearly defined and well understood before the occupation of their country."[77] Consequently, it is not surprising that a

---

75 *Historical Records of New South Wales*, II, 718 (1889), noted in Henry Reynolds, *Aboriginal Sovereignty: Reflections on Race, State and Nation* (St. Louis, 1996), 24–27, and 33; Dale, *A Descriptive Account of... King George's Land...* (London, 1834), 7, noted in Sylvia Hallam, *Fire and Hearth: A Study of Aboriginal Usage and European Usurpation in South-West Australia* (Cambridge, 1975), 32; King Papers, Mitchell Library MSS Coll., C/189, first noted by Henry Reynolds, *This Whispering in Our Hearts* (Sydney, 1999), 24.

76 Lyon, from a speech at Guildford, quoted in Reynolds, *This Whispering*, 73; Geo. Moore, Mar. 26, 1839, in *Diary of Ten Eventful Years in Western Australia* (London, 1884), 259.

77 See Hallam, 14, 28–31; Reynolds, *The Law of the Land*, 70; *Contested Ground*, ed. Ann McGrath, 244; Jan Critchett, *Distant Field of Murder*, 39. Cf. Peter Sutton, *Country Aboriginal Boundaries and Land Ownership in Australia* (Aboriginal History Monographs #3, Cambridge, 1995).

number of the Diaspora in Australia, in the 1790s and throughout the nineteenth century, spoke of "invading" aboriginal territory and of "conquest."[78] And a few, like Robert Lyon and George Robinson, argued that the Crown should act as the U.S. government had and purchase the land. ("What a contrast to the policy of the British, who act the part of the assassin and possess themselves of the lands they require [here] by powder and ball," Lyon wrote to the Secretary of State for Colonies in 1833.[79])

In the mid-1830s Lord Glenelg (nee Charles Grant), the newly appointed colonial secretary, appeared to be responding, for he went further than his predecessors had with respect to the rights of the indigenous people of Australia. He indicated that Australia's aborigines were subject to the Crown's "protection," and instructed the commissioners heading the new settlement in South Australia to set aside land for aboriginal use.[80] Critics of the South Australia Colonization Committee had noted the absence of any plan "respecting payment to the native inhabitants, the owners of the soil." The region to be colonized was the home of thousand of Aborigines who "must be paid for their lands."[81] The colony's promoters, however, secured parliamentary sanction for the undertaking in the summer of 1835, and the legislation contained the then-common legal language treating the region as *terra nullius*, and thus requiring no compensation be paid to anyone.

Despite the legislation, Glenelg advised the colony's planners in December that the Crown would not provide them with Letters Patent, transferring title and authority, unless they were to provide "reasonable assurance" that they would do no "act of injustice towards the aboriginal natives" of the region. This step led the chairman of the colony's commission, Robert Torrens, to delay the sailing of the first colonists. It was some seven months later that Torrens finally persuaded Glenelg to entrust him with the Letters Patent, at which time the ships sailed. By then Glenelg had appointed a protector of Aborigines who was to oversee the process of settlement and to insure that the property rights of the natives were purchased.[82]

---

78 Reynolds, *Aboriginal Sovereignty*, 97–101; *Contested Ground*, ed. Ann McGrath, 321.

79 Reynolds, *This Whispering*, 83.

80 Some forty-one sites, including the Boobra lagoon on the MacIntyre River (Rainbow Serpent site of the Bigambul people) and the Bruwarruia Fisheries site, were set aside in the New South Wales outback pastoral districts in 1850, mostly in one square mile "reserve" plots. Few were accepted by the Aborigines. *Contested Ground*, 67.

81 Anon.,"Review of R. Torrens, *Colonization of South Australia*," *Westminster Review* (July, 1835) 218, 239.

82 Henry Reynolds, *Law of the Land*, 104–07; *Contested Ground*, ed. Ann McGrath, 14–15, 221.

Glenelg was clearly a man who meant what he said. When Diaspora settlers in South Africa attacked the Xhosa, a Bantu people there, in the Frontier War of 1835, killing their leader, Huntza, the Cape Colony's Governor D'Urban proclaimed the annexation of the land between the Keiskamma and Kei Rivers (which he named "Queen Adelaide Province"). Glenelg was approached by officials of the London Missionary Society who had received complaints about "the abominations we practice abroad" from missionaries in South Africa. He was also advised (by R. W. Hay) against the Crown's sanctioning the annexation of more territory than could affordably and feasiblely be managed. Both arguments impressed Glenelg, and he reacted immediately. On December 26, 1835 he informed Governor D'Urban of the Cape Colony that the annexation had been renounced by the Crown, since it resulted "from a war" in which "the original justice" was "on the side of the conquered, not the victorious party." Governor D'Urban protested for some time that he was only trying to protect Bantu from Boer, but his own commander-on-the-scene, Sir Harry Smith, was leary of the annexation. Martial Law would have to come to an end and withdrawal begin, he reluctantly told the governor in August, 1836:[83]

> The sooner we march out of the Province the better, for how am I to 'eat up' the Kafirs, according to Blackstone?

With the exception of the Cape Colony's Governor D'Urban, Glenelg's "men on the scene" in the Antipodes were generally of his ilk (or those of his equally impressive successors, Normanby, Russell, Gladstone, and Stanley). Sir George Gipps, the governor of New South Wales, and his legislative council turned away an attempt by a syndicate headed by W. C. Wentworth to purchase one-third of the South Island of New Zealand in 1840 from "nine wandering Maoris picked up in the streets of Sydney" who, Gipps noted, had "no more right, by English law or Maori custom, to sell their country than they had to give a valid title to the surface of the surrounding Pacific." "Talk of corruption! Talk of jobbery!" Gipps raved before the colony's Legislative Council in July: Wentworth, he said, had "quoted largely from Vattel and the *Law of Nations* to prove the right of independent people to sell their lands," but "it was, in fact, necessary for him to show that the right existed in [these] nine savages...." Francis Allman, one of Governor Gibbs' district commissioners, refused to renew the licenses

---

[83] John S. Galbraith, *Reluctant Empire: British Policy on the South Africa Frontier, 1834–1854* (London, 1963), 126–28; Reynolds, *Law of the Land*, 98; Smith, noted in William M. Macmillan, *Bantu, Boer and Briton: The Making of the South Africa Problem* (1929), 130.

of "Squatters" who had extended their runs beyond the Bogan River, which separated the Diaspora from the Aborigines. Across the Tasman Sea in 1842 both New Zealand's chief justice and its police magistrate for the Auckland area refused requests that they order the arrest of Te Here Rangihaeata for that chief's destruction of an illegal British settlement at Porirua.[84]

These officials were inspired, in part, by humanitarians organized in the Aborigines' Protection Society, in part by that society's success in persuading the House of Commons to appoint a Select Committee on Aborigines. That committee in turn reported back to the House of Commons regarding the need for greater supervision and intervention by the Colonial Office to protect the customary property rights of native peoples in British colonies and possessions everywhere. In 1841, Justice John Walpole Willis ruled in Victoria that the indigenous people had "no right" to "trespass" on the Squattocracy's pastoral ranges unless there was a special clause in the Squatter's license to graze that required him to allow natives to continue "wandering" over land on which they had hunted, fished, and gathered for centuries. This provoked that colony's "Protector of Aborigines," George Robinson, to call upon the Crown to help Australia's native people secure "a reasonable share in the Soil of their fatherland. . . ."[85]

The new colonial secretary, Earl Grey, appears to have been persuaded: In February, 1848, he wrote to Governor Fitzroy in Sydney directing that pastoral leases "give the grantees only an exclusive right of pasturage for their cattle, and of cultivating such land as they may require," but were "not intended to deprive the natives of their former right to hunt over these Districts, or to wander over them in search of subsistence, in the manner to which they have been heretofore accustomed, from the spontaneous produce of the soil except over land actually cultivated or fenced in for that purpose." All pastoral leases issued thereafter in the Australian colonies were to contain a clause "conveying to the Natives the continuance of rights" (a legal privilege that was not of great practical use to Aborigines in the mid-nineteenth century but has become rather central to their legal cause in this day-and-age).[86] Parliament responded with legislation

---

[84] C. D. Rowley, *Destruction of Aboriginal Society: Vol. I: Policy and Practice* (Cambridge, 1970); Rev. J. D. Land Papers, "Reminiscences," p. 199 (on Gipps' speech), CY2188 (vol. 24), Mitchell Library; R. H. W. Reece, *Aborigines and Colonists* (1974), 183 (on Allman).

[85] Noted in Reynolds, *This Whispering*, 52–53.

[86] Reynolds, *This Whispering*, 58–60. Henry Reynolds and Jamie Dalziel, on the one hand, and Jonathan Fulcher, on the other, differ over how many rights Secretary Grey felt Aborigines retained and how many he intended to leave

(the Imperial Crown Land Sale Act) that provided for aboriginal reserves in the Australian colonies, and Secretary Grey added that it was the "duty" of Crown officials to do "whatever is possible" for "the preservation of the aboriginal race" in New South Wales and Victoria, as well as to create such reserves "where they do not exist." Funds for these purposes "ought to be the very first charge" on the colonial land revenues.[87]

None the less, the Crown did not trouble itself to enter into treaties with any of the continent's tribes, a fact regretted as "a great oversight" by Lt. Governor Arthur of Van Dieman's Land in 1832 in a memorandum to the Colonial Office urging such formal land purchases in the future.[88] (Qualifier: In the first years of the colony of Western Australia the local customary laws of the Aborigines were formally recognized by Governor Hutt in disputes between Aborigines).[89]

But while the Crown was reticent in recognizing the property rights of the Aboriginal tribes populating Australia, some individual Diaspora settlers were more willing to do so, for their own ends. As in the American colonies, title to land in the Antipodes was *supposed* to be acquired only from the Crown or its assignee-proprietors, not by individuals or private groups dealing directly with native inhabitants. Hence, officers of the Crown in Australia and New Zealand during the late 1830s and early 1840s checked attempts of both individual settlers and organized colonization companies to purchase land directly from native inhabitants. We have just noted Governor Gipps' rebuff to the efforts of W. C. Wentworth and his fellow New South Welsh

them. I find Fulcher's argument the more persuasive, but then he had the last word. Reynold & Dalziel, "Aborigines and Pastoral Leases – Imperial and Colonial Policy, 1826–1855," 19 *Univ. of New South Wales Law Journal* 315 (1996); Fulcher, "The Wik Judgement, Pastoral Leases and Colonial Office Policy in New South Wales in the 1840s," 4 *Australian Journal of Legal History* 33 (1998). But see also Robert Foster, "The Origins of the Protection of Aboriginal Rights in South Australian Postoral Leases," *Issues Paper #24, Land, Rights, Laws* (Australian Institute of Aboriginal . . . Studies, Aug. 1998).

[87] *Parliamentary Papers (House of Commons), 1837, no. 425 – Select Committee on Aborigines (British Settlements), Report, Evidence and Appendix,* 20; Henry Reynolds, *Law of the Land,* 131; Katherine Pettipas, *Severing the Ties that Bind* (Winnipeg, 1994), 21; Earl Grey, 11 Feb. 1848, noted in Reynolds, *This Whispering,* 57. See also Jamic Dalziel, "Pastoral Leases in the Northern Territory and The Reservation of Aboriginal Rights, 1863–1931," 22 *University of New South Wales Law Journal* 462 (1999).

[88] *Contested Ground,* ed. Ann McGrath, 321; John West, *The History of Tasmania* (1852), 289.

[89] Desmond Sweeney, "Australia's Forgotten Legal Pluralism: The Western Australia Experience under Governor Hutt," paper at an Australia-New Zealand Legal History Meeting, Melbourne, July, 1998.

entrepreneurs to buy tracts in New Zealand from "wandering Maoris" in Sydney. But when the Crown resisted the requests of enterprising groups that areas be acquired and made available for settlement, these groups treated directly with the native populations for such settlement rights. John Batman of Van Dieman's Land (Tasmania) and a number of his fellow Van Demonians sought permission to settle what would later become Victoria, but Batman's "Port Phillip Association" also took its own counsel. Preempting the Crown's response, the Association purchased some 500,000 acres north of today's Melbourne and an additional 100,000 acres to the west of modern Geelong from heads of bands of a number of aboriginal inhabitants, members of the Kulin (Dutigallar and Wathurong) people, in the vicinity of modern Melbourne and Geelong, in exchange for "protection" and annual payments of goods and money ("an annual tribute to those who are the real owners of the soil"). Batman and his associate, Charles Wedge, felt (not altogether correctly) that the native inhabitants of modern Victoria were "divided and wander about in families, and there is no such thing as Chieftainship among them."[90] But Wedge immediately wrote to an associate in Tasmania that this fact was "a secret that must, I suppose, be kept to ourselves or it may affect the deed of conveyance, if there is any validity in it." The clan heads they had in fact bargained with may have believed they were granting only a leaselike "use" of certain lands, or they may simply have thought they were being given rather elaborate "friendship" gifts. In any event, they were *not* likely to have felt that they had the authority to alienate permanently that much land of their clans outright.[91]

At the advice of Governor Bourke of New South Wales (Gipps' predecessor), Lord Glenelg rejected Batman's claim that the Aborigines with whom he had dealt were "the real owners of the soil" and that his payments (of "yearly rent or tribute" and a one-time payment of tools, weapons, blankets, shirts, and flour in exchange for 600,000 acres) constituted consideration for a lawful transfer of title. The Kulin did not possess any right to "alienate to private adventurers the Land of the Colony," the colonial secretary reminded his man-on-the-scene; but of equal significance, he added that, in the event, such a transaction

---

[90] Dianne Barwick has found that there *were* "clan heads of great status among the Kulin," and that five of the eight signatories of the Batman treaty were, indeed, "clan heads." "Mapping the Past," 8 *Aboriginal History* (1984).

[91] Alastair Campbell, *John Batman and the Aborigines* (Malmsbury, 1987), 101, 103–04, 120; J. Morgan, *Life and Adventures of William Buckley*, ed. C. E. Sayers (Melbourne, 1967), 87–88. (Buckley, an escaped convict living with the Wathurong, was aware of the transaction and is quoted as calling it "another hoax of the white man, to possess the inheritance of the uncivilized natives of the forest.")

would have proven "very ill for the real welfare of that hapless and unfortunate Race."[92] (Batman and the Port Phillip Association lobbied
on, but settled in a few years for a lesser grant of land in the same
regions in recognition of their gifts to the Aborigines.)

Simultaneously, Edward Gibbon Wakefield's New Zealand Company,
which had attracted the patronage and capital of Lord Durham, Lord
Petrie, and other notables, sought to buy land from the native Maoris
in 1839.[93] In that year, Captain Arthur Wakefield, the colonial theorist's brother, landed with a party of colonists in the vicinity of modern
Wellington and "bought" much land. This "sale" was soon repudiated,
both by Maoris (who claimed the "sellers" had "no commission from
the tribes and no title of their own to make the sale") and by the colonial secretary, who reminded the New Zealand Company, as it had
John Batman, that the Crown was in charge of British colonization,
and that the settlers would have to await an agreement between the
Crown and the Maoris.

This message was ignored. In 1843, these same New Zealand Company settlers "purchased" land in the northern reaches of the South
Island from a group of Maoris who claimed title to it by virtue of
conquest. When they proceeded to survey this land, they found themselves confronted at Wairau with Maori occupants who contested their
claim. A party led by Captain Wakefield attacked these Maoris and
was rebuffed with considerable loss of life. None the less, Governor
Robert Fitzroy declined demands from the New Zealand Company
settlers that these Maoris be prosecuted, since he believed that a truly
impartial jury would be obliged to acquit them, and he lacked confidence that such a jury could be empaneled. Fitzroy's report of the
incident to the Colonial Office prompted the secretary, Lord Stanley, to remark in his supportive response that the Wairau survey had
"needlessly violated the Rules of the Law of England...."[94]

[92] Reece, *Aborigines and Colonists: Aboriginal and Colonial Society in New South
Wales in the 1830s and '40s* (Sydney, 1974), 122, 124; Marie H. Fels, *Good
Men and True,* 8.

[93] A. Trollope, *Australia and New Zealand* (2 vols., London, 1873), I, 368,
370; II, 308–09, 311, 312–15; I. H. Kawharu, *Waitangi: Maori and Pakeha
Perspectives on the Treaty of Waitangi* (Auckland, 1989); Peter Taylor, *Station
Life in Australia: Pioneers and Pastoralists* (Sydney, 1988), ch. 6.
   Charles Terry offered another example of this unlawful direct purchase
of land from Maori in Hawke's Bay, by Captain Rhodes of the barque
Eleanor, in his account of New Zealand in 1842: *New Zealand: Its Advantages,*
99–100.

[94] Bruce Kercher, *An Unruly Child: A History of Australian Law* (Sydney, 1996),
12, 18; William Pember Reeves, *State Experiments in New Zealand and Australia*
(London, 1902), II, 226; Ian Wards, *The Shadow of the Land: A Study of British
Policy and Racial Conflict in New Zealand, 1832–1852* (Wellington, 1968),
60, 75, 88.

These acts of private initiative did, however, prod the reluctant Crown authorities to preemptive action. Thus by the mid-1840s Victoria was open for settlement, and in 1839, Lord Normanby, Glenelg's successor as Secretary of State for Colonies, dispatched Captain William Hobson, R.N., to New Zealand to enter into treaty negotiations with the Maoris. The colonial secretary and a parliamentary committee had come to agree, he told Hobson, that the unsupervised settling of New Zealand would prove to be "essentially unjust" to the Maoris, "a numerous and inoffensive people." Were the New Zealand Company and others like them to continue to function, "unrestrained by any [British] Law, and amenable to no [British] tribunals," they would eventually dispossess the Maori of much of their heritage. The Crown, through Hobson, must persuade the Maoris to cede their sovereignty in order to save their patrimony. "Laws administered by British Judges would far more than compensate for the sacrifice by the Natives of a National independence which they are no longer able to maintain." Hobson was to be "their official protector," and was to permit no Maori land to be transferred to settlers except via the Crown, and none to be acquired that was "essential, or highly conducive" to the Maori's "own comfort, safety or subsistence."

These instructions had been drafted in part by Permanent Undersecretary, James Stephen, who regarded the Maori not as "wandering Tribes," but men with "a settled form of Government" who "have divided and appropriated the whole Territory amongst them." They were not mere "huntsmen, but after their rude fashion, agriculturalists." Yet they were selling land to Diaspora adventurers:

> If nothing is done to check this abuse, New Zealand will ere long be like Prince Edward Island, the property of some 40 or 50 English absentees.[95]

For the first several years of contact with Diaspora settlers the Maori appear to have believed their "sale" of land was but the sale of a shared *use*, not full title and exclusive ownership. Thomas Cholmondeley was confident in 1854 that "until quite recently, when [the Maori] sold land to the stranger, they thought they only sold the right to do that which they had themselves been used to do with it, which was to use it in common with another to dwell and build upon."[96]

The Colonial Office's solicitude in the 1830s was due in part to the fact that the House of Commons had petitioned the Crown in 1834 to direct that office to treat natives with justice, and in part due to the character of those who served in it in those years.

95 Knaplund, *James Stephen*, 88, 90.
96 Thomas Cholmondeley in his *Ultima Thule* (1854), cited in Stuart Banner, "Two Properties, One Land," 24 *Law & Social Inquiry* 826 (1999).

Soon Under-Secretary Stephen would also worry about Diaspora magistrates subjecting Maoris to what he called "the yoke of Blackstone's Commentaries" – that is, putting their customs at the mercy of "the spirit of legal pedantry from which no English society is ever emancipated, and by the contempt and aversion with which the European race everywhere regard the Black races." Stephen added to one dispatch prepared for Captain Hobson that the natives "must be carefully defended in the observance of their own customs" (though the new secretary, Lord Russell, changed these to read that the native customs were to be "tolerated").[97]

In 1840, Captain Hobson arranged and signed a Treaty of Waitangi with some forty-six Maori tribal chiefs throughout Aotearoa (New Zealand), guaranteeing the Maoris the continued occupancy and use of their land in exchange for their fealty to Her Majesty, Queen Victoria.[98] The Maori chiefs appear to have regarded this surrender of

[97] Allan Ward, *A Show of Justice: Racial "Amalgamation" in Nineteenth Century New Zealand* (Toronto, 1973), 34, 62. In fact, the twenty-first editor of the first volume of Blackstone's Commentaries, published shortly after Stephen's comment, in 1843, was John Fletcher Hargrave, who would migrate to Sydney in 1856 and serve as a district court judge in 1858 before attaining higher legal positions as Attorney-General and Puisne Justice of the New South Wales Supreme Court.

[98] Major Bunbury, Hobson's representative at some of these signings, assured the Maori chiefs at Hawke's Bay that "Her Majesty's Government" had no intention of lowering "the chiefs in the estimation of their tribes," that a chief's signature "would only tend to increase his consequence by acknowledging his title." (Noted in David Williams, *Te Kooti Tango Whenua*, 117–18.) This foreshadowed a similar communication offered by a negotiator representing United States interests to Samoan chiefs in 1872: Acting under authority of Henry Pierce, U.S. Minister to Hawaii, Rear Admiral John Winslow sent Commander Richard Meade on the *U.S.S. Narragansett* to negotiate a coaling station at Pago Pago and U.S. protectorate-status over Samoa. The impetus behind this venture was the Great American Land and Steam Company of San Francisco, whose agent, Captain Edgar Wakeman, provided Commander Meade with two letters to deliver: One was addressed to "the Missionary, Rev. Powell," who was regarded as having considerable influence with the Samoan people generally. The second, for British Consul Williams at Apia, was intended for the ears of the Samoan chiefs: "Just as all Europe is on the Eve of throwing Kings & Imperialism to the dogs [a reference to the Paris Commune of 1871]," Wakeman told Consul Williams, "don't allow any one at your point to indulge in any such absurd notion. You have great power with the Chiefs and you must tell them that they must unite their future with the United States Government at Washington. . . . " Six years later a Samoan paramount chief traveled to Washington to sign such a treaty. See Dispatches from U.S. Consuls in Apia, Samoa, Microcopy T 27, Roll 3, Vol. III, 1867–1875, National Archives; 42nd

sovereignty as a symbolic but relatively meaningless gesture, perhaps in exchange for promised protection from alleged French designs on New Zealand, perhaps in order to retain continued access to British weapons and other trade goods. Nopera, a Kaitai Maori, is quoted as saying of the treaty at the time: "The shadow of the land goes to Queen Victoria, but the substance remains with us."[99] He and his country-men were, in time, to learn that, in fact, this surrender of sovereignty to one whose courts administered an English Common Law of prop-erty left *them* "the shadow," and vested its ultimate substance in the Crown.

In 1840, representatives of Wakefield's New Zealand Company pur-chased land from the Atiawa survivors of a recent raid by Waikato Maori in Taranaki. The company's English settlers were soon being located there. But in 1842, missionaries to the Waitako persuaded them to allow their Atiawa captives to return to their patrimony in Taranaki. Finding Pakeha strangers on their land, the Atiawa took "self-help," blocking roads and threatening the English settlers with violence. The company and the settlers turned to the land commis-sioner for redress, and that man (named Spain) held that the Atiawa had forfeited their title to 60,000 acres while in Waikato captivity. "This award," writes W. P. Morrell, "was unenforceable."[100] The Atiawa recov-ered most of their land by the "law" of *haka!* (that is, by intimidation and force).

In 1844, Hobson's successor, Governor Robert Fitzroy, overruled the land commissioner and repurchased 3,500 acres at New Plymouth, the site of the English settlement. But, feeling the pinch from a dearth of revenues, he also waived the Crown's preemptive right of acquisition and resale to the rest of the 60,000 acres, and permitted settlers to purchase land directly from the natives so long as they then paid a penny per acre tax on such land as was acquired. This spurred sales and added to the colonial government's income, but it was in violation of the Australian Waste Lands Act of 1842 (5 & 6 Vic. c. 36) and so up-set the Colonial Office that Fitzroy was recalled. The new governor,

Cong., 2nd Sess., *Executive Letters (Confidential) to U.S. Senate*, May 22, 1872; Piere to Meade, Jan. 19, 1872, U.S. Legation, Hawaii, Letters Sent, 1865–1897, Box 30–18, Record Group 84, National Archives; Wakeman to Rev. Powell [copy], Jan. 13, 1872, and Wakeman to British Consul Williams [copy], Jan. 13, 1872, RADM Richard Meade Papers, Box 1, N. Y. Histori-cal Society. Cf. George Rieman [Meade's clerk], *Papalangee, or, Uncle Sam in Samoa: A Narrative of the Cruise of the USS Narragansett Among the Samoan Islands* (Oakland, Cal., 1874).

99 Louis A. Chamerovzow, *The New Zealand Question* (London, 1848), 153.

100 W. P. Morrell, *British Colonial Policy in the Mid-Victorian Age* (Oxford, 1969), 209.

Sir George Grey, revoked the waiver immediately, in 1846, but no
sooner had Fitzroy's policy been reversed, a *new* colonial secretary, Earl
Grey, with a different perspective, took office. He and the New Zealand
Company secured from Parliament a Constitution Act for New Zealand
and in December, 1846, he dispatched royal instructions to his namesake in that colony that would have had the effect of dispossessing the
Maoris from all their "waste lands" – that is, all lands they were not ac-
tively cultivating at the time. The "opinion assumed" by "a large class of
writers" was that "the aboriginal inhabitants of any country are the proprietors of every part of the soil of which they have been accustomed
to make any use." But "from this doctrine" the noble Earl did "entirely
dissent." The Maori's right to those parts of New Zealand "unsubdued
to the uses of man" was "a vain and unfounded scruple." The colonial
secretary acknowledged that he was "well aware that in point of fact"
the governor was "not in a position" to ignore Maori claims to "the
waste," inasmuch as "past transactions" between Crown officials and
the Maori had given rise to "a state of things" (Maori expectations)
rendering "a strict application" of the principles he had just laid down
"impracticable." None the less, he insisted that, in Law, the Crown was
in sovereign possession, was "seized," of the "vast tracts of waste land"
that the Maori "pretended" to own, and to bargain for.[101]

Governor Grey saw either the injustice or the mischief in that, or
both. He responded to the colonial secretary in early April, 1847, that
the "position" that "we have . . . a right to take possession" of "tracts of
land . . . not in actual occupation or cultivation by Natives" appeared
to him "to require one important limitation":

> The natives do not support themselves solely by cultivation, but
> from fern-root, from fishing, from eel-ponds, from taking ducks,
> from hunting wild pigs, for which they require extensive runs. . . .
> To deprive them of their wild lands, and to limit them to lands for
> the purpose of cultivation, is to cut off from them some of their
> most important means of subsistence; and they cannot be readily
> and abruptly forced into becoming a solely agricultural people.
> Such an attempt would be unjust, and it must, for the present, fail,
> because the Natives would not submit to it; indeed, they could not
> do so, for they are not yet, to a sufficient extent, provided with the
> most simple agricultural implements. . . . To attempt to force sud-
> denly such a system upon them, must plunge the country . . . into
> distress and war; and there seems to be no sufficient reason why

---

[101] Grey to Grey, 23 Dec., 1846, Vol. 5, *British Parliamentary Papers/Colonies New
Zealand* (Irish Univ. Press, 1969), 523–25, noted in David Williams, *Te Kooti
Tango Whenua*, 110.

such an attempt should be made, as the Natives are now generally very willing to sell to the Government their waste lands at a price which ... affords the Natives (if paid under a judicious system) the means of rendering their position permanently far more comfortable than it was previously.... [102]

Not content with the registration of this protest, Governor Grey turned to his judicial allies in this matter, the two-member Supreme Court. A case concerning the former governor's proclamation regarding the purchase of Maori land by individuals served the purpose admirably. Citing the views of New York's Chancellor James Kent, U.S. Supreme Court Chief Justice John Marshall, and their counterparts in New South Wales, Chief Justice Martin and Justice Chapman held that the Maori's aboriginal title to "waste land" was protected by the Land Claims Ordinance of 1840, and that Governor Fitzroy's waiver of the Crown's preemptive rights was null and void. This gave Governor Grey the authority he sought to ignore Secretary Grey's instructions regarding "waste land," and he followed this up by setting aside a (modest) hunting reserve of ten acres per person for a Maori sub-tribe (*hapu*) in the Canterbury region. Glenelg's and the Aborigines Protection Society's long "shadows" was still managing to leave "the substance" of the land with the Maori as late as the mid-nineteenth century.[103]

When Edward Gibbon Wakefield arrived in New Zealand in early 1853 he immediately called upon Governor Grey to withdraw another proclamation barring the sale of waste land. Parliament had just granted Responsible Government to the New Zealand Diaspora, and, Wakefield wrote, "you tear off & trample upon a great piece of the Constitutional Act in its integrity" by issuing such a proclamation.

---

[102] Parliamentary Papers on New Zealand, 1847, quoted in Chamerovzow, 396–97.

Writing of the Maori in 1842, Charles Terry had sought to explain to a British readership "the laws and customs of the aboriginal chiefs and natives, regarding land." Their "various respective boundaries," he began, were "well-known" and could "easily be ascertained." They "possess their land either hereditarily, or by right of conquest," but "such dominions" were "not the property of one individual chief, but the property of the tribe in common, according to their grade." Maori moved "from one part of the property of the tribe to another," each family "occupy[ing] and cultivat[ing] a certain quantity of land," which was its "exclusive property for the time." Terry, *New Zealand; Its Advantages* (London, 1842), 98–99.

[103] *Regina v. Symonds*, NZPCC 387 (1847), citing *Attny. Gen. v. Brown*, 1 Legge (NSW) 312 (1847), *Johnson v. McIntosh*, 8 Wheat. (21 U.S.) 543 (1823); *Worcester v. Georgia*, 6 Peters (U.S.) 515 (1832), and James Kent, *Commentaries on American Law*, A. Ward, *Show of Justice*, 89.

Grey was unmoved. Wakefield thereupon wrote to his strongest ally, Lord Lyttleton, deeply involved in Wakefield's Canterbury settlement, complaining of the "Swanriverism" of Grey's governorship and asking for the assistance of "the friends of the colonies at home" in having Grey "reprimanded, if not recalled." (Wakefield was soon elected to the first Legislature under New Zealand's Responsible Government, created in June, 1852.[104])

Much the same sort of story played out in South Africa: Leaders of the Xhosa, the Basuto, and the Zulu were often either unable or disinclined to restrain those of their tribes from taking the cattle of British and Boer pastors, for, as Chief Makomo of the Xhosa told Governor Napier, the whites had "stolen the land with the pen." None the less, the Colonial Office continued to have little sympathy for those who "settle in the neighbourhood of marauding Tribes" like the Xhosa. As Undersecretary Steven put it, neither Boer nor British settlers should expect the Crown to "rescue" them "from the natural penalty of that improvidence any more than vine dressers and farmers at the foot of Vesuvius can expect indemnity against the effects of an eruption."[105]

Sir George Napier, D'Urban's replacement as Governor of the South African Cape Colony, worried constantly about the expansionist character of the Boer and their cattle: "They idolize their flocks," he told his brother, Richard: "[T]herefore if we follow them in all their wanderings and take possession as a colony of every foot of land which they seize[,] the colony must extend to the verge of the habitable ground." In 1842, he "proclaimed" a warning to the Boers: They were to halt their advance into the lands of the Griqua, Xhosa, Basuto, and Pondo or face penal sanctions and the "liveliest indignation" of Her Majesty's government.[106] Several months later, Justice William Menzies of the Cape Colony's Supreme Court, riding circuit on the colony's frontier, heard that a column of Boers under Jan Mocke was proceeding to Alleman's Drift on the Orange River, Griqua territory, to claim the region. The impulsive Menzies assembled a handful of British officials, outraced Mocke to the site, "planted the Union Jack," and "read a proclamation taking possession." When Mocke and his 300 armed Boers arrived two days later, "the judge delivered them a lecture on the law...." Despite the praise heaped on Menzies by the *Grahamstown Journal* (voice of the frontier British settlers), Napier reluctantly disavowed this annexation (he worried that it might be "the

---

[104] Wakefield to Grey, Mar. 10, 1853, Wakefield to Lyttleton, Mar. 24, 1853, Wakefield Letters to Sir George Grey, CY2870B, Mitchell Libr.
[105] Galbraith, *Reluctant Empire*, 49, 236–37.
[106] Sir George to Richard Napier, Aug. 1, 1839, quoted in Galbraith, *Reluctant Empire*, 186; Napier to Lord Stanley, July 26, 1842, Col. Off. 48/220, Pub. Rec. Off., noted in Galbraith, 200.

only means of averting calamitous consequences to the native tribes").
Lieutenant-Governor Hare then descended on frontier Colesberg with
850 troops, the vast majority of those available in the colony, to impress
upon the Boers that they were to leave Adam Kok's Griquas alone.[107]

Changes in Direction: The Age of Responsible Governments and State Sovereignty

"Things change." Later generations of officials, legislators, and jurists
in Canada, the United States, and the Antipodes eventually secured
independence from control by the Colonial Office and altered the
local ground-rules and balance-of-power.

North America

This process may be said to have begun as early as the eighteenth
century with regard to Nova Scotia's Micmacs, Upper Canada's and
New England's Abenakis, and New York's Mohawks. Despite Sir William
Johnson's protestation, a fraudulent land sale by minor Mohawk
sachems in 1703 to British speculator/developers, bitterly disputed
by leaders of the Mohawk in the early 1760s, was ultimately confirmed
as lawful in 1765 because Letters Patent (confirming title) had been issued over time by the royal governors involving land transactions flowing from this sale.[108] Abenakis complained as early as the 1720s that
Englishmen were taking their lands "contrary to the rights of men."[109]
Simultaneously, in Nova Scotia, Lieutenant Governor Belcher's Proclamation of 1762 granting the Micmacs "a common right to the Sea
Coast" and all land "reserved or claimed" was criticized as "silly and
too precipitate" by the Nova Scotia Assembly's London agent and an-
nulled by the Board of Trade.[110]

A century later, with the appointment of Indian Affairs Commissioner Joseph Trutch in 1866, natives throughout Canada suffered.
In particular, Trutch and the legislature of British Columbia's Responsible Government[111] undid in two decades (1866–1885) all that

---

[107] Galbriath, *Reluctant Empire*, 202–03; Macmillan, *Bantu, Boer & Briton*, 206,
220. Indeed, the leading Anglican missionary in the Cape Colony, Dr.
Phillips, felt that the only means of protecting the natives was "*annexation
up to the Tropics!*" (Macmillan, 202).

[108] Hulseboch, "Imperia in Imperio...," 360.

[109] Colin Calloway, *The Western Abenaki of Vermont*, 127.

[110] MacNutt, *The Atlantic Provinces: The Emergence of Colonial Society, 1712–1857*
(Toronto, 1965), 69.

[111] So called when Parliament granted to certain of a colony's Diaspora residents constitutional power to elect a legislative assembly with considerable
independent power to make Law, and to which the executive-branch officials of the colony would thereupon be "responsible," rather than to the
Crown.

Governor James Douglas had accomplished in the 1850s to protect
the property rights of the native inhabitants there. Thus, in 1865,
British Columbia's officials reduced the size of the reserve of the Head
of the Lake Okanagans by calling upon the authority of a non-Head
of the Lake Okanagan from the United States. In 1870, a native
belonging to one tribe located near Burrard Inlet stood before magistrate Edward Stamp, accused of theft. His chief told Stamp that, inasmuch as Stamp and his fellow newcomers "had stolen their land,"
he and his people "had a right to steal" from the logging company
that Stamp managed. These Indians might well have felt so, inasmuch
as the Crown had granted Stamp's lumber firm thousands of acres
of prime timber for a pittance, none of which went to the native inhabitants. Stamp's comment on the chief's remark was that, "unfortunately," he was not allowed to use "the necessary instrument of punishment" that would result in this chief receiving a "good flogging" for his
remarks.[112]

Things had improved very little by 1914, when commissioners representing British Columbia turned away claims advanced by Fraser
Canyon Indians who claimed "the free use of the mountainsides" based
on the law of "God Almighty." One commissioner replied that "if the
chief really understood his Bible he would know that 'God placed men
in authority – laws are therefore made for the benefit of us all and they
must be obeyed by us all'."[113]

Elsewhere the plight of Canada's "First Nations" took a serious turn
for the worse with the passage of the dominion of Canada's Indian
Act of 1876. Dominion oversight of Indian affairs began in Canada
under its terms, but questions immediately arose over the status of
earlier empowering statutes with regard to *provincial* authority over
native tribes and language groups within their borders, stipulated in
such language as found in section 13 of the British Columbia Terms of
Union Agreement of 1871. Designed to provide for the administration
of the affairs of aboriginal peoples, the Indian Act of 1876 voided the
powers of native courts and councils, excluded the half-native Metis
from native status, and regulated the rules for all Canadian Indians
regarding inheritance, family, and tax matters.

All the same, the Dominion's Indian Affairs officials were often more
solicitous of the rights of native peoples than their provincial counterparts, and the scope of their authority in these matters vis-a-vis the
provincial Responsible Governments was dealt a fatal blow in 1887

---

[112] Peter Carstens, *The Queen's People: A Study of Hegemony, Coercion and Accomodation among the Okanagan of Canada* (Toronto, 1991), 63; Cole Harris, *the
Resettlement of British Columbia*, 96–97, 131.
[113] Harris, *Resettlement*, 131.

when the Canadian Supreme Court decided in *St. Catherine's Milling v. Regina* that the title of all Indian land located within the borders of the preconfederation provinces was vested in those provincial governments, not in the Dominion of Canada, and when the Law Lords of Privy Council, in upholding this judgement, reminded their Canadian compeers that under the Law native tribes possessed no more than Common-Law usufructuary rights (those of occupancy), "dependant on the goodwill" of the provincial government. The Ontario judge (Boyd) who heard the case styled Indians "barbarians" and the particular tribe involved (the Saulteaux) to be a "nomadic" and "more than usually degraded Indian type." As Sidney Harring has said, evidence refuting this view could have been introduced had Indian witnesses been called to attest to "their extensive agricultural economy and well-established hunting, trapping, and fishing territories," but they were not.[114]

By the turn of the century, the Dominion of Canada briefly enjoyed a Superintendent General of Indian Affairs, Clifford Sifton, who turned away an unholy alliance of rapacious speculators and provincial trustees of native reserves sympathetic to their plans to open a portion of these reserves to white settlers. No reserve was to be opened for any use, Sifton held, without Indian consent. Thus, when Alberta M. P. Frank Oliver wanted to open the Stoney Plain Indian's reserves, Sifton refused to tolerate it. "The law is very specific and clear." But Sifton was gone by 1906, replaced by none other than Frank Oliver.[115]

Land disputes between Chief Peguis' Red River Indians at the St. Peters' settlement and Manitoba settlers in the late nineteenth century led in 1906 to a Royal Commission, headed by the Chief Justice of Manitoba's Court of Appeals, Hector Howell. Gerald Friesen tells us that, "rather than investigate, Howell suggested that the solution to the problem was simply to move the Indians." This led to "rigged meetings of questionable legality," led by "men who wished to speculate in forthcoming land sales," to "insider trading in lands by government officials," and "a rigged vote among St. Peters' residents." Indian complaints led to a second Royal Commission in 1912 which reported "the Surrender" to have been improperly executed and consequently

---

[114] *St Catherine's Milling v. Regina*, 10 Ont. R. 196 at 227 (1885); Harring, 138.

[115] Paul Tennant, *Aboriginal Peoples and Politics* (Vancouver, 1990), 39, 41; Leslie F. S. Upton, *Micmacs and Colonists: Indian-White Relations in the Maritimes, 1713–1867* (Vancouver, 1979), 62; D. J. Hall, "Clifford Sifton and Canadian Indian Administration, 1896–1905," in *As Long as the Sun Shines*, 120 at 134; Hamar Foster, "Letting Go the Bone: The Idea of Indian Title in British Columbia, 1849–1927," in Foster & John McLaren, eds., *Essays in the History of Canadian Law, Vol. V* (Toronto, 1995), 28–86.

"void," but the Dominion Parliament responded merely by confirming the removal and enacting legislation in 1916 that validated the titles of those who had purchased the surrendered St. Peters' land.[116] Similarly, in 1910 an unreported Dominion Supreme Court decision, "Rex v. Stoney Joe," held that natives in Alberta had the right to hunt under a federal statute, but the governments of Alberta and Manitoba continued to prosecute natives for violating their provincial game laws none the less.[117]

The process was much the same in the United States: President Thomas Jefferson was prepared to direct squatters away from resettled tribes on the distant banks of the Mississippi and Missouri, as we have seen, but when it came to the more accessible Indiana territory, he was of a different persuasion. He told that territory's governor to "push our trading uses, and be glad to see the good and influential individuals" among the tribes in that region "run in debt, because we observe that when these debts get beyond what the individuals can pay, they become willing to lop them off by a cession of lands." The ideological champion of Diaspora Agrarianism, Jefferson was eager to "promote this disposition to exchange lands which they have to spare and we want, for necessaries, which we have to spare and they want...."[118]

Apparently not enough Indians on the Missouri sank deeply into debt, and in 1816, the Missouri territorial legislature urged Congress to give "those Indians" living among them "lands some where Else," inasmuch as their current settlements were "the richest and most fertile part" of Missouri. Two years later, the Monroe Administration began to negotiate such a removal. In 1820, most of the Shawnee and Delaware

---

[116] Friesen, *River Road*, 64–65.

[117] Paul Tennant, *Aboriginal Peoples and Politics: The Indian Land Question in British Columbia, 1849–1989* (Vancouver, 1990), 19, 33–35; Leonard Rotman, *Parallel Paths: Fiduciary Doctrine and the Crown-Native Relationship in Canada (Toronto, 1996)*, 53; *St Catherine's Milling v. Regina*, 13 Can. S.C.R. 557 (1887); aff. 14 App. Cas. 46(1888); S. B. Cottam, "Indian Title as a 'Celestial Institution': David Mills & the St Catherine's Mill & Lumber Co v. the Queen: Indian Land Rights as a Factor in Federal-Provincial Relations in 19th Century Canada," in *Aboriginal Resource Use in Canada*, 247–65; D. Sprague, "Government Lawlessness in the Administration of Manitoba Land Claims, 1870–1887," 10 *Manitoba Law Journal* 415 at 426 (1980); Jean Friesen, "Grant me Wherewith to Make my Living," in *Aboriginal Resource Use in Canada*, ed. Kerry Abel & Jean Friesen (1991), 141.

[118] Jefferson to Governor William Henry Harrison, Feb. 27, 1803, in Andrew Lipscomb, ed., *The Writings of Thomas Jefferson* (17 vols., 1903), X, 368–70. See also Anthony F. C. Wallace, *Jefferson and the Indians: The Tragic Fate of the First Americans* (Cambridge, Mass., 1999).

agreed to move to the banks of the Arkansas, to land "not of equal quality by a great difference," or so Missouri's delegate to Congress informed Secretary of War John C. Calhoun. Those Indians who chose to remain in Missouri found themselves harassed and unable to gain redress for squatter trespasses and depredations from the new state's courts or legislature. That body of lawmakers memorialized the federal government in 1824 to arrange for the removal of these remnants of the two resettled tribes and offered this observation: "They must know... that the power of the State is against them; and that, sooner or later, they must go." In 1825, the last natives agreed to move to tracts on the Kansas River.[119]

In his first message to Congress, President Jackson maintained that the Cherokee's hunting grounds were not their own "merely because they have seen them from the mountain or passed them in the chase." The Cherokee Nation was subjected to the authority of the state of Georgia and the might of the United States Army and removed to the West in 1836 despite Chief Justice Marshall's decisions. By the late nineteenth century, Marshall's notion of "domestic dependent nations" had yielded to a newer "plenary powers" doctrine, which had it that the time for treaties had passed and that the Interior Secretary was empowered to lease or sell Indian land despite some explicit treaty language. It also yielded to federal legislation (the Dawes Severalty Act of 1887) that individualized Indian property rights and offered "surplus" Indian land to nonnative "homesteaders" (echoing measures adopted by New Zealand's legislature and Native Land Court in the same years), and to a doctrine of state sovereignty regarding Indian reserves, comparable to that announced by the Supreme Court of Canada in the St. Catherine's Milling case (1887). Thus, states were free to apply their game laws despite federal treaty provisions, ignoring existing Indian customary law courts, but state courts could simultaneously hold that they were not empowered to prosecute the theft of timber on Indian reservations, despite efforts of federal Indian agents to check such depredations. The prosecution of such criminal acts were beyond their jurisdiction, left to the weaker arms of tribal courts and law enforcement officers.[120]

---

[119] This paragraph relies on John Mack Faragher, "More Motley than Mackinaw," in *Contact Points*, ed. Andrew Cayton and Fredricka Teute (Chapel Hill, 1998), 316–23.

[120] *Lone Wolf v. Hitchcok*, 187 U.S. 553 (1903); *Ward v. Race Horse*, 163 U.S. 504 (1896); David Wishart, *An Unspeakable Sadness: The Dispossession of the Nebraska Indians* (Lincoln, 1994), 194–95. And see Sidney Harring, *Crow Dog's Case: American Indian Sovereignty, Tribal Law and U.S. Law in the Nineteenth Century* (N.Y., 1994); Jack Campisi, "From Stanwix to Canadaigua:

Arthur McEvoy tells us of one such tug-of-war between state and federal law authorities, over the fishing rights of northern California tribes on the Klamath, Trinity, Eel, and McCloud Rivers between 1850 and 1900. The first problem native salmon fishermen had was the placer gold-miners, whose efforts sent debris into the streams. The Chimariko fought them on the Trinity, but learned (in the words of contemporary ethnographer Stephen Powers) "that they must not presume to discuss with American miners the question of the proper color for the water in the Trinity River." By the 1870s the Trinity was devoid of fish and the Chimariko were virtually extinct.

Eventually the gold-mining died out on some of these spawning grounds, but the natives then faced the cannery firms who overfished the Eel and Sacramento Rivers, destroying the salmon culture of the Wiyot and Patwin peoples. In 1883, blasting by Central Pacific Railroad construction gangs drove the salmon run back from the Pit and McCloud Rivers, all but destroying the combined efforts of the Wintu and their Federal Fish Commission allies who had been creating a salmon hatchery on the McCloud.[121]

But the Klamath was not as hospitable to miners or railway construction. Consequently, the U.S. Interior Department managed to reserve the lower Klamath for the Yurok and Hupa tribal fisheries in 1877, calling upon the U.S. Army to evict Diaspora settlers from the reserve. The California legislature responded in 1880 by declaring the Klamath a navigable waterway, and Diaspora squatters reentered the reserve and in 1887, salmon-cannery tycoon R. D. Hume set up a floating cannery at the mouth of the Klamath, "and at gunpoint warned Captain Daugherty, the commander of the Army garrison at Requa, not to interfere." The Commissioner of Indian Affairs in Washington sought to bar Hume from the reserve, and asked the U.S. Attorney-General for a declaratory judgement on the matter. But that official deferred to California's declaration of the Klamath's navigability and offered his opinion that the Hupa "enjoyed no exclusive right to its fishery, but only the right in common with the public at large." The Indians then sued, and Captain Daugherty seized Hume's floating cannery. Hume won both the trial and appeal of the matter in the local federal district and circuit courts, but in 1891, President Harrison extended the boundaries of the Hoopa Valley Reservation to the ocean,

National Policy, States Rights and Indian Land," in Christine Vecsey & William Starna, eds., *Iroquois Land Claims* (Syracuse, 1988); and Charles Wilkinson, *American Indians, Time and the Law: Native Societies in a Modern Constitutional Democracy* (New Haven, 1987).

[121] Arthur McEvoy, *The Fisherman's Problem: Ecology and Law on the California Fisheries, 1850–1980* (N.Y., 1986), 47–50.

and the California legislature repealed its Klamath River navigability statute, "apparently in an effort to encourage mining upstream from the reservation." In this instance, the Indian's preferential right to the salmon had been protected; the "Center" may be said to have prevailed in these years over the "Periphery."[122] But this was not the way things usually played out in North America by the second half of the nineteenth century.

The Antipodes

While the first generation of Diaspora settlers in Australia generally recognized that the aboriginal tribes they were displacing had well-defined boundaries and property rules, the Colonial Office could never quite bring itself to deal with any of them in so formal and respectful a fashion as to enter into the sorts of treaties crafted in New Zealand and North America. In 1836, Justice Burton of the New South Wales Supreme Court held that Australia's aborigines were "not in such a position with regard to strength to be considered free and independent tribes." They possessed "no sovereignty."[123] In 1889, the Privy Council's Law Lords repeated (in *Cooper v. Stuart*) that Australia was "*terra nullius*" (vacant land). "The richest source of legal customs in early New South Wales," Bruce Kercher says of *Cooper*, "was ... in the minds and practices of the ancient peoples who had occupied the land for so long, but these customs were never recognized at an official British level."[124]

Similarly, the commander of New Zealand's military detachment, dispatched to the Hutt Valley (east of Wellington) in 1845, observed of the claims to the region of the Ngati Rangatahi Maoris: "No individual native or portion of the Tribe can substantiate a right to any part of this valley ... no ancient *pas* nor cultivations exist – the dense Forests remained undisturbed till the axe of the European and European labour and perseverance opened out and displayed the capability of the district." Ian Wards has aptly commented on Major Richmond's Locke-laced rhetoric: "He forgot, or had never known, that a tribe would fight for a cherished eel weir situated within an empty forest,

---

[122] McEvoy, 50–61.
[123] *R. v. Murrell*, 1 Legge (NSWSC) 2 at 73 (1836).
[124] *Cooper v. Stuart*, 14 App Cas 286 (1889); Kercher, *Debt and Seduction: the Birth of New South Wales Civil Law, 1788–1814* (Sydney, 1997), ch. 3, p. 65 in typescript. See also Julie Cassidy, "A Reappraisal of Aboriginal Policy in Colonial Australia: Imperial and Colonial Instruments and Legislative Recognition of the Special Rights and Status of the Australian Aborigine," 10 *Journal of Legal History* 365 (1989).

or for a sunny and well-favoured spot for growing early kumara in the midst of miles of seemingly waste land, or for the right to snare birds or pick the berries of the karaka or the kahikatea."[125]

The governments of New Zealand and the Australian colonies often did ignore such customary rights of the native inhabitants. In 1842, a New South Wales Act for Regulating the Sale of Waste Land dedicated half of the income derived from the sales to public expenses and half to fund new immigration (and, thereby, more sales); none was to be set aside in trust for the original inhabitants. The Ngai Tahu of the South Island of New Zealand released a huge block of their "waste land" to the Crown in 1848 in exchange for future reserves. Words in the Maori version of that deed promised them "the people's *mahinga kai*," or food-gathering places. These words did not appear in the English version, and the Ngai Tahu soon discovered at the hand of the government's young agent in the province of Canterbury, Walter Mandell, firstly that they were to receive a little less than 10 acres per person, and secondly, that the promise of food-gathering rights were not to be honored.[126]

Moreover, the Ngai Tahu had been selling the Diaspora newcomers in Dunedin seafood for several decades when, in the 1870s, several newcomer-run companies began to trawl outside of the Heads of Otago Harbor. Ann Parsonson tells us of the ensuing "tragedy of the commons": Within a few years fish in those waters were "described as 'less than scarce.' The new fishing-men had not taken any steps to conserve the resource that the industry [Pakeha and Maori] depended on." Just as seriously, the government did nothing to protect the Ngai Tahu in those rights to fish the fresh-water lakes and rivers, rights promised by the Crown in the Kemp purchase deed of 1848. The official involved (once again, Walter Mantell) explained his resistance: He "knew these [eel] weirs to be so great an impediment to the drainage of the country that in no case" would he "give way upon this point." Settlers, on the other hand, polluted the streams that fed Te Waihore (Lake Ellesmere), killing eels, flounder, and other Maori staples. The

---

[125] Prucha, *American Indian Policy*, 238; C. D. Rowley, *Destruction of Aboriginal Society*, I, 60; Wards, *Shadow of the Land*, 228.

[126] Mantell was told to "carry matters with a high hand" in his dealings with the Ngai Tahu, especially with regard to their rights on the Banks Peninsula. He overawed those at Port Cooper and Port Levy, but was less successful with the "insolent and turbulent" ones at Akaroa. In any event, by 1860 negotiations over their reserves had yielded the Ngai Tahu at Kaikoura, Akaroa, Otahou and Murichiku less than 5 percent of what they had ceded. Derived from figures in Ann Parsonson, "The Challenge to Mana Maori," in *The Oxford History of New Zealand*, ed. Geoffrey Rice (2nd ed., 1992).

process was much the same for the Ngai-te-Rangi, the Ngati Paoa, and the Ngati Whatua of the North Island.[127]

In both Queensland and New Zealand, disagreement arose over the use of tidal plains, customarily claimed by natives but considered Crown demesne under English Common Law. The Native Land Court's Chief Justice, Francis Fenton, tentatively declared that the Maori could well hold the rights to the foreshore of the Thames River goldfields (in the *Whakaharatau* and *Kauaeranga* cases (1870)), but his jurisdiction over "all that proportion of the Province [of Auckland] situated below high water mark" was thereupon simply suspended by government proclamation.[128]

A Maori Reserves Act of 1856, creating reserves in trust for Maori tribes upon the sale of other of their lands, quickly proved to be imperfect, inasmuch as the trust funds were controlled by the new provincial governments of the North and South Islands, not the Crown, and the trust commissioners leased the trust lands for insubstantial sums to settlers who often fell in arrears with impunity. Like the tribes of the North American Plains, the Maoris retained their own customary norms and tribal "courts" – that is, their *runangas*, or chief-led dispute settlement forums. One early British witness to these forums, Edward Shortland, reported that in each Maori community there were to be found important men who had devoted much time and effort to learning "their 'tikanga' or laws." "Persons so educated" were the Maori's "books of reference, and their lawyers," and "the form of words with which they invariably commence" all disputes over land ownership were the same.[129] Damage by settler cattle or pigs to Maori crops might prompt an act of Maori *utu*, a retaliatory measure, such as the holding of the offending animal, or one of a nearby and otherwise inoffensive fellow Pakeha (stranger).[130] Settler/pastoralist encroachment on Maori land or depredation of *kauri* timber might provoke a threat of *muru*, followed, if they proved ineffective, by the destruction of fences, crops, and structures or the killing of a shepherd or lumberman. Some British authorities allowed that this native law-enforcing resembled the "self-help" sanctioned by the Common Law and Equity with regard to nuisances, but many other Pakeha magistrates and legislators were as offended as most of their settler-compatriots by the notion that native legal norms and remedies could be imposed on British citizens located

---

[127] Ann Parsonson, "The Challenge to Mana Maori," in *The Oxford History of New Zealand*, ed. Geoffrey Rice (2nd ed., Auckland, 1992), 195–97.

[128] David V. Williams, *Te Kooti Tango Whenua*, 44.

[129] Edward Shortland, *The Southern Districts of New Zealand: A Journal* (1851), 95.

[130] For more on this see Chapter 4.

in what had been declared to be a Crown colony. Thus when an official argued in a memo to Native Minister Donald McLean that Maori customary laws of property were well-established and of long standing, McLean, or another reader, jotted in the margin.[131]

The simple plan that he should take who hath power & he should keep who can.

While *this* observer was making use of this Hobbesian aphorism to condemn Maori intertribal strife, recall that his Australian compeer had used the same aphorism to justify Diaspora behavior on that continent.

The solution Diaspora authorities in New Zealand settled upon was to win Maori acquiescence to the posting of British magistrates throughout the two islands, those in Maori domains to administer the law in concert with Maori chiefs, supported by Maori police (*karere*) and, in some instances, by Maori magistrate-assessors. In some regions this British resident-magistrate proved to be of an open-minded sort, willing to compromise and bend English rules here and there to accommodate Maori customs. In these regions the arrangement worked admirably, giving the appearance to British eyes that British Law had been imposed. While it appeared more rigid than a *runanga* to the Maori, with some strange outcomes at times, it was one close enough to their ways of resolving disputes for most of them to live with. But in other regions the magistrates behaved just as James Stephen had feared they would, imposing "the yoke of Blackstone's 'Commentaries' " with a "spirit of legal pedantry." This prompted one Maori chief to remark in 1848 that "when we adhered to our native customs [*ritangas*] we had light – but now the land is confused by the customs of the Europeans," and this was the nub of it: Aboriginal people saw their "customs" as being less "privileged" than the "law-custom" of the Diaspora/Pakeha newcomers. Another chief, Karaitana Takamoana of the Hawke's Bay Maoris, complained in 1867 that "in olden days disputes could be settled by discussion," while "now . . . everything is settled in courts of law."[132]

Individual decisions that struck Maoris as illogical or unfair began to emerge as patterns to them. In particular, disputes over the use of "waste" land, or of tracts sold under terms not fully comprehended by Maoris or not agreed to by all those with rights in those tracts,

---

[131] Noted in Stuart Banner's fine essay, "Two Properties, One Land," 24 *Law & Social Inquiry* 818 (1999).
[132] Richard Hill, *Policing the Colonial Frontier*, 213, 216; A. G. Price, *White Settlers and Native Peoples* (1940), 164; A. Ward, *A Show of Justice*, 205.

lay behind Hone Heke's early resistance to the Crown's assertion of sovereignty in 1844–45. It ultimately led to the "Kingi" movement (a vaunted Maori united front under an island paramount chief or "King," who would be subordinate to the Crown in certain regards, but not with regard to their unsold land). "Kingis" agreed among themselves at Lake Taupo in 1856 to relinquish no more of their land by sale or treaty grant.[133] This, in turn, was precisely contrary to the intent of the newly created Responsible Government, for not long after the Maori Lake Taupo agreement, the New Zealand Parliament enacted measures facilitating the privatizing of Maori-Pakeha land transfers.

And yet key figures in New Zealand's government were still of two minds about the question: In July 1856, a Board headed by Surveyor-General C. W. Ligar summarized the Diaspora's understanding of the nature of the Maori's own property law: "Each Native" held a "right in common" with "the whole tribe over the disposal of the land of the tribe, but also "has an individual right to such portions as he [sic] or his parents may have regularly used for cultivations, for dwellings, for gathering birds or rats, or as pig runs." This "individual claim," however, did "not amount to a right of disposal to Europeans as a general rule." (Ligar said little of the powers and rights of the chiefs in this process.) C. W. Richmond, the colony's Minister of Lands, commented on Maori tenure in May, 1857:

> If we were stronger we might take cognizance of and settle questions of territorial right between the Natives. It would be politic (and I think it would be just) to support any who might demand to have the lands of the tribe partitioned and their own share allotted to them to deal with as they thought good. I am not without hope that we may by degrees take hold of such questions – but not by the strong hand.[134]

In less than two years Richmond would have his wish: The Native Territorial Rights bill, individualizing Maori land tenure, was vetoed by the Crown in 1858, but in 1859 Governor Gore Browne, yielding to pressure from land-hungry settlers and speculators, authorized land sales by individual Maori occupants anyway. The governor remained sensitive to "the right of the minority" within a Maori *hapu* "to prevent the sale of land held in common," but he sought out and met

---

[133] Marshall Sahlins, *Islands of History* (Chicago, 1985), 60–61, 69–70; Price, *White Settlers and Native Peoples*, 164.

[134] W. P. Morrell, *British Colonial Policy in the Mid-Victorian Age* (Oxford, 1969), 232, 234.

with the Taranaki Maori and their paramount chief, Wiremu Kingi, in March, 1859. After the governor had urged the assembled to part with their "waste" land, one man, Teira, rose, offered to sell the land he "owned" individually in Waitara, and "laid a fine *parawai* mat at the Governor's feet." When Gore Browne picked the mat up, he reported hearing the cry: "Waitara is gone!" Wiremu Kingi, who actually lived in Teira's Waitara tract, thereupon jumped to his feet and warned that, as chief, he would "not give it up, Ekore [I will not]!, Ekore! Ekore!" "Waving his hand," Wiremu Kingi "and his people marched off without any salutation," or so Gore Browne reported with chagrin. None the less, the governor picked up the chief's gauntlet as quickly as he had Teira's symbolic *parawai* mat: A Maori chief had no right to bar individuals from selling "land belonging to themselves," for that "would be the means of keeping millions of acres waste and out of cultivation." He sent Colonel Murray to threaten Wiremu Kingi with military force. The chief reminded Murray that the governor had said himself at the meeting in March "that it is not right for one man to sell land to Europeans." "You," he told the colonel, "are disregarding the good law of the Governor, and adopting a bad law." Gore Browne ignored this face-saving rhetorical gesture ("the Governor can do no wrong"). W. P. Morrell feels that "Wiremu Kingi's veto was an assertion of independence irreconcilable with British soveriegnty." In any event, that appears to be the way Gore Browne saw things. The Taranaki War began within three weeks of the chief's response.[135]

By 1861, the British government's position had changed: In June of that year the new Secretary of State for the Colonies, the Duke of Newcastle, wrote to Sir George Grey (returning to New Zealand as governor), indicating that the Crown was "prepared to waive" the "serious objections" to the Native Territorial Rights Act that his predecessor, Lord Carnavon, had raised, and was "willing to assent to any prudent plan for the individualization of Native Title" as well as for "direct purchase" of Maori land by settlers ("under proper safeguards").[136] Thereupon, New Zealand's colonial legislature lost little time legitimizing Gore Browne's proclamation with another Native Lands Act allowing sales of land by individual Maoris as well as those of tribes. During the debate over this bill in the lower house, representatives Richmond, Fox, and Jollie argued that the title of the bill should include the phrase "to alter the Provisions of the Treaty of Waitangi." When the Cabinet's Minister for Native Affairs, Dillon Bell, objected that "the House would be interfering with the Royal [treaty-making]

---

[135] Morrell, 236, 240–41.
[136] D. Williams, 65.

prerogative," Mr Fox replied (correctly) that he "thought the Bill did that all along."[137] This bill received Crown approval and the Crown's Native Land Purchase office was disbanded.

Once again, war broke out almost immediately in the Waikato region over land tenure disputes. It spread to other parts of the North Island, resulting ultimately in the withdrawal of those Maori in-arms to a "King" country in the center of the North Island and, in due course, to the further acquisition of vast tracts of Maori land. Some of this acquisition flowed from the war: While the Maori in-arms against the newcomers "won" at least as many engagements as they "lost," the ranks of those anxious to continue the fight thinned. By 1865, the government enacted confiscatory legislation as well as a statute creating a Native Land Court, an institution to which the Maori were encouraged to turn (as the Irish had been in the early seventeenth century) to validate their land titles by having them reissued under "our law" (as the act's sponsor, Canterbury's first provincial superintendent, Fitzgerald, described the English-bred rule of individualized fee-simple title that was the product of the court's action).[138]

The Native Land Court and its Chief Judge, Francis Fenton, required personal appearances of Maori witnesses to the disadvantage of those located at great distances from its venue. In his opinion in *Papakura – Claim of Succession* (1867) Fenton ruled first that the deceased's cousins and members of his *hapu* were not entitled to their rights-of-succession under Maori customs (*mana* and *ahi ka*).

> It would be highly prejudicial to allow the tribal tenure to grow up and affect land that has once been clothed with a lawful [English] title.... Instead of subordinating English tenure to Maori customs, it will be the duty of the Court... to cause as rapid an introduction among the Maoris, not only of English tenure, but of the English rules of descent, as can be secured without violently shocking Maori prejudices.

He then addressed the rights of the deceased's daughter and two sons. Having rejected Maori customs, Fenton appears to have sought to accomplish what he may have thought would be an accommodative "middle ground," by altering the English Common-Law rule of primogeniture significantly. He would not assign all the land to the eldest son as this could not "be reconciled with native ideas of justice or Maori custom." Hence, the land was to pass to "all of the children equally." This judgement, "always followed in later Land Court decisions," had the "unfortunate outcome" that, "as one generation followed another,"

---

[137] 5 Sept. 1862, NZPD, 676, quoted at length in D. Williams, 66–67.
[138] D. Williams, 74.

there ensued "an extreme fragmentation of ownership rights in such pieces of Maori land as do remain."[139]

At least as serious a consequence of the Native Lands Acts of 1862, 1865, 1867, and 1873 was the steady erosion of land held by Maori *hapu* under Maori customary law, the steady increase in the partitioning-off of land from *hapu* control as individual Maori took advantage of offers made by government officials or private Pakeha buyers. Maoris, confounded by these statutes, turned again to *runanga* organized by tribal committees, such as the *Komiti Nui* at Rotorua. But Native Land Court judges "resolutely refused to recognize the standing" of such forums "or to implement decisions agreed in *hui* organized by them." When the New Zealand legislature granted limited powers to such committees in 1883, the Land Court "treated the findings and reports of the committees with contempt; they were immediately relegated to the waste paper basket," and the native committees, "finding . . . themselves despised, discontinued their action," or so one concerned M. P. reported to the Prime Minister in 1893. Thus, Maori found themselves forced to utilize the Native Land Court.[140]

[139] D. Williams, 179–81.
  The same phenomenon played out in the Cook Islands after the administration of those islands passed to New Zealand in 1901. A Land Titles Court was created which, under the leadership of Judge McCormick in 1914, awarded "title in common to all children of a previous owner," "owing to its misunderstanding of the significance of lineage affiliation in determining ownership of and succession to land rights," thus creating "excessive fragmentation of ownership," writes Ron Crocombe in *Land Tenure in the Pacific* (Melbourne, 1971), 62. (Cf. Crocombe, *Land Tenure in the Cook Islands* (Melbourne, 1964), 98–125. The central difference between New Zealand and the Cook Islands, however, is that, while the Maori lost most of their land under the Land Court there, Sir John Salmond's Cook Island Act of 1915 (sec. 422) stipulated that "every title to and interest in customary land shall be determined according to the ancient custom and usages of Natives of the Cook Islands," and (sec. 467) those native land interests were to be inalienable to foreigners (Alex Frame, *Southern Jurist*, 187). From 1909 through 1935, critical years, the ministers governing the Cook Islands were New Zealand Maori. By 1958 there were 27,084 acres of native customary land, 29,322 acres of native freehold land, 950 acres of Crown land, and only 270 acres of land owned by Diaspora interests (all of them religious bodies). Crocombe, *Land Tenure in the Cook Islands*, 106.
[140] Rees, M. P., quoted in David Williams, 95.
  But note that some Maori were at first uncertain of how they were to register objections to the surveying and partitioning of their land, "placing a letter in a notch cut into a tree on the survey line" in one instance. Williams, p. 5.

Illustration 6.   Petitioners and witnesses stand and wait, circa 1880, before the Native Land Court, Ahipara, New Zealand. (Alexander Turnbull Library, National Library of New Zealand/Te Puna Mātauranga o Aotearoa, F267801/2.)

Maori traditional leaders sought to prevent sales by individuals, because such sales generally required that the land of the *hapu* thereupon had to be surveyed and formally partitioned by Native Land Court assessor-judges, and by the 1870s Maori were being charged for the survey, the costs of court, and, of course, had to provide for their living expenses while awaiting their turn to testify at the lengthy court hearing, often held many miles from their village. In the words of one Waikato chief named Aporo, English Law was "a bad dog; it devours many."[141] Moreover, these expenses often had to be paid for by the sale of some of the land that had just been transformed from Maori to English legal form. (See Illustrations 6 and 7.)

The pressure of merchant debt and the appeal of ready cash and trade goods was too much for some Maori. Thus, the official charged with acquiring land for railway construction in "Kingi" country reported in 1890 on his successful negotiation with two Maori "who just disposed of their interests": The two "were fully a fortnight" before they "could screw up their courage to sell," and "instead of coming to see me in the day time," he wrote, "they waited upon me at 9 P.M.," having ridden "12 miles since sundown (they would not leave their own settlement until dark)." They "returned that night lest any of the

---

[141] Kercher, *Unruly Child*, 6–8; A. Ward, *Show of Justice*, 93, 121, 133, 151, 180, 212–13; Richard Hill, *Policing the Colonial Frontier*, I, 839, 856; II, 427.

Illustration 7.   A similar scene in northern Ontario, as members of one "First Nation" listen to the James Bay Treaty formalities at Flying Post, Sudbury, July, 1906. (Archives of Ontario, C275-2-0-3-S7627.)

local natives should see them and surmise that they had been selling land."[142] Maori-owned land fell from about 17.5 million acres in 1870 to about 7 million in 1915.[143]

As late as 1872, New Zealand's jurists held that the Crown was "bound by the Common Law of England and by its own solemn engagements" to give "a full recognition of native proprietary rights," which it defined as "whatever the extent of that right by established Native custom appears to be." But in 1877 the new chief justice, James Prendergast, perhaps recognizing the reality of what the Native Land Court had accomplished in the previous decade, led the court in a reversal of direction. He styled the Maori "primitive barbarians," denied that they had any "settled system of law," and held that colonial authorities possessed no power to interpret the terms of the Treaty of Waitangi, which

---

[142] Allan Ward, *A Show of Justice: Racial 'Amalgamation' in Nineteenth Century New Zealand* (Auckland, 1974), 299.

[143] D. Williams, 61. And see Bryan Gilling, "Engine of Destruction? An Introduction to the History of the Maori Land Court," 24 *Victoria University, Wellington, Law Review* 115 at 135 (1994).

the Maori and their remaining Pakeha supporters viewed as the sole remaining instrument that might be called upon to protect native customary rights. The treaty was now referred to as "a simple nullity," a dead letter unless the Crown chose to enforce its terms itself. A subsequent supreme court decision, in 1881 held that the treaty had not given to Maori customary rights the character of title. Thereafter, some trust reserves were sold in the late 1880s, and Lake Wairarapa was partially drained to benefit settler-farmers, damaging Maori eel fisheries, while these same settlers were allowed to hunt ducks with firearms in this same Maori preserve.[144] Maori property rights were diminished in this process. Few had been restored by the early 1990s when the process of restoration began under the Waitangi Tribunal.

North Island Maori *did* win a number of political fights in the 1890s, securing continued use of their eel weirs, access to their oyster beds, and freedom from license fees for trout fishing. But they faced a new challenge shortly after the turn of the century, when their rights to Lake Rotorua, a Maori domain on the North Island of New Zealand, became the subject of litigation. The local Te Arawa Maori had for many years divided the lakebed up among families,[145] the boundaries of these divisions marked with pegs, creating fishing rights that were "far more valuable to the old-time Maori than any equal area of land," as Te Rangi Hiroa put it. But in 1906, Prime Minister Richard Seddon told the Te Arawa that they had "no claim to the lakes." The Maori disagreed.

What prompted Seddon's remarks appeared to have been a judgement of Privy Council. In 1894, the New Zealand Court of Appeals had held (in *Tamaki v. Baker*) that a claim of title by the Crown to any land was "sufficient to oust the jurisdiction" of any and all of the courts in New Zealand. Maoris had disputed the Crown's title to land of theirs

---

[144] *Re Lundon & Whitaker Claims Act*, 2 NZCA 41 at 49 (1872); *Wi Parata v. Bishop of Wellington*, NZJR 72 (1877); *Mangakahia v. NZ Timber Co.*, 2 NZLR(SC) 345(1881); A. Ward, *Show of Justice*, 298. See also Richard Boast, "In re 90 Mile Beach Revisisted: The Native Land Court and the Foreshore in New Zealand," 23 *Victoria University of Wellington Law Review* 145 (1993); P. G. McHugh, "Aboriginal Title in New Zealand Courts," 2 *Canterbury Law Review* 235 at 245 (1986).

[145] Williams, *Politics of the New Zealand Maori*, 74–75. Similarly, among the Chippewa and Ottawa of the upper Great Lakes, beaver dams, cranberry patches, and sugar-making camps were reported to "all have owners . . . and are handed down from father to son." (Johann Kohl, writing in the late 1850s, cited in Robert Doherty, *Disputed Waters: Native Americans and the Great Lakes Fishery* (Lexington, 1990), 14.) This was also the case with tribes in British Columbia when it came to salmon-fishing sites, and with Aborigines in southeastern Australia when it came to quarries and individual trees!

that the Crown had never properly surveyed. They appealed the judgement, and in 1901, Privy Council reversed. Lord Davey explained that if a native could "succeed in proving that he and members of his tribe" were and had been in continual "possession and occupation of the lands in dispute under a Native title which had not been properly extinguished" (that is, not properly acquired by the Crown), he was free to maintain an action in New Zealand's courts to protect that title and occupation.[146]

In 1909, the colony's chief legal draftsman, John Salmond of the Solicitor-General's Office, met with the judges of the Native Land Court and prepared a consolidation of statutes pertaining to Maori customary rights and land titles. Soon after its passage, a Maori fisherwoman had her whitebait nets confiscated by a fisheries officer at the Waitara River in Taranaki. She sued, her attorney claiming customary rights to fishing under the provisions of the Treaty of Waitangi. Nonsuited, she appealed, and her case was eventually heard by the Court of Appeals. Now-Solicitor-General Salmond argued that the terms of the Native Land Act of 1909 that he had drafted effectively barred suits like this one, and that, in any event, such nonterritorial rights to tidal waters as the plaintiff claimed were vested in the Crown. The Court of Appeals agreed, thus discounting language in the Fisheries Act of 1908 that had guaranteed the continuation of "existing Maori fishing-rights."[147]

Salmond tried to persuade Maori leaders to accept the Native Land Act of 1909 and to rely on government offers of compensation rather than to pursue the judicial options reopened by Privy Council's *Tamaki* decision, but one Maori suit wound its way up to the Court of Appeals, which refused to cooperate with the Solicitor-General's efforts. In *Korokai v. Solicitor-General* (1912), following Privy Council's directions, the court held that the Maori had a right to have their customary rights determined by the Native Land Court. This cleared the way for the testing of Maori rights to the lakebed of Lake Rotorua in that court. When, after considerable testimony had been offered, the trial judge took ill and died, the parties entered into extensive negotiations, and

---

[146] *Tamaki v. Baker*, 12 NZLR 483 (1894); revs'd. in Same v. Same, NZPCC 371 (1901); AC 561 (1901).

[147] Alex Frame, *Salmond: Southern Jurist* (Wellington, 1995), 104; *Waipappakura v. Hempton*, 33 NZLR 1065 (1914). This restrictive general view of Maori fishing rights prevailed for over seventy-five years, until rejected by the court's President Judge, Robin Cooke (in *Te Rununga o Muriwhenua Inc. v. Attorney-Gen.*, 2 NZLR 641 (1990) (citing Privy Council's language in *Tijani v. Sec. St., Nigeria*, 2 AC 399 (1921) on "the principle of preservation of the Native's title after cession of sovereignty" – that is, though land might be ceded, customary fishing rights remained.)

the Maoris agreed to surrender their claim of customary title to all lakebeds and riverbeds in New Zealand to the Crown in exchange for retaining the right to *fish* those waters (as well as an annual payment of 6,000 pounds and title to some small islands).[148] The government had obtained the "title" to all of New Zealand's waters, while the Maori (some of whom may have wondered at what the difference was, and why the government had labored so mightily) continued to enjoy their fishing rights.

Hawaii

By the early nineteenth century the Hawaiian islanders had developed an elaborate set of regulating norms (*'Aikapu*), among them, rules regarding fishing rights and land tenure. Thus, it was forbidden to fish during the spawning season, and certain species of seafood were reserved for chiefs, others for males. Some land was held (by high chiefs) in perpetuity with rights of survivorship, but most was held by chiefs (*Ali'i Nui*) or land stewards (*Konohiki*) as trustees (*Kanaka*) for the use of others, including all commoners (*maka 'ainana*). Resembling those of the Fijians and Maori, Hawaiian land tenure was redistributed upon the ascendence of a new island high chief, but effectively it was held by the common Hawaiian cultivators, who may have found that he had a new *Konohiki* landlord/trustee from time to time, but rarely experienced "eviction."[149]

The arrival of Diaspora traders, missionaries, and planters, largely from the British Isles and the United States, in the early nineteenth century, all seeking "title" to land, prompted successive Hawaiian paramount chiefs to forbid any alienation of land to foreigners. In 1828, for example, Ka'ahumanu, consort of the late monarch Kamehameha I, halted one such transfer to pay a chief's debt to a trade by having the Hawaiian government assume that and all other debts of chiefs to traders. Later, in 1834, King Kauikeaouli directed chief Kaikio'ewa to give Diaspora newcomers seeking land leases "in the same manner" as he did on Oahu, by granting them a leasehold estate in certain property for their lifetimes or for as long as they stayed in Hawaii.[150]

---

[148] *Korokai v. Sol.-Gen.*, 32 NZLR 321 at 345 (1912); Frame, *Salmond*, 110, 112, 116, 119, 123.
[149] Norman Miller & Robert Horwitz, "Land Tenure in Hawaii," in *Land Tenure in the Pacific*, ed. Ron Crocombe (Melbourne, 1971), 21–39; and Lilikala Kame'eleihiwa, *Native Lands and Foreign Desires: Pehea La E Pono Ai?* (Honolulu, 1992), 54–58, 134–35, 204.
[150] Kame'eleihiwa, 28, 92, 171.

But successive epidemics weakened the faith of the chiefs in the spiritual strength of their *'Aikapu*, and by the 1840s many had become Christians and were prepared to adopt western norms, including those associated with land ownership. In December, 1845, Kamehameha III created a land commission (of three Hawaiians and two Americans) that recommended action by the chiefs that would formally divide all land into units held by individuals in fee simple. The Great *Mahele*, signed in 1848 by the monarch and the *Ali'i Nui*, accomplished such a division, into blocks held by the government, the king, the chiefs, and the common Hawaiian people. In 1850, the Hawaiian legislature sanctioned the purchase of such units by foreigners. Approximately 10,000 awards of land were made under the terms of the Great *Mahele*. Less than 20 percent were for over 100 acres; some 35 percent were for less than 10 acres. Yet the king, nobility, and government ended up with nearly four million acres, while the Hawaiian common people received only about thirty thousand acres, largely because so few of them came forward to make a formal claim.[151]

Common Hawaiians continued to cultivate the land as they always had, but steadily lost control, as their customary rights (such as their access to water) were deemed to be extinguished under Common-Law rules by Common-Law judges,[152] and as the fee simple title to the land of the *Ali'i Nui* and the king passed by sale to Diaspora planters.

South Africa

In 1848, the Cape Colony's Governor, Sir Harry Smith, chose to brow-beat Chief Adam Kok of the relatively weak Griquas into leasing much of his people's domain to Boer tenants for small annual quitrents in the hope that this would solve his Boer problem in that quarter. Simulta-neously, he secured the approval of Secretary Grey for the extension of the Cape Colony's northern border to the Orange River, though Grey reminded him that this would encourage the Boers to come into con-tact with natives once again when there was "no power in the colony" available "to restrain them." In early 1852, Governor George Cathcart signed the Sand River Convention, granting Transvaal Boers indepen-dence, and in early 1854, the Orange Free State's independence was recognized as well.[153]

Soon Boer settlers in the Northeast were encroaching on Chief Moshesh's Basuto. Smith assigned local colonial official Richard Southey the task of redrawing boundaries between the Boer and

---

[151] Miller & Horwitz, 29; Kame'eleihiwa, 200–15.
[152] As in *Maikai v. Hastings*, 5 Hawaii LR 133 (1884).
[153] Galbraith, *Reluctant Empire*, 248–49.

Basuto. John S. Galbraith tells us the resulting boundaries "could not have been more favorable to the Boers had a commission of burghers been invited to draw them." Similar treatment of the Gaika chief Sandile in 1850 led to the Kaffir War of 1850–53.[154] Local British and Boer editors had called for less "timorous hesitancy" on the part of Crown legal authorities (*Grahamstown Journal*) and for Responsible Government, as there was "no question" that "all would be better if the frontier population alone had the right and power of making laws for the security of the border." The Boer *Graaff Reinet Herald* agreed and added that the frontiersmen should be free to impose "that system of humane severity which alone can keep our restless neighbors in order." These views were echoed in Britain by the Conservative's voice, the *Times* of London: The Aborigines' Protection Society and their Whig allies were engaged in "mischievous meddling." The colonial secretary had "in every colony resisted to the utmost every attempt on the part of the colonists to manage their own affairs," and this was especially true in South Africa. The natives there were "barbarous and sanguinary wretches" incapable of civilizing. Enough was enough![155]

Between 1848 and 1851 several thousand British and other European emigrants descended on Natal, the coastal protectorate on the Cape colony's northeastern border, prompting Governor Smith to have Lieutenant-Governor Benjamin Pine assemble a Native Management Commission, dominated by Natal's white settlers. The commission's report called for a series of schools to teach native youth "habits of industry" and assign them to settlers on five-year apprenticeships. The Lieutenant-Governor was disappointed: "Too prominent a place" had been given to "the interests of the white Colonists, more especially as to the supply of native labour. . . . " Tribes "whose past avocations have been war and the chase" were not likely "in any short space of time to subside into regular agricultural labourers" or enjoy being domestic servants. Such a scheme ignored "the natural laws which govern the world." But Natal's necomers received their charter in 1856.

Chief Moshesh eventually asked for "the Queen" to "send a man to live with me" to teach the Basutos "to hear Magistrates. . . . " He and his council preferred to live "by our own laws," but other laws that "the Queen" wanted to introduce could be submitted to the council for approval. This was an invitation that would be followed by several years of painstaking negotiations, overseen by Governor Wodehouse, between the Colonial Office and Moshesh, eventually creating

---

[154] Galbraith, 248.
[155] *Grahamstown Journal*, Oct. 27, 1842; *Graaff Reinet Herald*, Feb. 9, 1853; *Times*, June 21, 1851; Nov. 12, 1851; all noted in Galbraith, 248–49.

the semisovereign state of Basutoland.[156] By comparison with what happened elsewhere in South Africa, to Australia's aborigines, the Maori, and many North American Indian tribes under the pressure of Responsible Governments and (in the United States) "state sovereignty," the creation of Basutoland stands out as one of the more impressive uses of the Crown's authority on behalf of indigenous people. (The same might be said of the Crown's creation of the Bechuanaland Protectorate in 1885.)

Fiji

But there is an even more impressive example of this: Law pronounced by the "Center" won out over the legal standards sought at the "Periphery" in another antipodal domain: Fiji. When British traders, missionaries, planters, and graziers wound their way to these islands in the second and third quarters of the nineteenth century, they found a feudal world of warring tribes dominated by chiefs with real authority. Many purchased land from the chiefs and other hereditary titleholders (*mata in vanua*), and by the 1860s, Diaspora newcomers (some from Australian colonies) had acquired most of the small westward Yasawa islands and a significant foothold on the two main islands of Viti Levu and Vanua Levu.[157]

Soon there was a British consul, and a western-style Fijian government with a paramount chief (Cakobau), ministers, and a legislative assembly. A local planter, Robert Swanston, would serve the Fijian Council of Chiefs as Minister for Native Affairs, and eventually a former consul, John Bates Thurston, would serve the Cakobau government as Chief Secretary and Minister for Foreign Affairs. Most of these Diaspora officials proved to be sympathetic to the Fijians when it came to land. Consuls W. T. Pritchard and H. M. Jones, in the 1860s, felt that

---

[156] A. F. Hattersley, *The British Settlement of Natal* (1950), 99; W. P. Morrell, *British Colonial Policy in the Mid-Victorian Age* (Oxford, 1969), 94–95, 104–05, 154, 171. And see Anthony Dacks, "Missionary Imperialism: The Case of Bechuanaland," 13 *Journal of African History* 650 (1972).

[157] Peter France, *The Charter of the Land: Custom and Colonization in Fiji* (Melbourne, 1969), 43–54. They soon learned that the land "must be openly bought," as J. B. Moss put it. "Secrecy" could be "fatal" since "some of the owners may have been left out" and the title would afterwards be disputed. Moss, *A Planter's Experience in Fiji* (Auckland, 1870), 62; Moss, *A Month in Fiji by a Recent Visitor* (Melbourne, 1868), 14; noted in France, 186. And see George Markham Diary, entry for Jan. 24, 1874 (on dispute with "the Vu Longa [or Tonga] people" who "lay claim to our 'wi' and breadfruit trees & have declared that if we take any more of them they will have war." YA 1462, Mitchell Library, Sydney.

"in the generality of cases where disputes arise between the natives and settlers, the latter will be found to be the aggressors." Swanston was troubled, however, by the thoughtlessness of Cakobau in granting Diaspora planters great tracts of land in Ba (western Viti Levu), the Yasawas, and Bua (southwestern Vanua Levu), displacing several thousands of Fijians whom he simply ordered to move. Secretary Thurston was equally appalled.[158]

In any event, the Fijians were persuaded in October, 1874 to sign a deed of cession and become a Crown colony. Fiji's first British governor arrived in June, 1875, Sir Arthur Gordon, a former Liberal M.P., former Governor of New Brunswick, Trinidad, and Mauritius, a former private secretary and personal friend of the British Prime Minister, William Gladstone, and a man of singular determination to do what he thought right. Diaspora residents soon learned that he viewed their land titles with suspicion. He produced instructions from the Colonial Office (now administered again by Lord Carnarvon, a Gladstone appointee). One of the conditions (which Gordon may have solicited) was that all foreigners claiming to hold valid land titles be required to "give satisfactory evidence of the transaction with natives" on which their claims relied, and proof that the land had been "acquired fairly, and at a fair price." The foreign planter-legislators in the Cakobau government had sought to protect themselves from just such a legal inquiry from the "Center" by excluding already-alienated lands from the cession of sovereignty (though the Colonial Office had managed to require this passage to read "shown to be alienated"). They felt that the deed of cession had placed this matter beyond Gordon's control. As Peter France puts it, they expected the governor to have "neither control over [these lands] nor the right to decide on their extent," except "properly," that is, in a court of Common Law. Their lawyers "drew attention to this fact," but when the Colonial Office's lawyers confirmed these contentions, Gordon still "refused to accept that the control of land alienation should pass from his hands." In 1878 he wrote to Sir Robert Herbert, the Colonial Office's Permanent Undersecretary, urging him to "find some means of overcoming the scruples of the gentlemen of the long robe" lest the colony "go to pieces." The Crown's legal beagles "became tractable," and Parliament soon gave Gordon the authority to create a Land Claims Commission to investigate all claims, recommend action to the governor-in-council, which would then render decisions appealable to a three-person panel consisting of the governor, his appointed-commissioner for native affairs,

---

[158] France, 63, 70, 98–100; Deryck Scarr, "John Bates Thurston, Commodore Goodenough, and Rampant Anglo-Saxons in Fiji," 11 *Historical Studies – Australia & New Zealand* 361–82 (1964).

and the colony's chief justice; the statute forbad appeals to Common-Law courts.[159]

Governor Gordon was determined to see the customary property rights of the Fijians preserved and protected by his and the commission's actions. (Thus, he privately told Chief Justice Sir John Gorrie in 1880 that his "great objective" was "to make the alienation of native land *as difficult as possible*," for their continued control of the land was "the only condition of any possible *progress* on the part of the natives.") Diaspora planters were well aware of this predisposition of Gordon's. "A Colonist" ranted about the governor's animosity toward "the pioneers of the country" in a pamphlet published at Levuka in 1879, complaining particularly that "Sir Arthur Gordon will not now sell an acre of Government land," and that "he wants Fiji for the Fijians." (But, in passing, this anonymous planter acknowledged that the governor was "the hardest-working man in the colony.")[160]

Gordon's solicitude mattered: The Land Claims Commission reduced Diaspora ownership from 850,000 acres to some 415,000 within a decade.[161] The problem was that Gordon formed his views of the property customs of "primitive people" largely on the strength of his reading of the work of pioneer anthropologist Lewis Henry Morgan (*Ancient Society*, 1877) and from the influence upon him of Morgan's local admirer, Lorimer Fison, a talented amateur anthropologist who shared Morgan's view that among "primitive" peoples all land was communally owned and was inalienable. Fison, and Gordon as well, appreciated that these "basic" property customs of "primitive" people did not seem to be in evidence in the Fiji of their day, but they attributed this to their having been corrupted by contact with the Diaspora newcomers. In any event, the governor decided that the *mataqali* (an agnatic family-tree clan much larger than the family unit) was the true "owner" under Fijian custom, and he set out, with eventual success, to have the council of chiefs agree to this and the land commissioners to use it as the basis of all surveys and recommendations.[162]

---

[159] France, 114–15. And see Bryan Farrell, *Fijian Land: A Basis for Inter-Cultural Variance* (Center for So. Pac. Studies, Univ. of Calif. at Santa Cruz, 1977), 97, 110.

[160] Gordon to Gorrie, Sept. 21, 1880, in J. D. Legge, *Britain in Fiji, 1858–1880* (London, 1958), 184; "A Colonist," *Remarks on the Address delivered by Governor... Gordon at the Colonial Institute, March 18, 1879* (Levuka, June, 1879), 9, 12, 14, copy at Mitchell Library.

[161] J. K. Chapman, *The Career of Arthur Hamilton Gordon, Lord Stanmore* (Toronto, 1964), 209.

[162] France, 111–20. And see Carl Resek, *Lewis Henry Morgan: American Anthropologist* (Chicago, 1960), 125–29 (on the active correspondence of Fison and Morgan from 1869 on).

Ultimately, this single-minded vision Gordon held was in significant measure responsible for the fact that most land today in Fiji is still owned by Fijians. The irony is that Gordon (and Fison) had it all wrong: In the first place, Fijian chiefs had sold much land to newcomers on their own hook, not because they misunderstood what the transaction amounted to, not because they were trying to wheedle guns and cash out of the Diaspora buyers with claims of ownership they lacked (though both of *these* things happened on occasion), but because *they held* sovereigns title to all the lands of their tribe (the *lewa*). Thus, most land sales had been "lawful" by the standards of both cultures. In the second place, successive land commissioners dutifully insisted on the *mataqali* as the ownership unit despite discovering substantial resistance to it from many quarters of Fiji. Land rights, it turned out, differed in different tribes. When Bau chief Tevita Raivalita impressed on the commission in Tailevu (eastern Viti Levu) in 1890 that simple family units rather than *mataqali* were the traditional customary feudal rightholders, the Secretary for Native Affairs ignored what he called this "somewhat singular statement." Consequently, when the government's surveyor sought to lay out the *mataqali*-based boundaries set by the commission, "he was met by a crowd of armed men painted for war and was forced to give up the attempt." Similar incidents were reported on other occasions in the Fijian-language press. None the less, Peter France tells us, "the social unit of the Fijian people" that commissioners like David Wilkinson, G. V. Maxwell, and Basil Thomson had found to be "most remote from the exercise of land rights" was gradually transformed between 1880 and 1918 "into the legally registered owner."[163] The "Center" and its agents hadn't gotten it quite right, but it *had* managed to protect the native land rights of 130,000 Fijians from the land lust of no more than 2,000 of Diaspora newcomers. In October, 1905, the governor reported to the legislative council that eleven twelfths of the land was owned by natives.[164] They had lost title to some valuable coastal and valley property, but had retained more than enough to sustain them throughout the twentieth century.

Sir Arthur Gordon figures in our story again in 1883, while serving both as Governor of New Zealand and High Commissioner for the South Pacific Islands. He had learned of the Queensland government's annexation-by-fiat of Papua/New Guinea. Appalled, Gordon wrote immediately to his friend, Gladstone. Queensland's government, he told the British prime minister, had been treating its aboriginal people with a unmatched savagery since it received its constitutional grant

---

[163] France, 121, 137, 173.
[164] Gov. to Council, Oct. 10, 1905, Fiji Miscellaneous Papers, CY2848, Mitchell Library.

of Responsible Government in 1859. Consequently the colony's annexation of a region filled with indigenous people was entirely inappropriate and immoral. Gladstone and his Liberals responded in *this*
instance in the manner of Glenelg. Britain voided Queensland's annexation, but extended protectorate status over the region.[165] Gordon
and the first Papua/New Guinean Governor Sir William MacGregor
sought out local chiefs and tried to create a colonial system sensitive
to the norms and traditions of the indigenous people. But Britain
had thrust the costs of the fledgling colony upon Australia, and this,
coupled with Australian racism, led to the end of such efforts to in-
volve Papua/New Guineans in local government with the appointment
of the utterly paternalistic Hubert Murray as the chief administrator
in 1908 (a post he relinquished only in death some thirty-two years
later).[166]

Similar complaints of abuses of aborigines in Western Australia by
pearl-diving companies in the same years prompted imperial officials
to write a clause creating an Aborigines protection board, responsible
to the Crown alone, into the act that granted the colony of Western
Australia Responsible Government in 1890. But in this case continued hectoring by the Western Australian leadership throughout the
1890s led to Parliament relinquishing this oversight board in 1897,
leaving aboriginal matters to that colony's quite irresponsible Responsible Government.[167]

Basutoland, Bechuanaland, and Fiji, then, can be thought of as "victories" in the late nineteenth century for the authorities and humanitarian interest groups at the "Center." But elsewhere, in Australia,
New Zealand, Canada, and the United States aboriginal people suffered at the hands of "Periphery" (local) lawmakers, without much
interference, generally speaking, from the Crown or its constitutional
"descendants" (the governments of the Dominion of Canada and the
United States). A major part of the reason for this was due to their relinquishing of powers over native peoples to state and provincial lawmakers, to the "devolution" of law-making authority to the Canadas, Nova
Scotia, Newfoundland, the Australian and South African colonies,

---

[165] Chapman, *Career of Gordon*, 294–301. This was, in part, to forestall German
ambitions in that quarter. See J. D. Legge, *Australian Colonial Policy: A Study
of Native Administration and European Development in Papua* (Sydney, 1956),
28–31.

[166] A. M. Healy, "Colonial Law as *Metropolitan* Defence: The Curious Case of
Australia in New Guinea," in *European Impact and Pacific Influence: British
and German Colonial Policy in the Pacific Islands and the Indigenous Response*,
ed. Hermann Hierry and John Mackenzie (London, 1997), 214–30.

[167] Reynolds, *This Whispering in Our Hearts*, 127, 131, 173–75.

New Zealand, Fiji, and the rest of the Canadian settlements, all in a few midcentury decades.[168] But this was, in turn, often due to the fact that the "center" authorities were themselves no longer as willing to exercise such "protectorship" of original people as they had been in previous years.

What became of the Colonial Office's humanitarian championing of aboriginal rights, so vibrant in the 1830s and 1840s? What became of the U.S. government's protection of tribal treaty rights as in the early nineteenth century? One explanation: A generation of British and American anthropologists writing in the mid-nineteenth century led a number of influential individuals on both sides of the Atlantic to doubt the wisdom of policies that had been designed to protect the customary rights of the Aborigines. A number of native peoples, who had been described as being "equal" to the Diaspora newcomers "under God's eyes" in the 1830s were increasingly described as "inferior" or "degraded." They might be worthy of solicitude, but only the sort that "uplifted" and "civilized" them by individualizing their land tenure and urging farming and grazing practices and other Western ways upon them.[169] The views of polygenesists like Charles White had, by the mid-nineteenth century, impressed many with their racist notions of "the regular gradations in Man," and in the 1860s and 1870s Charles Darwin's *Origins of Species* (1859) spawned a host of misrepresenting popularizers, the "Social Darwinists." In any event, "Social Darwinism" appears to have infected some jurists. By the turn of the century New Zealand's John Salmond would write of aboriginal customary laws: "They are not in themselves law" however much they might have been "primeval substitutes" for law. "There may have been a time in the past when man was not distinguishable from the anthropoid ape, but that is no reason for now defining man in such a manner as to include an ape."[170]

A second explanation: Many in Britain remained sympathetic champions of aboriginal customary property rights, as they understood them, but they ultimately counted for little. The Aborigines' Protection

[168] For one treatment of the process see Peter Burroughs, "Colonial Self-Government," in C. C. Eldridge, ed., *British Imperialism in the Nineteenth Century* (London, 1984), 58–60.

[169] See Charles White, *An Account of the Regular Gradations in Man* (1799); William Stanton, *The Leopard's Spots: Scientific Attitudes towards Race in America, 1815–1859* (Chicago, 1960); George Stocking, *Victorian Anthropology* (N.Y., 1987), and Douglas Lorimer, *Colour, Class and the Victorians* (Leicester Univ. Press, 1978). Darwin himself, mind you, was no "Social Darwinist" in this regard; he was sympathetic to the views of the Aborigines Protection Society.

[170] John Salmond, *Jurisprudence* (1st ed., London, 1902), ch. 2, sec. 19, 54–55.

Society and Anti-Slavery Society persisted and retained some influence, but their influence within the Colonial Office waxed and waned with successive changes in parliamentary leadership. In any event, Tories and Whigs, Conservatives and Liberals, agreed, from the 1840s on, that colonies were too expensive, and that they should devolve the costs of administration onto the colonists themselves by grants of Responsible Government. Laissez faire.[171]

In short, the leaders of the new Responsible Governments in Canada and the Antipodes rarely displayed the sort of sympathy with indigenous people that could be seen at the Colonial Office throughout most of the century. A steadily-rising flood of Diaspora settlers were thus granted a substantial share of the reins of government with the enfranchising of large segments of the adult male population and their ensuing legislative supremacy. And that combination of Social Darwinism and Responsible Government went a long way toward undoing aboriginal customary property rights.

But there was more to it than that.

THE POWER OF POPULAR NORMS AND FRONTIER JUSTICE: REDSKINS AND SETTLERS, ABORIGINES AND SQUATTERS

While Diaspora Law ultimately served to hedge in and virtually dispossess many of these native inhabitants, we have seen that this had not been the clear original intent of either the Crown, the U.S. Congress, or any of the first generation of governors or jurists in North America or the Antipodes. We have also seen that the waves of Diaspora newcomers that broke for decades over these lands eventually secured greater access to aboriginal property than governors or jurists had allowed, through their own legislative assemblies. But these British Diaspora "settlers" did not always wait for such legal ceremony. They appreciated statutes friendly to their purposes, to be sure, but until they could be obtained, *they took "self-help."* Some examples:

The United States

Yes, Virginia's colonial government had confirmed aboriginal title to "those seates of land that they now have" and had prohibited squatting by whites on these lands in 1652, but this statute "was ignored more

---

[171] Peter Cain has provided a useful collection of essays by such British and colonial statesmen as Gladstone, Lord Carnarvon, Dilke, Frounde, Dice, Lowe, and Julius Vogel debating the merits and demerits of "Greater Britain" in the 1870s in *Empire and Imperialism: The Debate of the 1870s* (South Bend, 1999).

often than it was enforced" (in Stephen Potter's words): Squatters steadily ate away at Indian reserves. This problem was common to all the North American colonies, and natives were quite aware that it was transpiring. The plight of the natives living in Natick in the late seventeenth century is a case in point. In the early 1680s, one John Grout bought fifty acres in that township from two natives "without the townes privity, or consent." Grout "afterwards altered the deed to read *five hundred acres.*" When the village sued, it recovered 400 of these acres, surrounded by lands owned by English settlers. Subsequently, the village decided to sell most of this land to another Englishman, Matthew Rice, to whom they also leased some meadowland. But Rice was no better than Grout; he tried to transform his lease into a kind of by-the-forelock fee simple title, and "when some of us have discoursed with him about it he says wee are poore creatures & have noe money, & if you goo to Law & I [ar]rest you might goe to prison & there Lyue & rott."[172] Pennsylvania's Indian agent, Conrad Weiser, told Ohio Valley chiefs in 1754 that their homes there were viewed by whites "as your hunting Cabbin only." He did not overstate the matter: General Edward Braddock frankly told the Delaware chief, Shingas, in 1755 that "No Savage Should Inherit the Land." This would account for why the Crown's Indian agent in New York, Sir William Johnson, was told by an Iroquois headman in 1753, "if we find a Bear in a Tree, there will immediately appear an Owner for the Land to Challenge the Property and hinder us from killing it."[173]

All title to aboriginal land was, as we know, supposed to be acquired from the Crown (or the U.S. government), and then resold to settlers; but this Law was sometimes ignored. The New Haven colonists, for example, bought the colony's land directly from local Indian bands (though the colony later registered that title with Crown officials when Charles II's administration insisted on that formality). Consequently, it is not surprising that many former Connecticut residents who moved to what is now northern New Jersey in the late seventeenth and early eighteenth centuries relied on documents establishing their purchase of land from local Indian tribes in the course of their long-term struggle with Crown-sanctioned proprietors (described at greater length in Chapter 3).[174]

---

[172] Jean O'Brien, *Dispossession by Degree*, 83.

[173] Potter, *Commoners, Tribute and Chiefs*, 196; Michael McConnell, *A Country Between: The Upper Ohio Valley and its Peoples, 1724–1774* (Lincoln, 1992), 106–07, 115, 119 and esp. 245.

[174] Kawashima, *Puritans and Indians*, 53, 67–68; Neal Salisbury, *Manitou and Providence: Indians, Europeans, and the Making of New England, 1500–1643* (1982), 200; Harry Wright, "The Techniques of 17th Century Indian-Land

These settlers had at least *bargained* with the native inhabitants for land; most Diaspora frontiersmen simply *squatted* on it. Sir William Johnson complained to the Board of Trade in 1766 of his inability ("I have it not yet in my power") to "take the necessary steps" to prevent these encroachments, "daily increasing, occasioned by the ill conduct of numbers of the Frontier Inhabitants" (whom he described elsewhere as "the lowest of the People"). They "seem regardless of the Laws, & not only perpetrate Murders whenever opportunity offers, but think themselves at liberty to make settlements where they please."[175] British military forces in western Pennsylvania did burn squatters out on the Monongahela and Cheat Rivers in 1761 and 1767, but they returned. Captain James Murray, commanding at Fort Pitt, wrote to General Thomas Gage that his efforts had been fruitless, and that both natives and whites were subsequently killing one another over settlements with impunity, being "under no Laws," inasmuch as he had insufficient force to police the frontier.[176] Similarly, throughout the eighteenth century in the foothills of the southern Appalachians, Diaspora frontiersmen and their families, described as "wild Peoples" by North Carolina officials, encroached upon the lands of the Catawbas and the Cherokee. "No officer of Justice from either [North or South Carolina] dare meddle" with these "people of desperate fortune." The[y] say the[y] will not Be Subject to our Laws," an Charleston agent wrote in the mid-eighteenth century. In March, 1775, a group of private speculators, the "Transylvannia Company," met with an assembly of some one thousand Cherokee at Sycamore Shoals to purchase the lands between the Kentucky and Cumberland Rivers for 10,000 pounds-worth of goods.[177]

These Diaspora squatters were bad enough, but at times those appointed as trustees for land duly acquired through title or government purchase and held for the benefit of the natives could prove to be just as destructive of their rights. Near the end of the century one such trustee deceptively secured from the Catawbas a ninety-nine-year lease for himself of a shoal in the Catawba River as a commercial shad fishery. At first he allowed the Catawbas to use the facility two of every seven nights, sufficient for their needs. Then, complaining that they had torn his nets, he converted their rights to a share of the catch doled out as he saw fit. "Every night and every morning Catawbas showed up at the shoal," James Merrell writes. "Sometimes they got

Purchases," 77 *Essex Institute Historical Collections 185 at 195* (1941), Brendan McConville, *infra*, ch. 3, note 50.
[175] Hulsebosch, 357.
[176] Richard White, *The Middle Ground*, 319, 344, 347.
[177] St. Aron, *How the West was Lost*, 62.

their fish, sometimes not." When the Catawba headmen complained of these and other depredations, they found that they were "not heard when we speak the truth on our trials," and that settlers took to raising "Quarrells with our people" and "little Slye crimes," using the courts to their advantage.[178]

Similarly, during the War for Independence the younger generation of Cherokee braves joined the Chickamaugas and British in waging war against their Diaspora neighbors to the east. As John Stuart reported the matter, the Cherokee were furious with the "amazing great settlements" made "upon tracts under titles obtained from individuals by taking advantage of their wants and poverty, or by forgeries and frauds of different sorts which the nation never acquiesced; for they are tenants in common and allow no person, however so great, to cede their lands without the consent of the nation obtained in general council."[179]

With the conclusion of the War of Independence, the British ceded the lands west of the Appalachians to the United States, and settlers began to pour through the passes. A number of adventurous speculators sought to create their own "State of Franklin" in Indian lands comprising what is now eastern Tennessee, ignoring the Treaty of Hopewell (1785–1786) with the local natives. When these settlers squatted on Indian treaty lands, Congress often reacted by buying those tracts from the tribes rather than enforcing their existing treaty rights. Some frontiersmen and women may well have sensed and anticipated this reaction. Federal Indian agent Return Meigs would later observe that "shrewd &... desperate" squatters often acted "in hopes the land will be purchased, when they will plead a right of preemption, making a merit of their crimes."[180]

General George Washington toured the recently acquired midwest in 1784 and reported that speculators "roam over the Country on the Indian side of the Ohio, mark out lands, Survey, and even settle them" in "defiance of the proclamation of Congress." This "gives great discontent to the Indians," and "unless measures are taken in time to prevent it," would "inevitably produce a war with the western Tribes." Despite similar warnings from Secretary of War Henry Knox and North Carolina's Senator Benjamin Hawkins, neither the Confederation government of the 1780s nor the new federal government that replaced

---

[178] James Merrell, *The Indians' New World: Catawbas and Their Neighbors from European Contact through the Era of Removal* (Chapel Hill, 1989), 185, 224.

[179] Colin Calloway, *The American Revolution in Indian Country: Crisis and Diversity in Native-American Communities* (Cambridge Press, 1995), 196.

[180] Prucha, *American Indian Policy in the Formative Years* (1962), 181.

it either could or would halt the flood of settlers, known to the Miami and Shawnee as the "Long Knives," and war did indeed ensue, to rage intermittently for the next several decades.[181] The Creek and Cherokee were forcibly removed west in the mid-1830s after President Jackson essentially made moot the import of the Supreme Court's verdict regarding the treaty rights of the Cherokee Nation *(Worcester v. Georgia)* by persuading Georgia's governor to pardon the missionary-plaintiff, Samuel Worcester. He thus obviated any need for federal force to be called upon to compel Georgia to respect the Court's views.[182]

This pattern of undermining the federal treaty rights of natives was played out by frontier ranchers, settlers, lumbermen, legislators, and jurists throughout the nineteenth and early twentieth centuries in the United States, using county courts to force land sales out of Indians indebted to local merchants.[183] Some of these measures led to violent clashes of the two cultures. Let one example suffice: The U.S. Supreme Court held in 1896 that Wyoming's legislature was free to bar the Bannock Indians from hunting elk on federal land despite a federal treaty that had provided them this right. When Wyoming officials thereupon sought to enforce their game laws, the result was the "Lighting Creek" shootout in 1903. Groups of Oglalla Sioux hunting antelope were stopped by a sheriff and a deputized posse. In a few moments the sheriff, one of his deputies, and five Oglalla lay dead.[184]

---

[181] Prucha, *Amer. Indian Policy*, 34–39, 160; Wiley Sword, *George Washington's Indian War: The Struggle for the Old Northwest, 1790–1795* (Norman, Okla., 1986), 203; Washington to Jacob Read, Nov. 3, 1784, in *Writings of George Washington*, ed. John C. Fitzpatrick (39 vols., Washington, D.C., 1931–1944), Vol. 27, p. 486.

[182] President Jackson was no deeply distressed friend of the Cherokee, to be sure, but he had been sympathetic to their plight in the past as military commander in the region (as we saw on p. 53). His primary rationale for the removal appears to have been a concern with South Carolina's Nullification Act and its possible adoption by its neighbors; hence the "deal" with Georgia. Alfred Kelly, Wilfred Harbison, and Herman Belz, *The American Constitution* (7th ed., New York, 1991), I, 205.

[183] Dunaway, *First American Frontier*, 252.

[184] Sidney Harring, *Crow Dog's Case: American Indian Sovereignty, Tribal Law and U.S. Law in the Nineteenth Century* (N.Y., 1994), 152n; Charles B. Wilkinson, *American Indians, Time & the Law: Native Societies in a Modern Constitutional Democracy* (Chapel Hill, 1989); Daniel Littlefield & Lonnie Underhill, "The 'Crazy Snake Uprising' of 1909," 20 *Arizona & the West* 308 (1978). And see the remark of one of the Catawba's neighbors in 1870: "For years the law among themselves was their own, and no white officer of justice thought of interfering with them. What was between themselves, was among themselves." Cited in James Merrell, *The Indians' New World*, 235.

None of this is remarkable now; Hollywood has recently discovered the profits to be made telling of the mistreatment of Indians and their lands in such venues as *Dances with Wolves, Little Big Man,* and *Soldier Blue.* What *is* remarkable is that American Indian concepts of customary law administered by tribal mechanisms have survived this century and a half of dishonor, to reemerge in viable form in the past generation.[185]

The Canadian Provinces

The story was much the same on the Canadian side of the border. Squatters steadily ate away at Micmac reserves in Nova Scotia, New Brunswick, and Prince Edward Island in the early and mid-nineteenth century. The colonial government in Nova Scotia made efforts to evict these squatters in 1810, the 1830s, and the 1850s, but "could only bluster," as Leslie Upton has put it, "for it had neither the money for the necessary court actions nor the force to remove undesirables." In 1859, the Nova Scotia legislature required squatters to buy the Micmac land they were on, the funds to go into a trust reserve for the tribe. But many squatters paid little or nothing. This proved to be the case in New Brunswick as well, despite the efforts of frustrated superintendents of Indian affairs there. And even when the Mills of the Law were set in motion, they ground Micmacs as often as they ground squatters. The Indian Commissioner for Cape Breton, H. W. Crawley, reported in 1849 that "under present circumstances" he was powerless to protect "Indian property." It was "vain to seek a verdict from any jury in this Island against the trespassers on the reserves; nor perhaps would a member of the Bar be found willing and effectually to advocate the cause of the Indians, inasmuch as he would thereby injure his own prospects, by damaging his popularity."[186]

Sidney Harring, who has pointed Crawley's views out, goes on to provide an example of the problem: *McLean v. McIsaac,* a suit for assault, false imprisonment, and trespass, filed by a squatter, David McLean, against the Indian Commissioner for Cape Breton, Donald McIsaac, who had been "trying to remove McLean and his son from the Whycocomagh reserve." McLean had been arrested, fined, and jailed on a warrant signed by McIsaac after "over twenty years" of defiance of Micmac demands that he depart. The trial court judge instructed the

---

[185] On the modern tribal court see Robert Cooter and Wolfgang Fifkentscher, "Indian Common Law: The Role of Custom in Indian Tribal Courts" (Pts. 1 & 2), 46 *American Journal of Comparative Law* 287ff & 509ff (1998); and James Zion, "The Navajo Peacemaker Court: Deference to the Old and Accommodation to the New," 11 *American Indian Law Review* 89 (1985).

[186] Harring, *White Man's Law,* 179–80.

jury to return a verdict for the Commissioner, but the jury defied him and awarded the squatter damages. McIsaac did finally prevail at Law, but only by pursuing an appeal before Nova Scotia's Supreme Court. Three Micmac chiefs wrote to Queen Victoria in 1842: "There seems to be a right and wrong with the white man which Indians cannot comprehend."[187]

As we have seen, the legal power of Governor Haldimand's Grand River grant to the Six Nations in Upper Canada/Ontario had been weakened by Chief Justice Robinson's *Doe ex d. Jackson v. Wilkes* opinion in 1835. This may have accelerated squatter encroachments; it could hardly have served to reduce them. In any event, a legislative committee report in 1847 confessed that they had failed to protect effectively the Indian reserves (any more than they had the clergy reserves) from "those natural laws of society to which even Governments must bend." They reported "the impossibility of exercising a surveillance over those vast tracts" to check the workings of those "natural laws" with regard to "the indigent emigrant" or "the fraudulent speculator."[188]

Mohawks living at Kanesatake in lower Canada (Quebec) confronted a different sort of encroacher – the Catholic Sulpician order, which had been awarded title to a large tract of Mohawk land in 1840. The Mohawks persisted in claiming rights to this land, frequently entering it to fell trees and remove timber. In 1868, their chiefs petitioned for a reconsideration of their property rights, but they also signaled to Quebec's secretary of state that, because of the "default of justice having been rendered us," they would "adopt such means as will ensure the removal of these priests" from their land. "Between 1870 and 1873 alone," Sidney Harring tells us, "about one third of the adult male Mohawks in the village were brought up on criminal charges for cutting wood without the permission of the Sulpicians." Repeated confrontations led to violence. Mohawks burned the Sulpician mission in 1877 and fifteen Mohawks were put on trial. Juries in all five trials (several were tried separately) failed to reach guilty verdicts. It appeared that the Protestant jurors would not convict anyone, even the "savage" Mohawks, for destroying the property of the even more-despised Catholic priests.[189]

On the Manitoba grasslands competition between natives, Metis, and whites for buffalo, fish, and especially for scarce stands of timber

---

[187] Upton, *Micmacs and Colonists*, 88, 95, 96, 108–11, 118, 133, 150; Harring, *White Man's Law*, 180; *McLean v. McIsaac*, 18 Nov. Sc. 304 (1885).

[188] Harring, *White Man's Law*, 37.

[189] Richard Daniel, "The Oka Indians v. The Seminary of St. Sulpice," in *A History of Native Claims Processes in Canada, 1867–1879* (Ottawa, 1980); Harring, 176.

grew steadily in the 1850s and 1860s. Lake Winnipeg was over-fished by a Detroit firm using seine nets. Gristmills and steamboats on the Red and Assiniboine Rivers killed off the sturgeon. Meti Joseph Royal complained to the province's governor in 1871 of the harvesting of timber on the Assiniboine and Sale Rivers: "Until now this timber was a commonly held resource where each limited the taking to what was necessary for his proper use." Ozawekwun, a Cree hunter, laughed when told by Indian Agent Ogletree in 1885 that he was not allowed to hunt deer in the Tiger Hills. He said "if he was starving and saw a Deer he would certainly shoot it. . . ."[190]

The invasion of the Diaspora resource-snatchers clearly led to the crisis, but Irene Spry shows that, at least on the Canadian plains, both cultural groups ultimately can be said to have shared responsibility for it. Unable to cooperate, they took what they could with increasing rapidity. One Indian band advised government negotiators in the 1870s "when timber becomes scarcer on the reserves we select for ourselves; we want to be free to take it anywhere on the common." The result was another ecological "tragedy of the commons" by the mid-1870s, and was one of the grounds leading Meti Louis Riel and his followers to declare Meti sovereignty in the 1880s.[191]

Another of the grounds for Meti resistance had to do with their treatment at the hands of the Diaspora newcomers. Lieutenant Governor Archibald wrote in 1871 that the Meti suffered both from the inadequacy of their land allotment and "the persistent ill-usage" they experienced from "newcomers who fill the town [of Winnepeg]." "They say that the bitter hatred" these newcomers expressed for them was "a yoke so intolerable that they would gladly escape it by any sacrifice." This "yoke," worse than "Blackstone's," led to Riel's "Rebellion" in 1885.[192]

In far Western Canada, natives and whites clashed over the rights to fisheries and campsites. In the early 1850s, Captain Walter Grant, RN, observed the Nootka and other tribes on Vancouver Island and wrote of them that "all of the tribes are singularly jealous of their fishing privileges, & guard their rights with the strictness of a manorial preserve." Many were protected in those rights by the efforts of the

[190] Jean Friesen, "Grant me Wherewith to Make my Living," in *Aboriginal Resource Use in Canada*, ed. Kelly Abel & Jean Friesen (Winnepeg, 1991), 146.

[191] Irene Spry, "The Tragedy of the Loss of the Commons in Western Canada," in *As Long as the Sun Shines and Water Flows*, ed. Ian Getty & Antoine Lussier (Vancouver, 1983), 210–13 (translation of Royal's remarks mine); Thomas Flanagan, "Louis Riel and Aboriginal Rights," in *Ibid.*, 247–62.

[192] Archibald to J. A. Macdonald, 9 Oct. 1871, Journal of the House of Commons of the Dominion of Canada, 1874, Appendix 6, quoted in Gerald Friesen, *River Road* (Winnepeg, 1996), 65.

Hudson's Bay Company's governor of the island, Sir James Douglas, but on the mainland of British Columbia commercial fisheries over-fished the salmon on the Fraser River in the mid-1860s at the expense of the Salish Indians. In 1878, after conferring with a number of tribal councils in the interior of British Columbia, Indian Affairs Commissioner Gilbert Sproat wrote to the superintendent-general that one consistent demand of these tribes was for access to their favorite tracts of land, "old 'places of fun' up in the mountains, or some places of fishing... where, at certain seasons, they assemble to fish, dig roots and race their horses." At Nass Harbour on the north coast, a Nisga chief expressed these sentiments to an Indian Commissioner in 1887:

> What we want is... our property – our land. We want to have... as much land as we need to use, and we want the words and hands of the Government, to make a promise on paper – a strong promise – that will be forever.... We are different from the whites. We don't all live in one place, but have to scatter all over the country to make a living. We want sufficient land for our numbers. We want food, salmon, berries, animals for food and furs, timber for houses, boxes and canoes, bark for mats. Now these things are got in different places, and we want land where we can get them....

This was what had been behind the killing of William Manning by Chilcotins in 1864. Manning had preempted one of their traditional seasonal campsites near Puntzi Lake; it was reported to Governor Frederick Seymour that the killers "went to the trouble of breaking up the ploughs and other agricultural implements."[193]

The Indians of British Columbia, then, had a clear sense of their rights to land as a vast commons. But despite the occasional government promise or the setting aside of tribal reserves, the British Diaspora and its continental European fellow settlers in that province relentlessly encroached upon these domains until many tribes had been forced into reservations barely sufficient for their subsistence and had been left without free use of those "places of fun."

The final indignity was the statutory outlawing of the practice of the "pagan" practice of potlatching, the ceremonial giving away of goods at specified times of the year or in celebration of noteworthy events in British Columbia, and of its counterparts, the Sun Dance and the Give-Away Dance, religious ceremonies of those native to the east on Canada's vast prairie. Many of the Kwakiutl people (among others) defied the potlatch statute. British Columbia's Chief Justice Matthew

---

[193] Robin Fisher, *Contact and Conflict: (Indian-European Relations in British Columbia, 1774–1890* (Vancouver, 1992)), 108, 207; Paul Tennant, *Aboriginal Peoples and Politics,* 60, 109, 194.

Begbie, in the first appeal from a prosecution under the statute, released a Kwakiutl man convicted of having engaged in potlatch. The Law, Begbie wrote, was imprecise, lacking a proper definition of the criminality in the act. So the legislature simply revised the statute, providing a more elaborate definition. Many Kwakiutl continued the custom none the less.[194]

Australia and New Zealand

In the Antipodes, British Diaspora settlers also sought to evade governmental interference with their demands on aboriginal property rights. But here there transpired something of a contrast in the results: The Aborigines inhabiting every corner of Australia that was of interest to whites quickly found themselves dispossessed, often ignored, and generally unprotected by the Crown and its Colonial Officers.[195] From the beginning, in New South Wales, aboriginal customs regarding dispute resolution were given virtually no status by the colony's jurists. Despite Lord Glenelg's specific stipulation in the South Australia Colonization Committee's Letters Patent that the new colony's government purchase land from the natives, the South Australians insisted that the natives were mere wanderers who "never held a single acre in permanent occupation."[196] Consequently, they purchased none from them.

---

[194] Fisher, *Contact and Conflict*, 207; Harring, *White Man's Law*, 203; and Katherine Pettipas, *Severing the Ties that Bind: Government Repression of Indian Religious Ceremonies on the Prairies* (Winnipeg, 1994). And see Joseph Masco, "It is a Strict Law that Bids us Dance: Cosmologies, Colonialism, Death and Ritual Authority in the Kwakwaka'wakw Potlatch, 1849–1922," 37 *Comparative Studies in Society and History* 41 (1995); and Douglas Cole & Ira Chaikin, *An Iron Hand upon the People: The Law against the Potlach on the West Coast* (Vancouver, 1990).

Distrust and fear of aboriginal dance was not confined to the western provinces of Canada, of course. One thinks of the dread and loathing that greeted the Lakota Sioux Ghost Dance, and of the Maori *Haka*. As the Wellington *Independent* put it, "scrape a Maori, the most civilized, and the savage shows distinctly underneath. The *Haka* [war challenge] is an *expose* of the evil which really lies at the root of their prostate condition, an exhibition of the substratum of utter immorality, depravity, and obscenity, which forms the ground work of their race." (K. Pettipas, *Severing the Ties that Bind*, 34.) This nineteenth-century view of the *Haka* reminds us today of the cultural distance we have been traveling since then, for the *Haka* is now danced by both Maori and Pakeha members of New Zealand's fabled "All Blacks" as they face their opponents at the onset of every "All Blacks" rugby match.

[195] For more on this subject see Chapter 4.

[196] Committee chairman Robert Torrens, cited in Henry Reynolds, *The Law of the Land*, 114.

Wherever land was coveted by whites, the Aborigines were seen as "savages," annoyances. In every corner of the continent, Diaspora shepherds, wranglers, and their employers lashed out at natives for wheat or sheep stolen or shepherds attacked. Henry Meyrick wrote his mother from the Goulburn in 1840 that natives were "shot like dogs," and in 1846, he told her that "no wild beast of the forest was ever hunted down with such unsparing perseverance as they are; men, women & children are shot whenever they can be met with." Meyrick "protested against it at every station I have been in in Gipps[land] in the strongest language." "No consideration on earth" would induce Meyrick "to ride into a camp & fire on them indiscriminately as is the custom here" (but he allowed that "for myself if I caught a black actually killing my sheep I would shoot him with as little remorse as I would a wild dog").[197] Edward Curr recalled that the Commissioner of Crown Lands in early Victoria would sanction force and "administer justice with sword & carbine to the wrong tribe in mistake [his underscoring]" when trying to settle "the frequent differences which occurred between the original lords of the soil & the Anglo-Saxon *parvenus*." Consequently, he was not surprised when an older Aborigine he came upon spearing fish on the Baala Creek "howled, abused, & spat at me, in a senile fury, asking (as Tommy afterwards explained) why I came to the Moira [a tract south of the Murray]?" The water, fish, and duck belonged to his tribe, the old man shouted, and added that "he hated me."[198] Protector of Aborigines Edward Eyre reported in May, 1842, from his post on the Murray River in South Australia that natives told him they had been fired upon "as soon as they have been seen, without the slightest previous provocation on their part."[199] Overseer T. W. Wills of a station in Queensland can be heard in 1861 requesting absentee-landlord H. C. Harrison to send him fresh station hands "who will shoot blacks."[200] In 1865, James Lang, one of the early pastoralist "Squatters" of South Australia, criticized his Diaspora countrymen in his new abode, southern Queensland, for their "cold-blooded cruelty," unchecked because it appeared to be the "rule and custom" there to deal with "the black question by killing them off."[201] And in 1880, station hand David Cormack wrote his sister Anne from Ravenswood, Queensland, that he had met Aborigines

---

[197] Henry Meyrick to his mother, Oct. 23, 1840, & April 30, 1846, Letters of H. Meyrick, MS 7959/654, Latrobe Library, Melbourne.

[198] Edward Curr, *Recollections of Squatting in Victoria* (Melbourne, 1883), 119–20, 176–77.

[199] Protector Edw. Eyre to Gov. George Grey, May 28, 1842, *Reports & Letters to Gov. Grey from E. J. Eyre at Moorinde* (Adelaide, 1985), 35.

[200] Wills to Harrison, Oct. 24, 1861, OM 66–2/2, Oxley Library, Brisbane.

[201] Quoted in Henry Reynolds, *This Whispering in Our Hearts* (Sydney, 1999), 97.

in the bush "but they never done me no harm." However, he told her that he had "knowen plenty of men in the Country that will shoot the poor things for Sport the same as we used to shoot rabbits in the old Countray at-home." Barrister George Moore of Western Australia was no blood-thirsty murderer, but he did complain to his brother of "that legal absurdity which is enjoined us by the mistaken humanity of those at home," namely, "the due course of the English law" that required warrants for the arrest of Aborigines for the killing of Diaspora settlers. "I wish they would give us credit for knowing as much of our affairs, and the necessities of our position, as they do."[202]

Australia's Aborigines fought bravely in defense of their "usufructory" rights (or as they put it, "our land"), but, armed with inferior weapons, and lacking the visceral traditions of warfare of the Diaspora settlers, they were dispatched, by Lawful means if possible, unlawful ones if not. In 1848, Western Australia's Colonial Secretary complained that "the wishes and intentions of the home government" toward the Aborigines had been "frequently frustrated, evaded, misrepresented and successfully counteracted" by "a dead weight" of settler "indisposition," a "persevering system of obstruction."[203] Had he been aware of the remark of Attorney Richard Windeyer, the man who had represented the men responsible for the Mynall massacre, offered in a public lecture in 1844, he might have quoted Windeyer: The Squattocracy's occupation of New South Wales was a case of the "grand, fundamental law," that "those who have should take the power and those should keep who can."[204]

The Maoris of New Zealand were an entirely different matter. They were divided, tribally, like the natives of Australia and North America. But, unlike the Australian Aborigines (but like the tribes inhabiting the North American Plains), they had acquired and had come to master

---

Lang had his counterpart in Fiji in 1871: John Hall James, a planter at Teidanu in western Viti Levu, wrote home of how he and his colleagues had just "shown the beasts" that they had no need for magistrates to punish local tribesmen for the killing of two fellow planters. James and his friends were "able to take care of ourselves." They had just retaliated by raiding a village. They shot "all we saw," "plundered it," "burned everything," and "then sat down and had a smoke." R. A. Derrick, ed., "Letters from a Planter in Fiji," 7 *Transactions and Proceedings of the Fiji Society* 76–77 (1968).

[202] David Cormack to his sister Anne, Nov. 24, 1880, Misc. Docs. 3167, Mitchell Library, Sydney; George Moore, *Diary of Ten Eventful Years in Western Australia* (1884), 318–19, 323 (he repeated the point in other letters). See also Diary of G. F. Read, Jr., Aug. 11 & 13, 1837, *Clyde Company Papers*, ed. P. L. Brown (8 vols., Oxford, 1952), II, 90 (on threats "to shoot every one" of a band of Aborigines deemed to have stolen from his Barwon station on the fringe of the Otway Ranges).

[203] H. Reynolds, *The Law of the Land*, 152–53.

[204] Reese, *Aborigines and Colonists*, 173.

Western firearms. And they were already quite proficient in the construction of well-fortified villages (*pas*) and sufficiently numerous to prevent the steadily-growing numbers of British settlers from facilely sweeping them and their customs aside.

The war that began in 1860 continued intermittently for a decade. But, even as a number of Maori tribal warriors fought alongside British regulars and New Zealand militia against the "rebels," merchants hungry for their land canceled their tribal credit arrangements, secured judgements against them, and required these Maori-allies to enter into "pre-title investigation transactions requiring debtor owners to agree to dispose of land...."[205]

After formal hostilities had ceased, individual acts of Maori resistance continued. In 1868, certain Ngati Ruanui warriors reacted in south Taranaki to the government's opening for settlement of land confiscated under a punitive war-time statute, by seizing the horses of settlers in *utu* (retribution under Maori customary law) and driving lumbermen off of Maori reserves. When magistrate James Booth arrested the "horse thieves," open warfare resumed. In 1876 and 1877, two Hawke's Bay Maori villages, in separate incidents, resisted with force the efforts of constables "seeking to execute an order of the Supreme Court to eject them from land claimed – unjustly, in fact – by settlers." Armed Te Arawa Maori forced the Land Court at Mahetu to adjourn a case in 1878. They resisted a survey of the Wanganui block in 1879; survey lines were obliterated. Surveyors were ambushed at Ohinenuri in that year, and followers of the prophet Te Whiti uprooted survey pegs on the confiscated Waimate Plains and upturned the crops of settler fields.

This prompted Pakehas in the region to organize a "Hawera Republic." The government intervened to forestall private bloodshed, but also to empower the Diaspora settlers. Sir Arthur Gordon, serving as the Crown's representative (that is, as governor), was disgusted by the treatment meted out to Te Whiti by the New Zealand government. While Gordon was on a visit to Fiji in his role of high commissioner, in September, 1881, Prime Minister John Hall sent Te Whiti an ultimatum: He had two weeks to evacuate Parihaka or face eviction by force. The *New Zealand Times* offered editorial applause: Te Whiti and his people should, indeed, be forced off "land they have so long and [more to the point] unprofitably encumbered." Upon his return Governor Gordon sought to secure the withdrawal of this ultimatum, without success. Hundreds of the passive Maori resistors

---

[205] M. P. K. Sorrenson, "The Purchase of Maori Lands, 1865–1892," MA thesis, Auckland University College, 1955, pp. 48–49, summarized in D. Williams, 144 (whose words I have quoted here).

were arrested. Armed constabularies building a strategic road linking New Plymouth and Hawera found their path blocked by new Maori fences every day; these "fencers" were also arrested; yet others took their places. Statutes enacted to permit the holding of these and other resistors were dead letters within a month, as "the old, the infirm, and children" now replaced the now imprisoned warriors "in the front line of resistence." As Richard Hill has observed, "the cost was becoming prohibitive, in terms both of money and public opinion at home and in England."[206]

Te Whiti and others were arrested and tried for treason in December, 1881. But a judge who followed the Rule-of-Law handed down by his predecessors dismissed the charges. Several hundred of those arrested were released and Prime Minister Hall forced to step down; in the next several months all the remaining prisoners were set free as well. Nevertheless, the government eventually managed to open the region to settlement, and Governor Sir Arthur Gordon left New Zealand in 1882, as frustrated and angry as his predecessor, Sir George Grey, had been.[207]

In 1886, another group of some 300 nonviolent Taranaki Maoris occupied the farm of one A. J. Hastie in a region that had been confiscated. They built a *whare* (Maori meeting house) and destroyed Hastie's paddock. Pakehas reacted by driving off their horses, and the leaders of this act of resistance were eventually arrested, the occupation ended. Thus, Pakeha law ultimately triumphed, but with something less of the finality than it had in Australia, Nova Scotia, British Columbia, or the original thirteen colonies: In 1891, Maoris still held sway on eleven of the twenty-eight million acres constituting the North Island.

"Kingis" continued to use traditional *runangas* to resolve property disputes in the Maori's domain, and there were Maori who sought to adapt English legal forms to their *tikanga* (customary law) when they adopted Pakeha ways of life. For example, when the Ngati Porou became sheep graziers, they found that the communal enterprise they sought was best managed "by forming a committee and turning the tribe into a sort of sheep-farming corporation." As this arrangement "lacked the protection of the Law," they sought to legitimize it no less than three times in the 1880s and 1890s.[208] But other Maori continued

---

[206] R. Hill, *Colonial Frontier Tamed*, 325–28; Belich, *I Shall not Die: Titokawaru's War, New Zealand, 1869–70* (Wellington, 1989), 290; J. K. Chapman, *Career of Gordon*, 245–60.

[207] A. Ward, *Show of Justice*, 224, 278; James Belich, *The New Zealand Wars and the Victorian Interpretation of Racial Conflict* (Auckland, 1986), 308.

[208] Williams, *Politics of the New Zealand Maori*, 85.

to resist "Blackstone's yoke": Kerei Kaihau, a follower of the Maori "King," Tawhaio, asserted Tawhaio's sovereignty over land occupied by Pakehas, tearing down survey markers. Arrested and briefly imprisoned, he repeated the act upon being released. Later, in 1894, he publicized a similar gesture that he planned with some twenty associates, to destroy the survey pegs of a road being cut into Maori land in the western Waikato. Forty constables were dispatched to stop them. John Williams tells us that "it took a wrestling match to complete the arrests." Jailed, Kaihaio and his associates "had discovered" that "the advance of settlement and government was inexorable. . . . " In 1893, a widespread *Kotahitanga* movement began a boycott of the Land Court and organized their own Maori legislative "Assembly."[209]

******

The story, then, was ultimately the same in New Zealand as it had been in North America. The property rights of the native inhabitants were, in the first generation of settlement, respected by the Crown and its officials, but eventually ignored by the Diaspora settlers and *their* Responsible Governments. (*Some* of these rights have at last been rediscovered and honored again in our lifetimes by both courts and legislatures in North America and the Antipodes, a story beyond the scope of this book, but one I can at least note and applaud as loudly as one can in a parenthetical phrase.)

SUMMARY

Customs sometimes had the force of law, and many of these customs were treated as law in Common-Law courts. Hunters, fishermen, and miners, indeed, the native inhabitants no less than the Diaspora newcomers, enjoyed vibrant customary property rights. But statutes, inspired by those who would benefit from the enclosing of common land (in Britain) or the "waste" and "uncultivated Crown demesne" (in the colonies), extinguished many customary rights. In the British

---

[209] Belich, *The New Zealand Wars*, 305; John A. Williams, *Politics of the New Zealand Maori*, 46; A. Ward, *Show of Justice*, 254, 306.

A Maori Lands Administration Act (1900) created Maori land councils for each district with Maori majorities, taking over some of the functions of the Native Land Court regarding ownership, trusteeship, and succession questions, but these were abolished in 1905. For the best accounts of the effect of Diaspora Law on the Maoris see the chapter by Richard Boast on the subject in Boast, Jeremy Finn, and Peter Spiller, *A New Zealand Legal History* (Wellington, 1996); and David V. Williams, *Te Kooti Tango Whenua*.

Isles those losing out were English cottagers, Scottish crofters, Welsh *pobol tai bach*, and Irish cottiers; in the colonies and dominions, they were the aboriginal peoples, *their* rights extinguished by the same men who had done in those of their counterparts in the British Isles, albeit some of their Diaspora servants and shepherds who participated in this theft of native property rights were the very cottagers who had been stripped of their rights to the commons in the mother country! Robert Brough Smyth's observation in the 1870s about the typical Aborigine in Victoria is telling in this regard: "He goes out in his canoe in the night and uses torches to attract the fish, exactly after the manner of the poachers of the North Tyne in England, who in their trows, and with lights burning . . . robbed that river of its salmon"[210] "exactly after the manner" of English poachers. But the Aborigine would be driven from that practice with greater thoroughness than had the English poacher.

Many of those losing their customary rights protested vigorously, sometimes violently. Their protests saved some of their rights, but most were lost. And for many of these losers the remaining options were leasing land, if they could arrange to do so, or working as the "hired hand" of another. (We will consider agricultural laborers and the Law in Chapter 6; the relations of landlord and tenant are the subject of the next chapter.)

While conflicts can be found between the Common Law and certain French, Spanish, and British customary rules that resurfaced (or were created) in North America and the Antipodes, it was generally uncommon for Common-Law jurists there to be asked to address questions of the customary-property rights of British or other European settlers. There were few customary property rules that could be said to have been created in the "New" World, given that one condition of customary law was that the custom had existed "from time immemorial."

But, of course, there was one enormous exception to this generalization: Those native to North America and the Antipodes had long enjoyed vibrant "customary rights." These were, at first, somewhat scrupulously protected by officers of the Crown, but were eventually largely extinguished by the Responsible Governments that supplanted them.

When the traditional way that aboriginal people used land and water resources came up against the ways of English Law, imposed by the agents of the Crown in the seventeenth, eighteenth, and nineteenth centuries, some of the discomfort with this notion of Law-imposed-from-the-top-down has been preserved: Thus, Moluntha of

---

[210] R. B. Smyth, *Aborigines of Victoria* (2 vols., Melbourne, 1878), xxxii.

the Shawnees told the U.S. commissioners during the American Revolution, "it is not with us as it is with you, for if you say to a man do so why it must be done, but consider that we are a lawless people and can do nothing with our people only but by fair words...."[211] In the early days of English settlement on the shores of the Chesapeake Bay, a Native American ambassador is reported to have told the Virginia Company's representatives "since that you are heere strangers, and come to our Countrey, you should rather conforme your selves to the Customes of our Countrey, then impose yours upon us."[212] But the English Diaspora were no more inclined to follow that norm in North America than they were in Ireland in the late sixteenth and early seventeenth centuries, nor would they be willing thereafter to follow such a norm elsewhere (for the most part).[213]

---

[211] Quoted in Colin Calloway, *The American Revolution in Indian Country*, 176.
[212] Noted in Karen Kupperman, *Settling with the Indians*, 55.
[213] "(for the most part)": In those reaches of the British Empire that were largely *unsettled* by British Diaspora (such as India, Fiji, and Nigeria), local law and customs *were* largely honored. But that is a story I will have to tell another time.

2

Corncribs, Manuring, Timber, and Sheep: Landlords, Tenants, and Reversioners

THE FORMAL LAW

Some of the British Diaspora newcomers to North America and the Antipodes had sufficient capital to acquire fee-simple title to land; those with less generally settled first for a tenancy agreement with a landlord in the fashion of the sorts of indentures many had held in the British Isles. Tenancy was a favored method of settlement in the quasifeudal visions of the founders of the "planting" of Elizabethan Ireland, those of Maryland, the Carolinas, Pennsylvania, and New Jersey in the seventeenth century, those of Prince Edward Island after the surrender of French sovereignty in 1763, the Squattocracy of New South Wales in the early nineteenth century, and the Grandees of New York and Lower Canada/Quebec (albeit in those provinces it had been Dutch patroons and French seigneurs who had been the first landlord–proprietors). Some tenants entered into relatively short-term agreements; others for twenty-one- or ninety-nine-year terms; still others for perpetual (999-year) "leases," obligating them and their heirs to annual "quit-rent" payments to landlord–proprietors, some of whom were identified in Crown grants as feudal "landgraves" or "barons."[1]

Most of the elements of the English Common Law with regard to landlord–tenant relationships were "received" in the lands of the British Diaspora without alterations, but at least two aspects of that Law were altered or abandoned there, for jurists in at least some of these lands either held them to be "inapplicable" to the "circumstances and conditions of a new country," or, in one case, to be unreasonable and unjust.

Landlord–Tenant Law, Generally, in the Lands of the British Diaspora

Savvy landlord–proprietors in the North American colonies wanted to have their woodland acreage cleared as quickly as possible for sale

[1] Beverley Bond, *The Quit-Rent System in the American Colonies* (New Haven, 1919).

to settler–farmers. To this end some of them sought short-term leases with lumbermen–tenants under arrangements for the cutting, sawing, and sale of the timber as lumber, fuel, and fence rails. Major grantee-Grandees built sawmills and leased them to skilled artisans to facilitate this process. They also leased less-arable uplands, complete with a stock of cattle, sheep, or hogs, to tenants who agreed to tend these animals for a share of the increase and profits "on such terms as are fair and just" (as one contract in western Virginia in 1843 read).[2] When such tenants could be found and set to work, that much of a proprietor's land was afforded *some* protection from the "swarm of squatters" who "infest[ed]" the frontier. It was also supposed to provide income to the landlord-Grandee (in the form of in-kind payments); and it "served as a stimulus for new inhabitants."[3]

Moreover, the tenant's improvements, such as they were, necessarily increased the value of the property. In the 1790s George Washington leased tracts of his land in western Virginia to "weak handed [i.e., poor] people," hoping to "have them restored to me at the expiration of the term for wch. they were granted, in good order and well improved." That expectation was not unrealistic. As one early nineteenth century visitor to eastern Tennessee put it, within two years a tenant's efforts increased the land's value "nearly thirty percent," and the land could then be sold to "a new emigrant" willing to pay the price of "improved" land.[4]

Suits between Diaspora settlers involving ordinary leases of property were not uncommon in the colonies and dominions[5]; and their disposition by CANZ jurists did not appear to me to favor either landlord or tenant.[6] All too often the same could not be said when the parties were Diaspora newcomers and the original people. For example,

---

[2] Wilma A. Dunaway, *The First American Frontier: Transition to Capitalism in Southern Appalachia, 1700–1860* (Chapel Hill, 1996), 98, 183, 237.

[3] Dunaway, 69.

[4] R. E. Harper, *Transformation of Western Pennsylvania* (1991), 64; Dunaway, 69.

[5] For examples of such actions in one jurisdiction, see the files of H. Hurry & Son, 13016/Box 1/10 (1 thru 12), Mss. Div., St. Lib. Of Victoria, which includes a number of leases and eviction notices, 1859–1860.

[6] In southern Appalachia landlord–tenant agreements appear to have been enforced to the advantage of the landlord. See Wilma Dunaway, 93.

This does not appear to have been the case simultaneously in New South Wales. There the instructions offered by the trial judges to the assessor-juries in these sorts of cases summarized the Common-Law English rules involved and called upon the assessor-juries to determine the facts. These juries were quite capable of finding facts advantageous to the tenant. Thus, in *Bucknall v. Moran* (1829) they awarded a tenant locked out of his leased farm some one hundred pounds in damages, despite some evidence that he had violated one of the terms of the agreement. In *Pilcher v. Cory* (1832) a landlord-"Settler on the Patterson's River" leased a farm to a tenant and

in colonial Massachusetts, some of the "landlords" complaining to the general court of the "Wasting of Timber" by their tenants were Indians, and some of these leases had not been provided by the native communities themselves, but by New England company commissioners after King Philip's War. The defeated Algonquins were relatively helpless, dependent upon an inadequate legal system to protect their lands. Nonetheless, they were not entirely without means of protecting them. Thus, Gay Head Indians protested the lease of 1,000 acres of their land to Ebenezer Allen in 1726 by impounding his cattle and pulling his fences down; the result of this "self-help" was that 200 of these acres were returned to them and an additional 800 set aside for their use elsewhere.[7]

included a provision that the tenant might live in his own house "whilst a house was building" for the tenant "on the Farm in question." When the landlord later forced the tenant to leave the house, a jury awarded the tenant forty shillings in damages, and the New South Wales Supreme Court distinguished the fact situation in *Pilcher* from the English case cited by the landlord's attorney and affirmed the judgement. In *Loane v. Perry* (1833) one man sublet two farms at Port Jackson for a seven-year term, and reoccupied one a year later. This was construed by the Supreme Court on appeal to have been a violation of the language of the sublease. He was found by a jury to have suffered no compensable damages when his subtenant thereupon abandoned the lease. See also *Barnett v. James* (1833). Similar tolerance of tenants, it could be argued, can be detected in *R. v. Wells* (1826). Tenant William Wells, "victualler," had refused to give up a leased house on Pitt Street, Sydney, despite his being served proper notice under the terms of the lease. When the landlord appeared, under the impression that Wells was ready to comply, Wells pushed him down the steps into the street and shut the door. The irate landlord, a man named Hodges, hammered in anger on the shop's windowpanes, breaking several. The tenant thereupon shot him dead through one of the panes. Tried before Chief Justice Francis Forbes and a jury, Wells' attorney sought to elicit from the attending physician the possibility that the pistol had contained nothing more than powder and wadding, and that it had been the glass from the windowpane that had produced the fatal wound on Hodges' skull. The physician resisted that interpretation, but Chief Justice Forbes left that question to the jury, and that body, "after a short consultation," returned a verdict of *not guilty*. These and hundreds of other cases before the Supreme Court of New South Wales in the 1820s and 1830s are now available to us all at www.law.mq.edu.au/scnsw due to the efforts of Professor Bruce Kercher.

[7] David Mandell, *Behind the Frontier: Indians in 18th Century Eastern Massachusetts* (Lincoln, Neb., 1996), 110, 115, 152.

In the mid-nineteenth century Hicoria Apaches complained to U. S. authorities that land claimed by those deriving title from the so-called Maxwell Grant were trespassers; the Hicoria insisted that they had only leased land to Maxwell. Maria Montoya. "Challenges to European Investment in the American West: The Lure of the Mythic West and the Reality of Local

Not all such native-newcomer lease arrangements were as unsatisfactory to the native landlords. In South Carolina in the late eighteenth century, for example, the Catawba "found it to our advantage" to grant long-term leases to settlers (who then complained that they were "Tributaries" to the Catawba). Similarly, in what is now Oklahoma, the Cherokee leased rangeland to Diaspora ranchers profitably in the 1870s and 1880s.[8] On the northern frontier of New England, a group of Abenakis leased some seven square miles of timberland near the Missisquoi River to James Robertson in 1765. Among the terms of this lease were stipulations that a tract of twelve farms on both sides of the river be reserved for their Abenaki owners, and that Robertson and his men were to plow the fields of these farms every spring "as shall be sufficient for them to plant their Indian corn every year." The parties appeared to have "lived in harmony," but, in time, as the Allen brothers carved Vermont out of the Abenaki domain, Diaspora tenants became less willing to pay rent; indeed, some didn't bother to lease at all, prompting some St. Francis Abenaki to visit these settlers in 1787 and 1788 in order to demand in-kind payments, it appears, of one-fourth of all "raised on said lands as Rent to them."[9]

In New Zealand, the newcomers' cattle and sheep grazed freely, and thus inevitably, on Maori land. When Maori sought compensation for the encroachments, the first generation of British newcomers often offered to lease the grasslands on which their animals were foraging. But ordinances in 1842 and 1846 made such leases illegal. A conference (*hui*) of Maori subtribes (*hapu*) at Taupo in 1856 was reported to have resolved to halt all land sales to the Crown and to use "every possible means to induce squatters to settle with flocks ... in the interior," there to "occupy the position of vassals to the Chiefs under whose protection they might live ... and to whom they are to afford a revenue, by way of rent for their runs, to assist in maintaining the power and influence of their landlords."[10] In 1861, four Ngati Kahungunu chiefs (*rangatira*) complained that the Diaspora ordinances were "wrong,

Resistance, ca. 1850," Forum on European Exapnsion and Global Interaction, Huntington Library, April, 1998.

[8] James Merrell, *The Indian's New World: Catawbas and Their Neighbors from European Contact to the Era of Removal* (N.Y., 1991), 210; Jeffrey Burton, *Indian Territory and the United States, 1866–1906* (Norman, Okla., 1995), 28, 115, 124; William Savage, "Leasing the Cherokee Outlet," 46 *Chronicles of Oklahoma* 285 (1968).

[9] Colin Calloway, *The Western Abenaki of Vermont, 1600–1800* (Norman, Okla., 1990), 194, 228, 244.

[10] Agent Cooper to Native Secretary (and chief land purchaser) Donald McLean, cited in David V. Williams, *'Te Kooti Tango Whenua': The Native Land Court, 1864–1909* (Wellington, 1999), 125.

incorrect." "The grass for which [we] asked payment belong[s] to [our]selves, not to the Europeans," and inasmuch as it was "impossible to keep the cattle and sheep off [our] lands so long as these were unfenced," the tribe "should receive payment." If not, the animals would have to be driven off, "although [we do] not wish to do so." Simultaneously, the Hawke's Bay Provincial Council, Diaspora neighbors and counterparts to these Ngati Kahungunu chiefs, also petitioned the government, urging repeal of the same Native Land Ordinance of 1846, and the statutory sanctioning of the common illegal grazier leases. Only thereby would "the prosperity of the Province" be promoted; only thus would "population and exports... rapidly increase;" only thus would "the peaceful relations between both races" be "secured" by "mutual interest."[11]

New Zealand's legislature responded with a statute sanctioning such leases in 1862. But there was an unstated rationale that lay behind this statute: Leases would lead to total land alienation. As New Zealand's Colonial Secretary, Dr. Pollen, put it to the legislative council in 1874: "It was perfectly well known that, in dealing with Native land, the first step was the lease, and that obtained, the freehold inevitably followed in time."[12] The 1846 ordinance had been applied quite selectively by Crown land purchase commissioners, ostensibly in defense of the Crown's preemption right, "to force the Maori into land sales by threatening to cut off lease revenue and other forms of exchange with grazers."[13] A different tack was taken in 1892 with the passage of Prime Minister John Ballance's West Coast Settlement Reserves Act, which created a public trusteeship for some 200,000 acres of Maori land, all of which was then offered in farm tracts to Pakeha settlers on twenty-one-year leases. The Maori "owned" the land and were paid rental fees which were to be adjusted according to settler improvements, but some Maori (followers of the Prophet Te Whiti) refused to accept these payments and ploughed the leased land as a challenge to the Law, while others (followers of the Maori king, Tawhiao) created a Constitution in 1894 that set out the conditions by which Pakehas might secure twenty-two-year leases of Maori land whereby Maoris controlled the process from start to finish.[14]

---

[11] Williams, 126.
[12] John A. Williams, *Politics of the New Zealand Maori: Protest and Cooperation, 1891–1909* (Seattle, 1969), 59.
[13] John Weaver, "The Construction of Property Rights on Imperial Frontiers: The Case of New Zealand Native Land Purchase Ordinance of 1846," 17th Annual Australia-New Zealand Law & History Conference, Melbourne, July, 1998.
[14] Williams, 40, 44. Much less fortunate were the Griquas of South Africa, who leased land to Boers under pressure in the 1830s and 1840s, only to see

Several hundred miles north, in Fiji, a form of farm tenancy had been customary for generations of native Fijians. Landlord-chiefs and subchiefs had been "leasing" land, breadfruit, ivi, and coconut trees to "tenants" for an unspecified share of the year's output, depending on the size and scope of the feasts that the overlord-chief felt called upon to provide each year. This might sound like a temptation to exploit the "tenant," but Basil Thomson, long-time magistrate and Native Lands Court Commissioner there, explained that the "safeguard against excessive demands lay in the fact that the tenant had always the power of deserting the land and offering himself as a tenant to a rival chief." Hence, "in practice" the "overlord" rarely "dared to make excessive demands upon his tenants."[15] Compare this to the agreement between one family-clan (mataqali) cultivating land in Naitasiri and a Diaspora newcomer who had purchased it from the former Fijian overlord: "[T]hey pay him something like a rent in kind," a Land Commission report read in 1900. "[A]bout 100 yams a year and from 50 to 100 dalo [taro root] each season, the owner of the land leaving it very much up to the people what they shall contribute from time to time, and up to the present both parties appear very well satisfied with the arrangement." The Fijian mataqali may well have preferred this arrangement, as it was sensitive to both their feast obligations and to the "success of the planting season." Thus, Isaac Driver reported quite contentedly in the 1870s that his Fijian tenants "were to give me some produce" as rent. "They pay me some years pigs, Fiji kava and yams. Some years I get a little, and sometimes a lot." Peter France tells us, by contrast, that when Diaspora planters (and some native chiefs) "introduced European precision" into these lease arrangements, specifying regular rental payments, "Fijians reacted less satisfactorily."[16]

Two Innovations: Agricultural-Tenant Improvements and Waste

English Common Law, not surprisingly, generally favored the interests of landlords. Consider first the tenant who over the course of time had erected a barn, shed, corncrib, pigsty, gin, or fence on the property.

it taken from them with the connivance of the British governor, Sir Harry Smith, in 1848. William M. Macmillan, *Bantu, Boer and Briton* (London, 1929), 192, 271.

[15] Basil Thomson, *The Fijians: A Study of the Decay of Custom* (1908), chapter 31, "The Tenure of Land," esp. pp. 379, 381.

[16] Peter France, *The Charter of the Land: Custom and Colonization in Fiji* (Melbourne, 1969), 46. 51, 186.

The English Common-Law rule was that, upon the termination of the lease, any such structures became the property of the landlord and could not be removed by the tenant.[17]

But this rule was rejected in the United States. New York's Chief Justice Ambrose Spencer "confess[ed]" that he "never could perceive the reason, justice [or] equity of the old cases which gave to the landlord such kind of erections." His peer and fellow New Yorker, Chancellor James Kent, praised the American rule allowing tenants to remove their improvements or be paid for their value as one that benefitted the public, and his counterpart on the U.S. Supreme Court, Justice Joseph Story, agreed with a rule that offered "every motive to encourage the tenant to devote himself to agriculture" in "the comparative poverty" of the underdeveloped American settlements. Retaining the English rule would result in the construction or addition of nothing "of much expense or value" to the land. At least in this instance, jurists in the United States preferred a rule with greater economic efficiency.[18]

English Common-Law rules also prohibited "waste": the damaging or removal of resources from land held by one without full title to that land (a tenant, a holder in fee tail, or a widow with a dower life estate) who typically cuts down more of the estate's timber than was necessary for his or her fencing or firewood (generally to sell it). One who "wasted" another's estate could be made to pay damages and might also be enjoined from further such behavior.

American courts in the eighteenth and early nineteenth century generally did not apply this rule mindlessly. They distinguished the English rule, often noting that it was inapplicable to the "conditions of this country" where timber was plentiful and the clearing of land for cultivation was "improvement" to an estate, not "waste."[19] After nearly

---

[17] *Elwes v. Maw*, 3 East 38 at 50, 102 ER 510 (K.B. 1802) (beast house, cart house, and pump house). (An exception, known as the Lincolnshire Custom, prevailed by the nineteenth century in that county, where most tenants held one-year, "at-will" leases and landlords were forced over time to agree to grant them recognized customary rights to their improvements (such as the construction of drainage ditches or the nitrating of the soil with chalk and bone matter). R. J. Olney, *Lincolnshire Politics, 1832–1885* (Oxford, 1973), 41–42.

[18] *Holmes v. Tremper*, 20 Johns. 29 at 30 (N.Y., 1822); James Kent, *Commentaries on American Law*, 3rd ed. (N.Y., 1836), II, 346; Joseph Story in *Van Ness v. Packard*, 2 Pet.(U.S.) 137 at 145 (1829) (a springhouse for a dairyman). See also *Whiting v. Brastow*, 21 Mass. 310 (1826) (a corncrib).

[19] See *Denwood v. Winder* (Md., 1770); Morton Horwitz, *The Transformation of American Law, 1780–1860* (Cambridge, Mass., 1977), 54–58.

200 years of settlement, the Massachusetts Supreme Judicial Court concluded in 1818 that the remaining stands of timber were, indeed, now quite valuable, and moved the standard for determining what was and wasn't "waste" back toward the English one,[20] but it employed the same pragmatic reasoning in the process: "Reasonable" use of timber was not "waste," and courts would decide what was "reasonable" based on the circumstances of the case and the prevailing economic conditions, for it was only by engaging in such an inquiry that one could decide whether the legal rights of the landlord, remainderman, or reversioner had been violated.

Did jurists of the other English settlement areas feel themselves bound by English rules here, or did they feel equally free to interpret those rules according to the "special circumstances" of frontier and settlement conditions? It appears that CANZ jurists felt bound by English principles, not simply English precedent. Jurists in Victoria (Australia) allowed a sheep grazer lessee at the Mt. Martha Station, Domana, to cut down timber not "used for building purposes."[21] A generation later that colony's supreme court similarly construed the word "timber" in a covenant to mean "trees" generally, and not just oak, ash, and elm, as in England.[22] The high courts of New Brunswick and Nova Scotia followed the "common sense" example of their counterparts to the south "in the United States, a country under similar circumstances with our own in respect to wilderness land." If timber was felled for cultivation purposes, these courts allowed a relaxation of the Common Law (though this was not to be understood to mean that a tenant could "range over the whole piece of land, calling here and there what trees may be fit for logs or timber").[23] Upper Canada's (Ontario's) high courts initially offered rather narrow interpretations of the English "waste" rule, enjoining tenants who cut certain valuable timber without express authority, and holding that the plea of another, that he had cut trees "for the purpose of clearing the . . . land and improving and cultivating the same" was bad, because the tenant had offered no proof of his having cultivated the land and may

[20] In *Conner v. Shepard,* 15 Mass. 164 (1818).
[21] *Bruce v. Atkins,* 1 W. & W. (Eq.) 141 (1861).
[22] *Campbell v. Kerr,* 12 V.L.R. (L) 384 (1886). None the less, in the same years, despite Crown efforts to protect scarce timber resources, Melbourne magistrates refused to fine anyone for felling trees in the protected areas, claiming a "public benefit" from such depredations. Raymond Wright, *The Bureaucrats' Domain: Space and the Public Interest in Victoria, 1834–84* (Melbourne, 1989), 45.
[23] *Rector of Hampton v. Titus,* 6 New Br. 278 at 324 (1849); *Titus v. Sulis,* 9 Nova Sc. 497, at 500 (citing the rule in New York state) (1875); *Titus v. Haines,* 11 Nova Sc. 542 at 546 (1877).

simply have been interested in harvesting valuable trees belonging to the landlord or reversioner.[24]

Most of these opinions were written by the Chief Justice of Upper Canada's Queen's Bench, Sir John Beverley Robinson, the son of a Loyalist refugee from New York. Robinson was a landowner in Upper Canada, the descendant of New York proprietor–landlords who had long wrestled with tenants over the "wasting" of timber. Hence he may well have been particularly sensitive on this issue, as Bernard Hibbitts has pointed out (though he also notes that in 1846 Robinson treated the burning of underbrush and scrub pine in what "was altogether a wilderness" as "indispensable" to "public good").[25] But Robinson's Equity counterpart, Chancellor Blake, was not as sure that the English rules regarding waste should inflexibly be applied "as to growing timber" in Upper Canada, since "the beneficial enjoyment of the land is ordinarily attained, and indeed can only be obtained, through the destruction of the growing timber." Similarly, he decided that "our different social condition" warranted the enjoining of one who had not been paid the remaining four fifths of the sale price for some land for four years from treating the sale as void under the laches rule and offering it for sale again. The first buyer had not made any of the remaining payments on the installment purchase and was said by the seller to have "committed depredations on the land by cutting down all the valuable timber. . . ." But Chancellor Blake pointed out that this told only half of the story: The errant installment buyer's situation was that of

> multitudes . . . by whose enterprise and labour the wastes of this vast province are rendered subservient to the purposes of civilization with unwarranted rapidity.

He had spent three times the value of his down payment in "improving" the land (largely by removing "the valuable timber"), and as a consequence his improvements were worth some £50. The application of the English waste rule in such a case would "outrage alike reason and justice." Similarly, in 1874 the counterpart and equal to Upper Canada's Queen's Bench, the Court of Common Pleas, adopted this more innovative view of its maritime and south-of-the-border compeers: "Many acts which would unquestionably be 'waste' under one

---

[24] *Lawrence v. Judge*, 2 Grant Ch. 301 (1851); *Weller v. Burnham*, 11 U.C.Q.B. 90 at 91 (1853). See also *Chestnut v. Day*, 6 U.C.Q.B. (O.S.) 637 (1843); and *Tayler v. Tayler*, 5 U.C.Q.B. (O.S.) 501 (1837).

[25] B. J. Hibbitts, "Progress and Principle: The Legal Thought of Sir John Beverley Robinson," 34 *McGill Law Journal* 454 at 475 (1989); *Dean v. McCartney*, 2 U.C.Q.B. 448 at 450 (1846).

state of circumstances would not be so under another," wrote Justice Galt. Holding too closely to the English standard would be "highly inexpedient and unjust," given "the natural state of lands in this Province. . . ." While the precedents of the various courts of the United States, collected in the published *American Reports*, were "not binding on us, yet they are entitled to the highest respect . . . because the state of landed property in that country is similar to our own."[26]

Thus, several (but not all) CANZ high courts engaged in some of the same acts of "bending" Common Law rules regarding waste and tenant improvements as had their counterparts in the United States. After all, the "receiving" statute that formally announced the adaption and applicability of English Common Law in each colony included such a phrase as "excepting only when inapplicable due to local climate or conditions." "New circumstances" and "special conditions of frontier settlements" were sometimes offered both in the American Republic and the British provinces in explaining the turning aside of English precedents in order to apply in commonsense fashion the *principle* behind the English waste rule. Hence the fact that these provinces were still subject to the Crown, their courts still subject to review by Privy Council, may have made a difference to Justice Sir John Beverley Robinson, but not to Justice Galt or Chancellor Blake.

THE INFORMAL LAW OF LANDLORDS AND TENANTS

England

English landlord–tenant relationships were sometimes enshrouded in layers of class and status. However successful a tenant might be, his or her financial and social future depended on the continued access to the land and such rights and amenities as might be associated with it. This was particularly true of tenants-at-will, who could, theoretically, be turned off the land within a year. Hence, we can detect clear evidence of deference in the English countryside, especially

---

[26] Blake, Ch., in *O'Keefe v. Taylor*, 2 Grant's Ch. 95 at 96, 100, 110 (1850); and in *Chisholm v. Sheldon*, 1 Grant's Ch. 318 at 320 (1850) (but he enjoined a mortgagee from further cutting of timber despite these *dicta*); Galt, J., in *Drake v. Wigle*, 24 U.C.C.P. 405 at 409, 410 (1874). See also the references to American cases by Hagarty, C. J., in his concurring opinion (418). And see the view of Boyd, Ch., in *Hixon v. Reaveley*, 9 Ont. L.R. 6 (1904): "All the niceties of the ancient learning as to waste which obtain in England are not to be transferred without discrimination to a new and comparatively unsettled country like this Province. . . . A like relaxation of the strict rule obtains in the United States, and the authorities of that country, so much alike in its territorial conditions to our own, may well be regarded by Canadian courts."

in such counties as Lincolnshire, where tenancy-at-will was common. Listen to Sir Charles Monck's message to his fifty pound franchised North Lincolnshire tenants on the eve of parliamentary elections in 1850:

> Nothing is more agreeable to the Constitution, and to all ancient usages of the Kingdom, or more advantageous to true liberty, than that landlords should endeavour by all fair means to lead their tenants. . . . I expect of my tenants that they shall not engage their votes before they have communicated with me and come to know my wishes. . . .

Sir Charles recommended a Free Trade Whig candidate, Sir Montagu Cholmeley, and his franchised tenants informed him that they would "plump" for Sir Montagu (that is, they would vote only for him).[27] Other tenants advised other landlords that their votes were "entirely under [your] direction." Consider, for example, William Dolby, tenant to Sir John Thorold. When he was told by the agent "receiving Sir J. Thorold's rents here" of Sir John's wishes in the upcoming election, he advised the candidate that "I consider every good landlord ought to direct one of his Tenant's votes, and under the circumstances I shall with much pleasure give you a Vote and also do what I can for your election. . . ."[28]

Lincolnshire's tenants, then, were deferential. Nevertheless, a landlord "would be extremely careful to avoid a precipitate action that might provoke the farming community," R. J. Olney writes of Lincolnshire. "Probably most . . . Lincolnshire fifty-pound [voting] tenants knew that the ultimate weapon of 'psychological coercion,' the threat of . . . eviction, was seldom employed and never implemented."[29]

Landlord–Tenant Relations in the Lands of the Diaspora

In the Diaspora colonies of the seventeenth, eighteenth, and nineteenth centuries, wherever Crown or proprietor landlords sought to utilize tenancy as the primary form of land tenure, there was little deference, and plenty of trouble for decades, at the very least.

Ireland

In Ireland, tensions between landlords and tenants, as well as tenants and subtenants, often gave rise to violence and political organizing, as early as the sixteenth century, and recurring every generation or so thereafter. English landlords seized almost at will (but "lawfully") the

---

[27] R. J. Olney, *Lincolnshire Politics*, 35–36.
[28] Olney, *Lincolnshire Politics*, 38.
[29] *Ibid.*, 42–43.

cattle of their English and Scottish tenants, and Gaelic-Irish tenants and subtenants struck back at these landlords, sometimes in the landlords' own imported English Common-Law courts (Attorney-General Sir John Davies reported the Munster landlords to be constantly "sued and vexed by the Irishrie"), sometimes in the court of "self-help." Irishmen expelled some of the new English, Scottish, and Welsh tenants of those "undertakers" of the "planting" of the new Munster and Ulster, recovered distrained animals and destroyed overdue-rent documents.[30]

David Konig related the tale of George Canning, an "undertaker by lease" of 3,210 acres in the Coleraine plantation created by the Ironmonger's Company. His local dominance of the Common-Law process allowed him to harass a tenant with whom he had fallen out. When the tenant, aptly named Samuel Pidgeon, complained, Canning responded that he "hath noe friend but his purse and the Lawe." These appeared to have been more than enough.[31] When a combination of circumstances led to a rise in the value of Irish land in 1760, Irish cottiers found themselves fenced and hedged out of plots that they had for years enjoyed for potatoes or grazing a milk cow. But the Irish tenantry was not supine. By 1761, their resistance had blossomed into a full-scale rising throughout the southern and western counties, as "Whiteboys" and "Levellers" destroyed fences, walls, and hedges, rescued imprisoned comrades, raided arsenals, and maimed their landlords' cattle. One of their leaders, writing as "Queen Sieve" in 1762, warned "Gentlemen . . . not to raise again either walls or ditches in the place of those we destroy, nor even to inquire about the destroyers of them. If they do, their cattle shall be houghed and their sheep laid open in the fields."[32]

This antilandlord turmoil persisted in the nineteenth century, even though farm income was then rising faster than rents and there were, in fact, few evictions. The threat of eviction was "the estate agents' maid-of-all-work, being used to collect arrears, to force tenants to pay increases of rent, to settle quarrels between tenants and to discourage

[30] Nicholas Canny, *Kingdom and Colony: Ireland in the Atlantic World, 1560–1800* (Baltimore, 1988), 44, 60–61; Hans Pawlisch, *Sir John Davies and the Conquest of Ireland*, 48.

[31] Konig, "Colonization and the Common Law in Ireland and Virginia, 1569–1634," in *The Transformation of Early American History*, ed. James Henretta, Michael Kammen and Stanlet Katz (N. Y., 1991), 80.

[32] See Peter Linebaugh and Marcus Rediker, "The Many-Headed Hydra," in Daniel Segal, ed., *Crossing Cultures: Essays in the Displacement of Western Civilization* (Tuscon, 1992), 120–21. And see Francis J. Biggers, *The Ulster Land War of 1770* (Dublin, 1910), for its "Oak Boy" counterpart some ten years later in the north of Ireland.

bad farming." But only about two of every thousand tenants experienced eviction, even in the doldrum years between the Famine and the "Land War," 1850–1878. The primary issues in these years were: firstly, the custom enjoyed by tenants in Ulster (but not in the south or west) – that is, the "custom of tenant-right" to receive the value of one's improvements in the sale of a tenancy. English law permitted a tenant in Ulster to reap such a benefit, as well as to bequeath a tenancy to a son, or to purchase such a tenancy from a neighbor, without approaching the landlord or paying either a fee or a tax. Tenants elsewhere in Ireland demanded this privilege as well, sometimes without success.[33]

Secondly, cottiers and laborers became embroiled in disputes with leaseholders, and leaseholders with landlords, over both conacre (small potato farms rented to laborers) and grazing land for the cottier's or laborers' cows. The legal system addressed these issues, and may have been adequate to the task in this instance. Common Law courts in Ireland "settled" issues involving conacre in the mid-nineteenth century, as David Moore has shown. In *Lord Westmeath v. Hogg* (1841),[34] *Dease v. O'Reilly* (1845),[35] and *Booth v. McManus* (1861)[36] the Irish Courts of Common Pleas and Queen's Bench held that the conacre arrangement was "only a mode of farming the land" according to "the usual custom of the country," and constituted a mere "license to till the land" for profit, "a temporary easement and not an estate in the land."[37] As such they were not viewed as subleases, prohibited by English landlords.

Thus, the English landlords lost in court, and losing "at law," they appear to have acquiesced, unable to "win" simply by litigating and harassing their tenants. Why? In the words of one landlord, "the costs to me" of litigating a case to bar the granting of conacre by one of his tenants "were upwards of 100 pounds." In the words of another, efforts "to enforce a [lease] was certain to incur an expense of £50, with scarcely the remotest prospect of success." This was so, in another's words, because some leaseholders were so behind in arrears that the

---

[33] W. E. Vaughan, "Landlord and Tenant Relations in Ireland between the Famine and the Land War, 1850–1878," in L. M. Cullen and T. C. Smout, eds., *Comparative Aspects of Scottish and Irish Economic and Social History, 1600–1900* (Edinburgh, 1978), 216–26; Joe Lee, "Patterns of Rural Unrest in 19th Century Ireland," in Francois Furet and L. M. Cullen, eds., *Irelande et France: XIX–XX siècles* (Dublin, 1980), 223–33; James Donnelly, Jr., *Landlord and Tenant in Nineteenth Century Ireland* (Dublin, 1973), 9, 20, 27, 61.

[34] 3 Ir. L R 27.

[35] 8 Ir. L R 52.

[36] 12 Ir. L R 418.

[37] 3 Ir. L R 27 at 32; 8 Ir. L R 52 at 58–59; 12 Ir. L R 418 at 435–36.

landlord "finds it a case of suing a beggar," and, in the case of a tenant able to pay:

> as tenants are naturally and rightly put on juries, it must be an extraordinary clear case indeed in which a landlord can get a verdict for breach of covenant.

Hence, the wise land agent advised the landlord to deal with unsatisfactory tenants "in the manner least objectionable to the habits and prejudices of the people."[38]

The North American Colonies and the United States

The English, Dutch, and Scottish grandees hoping to create manorial fiefdoms in New York, New Jersey, Maryland, Pennsylvania, Northern Virginia, and the Carolinas found courts to be inadequate and often inappropriate weapons to wield in the pursuit of their schemes. In New York, for example, they quickly lost their manorial powers to hold their own courts baron and leet – instruments in their own hands that would have enabled them to fine, amerce, and distrain goods – in power struggles with towns and counties.[39]

Moreover, by 1700 most of their tenants had acquired the vote, and, as such, they acquired leverage in the colonial legislature. By the 1720s, the New York legislature, like its Pennsylvania counterpart of the 1730s, was engaged in a bold-faced power struggle with proprietary interests over the issue of quitrent collection. Proprietors in both colonies sought to collect back quitrents by creating Equity courts that they would control to hear the cases. Legislators, reflecting tenant/lessee interests, placed substantial roadblocks in the path of this process, and Governor James Hamilton of Pennsylvania advised Proprietor Thomas Penn in 1736 that "Our lawyers" feared popular vilification were they to make "an application to the Court," unless it had been "established by Act of Assembly." Inasmuch as the Assembly insisted on juries in the Equity system, Penn dropped the idea, clearly sensing that a jury system would defeat his revenue-collecting purposes.[40]

---

[38] David Moore, "From Potatoes and Peasants to Quotas and Squires: The Endurability of Conacre from 1845 to 1995," in *One Hundred Years of Irish Law*, ed. Norma Dawson, et al. (Belfast, 1996), 204–07, esp. 205, n. 64; Homer Socolofsy, *Landlord William Scully* (Laurence, KS, 1979), 40–41. W. E. Vaughan, *Landlords and Tenants in Mid-Victorian Ireland* (Dublin, 1984).

[39] Sung Bok Kim, *Landlord and Tenant in Colonial New York: Manorial Society, 1664–1775* (Chapel Hill, 1978), 11, 90–91, 117. The "court baron" was the civil side of these; the "court leet," the criminal/misdemeanor side. Tenants were very much involved in the legal process in both such courts.

[40] Stanley Katz, "The Politics of Law in Colonial America: Chancery Courts and Equity in the 18th Century," in S. Katz, ed., *Colonial America* (Boston, 1976);

In Maryland, similar rent and quitrent delinquencies in the late eighteenth century were seen by one Loyalist claims commissioner as "partly owing to the laxness of the Steward[s], . . . the remissness of the Agent[s]," and "Tenants running away and selling their leases fraudulently." Maryland attorney Daniel Dulany, writing as such an agent to the province's chief landlord, Lord Baltimore, pointed to another problem landlords faced that courts were inadequate to prevent:

> [If] Landlords on the Spot find little profit, & suffer much from waste & Destruction of Timber, it may be easily imagined that his Lordship finds less, & suffers more.

Many tenants in Maryland stripped the land of its timber and built no buildings.[41] The typical landlord's recourse to the courts might have recouped the value of *some* of this "Pillage of Timber," but it clearly did not arrest it altogether.

Proprietors of tracts of land in Maine, Massachusetts' own province, found in the 1790s that those whom they leased land to, as well as those to whom they sold land adjacent any unsettled woodlands, stripped the timber as quickly as they could. The tenant might insist he was thereby "improving" the property, but many a landlord insisted that it was lumber-for-profit, not farming, that the errant tenant was after. David Cobb, agent to the vast estates of William Bingham and Henry Knox, wrote Bingham in 1797, "the farmer who setts down on a River in this Country, turns . . . naturally to a log stealer," and "a thousand such settlers will give no more value to the soil than so many Indians residing upon it. . . ."[42]

Landlords hoping to attract tenants to undeveloped regions felt "obliged" to build gristmills about every ten miles; some also built sawmills to provide lumber for home and barn construction, a purpose as important as the profits landlords expected from the export of lumber. The sensible landlord instructed his agent to "take pains to please tenants, as the propriety of my settlement [with them] will depend a good deal on their Being satisfied," or so James Duane wrote in the colony of New York in 1765. In the relatively open lands of

Mary Schweitzer, *Custom and Contract: Household, Government and the Economy in Colonial Pennsylvania* (N.Y., 1987), 94–95.

[41] Stiverson, *Poverty in Land of Plenty*, 20, 26. I am aware that the initial selection of farmland by freeholds and tenants in Chesapeake Maryland was often based on the very density of the timber stands, on the assumption that the presence of hardwood was a good predictor of rich topsoil, and that the girdling of these trees was viewed by all as an "improvement." I refer here only to those who harvested the timber and made no effort to farm, leaving the property of less value than it had been.

[42] Cited in Robert Moody, "Samuel Ely: Forerunner to Shays," 5 *New England Quarterly* 105 at 118–19 (1932).

colonial North America, the English adage – "the oak scorns to grow except on free land" – took on even greater meaning. Many landlords consequently also provided farm tools and animals in exchange for half of the resulting increase in stock (called a "praiseworthy custom" by one tenant in 1679). Often tenants were given a rent-free start-up period as well, and many acquired long-term leases on attractive terms and steadily acquired the ownership of their improvements until, "by degrees it became a custom," as one landlord put it in 1760. These leases, with improvements, they sold, on average, every nine years to new tenants for prices ranging from £40 to £400. Sung Bok Kim has calculated that some 1,800 tenants in New York in 1775 owned an average of £576 of property, compared to £554 owned by freeholders. Tenants, it would seem, had been provided with as much capital as freeholders.[43] Inasmuch as most settlers were interested in short-term profits, how were tenants at any disadvantage, and why might one rationally chose freehold status over tenantry? I have no answer to my question, but a consideration of comparative expenses (such as taxes and rent payments) may shed further light on the matter.

Despite the generally favorable terms offered to tenants and the general success these tenants enjoyed, most New York landlords of the eighteenth century received little or no return for their efforts.[44] Rent delinquency was widespread and substantial, back rent often running as high "as the value of their farms at Sheriff sales," as one of the Livingston family landlords put it in 1790. And when the arrears rose above those levels, suggesting eviction (by an action of ejectment) as an appropriate financial option, many landlords were reluctant to pursue such a course, either because it would "have this Effect that Most of them will leave the Farms," and to the costs of the suit would have to be joined the trouble of locating a suitable new tenant, or

[43] Kim, *Landlord & Tenant*, 164, 166, 168, 170, 179, 221, 250–62, 269, 274. See also the practice of rent abatement by the giant landlord of nineteenth century America, William Scully: Homer Socolofsky, *Landlord William Scully* (Lawrence, Kansas, 1979), 130. And see Daniel Unser, *Indians, Setters and Slaves*, 180, on similar leases of French colonial entrepreneurs in the 1760s in Louisiana, such as the one Antonie Bernard D'Auterive offered several Acadian immigrants, to furnish "five cows with calves and one bull" to each family "during each of six consecutive years," at the end of which time "they will return the same number of cows and calves, of the same age and kind, that they received initially; the remaining cattle and their increase" to be "divided equally between said Acadians and Mr Dauterive."

[44] Kim, *Landlord & Tenant*, makes this point, as does Gregory Stiverson in *Poverty in a Land of Plenty: Tenancy in 18th Century Maryland* (Baltimore, 1977), 26.

because such "harsh Measures" would "bring on Me some Disesteem in the Country I am always to live [in]," as Oliver DeLancey told his sister in 1755.[45]

Of course, some landlords did seek legal measures against recalcitrant tenants, but even where successful at trial, those efforts could be undone by a lenient executive branch. "Good God what an affair this is!" Robert Livingston complained in correspondence with Albany County's sheriff, Abraham Yates, in the winter of 1756–1757. "Pray how came it about" that one of his tenants, jailed after such a proceeding, "is sett at liberty[?]" Advised that the governor and Council had issued a proclamation of freedom for the man, Livingston warned that, it being "impossible for me to defend my Self against, a Government bent on my destruction," he would either have to "seek Some place of refuge," or shoot the liberated tenant, "which I am determined to do the first time I see him." This sort of confrontation would become widespread in parts of the eastern Hudson Valley in the 1760s.[46]

Eventually the balance of power shifted. As farmers, planters, and ranchers secured legislative power and the Common Law found its voice among professionally trained jurists, the landless poor found that squatting was not tolerated any longer, and began the steady movement toward tenancy or sharecropping. By 1860, over 20 percent of all those on the land in southern Appalachia were tenant farmers, and another 21 percent were sharecroppers; by 1880, the percentage of tenant farms ranged from a quarter to nearly a half of all such units in the states of the upper Mississippi Valley.[47]

In some of these regions tenants retained some political leverage over their often absentee landlords, voting for substantial property taxes to support local roads and schools and to subsidize the construction of spur lines from the nearest railroad in the vicinity. Indeed

45 Kim, *Landlord & Tenant*, 115, 210, 219, 221. On rent delinquency problems of landladies in late eighteenth century Philadelphia, see Karen A. Wulf, "A Marginal Independence: Unmarried Women in Colonial Philadelphia," unpublished Ph.D. thesis, Johns Hopkins University, 1993, 309 ff.

46 Livingston, quoted in Daniel Hulseboch, "Imperia in Imperio," 16 *Law & History Review* 352 (1998); Edw. Countryman, *A People in Revolution* (New York, 1981), 47–55; Irving Mark, *Agrarian Conflicts in Colonial New York, 1711–1775* (N.Y., 1940); Staughton Lynd, *Antifederalism in Dutchess Country, New York* (Chicago, 1962).

47 Wilma Dunaway, *The First American Frontier*, 75, 94; Paul Gates, *Landlords and Tenants on the Prarie Frontier* (Ithaca, 1973), 310.

Morever, in some "company towns" the mining, transport, or manufacturing firm's manager was known to shut the plant down for a time during election day and send supervisors to the polls with workers to whom homes had been leased "to control the vote ... in obedience to the company's interest." Duanway, 276.

one account of the phenomenon in a Nebraska local newspaper in
1874 claimed that "the speculators are getting tired of building school
houses, so that they are [now] offering their lands for sale very low
and on reasonable terms." But some legislatures were persuaded to
"shield" absentee landlords "from the burden of school tax," and, in
any event, others, like the Irishman William Scully, perhaps the largest
landlord–renter in Illinois, simply added the property tax to the cash
rent in the tenant's contract, collecting both at the same time, and
thus giving his tenants occasion to think twice before voting for hefty
tax levies.[48]

The Canadian Provinces

Tensions between landlords and tenants on Prince Edward Island
echoed those in Ireland and the middle colonies. Upon the French
cession of the island in 1763, the Crown granted great tracts to proprietors who offered leases with no option to purchase. Those tenants
who could be attracted to the site were not entitled either to remove
or to be paid the value of such improvements as they had made to
the property at the termination of their leases. Some of these leases
were of long duration, but some were not, and those improvements
they felt compelled to make could prompt the landlord to increase
their rental costs if and when they sought to renew the lease. But if
that legal rule was to their disadvantage, the reality appears to have
been that it was often rendered "moot," for they rarely paid all of their
rents; tenants were some £60,000 in arrears by 1800.

Seeking a measure of redress from the inefficient Common-Law
rule regarding tenant improvements, the Island's legislative council
proposed in 1827 that unimproved land should be taxed at twice the
rate as improved land (a precursor to Henry George's "single-tax"
scheme of the 1870s). A hesitant Governor John Harvey was eventually
persuaded to forward the proposal to the Colonial Office with his
endorsement, and Undersecretary Stephen recommended to Lord
Glenelg that it be approved, but the Island's absentee proprietors saw
to it that the proposal was rendered a dead letter.

Consequently, in the 1830s and 1840s recent Irish emigrants simply squatted, attacking the surveyors sent by proprietors. By the mid-
nineteenth century there were over 70,000 settlers, mostly from
Scotland and Ireland. Landlords of paying tenants continued to offer nothing for agricultural improvements. Tenants reacted with an
Escheat Movement in the 1840s, hoping to secure from Lord Russell's
Reform Government a revocation of proprietary grants on the grounds

[48] Gates, 278–79.

that many proprietors had failed to fulfill certain conditions (such as the construction of mills).

In this they were disappointed. No court of escheat was to hear their claims, and the ensuing resistance to rent collections in 1843 was met by force. One of the leading landlords, the Halifax-born shipping magnate, Sir Samuel Cunard, fought these "reformer" tenants (some of whom were Irish Land Leaguers, others "wild" English Chartists) every step of the way. Some tenants "began to come to terms," but Scottish tenants on Lot 45 "forcefully reinstated a dispossessed tenant" and burned the house of the landlord's agent, prompting the dispatch of troops. A disturbance orchestrated by Tenant Leagues in 1865 was also met with force. But upon Cunard's death, his heirs agreed to sell the land in 1866, and within a decade, upon the Island's absorption into the new Canadian Federation (in 1873), tenancy-without-option-to-purchase was finally abolished there (in 1875). Proprietors owning more than 500 acres were compelled to sell their excess to the Government whereby it was available for sale to the tenant-occupants.[49]

The status of quit-rents in Nova Scotia and New Brunswick resembled that of Prince Edward Island. By the early nineteenth century, the settlers in both colonies were over 50,000 pounds in arrears. In 1808, New Brunswick's Governor Guy Carleton, and in 1811 Nova Scotia's House of Assembly called upon the Crown to suspend further efforts to collect quit-rents, and the Crown's role as landlord in those Atlantic provinces "fell into abeyance."[50]

Most land in Upper Canada was freehold, but a fraction of all community land was set aside in the early nineteenth century for the support of the clergy of the established Anglican church. Much of the "Clergy Reserve" was leased to local residents, but by 1810 only about one-fifth of the rents due on these leases had been paid. Joseph Ryerson, the sheriff from the London district, reported in 1804 that he had "yet been very unsuccessful" in efforts to collect these fees, "owing

---

[49] Paul Knaplund, *James Stephen and British Colonial Policy, 1813–1847* (Madison, Wis., 195), 71–72; I. R. Robertson, "Highlanders, Irishmen, and the Land Question in 19th Century Prince Edward Island," in *Comparative Aspects of Scottish and Irish Economic and Social History, 1600–1900*, ed. L. M. Cullen and T. C. Smout (Edinburgh, 1978), 227–40; Robertson, *The Tenant League of Prince Edward Island, 1864–1867: Leasehold Tenure in the New World* (1996); W. S. MacNutt, *The Atlantic Provinces: Emergence of Colonial Society, 1712–1857* (Toronto, 1965), 173, 210, 231. A good re-examination of the question is Rusty Bitterman and Margaret McCallum, "When Private Rights became Public Wrongs: Property and the State in Prince Edward Isle in the 1830s," Colonia Law & Property Colloquium, Univ. of Victoria Law School, Feb. 2001.

[50] MacNutt, *Atlantic Provinces*, 149.

to the great scarcity of cash." When John Spencer, Newcastle's sheriff, tried to resell one Clergy Reserve leasehold whose owner had made no payments, that man insisted that "some of the Magistrates told him that [the sheriff] had no authority to take the property" and that he was free to "defend it, and the Law would bear him harmless." Hence he, "assisted by a number of others . . . drove the undersheriff and his assistants from the place and rescued the property from the intended Sale."[51]

Tenancy had been created by the conquering English in Ireland, Ontario, and on Prince Edward Island, but it had been the prevailing condition in Quebec long before the arrival of British law, and, as in Ireland and the American colonies, tenancy in French Quebec had bred trouble and this trouble warrants our (comparative) attention. The French seigneurial system of lords and vassals had sailed up the St. Lawrence with the first *Intendant* in the seventeenth century, but, as Richard Cole Harris has demonstrated, while its origin may have been feudal and its legal system very much alive in the French countryside, it was essentially an empty shell in Quebec. *Seigneurs* (landlords) had few of the privileges, much less of the income, and almost none of the social and political power possessed by their continental French counterparts. As in New York, tenants were hard to recruit, and the *seigneurs* were obliged to construct gristmills. Most lost money for a generation or more on these unprofitable enterprises. Worse, they were generally unable to collect all but a fraction of the rents due them, while some of the tenants (*censitaires*) were depleting the leasehold (*roture*) of its timber or fish, and others were taking their grain to the gristmill of a neighboring seigneury located closer to them. Thus the Jesuit seigneury on *l'Ile aux Ruaux* reported to the *Intendant* in 1708 that *censitaire* Charles Campagna had stripped his *roture* of timber and abandoned it, and complained more generally of "those who after having denuded and stripped a tract of its best wood, abandoned and deserted it."[52]

---

[51] Alan Wilson, *The Clergy Reserves of Upper Canada: A Canadian Mortmain* (Toronto, 1968), 40–44.

[52] Richard Cole Harris, *The Seigneurial System in Early Canada: A Geographical Study* (2nd ed. Kingston, Ontario, 1984), 5 ff, 13, 74, 80, 144, 163; A. L. Burt, "If Turner had looked to Canada, Australia, & New Zealand when he wrote about the West," in *The Frontier in Perspective*, ed. Walker Wyman and Clifton Kroeber (Madison, Wis., 1965), 61, 63.

Compare W. S. MacNutt, *The Atlantic Provinces: Emergence of Colonial Society, 1712–1857* (Toronto, 1965), 194 (on the stripping of timber in New Brunswick in the 1830s by those paying only the first installment of the purchase price), and Sidney Harring, *White Man's Law, Red Man's Land*, 50, 57 (on the leasing by chiefs and/or individual members of the Iroquois' Six Nations Grand River reservation in the 1820s and 1830s of tracts to

The seigneuries of the Catholic Church managed to collect their rents due, but resistance to the traditional church tithe (one thirteenth of income) led to its being reduced by 50 percent in the 1660s. When the Bishop of Quebec announced that the tithe would be raised back to its traditional level on all products of the soil, "un grand murmure" could be heard after church services, and the Council cancelled the edict.[53] In the words of the procurator of the St. Sulpice seigneury in Montreal in 1723, a Monsieur Magnieu, the difficulties *seigneurs* had in getting *censitaires* to pay rents "is common to all property owners, and one can safely say both in France and in Canada that land equals war."[54]

Some tenants acquired more than one *roture* (either for a child or as a speculative venture), and in 1682 the *Intendant* ordered *censitaires* to take up residence or have someone else do so on the *roture* they had leased (*tenir ou faire tenir feu et lieu*). This order was repeated by Louis XIV in his Edict of Marly in 1711, and hundreds of unfarmed *rotures* were recovered by *seigneurs*, but, according to Cole Harris, the holding of more than one *roture* by a single *censitaire* was still widespread in 1760. Tenants "were at their creative best in court" in explaining why their fees (*cens*), feudal lease-transfer taxes (*lods et ventes*), or rents should be reduced (though they found it difficult to evade the terms of *written* contracts).

The seigneurial system had been severely affected by the "law" of supply and demand. Being scarce, tenants were able to alter traditional property rules both formally and informally, to their advantage; thus while *rotures* were, by law, subject to partible inheritance upon the death of the *censitaire* until 1763, most *censitaires* in Montreal avoided this by means of gifts and wills, as division of many *rotures* would have produced subsidence-level plots.[55] These settlers altered social rules

---

"speculators from the United States" who stripped the land of its timber, paying nothing to the Iroquois).

53 Harris, *loc. cit.*, 81; Burt, *loc. cit.*, 64–65.

54 Magnieu, quoted in Louise Dechêne, *Habitants and Merchants in 17th Century Montreal* (Montreal, 1992), 138. (Similarly, in India, where British administrators espoused the "rent" theory of Ricardo and Mill and raised the peasantry's taxes, peasants hit particularly hard were among the first to join forces with the Sepoy mutineers in 1857. Eric Stokes, *The Peasant and the Raj: Studies in Agrarian Society and Peasant Rebellion in Colonial India* (Cambridge, 1978), 131. Indeed, some of those landlords in India who had been deprived of their status of lordship also joined the Rebellion (135–36).

55 Dechêne, *supra* note 54, 165. This was the case in Georgia and some Massachusetts towns as well. See Phillip Greven, *Four Generations: Population, Land, and Family in Colonial Andover* (Ithaca, 1970); and Kenneth Lockridge, *A New England Town: Dedham* (N.Y., 1970).

as well, rejecting the term *censitaire* as being feudal and degrading, and insisting on being called by the more dignified term, *habitant*[56] (which lives on, of course, today in the name by which the proud fans of the Montreal Canadiens call themselves, *Les Habs.*)

After the French capitulation and the cession of Quebec to Britain in 1763, the seigneurial system limped along for another eighty years before its abolition in 1854. Tenants continued to "waste" timber on their *rotures*; the Edict of Marly continued to be ignored, both by the *habitants* and often by the courts as well; tenant fees and rents remained in arrears.[57] Some *seigneurs* threatened to evict delinquent tenants, but they rarely followed through. Some felt "more repugnance in suing than they do in paying." And in any event, it was the *habitant's* merchant creditor who was "in reality the proprietor" of the land, for most indebted *habitants* owed their creditors "as much as the land is worth." Quebec's landlords must have had a saying akin to the English expression: "Sue a beggar and catch a louse." Moreover, *seigneurs* perceived an annoying quality, a *contrariété*, as one put it: litigation costs regarding matters of borders (*bornage*) and ditches, "the most common source of litigation where most of the proceedings... divided and ruined a great many rural *habitants*."

In short, *seigneurs* viewed litigation as a "last resort," indicating, in Evelyn Kolish's words, "how limited the intervention of the courts was in the private disputes of citizens in the late eighteenth and early nineteenth centuries" in Quebec. Most *seigneurs* preferred nonjudicial methods of persuasion in seeking to collect arrears. Those who took their tenants to court often got little for their pains, and, at one moment in time, in 1836, when their efforts "coincided with the growing radicalization of the *patriote* movement," they "undoubtedly contributed to the mobilization of these *censitaires* in support of the Rebellions" of 1837.[58]

---

[56] Harris, *op. cit.* 66, 128–29; Burt, *op. cit.*, 64.

[57] Richard Cole Harris and John Warkentin, *Canada before Confederation: A Study in Historical Geography* (N.Y., P74) 87; Evelyn Kolish, "The Impact of the Change in Legal Metropolis on the Development of Lower Canada's Legal System," 3 *Canadian Journal of Law and Society* 7 (1988); Richard Cole Harris, "Of Poverty and Helplessness in *Petite-Nation*," 52 *Canadian Historical Review* 23 at notes 67 and 68 (1971).

[58] Sung Bok Kim, *supra*, note 39, 219; R. Cole Harris, "Of Poverty," *supra* note 58, notes 67 and 71; Evelyn Kolish, "Some Aspects of Civil Litigation in Lower Canada, 1785–1825: Toward the Use of Court Records for Canadian Social History," 70 *Canadian Historical Review* 337 at 362, 365 (1989); Allan Greer, *Peasant, Lord and Merchant: Rural Society in Three Quebec Parishes* (Toronto, 1985), 128; Francois Noël, *The Christie Seigneuries:*

The Antipodes

Down under, in New South Wales, things were appropriately upside down: The "Squatters" were the large-scale pastoralist-graziers, "respectable Monied Men," using Crown land to the north, west, and south of the original generation of coastal settlements. By 1827 in New South Wales, they were expected to pay £1 per 100 acres of land in quit-rent to the Crown and acquired no claim for any "improvements" they might make. But they ignored this ordinance. After all, they intended to make few improvements, as their only interest in the land was as a source of grasses to fatten their cattle and grow wool on their sheep. One of their organs, the Sydney *Monitor*, argued on September 8, 1826, that "he who possesses and makes use of the land, and puts his labour into it," has a powerful claim to it, whereas "the king ... is merely the trustee of the land for the use of the colonists." Thus, the Crown's fees were both "unconstitutional" and absurd: "If the king has this absolute proprietorship of the land, he has by the same right ... to let out to rent the Pacific ocean which washes our shores." So they lobbied for a lower rate that would sanction their exclusive use of the vast tracts they sought, or already occupied. The Squatters Act of 1836, requiring only a flat lease-fee of £10 per run, and a half-penny per animal, crowned their efforts. The colonial secretary, Lord Glenelg, was disappointed with this concession to the Squattocracy, but, reluctantly, he accepted the colony's act, and the "Squatters'" actions. Under-Secretary Stephen regarded the Crown's inability to enforce the original terms of the Law (especially in the region that was to become Victoria) as justifying this capitulation, describing it as "an example and illustration of the prevailing triumph of popular feelings over Positive Law." Governor Gipps in New South Wales frankly confessed his incapacity to check the spread of these "Squatter"-graziers to Glenelg in April, 1839. It was "too late" to prevent their movements beyond the organized nineteen counties to the east: "All the power of Government, aided even by a Military force ten times stronger than that which is maintained in the Colony, would not suffice to bring back ... the Flocks and Herds, which now stray hundreds of miles beyond them," leaving as "the only question" whether the Crown was to "abandon all control over these distant regions, and have the occupiers of them unrestrained," or "make such efforts as are in our power to preserve order...."[59]

Estate Management and Settlement in the Upper Richelien Valley, 1760– 1854 (Montreal, 1992), 24, 60, 62–63 (on radicalization of *habitants* in 1836).

[59] Roger Milliss, *Waterloo Creek* (Sydney, 1994), 108. Stephen's remarks are reprinted in Stephen Roberts, *The Squatting Age in Australia, 1835–1847*

By 1840 these leaseholders had rights of occupancy good against all but the Crown (*Scott v. Dight* (NSW SC 1840)), and in cases of conflicting claims, the Colony's land commissioners were treating evidence of prior occupancy "as tantamount to possession" and were guided by local customs in the process.[60] By 1846, most of the area beyond the colony's original nineteen counties was held by enterprising pastoralists on long-term leases, some utilizing many thousands of acres. Pastoralists successfully lobbied in Sydney and London in the 1840s for an end to the condition of Governor Gipps that they be required to purchase 320 acre homesteads every 8 years in order to continue to be allowed to lease 20 square mile runs for £10 annual fees. Their leader, William Wentworth, told an assemblage of graziers in Sydney in April, 1844, that Gipps' plan to charge separate £10 fees for individual runs "tribute" and "intolerable." "All the value of this country" had been "imparted to it" by the Squattocracy and, "consequently, . . . these wilds belong to us, and not to the British Government."[61] They secured from Parliament the Imperial Waste Lands Act in 1846, implemented by Order-in-Council of March, 1847, authorizing renewable leasehold tenures of up to fourteen years for as many as 3,200 acres of New South Wales and what was to become Victoria. Lieutenant-Governor LaTrobe managed to squirrel away several inland tracts "to anticipate the public requirements" for townships and cultivated homesteads in Victoria "to provide for the ... consequent general settlement and improvement of the Colony," but the deed was done: the transformation of the Squatters into Great Leaseholder-Proprietors. (See Illustration 8.)

Despite Edward Gibbon Wakefield's success in getting the Colonial Office to require the sale of land in New Zealand at a minimum price of £3/acre, a group of these same sheep graziers from New South Wales descended on the Crown land agent in Canterbury in 1851 and persuaded him to lease them huge runs. It would be another forty years before a Liberal government in New Zealand would reassess grazier property leaseholds and order the repurchase of some of these runs for homesteads.[62]

(Melbourne, 1935), 83; Gipps' are in Bob Reece, *Aborigines and Colonists* (Sydney, 1974), 176.

[60] John Weaver, "Beyond the Fatal Shore: Pastoral Squatting and the Occupation of Australia, 1826–1852," 101 *American Historical Review* 981 at 999, 1002 (1996).

[61] Stephen Roberts, *The Squatting Age in Australia, 1835–1847* (Melbourne, 1935), 75, 80–81, 92, 269–72. Wentworth's remarks are reported in the *Sydney Morning Herald*, April 11, 1844.

[62] Burt, *supra* note 52, 73–76; J. D. N. McDonald, "New Zealand Land Legislation," 5 *Historical Studies: Australia & New Zealand* 195 (1952); John

Illustration 8. In 1863, Samuel Gill caricatured the "Squatter of New South Wales: Monarch of more than all he Surveys." (Mitchell Library, State Library of New South Wales, PXA1983f41.)

A number of these squatter-leaseholders (especially the absentee-partnerships) soon became landlords as well, subleasing chunks of their vast tracts to on-site pastoralists, or settling farm-laborers and their families on "cultivation paddocks or enclosed fields," providing seed, credit, and victuals in exchange for seasonal labor and a crop of wheat. One of these land-for-labor exchanges was gratefully described by an emancipated convict named Curry. In the 1830s he was provided with 30 acres by the MacArthur brothers. They "never took a shilling from me. I take a load to Sydney now and then . . . shear [sheep] . . . now and again. . . . You need not touch paper with them – they seem to like me to get on."[63] Thus, "Squatters" became "tenants" and, almost simultaneously, "landlords."

Norman, *Edward Gibbon Wakefield: A Political Reappraisal* (Fairfield, Ct.,1963), 7–18.

[63] Philip McMichael, *Settlers and the Agrarian Question: Foundations of Capitalism in Colonial Australia* (Cambridge Univ. Press, 1984), 142–43, 206; A. Atkinson, "Master and Servant at Camden Park, 1838," 6 *Push from the Bush* 55 (1980). For examples of one- to four-year leases of fifty acres for "cropping" (or, variously, "the share system"), where the tenant provided the seed, at the Chirnside station at Mt. Rothwell, see Chirnside Papers, MS 11127/2482/24/1, State Library of Victoria.

These "Squatter"-landlords would have identified with their seventeenth century predecessors in Quebec or New York's Hudson Valley: Tenants expected a great deal more than any English, Irish, or Scottish tenant that these "Squatters" gentry-fathers and uncles had ever enjoyed. One Anglo-Irish "pioneer" in Western Australia, George Moore, summed it up in 1839 for his family in Ireland: "[N]o rent is demanded for some years, and they have their proportion of the sheep which they keep besides. Think of having to give 4,000 or 5,000 acres for nothing, & to have to coax people to take it on the terms." (Moore had one tenant-applicant.)[64]

When the price of wool fell, as it did in the 1860s, such "Squatter"-landlords learned from their agents of the "great difficulty in getting some of the Tenants to pay." "In fact," Alexander Reid advised George Russell, Clyde Company's man in Victoria, "they have not got it to pay with." Russell's brother and partner, Robert, paid a visit to the Bothwell estate tenants and renegotiated their leases, reducing them by 10 percent for the next five years. When those years had passed, he "found Bedford complaining as usual about his rent." This time he told Mr. Bedford that "it was unreasonable to expect a reduction on account of the casual fluctuation of the market . . . that he must lay the tail of the sow to the head of the grice [small pig] and go on." Bedford thereupon proposed a "fresh lease on a *wool rent*" – that is, 500 pounds to be paid in-kind at a set price of 1s 6p per pound of wool, thus shifting the "casual fluctuation of the market" to his landlords. Robert recommended this arrangement to his partner. Bedford had been "a first rate Tenant: the fences and cribs are all in excellent order, and he annually expends something in the way of improvements." Given that these expenditures had enriched the Russell brothers (Clyde Company), they accepted his terms. One of their departing tenants, Phillip Lewis, does not appear to have been as fortunate; he expressed "regret" at "having expended so much in improvements – building huts, fencing, etc. – which are very expensive," for he knew he would now "reap no benefit from them."[65]

SUMMARY

Jurists in the lands of the British Diaspora were willing at times to search for the "principle" behind the English rule regarding a tenant's

---

[64] George F. Moore, *Diary of Ten Years' Eventful Life of an Early Settler in Western Australia* (London, 1885), 394.

[65] *Clyde Company Papers*, ed. P. L. Brown (8 vols., Oxford Univ. Press, 1959–1973), VIII, 27, 172–73, 212, 305, 318, 321. Phillip Lewis appeared to wear more than one hat for the Russells; he was a station manager, either leased or rented for a share, and may have owned a small share of Clyde Company.

agricultural improvements, the "wasting" of timber by a leaseholder, the custom of tenant-right in Ulster, or of conacre elsewhere in Ireland. Their decisions in the first two of these instances sounded as if some of these jurists were concerned with "economically efficient" outcomes. In some of those lands where landlords held sway, as in Ireland and Prince Edward Island, tenant protests eventually produced sought-after legal change (by statute). But "responsible" Diaspora legislatures and, at times, their judicial counterparts were sometimes not as "principled" when it came to the rights of Aboriginal landlords seeking to deal with Diaspora tenants who were cutting down all the timber, or not paying their rents, or both.

While it was interesting to learn more of the "formal" law of landlords and tenants, it was the story of the "informal" law that truly captured my attention. In most of the Diaspora, lands tenants showed little of the deference (at least in the first generation or two) toward landlords that their counterparts in England displayed. In the frontier conditions of early North America and the Antipodes, landlords had little leverage. In both regions tenants had to be recruited, and once on the site they had to be provided with considerable start-up capital and infrastructure. Their "wasting" of the leasehold's timber resources often could not be halted, nor could their rent payments be collected. In the Antipodes, the leasing of vast tracts of grasslands for sheep and cattle was accomplished by different sorts of "tenants" in spite of the Crown's initial policies and "the Law." Tenants generally held the upper hand, then, when the landlord was a "Great Proprietor" or the Crown itself; but the story was often different when the tenants were Diaspora newcomers and the landlords were aboriginals.

3

"They Seem To Argue that Custom Has Made a Higher Law": Squatters and Proprietors

One of the early struggles over rights to land between Diaspora newcomers, then, concerned the rights of landlords and tenants. But, throughout most of the lands settled by the British Diaspora, the more common struggle over property between Diaspora newcomers raged between those who purchased land directly from native inhabitants or simply moved onto land and began to use it (the "squatters") and those Crown favorites (the "Great Proprietors") who had been formally granted such land. Legislators addressed these struggles, as did jurists interpreting these statutes and applying the Common Law and Equity. Sometimes the squatters won the value of their "improvements," sometimes not. Sometimes squatters acquiesced in these decisions; sometimes they did not.

THE FORMAL LAW OF SQUATTERS, IMPROVEMENTS, RIPARIAN RIGHTS, AND TITLE

The *lawful* settlement of North America and the Antipodes by the British Diaspora in the seventeenth, eighteenth, and early nineteenth centuries proceeded by way of grants from the Crown to "proprietors" (and, in the United States after 1776, by way of grants by the states and federal government). Some of the larger grants went to "great proprietors" like the Virginia Company, William Penn, Colonel Thomas Talbot, the South Australia Company, and firms like the Union Pacific Railroad. Others were purchased by individuals or partnerships, and many of these were relatively small in size. But while many modest "homesteads" were acquired by direct purchase, most of the land transferred by the Crown went to a relatively small number of "great" or near-great proprietors. Land warrants and script had to be converted into actual title by way of registration of a claim to a particular tract of land with the proper government official. Inasmuch as few "great proprietors" had their claims surveyed and recorded promptly (for a number of reasons), and others recorded claims with imperfectly described boundaries, a number of colonial land offices were plagued with overlapping claims ("shingling"). Moreover, once one's claim *had* been legally established, a "proprietor" often faced a second, equally daunting task, that of evicting an "actual occupant," who might be a disappointed counterclaimant *or* an unabashed squatter. When the dust had settled from that confrontation, the ensuing "owner" eventually sought to exercise his right to bestow that property upon his (or, in some cases, her) "posterity." The Law with regard to such bestowing varied, depending upon where the individual interested in so bestowing lived.[1]

In the United States

Prior to the American Revolution, Thomas Jefferson called for a Law to benefit homesteaders, a statute to enable a Diaspora settler to "appropriate to himself such lands as he finds vacant," under the principle that "occupancy will give him title." At Virginia's Revolutionary Constitutional Convention in 1776 he recommended a provision entitling landless men to fifty free acres of Virginia's frontierland.

---

[1] In England, the Common-Law rule, until well into the nineteenth century, was that the real estate of one who died without having left a will went to the eldest son (primogeniture). That rule was abolished by statute in colonial New England and Pennsylvania, and a partible inheritance rule put in its place, whereby the eldest son inherited two portions and all other children, one. Privy Council disallowed Connecticut's partible inheritance statute in the 1730s (*Winthrop v. Lechmere*), but Connecticut continued to enforce it. When the Massachusetts version of this statute was challenged as well (*Phillips v. Savage*, 1733), Privy Council relented. Virginia and other states abolished both primogeniture and entail (the Common-Law rule permitting a testator to tie up the real estate for up to three generations) during the American War of Independence. Governor Thomas Jefferson defended the replacement of primogeniture with partible inheritance, "the best of all Agrarian law," as a measure that would remove "the feudal and unnatural distinctions which made one member of every family rich, and all the rest poor." This was not quite true, since most wealthy individuals created wills that left some land and personal estate to each child. Newfoundland ended primogeniture in 1833 with legislation heartily supported by Permanent Undersecretary James Stephen in the Colonial Office: "To transfer to the fishing stations & 'Ship Rooms' of Newfoundland, the ancient feudal Law of England, encumbered as it is, with that code of legal Metaphysics which the subtlety of our Jurists have devised," would not suit "the Exigencies of Modern Times." New South Wales abolished primogeniture in 1863. See Peter Hoffer, *Law and People in Colonial America* (Baltimore, 2nd ed., 1998), 105; *Autobiography of Thomas Jefferson*, ed. Paul L. Ford (1914), 77–78; Stanley Katz, "Thomas Jefferson and the Right to Property in Revolutionary America," 19 *Journal of Law & Economics* 467 (1976); Paul Knaplund, *James Stephen and the British Colonial System, 1813–1847* (Madison, Wis., 1953), 71; Andrew Buck, "Torrens Title, Intestate Estates and the Origins of Australian Property Law," 4 *Australian Journal of Legal History* (1996), 89–98.

Within six months, *Governor* Jefferson dismissed his recommendation as "a very hasty production." In 1779, he helped secure a land act that authorized "actual settlers" (including squatters) the right to *purchase* up to 400 acres "at a price below that available to non-residents, with the lowest charge to the earliest occupants," extending to them preemptive (first-refusal) rights to an additional 1,000 acres if they "improved" their tract by building a log cabin on it. A substantial fraction of the remaining land in Virginia's western reserves (present-day West Virginia and Kentucky) were given to Virginia's Revolutionary War veterans in the form of land script; the rest was offered for sale ("treasury warrants") for 40 shillings Virginia currency per 100 acres. Virginia currency declined in value, and many war veterans sold their land script. Millions of acres of this land passed into the hands of speculators. As many as 30 men acquired over 100,000 acres of Kentucky land-warrants apiece in the 1780s. By the early nineteenth century, some 90 percent of present-day West Virginia and Kentucky was "owned" by absentee land speculators.

In like fashion, North Carolina opened its frontierlands for sale in 1783 (the region later admitted to the Union as Tennessee), and by the early nineteenth century, some 70 percent of Tennessee was also absentee-owned. Other *resident* Tennessee landowners included Territorial Governor William Blount and members of his family, who had by 1795 acquired much of the upper portions of eastern Tennessee and were reselling millions of acres in the Northeastern states and Europe.[2]

Legislators thus concerned themselves in a number of ways, responding favorably to appeals for help from both the "Great Proprietors" and the actual occupants of the land. Nonresident, script-holding proprietors often took their time to file claims to specific tracts; once one had filed, one became subject to taxes on such tracts, and some legislatures passed "tax title" statutes designed to strip both owners and users of their land in a sheriff's sale if they had failed to pay their property taxes for a specific period of time.[3]

How did American courts react to these statutes in derogation of the Common Law of property? They accepted and applied most without much ado; others, such as tax title statutes, they accepted quite reluctantly.[4]

---

[2] Stephen Aron, *How the West was Lost: The Transformation of Kentucky from Daniel Boone to Henry Clay* (Chapel Hill, 1996), 70, 71; Wilma Dunaway, *The First American Frontier: Southern Appalachia, 1700–1860* (Chapel Hill, 1996), 57.

[3] Robert Swierenga, "The Odious Tax Title – A Study in 19th Century Legal History," 15 *American Journal of Legal History* 129.

[4] Some jurists clearly felt that for a legislative act to extinguish one's title to land by way of a sale of the property for failure to pay taxes required the

One issue was especially controversial. "Squatting" on land formally granted by the Crown to "proprietors" was widespread in colonial North America. Individuals and families bypassed the formal legal means of acquiring title by simply moving onto and "improving" tracts of land that had been granted to favorites of the Crown. And the practice continued after independence in the United States. How did the Law react?

In late eighteenth century Kentucky and Tennessee, and thereafter in thirteen states in the early nineteenth century legislatures ordered out-of-state claimants to record their claims for tax purposes and forgave squatter-occupants from paying rent until their squatting had been detected and an action of ejectment filed by the owner of the land, protected those who had purchased "improved" land from squatters and had further "improved" it, and treated such squatter occupancy as constituting "color of title," entitling the squatter to the equitable value of those improvements from the legal owner. A Kentucky statute in 1795 provided "relief" to squatters who had cleared and planted at least two acres "on the South side of Green River" by the end of that year to acquire title to upward of 200 acres at 30 cents per acre. It stipulated that no further squatting would be "granted the preference of settlement," but two years later another Kentucky statute dangled a similar, generous purchase option before both newcomers and older settlers who had failed to take advantage of the first statutory offer. Stephen Aron has found that "before the 1795 act, less than one in five heads of households in the Green River country owned any land; by 1800, a majority, about 5 out of 9 heads of household had gained legal possession of real estate," and in the counties south of that river "landowners accounted for an even higher proportion." The Green River's homesteaders constituted a sizable bloc of voters in early Kentucky; consequently their influence in the state legislature was considerable, and in 1798 and again in 1808 they secured statutes that enabled them to stretch out their land payments until the year 1820. This process of extending their deadline and restructuring their debt continued; in 1823, "a quarter century after the

clearest conditions of "notice" and sufficient passage of time to satisfy their sense of justice; they may have had in mind the "equity of redemption" rule, whereby one whose mortgage payment fell behind retained a window of time to undo any foreclosure that had ensued. Others appeared to fear that the "heartless speculator" would be the one to seize the advantage over "his neighbors misfortunes and necessities." See Justice George Wright in *McCready v. Sexton & Son*, 29 Iowa 356 at 400 (1870); and Swierenga, "The 'Odious Tax Title': A Study in Nineteenth Century Legal History," 15 *American Journal of Legal History* 124 at 135 (1971).

debts were supposed to have been retired," Aron tells us they still owed $33,000.[5]

In some cases (as with Kentucky in 1809) those legislatures also provided complete title to those holding land in adverse possession to the claims of others for at least seven years. Other southern and western state legislatures throughout the nineteenth century adopted similar "adverse possession" statutes, and several also adopted "replevin foreclosure" acts after the financial Panic of 1819 to delay creditor actions on settler land.[6] The high courts of these states generally found no fault with such statutes, nor could they be persuaded to interfere with the local juries of assessment created by the statutes to determine the value of squatter improvements unless "the most convincing evidence of the incorrectness of their estimate" was provided. Absentee proprietors might complain of assessments by Kentucky juries of "apple trees not bigger than a man's arm" valued at ten dollars, of "half-rotten fences" valued at "the full price of new rails," of "decrepit log houses judged equal to stone and brick mansions," but, as Stephen Aron has observed, such "absentee land claimants... could not vote" in Kentucky.[7]

Kentucky's Court of Appeals went *beyond* the legislature's Occupying Claimants Act in 1820 to protect the improvements of squatters holding without the least "color of title" (such as a "title" from a claims association or a "permit" or "signing right" acquired from a "possession" speculator who had cleared and fenced a field and then sold his "title" to it). The squatter in *Parker v. Stephens* could make no such "good faith" claims, but he was found to be entitled to the value of his improvements anyway.[8] The next year, when the same court less generously declared the legislature's replevin law postponing mortgage foreclosures to be unconstitutional, the legislature reacted by abolishing the court (in 1824) and replacing it with one more friendly to such farm debtor relief measures. The U.S. Supreme Court struck down the Kentucky Occupying Claimants Act regarding squatter improvements in 1823, but the reorganized Kentucky Court of Appeals simply ignored that decision in 1825 and enforced the squatter-friendly statute

---

[5] Donold Pisani, "Squatter Law in California," 25 *Western Historical Quarterly* 285 (1994); Aron, *How the West was Lost,* 153, 157–58.

[6] Paul Gates, "Tenants of the Log Cabin," in Gates, *Landlords and Tenants on the Prairie Frontier* (Ithaca, 1973), 18, 22–25, 42, 44–5.

　　The Congress added a federal statute in 1841 that gave squatters on federally owned land preemptive rights to purchase up to 160 acres of the federal land they occupied.

[7] Aron, *How the West was Lost: The Transformation of Kentucky from Daniel Boone to Henry Clay* (Chapel Hill, 1996), 97.

[8] In *Parker v. Stephens,* 10 Ky. 197 at 202 (1820).

until an "old court" party won control of the legislature in 1826 and replaced the high court once again. (Lo and behold, the U.S. Supreme Court thereupon reversed *itself* on the subject, in 1831).[9]

Of the rest of the American high courts, only California's appears to have insisted that the state's occupying claimants law was unconstitutional (but so did the U.S. Supreme Court, for that state's legislature was constrained by the terms of the Treaty of Guadalupe Hidalgo between the United States and Mexico, which had guaranteed the validity of all Mexican land grants throughout the ceded territory.)[10] This appears to explain the otherwise inexplicable story Frank Norris tells us in *The Octopus* (based on the true incident at Mussel Slough in Tulare County in 1878) of the "Pacific and Southwestern" (the Southern Pacific) Railroad's taking without compensation of the improvements (the houses, barns, and fields) of wheat farmers who had occupied the land as squatters for several years.

The Southern Pacific had advertised land at $2.50 an acre in pamphlets circulated in the mid-1870s. But it had attracted few buyers, and it had delayed taking title to its grant itself, something allowed under the relevant federal land-grant statute until the late 1870s, in order to avoid property taxes. Once title had been perfected by farmer-purchasers, the company demanded as much as $20 an acre from those in possession. A number of these squatters sought to create a rival "color of title" by filing land claims and organizing a land-claim club, the Settlers' Grand League. But both Congress and the local federal district court turned their petitions and legal arguments away. Soon thereafter a U.S. marshal and his party serving ejectment notices were confronted by armed members of the Settlers' League at Mussel Slough. A gunfight erupted, and several men fell dead. Seven League members were tried and convicted in federal court. (Their

---

9 *Green v. Biddle*, 8 Wheat. 1 (1823); *Bodley v. Gaither*, 19 Ky. 57 at 60 (1825); *Hawkins v. Barneys Lessee*, 5 Peters (30 U.S.) 457 at 466 (1831). Gates offers a slightly garbled treatment of the subject, *supra* note 5, 29–41.

10 Squatters on such grants, be they timber thieves, ranchers or farmers, thereupon resolved in August 1850 to "disregard all declarations of our courts in land cases and all summones and executions...touching the matter," and fought the Law for years, though many eventually agreed to long-term leases. *Billings v. Hall*, 7 Cal. l at 11 (relying on the overruled *Green v. Biddle*, and quoting John Locke) (1857); Paul Gates, "California's Embattled Settlers," 41 *California Historical Society Quarterly* 99 (1962); Gates, "The Land Business of Thomas Larkin," 54 *California Historical Quarterly* 333 (1975); Pisani, "Squatter Law in California," at 281, 291, 300; Karin Clay and Werner Troesken, "Squatting and the Settlement of the United States: New Evidence from Post-Gold Rush California," 1 *Advances in Agricultural Historical Economics* 202, at 231 (2000).

prison days were spent in relative comfort, however, with their families permitted free access to them on the top floor of the jail, and in little more than seven months they were reprieved to return to Tulare County "triumphantly," cheered on their arrival by a crowd of some 3,000.)[11]

The Southern Pacific's confrontation with outraged settlers at Mussel Slough is, perhaps, better known than the ways that other railroad companies in the West with federal land grants dealt with disgruntled settler–squatters. Many such railroads found squatters on the tracts that the road "selected" under the terms of the grant to help finance construction. The difference was that most of these companies avoided the legal disputes and bad blood of the Mussel Slough sort by coming to terms with these squatters quickly. The Illinois Central and the Burlington & Missouri River railroads, for example, found that "the easiest policy to follow" when squatters were detected was to rent the squatters the land "for one to three years at a nominal price of 20 cents an acre" in the hope that such improvements as the squatters made "would enable the land to bring a good price," either from the same tenant or another, or from a fee-simple purchaser, when the lease expired, as well as to establish clear legal grounds for eviction, "if necessary."[12]

In the Other Diaspora Lands

Jurists in the other "British settlement" regions of the eighteenth and nineteenth centuries considered here (Australia, New Zealand, and the Canadian provinces) were no less frequently called upon than Americans to address legal questions regarding land title and improvements with relation to English rules of Common Law and Equity, parliamentary statutes, or laws of their legislatures. These jurists sometimes turned the squatters' defenses away, while other times they granted them the value of their "improvements," if they had been occupants in "good faith."

[11] See Richard Orsi, "The Confrontation at Mussel Slough," in Orsi, Rice, and Bullough, *The Elusive Eden: A New History of California* (N.Y., 1988), 217–36; John Larimore, "Legal Questions arising from the Mussel Slough Land Dispute," 58 *Southern California Quarterly* 75 (1976); Richard Brown, *No Duty to Retreat: Violence and Value in American History and Society* (N.Y., 1991), 114, 222; *Southern Pacific RR v. Orton*, 32 Fed. 457 (1879); and David Bederman, "The Imagery of Injustice at Mussel Slough: Railroad Land Grants, Corporate Law and the 'Great Conglomerate West,'" 1 *Western Legal History* 237 (1988).

[12] Paul Gates, *Landlords and Tenants on the Prairie Frontier*, 309–10.

In the 1840s and 1850s, Sir John Beverley Robinson, Chief Justice of Upper Canada's Queen's Bench, showed little tolerance for "bad faith" squatters, but these miscreants were small-scale farmers and loggers, and Robinson was the son of a New York Loyalist Proprietor and the owner of large tracts of land in Upper Canada. Sir John opined in one case that government "policy" in Upper Canada had "for a long time, if not from the first," been that of "favouring these intruders," yet in this case his court upheld the ejectment of this "bad faith" squatter without providing any compensation for his improvements.[13]

But Chief Justice Robinson was not entirely consistent in this regard, despite his background. One squatter, who had been in possession of a lot in Chatham for only six years, was ejected by its owner after having spent £175 on improvements. The owner sued him for back rent ("mesne profits") and his costs for the ejectment action (£13). When the trial court jury gave him only nominal damages, he appealed. But Robinson, for his colleagues, held that the jury had properly taken into account the value of the squatter's improvements in denying damages. Moreover, Robinson was more generous in another case than the very officer of Upper Canada's courts from whom one might have expected generosity – the Chancellor, William Hume Blake. An individual had secured a land patent for some 200 acres of Clergy Reserve land from the Crown only to be told later by the chancellor that he was in effect no better than a squatter, holding the land in trust for another claimant. Robinson reversed this judgment. "Just such a patent as this is lies at the root of every man's title; thousands of them have been issuing annually, for nearly fifty years." Once the Crown had issued a patent, it would be inequitable, and unlawful, to cancel it in such a fashion as this.[14]

Blake's successor, Chancellor Phillip Vankoughnet, may have had a broader, more generously proportioned "chancellor's foot," for he was willing to ignore the commentary of John Dawson Mayne, the English treatise authority, on the question of whether a squatter-improver-defendant might establish, in an action for mesne profits (back rent), "the value of the improvements made by him upon the property" in

---

[13] *Fitzgerald v. Finn*, 1 U.C.Q.B. 70 (1844); *Henderson v. Seymour*, 9 U.C.Q.B. 47 at 53 (1853). See also *Bellows v. Condee*, 4 U.C.Q.B. 346 (1848) (jury award of £110 for timber taking affirmed).

Throughout the first half of the nineteenth century, many of Ontario's elite speculated in land (including Chief Justice Robinson's mentor, Archbishop John Strachan), making no improvements on their lots for ten years or more. Davig Gagan, *Hopeful Travellers: Families, Land and Social Change in Mid-Victorian Peel County, Canada West* (Toronto, 1981), 30.

[14] *Patterson v. Reardon*, 7 U.C.Q.B. 326 (1850); *Boulton v. Jeffrey*, 1 U.C.E.& A. 111 at 113 (1845).

mitigation of damages. The American treatise writer, Theodore Sedgwick, had recently indicated that this equitable rule was widely observed in the States, while his English predecessor, Mayne, had simply written: "no English authority can be found for such a doctrine." That left Chancellor Vankoughnet free to decide the matter by the measure of his own conscience, and he ruled that the jury had properly been at freedom to "make all proper allowances" for the defendant's improvements in awarding damages: "The course pursued in the American courts seems the more reasonable one, and not wrong on any principle of law."[15]

The New Brunswick Supreme Court used similar reasoning in 1842 while trying to decide whether a squatter in possession of another's land for over twenty years was entitled to *all* the land he had staked out, or only that which he had improved and fenced. "In the absence of any English case to direct our judgement," Justice Parker turned to American decisions for authority.[16]

But these were questions of Common Law and Equity. When an American *statute* was noted, the hint was rarely offered that a British colonial court might borrow from its language or spirit.[17] Thus, Chief Justice Hagarty of Ontario's Court of Appeals, had words of praise in 1888 for American "betterment" statutes regarding questions involving the valuation of improvements and mistakes effecting title, but confessed, in a case "of much hardship," and with "the strongest feeling of

---

[15] *Townsley v. Neil*, 10 Grant's Chancery R. 72 at 75 (1863). See also *Heck v. Knapp*, 20 U.C.Q.B. 360 (1861) (plaintiff not in actual possession cannot sue in trespass for defendant–squatter's removal of timber where defendant was in possession; must sue for mesne profits); *Henderson v. McLean*, 8 U.C.C.P. 42 (1858) (same); and see Macaulay, C. J., in *Glover v. Walker*, 5 U.C.C.P. 478 at 480 (1856): "To hold that even a squatter's house, . . . might be destroyed by strangers willfully felling trees upon them on the technical ground that the possession remained in the Crown [no transfer of title by land patent] . . . would, I think, be carrying the doctrine too far, or misapplying it to the wild lands of the Crown in Upper Canada." See R.C.B. Risk, "The Last Golden Age: Property and the Allocation of Losses in Ontario in the Nineteenth Century," 27 *University of Toronto Law Journal* 199 at 203 (1977) for a good general analysis.

[16] *Doe dem. Des Barres v. White*, 3 New Br. 595 at 626–27 (1842). The squatter got only the land he had cleared and fenced. See *Allison v. Rednor*, 14 UCQB 459 (1856) for a virtually identical fact situation with the same outcome.

[17] In *Church v. Fenton*, 5 Can. S.C. 239 at 254, 257 (1880), Justice Henry commented favorably on an Illinois statute in a case involving the sale of two acres of land by tax title, and then referred to "able" decisions of several American state supreme courts interpreting such statutes, adding that he felt "safe" in following them in the absence of English authorities on the subject. But this was uncommon, and Justice Henry was not a jurist of note.

regret," that his court could not draw upon any of these aspects of the American codes regarding squatter's rights, inasmuch as the Ontario legislature had failed to follow the example of their more enlightened counterparts to the south with regard to these questions in drafting its views on the subject.[18]

Compare Upper Canada's treatment of squatters with that of the courts of the essentially French settlement of Lower Canada (Quebec). Despite assurances in the Treaty of 1763 that the Quebecoise could retain their French law, and despite similar assurances of the Colonial Office's Under-Secretary Robert Wilmot Horton and its general counsel, James Stephen, in the 1820s, that the Crown had no intention of altering "your laws [and] usages," Francophone residents had cause to think otherwise. In the late eighteenth and early nineteenth centuries, English-bred, American Loyalist-exile jurists were appointed to Quebec's benches, soon outnumbering their French-Canadien counterparts three to one. Many of these men tried to tug that province's customs and French rules of land tenure into the English Common-Law system. Thus, in 1831, King's Bench Justice James Kerr incensed French-Canadiens when he called the law of Lower Canada "unworthy of an English judge" (and, it would appear, unfamiliar to him). More significantly, Judge Samuel Gale explained that even before the passage of the Canada Tenures Act of 1825, he had regarded French customary property law as being "illegal" in the Eastern Townships settled by Britons. Similarly, in 1831, Chief Justice Reid voided a notarial deed consisting of a general hypothec on the socage land (*franc aleu rotuier*) of a debtor, something that constituted a kind of secret mortgage, because it was inconsistent with the English rule regarding mortgages of land held in free and common socage.[19]

---

[18] *Beaty v. Shaw*, 14 Ont. A. 600 at 604, 606 (1888).
[19] See Evelyn Kolish, "The Impact of the Change in Legal Metropolis on the Development of Lower Canada's Legal System," 3 *Canadian Journal of Law and Society* 1 at 23 (1988); Brian Young, *Politics of Codification*, 31. This reading of the meaning of language in the Canada Tenures Act prevailed until the 1850s, when Lower Canada's Court of Appeals upheld the dower rights of a widow under *French* law, reasoning that Parliament had only introduced a limited version of English land law. *Wilcox v. Wilcox*, 2 LCJ 1 (1857); John E. C. Brierley, "The Co-existence of Legal Systems in Quebec: 'Free and Common Socage' in Canada's 'pays de droit civil'," 20 *Cahiers de Droit* 277 (1970).

Anglophone distrust of secret mortgages was at times echoed by similar confusion over the Law in such matters by both Diaspora settlers and French Canadiens. "No one knows what law regulates them" Johan Neilson complained to a committee of the assembly in 1838. He had lent money to

Responding to these Francophobic decisions, as well as to the petitions of a torrent of British Diaspora residents, the Diaspora-dominated assembly of Lower Canada granted the five eastern counties their own land registry offices in 1830.[20]

After the suppression of the Reform-led unrest of 1837, the Lower Canada Special Council passed an ordinance extinguishing some French property rules. All conveyances, mortgages, and land transfers were to be registered; there were to be no more hypothecary customs nor customary dower rights. Brian Young has fairly characterized this as an ordinance that favored the interests of capitalist investors, and he has also characterized the bankruptcy reform acts of 1842 and 1846, the bills of exchange and promissory note law of 1849, and the Seigneurial Act of 1854 in the same fashion, as they provided the means for the assembling of capital for the development of timber and water-power entrepreneurs.[21] But it is worth noting that by the early 1850s a new generation of British-bred and French Canadian jurists had largely abandoned the earlier effort of British and Loyalist jurists to impose an English Common-Law system on Lower Canada's property rules. The English rule that "livery of seisin" must be observed was deemed "an idle formality" that "has never been practiced" and would not protect a squatter who had fabricated a bill of sale (dating it "1813" on paper with a watermark of "1844"), from one who had bought the land from another with better "color of title." French, not English, property law now governed; hence another purchase was voided as it had "not . . . been followed by *tradition*" (even though this French act of delivery closely resembled the rejected "formality," livery of seisin).[22]

None the less, in 1857 Lower Canada's jurists *were* ready to abandon past precedent[23] and the respected work of Robert Joseph Pothier,

some younger sons of a French Canadien on the assumption that French law prevailed in that district and that they were lawful heirs, "but it appears now, that according to the English law it was the eldest son that had it all, and they had nothing, being younger sons, and I have no security for my money." (Young, *Politics of Codification*, 24.)

[20] Brian Young, *Politics of Codification*, 28, 29, 31.

[21] Young, *Politics of Codification*, 46, 59.

[22] *Stuart v. Ives*, 1 L.C.R. 193 at 203 (Q.B. 1851); *Stuart v. Bowman*, 2 L.C.R. 369 (Super. Ct. Montr. 1851); *Malloy v. Hart*, 2 L.C.R. 345 (Q.B. 1852); Brian Young, "Positive Law, Positive State: Realignment and the Transformation of Lower Canada, 1815–1866," in *Colonial Leviathan*, ed. Allan Greer and Ian Radforth (Toronto, 1992), 54. See also *MacDonald v. Lambe & Nickle*, 11 L.C.J. 335 (Privy Council, 1867), upholding *Same*, 9 L.C.J. 281 (1865) (proof that *bona* fide possessor had been in possession for thirty years a good bar to an ejectment proceeding by *seigneur*, using rules of French law).

[23] As late as 1856, Lower Canada's Superior Court distinguished between "good faith" squatter–possessors, who *were* entitled to the value of their

the eighteenth century French treatise authority (in his *Traite de Proprieté*) when it came to improvements (*ameliorations*) by so-called "bad faith" (*maivaise foi*) squatters. "The peculiar circumstances of this country as a new country," wrote Justice Short "the manner in which large tracts of land have been granted by which great uncertainty and difficulty attend in many cases the ascertaining of titles, and the encouragement always extended by our government to actual settlers, afford sufficient reasons to render the possession '*excusable*' to the extent necessary to enable the possessor to receive compensation for the excess of his improvements beyond the rents" (£130 in this case). The judicial act of transforming a "bad faith" possession into a "good faith" one ('*excusable*'), a simple legal fiction, was itself excusable because "it is founded in justice...,"[24] and this view was upheld by Quebec's high court for the rest of the century.[25]

Many of the first free settlers and emancipated convicts in New South Wales struggled within a capital-scarce economy to return profits through alternating years of floods and drought. Officials in 1806 used the failure of those holding 999-year leases to pay their quitrents as a means of reallocating some land, but the typical debtor was granted a stay of execution and an installment payment order. Only when such relief failed did the court order a debtor's land sold to pay the debts. All of this was very unEnglish, but it was precisely the way such matters had been handled for two generations in Pennsylvania and North Carolina. Similarly, despite both English and local New South Wales rules that land conveyances be in writing and be registered, many early settlers "simply handed over the original land grant document in return for payment," and the colony's early jurists accepted this procedure, "even accepting oral proof of titles to land when the crown granted document was lost," as Bruce Kercher has pointed out.[26]

Title to most settlers' land had been granted in the name of the governor rather than the monarch. This troubled no one terribly until the arrival of a new chief justice, Francis Forbes, in the 1820s. Forbes told attorneys, juries, and the governor that the formal English rule required the Great Seal of the Crown on the parchment of title, but, in *Rex v. Cooper* (1825) the jury ignored his instructions and

---

improvements, and "bad faith" ones who were not. See *Lane v. Deloge*, 1 L.C.J. 3 (1856).

[24] Short, J., in Circuit Ct. opinion, 1856, cited in *Stuart v. Eaton*, 8 L.C.R. 113 at 118 (Superior Ct., 1857).

[25] See *Ellice v. Courtemache*, 11 L.C.J. 325 (Q.B. 1867); *Handley v. Foran & Foran*, 5 Quebec Q.B. 44 (1894).

[26] Kercher, "Commerce and the Development of Contract Law in New South Wales," 9 *Law & History Review* 269 at 291 (1991); Kercher, 11 *Law & History Review* 454–55 (1993).

found for a defendant holding title based on a grant from a previous governor, lacking those proper legal accoutrements. Forbes yielded; he wrote Governor Brisbane that he "believe[d], with the Jury, that a very large Portion of the Town allotment and of other valuable Lands in the Colony, are at this moment held by no other title" than the one Cooper possessed, and he recommended that Brisbane issue a proper grant of title to him. Brisbane did so. Some five years later the Crown tried again in an action of ejectment drawn against a quarryman whose title consisted of a Letter of Occupancy grant issued to a former soldier. Barrister William C. Wentworth urged the jury to "look at this question of right with the eyes of colonists," and insisted that "it would be absurd to apply the technicalities of the laws of England here, respecting titles." Chief Justice Forbes directed the jury to find for the Crown, but intimated that they might come in with a special verdict if the defendant's "equitable claims" warranted it. The jury confounded those instructions and held that the defendant had proved his title. Forbes then ordered a retrial, before the Supreme Court judges, and the Court then rendered a "proper" verdict for the Crown.[27] This problem was eventually overcome by the legislature of New South Wales – that is, by the peers of those juries.

So was a similar problem: A number of settlers simply lost or misplaced such land grants as they had been given, and fell out with their neighbors when some of the original boundary marks (a tree, a boulder) were no longer evident. This could lead to boundary disputes and nasty lawsuits, where the outcome might turn on which party could produce the oldest witness to prove the claims, as in *Bushel v. Rose* (1827). To deal with these sorts of problems the legislature created a court of claims "to avoid the complexities and injustices of formal law and the courts" in Bruce Kercher's words.[28]

Graziers, it will be recalled from Chapter 2, descended on the plains of New South Wales, Tasmania, Victoria, South Australia, and New Zealand throughout the first half of the nineteenth century, first by "squatting," and then by leasing the land from the Crown for modest fees. Mere squatters acquired no rights to the value of their "improvements," even when the Crown's highest colonial officer, might intimate that they would. I have in mind the remarks of the Earl of Aberdeen, Secretary of State for the Colonies in March, 1835. Aberdeen had felt called upon to respond to appeals from Lord Surry,

[27] *Rex v. Payne* (1930). *Cooper, Payne,* and a case comparable in outcome to *Cooper, Martin v. Munn* (1833), are to be found on Bruce Kercher's website, *www.law.mq.edu.au/scnsw.*

[28] Brian Fletcher, *Landed Enterprise and Penal Society: A History of Farming and Grazing in New South Wales before 1821* (Sydney, 1976), 21; Kercher, *Unruly Child,* 119.

who had written on behalf of a large family of gentry-emigrants, the Hentys, who sought priority "rights of Settlement" to the land they were occupying in the Portland Bay region of what would become Victoria "in the event of the Districts of the Neighbourhood of Portland Bay ever becoming a permanent colony...." While declining to grant "the pledge" which [Mr. Henty] requires," Aberdeen did add that" Mr. Henty's pretensions to any *land actually brought into cultivation and surrounded by a proper fence"* (Aberdeen's emphasis) might well be "favorably looked upon by His Majesty's Government at a future period." The Hentys then proceeded to fence the dickens out of their holdings. When Major Thomas Mitchell happened upon their settlement in his exploration of western Victoria in 1836, he recorded that "from the magnitude and extent of the buildings, and the very substantial fencing erected, that both time and labour had been expended in their construction." The Hentys memorialized Governor Gipps in early 1840, describing their fencing of a total of 200 acres at four different homesteads, as well as their houses, sheds, barns, stables, cribs, and paddocks "grubbed of Stumps," and the construction of roads at a cost, they claimed, of about 9,000 pounds, "after the receipt" of Aberdeen's letter. But neither of Aberdeen's successors, Glenelg and Russell, nor their governors, Bourke and Gipps, chose to "look favorably" on their "properly-fenced" improvements. In Lord Russell's words, to reward the Hentys for their unauthorized settlement would "dispossess the public at large of Land which it is essential to reserve for public uses." The end result was that the Hentys were forced to purchase three of their tracts, amounting to only 48 acres, for nearly 2,000 pounds at a public sale.[29]

The governments of New South Wales and Victoria soon enacted "free selection" statutes to encourage the emmigration of farmers and the relocation to farms of the many miners who would be rendered redundant once Australian mines ceased to yield profitable ore. These sanctioned the selection of farms for purchase anywhere on the leased runs so long as the Squatters were compensated for any improvements they had made. In the event that the parties could not agree, the value of the improvements was left to a jury to decide. (The statutes did bar the purchase of specific units of land properly leased by pastoralists if these lessees had made £40 worth of improvements). These statutes were generally enforced by the courts when challenged.[30]

---

[29] Marnie Bassett, *The Hentys* (Oxford, 1961), 329, 393, 453–56, 462–65.

[30] *Ibid.*, 352. S. H. Roberts, *A History of Australian Land Settlement* (London, 1968), 151–211; A. R. Buck, "The Logic of Egalitarianism: Law, Property & Society in Mid-Nineteenth Century New South Wales," 5 *Law in Context* 18 (1987); *Blackwood v. Dobbin*, 1 NSWR (N.S.) (K.L. & F.) 75 (1878);

Farmers and miners thus acquired clear avenues to access and title, but the interests of their forerunners, the sheep station owners, were not ignored.

In the colony under the influence of the views of Edward Gibbons Wakefield, South Australia farmers had been encouraged from the beginning, and in *McKenzie v. Stocks* (1845), the colony's high court decided that pastoralist leaseholders had no claims for improvements or use against farmers (styled "cockatoos" by the squatters) holding location tickets of purchase down payment; further, such pastoralists could be "warned off."[31] Similarly, to Judge Wilson Gray of New Zealand's important Otago District (Dunedin) in the late 1860s, the matter seemed straightforward: The "squatters" on the South Island were sheep grazers, typically from New South Wales, England, and Scotland, with huge flocks. Gray tolerated them, but only in the absence of agrarian settlers: "As long as sheep and cattle require the land, let them have it to graze upon, but when men and women want it, let the sheep and cattle get out of the way."[32]

Despite Gray's sentiments, the fact is that most of these Squatters acquired "good faith" status in the 1850s, and most remained in possession until the Liberal governments of all the colonies in the Antipodes in the 1860 to 1890s bought a number of them out by statute for homesteaders.[33] (See Illustration 9.)

Riparian Rights

I don't want to give the impression here that jurists in the United States were habitual innovators. In fact, they were quite circumspect in revising Common-Law rules of property (as well as those of contract). A case in point is their treatment of suits involving riparian rights. With the exception of a handful of decisions of courts of the Rocky Mountain states (where the arid conditions clearly called for rules different from those of the rain-fed British Isles and the states east of the Great Plains), the courts of the United States adopted most of the rules regarding the sharing of water by upstream and downstream users entirely from English decisions and treatises.[34]

McBean v. Grieve, 2 NSWR (N.S.) (K.L. & F.) 153 (1879); *Peterson v. Prowse,* 2 NSWR (N.S.) (K.L. & F.) 191 (1879).

[31] *Ibid.,* 171.

[32] Reeves, *State Experiments,* I, 290–93.

[33] "Wilson Gray," 2 *Colonial Law Journal* 6, 13 (Nov. 1875). An M.P. in Victoria before taking the judicial post in New Zealand, Gray quoted Tom Mooney on the same subject to his fellow M.P.s in 1860 ("a vote, a rifle, a farm"). C. M. H. Clark, *A History of Australia* (Melbourne, 1978), IV, 123.

[34] See Karsten, *Heart v. Head,* 41–46.

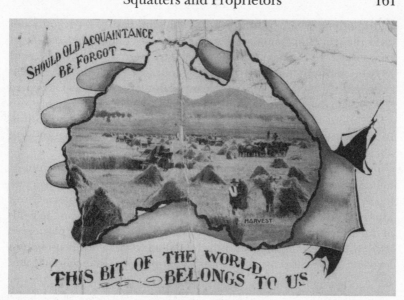

SHOULD OLD ACQUAINTANCE BE FORGOT —

HARVEST

THIS BIT OF THE WORLD BELONGS TO US

Illustration 9. This turn-of-the-century postcard celebrated the British Diaspora's "settling" of the Australian *"terra nullius."* (Oxley Library, State Library of Queensland, #146312.)

And, not surprisingly, so did the courts in New Brunswick, Prince Edward Island, Ontario, Quebec, and New South Wales. Thus, in 1849, Justice Chipman of New Brunswick's Supreme Court had no qualms about citing a decision of the next-door Maine Supreme Court as authority in refusing to allow a jury to decide "as to the balance of advantage or disadvantage to the public" in the case of a logger blocked by a milldam. Jurists on Prince Edward Island also cited U.S. cases in 1851 in deciding an appeal involving two mill owners.[35] Fourteen years later, in Upper Canada (Ontario) Vice Chancellor Esten thought the

Of course the special conditions of the arid western states led their legislatures to create county water commissioners with directions as to how to allocate this scarce resource among first and later users, farmers, ranchers, and miners. Similarly, in the arid regions of Australia, water was "parcelled out according to bureaucratic formulae." See Gorden Bakken, *The Development of Law on the Rocky Mountain Frontier: Civil Law and Society, 1850–1912* (Westport, Ct., 1983); Bruce Kercher, *An Unruly Child: A History of Law in Australia* (St. Leonards, 1995), 129.

[35] *Rowe v. Titus*, 6 New Br. 326 at 335 (1849); *Howat v. Laird*, Rpts. of SC of PEI (Haviland) 5, 15 113 (1850–51). See also *Beaver v. Reed*, 9 UCQB 152 (1852); *Gardiner v. Chapman*, 6 Ont. (Ch.) 272 (1884); *Stevens v. M'Clung*, 2 Legges R (NSW) 1226 (1859) (no prescriptive water rights existed in Australia because there had been no "immemorial possession" by British settlers; hence, the first milldam owner could abate the second dam where

damage done by a new, downstream milldam that had backed water
onto the wheel of a smaller, disused upstream dam to be "trifling as
compared with the damage that must result" were the Court of Equity
to issue an injunction and the larger mill to be shut down. And his
colleagues agreed that the upstream plaintiff should have accepted
the "reasonable compensation" offered him for the "not very grievous
injury" done to his property instead of insisting on "exorbitant" terms.
But when no settlement could be reached, Esten's colleagues went
ahead and issued a perpetual injunction.[36]

Jurists were not expansive in their reading of "developmentalist"
milldam statutes either, even when they had been involved in the crafting of the statutes themselves. As a legislator for Upper Canada, Oliver
Mowat sponsored a bill in 1859 to permit mill owners to flood the fields
of the upstream riparian for a fee, a developmental measure pioneered
by New England legislatures. But the bill was defeated, thirty-eight to
forty-four, and eleven years later as Ontario's Vice-Chancellor, Mowat

---

it had damaged his); *Hood v. Corp. of Sydney*, 2 NSW LR 1294 (1860); and
Lomax v. Jarvis, 6 NSW LR 237 (1885).

   The Common-Law rule of the *Cotumes de Paris* in Quebec acted, as in
England and New England, to permit an upstream owner of a disused mill
to prevent the downstream owner of a new mill from backing water onto the
disused mill's wheel, and, like their New Brunswick counterparts, Quebec's
jurists drew on the views of an American treatise (*Angell on Watercourses*) for
authority. See *Bussière v. Blais*, 7 Lower Can. R 245 (1857).

   But see *Queen v. Robertson*, 6 Can. S.C.R. 52 at 130 (1882) (Justice Gwynne:
Crown's right to grant salmon flyfishing licenses on Miramichi River governed by same rule as prevails in New York, Maine, and Pennsylvania; rule
regarding navigability of river not governed by ebb and flow of tide, as in
England).

[36] *Wright v. Turner*, 10 Grant's Ch. 67 at 70, 71 (1863). See also *Graham v.
Burr*, 4 Grant's Ch. 1 at 8 (1853) (same fact situation; Chancellor Blake
issued injunction, citing the "eminent jurists" from America, Kent, and
Story, as authority; Esten, V.C., dissenting here as well); *Dickson v. Burnham*,
14 Grant's Ch. 594 (1868) (the more developmentalist, soon-to-be Prime
Minister, Oliver Mowat, V.C., ordered a master's damage report in a similar
case, while inviting the legislature to enact law "to encourage the building
of mills and manufactories" and noting that such statutes had been passed
to good effect in several of the neighbouring states" as long ago as "when
they were Colonies of Great Britain"); *Wadsworth et al. v. McDougall*, 30
UCQB 369(1870); *In re Burnham*, 22 Ont. App. 40 at 43 (1895) (Justice
Osler denied the application of the "Peterborough Water Company," a
riparian "attempting to acquire the privilege" of building a 60 1/2 foot dam
downstream from a smaller milldam, "as a speculative [private] investment"
under the terms of the Water Privileges Act of 1873); and *Snure v. Great
Western Ry.*, 13 U.C.Q.B. 376 (1856) (Tannery entitled to damages when RR
bridge impedes navigation vessels delivering bark).

found a dam builder liable for damages "even though the proprietor above him suffers no material injury, and though the mill . . . is a public benefit." Mowat did, however, call for the legislature to reconsider its 1859 decision. When the legislature responded with the Water Privileges Act of 1873, the court construed its "public good" provision narrowly in *Parry Sound Lumbering Co. v. Ferris* (1882) and enjoined the operation of a mill.[37]

Similarly, Upper Canada/Ontario's high courts protected the riparian property rights of logslide, steamboat, and boathouse owners and operators against free-loading loggers and polluting sawmills, often citing U.S. decisions as significant elements of their authority.[38] Its jurists divided over the interpretation of the Rivers and Streams Act of 1849, narrowly sanctioning the use of "all streams" by loggers during freshets to include those made useable only by the efforts and expense of individual riparian owners.[39] There would be virtually no "balancing of the equities" with regard to riparian rights anywhere in the Common-Law world where rainfall produced navigable streams.[40]

[37] Mowat, V. Ch., in *Dickson v. Burnham*, 14 Grant's Chanc. 594 (1868); Ardagh, J., in *Parry Sound Lumbering Co. v. Ferris*, 18 Can. LJ 413 (1882), citing U.S. Treatises and cases on meaning of "public good" on watercourses. Excellent analyses of this subject, upon which I rely for part of this section, are Jamie Benidickson, "Private Rights and Public Purposes in the Lakes, Rivers and Streams of Ontario, 1870–1930," in *Essays in the History of Canadian Law*, ed. David Flaherty (Toronto, 1983), II, 365, at 369, 371; and John McLaren, "The Tribulations of Antoine Ratté: A Case Study of the Environmental Regulation of the Canadian Timbering Industry in the 19th Century," 33 *University of New Brunswick Law Journal* 203(1984).

[38] *Boale v. Dickson*, 13 UCCP 387 (1863) (log-slide owner can charge tolls); *Crandall v. Mooney*, 23 UCCP 212 at 221 (1873); *Ratté v. Booth*, 11 Ont. R. 491 at 500–01 (1886). Now-Premier Mowat reacted to the *Ratté* decision (finding against an Ottawa River sawmill as a polluter) by "introducing legislation" in 1885 "to protect the owners or operators of saw mills who threw sawdust and refuse into the Ottawa River from actions for injunctions when the Lt. Governor determined that the public interest so required." But the courts continued to be intolerant of polluters, reading the statute narrowly. Benidickson, *supra* note 35, 381; McLaren, *supra* note 35, 225.

[39] *Caldwell v. McLaren*, 9 HL 392 (1884), rev'g 8 Can. SCR 435 (1883), which had revs'd 6 OAR 456 (1881). Richard Risk and Robert Vipond, "Rights Talk in Canada in the Late 19th Century:'The Good Sense and Right Feeling of the People,'" 14 *Law and History Review* 1 at 10–11 (1996). The Candian Supreme Court (at 444) felt that the statutory sanctioning of logger activity that resulted in damages to improvements made by other riparians should be compensated "under and by virtue of the right of eminent domain."

[40] But see *Esson v. M'Master*, 3 New Br. 501 at 511 (1842), where Justice Botsford held that in "a new country" the "principle of public convenience" was what determined whether a river was navigable and could be used by loggers who

POSSESSION BY THE FIRELOCK: THE INFORMAL LAW
OF SQUATTERS AND PROPRIETORS

In the United States

Whether the land tenure offered by the Crown or its grantees was fee simple tenure, some combination of fee simple and commonly-held socage (as in New England), or "tail male" tenure (as in early Georgia),[41] proprietors who sought to sell land faced problems at least as formidable as those faced by those proprietors who preferred to lease: They had to mollify the native inhabitants, survey their own grants, register them,[42] and defend their titles and boundaries against others with conflicting or overlapping claims and registrations. But winning formal title to land "at Law" in this fashion was, for many, not the end of the line; they had managed to fend off these challenges to their titles, but they faced still greater threats to the success of their proprietary ambitions – the squatters occupying much of "their" land.

Some of those squatting on "owned" land claim one or another sort of quasi-lawful status, be it derived from a local Indian sachem and his fellow tribesmen, from a "possession" speculator who had acquired "signing rights," or a "permit" (which he then fraudulently transferred), or from someone else with a dubious claim to title at Common Law. These squatter–claimants could at least claim a "colour of title," and

damaged plaintiff's pier. But here Justices Parker and Botsford correctly cited Lord Hale's *De Juris Maris* in support of this argument.

[41] "Tail male" tenure, imposed by the Georgia proprietors, required that the land pass to male heirs and barred all encumbrances. The first settlers quickly secured a change to fee simple title, arguing that it was only by mortgaging their land that they could acquire slaves and compete effectively with their Carolina and Chesapeake Bay rivals in the tobacco trade. This confounded the humanitarian and policy objectives of Colonel James Oglethorpe and his fellow investors, but they yielded after a decade of debate. See Milton Heath, *Constructive Liberalism: The Role of the State in Economic Development in Georgia to 1860* (1954).

[42] Spanish officials in Louisiana offered grants to settlers who cultivated for three years, but there were few surveys and no formal registration of title. Spain secretly ceded the colony to France in 1800, and it passed to the United States by sale in 1803. The new American authorities required surveys and the registration of titles, but many settlers refused to submit their grant papers for review, fearing that they might somehow be deprived of their lands. Malcolm Rohrborough, *The Land Office Business* (N.Y., 1968), 38–50, 161–64; Harry Coles, "The Confirmation of Foreign Land Titles in Louisiana," 38 *Louisiana Historical Quarterly* 1(1955); George Dargo, *Jefferson's Louisiana: Politics and the Clash of Legal Traditions* (Cambridge, Mass., 1975), 18.

some of them surely could claim it in "good faith." Other squatters without such "legal" claims to make offered in their place the Lockean one: Their labor had created a "natural right" to work the land.[43] Some of the latter, styled by their contemporaries "daring disturbers of the peace," were, indeed, quite "daring" in their treatment of the Law of property.

Example one: Substantial conflict occurred in the Wyoming Valley of northeastern Pennsylvania in 1769 and 1770 between those close to the Penn family, holding large proprietary grants, and actual settlers, many of whom held title from the Susquehannah Company, which derived its claim from Connecticut, a colony that claimed the Wyoming Valley. Pennsylvania courts sometimes recognized the claims of the settler–improvers in these years, depending on the circumstances, but many dissatisfied settlers marched on Philadelphia demanding guarantees, while others burned the buildings of those holding title from the proprietor. Two of these incendiaries were arrested, but were released by a mob, and Sheriff John Jennings was killed in an attempt to recapture the two.

Though a Confederation tribunal at Trenton ruled for the Pennsylvania proprietors in December, 1782, the Yankee "militia"-settlers, led by John Franklin, drove the proprietors' tenants and supporters out of the Valley in 1784,[44] inspiring new speculator–owners of the Susquehannah Company to revive their efforts. They offered Ethan Allen twelve shares in 1785.

Allen was the son of one of the original Company men and the leader of a similar (but much more successful) alliance of speculators and squatters (the Arlington Junto and the Green Mountain Boys) in what would become Vermont.[45] When in 1771 New York's Governor William Tryon had proclaimed that land west of the Connecticut River (that is, present-day Vermont) was the territory of the Colony of New York, Allen told all who would listen that were Tryon to seek to give meaning to such a proclamation by dispatching officials to the area, "we shall Drive them two hundred miles and send them to hell."

[43] For examples, see A. G. Roeber, *Palatines, Liberty and Property: German Lutherans in Colonial British America* (Baltimore, 1993), 13; Alan Taylor, *Liberty Men and Great Proprietors*; and Brendan McConville, "Those Daring Disturbers of the Public Peace," *infra* note 50.

[44] G. S. Rowe, *Embattled Bench: The Pennsylvania Supreme Court and the Forging of a Democratic Society, 1684–1809* (Newark, Del., 1994), 113, 124–25, 192; M. Schweitzer, *Custom and Contract*, 98.

[45] See Michael Bellesiles, *Revolutionary Outlaws: Ethan Allen and the Struggle for Independence on the Early American Frontier* (Charlottesville, Va., 1993); and Oscar Handlin, "The Eastern Frontier of New York," 18 *New York History* 50 (1937).

Allen was soon touring the Wyoming Valley, telling the Company's settlers, who must have known of his reputation, that "Liberty & Property, or slavery and poverty, are before us," and urging them to "procure fire-arms, and ammunition, be united among yourselves." The Company recruited additional "Half-share Men," dispatching them to the Valley "to 'man their rights,' in the cant phrase of these people," as the Pennsylvania proprietors' Timothy Pickering put it in August, 1786. They and the original squatter–settlers managed to keep Pennsylvania surveyors at bay for some time, and in 1786 Pennsylvania's legislature responded to the demands of these actual settlers with a "confirming" act that favored their interests, but by 1806 the Pennsylvanians had won a qualified victory and were collecting an average of thirty-two cents per acre from the Valley's original Yankees, more from the more recent Half-share Men.[46]

Example two: In 1775, Judge Richard Henderson of North Carolina and a group of fellow adventurers financed Daniel Boone's exploration of lands they claimed as the Transylvania Company (see Illustration 10), bought 20 million acres of land in what is now Kentucky and northern Tennessee from Cherokee natives for £10,000 worth of goods, and offered settlers land at 20 shillings per hundred acres. But these speculator–proprietors overreached themselves when they altered the terms for title to land after the settlement's first year. Company arrogance, in Stephen Aron's words, "turned fence-sitters into foes." In March, 1776, nearly one hundred "aggrieved" Transylvanians petitioned the government of Virginia, disingenuously challenging the Company's land titles, by pointing out that they were derived from direct purchases from the Cherokee. Another group of dissident purchasers-turned-squatters argued three months later that a perfectly legitimate way to acquire title was "by Preoccupancy" (that is, squatting). One who labored on unimproved land by that act became entitled to "a subsistence for themselves and their Posterity." This they described as "ancient cultivation law."[47]

In any event, Transylvania Company claims and those of their disgruntled settlers-turned-squatters quickly came into conflict with the land grants and claims of others. "I'm afraid to loose sight of my House lest some Invader takes possession," John Todd wrote from "Week Kentucke" in 1776, commenting on the "clashing Interests" of speculator–surveyors like himself and "Cabining" squatters. The

---

[46] Alan Taylor, " 'To Man Their Rights': The Frontier Revolution," in *The Transforming Hand of Revolution*, ed. Ronald Hoffman and Peter Albert (Charlottesville, Va., 1995), 246–55; D. Hulseboch, "Imperia in Imperio," 353, n103.

[47] St. Aron, *How the West was Lost*, 68.

Illustration 10. George Caleb Bingham offered this romantic vision of heroic Diaspora newcomers to "Transylvania" in the late eighteenth century, "Daniel Boone Escorting Settlers Through the Cumberland Gap," in 1852. (Washington University Gallery of Art, St. Louis. Gift of Nathaniel Phillips, 1890.)

result, for decades, was overlapping surveys and legal chaos.[48] Similarly, in the region south of the Green River ("Southside") in western Kentucky speculator–proprietors employed agents like Robert Triplett to survey their land and eject squatters, but Triplett, for one, found the task both difficult and dangerous (he "carried a dirk for protection from menacing occupants"). "The occupants refused to surrender the land," Triplett advised his employer, and they also refused to pay rents as tenants. Knowing how difficult Kentucky's occupying-claimant statute made ejection actions, Triplett "sought to convince occupants to purchase lands for a reasonable price." Unfortunately, "prospective buyers almost always required credit," Stephen Aron writes, and they defaulted often enough "to make credit risky."[49]

By the time the titled landowner became aware that a squatter was in occupancy, "great waste" may have already "been made" by loggers

---

[48] Malcolm Rohrbough, *The Trans-Appalachian Frontier* (N.Y., 1978), 21–25; Thomas Abernathy, *Western Lands and the American Revolution* (1959), 123–34; Patricia Watlington, *The Partisan Spirit: Kentucky Politics, 1779–92* (N.Y., 1978), 21.

[49] Aron, *How the West was Lost*, 157.

"cutting down and destroying the timber," as one agent of a New Jersey proprietor put it in 1747. He found some one hundred "Gum Logs," cut from the Penn family's wetlands in Morris County at a sawmill operated by the local justice of the peace. Each log had its owner's initials cut into its base, but when the agent asked the justice of the peace to prosecute those squatter–loggers who had cut and removed them unlawfully, he received this response:

> If the Logs had been [taken] from a poor man or an honest man it had been another thing, but there was no such thing in nature as to wrong the Devilish Proprietors, for . . . I don't believe there's a drop of Honest blood amongst the whole Proprietors or their Council.[50]

With or without such moral justification, squatter–loggers mined the hills of colonial New England for the tall pines claimed by Parliament for the Royal Navy, as well as those of late eighteenth and early nineteenth century Maine and Kentucky. Few paid so much as a shilling in fees or fines to any Crown or state grantee for the privilege.[51]

The title holder might sue to eject a squatter, and many tried their legal remedy. But they found that such measures were imperfect weapons. In 1755, Robert Livingston, third lord of Livingston Manor, sought the assistance of the Law in the removal of "new England men" squatting "in my manor." The governor and Council issued a proclamation condemning the practice, but Livingston's squatters were no more

---

[50] Jonathan Whitaker, as reported by Penn agent, John Henry, in Brendan McConville, "Those Daring Disturbers of the Public Peace: Agrarian Unrest and the Struggle for Political Legitimacy in New Jersey, 1701–1783," Ph.D. dissertation, Brown University, 1992, 177, revised and published by Cornell University Press in 1999 with the same title. See also *Ibid.*, 41, 155, 247, 250, 256.

Compare the views of "the country people" bordering English Crown forests in 1729 who "everywhere think they have a sort of right to the wood & timber in the forests," a "notion" that "may have been delivered down to them by tradition from the times these forests were declared to be such by the Crown, when there were great struggles and contests about them . . . ," according to Surveyor-General of Woods, Charles Withers. E. P. Thompson, *Whigs and Hunters: A History of the Black Act* (N.Y., 1975), 136.

[51] Alan Taylor, *Liberty Men and Great Proprietors, supra* note 41, 25; Charles F. Carroll, *The Timber Economy of Puritan New England* (Providence, 1973), 104–14; Watlington, *supra* note, 22; David G. Allen, *In English Ways: The Movement of Societies and the Transferal of Local Laws and Custom To Massachusetts Bay in the Seventeenth Century* (New York, 1981), 115, 218 (squatting and timber theft in Newbury and Ipswich, two towns in the Massachusetts Bay Colony in the seventeenth century).

moved by it than his unruly tenants had been by more substantial legal measures (as noted in the previous chapter).[52]

The expenditure of resources to acquire effective counsel helped Maine's Kennebeck proprietors win fifty of fifty-five ejectment cases (including thirty-nine of forty-two tried before a jury) that had been sued to final judgement. But cases that went before juries were not foregone conclusions in some jurisdictions, despite the weight of the evidence. In 1677, the chief justices of England in Exchequer Chamber determined that Nathaniel Mason's proprietary claims in New Hampshire should be tried there "where those who occupied the land in question could defend themselves." Mason consequently lost several of these trials; others he won, but the "vast majority" of New Hampshire residents "refused to accept the various court verdicts rendered in...land tenure cases as anything which should alter their customary behavior." When he secured from Privy Council in 1679 an order that occupants of improved lands pay six pence per pound of annual income for secure titles, quitrent free, this order was ignored by the town councils he confronted in 1681. Samuel Allen then bought Mason's claim and *almost* secured a negotiated settlement from the settlers in 1705, but he died the day they were to present their offer; they thereupon withdrew it, created a fake Indian deed to the land, and secured a judgement in their favor from Privy Council in 1708.[53]

Squatters, like tenants, tended to "grow numerous" and were "Linkt by Marriages with their Neighbors." As such, "it will be scarcely practical to Remove them," James Alexander wrote in 1726 regarding property in New Jersey; this clustering of squatter networks sharply reduced the likelihood that an impartial jury could be impaneled in a trespass action. For that matter, it was at times no easier to prosecute squatters charged with killing surveyors, if the exoneration by a jury in Maine in 1809 of eight men charged with the murder of a surveyor for the Plymouth Land Company was at all characteristic. Moreover, by the late eighteenth century a squatter jailed for damages by a trespass judgement was free to "swear out" of "gaol" in some jurisdictions because he or she owned insufficient property to satisfy the judgement; he was "judgement proof."[54]

Jailed squatter–trespassers sometimes gained release extralegally. Several in East Jersey were liberated by their neighbors, relatives, and

[52] D. Hulseboch, "Imperia in Imperio," 16 *Law and History Review* 352 (1998).

[53] Jere Daniell, *Colonial New Hampshire: A History* (Millwood, N.Y., 1981), 75, 78, 85, 90, 91, 129–30.

[54] Taylor, *supra* note 41, 22, 56; Laura Ulrich, *A Midwife's Tale: The Life of Martha Ballard based on her Diary*, 1785–1812 (N.Y., 1990), 335; McConville, *supra* note 48, 83.

squatter sympathizers in the 1740s.[55] Surveyors and sheriffs in New Jersey, New York, and Maine were harassed, clubbed, and fired upon throughout the eighteenth and early nineteenth centuries. In the 1770s, squatters in northern New York claimed title from specious grants issued by New Hampshire's government, akin to those issued by Connecticut to Susquehannah Company settlers in Pennsylvania's Wyoming Valley. On this authority the "new England men" "tryed" the local New York justice of the peace who had the audacity to claim authority in their domain, sentenced him to 200 lashes, inflicted the penalty, and sent him packing with a threat of 500 additional lashes were he to reappear.[56] Squatter "clubmen" in New Jersey and Maine burnt barns, tore down fences, destroyed crops and wagons belonging to proprietors, their agents, and their tenants. As one agent reported to some of Maine's proprietors in 1801:

> The notion of the settlers is that they are the sole owners of such lands as they have made themselves the possessors of, & . . . have a good right to hold their possessions by the firelock & will kill any person who runs a compass thro' their possessions. This they say is no Murder.[57]

Notwithstanding their sometime use of force and violent rhetoric, disgruntled squatters generally preferred to vest their activities with august language, to simulate the Lawful measures their proprietor-foes were taking. Their pamphleteers cited or paraphrased the works of "the celebrated *Locke*": vis. – "he who makes any improvements on lands in a State of Nature has a better claim to it than any pretended purchaser can have" – and argued that any law denying the value of such improvements to one who had "bestowed his labour on it" was a violation of "the Rules of natural Justice." They spoke of "the peace-able Possession, especially of back waste vacant Lands," as a customary right exercised by landless Britons "from time out of mind" to "move out from the interior Parts to the back Lands, with their Families and find a Spot, whereon they built a Hut and made some improvements," thereby creating "a Kind of Right." Others told proprietary agents that "God gave the earth to the children," who "own no other proprietor." They maintained that "wild land ought to be as free as common air," that "these lands once belonged to King George" who "lost them by the American Revolution" whereby "they became the property of the

[55] McConville, *supra* note 48, 154–60. See also Taylor, *supra* note 49, 115.
[56] Hulseboch, "Imperia in Imperio," 353.
[57] McConville, *supra* note 48, 150–62; Taylor, *supra* note 49, 17, 96, 114, 117–30: Sung Bok Kim *Landlord and Tenant in Colonial New York* (Chapel Hill, 1978).

people who defended and won them." Others were reported to have said that "the bad acts of governments are not binding on the subject." These were revolutionary concepts, resonating for over a century since they were proposed by Diggers like Gerald Winstanley. Defrauded settlers in western North Carolina organized as "Regulators" and opposed "the Lawyer's Art" and the Law's courts. Squatter associations in Maine created "people's committees" to survey townships and regulate land transactions. Those in New Jersey and New York dispossessed those holding title or leases from proprietor–foes "by Club Law and called their proceedings a Court of equity and answerted [sic] that it was preferable to the Common law as it was now made use of."[58]

Many squatters thus managed to make "law" of their own that ultimately served to transform their mere occupancy to titled freehold estate at low cost. Others managed to secure a fair price for their "betterments" when they were ultimately dispossessed. Too many lawsuits would tax the resources of proprietors, while it took only one (averaging about $100 in 1810) to exhaust the resources of the typical squatter. But proprietors realized few profits when relying on legal measures alone in dealing with recalcitrant squatters. They, like landlords dealing with tenants, came to see that accommodation and fair play were ultimately more profitable. Hence "clubmen"-depredations were dealt with by plea bargain and leniency; claim association leaders and their kin were admitted to jury lists; jailed "clubmen," in turn, declined to be liberated by their comrades; squatter Indian purchase claims were abandoned with the passage of Betterment Acts that enabled occupants of six years duration to have juries of their peers substantially discount the price proprietors sought by the value of their improvements.

Consequently, the vast majority of Peapack New Jersey squatters in the mid-eighteenth century told proprietary agents that they "sought to buy," "agreed to l[ea]se," or "promised to p[a]y." In 1754, after some eight years of successful resistance to proprietor Andrew Johnston's efforts to dispossess him, William Todd told Johnston that "he ... now proposes to take a lease from us for the lott, or buy it." In 1787, squatters on Josiah Little's land in Bakerstown, Maine, told him they hoped to acquire title from "the State" government (of Massachusetts, but that "if we cannot git it any other way [we] will [buy it] of you." And in 1801, after persistent efforts to survey his land-grant domain, each

---

[58] Taylor, *supra* note 49, 101; Taylor, " 'The Seed Plot of Sedition': The Struggle for the Waldo Patents Backlands, 1800–1801," in Geoff Ely and William Hunt, eds., *Reviving the English Revolution* (London, 1988), 262; Stephen Aron, *How the West was Lost*, 60; Hulseboch, "Imperia in Imperio," 359; Kim, *supra*, note 55; McConville, *supra* note 48, 164, 191.

accompanied by a greater degree of armed protection than the previous one were met with vigorous resistance, proprietor Henry Knox finally produced a surveying party too large to resist. Subsequently all opposition ceased, and, anticipating by only a few years the similar submission of Yankee settler–squatters in the Wyoming Valley of northeastern Pennsylvania, some 136 squatters presented themselves at his estate to "post their note and mortgages" in exchange for the warranty deeds to their lots, as Alan Taylor writes of these "Liberty Men and Great Proprietors."[59]

The story in western New York was similar; in the 1790s a consortium of Dutch investors, the Holland Land Company, purchased 3.3 million acres of land from its Diaspora proprietary owners and its original owners, the Senecas. The company then surveyed the area, built roads, sawmills, and gristmills and began to attract settlers on lenient, long-term sales agreements.[60] According to several settlers, writing a generation later, "not one in a hundred ever read" these articles of agreement, but they constituted "color of title," and were privately traded for decades, sold along with such improvements as each settler had made, with the Company's agents serving as informal "referees" of such claims and counterclaims as sometimes arose between the parties after such informal "sales."

Others simply squatted, making some improvements, and then selling them, without any articles of agreement from the Company. Many of these squatters had found the harvesting of timber for potash and lumber more profitable than farming, a use of the property the Company objected to. But its threats to eject such persons were rarely carried out; the Law was too "troublesome," or so the Company's agent wrote.

In the late 1820s, a number of debt-ridden settlers, supported by an "Agrarian Convention" led by local politicians, refused to renegotiate their agreements and questioned the legitimacy of the Company's title. Five were served with writs of ejectment in 1835 and lost their cases in federal district court. One settled with the Company for costs of court and was allowed to stay on his lot. The other four were evicted. In short order, the Company's agency office at Mayville was destroyed and its records burned by 500 angry settlers. One of the evicted men reclaimed his farm, supported by his neighbors; it took a sheriff's posse

---

[59] Taylor, *supra* note 49; Taylor, " 'The Seed Plot of Sedition,' " 266; McConville, *supra* note 48. Taylor also notes that Knox's land company ultimately failed, but that was at least as much a function of the marginal quality of the land as it was of the strength of squatter resistance; after the collapse of their resistance in 1801 they paid over to him substantial sums for their titles.

[60] William Wyckoff, *The Developer's Frontier: The Making of the Western New York Landscape* (New Haven, 1988), 30, 81, 84–85, 92.

of 120 men to remove him a second time. "Many Settlers" thereupon wrote the Company's agent to warn of "the vengeance of an incensed God."

At this point the Dutch owners began to sell out to New Yorkers, who brought in William H. Seward as their agent and partner. Seward soon offered the rebellious farmers lower per acre prices and interest rates and redrafted many of their articles of agreement. But this peace was not permanent. In 1844, the new company secured eviction orders against two grazers in Cattarangus County, George and Jacob Learn, who had failed to meet their payments, and assigned their lots to others. When the local sheriff and his deputies appeared at their homes and served them with the eviction notices, they were confronted by 150 armed "Indians" who menaced them. After this incident, settlers at Machias resolved to resist "these pretended land owners" and spoke of violating "the letter," as opposed to the spirit, "of the law." Eleven of the identifiable "Indians" were in the meantime indicted by a grand jury, but the sheriff took no action on these until after the fall election, and then arrested only one. The arresting party was forced to flee the area, under "Indian" attack.

In late January, 1845, the sheriff secured the aid of 1,100 state militia to serve the Learn brothers, who thereupon agreed to sign new articles of agreement and were permitted to remain on their lots. Other indicted "Indians" surrendered to this massive show of force. "Settler on Dutch Hill" complained in a local paper of the use of citizen-soldiers "to compel settlers to take contracts at the point of a bayonet," and another force of 100 "Indians" resisted another effort of the sheriff to serve papers later in the year. Charles Brooks tells this story well, and notes that at this point the sheriff, "apparently chastened by the public outcry that followed his recent calling for the assistance of the militia," chose to negotiate an accommodation between these lot holders and the company. Brooks also observes that "none of the 'Dutch Hill boys,' including George and Jacob Learn, ever lost their land and improvements.... In the final analysis their agrarian vision had prevailed at least as much as [the] landlords' capitalist one."[61] The same may be said of their "informal" law.

A generation later, squatters in the West behaved in similar fashion. When a large enterprise, the Maxwell Land Grant & RR Company, purchased Spanish land grants in northern New Mexico and won a court battle with squatter–ranchers, –farmers, and –miners in the early 1870s, a Squatters Club defied the court. Sheriff O. K. Chittenden of Colfax County wrote Governor S. B. Axtell in 1875 that it was

---

[61] Charles E. Brooks, *Frontier Settlement and Market Revolution: The Holland Land Purchase* (Ithaca, 1996), 25, 57, 59, 92, 96, 135, 144, 180, 212, 216, 221, 225, 227–30.

"impossible" for him "to enforce the civil law." Some twelve years later, when the company finally got a grand jury hearing of its complaint against a number of these squatters, they sent word that they were prepared to settle for their improvements. But their theft of the company's timber continued, and when one squatter–rancher was ejected by the law, his neighbors reinstated him by force and sent the man who had taken up residence in the ranch packing. The last squatter did not settle with the company until 1899, some twenty-seven years after the Law had declared the company's title to be good.[62]

On the mid-western plains in the 1840s and 1850s, in Indiana, Illinois, Iowa, Wisconsin, Minnesota, and Nebraska, those who could not or would not wait for slower-moving federal land surveyors to lay out orderly tracts for purchase formed claim associations "to provide a quasi-legal land and title registration system in the absence of government action." Most then sold their claims before the survey and federal auction of the land; all covenanted to ensure that each would be able to purchase the section they claimed (and perhaps others they coveted as well) "at congress price, $1.25 pr. acre." A Methodist circuit rider described a claim association at Elkhorn Creek, Wisconsin, in 1835:

> They had, in the absence of all other law, met & made a law for themselves. . . . They . . . meted & bounded every mans wood land. . . . Timber being the great disideration of the country, they would not allow one man to monopolize . . . there was an understanding . . . equivalent to a law of the land, that the settlers should sustain each other against the speculator, & no settler should bid on anothers land.[63]

This account surely described the way *some* claim associations functioned, but it clearly cannot be said to speak for most of them. Allan Bogue's analysis of the numerous claim clubs in Iowa's central counties in the 1840s and 1850s makes clear that the typical midwestern "clubman" was far more of a speculator than an actual settler, and that these "claim Clubs" were essentially designed to force later-arriving actual farmers to deal with one of the local pack of federated speculators before they would be allowed to purchase federal land.[64] Here even the informal "law" worked in mysterious ways.

[62] Jim B. Pearson, *The Maxwell Land Grant* (Norman, 1961), 60–75, 118, 142.

[63] Gates, "Land Policy and Tenancy in Indiana," in Gates, *Landlords and Tenants, supra* note 6; James Willard Hurst, *Law and the Conditions of Freedom in the Nineteenth Century United States* (Madison, 1956), 3–5; Daniel Boorstin, *The Americans: The National Experience* (N.Y., 1965), 73–78.

[64] Bogue, "Iowa Claim Clubs: Symbol and Substance," 45 *Mississippi Valley Historical Review* 231 (1958).

It worked its wonders on the western range as well. In ways essentially the same as those employed by the graziers Squattocracy of eastern Australia a half century earlier, cattlemen in Montana and Wyoming advertised their "claims" in local newspapers in the decades after the close of the Civil War. In 1884, Charles S. Johnson authored one such announcement:

I, the undersigned, do hereby notify the public that I claim the valley, branching off Glendive Creek, four miles east of Allard [Montana], and extending to its source on the South side of the Northern Pacific Railroad as a stock range.

Johnson and his fellow cattlemen had no intention of *purchasing* this entire tract of land. They simply squatted on the range[65] (though a number eventually sent out their cowboys to claim "homesteads" along the riverbanks, the sources of water for his cattle, which was the only land he needed).[66] What his preemptive "claim" was intended to establish was his usufructary (use) rights. Many such ranchers acted pursuant to the federal Preemption, Desert Land, and Timber Culture Acts or similar statues passed by one or another territorial legislature, authorizing such preemptions. Others preempted such statutes, and a few preempted the formal acquisition by the federal government of those usufructary rights from the Indian inhabitants.[67]

Similarly, in the early 1880s dummy entrymen, falsely claiming that they had made the requisite improvements to their tracts, acquired title to quarter-sections in the Vermillion range of the Minnesota iron district and then sold their "homesteads" over to Charlemagne Towers' Minnesota Iron Company. When the government sought to prosecute such frauds upon the Homestead Act, land office agent Fred LeSueur wrote of the citizens who comprised the juries in the company town of Towers:

Public sympathy is with the entrymen & the property & persons of one who would testify against his neighbor would be in danger. When brought to the point, they will admit that none made the improvements contemplated by the law but they seem to argue that custom has made a higher law, & that they have a right to the land, and if they don't get it someone else will.[68]

---

[65] See Terry Jordan, *North American Cattle-Ranching Frontiers* (Albuquerque, 1993), 235–36.

[66] As described by Louis Pelzer, *The Cattleman's Frontier* (1936), 174.

[67] Ernest Osgood, *Day of the Cattlemen* (1929), 182–83, noted in Donald Pisani, "The Gold Rush and American Resource Law," 77 *California History* 123 (at 125) (1998).

[68] Fremont Wirth, "The Operation of the Land Laws in the Minnesota Iron District," 13 *Mississippi Valley Historical Review* 438 (1927).

In 1889, Congress threw open to settlement America's "last frontier," the unassigned lands west of Indian Territory, styled "Oklahoma Territory." Landseekers were to assemble on the territory's northern border with Kansas on April 22 and race south at the sound of the starter's gunshot to identify and stake their claims. But substantial numbers violated these rules by slipping across the border sooner than that date. (Celebrating this defiance of the Law, Oklahomans adopted the sobriquet "Sooners.") The result was that there arose claim conflicts, litigation, anger, and considerable violence. According to Payne County's first district attorney, no fewer than fifty murders in that county's early days were due to "sooner"/later claim fights. Anticipating trouble, Evan Barnard, his pal Ranicky Bill, and other "ex-cowboys" formed a "sooner's" land-claim protection league. Barnard drove one law-abiding landseeker from his own preselected claim, brandishing a rifle and a pistol and shouting that it would be "a hundred and sixty acres or six feet, and I did not give a damn which it was." After the protection league's threats led another latecomer to accept a $75 settlement for his overlapping claim, Ranicky Bill observed philosophically: "hits sure hell to get things regulated in a new country." Barnard, Bill and their outlaw-compeers in the Doolin-Dalton gang were only the more colorful characters in this saga; the first speaker-of-the-house in Oklahoma Territory's legislature, I. N. Terrill, ended his brief political career in 1891 when he murdered a man over such a claims dispute.[69]

In Canada, Australia, and New Zealand

In those British colonies where land was available for purchase – in Nova Scotia/New Brunswick, in Ontario and Manitoba, in Australia and New Zealand – there was less overt rejection of the "high court law" than one witnessed in Ireland or Prince Edward Island; there was no need to abolish tenancy, as in Prince Edward Island and Quebec. And yet the formal law of statute book and judicial opinion was still circumvented or ignored in significant ways.

Timber
Farmers complained of loggers stealing timber from their domains in early nineteenth century Quebec, once the timber industry had developed a lusty demand for logs. Logging companies continued to encroach on land they did not own, but some "settlers" in southern Quebec reciprocated. After acquiring location tickets from the Crown

---

[69] Evan Barnard, *A Rider of the Cherokee Strip* (1936), 141–43, 146, 192, noted in Richard White, "Outlaw Gangs of the Middle Border: American Social Bandits," 12 *Western Historical Quarterly* 387 at 399, 401 (1981).

or the lumber firm itself, they cut both their own and their corporate neighbors' trees. And some devised what appeared to be a low-labor, high-profit response to lumber company depredations on their lots. Thus, Romain Dellaire, a merchant "settler" in Lambton, secured a court order in 1859 for the seizure of some 2,500 logs that Clark & Co. had cut on five of Dellaire's lots. His timing was shrewd; he filed his action shortly before the spring high-water "roll-in" of the company's logs "when from the importance of time and the dangers of delay he would be most likely to coerce Clark & Co. into his terms," as the company's agent put it. When he and seventeen of his "guardian" friends prevented the company's men from rolling the logs in, Clark got the Crown timber agent to seize the logs for sale to be applied toward the remaining four installments on Dellaire's five lots. Since it was timber, not title, that Dellaire was after, he, three of his sons, and an employee threatened the deputy guarding the logs. For this act he was arrested and imprisoned by the local magistrate, an illiterate alcoholic friendly to Clark & Co., whereupon the mayor and fifty-eight inhabitants petitioned the government for the dismissal of their magistrate. (The man later resigned.)

After Quebec's virgin forests had been depleted of their mature trees, a second wave of plundering began with the technological advances in commercial pulp and paper production and the printing industry in the 1880s. Once again, settlers entered on lumber company lands. In 1897, the British-American Lumber Company's officers reported that "the expense of watching" for such trespassers had "increased," inasmuch as these second cuttings were not as valuable, "and in cases of trespass the costs of survey to prove trespass, together with the legal proceedings, almost invariably exceed the value of the timber stolen." Moreover, the poachers openly took the logs to local mills and lumber dealers and "no dishonour seems to attach to this class of stealing."[70]

Similarly, by 1815 there were "thousands of unlicensed squatters" clearing land in Nova Scotia and New Brunswick, or stripping it of its timber after paying only the first installment of the purchase price. By the 1830s, lumbermen from New Brunswick and Maine were stealing

---

[70] J. I. Little, *Nationalism, Capitalism, and Colonization in 19th Century Quebec* (Kingston, 1989), 113–14, 116, 118. For further examples of timber poaching on the Christie seigneuries in the 1770s, see Francoise Noël, *The Christie Seigneuries: Estate Management and Settlement in the Upper Richelieu Valley, 1760–1854* (Montreal, 1992), 22. And see Lorne Hammond, "Closing the Forest: The *Colon* and Quebec's Forest Tenure Debate" (on "bad" *colons* who proved to be mere timber thieves rather than the intended farmer-colonizers), "Property Law and History Conference, University of Victoria Law School, Victoria, British Columbia, February 23, 2001.

one another's logs on the St. Johns River, a disputed international border, a phenomenon known as the "Aroostook War" of 1839, resulting in a border treaty.[71] Such large-scale depredations can be detected at the microlevel. "Many persons" in early nineteenth century Western Ontario leased Clergy Reserve or "bought" land on credit, paying "only the first installment, then abandoned the land after stripping it of timber." Others merely trespassed to cut Crown or privately owned timber, and some of these threatened the landowners with firearms when detected. As Justice Hagarty put it in *Nicholson v. Page* (1868):

> We are well aware of the very high-handed manner in which timber is frequently taken by wrongdoers, in defiance of the true owner, and in fact by sheer force in many cases.

Juries consequently often awarded sums somewhat larger than the value of the timber loss that had been proved at trial in those instances when the culprits could be identified, as in *Nicholson Bellows v. Condee* (1848), and *Flint v. Bird* (1855), and Upper Canada's jurists upheld these awards. But the fact remains that "firelock" law governed much timber harvesting. And, once again, lands belonging to Aboriginal people suffered the greatest timber depredation.[72]

Title

By 1810, "local policy" in Newfoundland was turning a blind eye to the squatting of fishing families on Crown land. These were small plots "so that they could raise garden vegetables." By the end of that decade, there were food shortages and local riots against merchants. The colony's chief justice, Francis Forbes, held in locally popular decisions (*Williams v. Williams* (1818) and *Rex v. Keough* (1819)) that the customary local usages within the fishery allowed for title to a house and garden to be recognized by the Common Law, despite the government's policy.[73] Thereupon, the Board of Trade accepted this

---

[71] W. S. MacNutt, *The Atlantic Provinces,* 149, 194; A. R. M. Lower, *The North American Assault on the Canadian Forest* (Toronto, 1938), 84, 93.

[72] A. Wilson, *The Clergy Reserve,* 52, 193; F. C. Hamil, *The Valley of the Lower Thames, 1640 to 1850* (Toronto, 1951), 213, 259; Sidney Harring, *White Man's Law, Red Man's Land,* 50; *Heck v. Knapp,* 20 U.C.Q.B. 360 at 363 (1861) (firearms threat); *Bellows v. Condee* 4 U.C.Q.B. 346 (1848); *Flint v. Bird,* 11 UCQB 444 (1855); Hagarty, J., in *Nicholson v. Page,* 27 U.C.Q.B. 505 at 509 (1868). Compare the popular rejection of game laws in western Ontario to the rejection of similar laws a generation later in eastern Maine. See Edward Ives, *George Magoon and the Down East Game War: History, Folklore and the Law* (Urbana, 1988).

[73] Bruce Kercher, "Law Reports from a Non-Colony and a Penal Colony: The Australian Manuscript Decisions of Sir Francis Forbes as Chief Justice of Newfoundland," 19 *Dalhousie Law Journal* 417 at 420 (1996).

as a reality, ceased its efforts to relocate some of the population of Newfoundland in the Maritimes or British Isles, and began to encourage such small farms itself. These plots soon became held as a kind of conacre property right and were defended with vigor against all trespassers. Thus, in 1840, one woman threatened to kill another for stealing her son-in-law's scarce garden topsoil. Sean Cadigan has recounted other such threats and fights as the fishermen and their families created property rights with their labor.[74]

Resettled Loyalists and former solders, given "location tickets" and other generic titles to land in Nova Scotia and Ontario in the late eighteenth century, sometimes found themselves in title disputes with other settlers or proprietors. As in Maine, some surveyors in New Brunswick were "driven off by force" by squatters in the early and mid-nineteenth century. Squatters in Glenelg, Upper Canada, felled trees in 1855 onto the nearly completed house of a man who had purchased land they occupied, "which injured it so much that it took three men nearly one day to repair the damage.... The [squatter-] defendants were all there, and some had guns." Courts and administrators spent much time and energy, as in upper New England and Kentucky, in quieting titles.[75]

Some settlers in Ontario and New Brunswick simply occupied without color of title, and some Crown officials were said to have engaged in much "shutting an eye to squatting."[76] To his credit, Sir Isaac Brock, Upper Canada's chief administrator in 1812, issued a proclamation addressed to unlicensed Diaspora newcomers living on the Six Nations' Grand River reserves, threatening fines and warning that none could now "pretend ignorance of the law," but few removals ensued. Sidney Harring says appropriately of the failure of Brock to go beyond mere proclamation that the incident "highlights the ineffectiveness of government land policy" in these years in Canada. The Crown "was ignoring its own laws regarding squatters" on Indian land.[77]

Other officials were confronted with the problems of proprietor–entrepreneurs like Colonel Thomas Talbot of southwestern Ontario, who in the words of one of his freeholder's descendants, John Kenneth Galbraith, had been awarded "a vast fief" in 1803 of some

---

[74] Sean Cadigan, *Hope and Deception on Conception Bay* (Toronto, 1995), 56, 57, 59, 64.

[75] *Doe dem. Des Barres v. White*, 3 New Br. 595 at 626 (1842); *Glover v. Walker et al.*, 5 U.C.C.P. 478 (1856) (felled trees on house); Harris and Warkentin, *Canada Before Confederation*, 177; Graig, *Upper Canada*, 33.

[76] Hamil, *Lake Erie Baron*, 211; R. C. Harris and J. Warkentin, *Canada before Confederation*, 177–78; Gerald Graig, *Upper Canada: The Formative Years, 1784–1814* (London, 1963), 141; Paul Knaplund, "Arthur Mills' Experiment in Colonization," 34 *Canadian Historical Review* 139 at 147 (1953).

[77] Harring, *White Man's Law*, 43.

60,000 acres "by the English crown...for no discernible reason." Talbot was a sort of enlightened despot granting lots to "industrious" settlers. After interviewing them, he merely entered their names on his map of the Talbot lands in his estate. That pencilled entry, however, was the settler's only claim to the land for many years – a sort of "fee pencil." Were an individual to fail to fulfill his agreement steadily to improve the land for the first five years, or if he sought to sell his pencilled "title" and improvements, he might well find that Talbot had erased his name from the map and reassigned the land to another. The new occupant was required to pay the disseized individual for such improvements as he *had* made, but in 1822, the Governor's Council upheld Talbot's right to dispossess.

None the less, the *vox populi* was still capable of undoing some of Talbot's authority. In 1826, George Bateman "bought" one of Talbot's lots on the Longwoods Road from Samuel Alcock. When Talbot learned of this unauthorized transaction, he erased Alcock's name from his map and reassigned the lot to one Edward Jennings, who soon arrived at the lot with his brother and their possessions. Bateman and his four sons, however, drove the Jennings brothers off with axes and fists. Talbot thereupon had the local authorities remove the Batemans and put them on trial for assault. But Bateman was able "to make the stupid jury believe that the land was his," as Talbot put it to the attorney general in March, 1827, and Bateman won acquittal. Later in the 1840s, Talbot was finally stripped of his powers, and his settlers provided with titles to their lots by the Crown, after he tried to dispossess two settlers for having signed a Reform Party petition in 1832 (though the process took some ten years).[78] In 1833, the local St. Thomas *Liberal* editorialized of Colonel Talbot's service as a magistrate (justice of the peace) – he ruled "with a most absolute sway." When one recalls the ire of tenants in India, Ireland, and Prince Edward Island in the mid-nineteenth century, it comes as no surprise that in 1837, when Doctor Charles Dunscombe sought to raise a force of supporters of Mackenzie's Canadian rising, many of his volunteers came from Colonel Talbot's domain.[79]

[78] Fred C. Hamil, *Lake Erie Baron: The Story of Colonel Thomas Talbot* (Toronto, 1955), 136, 158, 162–65, 176, 213, 226.

[79] Galbraith, *The Scotch* (Boston, 1969), 3; Fred Landon, "The Common Man in the Era of Rebellion in Upper Canada," in *Aspects of 19th Century Ontario*, ed. F. Armstrong (Toronto, 1974), 162.

Even more ruthless was landlord Archibald McNab. His settlers refused to serve in the militia against Mackenzie in the Rebellion of 1837–1838. See Norman Macdonald, *Canada, 1763–1841: Immigration and Settlement: The Administration of the Imperial Land Regulations* (London, 1939), 189–201.

With the fatal statutory blows to the seigneurial system in Lower Canada in the 1850s, came the opening for settlement of new tracts, especially to the south of Montreal and Quebec. These were freehold estates, and in 1853, 100 acres were to be offered free to settlers who occupied and regularly improved their grants. By 1870, this had been altered to the sale by installments of land for twenty to sixty cents per acre, twenty percent down, possession to be taken within six months, a tenth of the purchase to be cleared within two years, and a house built.

The first targets of this beneficence were Scottish peasants ("crofters") from the Hebrides, especially from the Isle of Lewis. Families there, traditionally living on small plots leased year by year, had recently had "bitter experience" with "community-wide evictions" during the "Highland clearances" when landlords enclosed land. Many responded to invitations to emigrate to southeastern Quebec, where they were issued occupation permits. Functioning still within a clan culture, these Hebridean Scots selected their land collectively, by drawing lots and then forming a line. Beginning at a surveyor's mark, they "sang a survey," by singing the Twenty-third Psalm "so many times" per selector, as they strode along, marking off each family's plot. "They'd keep time walking through the woods," one descendant recalled, "and when that ended, the #1 man would make a mark on a tree, and that was his." (He would then break away from the others and walk-sing a square, deliniating his freehold.)[80]

These crofters sought grants specifically for the "poor people" among them, and engaged in much cooperative efforts ("bees"), pulling stumps, raising barns, threshing, cutting wood. Some chose to log their land, making few agricultural improvements; others made few or none of their installment payments for years. William Farrell, a Crown land agent told the authorities in the early 1860s that he found these Hebridean Scot immigrants to be "very poor and not disposed to make any payments" despite his urging upon them "the necessity of doing so . . . as it was useless to settle land unless they expected to pay ultimately." Agents like Farrell might remind the colonists behind in their payments of their obligations, some at the very doors of their

---

[80] J. I. Little, *Crofters and Habitants: Settler Societies, Economies and Culture in a Quebec Township, 1848–1881* (Montreal, 1991), 62; Sharon Bohn Gmelch, "A Social History of the Quebec Herbidean Settlements," in Margaret Bennett-Knight, "Folkways and Religion of the Hebredian Scots in the Eastern Townships," in *Cultural Retention and Demographic Change*, ed. Laurel Doucette (Ottawa, 1980), 46–47. This custom is comparable to, but should not be confused with another, the "procession" of church vestrymen in England, Virginia, and other British Diaspora lands along such existing survey lines each year to verify that no one had altered or moved any.

kirk, but they generally did not demand payments, sensing as did J. T.
LeBel, agent in the mid- and late 1850s in the Winslow area, that with
little capital, "they suffered and failed strictly by necessity, and were
not able to earn enough to make payments towards their lots."

None the less, improvements made by the mere squatters among
them were soon recognized and honored by the local Crown land
agent. Those armed only with occupation permits "who had proved
by their activity and their work that they were determined to establish
themselves" were granted the status of those holding location tickets,
and by 1855 the acts of those with informal claims who sold to third parties were honored, and Letters Patent issued to the buyers. Only nine
of the first twenty-seven settlers listed by the agent to receive Letters
Patent had been granted location tickets for the lots at issue. As elsewhere, squatters and selectors alike treated occupancy and improvements as evidence of ownership and adequate grounds for payment
in private sales; and as elsewhere, their presumptions were honored
whether or not they had been addressed in the land grant statute.[81]

By the 1860s, some of these Hebridean Scots had departed for better
land to the west (in Ontario or Alberta) or the southwest (in the United
States). Those who remained were finding new neighbors: French-
Canadiens from Montreal and Quebec to the north. Two of these
young men with location permits were driven from their lots on the
Megantic Road in 1853 by Scots who had intended these lots go to
relatives and friends due to arrive in the spring. "They intend to create
a new Guernsey," land agent Lupien reported with annoyance, urging
the intervention of the State "or the Canadiens of Winslow may pack
their bags."[82]

But the Crown exercised some restraint, recognizing the growing
tensions between the Scots, now no longer growing in numbers, and
the steadily growing communities of French-Canadiens. The Crown
land agent's reports in the early 1870s often came down on the side
of Scottish settlers complaining of French-Canadien squatters. For example, when Major William McMinn discovered in 1873 that Cyprien
Beaudoin had taken possession of one of McMinn's lots in Ditchfield,
McMinn posted trespass warnings on the lot within a few weeks of
Beaudoin's arrival and offered to pay him for such efforts as he had
undertaken in clearing the land. McMinn had paid all his location
ticket fees and was determined to end Beaudoin's entry. He dispatched
some men to begin to build a house on the lot. Beaudoin and six

---

[81] Little, *Crofters and Habitants, supra* note 78, 57, 59, 71 (translations mine);
Sharon Gmelch, "A Social History of the Quebec Hebridean Settlements,"
supra note 78, 21, 48.

[82] Little, *Crofters and Habitants,* 61.

armed colleagues ordered the men away, felled trees over the land they had cleared, chopped their house logs in half, and threw limbs and debris over the house site. The Crown land agent styled these acts the greatest "outrage" he had "ever known committed," and his recomendation to the commissioner that Beaudoin be ejected was approved.[83]

Thus, the formal Law of property generally prevailed in the eastern townships when title was at stake. But the stakes were often extremely high for the parties at odds themselves, and the Scots were not always the winners of these contests. Indeed, the most tragic of these tales was lost by Donald Morrison, the "Megantic outlaw."

Morrison, whose family farmed in the Lake Megantic area, worked on the prairie as a young man in the late 1870s and early 1880s, sending money home to his father to help pay debts due to a local merchant. Upon his return in 1883, young Morrison discovered that the merchant claimed he was still owed a substantial sum, and that his father had kept no receipts of his payments. The family became further indebted, the son "followed dubious legal advice," sued his father for the payments he had sent, and thus forced a sheriff's sale of the farm in 1886. To his chagrin, the merchant acquired the title. The Morrisons thereupon simply "squatted" for a year; but the merchant sold his title to one Auguste Duquette, who moved in during the winter of 1887–1888. That spring, Donald Morrison fired a shot through Duquette's window, and then burned the house and barn. When a deputy came to arrest Morrison, he shot and killed the man, and was harboured by his Scottish neighbors for the next ten months, gaining local fame as "the Megantic outlaw." The Quebec government declared martial law the next spring and soon captured Morrison. In the meantime, Duquette rebuilt his barn, only to lose it to flames again at the hands of Morrison's friends on the day his trial began. Imprisoned, Morrison died on a hunger strike. Duquette sold the farm at a loss and left the area. The Law had been imposed, but only after resistance to its workings had taken a toll of all involved.[84]

In New South Wales and the South Island of New Zealand there were "squatters" as well, confounding the Colonial Office's desire to create freehold farmsteads. But eventually most purchased the inexpensive leases noted in the previous chapter. When new pastoralists and grazers arrived, looking for runs and range, some found those already in occupancy to be uncooperative, unwilling to identify any land as being available for use. One, on the Murrinbigbee, advised

[83] Ibid., 139–41.
[84] See Ronald Rudin, "The Megantic Outlaw and His Times: Ethnic Tensions in Quebec in the 1880s," 18 Canadian Ethnic Studies 16 (1986).

the colonial secretary in 1837 of the way boundary disputes between old and new "squatters" were being settled: The rule, he explained, using a phrase others would employ as well, was "that he may hold, who gets; and he may get, who can." When "squatters" formally challenged the rights or boundaries of their neighbors, the Law in New South Wales tended to ignore their complaints, as John Weaver has shown.[85]

One exception to this that I detected in fact bears Weaver's point out: John Forde's turn-of-the-century celebration of Victoria's legal profession includes an account of two "squatter"-partners who became enraged by the encroachment of another on a well-watered section of their run. Unable to gain redress from the colony's officialdom, they paid solicitors and barristers 400 pounds to collect damages from the interloper. They won 300 pounds at trial, but their target thereupon declared insolvency, throwing the court costs upon them. All told, they paid out 1,000 pounds to drive the squatting "squatter" off; the well-watered tract at issue, they noted to Forde with chagrin, was worth only 200 pounds.[86]

So "squatters" in the Land of Oz were forced to turn away from the Not-So Powerful Wizard and settle matters informally. Some tried to "wedge" in between established runs, where the land was yet unleased or otherwise unoccupied (by the Diaspora invaders). Others moved on, preferring "neighbors with whom some agreement had been reached." Similarly, savvy owners of runs already in operation advised their station managers "not to embroil the Establishment by disputes with neighbors." As one such owner told his manager, located on the remote Goulburn Plains in 1833, "an extensive good Run, not subject to be encroached upon, may sometimes more than compensate for remoteness."[87]

Later, in the 1860s, after the Australian gold rush panned out, statutes overrode the Crown leases to these pastoralists and grazers and granted possessory rights to those who occupied and "improved" the land for three years and paid £1 per acre in installments. "Selectors" who were resourceful in the original sense of that word quickly located

[85] John C. Weaver, "Beyond the Fatal Shore: Pastoral Squatting and the Occupation of Australia, 1826 to 1852," 101 *American Historical Review* 981 at 989, 994 (1996).

[86] John L. Forde, *The Story of the Bar of Victoria* (Melbourne, 1906), 45–50.

[87] D. N. Jeans, "Crown Land Sales and the Accommodation of the Small Settler in New South Wales, 1825–42," 12 *Historical Studies: Australia and New Zealand* 205–10 (1966); K. Buckley, "Sir George Gipps and the Graziers of New South Wales, 1841–46," Pt 2, 7 *Historical Studies: Australia & New Zealand* 178–91 (1956); Stephen Roberts, *The Squatting Age in Australia, 1835–1847* (Melbourne, 1935), 278, 280.

at some of the colony's few available waterholes, sites they knew were indispensable to the pastoralists (a phenomenon known as "peacocking" in Australia, "spotting" or "gridironing" when it was later imitated in New Zealand). Some "peacocks" were content to sell their rights to the station owners at such profits as they could realize and more. There was little the government of New South Wales could do about it. When asked in that colony's legislature "Why did you not prosecute" dummy entrymen, the minister of lands responded: "How can you do so? You would have half the country in gaol if you prosecuted for all the false declarations in connection with land."[88]

But others were true settlers, dubbed "cockatoos" by the Squatters because these unfeathered bipeds were as annoying to them as the noisy feathered variety. Some Squatters "peacocked" as well to forestall settlers and ensure access for their animals to water. They selected and purchased (in their own names and those of each of the members of their families) the best of the land on their formerly leased runs, and thus, generally retained control of the runs, defeating in part the statute's apparent purpose. Indeed, in Victoria it was the Squattocracy who "selected" the lion's share of the acres alienated between 1860 and 1863. But where they had been beaten to the deed by a "cockatoo," some tried to intimidate these selectors and get them to sell out and move on, while a few more accommodating souls came to accept them and share resources, manpower, and ideas.[89] T. S. Hall, a Squatter leasing some 800 square miles near Yass in 1865 (and the district's magistrate), was an example of the more aggressive sort. When George Glendining and his sons selected lots on Hall's vast tract, Hall wrote this cordial greeting:

I am exceedingly sorry to hear and understand of the way you and your family are annoying and endeavouring to Injure Our St. Helier's property for I am quite sure you nor your Family never received any Injury at my Hands. And more than that, wile you kept away from me I was quite Determined not to Interfere with you – But Rest assured that If you continue to annoy us that we will take steps to protect Ourselves – All the Land Round about your First Selections is useful Greasing Land, as Good as a Good deal of the land we have bought, and there is nothing to prevent us From Buying Every inch of the Land in Neibourhud of your Selections – and take my word, this course will be adopted. And

---

[88] NSW Parl. Debates, Vol. 62, p. 3,590, quote in W. P. Reeves, *State Experiments*, 235.

[89] See, for example, the example of Squatter Samuel Shumack, noted in C. M. H. Clark, *A History of Australia* (Melbourne, 1978), IV, 166.

further, I will Find Shepherds that will not be afraid Even of your
Big Shelala – My motto has always been to live and let live and
I wish to continue in that course – I am your Obedient Servant,
Thomas S. Hall.[90]

Farther south, in Victoria, one of Hall's Squatter counterparts named
Bowen who ran cattle on the Ovens River harassed at least three
cockatoo-farmers like Glendining in 1867. Bowen had taken care to include a strip of land along the riverfront in his run and he impounded
the selectors' dairy cows when they strayed onto his run for a drink.
The Squatter-friendly magistrate ordered the selectors to fence their
crops in within fourteen days or tolerate Bowen turning his cattle "on
our little crops" to "feed them down," as Bowen himself threatened to
do. "By this means he will drive us of[f] the land," Thomas Carroll
wrote to the colony's responsible minister, "if your Honour refuse me
an additional time to erect the fince. [I] trow myself at your feet...."
A cockatoo-friendly Victorian government interceded, and by 1871
Thomas Carroll had purchased his selection, erected a house, shed,
stockyard, stable, and pigsty, fenced the property and had "improvements to the value of 405 pounds."[91]

SUMMARY

Diaspora jurists virtually everywhere tended to apply the English rules
regarding riparian rights as received from "the mother of all" Common
Law. But squatters often received generous treatment at the hands of
equity judges with regard to their improvements, and settlers with
imperfect titles often benefitted as well from such proceedings. Once
Responsible Governments were created, squatters tended to secure
favorable legislation protecting the value of their improvements and
providing prescriptive rights to purchase.

Diaspora settlers did not wait upon the generosity of Common-
Law jurists, however. They created their own "common law." Fishermen in Newfoundland created homes and gardens where the Law denied them the right to do so; entrepreneur-thieves in North America
stripped timber from land for which they had paid only the first small
installment-payment; dummy-entrymen deceived the State in the iron
ore fields of Minnesota and the vast grasslands of Australia; frontier
speculators in the Green Mountains, the Appalachians, the Wyoming

---

[90] *Yass Courier*, 23 Aug., 1865, reprinted in Stephen Roberts, *The Squatting Age
in Australia*, 169.
[91] John McQuilton, *The Kelly Outbreak: The Geographical Dimensions of Social
Banditry* (Melbourne, 1979), 194–95.

Valley of Pennsylvania, and New South Wales carved empires out of fraudulent land purchases, bribery, and sheer audacity; squatters in New Hampshire, Maine, and Upper Canada practiced "possession by the firelock" and "Club Law," proclaiming their "natural rights" to land they had mixed their labor with; "claim associations" protected squatters in the midwest. The Crown, its "Great Proprietors," and especially the Aboriginal people lost at *least* as often as they won whatever legal contest might ensue from these "bold frontiersmen."

4

Protecting One's Prope'ty:
Takings, Easements, Nuisances,
and Trespasses

Once you had acquired ("perfected") your title to land, your "quiet enjoyment" of that property could still be disturbed by a neighbor's blocking of your sunlight, or his polluting or diverting your watercourse, or his damaging your crops by failing to keep his cattle, horses, pigs, or fowls from your fields or garden, or by a railroad's "taking" a swath of your land for tracks or railway ties (to say nothing of the disturbance caused by the ensuing roar and soot of the passing trains).

The Common Law and Equity provided various civil remedies to one whose property had been thus encroached upon by others, either by compensation or injunction. But such measures took time and money, and one's resort to them was likely to be regarded as "uncivil" when the party being sued was one's neighbor rather than a "soulless" manufacturing or railway corporation. Law & Economics theorists predict that neighbors seek private, economically efficient resolution of trespass, nuisance, and easement disputes. How often did these neighbors turn to unlawful "self-help" rather than to Law when such "neighborly" efforts at dispute resolution failed, as they often did in the first generation or two of Diaspora settlements?

FRANCHISES

British and British-Diaspora legislators regularly granted franchises to corporate entities that offered to provide mills, ferries, bridges, toll roads, and railways to communities in need of such entities. Such enterprises would only stand a chance of profitablity if guaranteed monopoly rights, eminent domain "taking" powers appropriate to the task, and fixed prices for a substantial period of time, in the fashion of such franchises granted by the English Parliament in the past.

What did jurists have to say about franchises? American courts almost invariably honored the terms of such grants, so long as "the public" clearly appeared to be benefitted.[1] Indeed, they generally protected

---

[1] See Milton Klein and John Majewski, "Economy, Community and Law: The Turnpike Movement in New York, 1797–1845," 26 *Law & Society Review*

the original grantees from later legislative alterations of the original terms by new franchise grants to firms with newer technology or more dynamic corporate leadership.[2] Were CANZ jurists more willing than their American counterparts to favor more modern technologies or more "dynamic" bridge or railway companies in order to "release" new economic "energies" in the community? I reviewed such Canadian cases involving alleged infringements on milling, ferry, bridge, and railway franchises as I could detect in the nineteenth century reports of the various Canadian provinces, and found no infringements being permitted. Ferry owners collected damages from nascent competitors; tollbridge owners were allowed to tear down competitor's bridges or bar the construction of municipal bridges that would have been toll free; mill owners with seigneurial rights of *banalité* (the right to charge fees for services) were free to demolish private mills, be they for mere home consumption or for manufacturing or distilling "for export"; provincial governments and private shippers were able (as in the United States) to compel railways to continue to operate unprofitable lines under the terms of their charters and to carry freight at a "reasonable toll." Moreover, judges permitted juries to determine these rates (diverging from English practice), because, while the railways of England were "almost exclusively built by private means," those in Canadian provinces had received "large sums" from "the public exchequer," and were thereby subject to judicial oversight to prevent "their becoming monopolies" that might "leave at the mercy of the Company the fortune of every trader on the line of its railway."[3]

---

469 (1992); Charles Heckman, "Establishing the Basis for Local Financing of American Railroad Construction in the Nineteenth Century...," 32 *American Journal of Legal History* 236 (1988).

[2] See Peter Karsten, "Supervising the 'Spoiled Children of Legislation': Judicial Judgements involving Quasi-Public Corporations in Nineteenth Century America," 41 *American Journal of Legal History* 315 (1997), where I offer evidence refuting the claims of James Willard Hurst, *Law and the Conditions of Freedom in the Nineteenth Century United States* (Madison, 1956), esp. ch. 1, "The Release of Energy," and Morton J. Horwitz, *The Transformation of American Law, 1780–1860* (Cambridge, Mass., 1977), ch. 4.

[3] *Leprohon v. Globensky*, 3 Low. Can. J. 310 (1859); *Humberstone v. Dinner*, 2 Territor. L. R. 106 (1895); affmd., *Dinner v. Humberstone*, 26 Can. S. C. 252 (1896); *Girard v. Bélanger*, Ramsay's Digest, 712, 17 Low. Can. J. 263 (1872); *Corp. of Aubert-Galliou v. Roy*, 21 Can. S. C. 456 (1892); *Larue v. Dubord*, 1 L.C.R. 31 (1850); *Elwin v. Royston*, 4 Low. Can. J. 53 (1854); *Galarneau v. Guilbault*, 16 Can. S. C. (1886); *Monk v. Morris*, 3 Low. Can. R. 3 (1852); *Attny. Gen. v. New Bruns. & Can. Ry.*, 17 New Bruns. 667 (1878); *Greene v. St. John & Me.Ry.*, 22 New Br. 252 (1882); Dorion, C. J., in *Rutherford v. Grand Trunk Ry.*, 20 Low. Can. J. 11 at 16 (1875). Cf. *Lognon v. Audy*,

In one such opinion, Justice Day quoted New York Chancellor James Kent on the propriety of following precedent; in another, Justice Sanborn quoted from Isaac Redfield's treatise on railways and American cases on the "reasonableness" of freight rates; and in another, Justice Taschereau quoted from the *dissents* in the two Charles River Bridge decisions (Massachusetts and United States) to establish that a free bridge created by a local government in Quebec would not be tolerated when it infringed on a tollbridge's franchise.[4] The records of Brisbane's Tramways Company, Ltd., include correspondence with a key Queensland legislator who was proposing to regulate tramway rates. The company's solicitors drew his attention to two opinions of the U.S. Supreme Court regarding the propriety of legislation altering the terms of a carrier's charter with a state.[5] Thus, it appears that where American jurists had not parted company with their English compeers, or where they had addressed a problem closer to the one before a CANZ court than any English precedent, they could serve as viable judicial authority.

TAKINGS

The history of property in the lands of the British Diaspora is replete with restrictions and limitations imposed by the state on that "private enjoyment." While the abolition of tithes and many feudal obligations in the mid-seventeenth century had cut into the Crown's capacity to encumber property in England, the matter was different in the colonies. Purchases from the native inhabitants were forbidden, such purchases generally treated by the State as void at law. In most of the English colonies settled in the seventeenth and eighteen centuries land had to be acquired from the Crown or one of its "Great Proprietors" on long-term quitrent leases, which served as symbols of the sovereignty

---

4 Low. Can. R. 381 (1854); and Louise Dechêne, *Habitants and Merchants in 17th Century Montreal* (Montreal, 1992), 141 (grain not ground in the seigneury's mill subject to confiscation).

　　And see *The Queen v. Glenelg Ry. Co., Ltd.*, SALR 77 (1899) (the South Australian government, acting under the terms of its 1881 charter with the railway, can reclaim the company's property and pay it compensation).

4 Day, J., in *Monk v. Morris*, 3 Low. Can. R. 3 at 31 (1852); Sanborn, J., in *Rutherford v. Grand Trunk Ry*, 20 Low Can. J. 11 (1875); and Taschereau, J., in *Corp. of Aubert-Gallion v. Roy*, 21 Can. S. C. 456 (1892). See also Badgley, J., citing from a Louisiana opinion, in *Leprohon v. Globensky*, 3 Low. Can. J. 310 (1859) (ferry infringed on tollbridge); and the citation of American cases by both counsels in *Greene v. St. John & Me. Ry.* 22 New Br. 252 (1882).

5 J. S. Badger to Hon. D. F. Denham, Sept. 26, 1913, Brisbane Tramways Co. Records, Oxley Lib., Brisbane, OM 74–38.

and semisovereignty of those sources of land titles.[6] The Penn family encumbered all of their 999-year quitrent grants with "6% clauses," reserving up to that much of the grant for future public uses. Parklands were set aside in towns and cities; property was taxed for public purposes and "tax-title" statutes sanctioned the sale of property when taxes had for some years been unpaid; "nuisances" (such as "bawdyhouses," or any pigsty, tannery, rendering, or smelting plant in a congested area) could be enjoined and removed; ordinances regulated the materials used in urban construction; property in the path of an urban fire was subject to immediate destruction without compensation to protect "the greater good"; the relative rights of animal owners and cultivators were defined and sanctions created to be imposed on those who violated them.[7] It was not by chance that "free-born Englishmen," when speaking of their freedoms, sometimes defined them in terms of the "privileges" and "immunities" they enjoyed. "Privileges" and "immunities," however, have a source – grants (however grudgingly surrendered) from the Sovereign.

Perhaps the clearest examples of such encroachments on the rights of property owners in these years were the legislative grants of the state's "eminent domain" powers to public and quasi-public corporations to create milldams, roads, canals, and railroads. The practice of granting such "taking" powers for the construction of roads and milldams was centuries old, but it grew rapidly during the heyday of textile mills and in the years of "the Transportation Revolution," especially after Robert McAdam's invention of the improved roadbed and the development of the steam railway system.

English courts were perfectly prepared to allow companies "offsets" against "takings" damages where the property owner could be "considered compensated for by the public benefit expected to follow" in the

---

[6] Indeed, as late as 1836 the agent of the Port Phillip Association, in seeking title to land in what has become central and western Victoria from the Colonial Office, asked that it be in just such quitrent leases that would be "sufficient for the support of a small . . . establishment appointed by the Crown to superintend and protect all parties in . . . the colony." James Bonwick, *The Port Phillip Settlement* (London, 1883).

[7] See M. Williams, "Delimiting the Spread of Settlement: An Examination of Evidence in South Australia," *Economic Geography* Vol 42, No. 4 (Oct. 1966), 336–55; M. Williams, "The Parkland Towns of Australia and New Zealand," *Geographical Review* Vol 56, No. 1 (1966), 67–89; Georgina Whitehead, *Civilising the City: A History of Melbourne's Public Gardens* (State Library of Victoria, 1997); Robert Swierenga, "The 'Odious' Tax Title: A Study in 19th Century Legal History," 15 *American Journal of Legal History* 124 (1971); William Novak, *The People's Welfare: Law and Regulation in Nineteenth-Century America* (Chapel Hill, 1996).

path of the development. And they were also prepared to read the statute to permit damages only for actual lands taken, and not for "consequential" damage to the remaining property.[8] Courts in the States generally construed railway charters strictly, but where doubt as to the legislature's intent arose, they applied older Common-Law rules and reasoning as well as equitable standards to insure that the corporate beneficiaries of this legislative largesse paid a fair price for the "taking" and direct damages. Moreover, they sanctioned compensation for indirect ("consequential") damages as well when the offending party was a railroad or other for-profit corporation, not simply a municipality.[9] Thus, one southern high court found no fault in one trial judge's instructions to a jury regarding these direct and indirect damages for them to feel free to add consequential damages for a railroad "disturbing your farm with the scream of the whistle, the smoke of the engine, the rattle of the train, destroying the garden your wife and daughter have spent years tending and beautifying.... "[10] Only the courts of Illinois and Ohio failed to distinguish between municipal corporations, who were, elsewhere, *not* required to pay indirect damages, and for-profit railway, streetcar, and milldam corporations, who were. And those courts required *both* to pay indirect damages. Consider Justice Nathaniel Read's magisterial critique of the claim of Ohio's municipalities to this form of sovereign immunity:[11]

> A sort of transcendentalism, which enveloped both the courts and the profession in a mist growing out of the airy nothingness

---

[8] *Broadbent v. Imperial Gas Co.*, 7 DeG., M. & G. 436, at 459, 44 ER 170 (1856); *Hammersmith & City Ry. v. Brand*, LR 4 HL 171 (1869); *The Caledonian Ry. Co. v. Ogilvy*, 2 Macq. (Scot.) App. 229; *Mumford v. Oxford, etc. Ry.*, 1 H. & N. 36, 156 ER 1107 (1856) (no damages for noise); *Rickett v. Metropolitan Ry.*, LR 2 HL 198 (1867) (no damages for public house cut off from road by railway). But see *Lawrence v. Great Northern Ry.*, 16 QB 643, 117 ER 1026 (1851) (consequential-prospective damages OK for later flooding of lands); *Simpson v. South St. Waterworks Co.*, 13 Weekly Reporter 729 (1865) (statutes to be read strictly, limiting companies to such "takings" as are directly necessary for sanctioned operations).

[9] See Louis Hegyi, "Eminent Domain in Indiana, 1815–1865," 54 *Indiana Law Journal* 427–442 (1979); Karsten, "Supervising the 'Spoiled Children of Legislation: Judicial Judgements involving Quasi-Public Corporations in the Nineteenth Century United States,'" 41 *American Journal of Legal History* 315–67 (1997).

[10] Judge Aldrich, quoted in *Bowen v. Atlantic and French Broad RR*, 17 So. Car. 574 at 575 (1882).

[11] *McCombs v. Akron*, 15 Ohio 474 at 480 (1846). See also *Crawford v. Village of Delaware*, 7 Ohio St. 459 (1857) (regrading of street after announcing a different level for planning purposes, on the basis of which owner of lot had build house, actionable).

of the subject matter, enabled [municipal] corporations, like the pestilence which walketh unseen, to do their mischief and escape the responsibility.

Ohio had abandoned that "airy" practice and would hold all corporate entities to pay compensation for "takings," however consequential they might be.[12] Such a policy was not for "the public good."

Virtually all of the high courts in the States interpreted narrowly such statutory provisions as called for the offsetting of a landowner's compensation for such benefits as the railroad would provide him. Thus in *Isom v. Mississippi Central RR* (1858), Justice William Harris railed against the "moonshine standard of value" in one such offset provision. Such a standard served "these monopolies," the "interests or combinations of the many," who were misleadingly characterized in statutes as "the public necessity, public utility, [or] the public convenience." Railroad counsel's efforts to have the statute applied were the "pleas of despotism," against "the humblest, weakest citizen." Justice Harris regarded such allowances as contrary to natural justice and to the reading he and his colleagues gave to "compensation" in the state's constitution.[13]

Moreover, many state courts were prepared to set aside legislative grants of eminent-domain powers as unconstitutional if the public benefits of the taking were not obvious to them. Thus Georgia's Justice Euginius Nisbet commented expansively on the subject of "capital combinations" in a suit alleging the lack of compensation for a road to "a certain landing on Flint River." The alleged miscreants were road commissioners, a publican, and some local planters, but Nisbet spoke of "corporate influence" and capital, wielding "a power too potent for [legislative resistance] and the popular will. Degeneracy may seize the times, and the virtues of simple, honest revolutionary republicanism depart." Compensation for legitimate takings would always be required, and non-public takings would be prohibited, for "the right of accumulating, holding, and transmitting property lies at the foundation of civil liberty. Without it, man nowhere rises to the dignity of a freeman. . . . It is in vain that life and liberty are protected, . . . that the suffrage is free . . . if property be held at the will of the Legislature."[14] There appear to be fewer appellate cases involving "takings"[15] in the reports of the other lands of the British Diaspora; I detected a total of a

---

[12] *Nevins v. Peoria.* 41 Ill. 502 at 512 (1866).
[13] *Isom v. Miss. Central RR,* 36 Miss. 300 at 311 (1858).
[14] *Taylor v. Porter,* 4 Hill (N.Y.) 140 (1843); *Brewer v. Bowman,* 9 Ga. 37 (1850).
[15] They were called "expropriations" in Canada, when it was the Dominion doing the "taking" for an intercolonial railway, and "resumptions" or "reclamations" in Australia and New Zealand.

little over 100 (to 1910). But one can offer *some* generalizations about them and tender *some* comparisons with those of the United States.

Canada

Canadian jurists may have been *somewhat* less willing than were their counterparts in England and the United States to turn away corporate challenges to generous jury assessments for direct and consequential damages, but this was generally due to the constraints of the statutes they were interpreting and applying.[16] Let us consider those of Upper and Lower Canada (also known at other moments in the nineteenth century as Canada East/Canada West; Ontario/Quebec). Hagarty, Chief Justice of Upper Canada's Court of Common Pleas, allowed in 1876 that one landlady-cottager had been "really seriously injured" by

[16] Jurists in the Maritimes, however, *may* have been more like their peers south of the border: New Brunswick's Supreme Court upheld an award of £75 for two acres of land taken in 1853 for a highway, even though testimony had valued the land at only £5 per acre, and even though some jurors had been quoted as saying that the size of their award was deliberately intended "to prevent the road from being opened." The jury had taken into consideration the farmer's present and future fencing expenses that this road had created for him in their award, and the court was untroubled by this accounting. The same court sanctioned a jury award of £75 in 1870 for farmland actually taken by a railway for its tracks, as well as the truly substantial consequential damages of £275 for the inconvenience caused when this cut the farmer off from easy access to a portion of his fields. And their colleagues in Nova Scotia voided an arbitration award for an expropriation that they deemed inadequate. *ExParte Hebert*, 8 New Br. 108 at 114 (1854); *Queen v. Justices of Kent*, 8 New Br. 118 (1854); *Grazier v. Fredricton Branch Ry.*, 13 New Br. 3 (1870); *Askill v. Town of New Glasgow*, 40 Nova Sc. 58 (1895). See also *Koch v. Dauphinee*, 2 Nova Sc. 159 (1853) (court *almost* opted for the "sound policy" of the American state courts regarding the question of residual title to land taken as an easement for a road); and *Young v. Gr. River Navig. Co.*, 13 UCQB 506 (1856) (jury award of £100 upheld though witnesses valued loss of two acres at £50 and judge's disallowance of consideration of future loss consideration upheld).

The New Brunswick high court also declared unconstitutional the New Brunswick legislature's authorization of debentures to help build a railway linking New Brunswick and Maine. Justice Allen, allowed that this would produce "much disappointment and very serious inconvenience and loss," but explained that he and his colleagues were duty bound "in this, as in every other case that comes before us, ... to declare the law as we honestly believe it to be, wholly regardless of consequences," and in this case the British North American Act of 1867 had vested these powers of interprovincial development exclusively in the new Canadian Parliament. *Queen v. Dow*, 14 New Br. 300 at 310 (1873).

the vibrations of the Hamilton and Lake Erie Railway's trains passing by on her street (she lost tenants and sought consequential damages). But he none the less turned away her appeal with citations of English precedents and observed rather coolly: "Every dweller in large cities knows well that houses vibrate unpleasantly as heavy traffic rolls by." Similarly, his counterpart on Queens Bench, Chief Justice John Beverley Robinson, expressed unease about an award of damages to members of a community that suffered economic loss because of the construction of the Cornwall Canal in 1849. And five years later his court would not sanction the mulcting of some £10,487 from a railway for members of one of Montreal's leading families, the Babys, for one-and-a-third acre of their land.[17]

But while these (and a few other) judgments have been read as evidence that Robinson was no populist foe of corporations, they don't establish that he was a procorporate developmentalist either. Robinson and his court approved consequential damages associated with the construction of the Cornwall Canal because the statute allowed for them.[18] And cutting back Baby's £10,487 for only one-and-one-third acres in Montreal in 1854 was, I believe, no evidence of prodevelopmental behavior. The facts were these: The family had considered an offer of £1,125 for the property only two years before, two-thirds of the property was under water, and the arbitrators had improperly assessed the property, not at its current market value, but at what they thought it would have been worth after the railway was completed had it not been seized.[19]

Robinson's judgement benefitted the railway in this instance (to the detriment of a landowner of his own socioeconomic class). But Robinson was perfectly prepared to criticize railway corporations when they "embark in a contention about a trifle," forcing litigation on farmers "which must throw a considerable expense" upon the losing party instead of showing "consideration" and offering "to do whatever is fair," or when they blocked a farmer's drainage ditch, flooding his land after he had "amicably" sold them right-of-way without reservations instead of forcing the railway through the more expensive compulsory arbitration process.[20]

---

[17] In Re *Devlin v. the H & L E Ry*, 40 UCQB 160 at 162, 164 (1876); *Comms. of Public Works v. Daly*, 6 U.C.Q.B. 33 at 46–47 (1849); *Great Western Ry. v. Baby*, 12 U.C.Q.B. 106 (1854).

[18] *Comms. of Works v. Daly, supra* note 17, 45–46. For a different view see Bernard Hibbitts, "Progress and Principle: The Legal Thought of Sir John Beverley Robinson," 34 *McGill Law Journal* 454 at 507 (1989).

[19] *Great Western Ry. v. Baby*, 12 U.C.Q.B. 106 (1854).

[20] In *Nelson v. Cook*, 12 U.C.Q.B. 22 at 32 (1854) (railway entered land after

In any event, Robinson, Hagarty, and their successors generally interpreted the "takings" statutes in ways that favored individual property owners over canals and railway companies between 1849 and 1897 (by my count, by a margin of 15 to 8).[21]

agreeing to pay £27 10s., but before paying); and *L'Esperance v. Gr. W. Ry.*, 14 UCQB 173 (1856) (Robinson, C.J., diss.).

[21] The 15 plaintiff victories: *Janette v. Great Western Ry*, 4 U.C.C.P. 488 (1855) (award for damage to orchard and fields); *Nelson v. Cook*, 12 U.C.Q.B. 22 (1854); *Young v. Gr. River Navig. Co.*, 13 UCQB 506 (1856) (jury award twice that of witness valuations of loss, sanctioned); *Moison v. Gr. West. Ry.*, 14 UCQB 102 (1856) (five other cases joined to this also successful); *Wilkes v. Gzowski*, 13 U.C.Q.B. 308 (1857); *Cameron v. Ont., Simcoe, & Huron Ry.*, 14 UCQB 612 (1856); *Hugo v. Great Western Ry.*, 16 UCQB 506 (1858) (cattle-guards and fences in agreement must be maintained by railway); *Vanhorn v. Grand Trunk Ry*, 18 U.C.Q.B. 356 (1859) (£15 for damage to field from negligently build drain); *Clouse v. Canada So. Ry.* 4 Ont. (Ch.) 28 (1883) (Ry. must maintain all undercrossings agreed upon in arbitration 12 years before; reporter notes that "it seems that public convenience could not prevail over the plaintiff's private rights"); affirmed in *Clouse v. Ry.*, 11 Ont. (C. of A.) 287 (1884); *Fargey v. Grand Junction Ry..* 4 Ont. (C.P.) 232 (1883) (Ry. must build cattle pass for farmer); *Erwin v. Canada So. Ry.*, 11 Ont. (C. of A.) 306 (1884) (Ry. must pay compensation when it removes trestle bridge); *Hoskin v. Toronto Gen. Trusts Co.*, 12 Ont. (Ch.) 480 (1886) (consequential damage award for depreciation of remaining farm land affirmed); *James v. Ontario & Quebec Ry.*, 12 Ont. (Ch.) 624 (1886) ("taking" award); *Wells v. Northern Ry.*, 14 Ont. (Ch.) 594 (1887) (Ry. must pay compensation for filling up underpass landowner had enjoyed for 20 years); *Re Birely v. T H & B Ry Co*, 28 OR 468 (1897) (statute uncommonly said Ry should "do as little damage as possible and shall make full compensation . . . for all damage by them sustained by reason of the exercise of such powers"). The eight canal/railroad victories: *Com. of Public Works v. Daly*, supra note 17; *Great Western Ry. v. Baby*, supra note 17; *Carron v. Great Western Ry.*, 14 UCQB 191 (1856) (a "hard case"); *L'Esperance v. Great Western Ry.*, 14 UCQB 173 (1856); *Carroll v. Gr. Western Ry.*, 14 UCQB 614 (1856) (no special bridge necessary for farmer with alternative access to land); *Wallace v. Gr. Trunk Ry.*, 16 UCQB 551 (1858); *McGillwray v. Gr. W. Ry.*, 25 UCQB 69 (1865); *Powell v. T H & B Ry*, 25 OAR 209 (1897).

In 1903 the Canadian legislature created a Board of Railway Commissioners, and that Board began to hear a number of cases claiming that railways had a duty to construct safe crossings. Several of these decisions were appealed to the Supreme Court of Canada, and, as Bernard Hibbitts has shown, that court initially tended to defer to the Board's judgement and authority in its tendency to rule that such crossings need not be mandated. In one such case (*Grand Trunk Ry. v. McKay*) Justice Davies observed that to require a crossing gate in an uncrowded rural area "in a country such as Canada, could seriously impede railway development." But Hibbitts ultimately finds the court's behavior to have been more doctrinal than developmental in character. Hibbitts, "A Change of Mind: The Supreme

The court of Queen's Bench for Lower Canada/Quebec behaved just as had their Upper Canada/Ontario counterpart: Where arbitrators had allowed a landowner absolutely nothing for a substantial "taking" by a canal authority, an appellate court disagreed in 1859 and ordered that £8,575 be paid by the Crown, and Queen's Bench affirmed this judgement. Chief Justice Duval allowed that even though the property owner had experienced an "increased value of his property" due to the construction of the canal, he was still to be compensated for the land used at market value.[22] In other decisions the court held that road authorities and railways were to make payment before entering on the land being used, and in a separate case it concluded that even though the railway company's nominee arbitrator had proposed a sum substantially less than the other two arbitrators for farmland taken, the judiciary had no right to revise the award.[23]

With the creation of the Dominion of Canada in 1867 statutes emanating from that government's legislature created government-owned intercolonial railways, and expropriations of land and property for these entities were made subject to appeal to the federal government's Court of Exchequer. I read only a few dozen of the many reported judgements of this body.[24] I would not characterize its jurists as favoring one party or the other in these State-individual contests; they appeared to have functioned objectively, applying the statutory language and Common-Law rules where that language lacked clarity. But I want to

Court of Canada and the Board of Railway Commissioners, 1903–1929," 41 *Univ. of Toronto Law Journal* 60 at 70–72(1991).

[22] *Ellice v. The Queen,* 14 R. J. Quebec R. (Mathieu) 450 at 454 (1865). *Seigneurs* had been allowed to seize up to six *arpents* (about five acres) of a *censitaire's roture* for use as a mill by the 1720s, but they had also been obliged to compensate the *censitaire* for this privilege. Louise Dechêne, *Habitants and Merchants in 17th Century Montreal* (Montreal, 1992), 142.

[23] *Deal v. Corp. of Phillipsburg,* 15 Quebec 267 (1866); *Huot v. Q., M., & C. Ry.,* 10 Quebec Cour Sup. 373 (1896); *Atlantic & N.W. Ry. v. Leeming,* 3 Quebec Q.B. 165 (1894); *La Compagnie du Chemin de Fer de Montreal & Ottawa Ry. v. Castonguay,* 2 Quebec Q.B. 207 (1893). In *La Compagnie... Montreal & O. Ry. v. Bertrand,* 2 Quebec Q.B. 203 (1893) the rule cut the other way: A much larger sum had been proposed by the property owner's nominee arbitrator than by the other two. When the farmer appealed from the award, the Superior Court increased it by $200 (an 80% increase), but the Court of Queen's Bench reversed this. See also *Kierzkowski v. Grand Trunk Ry.,* 4 *Lower Can. J.* 86 (1857) (landowner cannot claim mutation fee (*lods et ventes*) from a railway that had taken over a railway with easement rights on his property).

[24] For those interested in the intersection of Quebec's Civil Law rules and the statutory and common law of the Dominion, I recommend in particular one typically excellent opinion of Justice Taschereau regarding the Dominion's Railway Act of 1881: *Paradis v. Regina,* 1 ExCR 191 (1887).

share a passage from one judgement of Justice Cassels (author of many Exchequer decisions). His Honor first held that farmer McDonald was entitled to about a third more than he had been offered (for a barn on land taken for an intercolonial railway to Sydney Mines). He then commented on farmer McDonald's remaining grievances – "the misery a cow would suffer by having to move her quarters," the same sort of distress a dozen hens would experience, and the "serious injury" the man would endure because he could no longer "have a continuous clothes line, 100 feet in length, to dry his washing." Wearily, Cassel found these efforts "to reach the sympathetic side of the court" to no avail.[25]

The Antipodes

The high courts of several Australian jurisdictions reported a total of some thirty-six "takings" appeals. For reasons that are not clear to me, jurists in Victoria, South Australia and Western Australia tended to treat the plaintiff/property owners *somewhat* more generously than did their more circumspect counterparts in New South Wales. A few illustrations: Following English practice, Victoria's Supreme Court allowed a jury in 1876 to assess the value of land seized by the Ballarat and Ararat Railway "liberally" because of the compulsory nature of the reclamation. In the words of Justice Stephen "although it is called compensation for compulsory purchase, it is merely another mode of expressing what should be a fair bargain as between man and man." Moreover, the court refused to allow a setoff of so much as a farthing from the direct damages ("the purchase money of the land taken") for such increase in the value of the remaining land as the jury had calculated.[26] In the following year the same court interpreted Victoria's Public Works Act of 1865 and its Land Compensation Act of 1869 strictly to warrant a jury award of the cost of fencing in a railway track passing through the plaintiff's land, even though he was free to chose to pocket the funds and throw the entire cost of fencing upon the railway itself (under the safety provisions (sec. 105) of the Public Works Act).[27] Later, in 1883, Justice Williams complained of a land compensation statute that allowed setoffs against the value of the land taken

[25] *R. v. McDonald*, 5 Eastern LR 431 at 433 (1908). But see *Malcolm v. R*, 2 ExCR 357 (1891) (significant victory for property-owner); and *Symonds v. R*, 8 Ex CR 319 (1903) (English rule-of-thumb that arbitrators could add 10% to award due to compulsory nature of expropriation OK).

[26] *Leslie v. Bd. Of Land & Works*, 2 VLR (L) 21 (1876).

[27] *Anderson v. Western Port Coal Co.*, 3 VLR (L) 276 (1877) (Stawell, CJ: "It may appear hard that the company may be compelled . . . to enclose this land although they have paid plaintiff a fair amount for the costs of fencing, but

based on the assessors' estimate of the benefit to the landowner to be derived from the improvement. "This set-off is not allowed in any other English-speaking country that I know of. . . . " he observed, but, the legislature having spoken, the court sanctioned the offset in this instance.[28] In two subsequent decisions also involving "offsets," however, Victoria's jurists cut into the State's powers in this regard.[29]

Further west, jurists in Western Australia and South Australia appeared to read "taking" statutes as liberally as were their compeers in the United States and Victoria. Thus Justice Hensman construed the language of Western Australia's Land Resumption Act of 1894 sanctioning the uncompensated taking of 5% of all land under Crown seal for roads and other works "of public utility and convenience" to exclude the colony's new Botanical Gardens. "This court," he explained, "will always adhere to a course which is just and equitable." He liked that so much he said it again: The court would pursue a course "not repugnant to justice and sense."[30] Similarly Justice Gordon of the South Australian Supreme Court held that the state's railway commissioners had behaved unjustly in relying on the terms of a 30-year old statute to limit compensation to no more than twice the value of the land at the time that statute was enacted. He cited English authority for his views, but his primary argument was that the older statute had simply not been intended to work the sort of hardship

we are not at liberty to consider such an argument.") And see *Smith v. Bd. Of Land & Works*, 4 Aus. Jur. Rpts. (Vic.) 134 (1873) (farmer deserves compensation for losses in value of both fee-simple and leasehold land traversed by railway). But see *Nosworthy v. Hallett*, 3 SALR 52 (1869) (no compensation for the fencing of previously unfenced land now traversed by a mere roadway).

[28] In *Harding v. Bd. Of Land & Works*, 9 VLR (L) 448 at 453 (1883). (The Law Lords went further than Williams and his colleagues, however: On appeal, they held that the statute should be read to allow offsets only against the consequential damage portion of the award, not the direct damages. *Harding v. Bd of Land & Works*, 11 App Cas 208 (1886).

[29] See *In Re Arbitration between Prahran & M. Tramways Trust and Ward*, VLR 656 (1914) ("offset" limited); and *In re Wildman Ex Parte The L. & W. Ry. Constr. Trust*, 27 VLR 43 (1901) (plaintiff wins on "offset" issue).

[30] *Dixon v. Throssell*, 1 WALR 193 at 196 (1899). Compare *Heppingstone v. Comms. Of Rys.*, 3 WALR 63 at 66 (1901) (plaintiff had proved twelve year "fee simple by [virtue of undisturbed] possession" in claiming compensation for land resumption. Chief Justice Stone turned away the Ry. counsel's appeal with the observation that, whether the plaintiff had the fee "or not," he did "undoubtedly" hold "a valuable [and] a marketable interest" in the land, warranting compensation.) But see Privy Council's reversal of a similarly proplaintiff judgement of the same court in *Thomas v. Sherwood*, 9 App Cas 142 (1883).

this particular reclamation amounted to. The railway commissioners' position, Gordon maintained, was "as simple as a highwayman's 'stand and deliver!"' and he was sure the legislature had not "intended to create such an ever-widening net of oppression" as counsel for the commissioners proposed.[31] His counterpart, Justice Boucaut sounded very much like the southern state court trial judge I referred to on page XXX in describing the consequential damages a dairyman faced when cut off from his sheds, machinery, and land by railway tracks: "The appearance of the place has been ruined, and life with the running of trains within a few yards of his house will be a daily torment.... " Perhaps members of this court had lived, indeed, may still have lived on such a farm. In any event, they held that the trial judge had correctly ordered that the Railway Commissioners must "take" and pay for both the land and the house and other improvements.[32]

The New South Wales Supreme Court did not appear to be quite as friendly to property owners as their western and southwestern compeers,[33] but it may be that the facts at issue in some of the reported cases explain this. A few examples: When a jury awarded £7,000 to a Mr O'Brien for three acres and a "portion of the frontage to the Bondi Beach" for the creation of the public park that exists there to this day, the Minister for Works appealed, and after visiting the site, that colony's supreme court held the award to be excessive. Cheif Justice Martin described the property: "It is a waste of sand, undulating,

---

[31] *Macdonald v. So Aus Ry Comms.*, SALR 135 at 154, 162 (1909). (Plaintiff had asked for 13,400 lbs; the Ry Comms. had offered 4,935.)

[32] *Draper v. South Aus. Ry Comms*, SALR 150 at 154 (1903). And see *In Re Reynell & the South Aus Ry Comm*, SALR 175 (1914) (consequential damages to vintner for taking of grapes crucial to a particular blended wine).

[33] "Unfriendly" decisions: *Douglass v. Robertson, 3 LR (NSW)* 57 (1882); *Forsyth v. Wright [Min. For Works]*, 5 LR (NSW) 251 (1884); *O'Brien v. Minister for Wks.*, 2 WN (NSW) 99 (1886); *Black v. Commissioners for Rys.*, 11 LR (NSW) 160 (1890); *Harris v. Lee*, 21 NSWLR 173 (1900); *Spencer v. Commonwealth*, 5 CLR 418 (1907).

"Friendly" decisions: *Phillips v. Comm for Rys*, 14 SCR (NSW) 360 (1876); *Kitchener v. Wachemo County Council*, LR 3SC 116 (1884); *Campbell v. Young [Min for Pub Wks]*, 18 LR (NSW) 171 (1897) (consequential damages, referred to as "sentimental"' damages by counsel, sanctioned for sewer line across property); *McQuade v. Whitfield*, 9 SR (NSW) 357 (affrmd 7 CLR 710 (1908); *Wilson v. Min for Pub Wks*, 8 SR (NSW) 427 (1908); *Brown & Others v. Commissioners for Railways*, 7 WN (NSW) 113 (1880); *Eckford v. Walker*, 2 SR (NSW) (L) 369 (1902) (sanctioning damages awarded a dairyman when railway construction workers damaged his fences and injured his cattle while blasting on his land for stone without having given notice of their intentions or negotiating for their reclamation).

rough, and not. . . . capable in its present state of being cultivated or being built upon. . . . " The same court rendered a similar verdict four years later: When a jury awarded a property owner at Lake Macquarie a sum for the coal seam beneath his land that was based on its anticipated value after the completion of the railway (when it might then be profitably mined), that colony's high court disagreed: The owner was to be awarded compensation on the basis of the property's prerailway value. Otherwise the Legislature "would invariably be frustrated in its intentions," inasmuch as virtually all properties on the path of new railways and roads experienced the same economic rising tides. And what was that prerailway value in this case? Chief Justice Darley was quite specific: "Here was an absolutely useless piece of land as could be found within the four corners of New South Wales; indeed, as one witness said, the whole 32 acres would not feed one goat."[34]

This colony's supreme court was by no means uniformly hard on property owners, however. Thus a stagecoach owner in Goulburn won an appeal from an unsatisfying award in 1875 due to the arbitrators' inappropriate comparison of English and New South Welsh "takings" statutes. As Justice Sir William Manning pointed out, "in England the whole system is different." Similarly, Justice Pring took issue with the views of two Law Lords (Halsbury and Watson) in a Privy Council decision that had been cited by counsel for the Ministry for Public Works. He and his colleagues then proceeded to affirm an award of £330 for *potential* consequential damage to a man's Bantry Bay property.[35]

Of the nine "takings" appeals that I detected in the New Zealand reports, there appear to be only four that could be said to reveal any evidence of judicial propensities in the interpretation of the relevant "takings/resumption" statute.[36] Of these, one, at most, could be read

[34] *O'Brien v. Min. for Works*, 2 WN (NSW) 99 (1886); *Black v. Comm. For Railways*, 11 LR (NSW) 160 at 162–3 (1890). And see *Spencer v. Commonwealth*, 5 CLR 418 (1907); *Macdonald v. So. Austr. Ry. Comm.*, SALR 135 (1909); But see *Brown & Others v Comm. For Rys.*, 7 WN (NSW) 113 (1880) (affirm'd by Privy Council on appeal, 15 AC 240) (jury's valuation of coal beneath land not adjudged to be excessive).

[35] *Phillips v. Com. For Rys.*, 14 SCR (NSW) 360 at 370 (1876); *Wilson v. Min. for Public Wks*, 8 SR (NSW) 427 at 436 (1908) (referring to *Cowper Essex v. Local Bd of Acton*, 14 App Cas 153).

[36] Among those that did *not* appear to do so were *Williams v. Mayor & Corp. of City of Wellington*, NZLR 3CA 210 (1881) (no compensation for loss suffered when street level altered unless former level appeared on official map as per statute); *Penn & Another v. Stratford Cty. Council*, 13 NZLR 33 (1894) (compensation due for loss due to alteration in road under provisions of statute); *Martin v. Westport Harbour Bd*, 14 NZLR (SC) 521 (1896) (statutes read *somewhat* liberally to sanction compensation for land "injuriously affected"

to suggest that the Kiwi high court inclined in the slightest toward the "developmentalist" point of view; the other three decidedly did not. In 1886 the New Zealand Court of Appeals would not read its Railway Construction Act in a fashion that limited the financial obligation of railway corporations to direct "takings." The Court considered a railway appeal from a jury award of £300, above and beyond the direct damage award for the land itself, for the cost of future fence maintenance. The company's counsel argued that inasmuch as the Act required the company to fence in the tracks, the company's own concern for its liability would force it to maintain the fence: "The danger caused by a train renders it compulsory on the company to see that the fences are in repair. If we do not, and any accident happens, we are liable for negligence." This reasoning might have persuaded a jurist of the "Law & Economics" persuasion, but it was no more convincing to the New Zealand Court of Appeals than a similar argument had been before their counterparts in Victoria nine years earlier. While the company might well be inclined to be the one to maintain the fencing, the adjoining landowner was, at least on paper, required to pay half the cost of such maintenance. It might be unlikely that the company would fine tune its accounting of such maintenance to know whom to send a bill for repairs made sometime down the chronological road, but it had the right to do so, and the court saw nothing illogical or inappropriate in an award of $300 for such charges, even though the landowner was, by law, "required to pay half the cost" himself![37]

Twenty years later, to be sure, one of New Zealand's jurists chose to offer an "economic-efficiency" rationale in a "takings" decision, but it was one that came down *against* urban development: The supreme court was asked by a property owner on a street being closed by the Foxton Borough Council (while a second was being opened) whether the action constituted a "construction of a public work" under the terms of the Public Works Act of 1894 (which would thus permit the plaintiff to seek damages). Chief Justice Stout held that the statute should indeed be read that way:[38]

> The court cannot, I think, be asked to assume that the Legislature meant to deprive persons of compensation whose frontages

by embankment construction); *Fitzgerald v. K & K Tramway Co*, 20 NZLR (SC) 406 (1901) (plaintiff wins retrial on all counts regard "offsets" and consequential damages for loss of ornamental trees, dampness, noise, and subsidence); *Public Trust v. Mayor & Corp. of Lower Hutt*, 28 NZLR (SC) 310 (1908) (no compensation for alteration of private road).

[37] *Walker v. Wellington & Manit. Ry.*, 4 N.Z.L.R. (C.A.) 127 at 129 (1886).
[38] *Symons v. Foxton Bor. Council*, 26 NZLR (SC) 698 at 701 (1906).

and access to their property has been taken away.... Magistrates would hesitate to give their consent to such schemes, and improvements in the arrangements of highways in a borough would in consequence be much impeded.

The other reported New Zealand cases of note involved the controversial Land for Settlements Act of 1894, which forced the great graziers to sell some of their runs back to the government for farm homesteads. Justice Christopher Richmond, a prominent Conservative Party figure and member of one of the earliest landed gentry on the North Island, had privately criticized the Liberal Government's earlier land reforms of 1891 in a note to his daughter dripping with sarcasm: It had been his "folly to have invested in land" that the legislature now declared "belongs to 'the people' and not to me."[39]

But when asked to apply the statute, New Zealand's jurists did so without any such expressions of distress. The leading case was *In Re The Land for Settlements Act, 1894, The New Zealand & Australian Land Co. v. The Minister for Lands* (1895). The Company's 4,266 acre Ardgowan estate in the Omaru district had been reclaimed. The Government had offered 29,000 pounds, but the reclamation adversely affected the value of the Company's nearby Totatara estate, and it asked for 45,800 pounds. The Company's counsel sought an extra 10% under what he called "the English rule-of-thumb" based on the compulsory nature of the taking, a claim that Justice Williams turned away with the observation that no such custom prevailed in New Zealand. Three years later the New Zealand Supreme Court (an intermediate court of appeals) again rejected the argument of counsel for three sheep-station owners that the English "custom" of an extra 10% be adopted in New Zealand, and they added that there was no appeal from the Compensation Court's award (though in dicta the court noted that the Compensation judge *could* be "liberal" in determining the sum due the former owners, which may have allowed for something approaching that additional 10%).[40]

The Role of Juries in the Informal Law of Takings

As we have seen, the Law generally did not prevent juries and assessment boards hearing "takings" appeals from behaving with great philanthropy toward their neighbors. These fact-finding bodies generally

---

[39] *The Richmond-Atkinson Papers,* ed. Guy Scholefield (2 vols., Wellington, 1960), II, 584.

[40] 13 NZLR (Comp. Ct.) 714 (1895) (the Company was awarded 34,600 pounds); *Russell v. Min. of Lands, Samsbury v. Same,* 17 NZLR (SC) 241 at 253 (1898).

awarded sums considerably above the market value of the property "taken," and, as we have seen, appellate jurists rarely held these awards to be excessive. Thus, the "customary law" of ordinary people managed to see to it that those doing the "taking" paid a pretty penny for the privilege, even if it could not *prevent* such "takings" altogether.[41]

In England, franchised railway developers had to pay for the support of landed gentry and aristocracy whose lands their tracks were to traverse in order to secure approval of their charters in Parliament. And the resulting enabling statutes, capped by the Land Clauses Consolidation Act of 1845, granted landowners with claims of fifty pounds or more either an arbitration hearing or a trial before a sheriff's jury. This jury, as well as most of the local "expert" witnesses, were persons "of the same class, pursuits, and sympathies" as the landowner–plaintiffs, or so the *Railway Chronicle* maintained in April, 1845. (Thus it is not surprising that one jury in 1846 gave 5,265 pounds for 12 acres of land (over 438 pounds per acre) taken from a 216 acre farm purchased seven years before for 78 pounds per acre.) The 1845 statute also stipulated that if any arbitration or jury award was greater than the settlement-sum that had been offered by the railway, the railway was to pay all the costs of court. The end result, Rande Kostal tells us, was a system that helped "humble yeomen" whose land had been encroached upon to "mobilize legal resources" and "maximize compensation awards."[42] English high courts sanctioned such "generous" awards in part because the statute allowed a *solatium* of 50 percent more than the current value of the land taken for "the indignity of compulsion."

Ultimately the costs of these "takings" came to some fourteen percent of all nineteenth century English railway capital expenditures, twice as much as at least one company had originally projected, and two to three times the cost per mile/kilometer of railway companies in France and Belgium where central governments and juryless courts provided developers with fewer impediments! But landowners had the capacity to subject railway companies to "crippling prices" because the original landowner's counteroffer often had to be tolerated and accepted (in the words of Henry Booth, supervisor of works for the

---

[41] See Tony Freyer, "Reassessing the Impact of Eminent Domain in Early American Economic Development," 1981 *Wisconsin Law Review*; and Karsten, "Supervising the 'Spoiled Children...,'" 8–30, for general discussion of the literature and cases on this subject.

[42] Kostal, *Law and English Railway Capitalism, 1825–1875* (Oxford, 1995), 145, 149, 150, 153, 158, 160,164, 364. See also S. Broadbridge, *Studies in Railway Expansion and the Capital Market in England, 1825–1873* (1970).

London & Northwestern Railway in 1849) because the property was "required for the immediate operations" of the company's construction engineers, and this was true throughout the United States as well, as Tony Freyer has shown.[43]

Compensation for takings in virtually all of the state constitutions in the United States was to be "just," and that was understood by jurists in the States to mean that the compensation was to be paid before the taking,[44] and that it was to be paid in cash, not company script or bonds.[45] The end result in the United States was a pattern of generous jury compensation awards, at least in the five mid-Atlantic jurisdictions where such awards have been analyzed. Tony Freyer has found that jury panels in Pennsylvania, Maryland, Delaware, the District of Columbia and New Jersey gave considerably more compensation per acre than canals or railroads paid to the landowners who came to a private agreement with them.[46] The attorneys of property owners who preferred to have their case heard by a jury would urge these assessors to "take care

[43] Kostal, 152, 171, 173n, 174, 333, 364; Freyer, *Ibid.*

[44] See, for example, *San Francisco v. Scott*, 4 Cal. 114 (1854); *McCam v. Sierra C o.*, 7 Cal. 121 (1857); *Chicago & Milwaukee RR v. Bull*, 20 Ill. 218 (1858); *Powers v. Bears*, 12 Wis. 214 (1860) (railroad act unconstitutional for permitting co. to enter land before compensation paid); *Shepardson v. Milwaukee & B. RR*, 6 Wis. 605 (1857) (same); *Bohlman v. Green Bay & L P. RR*, 30 Wis. 105 (1872) (cited in Robert Hunt, *Law and Locomotives*, 69–70); *Matter of Water Commissioners of Jersey City*, 31 N.J.L 72 (1864); and *Ross v. E. & S. RR*, 2 NJEq 422 (1841) (injunction halts construction until owners of land paid).

[45] See, for example, *State v. Beackmo*, 8 Blackf. (Ind.) 246 at 250 (1846) *Hamilton v. Annapolis & Elk Ridge Ry*, 1 Md. Ch. (Johnson) 107 (1847); *Burlington & C.RR v. Schweihart*, 10 Colo. 178, 14 Pac 329(1887); *Omaha v. Howell Lumber Co.*, 30 Neb. 633, 46 NW 919(1890); *Delaney v. Nolan County*, 85 Tex. 225, 20 SW 70(1892); and *Young v. Harrison*, 17 Ga. 30 at 43(1855).

[46] *Tidewater Canal Co. v. Archer*, 9 G. & J. (Md.) 479 at 499–500 (1839), cited in Freyer, *Producers versus Capitalists*, at 152–53. See also *RR v. Yeiser*, 8 Pa. St. 366 at 376 (1848) (for Justice Rogers' dicta). John Majewski offered a similar analysis of awards in counties in Virginia and Pennsylvania in the early nineteenth century, at a conference of the American Society for Legal History in Memphis, October, 1993. (Majewski has interesting observations as well on the links between the railroad corporations doing the taking and the landowners suing for damages (some were stockholders).)

Morton Horwitz notes that as early as 1795 juries were giving large awards in eminent domain "takings" for a canal in New York, and that this was evident as well in Pennsylvania, Connecticut, and Massachusetts in the first half of the nineteenth century, as well as in New York again in the 1820s, associated with the Erie Canal project. Horwitz, *The Transformation of American Law, 1780–1860* (Cambridge, Mass., 1977), 67–69.

of the people" in their struggle with a "corporation of foreigners" who were "taking their lands against their wishes and consent." The results were not lost on Justice Molton Rogers of Pennsylvania's Supreme Court:[47]

> Generally speaking, as we all know, the owners of land through which any public work passes, have very little reason to complain. They are usually benefitted by double the amount of the injury.

Cotton-textile mills faced a similar problem in New England; Josiah French, agent for the Boston-based Winnepisscogee Lake Cotton & Woolen Company, complained in 1871 that juror behavior in "any county" in New Hampshire "where the company have water rights. . . . It is impossible . . . to get a fair trial on any flowage case, as there are so many" affected, "or have relatives" who were, "that a jury cannot be got" that "will not be so prejudiced, as to go against the Company, right or wrong."[48]

Railways in the Canadian provinces faced jury assessments, sanctioned on appeal, that were at *least* as generous as those handed down in mid-nineteenth century England and the United States.[49] In the 1870s the original estimate of £35,000 for "takings" on Prince Edward Island to construct that province's railway had to be increased eight fold "as a result of incessant appeals for justice and generosity. . . ." Landowners demanded that numerous private crossings be provided them. The chief chronicler of the process concluded that these were

---

[47] Theodore Steinberg, *Nature Incorporated: Industrialization and the Waters of New England* (Cambridge, Mass, 1991), 247.

    Moreover, Jonathan Prude reports that townships and counties in which Massachusetts textile mills were located in the 1840s and 1850s were extremely unwilling to contribute towards any roads or fire companies for these factories or for any schools that might serve the children of their workers, and the factories lacked any legal means to force such payments from the locally influential farmers. Prude, *The Coming of Industrial Order: Town and Factory in Rural Massachusetts, 1810–1800* (Cambridge, Mass., 1983), 249–50.

[48] Noted in Theodore Steinberg, *Nature Incorporated: Industrialization and the Waters of New England* (Cambridge, Mass., 1991), 247.

[49] See, for example, *Daly v. Buffalo & Lake Huron Ry.*, 16 UCQB 235 (1859). For examples of railway negotiations with property owners for rights-of-way in the 1850s and 1870s see the records of William Chalk, Director of the Buffalo, Brantford & Goderich Railway in 1853, Chalk Collection, MU 527, Archives of Ontario, and the deposition of John G. Rideout of the Northern Extension Ry., regarding the "exorbitant" demands of Jesse T. Purdy of Meaford in 1872 (for $500 for twelve and one third acres), Miscellaneous MSS, MU 7148, Archives of Ontario.

essentially "status symbols."[50] An average of six such crossings were built for every mile of track laid down, and courts required railways to maintain these over time.[51] In New Brunswick, railway construction in the late 1880s cost three-and-one-half times the estimate. The property owners whose lands and buildings had been condemned "appealed with some success to the local politicians and swore one for the other as to value so ably" that the fourteen mile extension finally cost $2,000,000. One man from whom, it was said, no more than five dollars worth of sand and gravel had been taken by the construction crew without proper authority demanded $70,000. "Backed by the local politicians," he was given $16,000.[52]

In Toronto in 1853 Bishop John Strachan confided to Reverend Ernest Hawkins that, in the opinion of "the best judges" of such matters, the Society for the Propagation of the Gospel would "get double the price we shall ever get again" were they to sell the seven-and-one-half acres dedicated to endow Trinity College "on account of the increase in land values due to the coming of the railroad." There was "a great mania for railroads here." Similarly, Alex Lawe wrote to Richard Cartwright from Barrie in 1873 that "the value of land has gone up enormously, in consequence of its being a settled matter that the Hamilton & Northwestern RR is to come here."[53] One town council in Quebec approved a bonus of $10,000 for the Atlantic and North West Railway if the Railway's tracks passed through the town, but when the Railway acquiesced, the council refused to pay the bonus and successfully defended itself in court by pointing out that the relevant statute required a poll of the town's taxpayers before such a bonus could be made binding, something they had conveniently failed to order. Quebec's Court of Queen's Bench heard this self-serving reading of the statute with some reluctance, but they accepted the defense and upheld a lower court ruling exonerating the fortunate townsfolk from any payment.[54] An informal "law" had, quite simply, transferred wealth from private investors, many of them English or European, via a public utility, to private landowners, and the result was railway systems saddled with massive debt from the start and an investment community leery of making further loans.

---

[50] G. R. Stevens, *History of the Canadian National Railways* (N.Y., 1973), 96, 102.

[51] *Hugo v. Gr. Western Ry.*, 16 UCQB 506 (1859).

[52] Sam Dunn, "The Failure of Government Ownership in Canada," *Journal of Political Economy*, June, 1916, 5.

[53] Strachan to Hawkins, Feb. 4, 1853, Strachan Papers, MS 35 (11), Archives of Ontario; Lawe to Cartwright, June 2, 1873, Cartwright Papers, MU 508, Archives of Ontario.

[54] *A & N.W. Ry v. Corp. of Town of St. Johns*, 3 QQB 397 at 402–03 (1894).

The Informal Law with regard to Takings

The parties to a mandated arbitration hearing to award compensation in the event of an eminent-domain "taking" found themselves in court when one or the other rejected the award. These parties were not neighbors who would have to mend their fences and live side by side. One was a large corporate entity (be it public or private) with extensive resources; the other, typically, a farmer who did not look upon the corporation as a neighbor whom one was obliged to deal with in a conciliatory manner.

Statutes governed the process of compensating landowners for property lost by "takings" to a canal, road, or railway. And courts applied the language of those statutes without apparent bias.[55] But neither statute book nor jurist could prevent angry residents from defying the Law where a franchised company appeared to them to be behaving unreasonably, unfairly, or "unlawfully." One thinks of moments like the "Rebecca Riots" in Wales between 1839 and 1842 over the exacting of tolls on parish roads. While ultimately suppressed, these riots resulted in the government offering "major concessions over the turnpike system."[56]

Similar riotous objections were raised in the United States over the closing of milldams that impeded certain navigation, and over the rates to be collected of residents on local railway bonds. In the case of the former, the clash was between the interests of the powerful tobacco-growing interests in Kentucky's bluegrass region and the older, smaller-scale economy of corn whiskey in regions like Nelson and Bourbon Counties. Tobacco growers sought unimpeded river navigation in order to move their produce to downstream warehouses, but this could only come by removing the gristmill dams so vital to the sour-mash distilling process. When county courts in those homes of bourbon whiskey were persuaded by the petitions of tobacconists in 1825 to order the destruction of several of those "impediments," one observer, John Roche, reported that "the country people in the neighborhood" twice offered "resistance and threatened vengeance."[57]

The latter case (riotous objection to the raising of funds for railway bonds) flowed from the decision of state legislatures to sanction the raising of funds by county commissioners, or the holding of county referenda to purchase railroad bonds in the United States during

[55] See Heckman, "Establishing...Local Financing of American Railroad Construction."

[56] Hugh Kearney, *The British Isles: A History of Four Nations* (Cambridge Univ. Press, 1989), 218.

[57] Roche, noted in Stephen Aron, *How the West was Lost: Kentucky from Daniel Boone to Henry Clay* (Chapel Hill, 1996), 121.

the 1840s and 1850s. Many communities took the plunge in order to attract tracks to their county seats. Several of the roads that accepted such bonds in exchange for the promise to provide such tracks later defaulted, after having sold the bonds, often to foreign investors. When a number of communities balked at making payments on bonds they were receiving no benefits from, the bondholders sued, and the U.S. Supreme Court declared the counties liable and ordered them to pay.[58]

But such court orders were often hard to enforce. In Missouri, for example, county commissioners rather than voting taxpayers themselves had made the decisions to commit taxpayers to the bond issues. David Thelen has told us what ensued: Mobs of taxpayers opposed the issuances, and in one instance three "bond thieves" (one a judge, another a city councilman, a third an attorney) were actually murdered by such a mob. When petrified county officials reacted by suspending bond payments, the U.S. Supreme Court ordered them to continue paying in a series of cases in the 1870s. Subsequently, masked men destroyed tax records in St. Clair County in 1877. County officials thereupon resigned rather than comply and face local reaction. Missouri's governor refused to accept their resignations, and the bondholders offered various compromises. Federal marshals were finally called upon to arrest several county officials in 1878, leading to the imprisonment of Scotland County officials in 1881 and Cass County officials in 1882. By then some communities were helping their county officials to go into hiding. Knox County did not settle with bondholders until 1894; Jackson and Macon Counties until 1910 and 1911. Dallas County made its last payment in 1940. Thus, "compliance" was ultimately secured, but not the compliance that the Law had mandated.[59]

When the "taking" was for a city park rather than a railroad right-of-way in the countryside, the property owners whose land was seized were generally well compensated, but they were often not the only ones affected. For example, the owners of the 800 acres between 3rd and 7th Avenues and running from 57th to 106th Streets that was to become Central Park in New York City, "taken" by the city in 1856 and 1857, were quite content with their payments. But many of the over 1,000 African American, Irish, and German actual *inhabitants* of those tracts were neither property owners nor leaseholders. Most were squatters, raising pigs, goats, and chickens, selling stone for street

---

[58] *Gelpecke v. Dubuque*, 1 Wallace (U.S.) 175 (1864); Karsten, "Supervising the 'Spoiled Children...,'" 2–5.

[59] David Thelen, *Paths of Resistance: Tradition and Dignity in Industrializing Missouri* (N.Y. 1986), 64–67

paving, using its woods for cooking and heating, and living in simple dwellings of their own construction. These were torn down without compensation by the new park police to make way for the construction of a landscaped park crisscrossed by roadways with "ample room for...Horses & Carriages." The squatters, "left their homes," as Roy Rosenzweig and Elizabeth Blackmar tell us, somewhat bewildered by the abrupt change in their fortune, but, in this case, "quietly and without violence."[60]

Railway development in capital-scarce Australia followed a pattern not unlike that of the United States. Developers sought government aid, as in Sydney in 1848, where a group of such fellows resolved that since it was already "the duty of the Government to make and maintain the public roads and bridges of the colony," and "the cost of constructing and maintaining economical railways would not, in this country, equal that of macadamized roads," such railways "ought to be extensively assisted."[61] Some such railways funded by public revenues were popularly supported, of course, and some even managed to be profitable. But there were cases of resistance in the Land of Oz akin to the ones taken in the midwestern United States. Stefan Petrow has recounted one such moment, in Tasmania during the 1870s:

The Launceton & Western Railway was launched with some 100,000 pounds of pledged private capital and a government loan of 300,000 pounds. The charter stipulated that two-thirds of the landowners in the district to be served (northern Tasmania) duly vote their acceptance of the obligation to pay a substantial portion of the interest on the loan before the loan would vest. The requisite ballot was recorded, overwhelmingly in favor of the proposal, and railway construction proceeded apace. The Lauceston & Western opened for business in February, 1871.

But in the meantime the private investors, unable or unwilling to come up with their share of the capital (100,000 pounds), secured from the Tasmanian legislature a statute reducing to 50,000 pounds their obligation and increasing by 100,000 pounds the sum to be financed by government bonds. When the landowners learned of this new obligation, and the government began to collect the first 14,000 pounds of rates, they reacted in anger. A Mutual Defense Association was created in February, 1872, coinciding with the announcement signed by dozens of the district's magistrates "pledged to resist by every means in their power the levying of a rate, *be it legal or illegal* [sic]."

---

[60] Rosenzweig and Blackmar, *The Park and the People: A History of Central Park* (Ithaca, Cornell Univ. Press, 1992), 40–68, 80–85, 91.

[61] *Sydney Morning Herald*, Jan. 28, 1848, noted in Philip McMichael, *Settlers and the Agrarian Question* (Cambridge, 1984), 197.

The government sought to mollify the resistance by reducing the sum to be collected in the next levy substantially, but the district's M. P., Alex Clerke of Ringwood, publicly counseled further resistance, calling the rate unconstitutional. This drew praise from magistrate and railway commissioner Theodore Bartley, and payment in the Deloraine district ground almost came to a halt. Southern Tasmanians, annoyed that they were now expected to contribute some of the interest payment their northern compatriots were refusing to pay, won control of the legislature and moved to collect the rest of the rate. The northern ratepayers were, overwhelmingly, Nonconformists, and when they met in December, 1873, and agreed to engage in "passive resistance" (no further payments and no bids on any goods distrained by sheriffs), they began to use the rhetoric of their ancestors, invoking the memory of both John Hampden, whose opposition to King Charles' Ship-Money tax in 1635 made him an obvious political symbol, and Oliver Cromwell, who with his "Ironsides" were instrumental in securing victory for the Long Parliament over the King during the English Civil War. Some sixty-five of the seventy-nine magistrates in the northern districts petitioned the governor to delay the collection; when he refused, some twenty-eight resigned and most of the rest refused to hear the ensuing nonpayment cases or to issue summonses. Rate collectors and clerks of councils resigned, reporting the resistance "far more general and determined" than they were prepared to live with. Others were "hooted, hissed, tin-kettled, and threatened." On February 5, the colonial secretary was burnt in effigy and a riot ensued. But a handful of police magistrates and sheriffs carried out the distraints of goods and sales, protected by armed men. For decades northerners harbored resentment for what had been done to them.[62]

The Squattocracy in Australia and New Zealand reacted with both political efforts and a degree of violence to the reclamation of some of their sheep station tracts for homesteaders in the last forty years of the nineteenth century. And some of those homesteading "free selectors" struck back. John McQuilton argues convincingly that the "outbreak" of Ned Kelly and his gang in Victoria in the late 1870s was just such a reaction. But there were others who objected to "takings" in the Antipodes: "Takings" for roads in New Zealand produced fierce opposition on the North Island from Maori. The relevant legislation only provided compensation if the lands taken were "pahs, Native Villages, or cultivations." Maori "bush," left uncultivated but utilized for hunting, fishing, and timber, was "free for the Crown to take as it pleased." The Kingi government's newspaper reported the reaction of Tarei

---

[62] Stefan Petrow, "Resisting the Law: Opposition to the L & W Railway Rate, 1872–1874," 15 *University of Tasmania Law Review* 77 (1996).

Tukorehu in June, 1862, to word that Governor Grey was planning
a road from Auckland to Wellington. "If this road cuts through the
centre of this island, it . . . will die," just as a man dies "when you open
up [his] belly." The paper went on to assure readers that King Potatau
would not consent to such a project.[63]

Native department officials negotiated the acquiescence of Kingi
Maori for a road through land spiritually off-limits (*tapu*) west of Lake
Rotorua connecting Tauranga and Taupo in 1871 by pointing out the
benefits of seaport access, contracting for Maori labor with payments
in cash, and by promising to prevent Pakeha trespassing "in the pigeon-
trapping season." And in 1872 they provided advances to Maori in the
Napier region to repair a flour mill to secure their permission to built
a similar road that could serve to increase their access to markets for
their goods. But native department officials were not always as successful, nor as cooperative, as this. Some twenty Hauraki Maori expressed
their annoyance to the government in a petition in 1874. The presumption in English Law that the Crown possessed prerogatival rights
(of eminent domain) to seize up to five percent of one's land *without
compensation* offended them: "Now, friends, what harm is there in quietly asking the owner of property for his consent or refusal . . . ?" The
statute contained an "objectionable word: . . . 'take' [translated into
Maori as 'tango']." "Friends, amend this evil word which was at the
root of the Maori saying: 'If I am to die, I shall die upon my land.' This
expression gives an idea of trouble to come. If it does come, whose
fault will it be?"[64]

Maori resistance to the opening of roads and railways into or through
their lands was persistent, involving, at times, the destruction of survey
stakes and the harassing of surveyors and construction crews. Maori
resentment was exacerbated in the 1890s by efforts of the government
to charge the Maori property taxes for the maintenance of these roads
and bridges. In 1893, the Liberal government's minister for native
affairs sought to protect the Maori from such taxation by pointing
out (only *somewhat* speciously) that some road and bridge authorities
"carefully ignored" Maori land in order to keep its purchase price for

[63] David Williams, *'Te Kooti Tango Whenua: The Native Land Court, 1864–
1909* (Wellington, 1999), 196; McQuilton, *The Kelly Outbreak, 1878–1880*
(Mebourne, 1987); *Te Hokioi o Nui Tireni*, 15 June 1862; (I am indebted to
Ann Parsonson for this citation.).

For a comparable Aboriginal expression of annoyance over the "taking"
of land without asking, see the Fraser River Indian upset by the action
of the Canadian Pacific Railway, quoted in Cole Harris, *The Resettlement of
British Columbia*, 134.

[64] Ibid., 196–97. Cathy Marr, *Public Works Takings of Maori Land, 1870–1981*
(Wellington, Waitangi Tribunal Division, 1997), 92–93.

Diaspora newcomers low. But a Conservative government secured the tax in 1904.[65]

ANCIENT LIGHTS

Most state high courts in the United States abandoned the English common law easement of "ancient lights" in the mid-nineteenth century. This rule had it that if one owned a house with windows drawing light from over a neighbor's property for at least forty years, one acquired a prescriptive right to that light and could sue one whose construction blocked it. This sometimes led to preemptive action by a neighbor seeking to protect her future right to build; typically, one built a dead-wall some twenty-five to thirty feet in height near one's property line, blocking the lights at issue before the forty years had elapsed, a "most mischevous" and "wanton" act, but one flowing from the logic and nature of the English rule.[66] Jurists in the United States, no longer subject to review by Privy Council, signalled their independence from an "unneighborly" rule that seemed to them to have little to recommend it but its "ancient" lineage.[67]

Jurists in the CANZ domain felt they could do no such thing. One New Brunswick defendant's counsel cited the rule in the neighboring state of Maine, but plaintiff's counsel reminded the court that "your Honours cannot so hold" as had their colleagues in Maine. The court agreed. Chief Justice Carter of this same court had summed the matter up some twenty-one years earlier in another "ancient lights" case: This rule could not be challenged "without shaking important principles." And so said the courts of Ontario, Nova Scotia, South Australia, Victoria, New South Wales, the Australian High Court, and New Zealand.[68]

---

[65] John A. Williams, *Politics of the New Zealand Maori* (1969), 24–25. Convictions for such obstructions of surveyors in the Ngarara Block in the 1880s were affirmed in *Wi Parata v. Climate*, 8NZLR (SC) 7 (1889).

[66] Thus in *Cross v. Lewis*, 2 B. & C. 686, 107, ER 538 (1824), Justice Bayley observed that "if his neighbor objects to [his neighbor's window so near his property line as to constitute grounds for a future "ancient lights" easement claim], he may put up an obstruction, ... his only remedy...."

[67] See Karsten, *Heart versus Head*, Chapter 4, for discussion of the rule and its abandonment in the United States.

[68] *Ring v. Pugsley*, 18 New Br. 303 at 308, 310 (1878); *Longmaid v. McNichol*, 8 New Br. 497 (1857); *Carter v. Grasett*, 14 Ont. C. of A. 685 (1888), affirming *Same*, 11 Ont. R 331 (1887) (though here the matter was one of contract: the "implied grant of light."); *Renner v. Halifax Steamboat Co.*, 9 Nova Sc. 337 (1873); *Thwaites v. Brake*, 21 Vict. LR 729 (1895); *White v. McLean*, 24 So. Aus. R. 17 (1890); *Delohery v. Perm. Trustee Co. of NSW*, 1 CLR (Austr.) 283 at 311–13 (1904) (Griffith, C. J.: "American judges" might hold the

POLLUTION NUISANCES

As industrialization slowly proceeded in the mid- and late-nineteenth century, American courts were confronted with suits by property owners claiming that an industrial neighbor's air- or water-borne pollutants were nuisances, and asking that the firm either be enjoined from further pollution or be ordered to pay damages. Many state high courts simply adopted English rules and precedents to govern these matters, but a few engaged in a very un-English "balancing of the equities" to determine whether the polluter should be allowed to continue operations. Most courts did not allow polluters to defend themselves by arguing that they had been in operation before the plaintiff had established herself in the neighborhood (a defense sometimes allowed in England) and many also did not allow the polluter to use in his defense evidence of the "nature of the neighborhood" – that is, low-income, urban industrialized areas were not automatically treated as acceptable places to pollute (as they sometimes were in England).[69]

Jennifer Nedelsky has described the "judicial conservatism" of Canadian jurists deciding nuisance cases in the late nineteenth and early twentieth centuries. These admirers of all-things-Westminster showed *none* of the innovative propensities of their compeers south of the border; they did not even draw on the "flexibility to ease the burdens on industry" that appeared in a *few* English opinions in the late nineteenth century. However, of sixteen cases where the "local standards or character of the neighborhood" had been raised as an issue (three out of four times, by the defendant company), the complainant–plaintiff lost only once. Defenses based on a company's claim of the industry's importance, or of the lack of any proof that it had behaved "negligently" (a defense that had acquired some standing in England by the twentieth century), were also rejected. Canadian jurists of the early twentieth century said nothing in *dicta* of a need to adjust the law of nuisance to the industrial demands of a modernizing nation. On the contrary, they observed that only legislatures could change such rules.[70]

---

rule to be lacking "sound principles and natural justice. This, however, is not a matter on which we are called upon to express an opinion."); *New Zealand Loan & Merc. Ag. v. Wellington Corp.*, 9 N.Z.L.R. 10 (1893). (In 1894 a New Zealand statute abrogated all future ancient lights easements.)

[69] See Christine Rosen, "Differing Perspectives of Value: Cost-Benefit Analysis in Pollution Nuisance Law, 1840–1904," 11 *Law & History Review* 303 (1994); Karsten, *Heart versus Head*, 134–43; John McLaren, "Environmental Regulation of the Canadian Timber Industry of the 19th Century," 33 *Univ. of New Brunswick Law Journal* 203 (1984).

[70] J. Nedelsky, "Judicial Conservatism in an Age of Innovation: Comparative

Nedelsky's universe of cases included only three from the nineteenth century Canadian reports, and I wondered whether a reading of earlier evidence of judicial views on nuisance law among the various Canadian reports of the nineteenth century might find any benches more inclined to favor industrial entrepreneurs. I detected a total of fourteen reports of decisions involving pollution nuisances by appellate courts of one or another Canadian province, from 1849 to 1899. Polluters lost eleven of thirteen,[71] and there was virtually no sign of either a proentrepreneurial disposition or of an innovative propensity. Twice jurists rejected the defendant's defense that the plaintiff had "come to the nuisance" – that is, had moved into the neighborhood after the nuisance had existed for some time.[72] Twice they ruled that there would be no "balancing of the equities" either by judge or jury, no inquiry "as to the balance of advantage or disadvantage to the public" from the alleged nuisance. A fertilizer manufacturer in Quebec learned that the maxim *sic utere tuo, ut alienum non laedas* (use your property, but not to the injury of others) was a "beautiful" and "Christian" rule of "pure morality" that epitomized the law of nuisance both in England and the *Coutumes de Paris*, and that he must cease operation, "notwithstanding the value of the process" to the public and notwithstanding the fact that the sufferers were mere prisoners in "the common gaol."[73] An electric power plant was told that it had made the owner of an apartment building and shop suffer smoke damage "beyond what she is obliged to endure under the [Quebecoise] rules of

Perspectives on Canadian Nuisance Law, 1880–1930," in *Essays in the History of Canadian Law*, ed. David H. Flaherty (Toronto, 1981), I, 281–322, esp. 282, 287, 291, 293–94, 296–97, 306, 310, 311. (She notes that northern Ontario nickel smelters appeared to be the only polluters to be viewed by the courts (in 1917) as being entitled to proceed despite harm done to such farming as could be done in the area, because of the importance of the industry to Canada.)

71 These were: *Rowe v. Titus*, 6 New Br. 326 (1849); *Radenhurst v. Coate*, 6 Grant's Ch. 139 (1857); *Queen v. Brewster & Cook*, 8 U.C.C.P. 208 (1857); *Regina v. Bruce*, 10 Lower Can. R. 117 (1860); *Mitchell v. Barry*, 26 UCQB 416(1867); *St. Charles v. Doutre*, 26 Quebec 25 (1874); *Mayor of Sorel v. Vincent*, 32 Lower Can. J. 314 (1889); *Drysdale v. Dugas*, 16 Q.C.S. 195 (1893); *same*, 26 Can. S. C. R. 20 (1895) (Gwynne, J., diss.); *Gallery v. City of Montreal*, 8 Quebec C.S. 166 (1895); *Carpentier v. LaVille de Maisonneuve*, 11 Quebec S. C. 242 (1897); and *Francklyn v. People's Heat & Light*, 32 Nova Sc. R. 44 (1899).

In *Lawrason v. Paul*, 11 U.C.Q. B. 534 (1854), the court decided, procedurally, that the tenant suffering the pollution-smell of a nearby stable must sue, not his landlord.

72 *Queen v. Brewster & Cook*, 8 UCCP 208 (1857); *St.-Charles v. Doutre*, 26 Q 25 (1874).

73 Chipman J. in *Rowe v. Titus*, 6 New Br. 326 at 335 (1849); Aylwin J., *Regina v. Bruce*, 10 Lower Can. R. 117 at 120 (1860).

good neighborhood," notwithstanding the fact that her husband, a member of the town council, had voted for the creation of the power plant.[74]

The two victories for industry, both from the courts of late nineteenth century Quebec, were consistent with both English and French cases and treatises: Coal loading elevators in the Montreal ocean terminus were, by law, no nuisances according to the Superior Court for that city, for the law recognized "the dominating rights of a public harbour" in a "great port."[75] That same court fined a tannery $500 for polluting a stream and enjoined it from further operation as a consequence of the complaint of a riparian neighbor and "chemical analysis" of the water, despite the fact that the neighbor had just moved to the stream, that the tannery was one of several in the area, that it had been in operation for some fifty years, and that the municipal council had not taken public action against the tanneries. This combination of facts proved too much for Quebec's Appellate Court of Queen's Bench. They reversed. Tanneries should be regulated by the municipality and the courts, Justice Cross insisted, but there had to be a place for them somewhere, and this municipality's council had not chosen to regulate them. Moreover, those living even closer to the source than did this plaintiff had not joined in the complaint. In words that could easily be viewed as proentrepreneurial instrumentalism, Chief Justice Dorion offered a "worst case" rationale in *dicta* for the reversal:

> This is a matter of great importance to all the manufacturers in the country, for if Claude's establishment could be shut up for this cause, then anyone would have a right to close up any establishment because some inconvenience was suffered from it.... The inhabitants of Longue Pointe might compel the City of Montreal to close its drains. The mills on the rivers above us might be compelled to close because they polluted the river with sawdust.[76]

Viewed out of context, Chief Justice Dorion's remarks could make Quebec's judiciary of the late nineteenth century appear to be quite tolerant of municipal and industrial pollution, oblivious to English and French precedent. But we can see them in a larger context, one quite dominated by precedent, be it that of English Common Law or the Quebec-French *droit commun*. And this dominant legal system,

---

[74] Archibald J. in *Carpentier v. La Ville de Maisonneuve*, 11 Q.C.S. 242 at 244, 250 (1897).

[75] *Robins v. Dominion Coal Co.*, 16 Q.C.S. 195 at 199, 201 (1899).

[76] Dorion, C. J. in *Weir v. Claude*, 32 LCJ 213 at 220 (1888), reversing *Same*, 31 L.C.J. 39 (1886).

demanding of industry virtually the same behavior as of any other property-owing neighbor, could only be set aside to aid the forces of progress and development by either legislative intervention or private negotiation and a buyout of aggrieved plaintiffs downwind of the source of pollution.[77] Canada's judiciaries were very leery of judge-made innovation.[78]

TRESPASSES

Milldams, Drainage Ditches, Boundaries, Fences, and Rights-of-way

Disputes over milldams, drainage ditches, boundary lines, fences, and cattle in railroad rights-of-way were steady sources of tension throughout the lands of the British Diaspora. Such disputes could be handled in a neighborly fashion or they could lead to a unneighborly behavior and a lawsuit, or worse – to violence.

For example, George Howell, riparian owner of one side of a stretch of the Parramatta River, built a milldam in 1828, ignoring the protests of John Raine, owner of that part of the opposite bank that was adversely affected by the dam. After "many fruitless negotiations," Raine sought justice from the local magistrate, John MacArthur, a prominent Exclusivist magnate and member of New South Wales' legislative council. But MacArthur proved to be an ally of Howell's. Finding no help from that quarter, Raine took self-help by cutting a ditch to regain

---

[77] Jennifer Nedelsky offers evidence of precisely these two alternatives in Nova Scotia after the *St. Helens Smelting v. Tipping* sort of decision in *Francklyn v. People's Heat & Light*, 32 N.S.R. 44 (1899) in Nedelsky, *supra* note 60, 310.

   Another important way that the judiciary's propensity to curb polluters could be checked was for the attorney general to decline to bring public suits and bills forward, ignoring the appeals of townships, other businesses, and groups of individuals. For an example of this see J. I. Little, *Nationalism, Capitalism, and Colonization in 19th Century Quebec* (Kingston, 1989) 110–111 (on Govt. inaction against Clark and Co.)

[78] I detected very few such pollution nuisance cases in either the early, Kercher manuscript reports or the later, published appellate reports of New South Wales. But both *Munn v. Bettington* (NSWSC, Kercher, 1831) (no injunction granted to shipbuilder to prevent owner of wharfage property in Darling Harbour from construction that affected shipbuilder's access to deep water; referred to Common-Law remedy of damages) and *Hood v. Corp. of Sydney*, 2 Leg. R. (NSW) 1244 (1860) (barring so vital an activity in that colony as wool-washing, when that polluting activity was carried on in a stream that provided potable water to the community) suggest that jurists there were just as unwilling to ignore English precedent as their Canadian counterparts.

water for his field. MacArthur thereupon "employed his own men" and encouraged Howell and his supporters to join them in filling in Raine's ditch, not once, but twice (after Raine rebuilt it). MacArthur was quoted as saying that Howell was "making 500 pounds by his mill, and there is that fellow," Raine, "not worth two-pence, wanting to ruin him.... But I'll make him smart!"

Raine sought a criminal action against MacArthur for causing "a riot." This the colony's supreme court refused, "because they saw blame on both sides." Chief Justice Forbes lamented that "the more judicious course" had not been "resorted to," that of trying the legal questions "by civil action instead of resorting to violent measures," but the court was sufficiently annoyed with MacArthur's behavior to make him pay the costs of this unsuccessful action.[79]

Two more examples of drainage ditches that proved damaging to "good neighborhood," in other Diaspora domains: A farmer's ditch had produced flooding on another farmer's land in Livingston County, Michigan, in 1883. The cutting of this ditch first "led to a war of words" and then to violence as one farmer drew a knife and advanced on his neighbor and the other struck him, knocking him to the ground. The two men and their sons ended up in court where a jury heard their stories of property loss, bad blood, and assault.[80] Two neighboring farmers in Goulburn, Upper Canada, had a falling out in 1852 over a new boundary drainage ditch one had cut and the other had obstructed. First the town's fenceviewers, then a trial court and jury, and finally the appellate Court of Queen's Bench had to be called upon to settle the matter. Chief Justice Sir John Beverley Robinson began his opinion on the matter by commenting on the "captious" behavior of the parties in this "tedious and expensive law suit about so mere a trifle" when "a few hour's labor would have opened a passage for the water...."[81]

Robinson was certainly quite right in one sense: "Rational" neighbors would not squander their scarce resources and poison their relationships in such ways. But (as he may well have appreciated) he was quite wrong in another sense: Some neighbors behaved in quite "irrational" fashion when it came to trespasses (as, indeed, some still do).

---

[79] MacArthur thereupon threatened to initiate impeachment proceedings in the legislative council against the justices, prompting Forbes to write to the Colonial Office in their defense. Under-Secretary James Stephen commented on MacArthur's action subsequently with unveiled allusions to the "indiscretions and infirmities of temper" of such "Colonial Functionaries" as that magnate. *Rex v. MacArthur* (NSWSC, Kercher, 1828).

[80] *Daniel Newman v. Maynard Bowman*, Howell's Michigan Nisi Prius Cases 46 (1884).

[81] In *Malone v. Faulkner*, 11 U.C.Q. B. 116 at 122 (1853).

Again, two examples: When Andrew Sherk of southwestern Ontario decided to raise his milldam some two feet in the 1840s, he flooded a road used by the Wintermute farm, and destroyed forty acres of meadow and several fruit trees. Sherk and his father had for some time "been quarling" with neighbors "about the Roads which they flood." Wintermute complained to Sherk of the damage and Sherk responded in an obstinate and obstreperous manner. He and his associates appeared "out side of Wintermute's Door Yard Blaggarding and Abusing Wintermute's family...." " Wintermute responded with a lawsuit.[82] In the summer of 1849, two neighbors reached an impasse over their common boundary line, at the juncture of Portugal Cove Road and Torbay Road in St John's, Newfoundland. One put up a fence; the other threw it down. Later in the day the first put it up again with his hired hands, and the other "with 10 or 12 men, again knocked it down, and on this occasion, also, assaulted the plaintiff." This dispute produced a lawsuit and a jury verdict that the assailant pay £10 to his victim, as well as court costs and attorney fees.[83]

The wise settler sought to resolve such disputes informally, by direct negotiation with the neighbor, by town meeting as in Ontario,[84] or by calling upon another neighbor or local official to mediate the matter, as E. R. Chudleigh did in New Zealand, in 1868.[85] Later, Chudleigh became a magistrate himself, in Waitangi, Chatham Island, and by 1883 he was recording with annoyance the aggravation he and his fellow magistrates went through involving a single fencing dispute: He and a colleague had "a miserable day going through law & justice" with a Mr. Deighton, their colleague, the stipendary magistrate, who was "quite ignorant of all [such] law." This was particularly distressing for "as he is a paid officer there is a want of justice to the public in being ignorant." They fined one of the parties, who then demanded a viewing of the fences and boundaries at issue, and the three magistrates had to "spend 3 days inspecting roads because of Hay's Irish temper. He will be nasty," Chudleigh told his diary.[86]

---

[82] Statement of John Storne and John Peter, #5, Miscellaneous MSS, MU 7175, Archives of Ontario.

[83] Sean Madigan, *Hope and Deception at Conception Bay*, 76, 78; *McGill v. Morley*, 3 Newf.R. 146 (1850). The defendant learned little from this, for he appealed, winning a new trial on a pleading error of the plaintiff that could only have resulted in an even greater award for the plaintiff on retrial. See also *Curtiss v. Townsend*, 6 UCCP 255 (1857), a case with similar facts.

[84] G. P. de T. Glazebrook, "The Origins of Local Government," in *Aspects of 19th Century Ontario*, ed. F. H. Armstrong, et al. (Toronto, 1974), 44.

[85] E. R. Chudleigh, *The Diary of E. R. Chudleigh, 1862–1921* (Christchurch, 1950), 215.

[86] Three days later these magistrates functioned as arbitrators. They rode

In Victoria, Edward Curr and his fellow Squatters were regularly
visited as early as 1842 by a roving commissioner of Crown Lands whose
duties included the resolution of boundary disputes. Curr liked this
particular official's informality:

> Disagreements on this score, which in later times would have taken
> a judge, with his jurors, barristers, witnesses, and attaches of the
> court, a week to dispose of – Bah! The Commissioner settled them
> in half-an-hour, or less... [and] kept few records of his official
> acts, if any... his custom in cases of disputes... being to hear but
> short statements, give his decision in few words, change the con-
> versation, light his pipe & ride away.... [I]t was well enough suited
> to the times, & so gave great satisfaction.[87]

Conciliatory acts were less expensive, more neighborly, and more
likely to produce reciprocal behavior, as these and other incidents in
the historical record of New South Wales and Victoria make clear.[88]

Another common cause of disputes had to do with the responsibility to fence cattle grazing adjacent railroad rights-of-way. Some legislatures required railroad companies to fence their entire right-of-way;
some others imposed no such duty; most statutes were compromises,
drawing distinctions between rural and urban areas, requiring less of
the railroads in the former than the latter.

A case in point: The first major railroad in Michigan was owned and
operated by the state; it was also unfenced. When trains hit sheep, cattle, and horses, this state-owned entity simply paid full compensation
to the animals' owners, asking no questions of liability. When the railroad passed into private hands in 1846 and reemerged with some fresh
eastern capital as the Michigan Central, its charter imposed no more
duties to fence than had that of its predecessor. But the new management, feeling less sense of public responsibility, and less political heat,
offered only to split the cost of the value of animals hit on the tracks.

Aggrieved owners grew incensed at the change in policy and increasingly restless about their inability to reverse it. As one pointed out in a

---

"to the fence at Ocean Bay" where they "viewed the fences, roads &
creeks; read the evidence on the spot & soon fixed things." *Chudleigh Diary*,
316, 322.

[87] Edward Curr, *Recollections of a Squatter in Victoria* (Melbourne, 1883),
117–18. See also George F. Moore, *Diary of Ten Years' Eventful Life of an
Early Settler in Western Australia* (London, 1884), 58 (arbitrating a boundary
dispute in Western Australia in the 1830s).

[88] See C. M. H. Clark, *A History of Australia* (Melbourne, 1978), IV, 166 (on
some farmers and pastoralists sharing seed, machinery, workers, and ideas
in mid-century); Peter Taylor, *Station Life in Australia: Pioneers and Pastoralists* (Sydney, 1988), 75 (on station run neighbors fighting fires on one
another's land for two or three days running in the 1840s).

letter to a local paper in 1849, the policy effectively deprived graziers of rights, since "all cattle are by law free commoners" in Michigan, while trains ran "at the rate of 30 miles per hour" through their unfenced fields. And to sue the company for damages typically cost more than the animals were worth.

The Michigan Central's superintendent, confident of the company's legal rights, disingenuously offered to a committee of these aggrieved farmers and graziers $50 for their legal fees and costs were they to agree to bring a "test" case on appeal to the state's supreme court. That committee rejected the offer, but two years later another individual did pursue such an appeal, unsuccessfully. The railroad's charter imposed no duty to fence; hence it had no liability to animal owners. Unconvinced, angry settlers in Jackson County turned to violence, stoning trains and damaging tracks. Infiltrated by company agents and spies, over thirty of these "conspirators" were tried for criminal conspiracy and arson in 1851; twelve were convicted, despite the courtroom defense services of New York's Senator William Seward. But four years later, after the twelve had been pardoned, a Republican-dominated state legislature passed a statute requiring that all railroads construct and maintain fencing along the greater part of their rights-of-way or pay the price to those whose animals became victims of these modern engines of progress.[89]

Simultaneously, cattle owners in Upper Canada reported to a legislative committee in 1854 that the engineers of the Great Western Railway regarded the hitting of cattle on their tracks as "great sport." We do not know more of the specifics here. Perhaps some of the owners took action similar to their peers in Jackson County, but it is more probable that they stopped short of this, satisfied after having been heard by the legislative committee, whatever the results of its report may have been.[90]

Animal Trespasses and the Problem of Social Costs

In 1837, a Maori Bay-of-Islands chief asked missionary Samuel Marsden to "give us a Law" on a number of disputes common to Maori *runangas* (dispute settlement forums). He described four such issues. Fighting, adultery, and master-slave relations were three of these, but the first mentioned, and the one the chief devoted the most attention to was

---

[89] See *Williams v. Michigan Central RR*, 2 Mich. 259(1851); Charles Hirschfield, "The Great Railroad Conspiracy," 36 *Michigan History* 97 at 99–101, 103, 124, 217 (1952).

[90] Peter Baskerville, "Transportation, Social Change and State Formation, Upper Canada, 1841–1864," in *Colonial Leviathan*, ed. Allan Greer & Ian Radforth (Toronto, 1992), 238–39.

the problem of trespassing pigs. "My Law (*Ritenga*) is . . . that the Man who kills Pigs for trespassing on his Plantation, having neglected to fence, had rather pay for the Pigs so killed. . . . Fenced Cultivations, when trespassed on, should be paid for."[91]

That, in any event, was the way that Marsden represented this Bay-of-Islands chief's views of Maori law regarding animal trespasses. On the face of it, this rule does not seem terribly different from English law. But some of the other Maori and English rules regarding animal trespasses and fencing differed sharply, and these differences amounted to what economists call high transaction costs, which could have prevented the two cultures from reaching the sorts of "rational" agreements that members of a single culture often managed when faced with legal rules inconsistent with their own norms or mutual interests. How uncommon were disputes over animal trespasses among the British Diaspora themselves – that is, among settler neighbors in North America and the Antipodes who shared the same "high" and "low" legal cultures? These questions are significant because of the way that animal trespass law and human behavior have been linked by Law & Economics analysts. I think this is an important enough issue to begin this part of my story by telling you what these analysts have had to say.

The Law & Economics Model: Coase, Ellickson, and Cattle in the Corn
Legislatures, municipal councils, and courts (creators of "high" legal culture) have decided what the Law with regard to animal trespasses is, but the ways that people have resolved disputes over such trespasses have often not corresponded to the letter of that Law. Courts can and will enforce animal trespass statutes and ordinances when matters are brought before them, but animal trespass disputes were, and still are, generally settled "out of court," according to customary norms rather than by the formal letter of the Law. The Nobel Prize-winning economist Ronald Coase has argued in his famous essay, "The Problem of Social Costs," that those who suffer a loss of property due to a breach in a fence shared with a neighbor do not turn to the courts for relief. Instead, Coase tells us, the two parties bargain to terms reflecting the relative value each place on the property at stake in the dispute. The

---

[91] Alan Ward, *A Show of Justice: Racial "Amalgamation" in Nineteenth Century New Zealand* (Auckland, 1973), 27, 50. On more recent evidence that trespassing pigs in the gardens of South Pacific Islanders was (along with women-stealing and rape) a major cause of warfare (this time in New Guinea villages) see Roy Rappaport, *Pigs for the Ancestors: Ritual in the Ecology of a New Guinea People* (New Haven, 1967), 110. See also V. C. Wynne-Edwards, *Animal Dispersion in Relation to Social Behavior* (London, 1962).

Coase theorem assumes that ranchers and graziers will negotiate with farmers as rational profit maximizers, factoring the relevant legal rule extant on their lands into the bargaining like any other cost of doing business, and the one will buy out the other's legal entitlement at a figure that allows both to benefit financially. "If it is inevitable that some cattle will stray," he writes, "an increase in the supply of meat can only be obtained at the expense of a decrease in the supply of crops. The nature of the choice is clear: meat or crops." The rancher "will pay the market price for any crop damaged."[92]

Robert Ellickson has put Coase's theorem to the test by observing actual rancher-nonrancher behavior regarding animal trespasses in modern Shasta County, California. Most of Shasta County is subject to an open or "range" law, allowing ranchers to graze their cattle freely and requiring farmers and others who do not want damage to their crops, shrubs, or gardens to fence cattle out. But two significant portions of it, constituting about sixty square miles, have been zoned "closed," subject to "herd" law, which requires ranchers to fence their animals in to avoid liability. Hence, this county served as an ideal test for Coase's prediction that ranchers and farmers would take the applicable rule of law into account and bargain as rational actors.

Ellickson found rancher-other bargaining of sorts, but in forms that did not correspond to Coase's model. Firstly, ranch and ranchette owners (there were few farmers) simply split the costs of most animal trespasses and of any fencing constructed in the open, "range law" areas. Secondly, where ranchers fenced their cattle out of ranchette owners' shrubs and gardens in land zoned closed, the rancher paid all of the cost. Thirdly, the costs of repairing the boundary fences were never billed, despite the fact that the two parties rarely made the repairs together; they simply did what they felt ought to be done and assumed there would in time be forthcoming a reciprocal act. Finally, ranchers whose property was located in the open areas nevertheless acted quickly to remove their cattle from the property of a ranchette owner who had called them and often provided labor and equipment to replant or otherwise undo the damage.

Thus, one of Ellickson's findings was that the parties almost invariable behaved the same in both open and closed areas, as if the rule privileging one or the other party did not exist. Indeed, in one instance, after a heated political effort had resulted in the closing of a large tract of range to free-roaming cattle, the ranchette owners behaved as they had before they had gained this legal entitlement!

---

[92] Ronald Coase, "The Problem of Social Costs," 3 *Journal of Law & Economics* 1 at 4(1960). Cf. William Landes & Richard Posner, *The Economic Structure of Tort Law* (1987), 110–11 (economic analysis of fencing law).

This he attributes in *part* to their overestimation of the transaction costs of litigation. But he also points to a second finding, a kind of cultural norm: Being a "good neighbor." "Being good neighbors" was very important, one resident told him, and that meant cooperating, accomodating, and, above all, "no lawsuits."[93]

Ellickson explains this cooperative behavior with a rational-actor model he calls "welfare-maximizing." Thus, he relies on Law & Economics methodology and assumptions, while displaying great sensitivity to actual on-the-ground fact of life. But, in the process, he dismisses anthropological and sociological models of human behavior and dispute resolution.[94]

While some neighbors follow Coase's bargaining model and others behave as did Ellickson's Shasta County folk, that may still not exhaust the universe of experience nor of models of that experience. Ellickson's neighbors were, first and foremost, modern Euro-Americans, and may not be characteristic of how animal trespass and fencing matters were dealt with when and where the parties were not of similar cultural backgrounds. Moreover, his subjects were ranch and ranchette owners, not ranchers and farmers, and it is entirely possible that farmers using land for income crops might deal with animal trespasses in a manner more consistent with Coase's theorem. Ellickson wondered about this, and at one point he sought aid from the historical record. But he reports that his "search for evidence of animal trespass norms in the nineteenth century proved to be unavailing." Evidence about the norms that prevailed in the past "is inherently difficult to obtain." Nevertheless, for those inclined to try, he suggested that "old diaries, letters and newspaper stories may contain aspirational statements, descriptions of practices, and accounts of self-help enforcement."[95] He was right. Such sources of information provide us with insights into the informal norms people actually used in disputes over animal trespasses and fencing in the lands of the British Diaspora. Let us first summarize the formal Law of legislatures, councils, and courts with regard to these issues, and then let us turn to the evidence of those informal norms, distinguishing between settler-settler disputes, on the one hand, and native-settler disputes, on the other.

---

[93] Robert Ellickson, *Order Without Law: How Neighbors Settle Disputes* (1991), 60, 72–77.

[94] See Barbara Yngvesson, "Beastley Neighbors: Continuing Relations in Cattle Country," 102 *Yale Law Journal* 1787–1801 (1993); Mark Cooney, "Why is Economic Analysis so Appealing to Law Professors?" 45 *Stanford Law Review* 2211–30 (1993); and Lewis Kornhauser, "Are There Cracks in the Foundations of Spontaneous Order?" 51 *New York University Law Review* 647–73 (1992).

[95] Ellickson, 187, 188n.

The Formal Law

Fencing laws varied from region to region over the course of time. Early (pre-Norman) English Law favored animal husbandry over mere cultivators and put the burden of fencing animals out on the cultivator (which came to be known as "range" law). By 1600, however, the English agricultural landscape had developed to the point that the Law shifted the legal burden of fencing cattle out onto the owner of the animals ("herd" law). An aggrieved cultivator was free either to "distrain the cattle . . . doing damage, till the owner shall make his satisfaction," or simply to sue for damages.[96] English and Scottish settlers in Ulster in the seventeenth century, however, "allowed their animals to range over an unenclosed countryside," as did early New Englanders and most other colonists, favoring animal husbandry in the first stages of settlement. Thus, the burden of fencing cattle out was returned to the cultivator.[97]

The destructive pig was treated differently. Pigs were allowed to fodder on the commons and on the "waste" ("the woods" in America; the "bush" in the Antipodes), but they were to be yoked or ringed (to prevent their burrowing under simple fences and to facilitate their control), and as early as 1633, a Massachusetts ordinance stipulated that "it shal be lawfull for any man to kill any swine that comes into his corne."[98] Unringed and uncollared pigs were the subject of many

[96] William Blackstone, *Commentaries on the Law of England* (Oxford, 1769), Vol. 3, 211.

[97] On Ulster, see Nicholas Canny, *Kingdom and Colony: Ireland in the Atlantic World, 1560–1800* (Baltimore, 1988), 83.

The issue and its solution were the same in the Mississippi French community of St. Genevieve. When Charles Valle's oxen trampled M. Peyroux's garden in 1972, that neighbor's note to Valle, complaining of the damages, presumed Valle's obligation to fence the animals out under the custom of the region. Stuart Banner, "Written Law and Unwritten Norms in Colonial St. Louis," 14 *Law and History Review* 33 at 57 (1996).

[98] Where statutory duties were ambiguous or parties preferred other arrangements, neighbors sometimes recorded agreements regarding fencing with the town clerk, as in seventeenth century Hingham, Massachusetts. The pig-trespass ordinance of 1633 was inspired by the killing of such animals by native American neighbors of Puritan farmers. See David Grayson Allen, *In English Ways: The Movement of Societies and the Transformation of English Local Law and Custom to Massachusetts Bay in the 17th Century* (Chapel Hill, 1981), 43, 49, 50, 56, 76, 158, 221; William Cronon, *Changes in the Land: Indians, Colonists and the Ecology of New England* (N.Y., 1983), 135–37. See also Alvin Peters, "Posts & Palings, Posts & Planks," *12 Kansas History* 222 (1990); Yasuhide Kawashima, "Fence Laws on the Great Plains, 1865–1900," in *Essays on English Law and the American Experience*, ed. Elizabeth Cawthon and David Narrett (College Sta., Tex., 1994); *Cole v. Tucker*, 6 Texas 266 (1851); *Aylesworth v. Herrington*, 17 Mich. 416 (1868); *Cameron v. Reed*, 2 Mich.

lawsuits in seventeenth and eighteenth century Montreal. One ordinance in that city, as in its southern New England counterparts, allowed one who found a pig on her field at an unsanctioned time of year to kill the animal. After several *habitants* took full advantage of that recourse, however, their swine-owning neighbors angrily objected, and in 1687, a new ordinance forbade them from "killing more than one pig at a time." Later, the government sought to reduce the problem by encouraging the fencing of fields. Any *habitant* could "ask that a fence and a ditch be built at his and his neighbor's expense." If the latter refused, "he was forced to repay his share." But this process "advanced extremely slowly," and the local court continued to honor *vaine pâture* (the communal right to graze animals on the unfenced fallow of others after harvest and before replanting) long after it was abolished by decree in 1725, as Louise Dechene explains.[99]

The same Law of fencing was not required of the Aboriginal people. The Plymouth and Massachusetts governments and the Virginia House of Burgesses, for example, required newcomer–settlers either to keep their hogs and cattle away from the unfenced crops of the natives or to help natives who were without tools and skills "in feling of Trees, . . . sharpning railes, and holing of posts" for fencing. In exchange natives so protected would maintain the fence and surrender

Nisi Prius (Brown) 150 (1871); *Wellis v. Beal*, 9 Kans. 406 (1872); Charles Carroll, *The Timber Industry in Puritan New England* (Providence, 1973), 63.

99 Louise Dechêne, *Habitants and Merchants in 17th Century Montreal*, 176–77 (pigs); *Les Curé et Marguilliers de l'OEuvre et Fabrique de l'Isle Perrot v. Ricard*, 9 Lower C. J. 99 (1864) (no prescriptive right created by fence on neighbor's land for some forty years with his acquiescence); *Ricard v. La Fabrique de la paroisse St. Jeanne . . .* (unreported, Q. B. Montreal, 1868) (reversing *Les Curé v. Ricard*; prescriptive right created by such a fence); *Martin v. Jones*, 15 Lower C. J. 6 (1869) (Martin, J., Ct. of Review, Montreal, relying on plaintiff's having "acquised in, and even highly approved of" the defendant's construction of a boundary fence and his promise "to pay half the price of building it . . . operated as a kind of *fin de non recevoir* against the plaintiff"); *Pattenaude v. Charron*, 17 Lower C. J. 85 (1870) (Same, citing *Ricard II*); *Whitman v. Corp.of Town of Stanbridge*, 26 Lower C. J. 144 (1881) (Queen's Bench, Montreal: The Civil Code required proprietors "to make, in equal portions or at common expense, between their respective lands, a fence . . . according to the custom . . . of the locality," but the fencing of a municipality's front road was entirely at the expense of the private landowner, a "most economical" practice (Cross, J., 147).

Similarly, in French-colonial Louisiana cattleowners were, by an ordinance in 1770, granted *vaine pâture* "from the eleventh of November one year, to the fifteenth of March the next." Daniel Unser, *Indians, Settlers and Slaves in a Frontier Exchange: The Lower Mississippi Valley before 1783* (Chapel Hill, 1992), 188.

the right to sue for damages to their corn unless they could establish that the animal trespass had come through no fault of theirs. Some laws held the towns in which such animal owners resided to be responsible for securing compensation.[100] The seasonally mobile Algonquins had little experience with such tame herbivores; hence this rule *seemed* a sensible way to keep peace.

Later, by the nineteenth century, in some regions of North America, the rule of Law was that animals should be fenced in, and there natives who had acquired herds of their own, used to letting those animals forage on the vast "commons" that surrounded their campsites, were called to task, as in British Columbia, where Nicola tribesmen suffered "heavy fines" in 1871 when their cattle pillaged a British settler's grainfield, and in Oklahoma in the early twentieth century, where Creek animals trespassing on the fields of nonnative farmers were subjected to impoundment.[101] Moreover, in those same years the Massachusetts Supreme Judicial Court "rediscovered" English Common-Law rules that weakened the ordinances favoring herdsmen. But while Massachusetts was closing the range, the South's antebellum courts continued to uphold as constitutional those ordinances and statutes requiring landowners to fence animals out. The Southern range was not closed to the herdsman's wandering cattle until legislatures, voters, and county officials changed the rules in the late nineteenth century.[102] (See Illustrations 11 through 15.)

The governments of Ontario, New South Wales, New Zealand, and Fiji also created ordinances regarding animals and fencing, and their courts heard a number of cases involving, animal trespasses, and the

[100] See, for example, Virginia DeJohn Anderson, "King Philip's Herds: Indians, Colonists, and the Problem of Livestock in Early New England," 51 *William & Mary Quarterly* 601 at 608, 611 (1994). Thus, in 1662 the Virginians ordered the Rappahannocks and their white neighbors to maintain one hog keeper on each side to reduce that source of friction. Gwenda Morgan, *The Hegemony of the Law: Richmond County, Virginia* (N.Y., 1989), 28.

[101] Stephen Potter, *Commoners, Tribute and Chiefs: Algonquians in the Potomac Valley* (Charlottesville, Univ. Of Virginia Press, 1993), 196; Sidney Harring, *Crow Dog's Case* (N.Y., Cambridge Univ. Press, 1994), 96–97; Robin Fisher, *Contact and Conflict: Indian-European Relations in British Columbia, 1774–1890* (Vancouver, Univ. Of British Columbia Press, 1977), 200.

[102] Stephen Hahn, "Hunting, Fishing and Foraging: Common Rights and Class Relations in the Postbellum South," 26 *Radical History Review* 37 (1982); Shawn Kantor and Morgan Kousser, "Common Sense or Commonwealth? The Fence Law and Institutional Change in the Postbellum South," with Reply by Hahn and Rejoinder by Kantor and Kousser, 59 *Journal of Southern History* 201 (1983); R. Ben Brown, *Closing the Southern Range: A Chapter in the Decline of Southern Yeomanry* (Amer. Bar Found. Working Paper, 1990), 3; *Cantrell v. Adderholt*, 28 Ga. 239(1858); R. Ben Brown, "*Let Us Confound Them*" (Amer. Bar Found. Work. Paper, 1989).

misuse of tubary (the right to graze animals on the unfenced fallow of others after harvest and before planting).[103] In New South Wales, before the creation of Responsible Government, the governors of this penal colony often created ordinances by proclamation, but when Governor Lachlan Macquarie decided in 1820 that farmers were to fence cattle out of their crops, the colony's sole justice, Barron Field, objected to this very un-English decree and prepared a proclamation for the governor announcing its recission. Shortly after the beginnings of the Diaspora's use of New South Wales for cultivation and grazing, magistrates heard complaints of damage to crops by trespassing horses and cattle,[104] and in the 1820s that colony's newly minted Supreme Court dealt with a number of appeals involving damages for the loss of animals killed while trespassing on someone's land, as well as those for fees due to poundkeepers for cattle or horses they had maintained as a consequence of the animal's having trespassed upon someone's farm.[105]

[103] *Firth v. Martin*, Nov. 1858, Wellington, N. Z., Magistrate's Court, reported in *N. Z. Spectator*, Nov. 13, 1858, p. 2 (damages for cow trespassing); *Challoner & Another v. McPhail & Another*, NSW SCR (Knox) 157 (1877) (trespass by sheep during drought the cause of the death of 2,000 sheep); *Mackay Bros. v. Wellington-M. Ry.*, 6 N.Z.L.R. (C.A.) 185 (1887) (stock lost, statute imposed obligation on Ry. to fence but a mutual obligation to maintain fence; plaintiffs negligent in failing to help maintain fence); *Malone v. Faulkner*, 11 U.C.Q.B. 116 (1853) (def. obstructed new drain; fence-viewers called in by plaintiff. Jury awards 6 p. to plaintiff).

[104] Bruce Kercher, *Debt, Seduction and Other Diasasters: The Birth of Civil Law in Convict New South Wales* (Sydney, 1996), 108–11; John Pickard, "Trespass, Common Law, Government Regulation and Fences in Colonial New South Wales, 1788–1828," 84 *Journal of the Royal Australian Historical Society* 131 at 134–35 (1998).

[105] See *Lawliss v. Kniffe* (NSWSC, Kercher, 1824); *Nash v. Purcell* (NSWSC, Kercher, 1828); *Honey v. Blake* (NSWSC, Kercher, 1829); *Donnison v. Sharpe* (NSWSC, Kercher, 1830). The post of poundkeeper was "a valued position in Colonial Tasmania," Alastair Campbell tells us. "Settlers sought these appointments, as they allowed incumbents to protect their own herds" while harassing "their competitors." Campbell, *John Batman and the Aborigines* (Melbourne, 1987), 21.

Illustrations 11 and 12.   On the "frontiers" in North America and the Antipodes, the British Diaspora grazed their animals on partially cleared but unfenced land, as on this range in Muskoga, Ontario (top). This prompted frontier farmers to fence their crops in, until the fencing of cattle was mandated by colonial government. In the event much lumber and labor was consumed, as in these "worm" fences, Bond Head, Beeton Road, Simcoe County, Ontario. (Archives of Ontario, S14723; S4817.)

Illustrations 13 and 14.   Note as well the split-rail fences lining the pathway to Mt. Torrens in William Cawthorne's sketch of 1856 (top), and the elaborate fencing in the engraving for the *Canadian Illustrated News* of "A Farm in the Eastern Townships of Quebec," 1833. (Mitchell Library, State Library of New South Wales, ZPXD39f25; Archives of Quebec.)

Illustration 15.   In Australia and New Zealand fencing kept rabbits and dingoes out of pastureland. "The Long Road, No. 1," is in Western Australia. (F. H. Broomhall Collection, National Library of Australia, Canberra.)

Similarly, during the British settlement of New Zealand, in 1842, the colony's Legislative Council created a Cattle Trespass Ordinance requiring the fencing-in of crops. The Reverend George Clarke, the Crown's appointed "Protector" of the rights and interests of the native Maori, reported to the Council that the Maoris rarely fenced their land, and that consequently the cattle of British settlers were doing considerable damage to their crops, while trespassing Maori hogs were being killed at will by these same settlers. As this struck both Clarke and the Council as unfair and impolitic, the Council amended the ordinance to the Maori's advantage, as their predecessors had in Massachusetts.[106]

King Cacobau's Fijian government created an Animal Trespass ordinance in 1872, providing fines of $1 "for pigs goats sheep and small animals" and $5 for cattle and horses, and provided for hearings before two magistrates who were empowered to "order that compensation be made for the harm done and how it is to be paid and how future trespass is to be prevented...."[107]

[106] J. M. Bennett, "The Day of Retribution: Commissioner Bigge's Inquiries in Colonial New South Wales," 15 *American Journal of Legal History* 85 at 103(1971); Peter Adams, *Fatal Necessity: British Intervention in New Zealand, 1830–1847* (Oxford, 1977), 222.

[107] Act #35, 23 July 1872, copy in S. W. Dutton, comp., "Historical Records of Fiji, 1860–1910," MS CY2591, Mitchell Library, Sydney.

The Informal Law of Animal Trespasses in North America
and the Antipodes

Evidence of Rational Behavior. We begin in Upper Canada/ Ontario.
By the 1830s and 1840s many, perhaps most of Ontario's newcomer–
settlers appear to have behaved like Ellickson's "rational welfare-
maximizers" when it came to animal trespasses. For example, John
Malloch, an attorney and farmer from the Bathurst area in the early
1840s, was immediately prepared to control his newly acquired oxen
when "Cpt. McMillan sent his man down with the oxen tonight, saying
they were breechy – Had broken into his oats." So was Walter Hope
of Sydenham, whose cow had "begun to go with Malcolm's Cattle" in
May of 1848.[108] John Galbraith, a farmer in Blenheim, often recorded
"much provoking abuse" that he had received in the 1830s from neighbors; one "cut a fine sugar tree" on his property; another "twice took
horse & sleigh without my consent or privilege." A third was asked to
keep his horses "out of my orchard;" a fourth was asked "to take [his]
Calves out of the Orchard after they had done considerable injury,"
something that the neighbor did quite reluctantly ("Got Mackenzie
against the grain"). Galbraith made no further mention of any of
these disagreeable moments, and my comparison of this fact with the
evidence available in the many other farm diaries from this region in
these years tells me that Galbraith, like the majority of his fellow early
Diaspora settlers in Ontario, was of a conciliatory disposition, predisposed to organize and participate in barn raisings, threshing bees and
the like (See Illustration 16). He may have expressed annoyance from
time to time to his diary, but that was where he felt that annoyance
belonged, in a private, personal corner of his life and world.[109]

Galbraith may well have been a great-grandfather of economist John
Kenneth Galbraith, who wrote of farm society in his ancestral homeland of western Ontario: "Men stuck to their bargains and negotiated
their disputes. . . . A man would have been excluded [from society] if

---

[108] Malloch kept them "in the yard all night" and "mended" his fences. June 14
and 15, 1841, Journal of Judge John Malloch, MS Diaries, MI 842, Archives
of Ontario; Entries for June 17, and 19, 1848, Diary of Walter Hope, MS
338, Archives of Ontario.

[109] Entries for Dec. 26, 1834, Aug. 19 1836, Sept. 3, 1836, Dec. 17, 1836, John
Galbraith Diary, MS 450, Archives of Ontario.

See also Graeme Wynne, "Ideology, Society and State in the Maritime
Colonies of British North America, 1840–60," in *Colonial Leviathan*, 294–97,
for a good account of the cooperative behavior of farmer John Murray and
his neighbors near Pictou, Nova Scotia. And see Daniel Vickers, *Farmers and
Fishermen: Two Centuries of Work in Essex County, Massachusetts, 1630–1850*
(Chapel Hill, 1994), 60–61, 237–240, 299, on cooperative labor exchanges
between farm families.

Illustration 16. Once settlements of the British Diaspora had matured, neighbors and fellow parishioners accommodated one another and cooperated in efforts such as this barn raising in Kincardine, Ontario. (Archives of Ontario, S1893.)

he had shown himself to be unneighborly.... The Common law on these matters was clear and well enforced. A man was obliged to put his neighbor's need ahead of his own and everyone did.... No one ever declined.... The social penalty would have been too severe."[110] Galbraith's phrase "the Common law on these matters" is a nice play on words that is precisely on target. The *formal* Common Law was not what made people in western Ontario behave in a neighborly fashion in the *fin de siècle*; rather it was the informal law, common to all in the community, that was observed. Some of the rules of the two systems of norms overlapped; many of the rules in the formal Law had, after all, been derived from long-standing customs. But Galbraith had in mind community *observance* of popular norms. Neighborhoods of like-minded Ontario farmers relied on one another, and that co-dependence created a kind of local "law" of popular norms.

In the early days of settlement in New South Wales those who suffered damages to their unfenced crops from free-ranging cattle had a fairly simple remedy: They reported the losses to the largest single owner of such animals, the government itself. John and Thomas Pickard have discovered accounts of payment made from the Colonial Police Fund to such farmers in the pages of the Sydney *Gazette*. It

[110] John Kenneth Galbraith, *The Scotch* (Boston, 1964), 47–48.

was "easier to sue" the Crown "than private stock-owners," they conclude,[111] and this may be read as evidence of just such a cost-benefit "bargaining" as Ronald Coase posits. When it came to *private* stockowners (who by the 1820s were the only pastoralists in town), conciliatory acts such as those just noted in the United States and Ontario appear to have been seen as less expensive, more neighborly, and more likely to produce reciprocal behavior in Australia[112] and New Zealand as well. The Law called upon neighbors to share fencing costs, but since one runholder might well decide to fence before his neighbor was prepared to assist, the former might find his polite appeal for the neighbor's share of his expenses ignored. A second letter was likely to be worded quite formally, like the one John Docker of Wangaratta received on January 8, 1856, announcing that the fence was under construction and "requiring" him "within seven days from this service" to name an arbitrator to meet with the one his neighbor had named and threatening "legal proceedings against you" under the terms of the Act of Council if he failed to respond. Some employed solicitors to convey such formal messages; these gentlemen often employed more velvet in wording these communications: arbitration would "avoid law expenses" and was "a much more amicable mode of settlement."[113]

[111] John Pickard, "Trespass, Common Law, Government Regulations, and Fences in Colinal New South Wales, 1788–1828," 84 *Journal of the Royal Australian Historical Society* 135.

[112] Thus, Captain G. Griffin of Whiteside, Moreton Bay, lent a neighbor a horse to separate his bullocks from some wild cattle (Diary of G. Griffin, June 2, 1848, MS 72–42/1, Oxley Library, Brisbane. See also C. M. H. Clark, *A History of Australia* (Melbourne, 1978), IV, 166 (on some farmers and pastoralists sharing seed, machinery, workers and ideas in midcentury); Peter Taylor, *Station Life in Australia: Pioneers and Pastoralists* (Sydney, 1988), 75 (on sheep station neighbors fighting fires on one another's land for two or three days running in the 1840s).

[113] Unknown Author, to Docker, Jan. 8, 1856, Docker MS 10437/Box 1459/13, St. Library of Victoria; Anderson & Shaw, Esq., to Neil Black & Co., Jan. 13, 1856, Neil Black MS, Latrobe Library, Melbourne. See also James Ross, Esq., representing James Brown, seeking "an offer" for trespass damages, May 1845, from Neil Black (Black agreed to arbitration); H Hurry & Son, Esq., April, 1904, to M. Commons (on behalf of J. A. Johnston), for his share of fencing costs (after Commons declined to pay because he had not received "a notice from you to fence under the [terms of] the fencing act. I therefore cannot acknowledge your account"), MS13016/39(3), MS Div., St. Library of Victoria; and Lewis, Orr & Gibson, Esq., Records, Baillieu Library Special Collections, University of Melbourne, 186/9(iv)/file #910 (for an agreement between Charles Reynolds and Florence Morris to fence land purchased from R. E. Lewis, Nov. 16, 1914).

Yvonne du Fresne of the North Island of New Zealand recalled one of her father's conciliatory acts toward a neighbor in this regard in her autobiography: The neighbor, a Major Gore, trotted up to her Danish Grandmother Westergard's home and announced, with his polite but formally firm English manner:

> Just thought I'd let you know that one of your heifers wandered down the road. Ha ha! Been in my maize patch all morning. Ha ha! One of my chaps is bringing it back now.

Her grandmother responded:

> 'Thank you. Your fences are a disgrace; therefore my poor old heifer goes into your maize patch.' But not in English she spoke. Nej. She spoke in ... the Danish of a frost-droning. We were saved by dear [father]. He strolled up ... 'Good heavens,' he said. 'That stupid old heifer again? I will come down in a tick and see to your fence.'[114]

The diaries of Oraru Gorge sheep-station owner Charles Tripp in the 1860s, 1870s, and 1880s are evidence of a somewhat less generous behavior when it came to fencing disputes than that of Yvonne du Fresne's father, but Tripp's was no less successful, and his may well have been the way that most owners of New Zealand sheep runs managed to persuade recalcitrant neighbors to share the costs of fencing and the like. In 1867, Tripp was having difficulty in arranging with a fellow rancher and neighbor, a Captain Jollie of Peel Forest, to fence their boundary. On December 19 (early summer Down Under) Tripp wrote Jollie rather sharply: "I now make this formal application to you to join me in fencing the boundary where sheep are likely to cross." All told, Tripp would have to erect some sixty miles of fencing, at a cost of about fifty pounds per mile, to bound his seven thousand acres. Jollie's boundary was the most extensive of those he bordered, and Tripp was clearly apprehensive. But Jollie had similar prospects, and on Christmas Day Tripp received Jollie's agreement to cooperate. Tripp immediately responded, on December 26, with relief, and a friendlier tone: "I think I can make the [fencing] trip pleasant & agreeable for you...."

Several years later the problem was rabbits, not the fences that many of these prolific nibblers of green pastures bounded over or through. New Zealand's sheep grazers were devoting substantial resources to rabbit killing. Each run dispatched its own rabbit killing parties; but cooperation was important here as well. Another of Tripp's neighbors, J. M. Barker, had put in the field some men with dogs, but without

[114] Yvonne du Fresne, *The Bear from the North: Tales of a New Zealand Childhood* (London, 1989), 140.

mules. One or more of these fellows had come upon one of Tripp's boundary huts, built for shepherds and rabbit killers to take refuge. A mule was tethered to the hut, left by someone on a chore in the bush, and one of Barker's people decided the hut was on Barker's land and proceeded to kill the mule and burn the hut. Tripp's reaction to this, while cool (indeed, sarcastic), was conciliatory. "You will oblige me by saying where your rabbit-killers *are* living," he asked. If, as reported, they were sleeping several miles from the infested area, the dogs would have too great a distance to travel to be of much use. Wouldn't Barker's man like the use of Tripp's boundary huts and mules, for greater mobility? "All I ask is, if you *will* kill another mule or burn the hut again, to share with me the cost of replacing it, as mules & huts cost money."[115]

Robert Ellickson would recognize many of these settler–settler "bargains" as "welfare-maximizing" ones, and I would agree with such a characterization. Indeed, his "neighborly" norm may also have been a standard for many in the United States. In "Mending Wall," Robert Frost has his New Hampshire neighbor tell him, as they rebuild their borderwall each spring, "Good fences make good neighbors." Frost

[115] Letters of Charles G. Tripp of Oraru Gorge, Canterbury, Dec. 19, 1867, Dec. 26, 1867, Feb., 1874, June 18, 1881, Mss. Div., Turnbull Library, Wellington (originals in Canterbury Museum archives, New Zealand, but originals for 1867 missing). (But see Miles Fairburn, *The Ideal Society and its Enemies*, 170ff (few New Zealanders before the 1890s behaved in reciprocal ways with neighbors with regard to fencing, harvesting, or other activities).)

Tripp's experience was echoed in the diaries for 1898 and 1899 of Duncan McRae, Jr., of Wyndham Station, South Island: "Mar. 17, 1898 – Sent a letter to Murray demanding £3.15.0 for clearing boundary line & damages for trespassing . . . Sept. 12, 1898 – Went & mended Beange's Fence up at the young grass. . . . Oct. 18, 1898 – Gave Colin McPhail a hand with the garden fence."

Entries for November 14 and December 1 report the damage done by the McRae horse and buggy to neighbor James Foster's gate and the arrival of Mr. Foster at the McRae house "to settle with uncle." McRae, Mss #1391, Alex. Turnbull Library, Wellington.

And, of course, Tripp's experience was also echoed in the diaries of Ontario farmers: "May 1, 1885 – Fixing Fence in Bush Between Sargent and us. . . . May 19 – Fixing fence Between Bob Sargent and us. . . . April 27 – Fixed Fence Between McCagherty and us. . . . Aug. 14 – Put up wire Fence along orchard." Thomas Thompson Diary, Tullamore, MSS Diaries Coll., MU 871, Arch. of Ontario; "Sept. 12, 1836 – Forenoon fencing the west orchard. . . . Sept. 13 – fixing fences. . . . Sept. 22 – mending fences [due to trespasses by horses and calves of Thomas Mackenzie]," John Galbraith Diary, MU 450, Arch. of Ontario; "May 8, 1848 – Split a few rails and began a fence between McCallem & me. . . . June 17 – cow arrived. . . . June 19 – the cow has begun to go with Malcolm's cattle," Diary of Walter Hope of Sydenham, MU 338, Arch of Ontario.

found this aphorism to be innane, given that "my apple trees will never get across/And eat the cones under his pines." But this aphorism, or maxim, had made much common sense when animal husbandry had been prevalent in New England.

My evidence of rational "welfare-maximizing" notwithstanding, the fact is that I detected considerable evidence, for each of the lands settled by the British Diaspora, that such behavior may not have been the norm, at least during the first half century of Diaspora settlement.

Evidence of Irrational Behavior. The problem with the Coase and Ellickson models is that few of the early colonists (outside of first-generation New England and Pennsylvania) were neighborly *most* of the time, and some were not very rational or neighborly *any* of the time (as John Demos and David Konig have demonstrated for seventeenth century New England and Sean Cadigan and Tina Loo have for nineteenth century Newfoundland and Vancouver Island).[116] Consider the case of John Conklin's slander suit in seventeenth century New Haven against one who had called him "a neighboure not fitt for an Indian to live by" in front of "the greater part" of the local militia company, because he had killed one of his neighbor's hogs (however lawfully). Or consider the account offered by Sarah Holton of Salem Village in 1692 regarding the behavior of Rebecca Nurse in or about 1689:

> Rebecca Nurse came to our house & fell a railing at [my husband] because our pigs got into her field, tho our pigs were sufficiently yoaked & their fence was down in several places, yet all we could say to hir coundt no ways passife her, but she continued Railing & scolding a grat while together calling to hir son Benj. Nurs to go & git a gun & kill our piggs & let non of them to our of the field.

Inasmuch as the Holtons and Nurses were either unable or unwilling to litigate this dispute, it simmered. Sarah Holton believed that Rebecca Nurse had called upon the Devil to punish her husband, Benjamin, and when he became blind and then died, she accused Goody Nurse of witchcraft. What may have happened was that Rebecca Nurse had, indeed, prayed that Benjamin Holton be punished; but she probably prayed to God, not the Devil. Be that as it may; whichever

---

[116] See John Demos, *Entertaining Satan* (1982), David Konig, *Law and Society in Puritan Massachusetts: Essex County, 1629–1692* (1979); Sean Cadigan, *Hope and Deception in Conception Bay: Merchant-Settler Relations in Newfoundland, 1785–1855* (Toronto, 1995); Tina Loo, *Making Law, Order, and Authority in British Columbia, 1821–1871* (Toronto, 1994). And see Yasuhide Kawashima, *Puritan Law and Indians* (New York, 1966), 63, for an earlier, and Francis Prucha, *American Indian Policy* (1971), 158, for a later example.

supernatural power she turned to, it was not a temporal, judicial one. It was not *the Law.*

Neither was the power that Rebecca Nurse's coreligionist and Salem Village neighbor, Sarah Cole, turned to. She "thretened" John Browne "for medling" after he had served as an arbitrator to "adjust sum Damages Don by said Sarah Coles hogs... to Abraham Welman['s crops]," saying to Browne "he had better not to have done" the awarding of damages. Later, when Browne asked Sarah Cole to make him "an Indian puding," she produced one that "was red like a blud puding w'ch he believes was done by Sarah Cole" to punish him. Similarly, Edward Hooper reported that he went with John Neal to the home of Dorcas Hoar "when the s'd. neal brought a [hen] of the s'd whors which he had kiled doing damagee in his master witedg's Corn," whereupon "the s'd whore [sic] did say then to the s'd John Neall that he should be never the beter for it before the weak was out." Another complainant, John Louder, deposed to the same Court of Oyer and Terminer investigating the charges of witchcraft in Salem Village in 1692, that he had "had some Controversy with Bridgett B[i]shop... aboute her fowles that used to Come into our orchard or garden." "Some little tyme after" this meeting, Louder awoke "aboute the dead of the night" oppressed by a "Beast" that looked like Bridget Bishop and "choaked" him.[117] In short, some fencing and animal-trespass disputes in 1692 could lead in Massachusetts to accusations of witchcraft if they were not successfully arbitrated or adjudicated.

By the eighteenth and nineteenth centuries animal trespasses no longer led to charges of witchcraft, but some resulted in the same peremptory killing of the animal, be it a transient longhorn that might carry splenic fever, a horse, a mule, a ram, or, more commonly, a pig. Neither statutory threats of triple damages nor more open-ended punitive damages served to curb these acts completely. Once hogs had rooted under one's garden enclosure, for example, they were hard to dissuade in the future, and a breakdown in what one jurist called "the offices of good neighborhood" could result in "bad feelings" between neighbors. Horses or cattle straying into a neighbor's pasture in the event of a downed fence led to trouble when the aggrieved farmer took "self-help," maiming the animal or cutting the mane of a trespassing horse as a warning to its owner of more serious measures that

---

[117] See Cornelia H. Dayton, *Women before the Bar: Gender, Law and Society in Connecticut, 1639–1850* (Chapel Hill, 1995), 296; *Bliss v. Dorchester* (March 2, 1653), *Colonial Justice in Western Massachusetts, 1639–1702: The Pyncheon Court Record,* ed. Joseph H. Smith (Cambridge, Harvard Univ. Press, 1961), 230; Paul Boyer and Steven Nissenbaum, eds., *The Salem Village Witchcraft Papers* (3 vols., N.Y., 1977), I, 99, 231; II, 399–400, 430.

might be taken the next time. We can find evidence of what might happen "the next time" in many crannies of the historical record, as in Lancaster County, Pennsylvania, where a sheriff and posse were called upon to arrest two of John Lowe's sons for killing horses near their fields and assaulting two of the animals' angry owners, and as in tidewater Virginia when Edward Pridham shot a horse belonging to "Parson Giberne" in September, 1772. The animal had encroached on Pridham's cornfield after a windfall in the Giberne-Pridham fence. (The parson sued.)[118]

When the fence was a "bad" one, inadequate to the task, it "often" became "the means of the most unhappy disputes and downright quarrels amongst neighbors, from which have flowed assaults, batteries, lawsuits, and ill-will for life, and after – for the quarrel has often been entailed with the property to the son – amongst those who would otherwise have lived . . . friendly . . . all their days," as the *Farmer's Cabinet & American Herd Book* put it in 1841.[119] Lawsuits for recovery of losses to crops generally "had little chance before a jury," or so one nineteenth century observer maintained. Only about one in twenty suits ever resulted in any recoverable damages. According to the *Farmer's Review*, "only in rare cases" did the owners of trespassing animals "ever offer to make good the loss occasioned by them." This may have been the jaundiced view of an advocate for cultivators, but it sounds plausible: Trespasser defendants would have known that they might convince a jury that the plaintiff's own fence was in disrepair and that the plaintiff's court costs might well exceed his recoverable damages. This is borne out by testimony offered by a Minister named Damer who told a court in South Carolina that when the offending railroad company had, after much delay, finally paid the judgement award in the loss of his cattle throughout 1849 and 1850 he discovered that "it cost more to recover the damage by suit than the cattle killed were worth."[120]

---

[118] Lowe incident noted in Thomas Slaughter, "Crowds in 18th Century America," 115 Pa. *Mag. Of Hist. & Biog.* 1 at 15 (1991); *The Diary of Colonel Landon Carter [J. P.]*, ed. Jack P. Greene (Charlottesville, Va., 1965), II, 732. And see the complaint of Anna Chenal in 1773 that "residents of Opelousas have been killing much of my live-stock at my dairy farm giving as a reason that they are straying." Noted in Daniel Unser, *Indians, Settler's and Slaves*, 189.

[119] *Farmer's Cabinet & American Herd Book*, VI (Phila. 1841), 59, noted in Earl Hayter, "Livestock-Fencing Conflicts in Rural America," 37 *Agricultural History* 11 (1963).

[120] *The Farmer's Review*, VIII (Chicago, 1882), 54; *NE RR v. Sineath*, 41 So. Car. (8 Rich. L) 185 at 187 (1855), noted in James Hunt, "Legislatures, Courts, and 19th Century Negligence," paper delivered at October 1997 conference of the American Society for Legal History. See *Damer v. SSRR*, 38 So.

In any event, as late as 1903 a state representative told his colleagues in the Alabama legislature that "shotguns were playing an important part" in the resolution of animal trespass controversies in his district.[121] And, of course, it is well known that in the American West both county adoptions of herd laws and seasonal cattle drives sometimes resulted in the cutting of fences despite statutes prohibiting this behavior and court decisions enforcing those statutes. Cattlemen, sheep grazers, and "homesteaders" there had different notions of land use, and these were often profound enough to lead to violence rather than accommodation. Large-scale stockmen illegally fenced the public lands around creeks and meadows they sought to deny smaller-scale stockmen and homesteaders throughout the prairies in the 1880s. One posted a sign on his fencing: "The son of a bitch who opens the fence had better look out for his scalp."

These same stockmen pulled down the fences of homesteaders on the Powder River in Montana and lynched two who had encroached on Albert Bothwell's ranch. Some judges (including Willis Van Devanter, the future U.S. Supreme Court Justice) seem to have favored big stockmen; others the smaller stockmen. But it was not statutes, such as Wyoming's "Maverick" Law of 1884, or individual court decisions that decided matters on the grasslands of the late nineteenth century. Texas gunslingers, employed by the big stockmen, sometimes simply fought it out with the smaller stockmen and their hands. And eventually dry-farm homesteaders, moving into the West in sufficient numbers, threw up "their fences, chased, dogged, and stol[e] cattle, and generally so interfered with ranching" that the directors of the Swan Land & Cattle Company, Ltd., one of the giants, "decided to sell all the cattle and buy more sheep."[122]

Car. (4 Rich. L) 329 (1851), for the original judgement and appeal the Reverend Damer was referring to.

[121] R. Ben Brown, *Closing the Southern Range: A Chapter in the Decline of the Southern Yeomanry* (Amer. Bar Found. Work. Papers, 1990), 18. See also Hahn, "Hunting, Fishing and Foraging," and Kantor and Kousser, "Common Sense or Commonwealth?" *supra* note 6.

[122] See Kawashima, *supra* note 96; *Cole v. Tucker*, 6 Tex. 266 (1851); *Champion v. Vincent*, 20 Tex. 812 at 817 (1859); *Fugate v. Smith*, 4 Col. App. 201, 35 Pac. 283 (1894); Harmon Mothershead, *The Swan Land & Cattle Company, Ltd.* (Norman, Okla., 1971), 114, 123; Helena H. Smith, *The War on the Powder River* (N.Y., 1966), 60–62, 66, 78, 85, 96, 121ff., 117, 190, 275; Louis Pelzer, *The Cattleman's Frontier* (1936), 173–90; Walter Prescott Webb, *The Great Plains* (Boston, 1931), 314; Thad Sitton, *Backwoodsmen: Stockmen and Hunters along a Big Thicket River Valley* (Norman, Ok., 1995); Robert McMath, "Sandy Land and Hogs in Timber: Farmers Alliance in Texas," in Jonathan Prude and Stephen Hahn, eds., *The Countryside in the Age of*

Similarly, many neighbors in both the Canadian and Atlantic Maritime provinces and the Antipodes appear to have squandered their scarce resources and poisoned their relationships over the occasion of animal trespasses. Thus, when James Counsell's pig got into Catherine Callahan's garden at Conception Bay, Newfoundland, in 1836, she yoked and retained it, and threatened Counsell's wife, Mary, with a beating if she tried to reclaim the animal. Later, in Harbour Grace Thomas Pine killed the trespassing goat of George and Sophie Heater when the animal plundered his garden. Two brothers began slugging it out in the same year at Broad Cove when one's horse was discovered in the other's potato garden. Their wives joined in; one knocked the other down with a spade. A third brother exercised remarkable restraint; watching all of this impassively, he called to his wife to assist her downed sister-in-law "while he returned to digging his potatoes."[123]

On Vancouver Island a political confrontation of sorts began with another case of trespassing pigs. Robert Staines, the Hudson's Bay Company's chaplain for that island, sent his bailiff to the estate of William Tolmie, the Company's local surgeon, when he discovered that Tolmie's bailiff was holding a number of his pigs. Staines' bailiff returned with two, but claimed that several others were being wrongfully detained. Later in the week Staines descended on the Tolmie property himself, armed with a warrant and several employees, in a "wrathy" mood. He left with five more hogs. Tolmie then sued Staines, complaining that the warrant Staines had obtained from magistrate Thomas

Capitalist Transformation (Chapel Hill, 1985), 216; and Robert Dykstra, *The Cattle Towns* (1968), 301–02.

Rural fencing disputes over animals were the most important ones in nineteenth century America, but "spite" fences, built by urbanites to harass their neighbors, are also worthy of note. The most famous of these may have been the one, thirty feet high, erected by San Francisco railroad plutocrat Charles Crocker around three sides of a neighbor's property to induce him to sell out. William Deverell, *Railroad Crossing: Californians and the Railroad, 1850–1910* (Berkeley, 1994), 44.

For evidence of fencing and boundary disputes in working class neighborhoods in Massachusetts in the 1980s, see Sally Engle Merry, *Getting Justice and Getting Even: Legal Consciousness Among Working-Class Americans* (Chicago, 1990), 42–46.

[123] Eight years later, at Marshall's Folly, Rebecca and Ann Slade were cited for poking one another over "a fowl laying an egg in the garden." Sean Cadigan, *Hope and Deception at Conception Bay*, 76, 78; *McGill v. Morley*, 3 Newf.R. 146 (1850). The defendant learned little from this, for he appealed, winning a new trial on a pleading error of the plaintiff that could only have resulted in an even greater award for the plaintiff on retrial. See also *Curtiss v. Townsend*, 6 UCCP 255 (1857), a case with similar facts.

Shriner lacked the "forms prescribed by the Law" in that there had been no hearing before its issuance. The Island's recently appointed chief justice, David Cameron, agreed, and Chaplain Staines was as a consequence briefly detained by order of the court. Upon his release the outraged chaplain initiated countercharges of theft against Tolmie and his bailiff and organized a petition objecting to Justice Cameron's action. This prompted others to rise to Cameron's defense. The story, complicated and embellished by the political positions of the litigants and their supporters regarding the monopolistic Company, is well told by Tina Loo.[124] I retell to it here as another example of the many ways that stray porkers could lead to trouble between neighbors.

Animal trespasses raised hackles in early Ontario as well. John Thomson of Burford complained to the local magistrate in 1839 that Allan Muir and William Cruden had "removed a fence so that a young orchard on my Farm was exposed to the depredations of Crudens cattle." Thomson had purchased his farm from Cruden, but Cruden persisted in the use of its barn and meadow for his animals, destroying Thomson's gates and locks in the process, and the local magistrate was unable to stop this behavior. The rule of Law and the arbitration process were only so strong in early rural Ontario as its inhabitants allowed, as Susan Lewthwaite has argued.[125] My reading of the diaries of early nineteenth century Ontario farmers confirms this view. For example, When William Oliver of Drummond, in Eastern Ontario, quarreled in July of 1842 with "one Toomy" on Toomy's farm "about some cattle," the results were tragic. As John Malloch, a neighboring farmer noted in his diary: "Toomy took a gun from the house & told Oliver to keep off or he would shoot – Oliver advanced . . . the other shot him [;] died on the spot."[126]

One who chose to take the sort of preemptive action John Neal had taken in Salem Village, an action sanctioned by ordinance in Montreal until 1687 and in Sydney briefly in the 1790s, might find himself in court with all of the attendant costs. There were a number of incidents in the early history of New South Wales of trespassing goats or pigs rooting in a neighbor's garden that led those displaying negativism to experience costly fights in court, and evidence of the same phenomenon in the other Australian colonies. A few examples:

[124] Loo, *Making Law, Order and Authority in British Columbia, 1821–1871* (Toronto, 1994), 45–47.
[125] Susan Lewthwaite offers the Thomson-Cruden story in "Violence, Law and Community in Rural Upper Canada," in *Essays in the History of Canadian Law*, ed. Jim Phillips *et al.*, (Toronto, 1994), 353, 359.
[126] Entry for 19 July 1842, Journal of Judge John Malloch, MSS Diaries Collection, MU 842, Archives of Ontario.

First, Gregory Blaxland's sow repeatedly invaded John Bennett's crops in Sydney throughout 1806 and 1807 until Bennett shot the animal. Blaxland sought damages. Bennett explained to the court that he had had no other recourse, inasmuch as the cost of suing for the damages in any single incident had not been "worth the trouble" and that he had warned Blaxland that he would take "self-help" were the sow to trespass again. The Court of Civil Jurisdiction awarded Blaxland the value of the sow, but then creatively deducted from it the damages done over the course of time to Bennett's crops.

Second, twenty-three years later, on Sydney's North Shore, "certain pigs" belonging to merchant Henry Donnison ravaged the garden of a farmer named Sharpe once too often. Sharpe shot them, and refused to apologize or to offer compensation. Donnison thereupon sued Sharpe. The trial court judge told the jury that the "self-help" permitted under the Law was limited to a civil lawsuit or the impounding of the offending animals, not their destruction, but he also advised them that, in calculating the cost of the pigs in assessing damages, they were free to deduct from that figure such damages to Sharpe's garden that they had done, echoing the step taken by the Court of Civil Jurisdiction twenty-three years before. Donnison was awarded only forty shillings, and Sharpe made to pay costs of court. Both had "lost" financially from the suit.

Third, in 1790 Surgeon John White's goat invaded the vegetable garden of convict-carpenter John Fuller in Sydney; unable to obtain satisfaction from either White or other "Gentlemen whose Goats had strayed and broken into" his garden, Fuller sued for damages. Magistrates David Collins and Augustus Alt turned him away, his "Hedge being proved not sufficient to keep any Animals such as Hogs or goats out," a central condition of the Law. Thus, Fuller lost; but the magistrates went on to appeal to White and the other unnamed "Gentlemen" to provide Fuller with "some Satisfaction equal to the Loss he has sustained by their Goats, either in a daily Allowance of Vegetables, or by new stocking his Garden, or assisting him in new fencing it." After all, they argued, convict-carpenter Fuller was "very much employed for the Publick" and thus had "not much Time to work for himself." He had "therefore ... made the best Fence in his Power" and ought to be accommodated by his more powerful free neighbors.

Fourth, Edward Henty, member of the first British settler–family in what would become Victoria, recorded a falling out he'd had with a whaler employee named Hubbard in March of 1835. Hubbard's pig, and that of another employee, had "got into the Garden" and had "rooted up all the Potatoes with some Turnips." Edward and his brother "drove them off," with buckshot "at about 40 yards" and "thrashed ...

them with sticks. . . . " Hubbard reacted in a "very insolent" way, telling Henty that if he killed his pig "he would shoot my dogs." "I retaliated by threatening to shoot him if he did[.] [W]e were both in a Passion but at last got cool and parted good friends." Indeed, Hubbard allowed to Henty that he wished he had "not bought the Pig" as it had become more of a nuisance than it was worth."

Fifth, in 1824 William Hovell's cattle invaded the wheat-field of a "ticket-of-leave" convict, Robert Brierson. Only two years before Hovell had expressed outrage to one of the Minto magistrates, a man named Howe, whose "cattle destroyed my wheat." Consequently, in 1824 he offered Brierson the equivalent of the fine he would have to pay the magistrates for his cattle's trespass, a "welfare-maximizing" measure. "I am no poundkeeper!" Brierson replied and caused Hovell to be brought before the magistrates.[127]

Colonial Australian legal districts might find it hard to recruit folks willing to risk life, fortune, and respect as a sheriff,[128] but the office of poundkeeper was an altogether different matter. The impounding of trespassing cattle under the terms of the impounding ordinances gave the poundkeeper "great power," often "corruptly exercised." The pound might be quite distant from the property from which the animals had strayed. And the subsequent fees charged by

---

[127] The Fuller-White decision was hailed by the Sydney *Gazette* as "highly consequential" to the future of such animal trespass disputes, and has been legitimately styled by Kercher as "a characteristically creative" decision of this somewhat innovative early New South Wales judiciary. Kercher, *Unruly Child*, 46, 127; Kercher, *Debt, Seduction and Other Disasters: The Birth of Civil Law in New South Wales* (Sydney, 1996), 108–10; T. G. Parsons, "Was John Boston's Pig a Political Martyr? The Reaction to Popular Radicalism in Early New South Wales," 71 *Journal of the Royal Australian Historical Society* 170 (1985); Marnie Bassett, *The Hentys* (Oxford, 1961), 309; *Donnison v. Sharpe* (NSWSC, Kercher, 1830); Paula J. Byrne, *Criminal Law and Colonial Subject: New South Wales, 1810–1830* (Sydney, 1993), 222, 223–24 (on the Hovell-Brierson dispute), 239; J. F. Nagle, *Collins, the Courts and the Colony: Law and Society in Colonial New South Wales, 1788–1796* (Sydney, 1996), 164–65. See Alastair Campbell, *John Batman and the Aborigines* (Malmsbury, 1987), 160, for an account of the feud between Henry Batman and John Pascoe Fawkner, early Melbourne settlers, over dogs and rabbits shot by Batman's servant and attacks on one of Fawkner's calves by a bulldog "encouraged" by Batman's wife. The dispute went to compulsory arbitration; a panel of three arbitrators fined Batman a total of sixty shillings and commended Fawkner for "a degree of forbearance" that was "highly gratifying." Fawkner MS, May 2, 1836, 3662/5, St. Library of Victoria. And see Michael Sturma, *Vice in a Viscious Society: Crime and Convicts in Mid-Nineteenth Century New South Wales* (St. Lucia, 1983), 133, for mention of a threat to "wring Howe's neck off" over a straying horse in Sydney in 1840.

[128] George Moore, Jan. 1, 1833, *Diary of Ten Years*, 155.

the poundkeeper could mount quickly and soon approach or exceed their value. Hence, a number of tense confrontations in early New South Wales, Van Dieman's Land/Tasmania, and Victoria involved the impounding of sheep, cattle, and pigs.[129] John McQuilton has persuaded me that the impounding by Squatters and their allies of the milk cows of selector-farmers on the Ovens and King Rivers in eastern Victoria in the 1860s and 1870s was one of the causes of the "outbreak" of the fabled bandit Ned Kelly and his gang in 1878. Indeed, most of the gang were the sons of such harassed selector-farmers, and Kelly, for example, had been thrashed by the Noyhu pound-keeper for setting free cows belonging to his family when he was fifteen years old.

The duty to fence could produce fights between neighbors as well. Henry Lawson's fictional account of "The Little World Left Behind" in "a western agricultural district in Australia" virtually begins with these lines:

The row about the boundary fence between the Sweeneys and the Joneses was unfinished still, and the old feud between the Dunderblitzens and the Blitzendunders was more deadly than ever – it started three generations ago over a stray bull. The O'Dunn was still fighting for his great object in life, which was not to be "onneighborly," as he put it. "I don't want to be onneighborly," he said, "but I'll be aven wid some of 'em yit...." Jones' red steer... was continually breaking into Rooney's "whate an' bringin' ivery head av the other cattle afhter him, and ruinin' him intirely." The Rooneys and M'Kenzies were at daggers drawn, even to the youngest child, over the impounding of a horse belonging to Pat Rooney's brother-in-law, by a distant relation of the M'Kenzies, which had happened nine years ago.[130]

On the vast tracts of grazing land in southeastern Australia the need for fencing only arose "when my flocks met those of my neighbors in the bush." Even then there was "time enough to move on the matter" in the first few decades of pastoral expansion. But by 1840, there

---

[129] "Major Schaw & Garrett have had a great feud about pigs: Mr. Garrett put the Major's pigs in Pound; he was afterward tried for cruelty to animals." Phillip Russell to George Russell, July 4, 1838, *Clyde Co. Papers* (8 vols. Oxford, 1959–73), II, 155; A. Watt, Supt., to Neil Black, Feb. and Mar., 1845, warning him he has the land commissioner, Captain Fyans', authority to impound his sheep on the Brown dairy farm, Neil Black Papers, Latrobe Lib; John West, *The History of Tasmania (1852)*, ed. A. G. L. Shaw (Sydney, 1971), 104; John McQuilton, *The Kelly Outbreak, 1878–1880: The Geographical Dimensions of Social Banditry* (Melbourne, 1979), 27, 51, 78.

[130] Henry Lawson, "The Little World Left Behind," in *Joe Wilson and His Mates* (1901).

were some 673 such runs in New South Wales with three hundred fifty thousand cattle and one and a quarter million sheep. Furthermore, these "squatter"-station owners soon learned (during the region's Gold Rush) that with a wire fence there was no further need of costly outstations, each with two shepherds and a hutkeeper. So they fenced their runs and formed vigilante associations in an effort to deal with both the persistence of sheep- and cattle-rustling and the lack of sympathy displayed by settler and emancipist-dominated juries.[131] Throughout the nineteenth century in Australia and New Zealand, as in North America, squatter–pastoralists and farmer–selectors fought over trespassing herbivores until fences criscrossed the land (a comparativist's celluloid dream starring John Wayne and Paul Hogan?).

In New Zealand there were more than a few moments in which settlers proved to be unable to accept the Law with regard to such trespasses. W. M. Smith wrote in the *New Zealand Gazette & Wellington Spectator* in January, 1843, of "experiencing the grossest outrage which has yet been committed in the name of the law." What was this? "The chickens of a Mrs. Wakefield repeatedly injured plants" in Smith's garden. "Finding complaint of no avail," he "shot some of them." But this "led her to apply to her solicitor." Smith had to turn to one himself, and the upshot was that the resident magistrate found for Mrs. Wakefield and ordered Smith to pay £2 10s. Similarly, Dunedin businessman William Cullen was summoned to court in 1858 for letting his dairy cows "vegetate feed and fatten" on his neighbor's "rich cabbage gardens," to his judicial regret.[132]

This sort of behavior was not only expensive; it was divisive. For some forty years in late nineteenth century New Zealand, two South Island families, the Shands and the Deans, treated one another to sullenness and incivility. According to a Mrs. Foster, a descendant of one of these families, the cause of this feud was not unlike that which had separated Mr. Smith of Wellington from several pounds and his dignity: "The Dean's pig had crossed over from their farm and the gardener had reported that he was eating the vegetables." The gardener was told "to get a gun and shoot." This he did "promptly," and "too successfully." Time and the lapse of memories eventually healed

---

[131]   Peter Taylor, *Station Life in Australia: Pioneers and Pastoralists* (Sydney, 1988), 32, 34, 35; Stephen Roberts, *The Squatting Age in Australia, 1835–1847* (Melbourne, 1935), 26, 53–55, 78; Philip McMichael, *Settlers and the Agrarian Question* (Cambridge, 1984), 217, 219.

[132]   *N. Z. Gazette & Wellington Spectator*, #214, Jan. 25, 1843, p.3; Richard Hill, *Policing the Colonial Frontier*, I, Pt. 2, 542. Query: was Mrs. Wakefield related to Colonel William Wakefield, to Captain Arthur Wakefield, or to their brother, E. G. Wakefield, all of whom had led the migration to Wellington in these years?

the wound. Three generations later, when members of the Shand and Dean families greeted one another, according to Mrs. Foster:

the remark is often heard: 'Did you shoot the pig or did we?' amid laughter. In those days a pig must have been quite an item of capital stock. [As, indeed, it was.][133]

Another example of a less than productive dispute resolution technique was recorded in the early 1870s in Pukaki, South Island. Edward Dark of Glentanner Run became angered when rams from Henry Dawson's adjacent run breached the boundary fence and socialized with Dark's ewes. Dark's reaction was to challenge Dawson to a fistfight; the result was that Dawson darkened Dark's lights.[134] All in all, Smith, Shand, Dean, and Dark had opted for actions that left them worse off than they had been when the conflict surfaced.

In 1828, the New South Wales Legislative Council created an ordinance requiring "adjacent landowners to contribute equally to the erection and repair of boundary fences, and provided arbitration to resolve disputes," but John Pickard tells us that tensions over such fences have continued "to the present day."[135]

The Native-Settler Cultural Impasse over Animal Trespasses

In Colonial America. The rule requiring white settlers to fence animals away from native crops, as I have said, *seemed* a sensible way to keep the peace, but it was widely ignored by those at whom it was aimed. In the early days of British settlements, when the settler Diaspora were minority communities, the unfenced field crops of aboriginals were provided with some protection from marauding animals owned by the interlopers. Thus in 1632, Sir Richard Saltonstall was ordered by Massachusetts Bay authorities to give "Saggamore John a hogshead of corne for the hurt his cattell did him in his corne." In 1656, the townfolk of Rehoboth, in the Plymouth colony, constructed an extensive fence along the town's border.[136] And further south, in 1725, Carolina's Indian Trade Commissioner, Colonel George Chicken, promulgated an "Order to all White men Traders and Men in the Cherokee Nation" to stop their horses from foraging on the unfenced

---

[133] Shand-Dean Papers, Alexander Turnbull Library, Wellington, N. Z. See Eugen Weber, *Peasants into Frenchmen: The Modernization of Rural France, 1870–1914* (Stanford, 1976), 401n, for evidence of similar feuds (*faires des reproches*) in the Loire Valley over "the loss of a sow, or a boundary dispute" as late as the 1890s.

[134] Robert Pinney, *Early South Canterbury Runs* (Wellington, N. Z. 1971), 95.

[135] Pickard, "Trespass, Common Law, Government Regulation and Fences," 138.

[136] Anderson, "King Philip's Herds," 608, 610.

crops of the Cherokee, he "having given the Indians a particular Charge to Shoot any Such Horses as may at any time hereafter be seen in their Cornfields...."[137]

But when colonial authorities called for joint use of "unimproved" (and thus unfenced) land, they intended that the settlers' cattle, sheep, goats, and hogs forage on the same "waste" that the natives treated as their hunting grounds. And this soon led to trouble. Some natives initially feared the spiritual nature of cattle; others initially regarded the Diaspora's tame fowl as sacred, and were upset when told they were raised for food.[138] *All* eventually came to fear the voracious appetites and destructive propensities of pigs, goats, cattle, and horses. John Easton of Rhode Island noted in 1675 that "when the English [bought] land of them," the Wampanoags and Narragansetts expected "that they would have kept their catell upone ther owne land," and were increasingly alienated from their new neighbors due to the damage done by the ranging "English catell and horses."[139] New England natives were "not willing" to enclose their corn, as the missionary to them, John Eliot, put it in the 1640s, "because they have neither tooles, nor skill, nor heart to fence their grounds.... And if it be not well fenced, their Corne is so spoyled by the English Cattell... that its a very great discouragement to them...." Nantucket Indians complained of English sheep in their cornfields. In Maryland native appealed to the General Assembly in the 1690s: "Your hogs & Cattle injure Us. We can fly no farther[;] let us know where to live & how to be secured for the future from the Hogs & Cattle." And that was not all. In 1642, the Narragansett sachem Miantonomo complained that settlers' "hogs spoil our clam banks, and we shall be starved."[140]

From the settler's perspective, the sharing of unenclosed land by foraging animals and hunting natives also proved to be less than satisfactory. Horses and cattle were injured in Indian deer traps or "torn

---

[137] George Chicken Journal, 12 Oct. 1725, cited in John Phillip Reid, *A Better Kind of Hatchet: Law, Trade, and Diplomacy in the Cherokee Nation during the Early Years of European Contact* (Penn State Univ. Press, 1976), 191–92.

[138] See Rebecca Kugel, "Of Missionaries and their Cattle: Ojibwa Perceptions of a Missionary as Evil Shaman," 41 *Ethnohistory* 227 (on Minnesota territory in 1871) (1994); Daniel Unser, *Indians, Settlers and Slaves*, 195 (on Houma Indians and sacred chicken in 1700).

[139] Anderson, "King Philip's Herds," 621.

[140] Jean O'Brien, *Dispossession by Degrees: Indian Land and Identity in Natick, Massachusetts, 1650–1790* (Cambridge Univ. Press, 1997), 28; Daniel Mandell, *Behind the Frontier: Indians in Eighteenth Century Eastern Massachusetts* (Lincoln, Neb., 1996), 23, 110; Anderson, "King Philip's Herds," 608; Colin Calloway, *The American Revolution in Indian Country* (Cambridge Univ. Press, 1995), 4.

by their dogs."[141] From the Indians' perspective, hogs consumed the nuts, wild tubers, and clams that served to supplement native diets, and cattle depleted the forage that sustained deer populations, and frightened the deer off. Moreover, settlers hunted deer, turkey, buffalo, and other game with abandon, and without asking permission of the Original People. "When you white men buy a farm," Ohio Valley warriors told David McClure in 1769, "you buy only the land; you don't buy the horses and cows and sheep. The elks are our horses, the buffaloes are our cows, the deer are our sheep, and the whites shan't have them." On one occasion in the early 1770s Shawnee warriors "relieved" some Virginia hunters of 1,100 deerskins. Michael McConnell observes of this action that the Shawnee would have called this justice "for poachers who had . . . robbed native hunters of their livelihood."[142]

In Cherokee country, Commissioner George Chicken told natives with whom he conferred at the Ellijay Council in 1720 that "the English did not Suffer" persistent ravaging of their crops by a neighbor's horses, and if the horses belonging to Carolina traders continued to consume their crops "they would take more care of them in the future" if the Cherokee "would Shoot some." And we have just seen that he was true to his word in warning all colonial British traders to this effect. But at this point in their relations with the British, the Cherokee were disinclined to take such a self-help measure as to kill "any White Man's horse." John Reid argues that the Cherokee viewed such a drastic act as being unacceptable behavior, disruptive to the "harmonious relations" they sought in their lives and their towns. And this sounds right. Similarly, "praying" Indians in the town of Okommakamesit, some thirty

---

[141] Anderson, "King Philip's Herds," 608; Mandell, *Behind the Frontier*, 34.

[142] Mandell, *Behing the Frontier*, 13. And see James Merrell, *The Indian's New World: Catawbas and Their Neighbors from European Contact through the Era of Removal* (Chapel Hill, 1989), 100, 175, 184 (on similar tensions in Catawba Valley over foraging settler animals in deer country, the accidental destruction of settler fences by Catawbas using fire to hunt, and the killing for consumption of settler hogs or cattle); Thomas Sugrue, "The Peopling and Depeopling of Early Pennsylvania: Indians and Colonists, 1680–1720," 116 *Pa. Mag. of History & Biog.* At 23 (1992) (Diaspora pigs a problem to the Lenape); *Diary of David McClure*, ed. Franklin Dexter (1899), 83–85; McConnell, *A Country Between*, 259, 262. See also Elizabeth Perkins, *Border Life* (Chapel Hill, 1998), 14–15, 77 (Ohio Valley natives complaining that "the whites were killing off their turkies[sic], deer and etc."); and Colin Calloway, *The Western Abenakis of Vermont, 1600–1800* (Norman, Okla., 1990), 231 (on the suffering of Abenaki at the headwaters of the Missiquoi River in the late eighteenth century due in part to "the moose and deer (which formerly abounded here) being destroyed by the settlers.").

miles from Boston, simply abandoned some 150 acres to English settlers: "It brings little or no profit to them, nor is it ever like to do[,] because the Englishmen's cattle, &c. devour all in it, because it lies open and unfenced."[143] Virginia Anderson writes that these natives "clearly expected no redress." Thus, like the Cherokee, these Algonquins engaged in no "bargaining" with British colonists; they simply accomodated them unilaterally.

English settlers understood property rights to encompass the "improving" of land "by enclosing and peculiar manurance," in the words of Governor John Winthrop of the Massachusetts Bay colony. Winthrop faulted the native inhabitants: "They inclose no ground; neither have they cattell to maintain it." This need for cattle to plough and fertilize settler fields, as well as to provide them with dairy products, meat, and hides, led the newcomers to seek new, inland towns as the meadows of the first communities became overcrowded. "No man now thought he could live except he had cattle and a great deal of ground to keep them," Plymouth's Governor William Bradford complained in 1632.[144]

Both cultural groups eventually acted to defend their own notion of what was fair and right. Newcomer-settlers in Warwick, Rhode Island, complained to the local sachem that "his people were killing their swine." The sachem promised to "come to court to resolve the issue." Iroquois at Sillery, Quebec, killed a newcomer's cow in their corn in 1646 and, when told by the French authorities that they must pay six beaver skins in restitution, they complied once they had been assured "that when they should complain, Justice would be done them" for such damage to their crops in the future. In 1636 Massachusetts Bay commissioners in Saco made the killing by angry Abenakis of "any swyne of the Inglishe" a capital offense. Abenakis were killing pigs; Shawomets, cattle, when complaints of their destructive behavior went unheeded in 1688. Both sides then began to seize hostages, and in short order the "Eastern" front of King William's War had opened.[145] Choctaw and Natchez warrior-hunters "raided livestock" throughout the eighteenth century in the South, "hunting them like a new species

[143] Reid, *A Better Kind of Hatchet*, 185–86; Anderson, "King Philip's Herds," 611.

[144] *Of Plymouth Plantation, 1620–1647*, ed. Samuel Eliot Morrison (N.Y., 1952), 253.

[145] Katherine Hermes, "Jurisdiction in the Colonial Northeast: Algonquin, English, and French Governance," 43 *American Journal of Legal History* 71 (1999); Alfred Bailey, *The Conflict of European and Algonquin Cultures, 1504–1700* (2nd ed, 1969), 94; Anderson, "King Philip's Herds," 612; Kenneth Morrison, *The Embattled Northeast: The Elusive Ideal of Alliance in Abenaki-Euramerican Relations* (Berkeley, 1984), 113.

of game." When their newcomer-owners fatally beat one Choctaw for killing cattle near Galveztown in 1782, vengeful warriors attacked that settlement.[146] Rhode Island and Nantucket natives seeking to graze their hogs and cattle on various town commons were turned away in the 1660s and thereafter. Virginia DeJohn Anderson has aptly observed that "no problem vexed relations between settlers and Indians more frequently in the years before King Philip's War (1675–1676) than the control of livestock," and she points out that in the course of that brief war Indian forces ruthlessly killed some eight thousand head of English cattle.[147]

This cultural conflict over animals and crops was not limited in time and place to the *colonial* American world, of course. I offer five examples of its existence in the nineteenth century: We have already met my first (in Chapter 1) – the widespread trespassing of newcomer cattle on lands of the Cherokee Nation. General Andrew Jackson and his successor-military commanders in the region would drive the intruders off in the 1820s, but Commissioner Return Meigs reported to John C. Calhoun in 1819 that they "returned as thick as crows that are scattered . . . by a person passing on the road, but as soon as he is passed they return. . . ."[148] Secondly: When the beleaguered Shawnee of the Ohio Valley turned to their visionaries for direction in the early nineteenth century, they were advised to shed Diaspora ways by killing such cattle as they had acquired and destroying such fencing as they had built. Then "you will have wild game enough, and the deer will come in front of your huts."[149] Thirdly: In the early 1820s, Black Hawk, the war leader of the Sauks on the Mississippi River, recalled white settlers "beating me with sticks. . . . They accused me of killing their pigs." He told of "another time" when "one of our young men was beaten with clubs by two white men" over a breach in a fence. "His shoulder blade was broken, and his body badly bruised, from which he soon after died."[150] Finally: In 1854, a Mormon immigrant complained to

[146] Daniel Unser, *Indians, Settlers and Slaves in a Frontier Exchange: The Lower Mississippi Valley before 1783* (Chapel Hill, 1992), 67, 128–29, 186.

[147] Anderson, "King Philip's Herds," 602, 622; Mandell, *Behind the Frontier*, 74. And see Calloway, *Western Abenaki*, 150, 152, for three reports in the 1740s of Abenaki killing settler cattle.

[148] Return Meigs cited in Wilma Dunaway, *The First American Frontier*, 71.

[149] Stephen Aron, *How the West was Lost*, 110–11.

[150] William Cronon, *Changes in the Land*; Gwenda Morgan, *The Hegemony of the Law: Richmond County, Virginia, 1692–1776* (N.Y., 1989), 28; *Black Hawk: An Autobiography*, ed. Donald Jackson (Urbana, Ill., 1964), 97, 102. See also Jeffrey Burton, *Indian Territory and the United States, 1866–1906: Courts, Government and the Movement for Oklahoma Statehood* (Norman, Okla., 1995), 124.

the U.S. Army commander at Ft. Laramie that someone in a nearby encampment of Brule Sioux had stolen one of his oxen. The Brules claimed that the animal was wandering and had been abandoned. When a lieutenant and eighteen men were dispatched to the camp to arrest a Brule suspect, their attempt met with fierce resistance; all perished and more blood was shed in "punishing" the Brules.[151] Finally, in British Columbia's Fraser Canyon a Diaspora settler at Kwi.owh.um by the name of Tim Ryan acquired title to land with "the only water that could be used for irrigation" in the area, and was reported in the 1870s to be making the native people "pay for trespass" when their horses passed through his "bad fences."[152]

Maoris and Pakehas:the Cultural Impasse in New Zealand. The problem in New Zealand was similar to those in colonial America and Australia: While Maoris generally found ways to resolve animal trespass disputes with fellow Maoris, and Pakehas with fellow Pakehas, the cultural barriers between the two peoples were such that few individuals surmounted them.

Trespassing pigs were a constant source of trouble. Where Maoris were in the minority, as in the South Island, whalers and settlers shot native pigs with relative impunity, and Maoris had to appeal to British magistrates for redress; but where Maoris predominated, throughout most of the North Island for the first thirty or so years of interaction and colonization, their *runangas* functioned, and native police (*karere*) and assesors fined Pakeha runholders and farmers for killing native pigs. In 1835, the two North Island cultures engaged in what was styled "the battle of the pork"; Pakehas in that year seized crop-damaging native pigs at Hokianga. Within a decade Hone Heke and his men engaged in the first formal acts of resistance to British sovereignty – the stealing and killing of Pakeha pigs in the Bay of Islands.[153]

At least as serious a problem was the resolving of disputes flowing from the importation of British cattle. On the issue of trespasses to crops by cattle the two cultures were poles apart, one favoring "range" law, the other "herd" law. As magistrate John Gorst put it in 1842, "so long as Europeans and Maoris continue to farm on antagonistic principles – the one fencing their crops and letting their cattle run at large, the other tying up their cattle or driving them to other regions, and leaving their crops exposed – there will be disputes whenever the two races come in contact."

[151] J. P. Dunn, *Massacres of the Mountains* (N.Y., 1886), 194.
[152] Cole Harris, *The Resettlement of British Columbia*, 122.
[153] R. Hill, *Policing the Colonial Frontier*, 74, 152, 839, 882–83; A. Ward, *Show of Justice*, 27, 50, 79, 80; Ian Wards, *Shadow of the Land*, 102.

The early governors and their councils, you will recall, sought to accomodate this difference by requiring settlers to fence *Maori* animals out of their crops *and* requiring them to pay damages to Maoris when unfenced *settler* cattle ruined unfenced Maori field crops.[154] But this meant that Pakehas adjacent Maori land might have to pay the full cost of their fencing, a condition foreign to their customs and offensive to their pride. Some Maoris must have offered to contribute some of the costs or labor necessary for the construction of their Pakeha neighbor's fence,[155] but the behavior that was commonly reported was otherwise. Minister for Lands C. W. Richmond described the "daily provocations" British colonists faced in 1860: "His cattle . . . stray from his paddock; he follows them to a neighboring *pa*, and is compelled to redeem them by an exhorbitant payment. . . . On the other hand should he try the experiment of driving Native cattle to the public pound for trespass on his cultivations, a strong party of Maoris, with loaded muskets, breaks down the pound and rescues them. He has to maintain party fences without contribution from his Maori neighbor." Moreover, "redress in the Courts of Law is not to be attained because it would be dangerous to the peace of the country to enforce the judgement," while "Natives freely avail themselves of their legal remedies against Europeans."[156] Similarly, Resident Magistrate Herbert Wardell claimed, regarding the entire East Coast region in 1856, that the Maoris "did not recognize the authority of [British] law, & yielded obedience

---

[154] A. Ward, *Show of Justice*, 50; R. Hill, *Policing the Colonial Frontier*, 226 (Governor Hobson ordering M. de Thierry to pay damages in Hokianga).

[155] I found no evidence of this in New Zealand, but in Fiji George Markham appears to have found a sensible way of drawing some of his Fijian neighbors into reciprocal fence building: Over a period of several days in late January and early February, 1877, he noted in his dairy the playing out of "arrangements" he had made "with the natives of Tei Damu" to "plough their Government plantation in consideration of their putting up a horse-proof fence a quarter of a mile in length." Later, in early March, he recorded a similar arrangement "with the Na Wesi people" to plough their fields "in consideration of their building us a new corn house." When Markham arrived at Na Wesi and began to plough, he noted that he worked "amidst the plaudits of an admiring crowd of mountaineers" who "Brought me a quantity of yams, paw paws, sugar cane & a fowl." Markham Diary, YA1422, Mitchell Lib.

[156] A. Ward, *Show of Justice*, 119–20. Richmond may simply have been alluding here to Maori occasional use of the resident magistrates; or he may have been referring to their use of *runangas* to fine Pakeha, to *utu* or even *muru* (retributive plundering), for Maori did indeed depasture or impound Pakeha cattle and sheep throughout the North Island. I noted evidence of this at Porirua in 1847, Poverty Bay in 1856, Taranaki in 1857, and Hawke's Bay in 1861.

or refused it as suited their purpose," while noting particularly that they "helped themselves" to his own cattle after their *runanga* decided that his distraint of some of their cattle had been improper.[157] (See Illustrations 17 and 18.)

That was the Pakeha view. The Maori saw things from a different perspective. In April, 1857, the Tu Wharetoa chief, Te Heuheu Iwikau, complained to Governor Thomas Gore Browne that "Englishmen among the Maoris were often men of desperate character," and that "their cattle trespassed on Maori lands." "Instead of compensation" for these trespasses, the Maori "received abuse" and "could get no redress." The first speech delivered by a Maori legislator before his colleagues in the General Assembly, that of Tareha Te Moananui of Hawke's Bay in 1868, echoed this theme: The Native Land Court, he explained, had impounded his cattle for trespasses, yet when he impounded Pakeha cattle on his land, he was "taken to court." When the unfenced cattle of Pakeha settlers at Kaiwharawhara destroyed crops belonging to Ngati Tamas in the 1840s, this tribe of Maoris, unable to obtain relief or redress, moved en masse away from the four-legged plunderers, as had their counterparts in southern Appalachia and Massachusetts. Later in the century Maori were made to pay a dog tax by the County Councils. Those councils were unmoved by the appeals of those Maori who had moved away from the Pakeha's animals and insisted that, inasmuch as they were now "miles away from European sheep runs," their dogs could "not annoy the public." In the early 1890s, a "Maori Parliament" petitioned the Pakeha Government for repeal or exemption from this tax, and for years North Auckland Maori refused to pay it and resisted arrest.[158]

What happened when those pushed preferred to shove back? In 1852, a settler in Taranaki named Bayley tried to get his Maori neighbors to split the cost of his fencing. When they refused, he simply left his wheat unprotected. Bayley "wouldn't fence for natives," as he later explained. When the crop was ravaged by native cattle, he took "self-help" by injuring some of the trespassing beasts. Their owners sought compensation, and when Bayley refused to pay, they seized some of his household goods in *muru*, depositing them with a Maori assesor. The matter was finally pleaded before Resident Magistrate Joseph Flight who awarded Bayley ten shillings, to go along with the lasting enmity both he and his neighbors had already earned for one another. Cattle, then were a constant source of problems and tensions, rarely solved by compromise. Stubborn behavior like Bayley's and that of his Maori

---

[157] Ian Wards, *Shadow of the Land*, 290; R. Hill, *Policing the Colonial Frontier*, 423, 426, 462, 828.
[158] D. Williams, *Politics of the New Zealand Maori*, 76–77.

Illustrations 17 and 18. Aboriginal people often had different norms regarding the fencing in or out of crops and animals. The first illustration, for a story on "The Impact of Sanitary Advice," in *The Illustrated New Zealand News* (1883), depicts a "modern Maori Pa [group of dwellings], complete with fenced yards that kept pigs under control" (top). But the second, a photo from the same period of a Maori dwelling in Urewera, showing an unfenced Pa and free-roaming pigs, appears to have been closer to the reality for most of the nineteenth century. (Alexander Turnbull Library, National Library of New Zealand/Te Puna Mātauranga o Aotearoa, C-208210-; F-570251/2.)

neighbors helped bring the two peoples to war in Taranaki within a decade.[159]

Aborigines and Squatters: the Cultural Impasse in Australia. Perhaps nowhere in these British colonies were tensions over the Diaspora's herbivores more pronounced than in Australia. Justice Field, it will be recalled, had insisted in 1817 on the Common-Law rule that cattle in New South Wales be fenced in. There is some evidence that "substantial" fences were built along some of that colony's roads and around many small farms and gardens, and that some leaseholders "fenced in" their "cultivated ground," conceivably at the instructions of their landlords.[160] Perhaps the *custom* was range law, though the Law was herd law. In any event, the requirement in Governor Gipps' proclamation that selectors build "good and substantial" fences within two years of settlement was widely ignored, because "no selector in his right mind would attempt to enclose his property" with what then and there was, necessarily, a wooden fence until both he and his neighbors had cleared their property of all brush and scrub, in order to avoid "the risk of the fences being promptly burnt to the ground when clearing by fire got underway," as one such selector put it.[161]

But selectors burning the dense scrub to be found in some regions were not the major cause of fire hazards to Diaspora fences, crops, and buildings in the nineteenth century: The Aboriginal people of Australia had for centuries cleared the brush by periodic burning in order to create grassy pastures and openings at water holes for the kangaroo and emu they hunted on their land. "Every tribe has its own district," one early Diaspora observer noted, "and within that district all the wild animals are considered as much the property of the tribe" as "flocks of sheep and herds of cattle" were to the British. "Squatters" felt that they had "discovered" these "grasslands so well adapted for

[159] A. Ward, *Show of Justice*, 79,221; Ian Wards, *Shadow of the Land*, 224; W. P. Morrell, *British Colonial Policy in the Mid-Victorian Age* (Oxford, 1969), 224.

    The same tensions between British settlers and Polynesian people over trespassing cattle can be detected in Hawaii in the 1840s as well: Cows belonging to Richard Charlton, the British Consul in Honolulu, had repeatedly ravaged the crops of natives. When one of these men shot one of Charlton's offending cows, Charlton dragged him by the neck from his horse until the farmer died. E. W. Joesting, *Hawaii: An Uncommon History* (N.Y., 1972), 127–29.

[160] John Pickard, "Trespass, Common Law, Government Regulations, and Fences in Colinal New South Wales, 1788–1828," 84 *Journal of the Royal Australian Historical Society* 135; John Lhotosky, *A Journey from Sydney to the Australian Alps* (Sydney, 1835), 16; testimony of William Muston in *Bucknall v. Moral* (NSWSC, Kercher, 1829).

[161] Ross Hartnell, *Pack Tracks to Pasture* (Poowong, 1974), 29.

cattle. They soon learned of the systematic burning that had produced them (sometimes to their distress, when the fires destroyed all or parts of their homesteads, barns, crops, and fences).[162]

Aboriginal-Squatter tensions were inevitable, and had less to do with this firing of the brush than with the conflict over the use of the resulting grassland. Settler sheep and cattle were turned loose on their grasslands, lands generally insufficient in nutrients and water for both these western herbivores and the native kangaroos. In 1838, the Sydney *Herald* echoed the Swiss jurist Emmerich Vattel, the English political philosopher John Locke, and the Massachusetts Bay Colony's first governor, John Winthrop, in dismissing the notion that Aborigines possessed any property in the land: "This vast country was to them a common – they bestowed no labour upon the land – their ownership, their right, was nothing more than that of the Emu or the Kangaroo." The British Diaspora "took possession," and "they had a perfect right to do so, under the Divine authority, by which man was commanded to go forth and people, *till* the land."[163]

With this sort of perspective, the typical Diaspora newcomer had little patience with aboriginals he confronted while leading "his flocks, and his herds, and his men" into what the Murray River's Resident Magistrate Edward John Eyre called "the patrimony that has descended" to the natives "through many generations." "Met with repulsion, and sometimes by violence," the natives were made to feel they were "strangers in their own land." Eyre was not surprised that they soon took to stealing, or merely killing, sheep.[164] "Old Dalaipi," an Aborigine living near Brisbane in the 1850s, later recalled the consequences of this view of relative rights: "They stole our ground where we used to get food, and when we got hungry and took a bit of flour or killed a bullock to eat, they shot us or poisoned us." Given these circumstances, Sir Thomas Mitchell observed in 1848, the Aboriginal bands were likely to "feel disposed . . . to help themselves to some of the cattle or sheep that have fattened on the green pastures kept clear for kangaroos from time immemorial by the fires of the natives and their forefathers. . . ." Moreover, Diaspora cattle "trample out the signs of turtles found in dried-up swamps, the trail of the crocodile to his nest, they eat the tops of yams, and eat and destroy the lilies, all of which make natural food scarcer and harder to find," one Aborigine explained.[165]

---

[162] Sylvia J. Hallam, *Fire and Hearth: A Study of Aboriginal Usage and European Usurpation in Southwestern Australia* (Cambridge, 1975), 15, 47, 75.

[163] 7 November 1838.

[164] Edward Eyre, *Journals of Exploration and Discovery into Central Australia* (2 vols., London, 1845), I, 169, 172.

[165] Henry Reynolds, *The Other Side of the Frontier* (Ringwood, 1983), 159. The problem was evident in French Melanesia as well, where free-ranging

The Law allowed Aborigines the customary right to enter unfenced Crown land (as most Squatter pastureland was in the first generation) to hunt kangaroo, but the Squatters on such land often ignored that Law and took to warning Aborigines off "their" land, to killing kangaroos and emu as "pests," and, all too often, to killing Aborigines as well. Louis Chamerovzow described the cultural impasse well in the mid-1840s:

> The white man hunts down for sport or for purposes of trade, the animals and the fowl which constitute the native's food; their ordinary subsistence failing them, [they] who are unable to understand by what right the stranger despoils them, then fall upon the flocks of the Settler, or rob his homestead, and suddenly find themselves entrammeled within the meshes of a law which teaches them that they must not steal from the white man, but which casts not its protection over *them* from whom *he* has first stolen.[166]

Edward Curr, who observed some of the ways of Aboriginal people in Victoria, could see the problem: The animals imported from Britain "devour wholesale the roots and vegetables" which constituted the Aborigines' "principal food, and drive off the game they formally hunted." But, less sympathetically, Curr also wrote of a "plague" of kangaroos in Victoria that had the temerity to "consume as much grass as sheep," so many "that, in some places, they threatened to jostle the sheep and his master out of the land." Consequently, "energetic and costly steps had to be taken to reduce their numbers." On one large run of some 70,000 acres "ten thousand of these animals were killed and skinned annually for 6 years." Elsewhere, "by means of long lines of fencing and high yards, specially erected for the purpose, as many as two thousand have been destroyed in a single day." Similarly, Charles Blomfield recalled that by the late 1860s kangaroos had been declared "a noxious animal & 6p apiece given for their scalps" by governments influenced by graziers who "thought [the kangaroo] were making a considerable difference to the grass for their stock...."

Aborigines responded by spearing sheep, cattle, and horses, destroying fences, and (selectively) killing those suspected of having killed one of their clan.[167] Within a decade of Squatter settlement a Jiman

---

European-owned cattle damaged cane, bananas, and other crops. Robert Aldrich, *The French Presence in the South Pacific* (Honolulu, 1990), 188, 190.

[166] Edward Curr, *The Australian Race* (4 vols. Melbourne, 1886–87), I, 106; Edward Curr, *Recollections of Squatting in Victoria*, 184; Charles Blomfield, "Reminiscences of Early New England, 1868-" pp. 14–15, CY373, Mitchell Lib.; L. Chamerovzow, *The New Zealand Question and the Rights of the Aborigine* (London, 1848), 212–13.

[167] Henry Reynolds, *The Other Side of the Frontier: Aboriginal Resistance to the*

band in central Queensland were indeed poaching settler flocks and herds. When they killed a protesting shepherd in 1854, and massacred a family of pastoralists at Hornet's Bend station in 1857, they and their fellow tribesmen were tracked and killed by the colony's mounted constabulary.[168]

"Squatters" and their stockmen, mounted and armed with superior weapons, retaliated with ruthless abandon, despite the efforts of some government officials to curb and punish such behavior. "In want of a fresh run for his stock," James Coutts Crawford, a Squatter headed southwest with a herd toward South Australia on the Murrumbidgee. In February, 1839, he complained to his diary that he who ventures beyond "his [British] neighbors" soon comes "in contact with an un-civilized tribe of blacks" who cannot understand why his (unfenced) bullocks could not be speared the same as native kangaroos. One of his bullocks had been speared and roasted by a local tribe, and he noted that he was likely to be condemned in High Places for such "self-help" as he were to take by way of retaliation: "All our colonies are more or less plagued with so-called Philanthropists... at Exeter Hall and elsewhere."[169] Another Squatter in Victoria who had been losing sheep to Aborigines wrote to his relations in Scotland that the natives were "one link removed from the 'ourang-outang' and should be exter-minated." Seven stockmen who *were* punished (executed for the Myall Creek massacre in 1838) claimed that they had acted "solely in defense of their Masters' property."[170] The Diaspora equation: The lives of Abo-rigines for the lives of sheep or cattle. (See Illustrations 19 and 20.)

European Invasion of Australia (1982), 106–09; Jan Critchett, *"A Distant Field of Murder": Western [Victoria] District Frontiers, 1834–1848* (Melbourne, 1990), 90–91, 97–108; R. H. W. Reese, *Aborigines and Colonists:... Society in New South Wales, in the 1830s and '40s* (Sydney, 1974), 28; Sylvia Hallam, "Aboriginal Women as Providers: The 1830s on the Swan," 15 *Aboriginal History* 38 at 43 (1991); Ann McGrath, ed., *Contested Ground*, 183.

[168] Kercher, *Unruly Child*, 6–11; Constance C. Petrie, *Tom Petrie's Reminiscences of Early Queensland* (Brisbane, 1904), 182–83, quoted in C. Rowley, *The Destruction of Aboriginal Society, Vol. I*, 158; C. W. Rowley, *The Destruction of Aboriginal Society: Vol. I* (Cambridge, 1970), 112–14; Gordon Reid, *A Nest of Hornets: The Massacre of the Fraser Family at Hornet's Bend... 1857* (Melbourne, 1982), 6, 25, 55, passim; Michael Roe, *The Quest for Authority in Eastern Australia, 1835–1851* (Melbourne, 1965), 66–67.

[169] D. H. Pike, "The Diary of James Coutts Crawford...'" 4 *South Australiana* 4–5 (March, 1965). ("Exeter Hall" = Aborigines' Protection Society.)

[170] *Contested Ground*, ed. Ann McGrath (St. Leonards, NSW, Allen & Unwin, 1995), 131, 244; Critchett, *"Distant Field of Murder,"* 29; Reece, *Aborigines and Colonists*, 30, 94,158, 195; "Philanthropus," in the *Sydney Gazette*, 5 Aug. 1824, reprinted in Henry Reynolds, *Dispossession* (Sydney, 1990), 54 (ob-jecting to the equating of the lives of animals and Aborigines).

Illustrations 19 and 20.   George Hamilton depicted "Natives Spearing the Overlanders' Cattle" (note the native dogs in the lower left)
and "Overlanders Attacking the Natives" in 1846. (Mitchell Library,
State Library of New South Wales,V/AUS/ABO/CIV/30 and 31.)

Men like Eyre, Curr, and Mitchell appreciated what was happening
and expressed sympathy for the Aborigines, but they did not protest
mightily against that process that weighed so heavily against the future
of Aboriginal rights and culture, because their core value systems were
western. They accepted the "need" to put the Australian grasslands to
more "productive" use: Wool for the textile mills of Yorkshire. This failure to "cross-over" the cultural divide is clear in the dairy and letters of

another sympathetic Diaspora figure, George Moore, a trained Anglo-Irish barrister who migrated to Western Australia in 1830, served as a magistrate and member of the colony's Legislative Council, managed a successful farm/ranch, and was a sympathetic friend and informal protector to the vicinity's native people. That much is clear from the accounts he left us and from the fact that he completed a thorough glossary of Aborigine terms and syntax and an Aborigine-to-English dictionary. And yet, in one crucial regard, Moore was virtually as much a threat to the future of the Aborigines as those Squatters and station hands throughout the continent who cut Aborigines down for the slightest offense. How so? As a landowner and magistrate, Moore had little patience with Aborigines who hunted sheep with their dogs (dingoes), or who tolerated their dogs getting among the sheep or pigs on their own. "These uninformed creatures think that they have as good a right to our swine as we have to their kangaroos," he wrote in June, 1832. Yet he simultaneously reveled in hunting the native's chief source of protein, the kangaroos, with his own imported hounds.[171] And this form of recreation was so common as to be the subject of numerous engravings and watercolors in Australia throughout the nineteenth century. (See Illustration 21.)

South Africa. The tension at the Cape over animals had a different character, for the natives there had for centuries been herdsmen. From the first days of contact, when the Dutch in the 1650s introduced their own cattle to the region, the Hottentot (Khoi) chiefs attacked in 1659. After an uneasy truce had been declared, they complained in 1660 that "you come and occupy our pasture" with your cattle, "and then say the land is not wide enough for both! Who then can be required with the greatest degree of justice to give way, the natural owner or the invader?" Governor Van Riebeck maintained that he "would not restore the land, as it had now become the property of the Company by the sword and the laws of war," but the Dutch Company's directors directed him to purchase the land, as the chiefs' "discontent" had been "neither surprising nor groundless," and this was eventually done, in 1672.

None the less, the steady growth in numbers of the Boer herdsmen caused constant tension in the region. In the late 1820s, several decades after the Cape Colony had been taken by the British,

---

[171] See, for example, Moore, *Diary of Ten Years,* 120 (entry for June 28, 1832), 280 (entry for Sept. 15, 1835). But there were many other entries like these. And see the casual diary entry of New South Wales Judge-Advocate Richard Atkins for August 9, 1794: "The dogs ran down an Emue." (Www.law.mq.au/scnsw/atkins_1794.html)

Illustration 21. This engraving for *The Picturesque Atlas of Australasia* (circa 1888) celebrates a popular pastime of "squatters," their overseers, and their station hands alike: a kangaroo hunt, complete with English hounds. (In possession of author.)

missionary James Clark worried in his journal about the pressure on another band of natives much closer culturally to Australian aboriginals than the pastoral Khoi and Bantu – namely, the Bushmen. Boers "come over the Craddock [the Orange] to pasture ... are not only driving the Bushmen from their fountains, and the wild game, their principle support, but they have thus reduced them to the necessity either to steal the farmers' cattle, or perish from hunger." The Frontier War of 1834–1835, referred to in Chapter 1, involved the slaughter of some 112,000 Boer cattle and 162,000 sheep by their Bantu competitors for pastureland.[172]

Cattle and Negativism: a Note on Animal-Trespass Public Nuisances. All of the examples of disputes over animal trespasses described thus far concerned trespasses onto *private* property. What of *public* trespasses ("public nuisances")? Each Diaspora community created ordinances regarding the "public nuisance" committed by animals trespassing in public places, which were then, at times, invoked against those who allowed their pigs or cattle to wander in towns and settled communities.

[172] W. Basil Warsfold, *South Africa* (1895), 13, 31; William M. Macmillan, *Bantu, Boer & Briton*, 42.

Let New Zealand serve as an example: In one year in the early 1870s some 84 of 110 convictions before the resident magistrate's court in New Plymouth, Taranaki, were for allowing cattle to be at large. Another way to put this is to say that a full generation after the first settlers and their cattle had appeared on the scene, wandering herbivores were still the greatest public problem in the towns. Conversely, in the city of Auckland Mayor P. A. Philips remarked in the same year (1871) that the Impounding Act was "almost a dead letter," largely unenforced by the Armed Constabulary who served in that era as its police force.[173] All of this sounds similar to Dirk Hartog's description of the inability of New York City's authorities to keep pigs off the streets in the first half of the nineteenth century.[174] And it is, but there was a cultural dimension to animal trespasses in New Zealand, as we have just seen, that caused these scenes of popular disregard for the formal Law to assume truly tragic dimensions at times.

SUMMARY

As was the case with legal issues involving leaseholds, riparian rights, and challenges to title, CANZ jurists tended to follow English Common-Law precedents rather scrupulously when it came to pollution nuisances or the ancient-lights easement rule. While some were aware of the fact that a number of state jurisdictions in the United States had abrogated the ancient-lights doctrine, or altered some aspects of the Law with regard to pollution nuisances, CANZ jurists simply did not feel either empowered or inclined to follow the example of their republican compeers in these instances.

When it came to interpreting statutes that had brought franchised corporations into being, both U.S. and CANZ jurists generally interpreted these quite "strictly," protecting the rights granted therein from challenges from those seeking to infringe on the franchise granted, while limiting the enfranchised corporations to the terms of their charters. But when it came to the eminent-domain ("takings") provisions in many of these charters, our attention is drawn to both the modest, "liberal" interpretations courts sometimes gave them, out of respect for the property rights of those whose land, or its "quiet enjoyment" was

---

[173] R. Hill, *The Colonial Frontier Tamed: New Zealand Policing in Transition, 1867–1886* (Wellington, 1989), 188, 246. See also the Wellington police report in 1851 indicating that wandering cattle were "one of the greatest nuisances in this Town"(*Ibid.*, 387). And see the evidence that a prosecution for infanticide of a young Hawera woman in the 1880s failed because "pigs ate the corpse" (*Ibid.*, 306).

[174] Hendrik Hartog, "Pigs and Positivism," 1985 *Wisconsin Law Review* 899.

being disturbed, and to the more aggressively prolandowner actions of that *Vox Populi*, the jury of assessors. Whether one is speaking of the actions of juries in England, the United States, the Canadian Maritime provinces, Upper or Lower Canada, or New Zealand, the story is the same: Juries displayed considerable generosity toward those who had been encroached on; and jurists rarely interfered with these awards.

The Law and popular norms came to loggerheads over encroachments on property rights, in Wales, Tasmania, and the United States, when it came to tolls, taxes, cattle killed on railroad rights-of-way, or the collection of defaulted railroad bonds (affecting farm mortgages). In each instance, the offender was a distant corporation or an arm of the state – not one's neighbor.

Those who did behave in conciliatory ways fared better than those who went to private Law or private war, but that social fact did not prevent some members of the British Diaspora from taking costly or violent measures when trespassed upon.[175] While the Law was virtually

---

[175] It seems clear from this comparative look at animal trespasses that the bargaining process described by Ronald Coase often did not take place. One problem is that Law & Economics theory employs an amorphous catch-all term, *transaction costs*, to capture every-and-all intervening variable interfering with the smooth flow of "rational" economic exchanges. To Law & Economics folk the term *transaction costs* usually means the costs of obtaining information in the bargaining process as well as those associated with the actual negotiation or litigation. But where cultural barriers are high, the term also has to be used to refer to the costs needed to surmount those barriers of language, symbols, meaning, and values. This amounts to a rather clumsy way of establishing that cooperation is difficult to arrange when the parties come to the issues wearing different cultural glasses. Law & Economics theorists can claim that they can "account for" those differences and all they entail in calculating the bargaining process or the transaction costs, but the accounting may not be as useful as they would like to believe.

As we have seen, "irrational" behavior sometimes prevented rational bargaining and neighborly sharing of costs among the British Diaspora. Law & Economics theory does not work well when neighbors are simply "irrational" (or "abnormal" as the psychologist would have it). I found very little bargaining when it came to native-settler interactions, and very many failed bargains when it came to settler–settler interactions during the first generation or two of settlement. The percentage of "irrational" folk in the lands of the British Diaspora of the past was not insignificant. That ought to signal to us that rational-actor models of dispute resolution should be supplemented with those of anthropology, psychology, and sociology. Such theory also does not work very well to explain behavior when the parties to a dispute were from strikingly different cultures, since such theory does not give sufficient weight to ordinary perceptions of "fairness," a crucial motivating force that can get in the way of "logical" solutions to disputes.

useless in restoring neighborly relations in these sorts of disputes, that did not mean that it was unutilized. All too often neighbors (especially in those first two generations of settlement) engaged in expensive litigation, or resorted to the worst "self-help," violence. In the first stages of frontier life, when neighbors were not well known to one another, where those on the two sides of a boundary fence were not yet likely to be the offspring of established members of the community or church, the sort of social isolation that Lois Carr and Miles Fairburn detected in the first generation of Maryland's and New Zealand's settlers could get in the way of accommodation and cooperation.[176] This was surely the case in the first decade or two of settlement life in Victoria, where the Diaspora population in 1841 numbered 1,102 males and 158 females, and there was evidence of considerable social tension within the Diaspora's ranks.[177] Similarly, Ann Herraman's analysis of the records of magistrates in South Australia's Mt. Barker district in the 1850s indicates that, despite the beginnings of churches and neighborly behavior, and the scarcity of constables to enforce the Law, over half of some 1,520 entries in these records were for acts of violence, public disorder, or property disputes, whereas the litigation before magistrates in more settled communities was largely that of debt collection.[178]

Eventually social bonds developed, and the relatively equal resources and claims of the parties in the inevitable disputes over animal trespasses lent themselves to informal, "neighborly" adjustments, just as Robert Ellickson had found in modern Shasta County, California. The "common law" of good neighborliness was sufficient in most

Those of the Law & Economics persuasion can claim to accommodate such cultural collisions as those of Algonquins and Puritans, Aborigines and "squatters," Maoris and Pakehas, but only by insisting on inappropriate language and terms. They must make room for both the psychologist's concept of abnormal behavior and the anthropologist's concept of culture and for what they represent – the "irrational" and less-than-pecuniary domains of personality traits, norms, symbols, and values.

[176] Miles Fairburn, *The Ideal Society and its Enemies: The Foundations of Modern New Zealand Society, 1850–1900* (Auckland, 1989); Lois Carr, "The Development of the Maryland Orphan's Court, 1654–1715," in Carr and Aubrey Land, eds., *Law, Society & Politics in Early Maryland* (Baltimore, 1977), 41ff. See also William Wyckoff, *The Developers' Frontier*, 129–30 (No churches in the Holland Land Company's domain in western New York for several years; the individual and the nuclear family the central social units for some time).

[177] Critchett, *A Distant Field of Murder*, 26; Alastair Campbell, *John Batman and the Aborigines*, 150–70.

[178] A. Herraman, "Crime and Social Conflict in Nineteenth Century Rural South Australia," Australian Historical Association Conference, Sydney, July, 1998.

instances when settlers in mature communities with churches, schools, and social organizations came to dispute a boundary line, irrigation ditch, fence, or animal trespass, though such neighbors could still fall out over the overflowing of a milldam, or a pig or bullock who had ravaged a garden.

But there was less willingness to accept either the "high" or "low" law when the trespass involved members of such strikingly different peoples as the Aboriginal people and British Diaspora immigrants. Settlers could not easily assume the costs of fencing both their own animals *out* of Algonquin or Maori crops and their own crops *in* from Algonquin or Maori animals, and, in any event, they refused to do so. Nor were they willing to provide forage and protection for the deer and kangaroo who shared the open pasture and meadows of North America and Australia. These different cultures were often unable to accommodate one another's claims; their differing perceptions of the proper rules regarding the fencing in or out of crops and animals, on the one hand, and the low opinion of natives held by most British settlers, and of settlers by aboriginals, in both North America and the Antipodes, on the other, led to widespread ignoring of the Law and to the imposition by both parties of an often bloody "informal law."

PART TWO

Agreements

5

We Have An Agreement: The Formal and Informal Law of Sales, Third-Party Beneficiary, Common Carrier, and Contingency-Fee Contracts

The nineteenth century statute books were filled with Laws affecting property. Those same books were virtually silent on agreements not involving real estate until the late nineteenth century. With the exception of some aspects of contracts for personal service which were governed by a number of 'Master and Servant' Acts, and the Statute of Frauds (1677), contract Law was "private," and it was sometimes said that when two people came to an agreement about the transfer of commercial paper or the sale of a commodity, or, indeed, the sale of one's labor to the other, they had "made law" between them.

When agreements between parties with long-standing trade and credit relationships are broken, the parties generally do not resort to litigation to secure relief or compensation.[1] But other agreements, especially those one-time agreements between strangers, or between employers ("masters") and employees ("servants"), are not as easily renegotiated or arbitrated when one party defaults in whole or part. These were the chief candidates for litigation, and it is with these that the Law was primarily concerned. This chapter and the next (on labor contracts) ask whether and to what extent these generalizations apply to the formal and informal laws of agreements between parties in the lands of the British Diaspora prior to the twentieth century.

SALES CONTRACTS

Were there any differences between the behavior of jurists in England, The United States, Canada, and Australasia when contract cases came to the courts? Jurists in the United States were not as innovative in

---

[1] The classic study of the phenomenon in the twentieth century is Stewart Macaulay, "Non-Contractual Relations in Business," 28 *American Sociological Review* 55 (1963).

this field as they were in others; they followed English rules and cited English precedents with regard to most contract issues. They appear to have been quite comfortable with virtually all of the English Common-Law rules regarding sales and credit, but did strike out on their own on a few issues, chiefly regarding personal service contracts.[2] How did CANZ jurists behave?

The Formal Law of Sales Contracts

Those who tell us about contracts for sale in nineteenth century America do not say the same things. Some believe that jurists in the United States "transformed" English rules in response to the needs of commerce, holding parties to the terms of contracts in un-English ways and imposing new expectation damages on those who breached contracts for future delivery.[3] Others (and I count myself as being firmly in this camp) dispute these claims and argue that all of the allegedly "new" doctrines were quite old and quite English, that there was nothing new to the practice of courts ordering the payment of expectation damages in breaches of futures contracts, that the parties had always been held to their agreements at Common Law, so long as consideration had moved in exchange for a promise, neither party had engaged in fraud, and no practice against good public policy (such as prostitution) was the subject of the contract.[4]

Inasmuch as I am convinced that jurists in the United States had not tinkered with the rules regarding contracts for sale in the nineteenth century, and inasmuch as R. C. B. Risk has made the case that Ontario's jurists in the nineteenth century had not tinkered with such rules either,[5] I did not regard cases involving sales contracts in Australia, New Zealand, or the other Canadian provinces as being particularly fruitful subjects of exhaustive study, since we are searching for the moments that CANZ jurists might have felt inclined to veer away somehow from

---

[2] See Karsten, *Heart versus Head*, ch. 2, 5, 6.

[3] See, especially, Morton Horwitz, *The Transformation of American Law, 1780–1860* (Cambridge, Mass., 1977), ch. 6, "The Triumph of Contract"; and Kermit Hall, *The Magic Mirror: Law in American History* (N.Y., 1989), 119–23.

[4] See A. W. B. Simpson, "The Horwitz Thesis and the History of Contracts", 48 *University of Chicago Law Review* (1979); Kim Scheppelle, *Legal Secrets:* (Chicago, 1988), 269–98; Karsten, *supra* note 2, ch. 2.

[5] R. W. B. Risk, "The Golden Age: The Law about the Market in Ontario in the 19th Century," 26 *Univ. of Toronto Law Journal* 307 (1976); but see Bernard Tibbitts, "Progress and Principle: The Legal Thought of Sir John Beverley Robinson," 34 *McGill Law Journal* 454 (1989), who seeks to make the case that this Chief Justice of Upper Canada's Queen's Bench was innovative in the fashion of Horwitz's "transformation" of contract law (supra note 1).

an unappealing English rule. But I did sample them and offer a few observations.

By the 1820s, experienced jurists were made available to hear cases before juries in New South Wales. The instructions they provided jurors and assessors with in suits involving sales contracts were faithful to English legal authority.[6] Quebec's jurists seem to have the same rule as those of New York and New South Wales regarding implied warranties: If the buyer had more information about the product than the seller (an agent, factor, or wholesaler), then the rule was "let the buyer beware"[7]; whereas, if the seller had more information than the buyer, then the rule was "let the seller beware" (*caveat venditor*).[8]

In 1807, Richard Atkins, the Judge-Advocate of New South Wales, had been unwilling to award expectation damages to the creditor of an Emancipist farmer caught by rising prices. Atkins was as man without legal training, and was taken to task in the pages of the Sydney *Gazette* for this decision. Within a few years his Westminster-trained successors ordered such damages in a similar case.[9] Later judgements of the high courts of Quebec, Manitoba, and New Zealand joined their English, New South Wales, and U.S. counterparts in upholding awards of expectation damage against defendants who had failed to deliver hops, clover seed, wheat, or railway-company stock at the agreed-upon time and price.[10] And, inasmuch as the decisions of U.S. state courts on

---

[6] As in *Macqueen v. Lamb* (ed. Kercher, 1824) (if no warranty and no fraud in sale of horse, balance due seller; jury awards forty-five pounds); *Henderson v. Colls* (ed. Kercher, 1828) (sound price for horse not a warranty without express language, citing Lord Mansfield; jury awards seller forty pounds); *Levey v. Bennett* (ed. Kercher, 1826) (no warranty for glassware if note given before boxes opened to detect breakage; jury awards seller thirty-two pounds).

[7] See Kim Lane Scheppelle, *Legal Secrets: Equality and Efficiency in the Common Law* (Chicago, 1988), ch. 14, "The Rule of *Caveat Emptor* in Nineteenth Century New York;" and *Latter v. Brogden*, 1 O., B., & F. (Ct. of Appeals, N.Z.) 116 (1879).

[8] See *Fallon v. Smith*, 18 Quebec 113 (1865); and *Benson v. Mulholland*, 18 Quebec 372 (1866). In *Fallon*, the Chief Justice of Quebec's Queen's Bench observed that "our rule of law" was "more favorable to the purchaser," and spoke of Quebec's "*garantie de droit*" in addition to "a *garantie convention-nelle.*" This may be compared with the rule in Louisiana, another jurisdiction with a Civil Law past (and lingering presence). See *Melancon v. Robichaux*, 17 La. (O.S.) 97 (1841).

[9] Bain, J., in *McCuaig v. Phillips*, 10 Manitoba LR 694 at 698 (1895); Bruce Kercher, *Jurisprudence*, ch. 7, p. 2.

[10] *Grand Trunk Ry v. Webster*, 6 Low. Can. J. 178 (1861); *Boswell v. Kilborn*, 6 Low. Can. J. 108 (1862); *Campbell v. Fox*, Maccassey's R. (N.Z.) 664 (1867); *Anderson v. Shand*, 3 J.R. (N.S.) (N.Z.S.C.) 130 (1878); *McCuaig v. Phillips*, 10 Manitoba LR 694 (1895).

expectation damages were consistent with those of Westminster, the
Manitoba court in one such case felt quite comfortable in relying on
American cases for one key question of contractual interpretation.[11]

I did notice (simple) alterations in the Law with regard to mercantile rules (regarding credit and insurance). One: In the early 1840s,
attorney Roger Therry explained, settlers in New South Wales could
secure "an advance usually of 8d. per lb." on his wool "in the early
part of the year" by "giving a guarantee to a merchant" that he would
"deliver his wool at the end of it." This amounted to a lien on the wool,
and Therry added that this amounted to an "innovation on the strict
principle of English law" that such advances were to be limited to rent
or a lien on the crops of one's real estate. "Pastoral land is only valuable
for the wool it yields, and the stock it feeds," Therry wrote. "There is no
money-rental from the greater part of the land, as in England, where
rents are applied to the payment of mortgage-debts. Wool and stock
may, therefore, be considered in Australia as an equivalent for rent,"
and it had been "found necessary" in New South Wales "to mould the
laws of England agreeably to the nature and peculiarities of property
there."[12] Two: In 1856, the high court for New South Wales held that a
policy of marine insurance contained an implied warranty of the vessel's seaworthiness. Within days of this decision, word reached Sydney
of a twelve to four decision of the Law Lords, affirming a decision
of England's Queen's Bench, in a four-square case involving a similar
marine insurance policy. Both had held that the policy did *not* contain
any implied warranty of seaworthiness. The jurists of New South Wales
added to their previous judgement the observation that, while such
"Superior Courts in the United Kingdom" as Queen's Bench were entitled to "the greatest respect," only Privy Council's views were binding
in Sydney, and these decisions "did not amount to a sufficient reason
why the Court here should alter its judgement."[13]

There was also some disagreement among the various courts of the
American states and British colonies, provinces, and dominions with
regard to certain contracts made with stock brokers: Some American

---

[11] Justice Bain in *McCuaig v. Phillips*, 10 Manitoba LR 694 at 698 (1895). Similarly, a Scottish-bred judge named John McCord, sitting at Bedford in southeastern Quebec, near the border with Vermont, felt comfortable drawing
on Nathaniel Chipman's treatise on contacts, published in Middlebury,
Vermont in 1822, to answer questions of where bills were payable and what
the duties of the parties where payment was specified to be of an "in kind"
sort (cattle or grain), rather than relying on an English treatise or one on
the French law of obligations. Brian Young, *The Politics of Codification: The
Lower Canadian Civil Code of 1866* (Montreal 1994), 30.

[12] Philip McMichael, *Settlers and the Agrarian Question*, 196.

[13] *Williamson v. NSW Marine Assurance Co.*, 2 Legge (NSW) 975 (1856).

courts were less tolerant than were their English counterparts of speculative transactions – purchases on "margin," or "options." In Illinois, home of the Chicago Board of Trade, the Supreme Court regarded such transactions as being contrary to "good public policy" in that they were mere "gaming" arrangements that undermined morals and risked family resources and community stability and well-being.[14] Jurists in Ontario were more tolerant of such transactions, in the fashion of English courts, and some of the British-bred members of the courts of Lower Canada/Quebec in the second half of the nineteenth century took the same view. Thus, Justice Hall insisted that the contract a client made with a broker for shares of stock on speculation with no delivery of the shares actually intended ought still to be honored. Any other rule, he argued, in what could later be styled proper Law & Economics fashion, would "hamper legitimate trade," "intimidate the use of capital, and check the spirit of enterprise." But Chief Justice Sir Alexandre Lacoste and the rest of his colleagues on Quebec's Queen's Bench did not agree. Such "unrestrained passion for becoming rich without work at the expense of others, entails disaster and ruin to the family, and brings about...financial crises...."[15] And the chief justice and his colleagues were essentially echoing the views of their predecessors over the previous two decades.[16]

Privy Council overruled Quebec's Queen's Bench in this instance, concluding that, since the broker had faced no prospect of loss himself, the contract could not be said to have been a gambling one, and Quebec's jurists responded by permitting such a contract two years later. But, simultaneously, the province's superior court judges refused to permit a speculator who had bought and sold stock in the same day to recover his profits from the Montreal Metropolitan Stock Exchange. This had been a mere "gaming transaction" and was void. Quebec's French legal roots proved to be resistant for some time to speculation

---

[14] See discussion in Karsten, *Heart v. Head*, 302–03.

[15] In *Forget v. Ostigny*, 4 Q.Q.B. (1895), 118 at 156–59, 161, 163. See also Justices Ramsay and Monk, dissenting in *Macdougall v. Demers*, 30 LCJ 168 at 171 (1886) (arguing that a broker should be able to get commission fees and recover any losses in contract for purchase of grain on margin, even though no delivery of grain had been intended since "the decisions of the English courts" allowed this).

[16] *Shaw v. Carter*, 26 L.C.J. 151 (1876) (sale of grain futures without intent to deliver grain illegal as a "*contrat de jeu*" (gaming). Justice Ranville: "Le principe général base sur les notions...les plus sacrées de la justice et de la morale publique" and was "spéculation périlleuse et illicite"; *Allison v. Macdougall*, 27 L.C.J. 355 (1883) (sale of telegraph stock on margin illegal); *Macdougall v. Demers*, 30 L.C.J. 168 (1886) (sale of grain on margin with no delivery void; Justice Cross and majority rely on Pothier and old French law).

in the exchange markets sanctioned by Westminster's Common-Law courts.[17]

These French roots were more receptive to contracts made for the benefit of a third-party gift beneficiary. Though such beneficiaries had for centuries been granted access to English courts to enforce the bargains other parties had made for their benefit, such beneficiaries were no longer permitted standing by the mid-nineteenth century. They were now seen as lacking any "privity" with the parties who had agreed to act in some fashion to their benefit. Further "no consideration had moved from them" to the defendant that would warrant their action. Most of the courts of the United States did not follow this new English twist in the Common Law; neither did those of Quebec, but that was because they followed the French codified Law here, not the early English precedents that the jurists of the United States had preferred.[18] And, once again, while Quebec's courts proved (however accidentally) to be in accord with the views of most of their U.S. counterparts in this regard, they were out of step with the courts of New Zealand and the other Canadian provinces with regard to the rights of third party beneficiaries to sue on a contract, in that these courts first sanctioned such suits in the early nineteenth century (citing English precedent), and then, followed the new English judiciary's "privity" rule and refused to allow them.[19]

[17] *Ostigny v. Forget,* LR (H of L & PC) 318 (1895); *Stevenson v. Brais,* 7 QQB 77 (1897); *Brand v. Metrop. Stock Exch.,* 11 Q.C.S. 303 (1897). Lower Canada's Circuit Court also upheld the enforcement of market regulations by the city of Quebec in *Dumontier v. Baudon dit Lariviere,* 1 L.C.R. 473 (1851).

[18] See esp. *Tweedle v. Atkinson,* 1 B. & S. 396, 121 ER 762 (Q.B., 1861); and Peter Karsten, "The Discovery of Law by English and American Jurists...: Third-Party Beneficiaries as a Test Case," 9 *Law & History Review* 327 (1991), on the English and U.S. story; see *Dupuis et vir. v. Cédillot et Kelly,* 10 L.C.J. 338 (1866); *Fraser v. Dupres,* 15 L.C.J. 111 (1870); *Robitaille v. Trudel,* 16 QCS 39 (1899); and *Baron v. Lemieux,* 17 QKB 177 (1908), for the Quebec rule.

[19] Karsten, *Heart versus Head,* 62–78; *Teschemacher v. McLean,* Macassey (NZLR(SC)) 1 (1861); *Tyrill v. Annis,* 1 UCQB 299 (1842) (3rd party suit allowed, Chief Justice Robinson citing older English authority); *Thomas v. Grace,* 15 UCCP 462 (1865) (defendants not obliged to honor promise to pay $100 to bank for benefit of Episcopal Church of Goderich; Chief Justice Richards: "no privity between plaintiff and defendant" and consideration hadn't moved from him "but from others.... Plaintiff cannot sue on the promise" (citing recent English authority), but plaintiff *can* sue on the defendant's promissory *note*); *Abbinett v. N. W. Mutual Life Ins. Co.,* 21 New Bruns. 216 (1881) (wife can't sue on life insurance policy for her benefit; administrator of estate must do so (citing English precedent)). See *Trident Gen. Ins. v. McNiese Bros.* (1985) for a recent rejection of this requirement by Australia's High Court.

I'm Canceling my Order! The Informal Law
of Sales Agreements

We have seen that many people in the nineteenth century world of
North America and the Antipodes ignored some of the rules of property law, settling some disputes informally with their own "rules." So it
was (and is) as well with contracts, or as they are often called, "orders,"
"bargains," or "agreements." The sale of a horse, one of the commoner
sort of transactions, was *legally* regulated by Common-Law rules, and
sometimes local statutes, but a disappointed buyer was more likely
to use personal persuasion, seek arbitration, or simply chalk it up as
"a learning experience," than to hire an attorney and finance a lawsuit.
After all, the "horse trade" was the epitome of one's freedom of contract: One of the first things a young man, and many a young woman,
of the yeoman and gentry classes learned in early modern Britain
and her colonies was how one assessed a pony, mare, gelding, or stal-
lion. One checked the horse's mouth, joints, withers, coat, gait, and
so on. An earnest buyer might then form an estimate of the animal's
worth with which to begin the bargaining process, and, as such, he
might well conclude that he had no one to blame but himself if the
purchase did not live up to expectation. In the process, the party's
final offers were generally "split" in order to reach a final agreement,
but there were interesting variations. I relate but one: In the early
1850s, Joseph Raven drove a mob of unbroken horses toward the goldfields on a speculation. In Wagga Wagga, he was overtaken by Henry
Rickettson of Barratta Station on the Edward River, who began to bargain for them. Rickettson made a final offer of twenty-three pounds
per head; Raven would take no less than twenty-five pounds. He later
recalled that Rickettson began to ride away, but after "a few yards he
pulled up & shouted back 'I'll toss you whether I'll give you #23 or
#25.' I accepted his offer & he took a halfcrown out of his pocket &
spun it up. I called 'Heads' & won & he agreed to pay me #25 a
head...."[20]

Merchants, shopkeepers, and farmers often accommodated one
another after-the-fact as to prices, quantities, time of delivery, and
time of payment. Long-standing credit and trade relations between
farmers and merchants, merchants and other merchants, indeed, between neighbor and neighbor, could remain sound and long-standing
precisely *because* one party allowed the other to "cancel my order"
now and then, to renegotiate the repayment date of a note, or to
agree to arbitration of the amount of the note at issue. An ongoing

[20] Joseph W. Raven, "Reminiscences of a Queensland Pioneer, 1851–1900,"
p. 2, YA2692, Mitchell Library, Sydney.

trade relationship was, and still is, generally worth far more than what might be gained by a lawsuit when one party failed to meet one or more of the terms of a contract. Lawsuits were rancorous, expensive, and time-consuming. And even when a potential plaintiff was confident that he had the Law on his side, the outcome was not always predictable.[21]

The first forms of "sales agreements" the Diaspora newcomers entered into in the colonies were those involving the fur trade with the North American natives. These Diaspora traders quickly discovered that gift-giving, a measure to the natives of mutual respect, was an essential preliminary to any transaction. Some traders also came to appreciate that, for many natives, the acquisition of European goods was inspired by more than a simple desire to achieve "economic" benefit. (Indeed, Joseph Banks found Aborigines on Australia's east coast in the 1770s to "have no Idea of traffick" in goods at all, "nor could we teach them." They "readily received the things we gave them but never would understand our signs when we asked for returns." But Banks may have partially grasped what the Aborigines probably thought was happening when he noted that they *had* brought one small fish "as a kind of token of peace.")[22] The acquisition of British goods could improve one's local reputation, and provide evidence that one had influence with the British traders. Thus, some of the more valued foreign goods were often buried with the dead Aboriginal trader.

Moreover, for many native tribes the trade *relationship* was as important as the trade itself, inasmuch as the process constituted a kind of alliance with a source of foreign power. Thus, the Cherokee were quite upset by the paltry nature of British gift-giving during their joint campaign against the French in 1757–1758. They were rewarded for their service, information, and enemy scalps, but the payments were doled out in the fashion of one paying wages to mercenaries (as, indeed, the British commanders looked upon the Cherokee), instead

---

[21] Among studies of this phenomenon in the nineteenth century see John Phillip Reid, "Binding the Elephant: Contracts and Legal Obligations on the Overland Trail," 21 *American Journal of Legal History* 285 (1977); Lawrence Friedman, *Contract Law in America: A Social and Economic Case Study* (Madison, Wis., 1965); William C. Jones, "An Inquiry into the History of the Adjudication of Mercantile Disputes in Great Britain and the United States," 25 *University of Chicago Law Review* 445 (1958); and David J. Langum, *Law and Community on the Mexican California Frontier: Anglo-American Expatriates and the Clash of Legal Traditions, 1821–1846* (Norman, OK, 1987), esp. chs. 5 and 8.

[22] Joseph Banks, *The Endeavour Journal of Joseph Banks, 1768–1771*, ed. J. C. Beaglehole (Sydney, 1962), II, 125.

of with the gift-giving rituals appropriate for a treasured ally (as the Cherokee saw themselves). Gregory Dowd aptly regards these cultural misunderstandings as the grounds for the Cherokee decision to turn and wage war upon the offending British in 1759.[23]

This is not to say that native hunters and traders were uniformly indifferent to the relative value of the objects of trade; many impressed their Diaspora trade partners with being especially shrewd or hard-driving. Thus in the 1640s, Roger Williams maintained that the Ninnimissi-maks of New England were "marvailous subtle in their bargaines to save a penny," would "beate all markts and try all places . . . to save six pence." Just so, a Cree hunt captain of the early eigthteenth century told his Hudson's Bay Company factor to "tell your Servants to fill the [gunpowder] measure and not to put their fingers within the Brimm," to "Give us good black tobacco (brazl. tobacco) moist & hard twisted, [&] Let us see itt before op'n'd," and to "Give us Good measure in cloth [&] Let us see the old measures. Do you mind me!"[24]

Throughout the South Pacific, in places like Tonga, Samoa, and Fiji, Diaspora traders managed to establish beach-hold niches by building local trust in their quest for sandalwood, beche-de-mer, and pearls. Among the more conscientious, and sensible, of these traders in the mid-nineteenth century were Robert Towns, an Australian, and

[23] Gregory Dowd, " 'Insidious Friends': Gift-Giving and the Cherokee-British Alliance in the Seven Years' War," in Andrew Cayton and Frederika Teute, eds., *Contact Points* (Chapel Hill, 1998), 132–40; Marcel Mauss, *The Gift: Forms and Functions of Exchange in Archaic Societies* (trans. N.Y., 1967). Cf. David Cheal, *The Gift Economy* (1988); Annette Weiner, *Inalienable Possessions: The Paradox of Keeping-While-Giving* (1992); Bruce Trigger, *Natives and Newcomers* (Kingston, 1985), 186.

[24] Neal Salisbury, *Manitou and Providence: Indians, Europeans, & the Making of New England, 1500–1643* (1982), 59; Robin Fisher, *Contact and Conflict: Indo-European Relations in British Columbia, 1774–1890* (2nd ed., Vancouver, 1992), 10; Michael McConnell, *A Country Between: The Upper Ohio Valley and its Peoples, 1724–1774* (Lincoln, 1992), 35, 41; Richard White, *The Middle Ground: Indians, Empires and Republics in the Great Lakes Region, 1650–1815* (N.Y., 1991), 98–102, 117; Roger Williams, *A Key into the Language of America* (1643, repr. 1936), 120–21; Arthur Ray, "Indians as Consumers in the Eighteenth Century," in *Out of the Background: Readings on Canadian Native History* (1988), citing E. E. Rich, ed., *James Isham's Observations on Hudson's Bay, 1743* (1949), 83–87; Colin Calloway, *The American Revolution in Indian Country* (Cambridge, 1995), 268; James Merrell, *The Indians' New World: Catawbas and their Neighbors* (Chapel Hill, 1989), 149; David Wishart, *The Fur Trade of the American West, 1807–1840* (Lincoln, 1979), 98–99; Colin Calloway, *The American Revolution in Indian Country* (Cambridge U. Pr., 1995), 268; James Merrell, *The Indians' New World: Catawbas and their Neighbors* (Chapel Hill, 1989), 149; McConnell, *A Country Between*, 155.

Andrew Cheyne, an Englishman. Towns told the captains of his trading vessels that he would "sooner abandon the Trade altogether" than tolerate "any act of cruelty or hostility towards the Natives." Cheyne advised those interested in the South Sea Island trade to keep "on peaceable terms with the natives of the different islands. . . . [T]ake nothing from them without payment, not even a cocoa-nut, not so much as a bundle of grass."[25] The cultural tradebridge was no easier to cross there than it had been in North America: George H. W. Markham, a trader, planter, and surveyor in Fiji, boasted in his diary in 1873 that, while he had experienced "a little trouble today with some of the people" in trading for some 2000 yams, "a little firmness on my part soon made it all right again." But another in the same island kingdom was less fortunate. Tovata's native magistrate's court imposed a Tabu Levu (legal ban) in the 1860s upon one obstreperous Diaspora trader, barring him from entering into any commercial transactions with any parties "until such time as he shall adopt a different course, and abandon his factious conduct."[26]

None the less, "trade-for-profit" sometimes had a very different meaning to Aboriginal hunter–traders than it did to their Diaspora counterparts. The ordinary "laws" of supply and demand did not seem to apply to many native hunters. Gabriel Archer, one of the first Virginia colonists, felt that the natives in the vicinity of Jamestown had "no respect of profitt, neither is there scare that we call meum et tuum [a sense of private property] among them save only the . . . people [know] their severall gardens."[27] The economic objective of many native traders was not so much the acquisition of wealth, but that of comfortable subsistence. Their strategy was to exchange enough beaver to acquire a relatively fixed passel of trade goods, and to acquire these goods with the least expenditure of effort. Hence, "Giving Indians [a] larger Price" for their pelts when they were scarce "would occasion the Decrease of Trade," not its increase, or so several Hudson's Bay Company officials put it in 1749.[28] The Company's chief factor at Fort Nez Perces in 1830 offered a similar judgement.

---

[25] Both noted in Jane Samson, *Imperial Benevolence: Making British Authority in the Pacific Islands* (Honolulu, 1998), 86.

[26] Geo. H. W. Markham Diary, Mar. 11, 1873, MS YA1462, Mitchell Lib; Peter France, *The Charter of the Land* (1969), 89.

[27] Karen Kupperman, *Settling with the Indians: The Meeting of English and Indian Cultures in America, 1580–1640* (Totona, N. J., 1980), 57.

[28] Thistle, *Indo-European, Trade Relations*, 12, 23; Harvey Feit, "The Ethno-Ecology of the Waswanipi Crees: How Hunters can Manage Their Resources," in *Cultural Ecology: Readings in Canadian Indians & Eskimos*, ed. B. Cox (1973), 115; William Coker and Thomas D. Watson, *Indian Traders of*

(But note that this phenomenon was a characteristic of Diaspora hunters as well: James Finley recalled of hunters he had known as a boy in late-eighteenth-century Appalachia that they had "no artificial wants which wealth" could "gratify," that they had not been "animated" by economic "stimulus.")[29]

One recurrent problem with the fur trade flowed from the "firewater" that served to lubricate much of it. Many Indians felt that liquor helped them to get in touch with the Spirit World. But inasmuch as alcohol is both an intoxicant and a depressant, its consumption can produce both irrational and antisocial behavior, and the U.S. Congress, following the lead of some of the colonial legislatures, sought to curb this part of the trade with a series of Intercourse Acts. As both James Merrell and Francis Prucha have shown, such efforts were almost total failures, "impossible" to observe, as South Carolina's Indian Trade Commissioners put it in 1710. John Jacob Astor's American Fur Company originally obeyed the law, but reversed its policy when it became clear that the availability of liquor was "essential" to the trade, as the U.S. Superintendent of Indian Affairs put it himself in 1826. Similarly, S. C. Stambaugh, the Indian agent at Green Bay, told Territorial Governor Lewis Cass in 1831 that the Law, "as custom has rendered it, only serves to retain bad men [that is, licensed but unscrupulous traders] among the Indians. . . . " Captain John Stuart, writing the secretary of war from Fort Smith on the Arkansas River in 1833, complained of the biases of "Justices of the Peace and Jurors, under the control of the Lawless traders, and Neighbourhood opinions," who made it "impossible to get a Legal Decision made against an offender, where Neighbourhood Interest[s] are involved. . . . "[30] And later, in 1870, John Craig, Indian agent to the Cherokee, reported that much liquor had been "brought into the country" despite efforts of "the United

the Southeastern Spanish Borderlands (1986), 60; E. E. Rich, "Trade Habits and Economic Motivations among the Indians of North America," in Sweet Promises:. . . Indian-white Relations in Canada, ed. J. R. Miller (1991), 170–72; George Dalton, "Economic Theory and Primitive Society," 63 American Anthropolog. 1 (1961).

29 Theodore Stern, Chiefs and Chief Traders: Indian Relations at Fort Nez Perces, 1818–1855 (Corvallis, ove., 1993), 136; Autobiography of Rev. James Finley, or Pioneer Life in the West (Cincinnati, 1853), 36, cited in Stephen Aron, How the West was Lost (Baltimore, 1996).

30 Merrell, Indians' New World, 66; Prucha, American Indian Policy: The Formative Years (Cambridge, Mass., 1962), 97, 111, 128. Cf. P. C. Mancall, Deadly Medicine: Indians and Alcohol in Early America (Ithaca, 1995); and Willaim E. Unrau, White Man's Wicked Water: The Alcohol Trade and Prohibition in Indian Country, 1802–1892 (Lawrence, Kansas, 1996) (documenting defiance of federal Law against the liquor trade with Indians).

States authorities to check its introduction." On-the-scene Cherokee law enforcement officers could "suppress its introduction," he felt certain, but they would "make no systematic efforts to that end."[31]

Another aspect of the fur trade, in both the United States and Canada, was that of the construction of what might be called a *debt chain*. The English legal rules of debt collection, particularly those pertaining to the seizure and sale of the debtor's property, were foreign and troubling to the Cherokee and could lead to grief. Indians had notions of indebtedness that were similar to those of the Diaspora newcomer–traders, but they were not identical ones, as John Phillip Reid has explained in his account of Carolina traders and the Cherokee people in the first two generations of their interaction. English capitalist–merchants extended credit to Charleston merchants "who in turn credited the Carolina trader." That trader, "needing skins to meet his debts, could not resist the temptation of obtaining a lien on the next winter's kill by extending credit to the Cherokee hunter," which often led to "ill Consequences," such as those "fatally Experienced" in bloodshed with a neighbor of the Cherokee, the Yamasees, in 1715, or so Indian Trade Commissioner George Chicken put it in 1727.[32]

---

[31] Jeffrey Burton, *Indian Territory and the United States, 1866–1906* (Norman, 1995), 32. Cf. Paul Thistle, *Indo-European Trade Relations in the Lower Saskatchwan River Region to 1810* (1986), 30. And see the similar complaint of Indian agent Street in Wisconsin, Prucha, 184.

For that matter, the Law was unable to keep liquor out of the hands of another subgroup of the population in nineteenth century America; the Baltimore & Ohio Railroad had a "no whisky" clause in the contracts it entered into with its Irish navvies, but Benjamin Latrobe, the company's chief engineer, reported from the west of Virginia in 1849 that the clause was unenforceable there because whiskey sellers were "so readily found in that wild [and wonderful?] country." James Dilts, *The Great Road: The Building of the Baltimore & Ohio, the Nation's First Railroad, 1828–1853* (Stanford Univ. Press, 1993), 345.

Ellen Clancy offered a similar verdict on the efforts of Victoria's lawmakers in the early 1850s to keep spiritous liquor out of the gold diggings. Publicans were licensed to sell such spirits on the highways, but "resolutely refused on the diggings. The result was the opposite of that ... intended. ... There is more drinking & rioting at the diggings than elsewhere. ... Some of the stores ... managed to evade the law rather cleverly – as spirits are not sold, 'my friend' pays a shilling more for his fig of tobacco. ... then glasses are brought out, and a bottle produced, which sends forth not a fragrant perfume on the sultry air." Clancy, *A Lady's Visits to the Gold Diggings in Australia, 1852–53* (London, 1853).

[32] John P. Reid, *A Better Kind of Hatchet* (1976), 172. On the unfamiliarity of New England Algonquins with the principles of English contract law

But, for their part, Indians soon discovered that they could manipulate traders who refused to provide them with additional credit, either by attacking and beating that trader (in which case the relationship usually came to an abrupt end), or by threatening to shift their business to others. This latter course often resulted in their being extended credit, until that trader found himself inexorably bound to those native suppliers.[33] Peter Skene Ogden was in charge of the Hudson's Bay Company's trapping parties on the Snake River in the 1820s when his Indian and Meti hunter–trappers began to ignore and disobey his orders. He reported that, with American competitors in the vicinity, "I did not think it good policy to use any threats towards them" (though he longed to "make an example" of "some of them" once they returned to the trading post in the fall). He had been correct; some of his Iroquois trappers soon left him for the American competition with these words: "Now we go and all you can say or do will not prevent us from going." Throughout the early nineteenth century Company officials sought informal, non-judicial means of resolving disputes, and displayed respect for the laws, customs, and norms of the native peoples in what they often referred to as "Indian Country."[34] Later, in the 1840s, the Company (an organization perfectly capable of using violence to obtain its ends) limited its response to the murder of two of their traders to non-lethal measures. Ogden, now serving the Company in a more elevated position, explained this with a kind of cost-benefit rationale: "We have nothing to gain. On the contrary, everything to lose." Similarly, when the Company prosecuted a Meti in its General Quarterly Court of Assiniboia for trading with its American competition, a mob of Metis surrounded the courthouse. The man was found guilty, but the judge took the advice of the jury that there be no penalty imposed and immediately set the man free, prompting one of the Meti jurors to shout to the jubilant crowd, "Le commerce est libre!"

---

and debt see Calloway, *Western Abenaki of Vermont,* 139; and Y. Kawashima, *Puritan Law and the Indian, passim.*

[33] Daniel Francis and Toby Morantz, *Partners in Furs: A History of the Fur Trade in Eastern James Bay, 1600–1870* (1983), 44–45; McConnell, *A Country Between,* 41; Royce Kurtz, "Looking at the Ledgers: Sauk & Mesquakie Trade Debts, 1820–1840," in *The Fur Trade Revisited,* ed. Jennifer Brown, et al. (1994), 143; Thistle, 12, 67.

[34] Cole Harris, *The Resettlement of British Columbia,* 47–48; Hamar Foster, "Conflict Resolution during the Fur Trade in the Canadian Northwest, 1803–1859," 25 *Cambrian Law Review* 127 (1994). And see Arthur McEvoy, *The Fisherman's Problem,* 57, on the settling of debts between natives and Diaspora miners and salmon packers in California in the 1850s and 1860s.

Dale Gibson notes that the Company made no further attempts to prosecute "freetraders."[35]

Needless to say, this binding of creditor and debtor occurred within the bounds of British settler society as well. In the early stages of frontier life and of mining communities, a kind of "agreements" ethic was widely held – that "debts would be paid as means were available, and that legal action circumvented the normal process of negotiation and accommodation that should occur between creditor and debtor."[36] Miners in the American West "felt and said that it was disgraceful to dun a man for money." They believed that "honor between men, and the strength of society and business relations," were "far better protection to the lender than bond of Shylock and execution of sheriff," as Charles Shinn put it in 1880. He claimed that no court of miners "ever collected debts...."[37]

Moreover, when an insolvent farmer owed a merchant for goods received in Virginia, for example, the merchant–creditor knew that the farmer–debtor was entitled to a jury trial, and such juries often included men who were available for duty because they were themselves defendants in a debt action in the same court on the same day! Such juries in early nineteenth century Virginia were given considerable authority with regard to findings of fact and some questions of law. They often reduced the debt and required no interest from the date of default to the date of judgment. Similarly, judges and juries in Pennsylvania in the same years engaged in an "indulgence" toward debtors, giving them time after the issuance of a *fieri facias* to the local sheriff and the formal "attachment" of their property. This "indulgence," Justice Hugh Henry Brackenridge explained, was "the practice of the country." It was "founded in humanity," and was not to be "superceded by a rigid common law. And the *salus populi suprema lex est* [the voice of the people is the supreme law],... for the tearing away property by an execution amongst the groans of the distressed, and the tears of families, is hard enough even with all the softening that can be

---

35 McConnell, *A Country Between*, 41; Fisher, *Contact and Conflict*, 38; Date Gibson, "Company Justice: Origins of Legal Institutions in Pre-Confereration Manitoba," 23 *Manitoba Law Journal* 247 at 250 (1996).
36 Christopher Clark, *The Roots of Rural Capitalism: Western Massachusetts, 1800–1860* (Ithaca, 1990), 33–38, 47.
37 Shinn, *Mining Camps: A Study of American Frontier Government*, 126. This is to say nothing of the earlier debtor relief statutes of the 1780s in North Carolina (the Pine Barrens Act of 1785) and Rhode Island (the Force Act of 1785) that compelled creditors to accept something other than the specie bargained for (Rhode Island) or forced upon them barren pine lands in exhange for the more valuable property the creditors were prevented from forcing to a sheriff's sale.

given it." The "Shylock that would say to the officer, 'I stand upon my bond; remove and sell instantly,' would be considered in most cases, an unfeeling creditor."[38]

This "indulgence" had been challenged in the 1780s when the government of Pennsylvania set its sights on the full redemption of the state's Revolutionary War bonds at par value. By 1782, most of these bonds were in the hands of prominent politically-connected men from the eastern region in and around Philadelphia. When the legislature imposed new taxes in order to meet the state's dividend payments on these bonds, their collection officials met widespread resistence. Constables were still held liable for negligent failure to collect funds by attaching personal property of delinquents for sheriff's sales, but most constables were poor and thus "judgement-proof." Therefore many constables chose to "Indulge their neighbors" by forgoing the service of legal papers. When foreclosures did lead to sheriff's sales, farmer-neighbors of the debtors intimidated potential bidders and closed local roads to prevent the removal of the chattels being sold. "The laws are eluded without being openly defied," one Fayette County official wrote in 1787. By 1794, arbitration societies had emerged in central and western Pennsylvania, whose leaders warned creditors to "apply to the society for redress" rather than to the courts, and Terry Boulton feels that the societies proved to be effective in arbitrating reasonable settlements of many debts actions. It was this experience with war-bond dividend collection, then, that led both to the Whiskey Rebellion (against federal excise tax collectors) and to Justice Brackenridge's observations.[39]

When creditors in Newfoundland turned to legal proceedings, those called upon to attach the debtor's property also faced stiff resistance. A constable in there who sought to attach the property of fishermen and "planter"-middlemen for their debts in the eighteenth and nineteenth

---

[38] For the observations on Virginia see F. Thornton Miller, *Juries and Judges Versus the Law: Virginia's Provincial Legal Perspective, 1783–1828* (Charlottesville, 1994), 7, 30, 37, 99. See H. H. Brackenridge, *Law Miscellanies* (Phila., 1814), 205–07, on Pennsylvania.

The situation was quite different in Greene County, Georgia, between 1868 and 1872 (during Reconstruction), where white Republicans of all sorts who had aided the former slaves were sued vindictively by their "un-Reconstructed" Democratic creditors in efforts (often successful) to force them into bankruptcy. "In every case," Jonathan Bryant tells us, these Republican debtors "lost in jury trials." Bryant, *How Curious a Land: Conflict and Change in Greene County, Georgia, 1850–1885* (Chapel Hill, 1996), 139.

[39] Terry Boulton, "A Road Closed: Rural Insurgency in Post-Independence Pennsylania," *The Journal of American History* 855, at 873–84, 878–81 (2000).

centuries could well face a threat to "blow his brains out." One debtor's angry wife, Ann Earles, told a constable that she "shit on the King's Writ," and to drive the point home "she took up a Hatchet in her hand in defiance of this Deponent...." Later, in 1848, men with blackened faces overpowered a bailiff guarding the attached property of an insolvent Newfoundland "planter" to prevent its being sold to pay overseas "merchants." In any event, as Sean Cadigan puts it, "there was much room for popular negotiation and adaptation before disputes might end up in court."[40]

A frontier ethic of creditor forebearance and trust survived in New England for the first generation or two of Puritan settlement. But it had largely vanished from the country stores of Connecticut by 1720, from the dealings of Plymouth County merchants by the early nineteenth century, replaced by the promissory note, which made debts transferable as credit by the early eighteen century in England and was soon in widespread use throughout the Diaspora lands to avoid some of the legal problems that the action of debt could pose in court.[41] Promissory notes made a lot of sense, both in places where debtors could no longer be trusted to respect a storekeeper's mere "book account" of a debt, and in cash-scarce places like early New South Wales where everyone's notes circulated and served as a primitive currency medium. Throughout the first several decades of settlement, the governors of New South Wales sought to prohibit the use of notes drafted by convicts and those written for any value but sterling, since they were contrary to English Law and, in any event, the negotiable value of such notes were often difficult to assess. Nevertheless, the colony's chief jurist, Ellis Bent, found their customary use to be so pervasive as to warrant ignoring the gubernatorial proclamations.[42]

None the less, when the promissor refused to honor his note, the costs of court proceedings, of the legal counsel accompanying them, and of the prospect of appeals from an initial decision, prompted most New York merchants, as well as their smaller-scale counterparts on the Wisconsin frontier, to insist on commercial arbitration of their disputes.[43] Moreover, by the 1820s and 1830s merchants, contractors,

---

[40] Madigan, *Hope and Deception at Conception Bay*, 72–73, 100, 118–19.
[41] C. W. Brooks, "Interpersonal Conflict and Social Tension: Civil Litigation in England, 1640–1830," in *The First Modern Society*, eds. A. L. Beier, D Carnadine and J. Rosenheim (Cambs. 1989), 87–89; Bruce Mann, *Neighbors and Strangers: Law and Community in Early Connecticut* (Chapel Hill, 1987); William E. Nelson, *Dispute and Conflict Resolution in Plymouth County, Massachusetts, 1725–1825* (1981).
[42] Bruce Kercher, *Unruly Child*, 53–54.
[43] William Jones, "Three Centuries of Commercial Arbitration in New York," 1956 *Washington University Law Quarterly* 193 at 206–7, 215–19;

and their farmer counterparts had available to them in the United States insolvency statutes that made accommodation and out-of-court settlement an even more attractive avenue for debtors to follow than the Common-Law remedies. Hence, when one such merchant in Baltimore, James Partridge, was deemed in 1819 to be "in quite an embarrassed situation," his primary creditor, a member of the DuPont family, was advised by an agent that he "had best make a settlement with him by getting what he can from him" since Partridge would find "little difficulty in getting discharged by our insolvency law...." Joseph Ellicott, the Holland Land Company's first agent in western New York, reported in 1818 that "the whole of this community is Debtor & Creditor, Creditor & Debtor," and Ellicott persistently advised the Company officers not to threaten its many indebted lotholders with legal action, since the fruits of such suits were notoriously bitter. Merchants in the Green River country of Kentucky "initially adapted their trade to the rules of the countryside, to the barter arrangements that characterized exchange among neighboring households," Stephen Aron tells us. They "sold their commodities on loose terms – loose, not only in the time stipulated for making payment but also... vague as to the type of payment."[44] (See Illustration 22.)

Similarly, a supplier of farm equipment in Ontario, and thus a creditor of many farmers, wrote a colleague during financial "hard times" in June, 1838, that "very few feel under any obligation to pay," and "to sue is worse than useless." Rural Ontario's manufacturers and storekeepers knew that they had to provide credit, especially during "hard times," if they were to survive, for were they to press their debtors for payment, both their credit assets and their local reputation might well be lost. The result of taking a debtor to court was that he was forced into bankruptcy, as land, supply, and seed creditors all jumped in, accompanied by attorneys and court costs. "Sue a beggar, catch a louse" was the maxim; the merchant was better off pressing his own credit limits than pressing those of his or her debtors. Douglas McCalla has documented these kinds of credit arrangements for Upper Canada in the first half of the nineteenth century, and he notes the price that merchant–creditors were prepared to pay in this business – an average of 20 percent of one's debtors defaulting in a given year. Moreover, despite the English Common-Law rule, enforced in Canada's

Donald Kommers, "The Emergence of Law & Justice in Pre-Territorial Wisconsin," 8 *Amer. Journal of Legal Hist.* 20 at 28 (1964).

[44] Tony Freyer, *Producers versus Capitalists: Constitutional Conflict in Antebellum America* (Charlottesville, 1994), 65; Charles E. Brooks, *Frontier Settlement and Market Revolution: The Holland Land Company* (Ithaca, 1996), 112; Aron, *How the West was Lost,* 167. Aron does add that they did eventually impose "the rules of the market on all manner of exchanges."

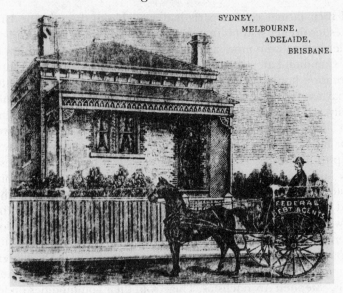

SYDNEY,
MELBOURNE,
ADELAIDE,
BRISBANE.

OUR MODE OF COLLECTING.

If you do not wish our Debt Collecting Cart to call, please
come and arrange payment.

Illustration 22.   Seeking to avoid the costs of formal litigation, some
creditors employed such debt-collecting firms as Australia's "Federal
Debt Collecting Society," a firm that served an official-looking "Final
Notice" on debtors and depicted an intimidating "Mode of Collect-
ing," intended to look like a sheriff's process server, come to seize
enough of the debtor's movables to satisfy the judgement. (In the
"Correspondence of Clients" file of the Papers of Sir James Martin,
CY2535, Mitchell Library, State Library of New South Wales.)

courts, that third party beneficiaries of contracts had no standing
to sue to enforce the terms of those contracts made for their benefit, the fact is that in the cash-scarce economy of early rural Canada,
farmers with a momentary credit balance at a local merchant's store
often contracted with that merchant to have some or all of that credit
transferred to one of their creditors who also had a line of credit with
the merchant.[45]

Merchants lending to farmers have always had to factor into their
lending costs the constant risk of defaulters and absconders. But

45 D. McCalla, "Rural Credit and Rural Developement in Upper Canada,
    1790–1850," in *Patterns of the Past: Interpreting Ontario's History*, ed. Roger
    Hall et al. (Toronto, 1988), 40, 43, 49.

NO. 5 QUEEN'S CHAMBERS, BARRACK ST., SYDNEY,
(Second Floor), Opposite David Jones & Co.

THE FEDERAL DEBT COLLECTING SOCIETY,
WHITTINGTON & CO., PROPRIETORS.

FINAL NOTICE.

Dated this *Feb* day of *14th* 189*4*

. The undermentioned debt MUST BE PAID AT THIS OFFICE and not at

Mr. *Shying*

Mr. *Moxon*

We have to inform you that Mr. *Shying*

of *Sydney*

has placed in our hands this account amounting to £ *1 : 12 : 0* against you for collection, and our instructions are (that unless the said amount is paid or remitted to this office, together with our expenses, or satisfactory arrangements made with us within seven days from the service of this notice upon you) to **IMMEDIATELY** take such steps as the law directs for its recovery without further notice, and you will be subject to all costs and expenses consequent thereon.

☞ The costs of an action at law with you will probably amount to £3 3s., as we proceed through our own solicitor.

Yours, &c.,

WHITTINGTON & CO.

To Account Rendered   £ *1 : 12 : 0*
To Expenses   ....   £ *: 5 : 0*   Money Order to Whittington & Co.

Total   ...   £ *1 : 17 : 0*   Office Hours—9 till 5.   Saturdays, 9 till 1.

Cheques and Post Office Orders to be crossed and made payable to WHITTINGTON & CO., and also state the name of the person the money is for.

WHEN PAYING, PLEASE BRING OR SEND THIS FORM.

Illustration 22.   (*continued*)

merchants who buy from and sell to one another in established markets and mercantile exchanges have for centuries enjoyed a dispute-resolution system that works, the customary law of merchants (the law merchant), with its informal hearings of disputes and speedy judgements rendered by fellow merchants. This customary law of contracts was celebrated in Chicago in 1885, for example, at the dedication of the new Chicago Board of Trade building when attorney Emery Storrs praised these customs, "stronger" as they were "than any mere legal technicalities." Before them "the [Common] Law must bend," Storrs remarked, "and if it does not it will break."[46]

[46] Noted in Jonathan Lurie, *The Chicago Board of Trade: The Dynamics of Self-Regulation, 1859–1905* (Urbana, 1979), 17.

The Gentleman's Wager

As I indicated earlier in this chapter, gambling debts could be collected in English legal proceedings until the 1840s because they were based upon an exchange of promises for good consideration and thus conformed to the conditions of classical contract law.[47] Gambling was common throughout the lands of the British Diaspora. Thus, "gentlemen" staked substantial sums on point-to-point horse races in colonial Virginia, and wagers on these and other matters were enforceable in the colony's courts until the passage of a statute by the House of Burgesses in 1740, which rendered them void and unenforceable. But George Chumbley insisted that "the feeling against anyone who would plead the gaming statute" in order to escape such a debt "was very strong," inasmuch as the Virginia gentry's self-image was "based on a code of honor."[48] Cockfights, prizefights, footraces, and steamboat races all attracted wagers in North America and the Antipodes. Indeed, Helenus Scott, Jr., Police Magistrate in Newcastle, New South Wales, in the 1860s, owned, and presumably made use of, a pamphlet, *Laws of Racing*, which described the rules of betting, odds-calculating, and racetrack complaint-lodging.[49] By the nineteenth century, gambling was being made unlawful by the British Parliament and the legislatures of the Responsible Governments of the lands of the Diaspora.[50] All the same, folks everywhere in those lands continued to gamble.[51]

Personal honor generally sufficed to "enforce" these sorts of agreements. But when losers refused to pay, at least *one* frontier community that lacked established Common-Law courts, town meetings, and religious institutions (that of the ranchers, farmers, and caravan wagoners of the Great Plains in the 1860s) turned to the commanders of army

---

[47] See, for example, *Sherbon v Colebach*, 2 Vent. 175, 86 ER 377 (C. P. 1690).

[48] See George Chumbley, *Colonial Justice in Virginia* (Richmond, 1938), 113–16; and Timothy Breen, "Horses and Gentlemen: The Cultural Significance of Gambling among the Gentry of Virginia," 34 *William & Mary Quarterly*, pp. 239–57 (1977).

[49] Helenus Scott the Younger Pers. Papers, MS 38/11X, Mitchell Lib.

[50] But see *Guise v. Klensendorlffe*, NSW (Kercher, 1827) (loser of mare in wager sought recovery in action of trover; court instructs jury that gambling not at issue because mare transferred by loser–plaintiff by paper title to winner–defendant; jury finds for def.); and *Bailey v. McDuffee*, 18 New Bruns. R. 26 (1878) (old common law rule sanctioned gambling contracts; New Brunswick statute of 1854 (c. 103) made all *signed* gambling contracts void, but oral contracts still had force of law). And see Beverley Smith, "Enforcability of Wagers in New Brunswick," 6(1) *Univ. of New Brunswick Law Review* 10 (1953).

[51] Many native people gambled as well, with one another and with Diaspora traders. See Theodore Stern, *Chiefs and Chief Traders*, 129–30.

outposts in Kansas and Nebraska. According to Army Captain Eugene Ware,

> people applied to the post to enforce the payment of bets which they had made. It was a betting age, and a betting country. We did not go according to the statute law in this matter. We recognized that the payment of bets was an obligation which persons should honor; that betting was recognized by the community as legitimate, and the non-payment of bets tended to disturb social conditions and make enemies, and bring about aggressions.

To be enforced by the post commander, to be sure, the bet "had to be proven in writing or admitted," but that having been accomplished, gambling debtors "had the alternative given them of paying..., or else going to the guard house. If they didn't have the money, they went to the guard-house anyway. There had to be some punishment."[52] I can't say how *often* this sort of military "enforcement" of an unlawful "obligation" that the "community" regarded as a "legitimate" way to reduce "aggressions" took place, but I suspect that Captain Ware's story was not unique.

TWO CONTRACTS FOR SERVICES: THE LAW OF COMMON CARRIER AND CONTINGENCY-FEE AGREEMENTS

Jurists on most American state supreme courts in the nineteenth century abandoned one or more of three English rules involving contracts for service: By the 1870s, they began to void special contracts made by common carriers to limit their liability for loss of or damage to freight or baggage; in the 1830s, they began to sanction contingency fee contracts between attorneys and their clients, consigning the English champerty doctrine to the ashbin; and in the 1850s and

---

[52] Eugene Ware, *The Indian War of 1864* (reprinted, New York, 1960), 123. Similarly Ware tells us (278–79) that a wagonmaster of a transcontinental "caravan" who "requisitioned" goods and services from a farmer, rancher, or merchant would be hauled before Ware's court, tried, and if unwilling to pay, "would have to stay in the guard-house until he paid the money in cash."

John Phillip Reid has shown us that sojourners on the Overland Trail in the mid-nineteenth century created and dissolved partnerships, transferred property rights, and contracted with one another in a number of ways quite successfully, without the existence of any but a tiny handful of law-enforcement officials, such as Captain Ware's commanding officer turned himself into. But once such a magistrate hove into view, it appears his services were sought.

thereafter they allowed juries to offer laborers who quit "entire" contracts awards of *quantum meruit* (what their labor had been worth to their employers). (This latter issue is explored in the next chapter, on the formal and informal law of labor contracts.)

The first, disallowing steamboats and railroads the right to "contract out" of their common carrier liability, was defended as being a response to the lack of mutuality in the contract process; shippers were at a disadvantage in a world that often lacked substantial carrier competition. The second, contingency fee contracts, were justified in American courts as being the only way that many poor Americans could enjoy their "day in court," while the third, *quantum meruit* recovery, was allowed to be in conflict with the harsh "all or nothing" rule of "the old cases" in the English reports, but was defended as being "more equitable," as being "bottomed on justice."[53] Were jurists in the CANZ courts aware of these American innovations, and, if so, how did they react to them? If not, did they create anything like them?

Contracting Out of Common Carrier Liability in Canada, Australia, and New Zealand

CANZ jurists had no difficulty in applying the English rules regarding common carrier liability when a passenger had informed a ship's mate, or a railroad's freight agent, of certain "valuables" in her luggage, or when a railway passenger left his travelling bag on his seat while he visited the restroom, and these objects were lost or stolen.[54] A passenger's luggage was protected by an implied contract that it would be safeguarded with care. But shippers of hogs, cattle, oil barrels, machinery, and other freight were generally offered, and generally agreed to, "special" contracts offering lower fares in exchange for the waiver by the shipper of some or all of the ship's or train's common carrier liability. And these contracts were held to be binding in all but one Canadian jurisdiction when carrier negligence led to loss or damage to the shipper's goods and the angry shipper sued.[55]

The Canadian jurists who upheld the validity of this "contracting out" of common carrier liability were not "progrowth" friends of the

---

[53] See Karsten, *Heart versus Head*, chs. 5, 6; and *RR v. Lockwood*, 17 Wall. (84 U.S.) 357 (1871).

[54] See *Macdougall v. Torrance*, 4 Low. Can. J. 132 (1860); *Cadwallader v. Grand Trunk Ry*, 9 Low. Can. R 169 (1858); *Gamble v. Great Western Ry.*, 24 UCQB 407 (1865).

[55] See; *Hood v. Grand Trunk Ry*, 20 UCCP 361 (1870); *Hamilton v. Grand Trunk Ry*, 23 UCQB 600 (1864); *Spettigue v. Great Western Ry*, 15 UCCP 315 (1865); *Dodson v. Grand Trunk Ry*, 8 Nova Sc. 405 (1871); *McDougall v. Allan*, 6 Low. Can. J. 233 (1862).

railways, but *critics* of the English rule permitting its validity. They sanctioned the "contracting out" reluctantly, with airs of resignation. Thus, Chief Justice Draper and Justice Morrison of Upper Canada's Queen's Bench were clearly troubled by a special contract to carry plate glass, essentially at the shipper's risk, viewing the arrangement as "destructive of the common law." They both indicated that, were it not for English precedent that they were compelled to follow, they would not have sanctioned the "contracting out." Similarly, Justice Wilson indicated in 1865 that he and his colleagues on Upper Canada's Court of Common Pleas "feel the same difficulty" with the rule as did their counterparts in Upper Canada's Court of Queen's Bench, in that

> we shall be encouraging the servants of companies ... in being careless and negligent in the transport and handling of goods; but we are bound by these authorities and contrary to our conviction of what would be really right, but for these [English] decisions.

Nova Scotia's Chief Justice, Sir William Young, echoed these sentiments six years later (on the eve of the decision of the U.S. Supreme Court that abrogated the rule permitting such "contracting out"). He and his colleagues were "constrained by the authorities." So he called on the legislature of the new Dominion of Canada "to enact a law" limiting this right.[56] These legislators may be said to have responded immediately, for they passed just such a law the same year (1871), prohibiting the "contracting out" of negligence liability. This statute was thereupon applied by the courts in such interprovincial railway cases as *Grand Trunk v. Vogel.*[57]

In Lower Canada/Quebec jurists eventually denied carriers the right to "contract out" for the same reason that their counterparts on the Canadian Supreme Court would – that is, Article 1676 of Quebec's Civil Code of 1866 prohibited such "contracting out" by common carriers, and the French-Canadian members of the court, generally joined by Justice Drummond consistently found for the plaintiffs in such cases. Justice Badgley just as consistently argued that the parties

---

[56] Justices Draper and Morrison in *Hamilton v. Grand Trunk Ry.*, 23 UCQB 600 at 608–10 (1864); Justice Wilson in *Spettigue v. Great Western Ry*, 15 UCCP 315 at 319 (1865); Chief Justice Young in *Dodson v. Grand Trunk Ry*, 8 Nova Sc. 405 at 412 (1871). But see *Sutherland v. Great Western Ry.*, 7 UCCP 409 (1857), where the executor of a man who had been issued a free ticket with a condition that the recipient assumed "the risks of accidents and damage" and had died in the collapse of a bridge caused by negligence of the company was barred from suing in a wrongful death action by virtue of the special contract, and no jurist objected.

[57] 11 Canadian Sup. Ct. Rep. 612 (1886).

were entitled to make such agreements, but he invariably spoke in dissent.[58]

Jurists in New South Wales, Queensland, and New Zealand operated under the same conditions as their pre-1871 counterparts in Ontario and Nova Scotia – that is, none of their legislatures had prohibited a "contracting out." But in all of their decisions but one the railway companies were ordered to pay damages. In one instance, a racehorse shipped in 1860 was injured in a collision. The railway had posted its exemption from liability for horses and dogs, but had made no such entry on the shipping voucher. The high court of New South Wales held that the mere posting of railway exemption from liability was not binding upon the shipper, and upheld a jury verdict for the shipper of £500. The court *did* allow that the railway was free to write exemptions into special contracts, though it added a barbed comment – "however unreasonable" such exemptions might be. Eight years later, the same court held that while the railway might offer contracts holding owners of race horses being shipped to assume the "risk of accidents," they could not escape liability for injury to such animals when their employees' "willful misfeasance" had led to a collision. Here the company was held to have breached the contract; the collision was not deemed an "accident." But this court was not incapable of finding for the province's Commissioners of Railways where the value being claimed for lost goods had not been declared by the shipper; in such a case their by-laws limiting liability was regarded as sufficient notice.[59]

Queensland's Supreme Court upheld a jury finding for the defendant railway commissioners. In 1876, in a case where bulls being shipped to Ipswich had been injured, the carrier had contracted out of all liability except the "gross negligence" of its agents. This jury had not regarded the evidence to warrant a finding of that sort.[60] But the same court was just as ready to affirm damage awards to shippers where the steamship or railway commissioners' appeal challenged the jury's finding that the evidence had warranted a finding of "gross" negligence. Such questions, Chief Justice Cockle pointed out, were for juries to decide. While he allowed that "all would suffer by any injury to the

---

[58] See *Harris v. Edmonstone*, 4 Low. Can. J. 40 (1859); *Huston v. Grand Trunk Ry*, 2 Low. Can J. 269 (1859); *Grand Trunk Ry v. Mountains and Huston*, 6 Low. Can. J. 173 (1860); *Grand Trunk Ry v. Campbell*, 24 Quebec 125 (1872).

[59] *Bell v. Ry. Comm.*, 2 Legge's R (NSW) 1398 (1861); *Cheeke v. Comm. of Rys.*, 8 NSWSLR 111 (1869); *Alcorn v. Com. Of Rys.*, 1 NSWR(L) 196 (1880). And see *Christchurch Finance Co. v. Black*, 10 NZR(CA) 238 (1891).

[60] *Kirk v. Comm. for Rys.*, 4 Queens. SCR 160 (1876) (Justice Lilley citing U.S. opinions and treatises).

commercial interest," he added that "all" would also "suffer if these contracts were not fairly interpreted by the Courts, and acted upon by juries."[61]

Champerty versus Contingency Fees in North America and the Antipodes

Since the Middle Ages in England, those who offered to assist the lawsuit of a stranger for a portion of the spoils were regarded as *champertors* and barred from such action by both penal statutes and common-law rule. The "stirring up" of lawsuits against others for a stake in the outcome was regarded by the leaders of the legal profession in England as being odious and unethical, and they regularly declaimed against it. By the nineteenth century, some seem to have recognized that this rule disadvantaged the poor. In 1843, for example, Lord Abinger appeared impatient with a rule that left "a poor person in the street oppressed and abused, and without the means of obtaining redress." It "would take a very strong argument" to convince him that a friend who provided funds for an attorney "could be said to be stirring up litigation or strife." Abinger was describing a good samaritan, not an attorney advancing funds for affidavits and court fees in exchange for a contingent percentage of the prospective award. His remarks did not sanction contingency fee contracts. And the problems that even those suitors with good samaritans as friends faced without such contracts were significant. Convinced by government coal mine inspectors that "all interests are arrayed" against those widowed by the negligence of coal mine owners, the Home Office financed one widow's suit and appeal in 1854 under the terms of Lord Campbell's Act (permitting surviving spouses to sue in actions of wrongful death). The government's legal costs of this experiment ran to £187 13s. 11d. It was, consequently, not repeated. Between 1851 and 1854, the inspectors reported, some three thousand fatal accidents had occurred in the mines; no cases of compensation recovered could be identified. The situation prompted one inspector to lament that the statute was

---

[61] *Pettigrew v. Australasian Steam Navigation Co.*, 1 Queens. SCR 113 (1864); *Wing Wah v. Austr. Steam Nav. Co*, 2 Queens. SCR 36 (1869); *Tough v. Aust. S.N. Co.*, 2 Queens. SCR 75 (1870). Similarly, in 1906, Western Australia's Supreme Court cited a decision of a British high court that disallowed the contracting out of liability for lost freight by a common carrier as authority for holding its own state's Commissioner of Railways liable for the loss of apple crates. *Silbert & Sharp v. Comm. Of Rys.*, 8 WALR 77 (1906) (citing *Curran v. Midland Gr. West. Ry.*, an Irish Exchequer Division case).

"comparatively inoperative, as regards collieries, owing to the poverty of the suitor."[62]

By the late eighteenth century in the new United States, arrangements between attorneys and clients on contingency fee bases were relatively common. Hugh Henry Brackenridge claimed that in colonial Pennsylvania "the scarcity of circulating medium" had led attorneys to enter into "what are called contingent fees" with "parties not monied" who sought legal assistance"for something out of what was recoverable." Others reported such arrangements in Ohio, Kentucky, New York, Massachusetts, and Louisiana. Confirmation of the practice can be found as well in the records generated by those dissatisfied with it. Thus, some of the Diaspora settlers in early Fayette County, Kentucky, who must have felt compelled to agree to such terms in order to find legal assistance in establishing title to their claims, resolved in 1798 that the prevailing "custom of the country in giving one half" of the land one sought title to "to save the other [half]" was "too large" a contingent fee arrangement.[63] Between 1824 and the 1850s, jurists in the state courts of the United States came to reject the champerty rule as inhumane, in that it "shut the door of justice to the poor,"[64] and by the late nineteenth century, the sanctioned American practice of attorneys working for contingency fees was well known in the Canadian and Australasian lands of the British Diaspora.

In Ontario, Quebec, New Zealand, Victoria, and New South Wales some solicitors tried to use contingency fee arrangements, and the practice, *soto voce,* may have become commonplace in England and elsewhere, but nowhere were they sanctioned by the courts (except for a brief span of time in *fin de siecle* Quebec).[65] Justice Manning of

---

[62] See Bartrip and Burnam, *The Wounded Soldiers of Industry,* 110–11; and Karsten, *Heart versus Head,* 191–93.

[63] Stephen Aron, *How the West was Lost,* 85; Peter Karsten, "Enabling the Poor to Have Their Day in Court: The Sanctioning of Contingency Fee Contracts, A History to 1940," 47 *DePaul Law Review* 231 (1998).

[64] Karsten, *Heart versus Head,* 194–99.

[65] See *O'Connor v. Gemmill,* 26 Ont. C. of A. 27 (1899); *Dorion v. Brom,* 27 L.C.J. 47 (1879); *Mills v. Rogers & Another,* 18 NZLR 291 (1899); *Ex Parte Davidson in the Insolvency of Little,* 2 NSWLR 276 (1881); and *Reilly v. Melbourne Tramway & Omnibus Co., Conway v. Same,* 19 Vict. LR 75 (1893) (a contract for 50 percent of the personal injury award plus costs void as champertous; Mr. Kidston, the attorney in question, testified that his *clerk* had drawn up the champertous agreement with Reilly and Conway, and he "immediately pointed out that the agreement was unlawful and could not be enforced, and would not accept it." He "treated it as if of no use and returned it" to his clerk. The court wondered, however, why the clerk had felt it appropriate to draw such a contract up in the first place, and why it had been filed and not simply destroyed).

the high court of New South Wales lamented the fact that the champerty rule "might often defeat justice being done to a poor litigant, who has not ready money," but in the absence of a statute in New South Wales sanctioning such arrangements, he could not permit them since the champerty precedents were "too strong to be reasoned with."[66] In a New Zealand case, the solicitor's barrister pointed out that American jurists had sanctioned such contracts, but neither Justice Denniston nor any of his colleagues made the slightest reference to the American cases that had been cited in voiding this contract.[67] Justice Ramsay of Lower Canada's Queen's Bench took the equally cold view that contingency fee arrangements were simply "incompatible with the existence of a respectable bar"; there would be no "trafficking by solicitors in speculative actions, or stipulating for payments by results." But while Ramsay was joined by both Justice Cross and the Chief Justice, both Justices Tessier and Monk were willing to sanction these arrangements.[68] In 1886, this same court finally appeared to have actually sanctioned a contingency fee contract. Six years later, Justice Robert Hill of Quebec's Queen's Bench held that the financial assistance that a friend of the plaintiff provided her "to prosecute this action, upon condition that he should have a share of whatever amount might be realized" was not to be deemed champerty or grounds for interfering with an award to her of $1,230 from the Canadian Pacific Railway for the negligent killing of her husband at a crossing. This friend, however, had been Lord Abinger's "good samaritan," not a champertous attorney. And when Quebec's Court of King's Bench sanctioned a contingency fee contract in 1903, it was reversed by the Canadian Supreme Court that held such contracts to be void at law there as elsewhere throughout Canada.[69]

Manitoba's high court ignored this decision. In 1890, Manitoba's legislature sanctioned contingency fee contracts, and Manitoba's Supreme Court turned away a challenge of the constitutionality of that statute. In 1910, Justice Perdue called the sweeping language in

Some plaintiffs were, of course, able to secure attorneys in civil actions *in forma pauperis* in Quebec. See, for example, *Bastien v. Forget*, 12 Quebec C. S. 425 (1897).

66 *Ex Parte Davidson, supra* note 19, at 278.
67 *Mills v. Rogers & Another*, 18 NZLR 291 at 297, 303 (1899).
68 *Dorion v. Brom*, 27 L.C.J. 47 at 52 (1879).
69 *Dussault v. Le Ch. de fer de la Rive-Nord* (QB), 12 Rap. Jud. de Q 50, 14 Revue Legale 207 (1886); *La Comp. du Ch. de Fer Can. du Pacifique v. Birabin dit St. Denis*, 4 QQB 516 at 523 (1894); *Ritchot v. Cardinal*, 3 QQB 55 (1893), and *Meloche v. Deguire*, 12 Queb. B. du Roi 298 (1903) (Justice Hall at 309: "The term 'champerty' seems almost as barbaric as 'wager by battle' and should be banished from modern procedure."); reversed by the Canadian Supreme Court in *Meloche v. Deguire*, 34 Can. SC 24 (1903).

the Canadian Supreme Court decision of 1903 to be "mere *obiter dictum* is so far as Manitoba is concerned," in light of Manitoba's statute.[70]

But if this was the Law with regard to contingency fee contracts as pronounced by English and CANZ jurists, we need not conclude from this that poor plaintiffs were unable to obtain legal assistance on a contingency fee basis in nineteenth century Britain or her Diaspora lands. Both counsel and jurists in those cases in the courts of the United States that finally resulted in the sanctioning of these sorts of contracts constantly referred to the arrangement as a widespread and "common" "habit," as did others.[71] And this was clearly the case by the mid-nineteenth century in England as well. Rande Kostal argues that the plaintiff in *Priestley v. Fowler* (1837) was probably represented under a "kind of *de facto* 'contingency fee' arrangement" whereby solicitor and barrister took a case they felt might be winnable without receipt of any retainer or other fees, and he regards the arrangement as "commonplace" by the 1860s in litigation involving injured railway passengers. Moreover, he quotes the London & Northwestern Railway's general counsel who told a parliamentary committee in 1870 that injured passengers routinely found attorneys willing to take their cases "upon speculation," and that "touters" appeared at the scene of accidents soliciting business for these lawyers. Thus, some 400 claims were filed within 48 hours of the New Cross accident on the London & Brighton Line and over 100 of these went to trial.[72] Contingency fee contracts may have been void in Law throughout most of the lands of the British Diaspora, but they were generally voidable only by one or the other of the parties, *not* by the pleas of railway-company attorneys

[70] Bora Laskin, *The British Tradition in Canadian Law* (London, 1969), 27, Justice Perdue in *Thompson v. Wishart*, 19 Man. R 340 at 348 (1910); Kenneth Gifford and Arthur Heymanson, *The Victorian Solicitor* (3rd ed., Sydney, 1974), 311; *Clyne v. NSW Bar Assoc.*, 104 CLR 186, 34 ALJR 87 (1960).

It would not be until 1960 that they would be sanctioned in part in the Australian province of Victoria, and more recently before they would be sanctioned elsewhere. The British Court and Legal Services Act of 1990 and the Conditional Fee Arrangements Regulations of 1995 (Sl No 1675), for example, sanction some such arrangement, but attorneys acting under such agreements can be made personally liable for the winning party's costs of an action. *Hodgson & Others v. Imperial Tobacco Ltd. & Others*, rptd. *The Times* (London), Feb. 13, 1998.

One of India's British courts sanctioned contingency fee contracts in 1875 in *Coondoo v. Mokerjee*, 2 A.C. 186 at 210 (1876) (Justice Sir Montague Smith: "in furtherance of right and justice" and "to resist oppression").

[71] See Peter Karsten, "Enabling the Poor to Have Their Day in Court: The Sanctioning of Contingency Fee Contracts, A History to 1940," 47 *Depaul Law Review* 231–60 (1998).

[72] Kostal, *Law and English Railway Capitalism*, 261, 378.

who had become aware of their existence. And most plaintiffs whose attorneys had succeeded in winning awards for them appear to have been satisfied that they should stick to the agreement and not seek to reduce their attorney's share to a court-imposed quantum meruit. Thus, once again, the formal Law and the ways that ordinary people behaved when it came to contracts of this sort were not in synch. At least *some* Brits, Canadians, Aussies, and Kiwis found attorneys who offered informal contingency fee contracts.

SUMMARY

Most of the Diaspora's courts followed English, not American Common-Law rules with regard to contract law. The exception was those of Lower Canada/Quebec, whose jurists adopted the same course as many of the state courts south of the border when it came to implied warranties, stock futures and options, third party beneficiary contracts, efforts of common carriers to contract out of liability, contingency fees, and (as we will see in the next chapter) *quantum meruit* recovery off of "entire" contracts when the employee quit. Whereas American jurists had found their ways to new positions on these issues by rejecting English precedents (something they were free to do) and substituting rules of their own fashioning that they deemed more equitable, Lower Canada/Quebec's jurists were coincidentally led to the same views largely because by 1866 they happened to be the rules of their largely French Civil Code.

Ultimately, popular norms and customs were more important than what the Common Law had to say when it came to the way stockbrokers, commodity traders, and quite ordinary merchants and settlers conducted themselves from day to day when it came to sales transactions. Similarly, despite the voiding of gambling contracts by legislative fiat, many of the British Diaspora continued to gamble, and continued to expect the loser to "act honorably."

When the contract was one between a Diaspora fur trader and a North American Indian, often neither the rules of the Common Law, nor the customary-law expectations of the Diaspora trader were satisfied. Indians were simply not on the same cultural wavelength as Diaspora traders when it came to sharing an understanding of debt obligations, payments-qua-"gifts," or, for that matter, the "law" of supply and demand. And the regular inclusion of hard liquor in the fur trade often complicated the resolution of differences born of this cultural gap.

6

Work: The Formal and Informal Law of Labor Contracts

The plight of those who offered their services to others has, for millennia, been captured by terms which translate into English as "master" and "servant" relationships. Once a labor contract was agreed upon, the "servant" surrendered several of his or her freedoms to the "master" for so many days, weeks, or months, for "the season," "the voyage," or "the term of apprenticeship." Moreover, in many of the rebellious American colonies and their successor, the United States, there existed *involuntary* labor relations, governed by statute, for some Native and most African Americans – that is, lifetime servitude, slavery.

Throughout the years addressed in this book, the common and statutory Law of labor contracts was formally administered by courts of Law, and there were developments in, and variations between, these Laws in the lands of the British Diaspora that deserve attention. But deserving of at least equal attention is the story of the *informal* "law" that "regulated" many disagreements between "master" and "servant." We explore a number of these issues in this chapter, but I offer the views of Reverend C. F. Sturgis, penned in Alabama in 1850, to serve as one illustration of what I mean by this latter, *informal* "law":

> Black people [slaves] expect, and, by a kind of conventional usage, almost demand, a number of little rights and privileges, which, although like the "common law," not referable to any positive enactments, are, like it, also of very binding influence.... One of the most effectual modes of inducing servants to perform their duties with cheerfulness, is to recognize all those little points; not, perhaps, as matters of right, but as concessions cheerfully made ... [from] master to servant.[1]

---

[1] Holland McTyeire and C. F. Sturgis, *Duties of Masters to Servants* (Charleston, S. C., 1851).

I remind you that, while I illustrate the "informal" nature of "master-servant" relations with this passage, I will not be treating slavery in this chapter as one of my subjects (except where it touches peripherally on my

THE FORMAL LAW

Ever since the days of the Black Death in the mid-fourteenth century, laborers in England had been compelled to work at rates set by local magistrates and compelled to complete any contracts they had entered into or suffer fines, imprisonment, and corporal punishment. And those who quit "entire" contracts (that is, contracts for a specific sum for a specific period of time) and sought to be paid "what their labor had been worth" their employers (*quantum meruit* payments) invariably failed in British courts throughout the seventeenth, eighteenth, and nineteenth centuries. By contrast, in the United States laborers won the right to quit without criminal penalties by the early nineteenth century, and, beginning in 1834 (in New Hampshire), an increasing number of state courts allowed them what their labor had been worth their employer "off" the contract that they had entered into with him or her. Moreover, juries in the States tended to award workers what they had claimed despite employer counter-claims for the costs of finding a replacement.[2] How did CANZ jurists deal with employee–employer suits?

In a nutshell, what I found was that workers suing their employers for wages or *quantum meruit* were more successful when their cases reached the appellate courts of the Antipodes than when they reached those of one or another of the Canadian provinces. They won thirteen and lost only two such appeals in Australia and New Zealand, while they won twenty two, but lost fourteen decisions in the high courts of the Canadian provinces. When we combine these figures, we see that workers won over twice as often in these appellate decisions as they lost (thirty five to sixteen). Furthermore, they were held to be criminally liable under the Master and Servant Act for abandoning their work in only one of sixteen appellate cases interpreting such a statute.

Workers in Canada, Australia, and New Zealand thus enjoyed some of the same rights to recover "what their labor was worth" as workers in half of the American states had acquired at the hands of common law jurists by 1900. And, if they had not acquired all of the American

---

primary topic of free labor agreements, as it does with regard to Bantu-Boer relations in Natal and the recruiting of South Seas Islanders for the sugar fields of Queensland and Fiji).

[2] See Robert Steinfeld, *The Invention of Free Labor* (Chapel Hill, 1994); Peter Karsten, "'Bottomed on Justice':... Breaches of Labor Contracts by Quitting or Firing in Britain and the U.S., 1630–1880," 34 *American Journal of Legal History* 213 (1990); and Karsten, *Heart versus Head*, ch. 5, on this issue.

rights to quit "at will," conversely, they were not subjected to a less desirable late nineteenth century American innovation, the "employment at will" doctrine – the right of the employer to fire them "at will."[3] They were overwhelmingly successful in both Canada and the Antipodes against employers when they charged that they had been wrongfully discharged, winning thirty-five of forty-two such appellate cases. Thus, overall, workers won 85 of 109 appellate decisions (78 percent) pertaining to breach of labor contracts. They clearly appear to have fared rather well at the hands of Canadian and Antipodal jurists.

Sheer numbers can be deceiving; so we must look more closely at the decisions, beginning with those concerning merchant seamen.

Seamen

Merchant seamen were viewed in English (and American) Law as being particularly vulnerable in labor contracts. "Mutuality" – a level field for both parties to the contract with neither being able to "leverage" the other – was often absent on the docks of the early modern English maritime labor marketplace. Seamen suffered from "crimping" (indebtedness to a waterfront landlord or publican) and "shanghaiing" (the taking aboard a vessel of one in a drugged or intoxicated state);[4] in both cases, the seaman might find himself "bound" without his having truly consented. Parliament addressed these injustices with statutes regulating many of the terms of a merchant seaman's labor contract. As such, these workers were protected in ways unlike most other laborers.

Consequently, I was not terribly surprised to find that merchant seamen won eight of the nine appealed cases I managed to find involving their labor contracts in the Canadian and Antipodal courts of the nineteenth century. In maritime New Brunswick, a seaman quit and sued for his wages in 1892 after the ship's master struck him with his fist, called him "a son of a whore," and threatened to "knock your brains out" with a hammer. He won at the stipendiary magistrate's hearing, but, on appeal, these admittedly "crude" and "brutal" remarks were discounted by Chief Justice Sir John Allen. "Sailors," he observed, "are

---

[3] Jay Feinman, "The Development of the Employment at Will Rule," 20 *American Journal of Legal History* 118 (1976).

[4] See Marcus Rediker, *Between the Devil and the Deep Blue Sea: Merchant Seamen, Pirates, and the Anglo-American Maritime World, 1700–1750* (Cambridge, 1987); Peter Karsten *The Naval Aristocracy* (N.Y., 1972), 76–88; and J. C. Healey, *Foc's'le and Glory Hole: A Study of the Merchant Seaman and his Occupation* (N.Y., 1936).

not much alarmed by abusive language." Justice Tuck excused the master's behavior as well. The seaman's carelessness had led to the breaking of the ship's boom:

What more natural than for [the master] to get angry and excited under the circumstances. The wonder is, with the knowledge one has of those who follow the seas, that the master did and said so little.[5]

This New Brunswick seaman's action failed, but all the others that I detected in the reports of the high courts of the other maritime provinces of New South Wales, Nova Scotia, Lower Canada, Newfoundland, and New Zealand were successful.[6] This is in large measure due to the solicitude that the international maritime codes, Parliament, the Vice-Admiralty Courts, and the Common Law itself had long extended to sailors. But shipowners and masters were surely as aware of this custom as were seamen; hence it is noteworthy that these defendants lost cases fought out at the appellate level as often as they did.

The sympathy that many British colonial jurists had for sailors in the nineteenth century is captured beautifully in one of these decisions from the high court of New Brunswick's parent province, Nova Scotia. *Ralston v. Barss* was decided there in 1837, the same year that the English Court of Exchequer shaped the assumption of risk rule in *Priestley v. Fowler*.[7] In *Ralston*, Justices Hill and Bliss not only offer an eloquent statement of the rights of injured seamen to the whole of his wages; they also offer an alternative vision of employer responsibility to workers injured on the job. The plaintiff had contracted for a voyage from New York to Liverpool via Pt. Medway, Nova Scotia. While in Pt. Medway, the plaintiff's leg had been broken while loading freight.

---

[5] *Ex Parte Lowery*, 32 New Br. 76 at 79–82 (1893). Judith Fingard also quotes the proemployer decision of Justice Tuck in an unreported New Brunswick high court case in 1887: Fingard, *Jack in Port* (Toronto, 1982), 192.

[6] *Hourston v. Norris* (NSWSC, Kercher, 1825); *Sims & Foster v. The Cumberland & Rbt. Carns, Master* (NSWSC, Kercher, 1827); *Geary v. Vivian*, 1 Legge's R (NSW) 1 (1830); *Ralson v. Brass*, 1 Nova Sc. R 75 (1837); *Frechette v. Gosselin*, 1 Low. Can. R 145 (1851); *Dunn v. McLoughlan*, 4 Newf. R 177 (1857); *Cousineau & Divers v. Opposants*, 7 Low. Can. J. 218 (1858); *Parlow v. Worsp*, Res. Mag., Dunedin, 1 N.Z. Jur., Pt. 9, 78–80 (1876). And see *Thornton v. Hurley* NZ Te Kopuru Magistrates' Court, 1876 (master of *Wild Wave* fined 3 pounds 8 shilling for "collaring and shaking the mate," noted in Judith Bassett, "Abstemious Millhands and Bush Lawyers: The Te Kopuru Magistraes' Court, 1875–78," 1 *Austr. Journal of Legal History* 221 at 233 (1995)).

[7] *Ralston v. Barss*, 1 N.S.L.R. 75 (1837); *Priestley v. Fowler*, 3 M.&W. 1 (Ex. 1837).

He had been left in that port and cared for by the owner's physician. Upon recovery, he asked for wages due him for the entire voyage, a maritime custom. The owner contested this and also demanded an offset against such wages as were lawfully due the plaintiff to cover the costs of his medical care.

With references to the Laws of Oleron as well as "the laws of humanity" and the treatises of New York's Chancellor James Kent and U.S. Supreme Court Justice Joseph Story, Justices Hill and Bliss both insisted that the plaintiff should receive the full amount of his wages for the New York to Liverpool voyage, and that no offset should be permitted for the medical care provided. They acknowledged that the English cases did not require that the master pay for the medical care of an injured servant unless he or she was living under the master's roof, and they offered a full and accurate discussion of these cases. Neither suggested that the seaman's injury was a risk he had assumed in the wages he was being paid. They acknowledged in the fashion of Lord Mansfield, that the master had no more than "a moral obligation" to care for the injured seaman. But they held that, since the master had acted voluntarily – that is, without formal prompting by the plaintiff – the plaintiff was therefore not obliged to reimburse him.

In light of the views of certain economic-oriented scholars that jurists were particularly concerned with the well-being of commercial entrepreneurs in the nineteenth century, I found the *dicta* of Justice Hill of considerable interest. This jurist seemed anxious to signal that he, too, was concerned with "the interest of the mercantile world," as he put it. And I have no reason to doubt that he was. But note that Justice Hill's "mercantile" rationale for his judgment, reasonable as it may well be, was not the sort that the defendant–shipowner had hoped for. Hill asked, rhetorically, whether it was not "good policy" to find for the plaintiff:

> In upholding and protecting the interests of seamen we best subserve the interest of the mercantile world who employ them; for what can be a greater inducement to a sailor to enter the merchant service than if he should be disabled in the performance of his duty in the course of a voyage, he is still entitled to his full wages.[8]

Had *Ralston* stood alone in its defense of sailor–workers, we would treat it only as an interesting aberration. It did not, but I offer only one more of the other cases consistent with it: John Dunn had been a stowaway on the *Wyoming*, a vessel hunting seals in Labrador in 1856. While first told to operate a bilge pump for his keep, he was fitted out for the seal hunt when the vessel reached its destination and a shipboard relation of the defendant promised him a share of the ship's bloody

---

[8] *Ralston v. Barss*, 1 Nova Sc. L.R. 75 at 78 and 82 (1837).

booty in exchange for his participation. When denied this share on the ship's return to Newfoundland, the plaintiff–stowaway sued (*Dunn v. McLoughlan* (Newfoundland, 1857)) and enjoyed a trial before a judge and jury willing to interpret a Common Law rule liberally to his advantage. Judge Des Barres told the jury that, inasmuch as the man's labor had been "accepted" by the *Wyoming's* skipper, he was indeed entitled to be paid what his labor had been worth to the defendant-shipowner. The jury thereupon awarded him £26, 5s. These instructions were liberal in their interpretation of what amounted to *quantum meruit* recovery on the "common counts."[9]

Nautical Labor Agreements from the Law and Society Perspective

Merchant Seamen

My evidence of the formal treatment meted out by the Law to merchant seamen in nineteenth century CANZ courts was largely limited to what I detected in appellate reports and legal journals. Briton Busch has tracked the disputes between masters and sailors aboard American whalers throughout the ports frequented by these vessels in the nineteenth century, and Judith Fingard has provided us with a complete account of their treatment in the vice-admiralty and police magistrate's courts of the maritime cities of eastern Canada from the 1830s to the 1890s. Busch offers us a number of examples of tyrannical Captain Ahabs, and he tells us that whalers lost their suits more often than they won them when they initiated grievance procedures against their whaling masters before U.S. consuls overseas. But the ledger is not a lopsided one; Busch provides plenty of evidence of consular sympathy with these whalers, and animosity for the masters who "perjure themselves" to shift the costs of caring for abandoned sailors from off of the ship owners onto the U.S. government. "Masters promise much at home, in order to get a Crew," one consul reported in 1824, "but never perform abroad." "The only way to reach them," another wrote in 1862, "is through the pockets of their owners."[10]

Judith Fingard found that merchant seamen in the Maritimes generally lost cases where it was established that they had "jumped ship" (had no "ticket of leave") to sign on in the Canadian ports where salaries were often two to three times higher than in the British Isles.

---

[9] *Dunn v. McLoughlan*, 4 Newf. 177 (1857).

[10] Briton Busch, *"Whaling will Never do for Me": The American Whaleman in the Nineteenth Century* (Lexington, Ky., 1994), 70–84, esp. 75–76. And see Susan Chamberlain, "The Hobart Whaling Industry, 1830–1900," unpub. Ph.D. thesis, LaTrobe Univ., 1988, on whaler use of Master & Servant legislation.

(They were thereupon generally held in jail until their original vessel was about to leave port; the Master and Servant Acts clearly reached merchant seamen in the Maritime Provinces who had signed their ship's articles of agreement.) But she also found those who sued their ships' master or owner for unpaid wages were generally successful, and that in the 1840s, Maritime legal officials were reading the ancient maxim "freight is the mother of wages" to require the sale of vessels to meet seamen wage demands whether there had been a profit gener-ated by the voyage or not, which was a recasting of an old English rule, "decidedly in the sailor's favour."[11] Police magistrates prior to the mid-1850s relied on the fees they collected from the parties before them, Fingard also points out. And the merchant seaman who lost his case generally could not pay any fees. This appears to have been the cause of the proseaman bias of these magistrates, and thus the creation of stipendiary (salaried) magistrates and other statutory changes in 1873 resulted in police courts less friendly to seamen.[12]

For many years, the managers of the Hudson's Bay Company were empowered by Crown and Parliament to administer the Company's version of English Law to its employees and other British citizens in "Rupert's Land," a region that included virtually everything from the Pacific Northwest coast to those lands whose rivers fed into Hudson's Bay. Company employees who chose to engage in work stoppages or other forms of labor protest, be they miners, traders, or seamen on the Company's tiny "fur trade navy," could find themselves clapped into irons and put on bread-and-water rations for a week by its officials, as Hamar Foster has shown.[13] But this treatment was very idiosyn-cratic: One "captain," such as David Home, might treat seamen who had absented themselves without leave leniently; another, like William McNeill, might lash or confine "mutinous" strikers. In any event, the Company's Law was not administered consistently. Labor contracts contained penal clauses, entitling the Company to several of the mea-sures "Captain" McNeill took, as well as to the loss of all wages. But when McNeill took action against four work-stoppage leaders in 1837, three of the men sued for their back wages anyway, and, lo and behold, the Company's governor and council ordered them to be paid![14]

[11] Judigh Fingard, *Jack in Port: Sailortowns in Eastern Canada* (Toronto, 1982), 4, 140, 142–45, 152, 176–86.
[12] *Ibid.*, 187–88. See also Greg Marquis, "'A Machine of Oppression under the Guise of Law': The St. John Police Establishment, 1860–1890," in *Historical Perspectives on Law and Society in Canada*, ed. Tina Loo and Lorna McLean (Toronto, 1994), 205.
[13] Hamar Foster, "Mutiny on the *Beaver*: Law and Authority in the Fur-Trade Navy, 1835–1840," 20 *Manitoba Law Journal* 15 (1991).
[14] Foster, "Mutiny on the *Beaver*," 27ff.

Cod Fishermen and Sealers

An issue that can be related to the rights of merchant seamen in the maritime provinces to their wages was once associated with the Newfoundland cod and seal fisheries. The legal issue regarding the wages of cod fishermen and sealers in Newfoundland was this: When the storekeeper–supplier ("planter") to the fishermen became insolvent (as sometimes occurred), were the fishermen entitled under the Law to "follow the fish and oil" to their "planter"–supplier's capitalist–creditor in Britain (called the "merchant") for their wages, or were they bound to stand in line among the creditors of the insolvent? This was a question batted about in the Newfoundland high court for a *century*. Although it is a complicated story, I think it worth bearing with me for the next few pages as I tell it:

The storekeeper–suppliers ("planters") were, in fact, mere middlemen throughout the eighteenth and nineteenth centuries for British-based capitalist investors ("merchants") who put up the funds managed locally by "planters" to finance the cod fishery. Since everything depended upon the adequacy of the catch, a season in which the cod were harder than usual to locate on the Outer Banks could prove disastrous to both the "planters" and the "merchants." By the eighteenth century, the fishermen appear to have been the first creditors to be paid out of the catch, even if it had already been sent on to the overseas "merchant." Since the fishermen were always in one degree of debt or another to the "planters" for various and sundry supplies, this "custom" of the trade gave them an advantage in the event their "planter" had become insolvent. Since the "planter's" primary creditor was the "merchant," and his primary debtors were the cod fishermen themselves, this practice of allowing the fishermen to "follow the fish and oil" as first creditors to the capitalist–investors who now held them, placed them in the same favored status as a merchantman's crew suing in an Admiralty proceeding for its wages upon the sale/liquidation of the ship and its cargo.

In 1768, Newfoundland's Governor, Sir Hugh Palliser, ordered all fish to be held by "planters" until their fishermen–"servants" had been paid, and he warned "merchants" to follow this rule or lose their rights. Seven years later Parliament formalized the practice.[15] Fishermen in Newfoundland were to be offered terms in writing. Funds were to be set aside from these wages for their possible return passage, and half of

---

[15] In 15 Geo. III, cap. 31, sec. 16 (1775). Gerald Sider, *Culture and Class in Anthropology and History: A Newfoundland Illustration* (Cambridge, 1986), 47–50; John Crowley "Empire versus Truck: The Official Interpretation of Debt and Labour in the 18th Century Newfoundland Fishery," 70 *Canadian Historical Review* 311 at 325–27 (1989).

the fishermen's wages were to be free from any "truck" indebtedness
for liquor, goods, or advances. The balance was to be paid in bills of
exchange drawn on British merchants of good standing. Seamen were
granted a preferred lien which was to follow the catch into the hands
of the middlemen–"planters" and the British "merchants." Palliser's
Act, as it came to be known, thus forced "merchants" to negotiate and
commit themselves to paying fishermen's seasonal wages *before* the cod
crop's profitability could be known.

Newfoundland's courts originally chose to ignore the more severe
features of Palliser's Act – that is, the use of the lash and the imposition
of gaol terms for fishermen who broke their labor contracts. They also
tended to ignore the "entire" nature of these contracts – that is, they
tended not to require the total forfeiture of wages in the event of a failure to fulfill a portion of the contract's provisions. According to Sean
Cadigan, fishermen "almost always won suits for wages against evasive
masters" in both the Surrogate Court and the Court of Session.[16]

They won appeals, at first, in the Newfoundland Supreme Court as
well. In 1809, Chief Justice Thomas Tremlett refused to allow "planters"
and "merchants" to fob off any doubtful bills of exchange on fishermen as part of their wage package, inasmuch as they, and not the fishermen, possessed the information that might enable one to assess the
value of such bills. Upset by this judgement, the Board of Trade recommended Tremlett's replacement, without initial success. But when
Francis Forbes was named chief justice several years later, he proved
to be a bit more accommodating: In 1818, he allowed "merchants"
to insist that their "planter"–middlemen hire fishermen on shares
rather than fixed-voyage wages, and in 1819, he held that a fisherman-
creditor working on such a "shares" agreement was not entitled to the
preferred lien that Palliser's Act provided for wage–fishermen against
the assets of an insolvent "planter" who had arranged the fishing expedition. Forbes also ruled that the "merchant" who had provided the
capital for the expedition was thereby entitled to stand at the head
of the line of the insolvent's creditors. This was understandably unpopular with the fishermen, but the confidence it provided capitalist–
"merchants" *could* have resulted in attracting more capital investment
to their industry. In any event, in 1819, Forbes yielded on one issue.
He held in *Dooley v. Burke & Hackett* that the English legal view of the
fisherman's lien was not expansive enough. English jurists had held
that a "merchant" was not to be presumed to have known all of the
contractual agreements his "planter" had entered into with fishermen,
and that, as a consequence, fish and oil that had reached the hands

[16] Sean Cadigan, *Hope and Deception on Conception Bay: Merchant-Settler Relations in Newfoundland, 1785–1855* (Toronto, 1995), 84.

of such a "merchant" were not subject to the lien of such an unknown "servant." Forbes disagreed; Palliser's Act, he explained, had to be interpreted liberally, by those attentive to the special circumstances of the fishing industry. The "correct interpretation of the law" would "depend upon a practical knowledge of the subject to which the law is intended to be applied." Forbes would "always bend to the superior wisdom of English lawyers upon a point of English law" but the Chief Justice bent ever so slightly: It was notoriously known in Newfoundland, he explained, that "there is an intimacy of connexion approaching to identity" between "merchants" and their "planters." Consequently, unless the "merchant" could prove that some fraud had been perpetrated, the court would accept the slightest evidence to establish that the "merchant" had known or ought to have known of the lien.[17]

Forbes elaborated on the primacy of "merchants" in a case involving a "planter's" insolvency, decided in 1821, of considerable interest to all in the trade. Archibald Graham, a "planter" in Newfoundland was indebted to Hunters & Company,[18] British "merchants." After communicating his intentions and securing the company's sanction, he sent the season's cod directly to the company's agent in Oporto, intending to generate dollars that could be remitted to him to pay ("for the benefit of") the fishermen. But by 1821, English Common Law no longer honored the claims of third-party creditor beneficiaries, and the company's agent ignored his request and applied the entire value of the catch against his ledger debt. After Graham's death and his estate's declaration of insolvency, a local provider to the fishermen, Archibald Hunter (no relation to the company), claimed that the Bills of Credit Graham had written for his "Servant's wages & other Bills on him, which bills [Hunter] paid," should be repaid out of the insolvency funds with the priority that was due a "Servant" (that is, at the head of the line of creditors). Forbes acknowledged that it "had been the practice" to "allow persons holding Bills drawn in favour of Servants, and passed away from them, to rank as *wages*, which in effect they represented, and without which Servants who had received Bills would not only be deprived of the benefits of the preferences given them by law, but also saddled with the expenses of Protest, and other charges on Bills." But, Forbes explained, the question before him had primacy: Did the man who had honored these bills stand, so to speak, in the shoes of the fishermen? Forbes held that

---

[17] *Stuarts & Rennie v. Walsh*, 1 Newf. R. 82 (1818); *Dooley v. Burke & Hackett*, 1 Newf. R 190 (1819). See also *Lahy v. Tree*, 1 Newf. R. 129 (1818); and *Doyle's Servants v. Receivers*, 1 Newf. R. 261 (1821).

[18] Or perhaps it is "Hunt, McCoy & Co." Forbes' manuscript text at the Mitchell Library is hard to decipher.

he did not. Six months later Hunter tried a different tack, arguing that Graham had really been a "merchant" when he sent the catch directly to Portugal, thus rendering unlawful the company's agent in Oporto. Forbes reviewed the evidence and disagreed: "As the suppliers of Graham," the company "had a lien upon the fish," a "primary right to the Cargo."[19] The "servant"–fishermen were thus placed at future disadvantage, inasmuch as much of their pay was provided them in the form of bills of credit.

Forbes' earlier unpopular judgement regarding the rights of "shares"–fishermen was immediately ignored by the separate Surrogate Court, run by officers of the Royal Navy. This institution continued to treat fishermen–"planter" contracts for shares as if they were wage contracts under the Act, entitling fishermen to preferred liens. The colony's governor, probably under advice from Forbes, thereupon proclaimed, to the contrary, that fishermen on "shares" were only entitled to preferred-creditor status, up to the forty shillings reserved in the Act to pay for their return trip to the British Isles (now a fiction for nearly all resident fishermen). But the region's naval commander disagreed, and upheld his officers' views regarding the law, telling Crown authorities that both the fishermen and the local middlemen–"planters" "appear to me to be more like the slaves of a feudal lord, than the free subjects of a Great Nation." Parliament responded to the arguments of those with influence in the British Isles, the "merchant"–capitalists: The Fisheries and Judicature Act of 1824 removed the naval courts from the picture, gave the "merchants" a lien of current supply, and tied the fisherman's lien to shares of the fish caught rather than the fixed wages agreed upon. This "piece-rate" system appeared more economically efficient, encouraging greater work effort while on the Banks and coasts, but it was unpopular and led to resistance.[20]

In the early 1830s, a new Chief Justice was named, a Tory, Henry John Boulton, removed from the post of Attorney-General for Upper Canada for biases he had displayed. In Newfoundland Boulton altered the writ of attachment in debt actions in order that sheriffs could attach the boats and tackle of debtor fishermen and, following a drift in the English Common-Law of Contract, ruled that they should receive pay only from the "planter" with whom they were in privity, and not from the "merchant" who acquired the fish. Most of these fishermen were Irish Catholics, and the island's Catholic "reform" spokesmen

[19] "In the Matter of Archibald Graham's Insolvency," June 11, 1821, and "Archibald Hunter v Hunters & Co.," Dec. 13, 1821, Sir Francis Forbes Decisions of the Supreme Court of Judicature of Newfoundland, CYA 740, pp. 244ff, Mitchell Library.

[20] Sean Cadigan, *Hope and Deception in Conception Bay: Merchant-Settler Relations in Newfoundland, 1785–1855* (Toronto, 1995), 30, 83–4, 89.

criticized these decisions,[21] while styling those of the dissenting Justice
Tucker, the views of "the Poor Man's Judge." Petitions for Boulton's
removal from office appear to have led to his replacement in 1838.[22]

By the 1840s, Justice Augustus Des Barres broke ranks and helped
return the court to the practice of letting fishermen "follow the fish
and oil" to "merchants" for their wages. (Des Barres, unlike his contemporary, John Walpole Willis, did not appear blindly to adhere to
English Common-Law rules or practices. In one exchange with a barrister quoting from one of Joseph Chitty's treatises, he once remarked,
"Chitty, Mr. Hayward! Goodness me, what does Mr. Chitty know about
this country? He was never in Newfoundland.") But the court reversed
direction again in 1854, holding that the practice rested upon positive
Law alone, that there had been no custom "from time immemorial"
sanctioning it without the Parliament's voice which was now silent
(with its repeal of those aspects of Palliser's Act).[23] In the late nineteenth century, Newfoundland's jurists abandoned this position and
returned to the view that the practice *had* acquired the status of customary law. They turned away another challenge to the custom in 1885
when they ruled against the argument of a "merchant"–investor's attorney that he was not responsible for hiring contracts made by his
debtor, the "planter." The court fended off this "lack of privity" claim
(which could well have succeeded in a court within the British Isles in
these years) by ruling that the "merchant"–investor had "constructive"
privity with regard to the hiring by his "planter" of virtually any and all
fishermen–employees.[24]

[21] "Boulton, Henry John" in *Provincial Justice: Upper Canada Legal Portraits from the Dictionary of Canadian Biography*, ed. Robert Fraser (Toronto, 1992), 46; Cadigan, *Hope and Deception*, 144, 148, 150, 153.

In fact, one capitalist–merchant, Thomas Holdsworth Brooking, told a parliamentary committee in 1837 the Boulton's judgement "seemed to be very hard on the working man. It gave the merchant a power he never had before, of seizing the fisherman's nets and tackle for debts." Sider, *Culture and Class*, 136.

[22] MacNutt, *Atlantic Provinces*, 209. What these reform-minded folk may not have appreciated was that Justice Tucker joined two of his colleagues in recommending the end of all profisherman legislation to the Colonial Office in 1831, and that he resigned in 1832 in protest against the grant of Responsible Government. *In Re Insolvent Estate of Alexander*, 2 Newf. R. 29 (1831); MacNutt, *Ibid.*, 206.

[23] *In Re Insolvent Estate of Sullivan*, 3 Newf. R. 1 (1846); *Moreen v. Ridley*, 3 Newf. 4 (1846); *Hanrahan v. Barron & Doody*, 3 Newf. 102 (1849); *In Re Fishery Servants of Cashman*, 4 Newf. R. 11 (1854); Cadigan, *Hope and Deception*, 157; D. W. Prowse, *History of Newfoundland from the English Colonial and Foreign Office Records* (1895), 423n.

[24] *Antle v. Baine, Johnston & Co.*, 7 Newf. R. 99 (1885); *Parsons v. Fox*, 8 Newf. R. 20 (1898).

In large measure, most of these decisions were based on close and reasonable readings of parliamentary statutes, giving fishermen a lien on their catch. But several relied not on statutes, but "custom," and even those cases involving statutes could have been decided differently. This (generally) profisherman pattern of appellate judging may be dismissed as judicial "paternalism;" but it helped Irish and west-country families endure on the harsh Newfoundland shores for over a century.

Landlubber–Laborers and Builders

Merchant seamen and cod fishermen aside, how did the rest of labor fare at the hands of high court CANZ jurists? Cod fishermen may have been favored in Newfoundland, but miners in New South Wales in 1848, for example, were not similarly judged to be preferential creditors of insolvent employers for back wages.[25] Statutes and customary law varied widely with regard to such status. When apprentices, masons, carpenters, teachers, hired hands, clerks, sheep shearers, and stone cutters quit "entire" contracts and sought what their labor had been worth to their employers, or when these workers were fired and claimed that the firing was "wrongful," how did CANZ jurists deal with the issues? Did they simply follow English precedent?

Punishing Apprentices and Indentured Servants

Let's take up the question of punitive measures against apprentices and indentured servants first. The rule in early Quebec as well as the other Canadian and Australasian provinces was that those who entered into indentured servitude, apprenticeship, or other menial trades governed by the Master and Servants Acts were to fulfill the terms of their contracts or suffer short-term coercive imprisonment and additional periods of service. This was the Law in England,[26] and it was the Law in Canada and Australia, both in theory and in practice. Apprentices, indentured servants, convicts in Australia on "tickets of leave," blacksmiths, "station hands" (typically shepherds) in Australia

[25] *In re Whittell*, 1 Legge's R. (NSW) 441 (1848).
[26] Where a "huntsman" on a yearly salary of £100 was adjudged to be a menial servant, subject to the Acts. The man had been fired after four months; a jury had viewed the "custom" to be a yearly hire and had awarded him £80, but Common Pleas reversed, viewing a man paid as much as £100 per annum as a "menial," subject to the Acts, and hence subject to a month's notice. See *Nicoll v. Greaves*, 17CB (N.S.) 27, 144 ER11 (C.P. 1864) (questioned in *Fleming v. Hill*, 10 Nova Sc. 268 at 273 (1876)). The rule was abrogated in England in the Employer & Workmen Act of 1875, ending the penal treatment of those who quit most occupations.

and New Zealand, indeed, many sailors as well, were often held by magistrates in the early and mid-nineteenth century to be subject to the prevailing Masters and Servants Act – that is, to be subject to punishment for having quit work without permission.[27] These terms may have become dead letters by the turn of the nineteenth century in America,[28] but they were still in place in Canada and Australia (and possibly New Zealand as well) as late as the early twentieth century. Thus, indentured servants of all descriptions and trades in Van Dieman's Land (Tasmania) in the 1830s were imprisoned for cause when they disobeyed orders, refused to work, were inattentive to their duties, drunk, or absent from their appointed places.[29]

Similarly, Hudson's Bay Company employees who "deserted" their jobs in the nineteenth century were tracked down and compelled to return to work by the Law, as administered by the Company in its domain. In 1877, the Dominion of Canada's Parliament repealed the criminal aspects of all private breaches of labor contracts (they being "in general civil wrongs only"), but "wilful" breaches of contracts by public employees as well as those causing "danger" or "grave public inconvenience" remained criminal. The Northwest Mounted Police were employed to check the "cessation of the work of construction" of the Canadian Pacific Railway in the Kootenay district of British Columbia in 1885. And when four men quit construction work on the Grand Trunk Pacific line in western Canada as recently as 1907, the Division Engineer wrote the company's Assistant Solicitor, seeking "action" against those "shirking" their duties:

> We are having considerable difficulty by men refusing to work, and our work is very expensive on account of not being able to line men up as they should be.

The four, Herbert Haines, James Thompson, Donald Morrison, and William Fairburn, were thereupon hauled before the Portage la Prairie

---

[27] Sigmund Diamond, "An Experiment in Feudalism: French Canada in the 17th Century," 18 *William & Mary Quarterly*, 3rd S., 1 at 24 (1961); Bruce Kercher, "Commerce and the Development of Contract Law in New South Wales," 9 *Law & History Review* 269 at 299, 310–11 (1991); Michael Cannon, *Life in the Country: Australia in the Victorian Age* (Melbourne, 1973), II, 43–44; John E. Martin, *The Forgotten Worker: The Rural Wage Earner in 19th Century New Zealand* (Wellington, 1990), 94.

[28] For a good account of the movement away from these practices in America in the late-eighteenth and early-nineteenth centuries to a "right to quit" see Robert Steinfeld, *Invention of Free Labor.*

[29] Alastair Campbell, *John Batman and the Aborigines* (Malmsbury, 1987), 192, 217.

Police-Court magistrate who sentenced them to one month in prison, suspended if they returned to work.[30]

None the less, CANZ courts scrutinized these sorts of labor contracts with great care before permitting punitive action. Thus, a Toronto magistrate took his domestic servant to a colleague's court, seeking to have her sentenced to the statutory week of jail for having been away from her work without permission for more than a day. But that magistrate, George Gurnett, a former mayor of the city, infuriated his colleague. The sentence "might ruin" the young woman's "future prospects in life," and Gurnett refused to punish her. This might well be dismissed as the idiosyncratic (or political) behavior of one lower-level legal figure. But the action of Upper Canada's Court of Queen's Bench some two years later is consistent with what I feel was a pattern of behavior from this and other CANZ benches with regard to Master-&-Servant-Act questions. In *Dillingham v. Wilson* an apprentice was enticed to leave his master for a higher-paying employer. When the aggrieved master sought damages, and the trial court decision was appealed, Justice Henry Sherwood, ruled that the relevant statute ("the statute of 5 Eliz 4") was a mere "local act which was probably adopted to the state of society in England three hundred years ago, but is not now, and never was adapted to [this] colony, and was never in force here." *Mitchell v. Defries* (1846) was of the same character. An employee sued his employer for assault and battery and release from the employment contract; the employer responded that he had merely administered the kind of correction he was allowed under the Master & Servant Act. The Queen's Bench jurists did not buy that, if only by distinguishing the correction of an adolescent servant from that of an adult. "The beating of a servant of full age cannot be justified," Justice Archibald McLean observed.[31] In the same year that court's chief

---

[30] John Phillip Reid, "The Layers of Western Legal History," in *Law for the Elephant, Law for the Beaver*, ed. John McLaren et al., (Regina, 1992), 23 at 27; Breaches of Labour Contract Act, SC, 1877, ch. 35; Walter Sage, "The Northwest Mounted Police and British Columbia," 18 *Pacific Historical Review* 352 (1949); Grand Trunk legal dept. records, R.G. 30, Vol. 3486, File 72, National Archives of Canada.

[31] Susan Lewthwaite, "Violence, Law, and Community in Rural Upper Canada," in *Essays in the History of Canadian Law*, ed. Jim Phillips et al., V (Toronto, 1994), 356; Paul Craven, "The Law of Master & Servant in Mid-19th Century Ontario," in *Essays in the History of Canadian Law*, Vol. I, ed. David Flaherty (Toronto, 1981), 174 at 183, 204; *Dillingham v. Wilson*, 6 UCQB (O.S.) 85 at 87 (1841); *Mitchell v. Defries*, 2 UCQB 430 (1846), noted in Craven, p. 185. (Justice McLean cited Burns' *Justice of the Peace* here. In other words, this was not at variance with English law, however much it might have been from English practice.)

justice, Sir John Beverley Robinson, held that the relevant Elizabethan Master & Servant statute was not in force in the colony (in the case of an apprentice tinsmith who had been imprisoned for quitting). Such a rule was "wholly foreign to the nature of our institutions," wrote this Conservative jurist.[32]

Similarly, high-court jurists in Lower Canada and the Northwest Territories upheld the criminal convictions of masters who had, in one case, hit an eight year-old female servant and in the other, left an injured fifteen year-old farm hand so "utterly helpless" that he developed gangrene and died.[33] In fact, I found only one such case that could be said to have been won on appeal by an employer where punitive measures were at issue in Canada.[34]

The Supreme Courts of New South Wales and Queensland took the same position as had their Canadian compeers. In New South Wales,

[32] *Whelan v. Stevens,* UC (Taylor's) 439 (1827) (cited in Paul Craven, "The Law of Master & Servant," *supra* note 31, 184) (man with oxen not a "servant"); *Shea v. Choat,* 2 UCQB 211 (1846) (apprentice tinsmith not a servant under Elizabethan statute); see *Regina v. Tiffidge,* 1 Legge's R. (NSW) 793 (1853) (drovers not "servants" subject to coercive terms of Master & Servants Act); *Ex Parte Evernett,* 2 LRNSW 813 (1853); *Ex Parte Tighe,* 2 LRNSW 1100 (1853); *Newland v. Humphrey,* 2 Legge's R 1167 (1854); *Ex Parte Erwin,* 2 Legge's R 816 (1854); *Ex Parte Zahn,* 1 Queensland SCR 77 (1862 blacksmith subject to Act, but commitment warrant bad); *Regina v. Mollison, Ex Parte Crichton,* 2 Vict. LR (L) 144 (1876) (glass worker quit work "in the middle of the day" after making sixty-three dozen bottles, later claiming this a privilege under "the usages of the glass trade in England." Foreman objected, and man fired next day. Convicted and imprisoned by J.P. under Master & Servant Act. On appeal, Chief Justice Stawell reversed, with the observation (146): "A man is not to be treated as a criminal if he really believes that his contract gives him the right which he insists on exercising."); *Mete Kingi v. Davis,* 1 NZ Jurist (NZ) (NZCS) 117 (1875) (magistrate had awarded £10 to Maori laborer for his wrongful imprisonment by defendant's servant despite divergence of facts with common law liability rule "on grounds of equity and good conscience"; Supreme Court approved this.)

Not surprisingly, Paul Craven, who has studied the law of master and servant in mid-nineteenth century Ontario closely, concluded that the legislature there "reinvented" that law only after the high court jurists had abandoned it. Craven, "The Law of Master and Servant in Mid-19th Century Ontario," in *Essays in the History of Canadian Law,* Vol. 1, ed. David Flaherty (Toronto, 1981), 174, at 183, 204. On balance, however, Craven believes that magistrates followed the English legal rules with equanimity, rules that "favored the employer's part of the bargain." (181, 201–05)

[33] *Queen v. Bissonette,* 23 Lower Can. J. 249 (1879); *Queen v. Brown,* 1 Terr. LR 475 at 481 (1893). But see *Queen v. Coventry,* 3 Terr. LR 95 (1898).

[34] This was *Queen v. Coventry,* 3 Terr. LR 95 (1898), a case in which the employer was defending himself against a charge of abusing a servant.

jury awards of substantial sums in two separate cases in 1827 were sanctioned, the first to an indentured blacksmith (50 pounds), the second to a cook at an orphan's school and her husband (290 pounds), after the blacksmith and the cook had been wrongfully imprisoned by their magistrate–employers. David Leighton was fined ten pounds two years later in Sydney, ordered to pay another ten pounds to his servant, Margaret Thugate, and made to post a good-behavior bond of forty pounds for hitting her several times and driving her from the house after she had taken too long in buying a goose for dinner. Similarly, in 1862, a shepherd who had been beaten by his employer charged him with assault, and the employer acknowledged the act before a police magistrate. The shepherd sought legal release from his employment contract and his employer contested the action. Justice Lutwyche held that in Master-Servant Law cases regarding such employees as shepherds, "it ought to be well understood by all classes, that a master may not beat his servant," and that were he to do so, "such conduct" would constitute "lawful cause" for the servant to quit.[35] Later Queensland's Supreme Court threw out the conviction of George Groshanig, a sheep shearer, who had quit (along with others) when the station owner refused to pay union rates. The owner insisted that the men had agreed to continue working "till the sheep are shorn," while the shearer testified that he had said nothing in response to this term of the contract, agreeing only to work piece rate, "by the score." Chief Justice Lilley criticized the lower court's ten pound fine as "highly penal" and took issue with the trial judge's interpretation of the evidence: As the shearer had not responded to the station owner's terms that the men continue work "till the sheep are shorn," Lilley held that he could not "regard his silence as positive assent" and treated the agreement as a piece rate, one that the shearer was free to terminate at will. The same court threw out a similar conviction the following year. This shearer, one James Neighbour, clearly had agreed to shear "for the season," but he and his mates had complained without effect of the unfit beef they had been provided at excessive rates; they demanded mutton, and Neighbour quit. A lower court fined Neighbour £6, 16s for absenting himself from the Mt. Morris Station without proper leave, but Queensland's high court held that the station owner had violated the terms of the provisions portion of the contract and threw out the conviction.[36]

[35] *Broadbear & Broadbear v. Mac Arthur* (NSWSC Kercher 1827); *Adams v. Dawson* (NSWSC, Kercher, 1827); *Rex v. Leighton* (NSWSC, Kercher, 1829); *Walsh v. Kent,* 1 QSCR 44 at 47 (1862).

[36] *Groshanig v. Vaughan,* 4 Queens. LJ 50 (1891); *Neighbour v. Moore,* 4 Queens. LJ 145 (1892).

Five apprentices were involved in nonpunitive actions concerning the terms of their agreements in Newfoundland, Lower Canada/ Quebec, Victoria, and New Zealand; the apprentices won all five. A lad apprenticed to a contractor to learn cabinet making in Newfoundland objected that he had been made to do general carpentry work on a church at Harbor Grace in 1817. Newfoundland's judiciary ordered him released from his indenture. Thirteen years later Justice Johnson held in Montreal's Superior Court that the master of an apprentice who had been ill for over a month was not to be permitted to extend his apprenticeship for the time he had been ill, and called the attempt "a monstrous case of oppression by a master." The magistrate's ruling that the apprentice *was* to make up the time lost was dismissed by Justice Johnson as one characterized by "ignorance" and "inhumanity."[37] An apprentice to a silk-hat maker in Victoria in the 1870s quit working after being convinced that his master had not and was not going to offer him the sort of instruction in the trade that had been agreed upon. The master hauled him before a magistrate to force him back to work; he countersued for damages for breach of contract. The magistrate's ruling for the apprentice was appealed by the master, and the appeal was heard by Victoria's Supreme Court in 1881. Justice Williams held that "it would be monstrous if an apprentice was bound to serve the whole term of his apprenticeship to one who refused to teach him his trade, and that his only remedy should be an action for damages at the end of the term." It was "but justice" to award the apprentice £52 damages and costs. New Zealand's Justice Theopolis Cooper cited Justice Williams' language twenty-six years later in a virtually identical decision, reversing a magistrate's ruling and awarding £124 to a blacksmith's apprentice in Hanera who had quit work after two years without proper instruction.[38] The number of cases I detected involving apprentices in Diaspora lands of the nineteenth century is not so substantial as to warrant confident generalizations, and the cases tell us little of how most workers fared at the hands of magistrates, but this much may be said: These cases are consistent with the larger body of provincial appellate case Law concerning worker contracts in these years, in that the employer generally lost.

---

[37] *Ex Parte David & Collerette*, 19 Lower Can. J. 111 (1875). See also *Ex Parte Rose*, 3 Lower Can. R. 495 (1853).

[38] *Barter v. Johnston*, 1 Newf. 33 (1817); *Fletcher v. Bizolich*, 7 Vic. LR (L) 348 (1881); *Maunder v. Taylor*, 9 Gaz. LR (NZ, Wel. S.C.) 369 at 371 (1907). In *Ex Parte Costigan v. Murphy*, 7 Newf. 414 (1889), a group of lobstermen who stopped attending their traps in a dispute with their "planter" successfully appealed a fine at a magistrate's hearing; the court held that they were contractors, not servants subject to the Master & Servant Act.

Laborers and Builders who Quit

This was not the case when it came to another mainstream issue involving the labor contracts of hired hands, masons, quarrymen, clerks, and teachers: When these sorts of workers quit "entire" contracts and sued for what their labor was worth to their employer, they lost on appeal as often as they won. The Law in the colonies with regard to these sorts of breaches of labor contracts may not have been rendered quite as harshly as it was in Britain, but it was not served up as generously to employee–plaintiffs as it was in about half of the state courts of the United States.[39] Workers in the other Diaspora lands could well be held to the terms of "entire" contracts – that is, denied *quantum meruit* recovery "off the contract."

A few illustrations: A merchant's clerk in St. Catherine's, Ontario, served ten months of his second year of service until "gold fever" took hold of him. He "went to California" and sent a relative to his employer to ask for wages. The annual agreement had been for £60. The employer offered £25, a little over half of what the clerk felt he was entitled to; hence he sued. At trial, a fellow clerk testified that "if he were to leave in the same manner, he should expect to lose his wages." The jury awarded the clerk £25; the case went to Upper Canada's Queen's Bench on appeal, where Chief Justice Robinson ordered a new trial. "It may be said, and perhaps thought," the chief justice allowed, "that the verdict is consistent with justice," but *he* did not think it was. Courts had clerks too, and jurists like Robinson might have appreciated the rule more readily than jurors that "courts of justice" had expressed "strongly on the importance to society of enforcing such engagements, by making parties bear the legal consequences of breaking them."[40] Five years later the chief justice elaborated on the public-policy rationale of this "all-or-nothing" rule. A man had agreed to clear and fence twenty acres for £60. He was paid £30, cleared sixteen acres, and then quit. Robinson and his colleagues would not hear his plea for *quantum meruit* recovery:

> Otherwise, whenever a man has taken a job at a low price, or when [labor] prices have risen greatly after he took it, he would feel himself at liberty to abandon his special contract [and sue for what his labor had been worth].

[39] See Karsten, " ... Breaches of Labor Contracts ... "

[40] *Blake v. Shaw*, 10 UCQB 180 at 182 (1851). See also *O'Neill, et al. v. Leight*, 2 UCQB 204 (1846).

Victoria's Chief Justice William a'Beckett similarly condemned "gold fever" and those employees who had breached their contracts with employers (typically sheep station owners) in the first throes of Victoria's gold rush. a'Beckett's view appeared in a pamphlet he published, not an opinion. C. M. H. Clark, *A History of Australia* (Melbourne, 1978), IV, 19.

As Justice Wetmore of the Supreme Court for the Northwest Territories put it forty-eight years later: "Some men have the idea that if their employer looks crooked at them, they are at liberty to quit the most binding agreement."[41]

This was the way jurists treated the suits of several farm tenants, domestic servants, salesmen, house builders, and construction engineers over the next half century in both Upper and Lower Canada, New Brunswick, Manitoba, the Northwest Territories, and New South Wales.[42] And in two of these opinions, from the courts of Manitoba and Ontario, jurists specifically rejected "the doctrine of 'substantial performance'... held in the courts of many of the states of the neighboring Union" in favor of harsher English precedents.[43]

But these CANZ courts appear at times to be inconsistent. The same jurists from Canadian courts who had followed the "all or nothing"

[41] *Orser v. Gamble*, 14 UCQB 576 at 579 (1856); *Owen v. James*, 4 Terr. LR 174 (1899).

[42] See *Parnell v. Martin*, 5 UCCP 473 (1855) (tenant agreed under seal to cultivate farm for one year for £95; "left after nine months at the defendant's request, and upon his promise... to pay or settle with him"; Chief Justice Macaulay held that the tenant's plea for recovery of what his labor had been worth, off the covenant, was bad, but he intimated that a different plea might have been good); *Berlinguette v. Judah*, 17 Low.Can. J. xiv (index) (1872) (domestic servant who leaves three days before end of month received nothing); *Cyr v. Cadieux*, 17 Low.Can. J. 173 (1872) (domestic servant who quit one year contract after two and a half months for $185 gets nothing because of the wording of the Quebec Code ("*Le texte de la loi est formel....*"); *Clarke v. City of Winnepeg*, Manitoba R. (Temp. Wood) 56 (1876) (contractor excavating water tanks to be paid weekly sums for his employees); *Owen v. James*, 4 Terr. LR 174 (1899); *White v. Belliveau*, 16 New Br. 109 (1875); *Nixon v. Darling*, 27 Low. Can.J. 78 (1883); *Smith v. Strange*, 2 Manitoba LR 101 (1885) (two workers who pressed and baled hay to be paid); *Sherlock v. Powell*, 26 Ont. C. of A 407 (1899).

Sir Zelmen Cowen reports in his biography of Isaac Isaacs that, at the age of twenty, in 1875, the future chief justice of Australia's High Court lost an action for wages in a county court of Victoria when he resigned from a teaching position before completing his contractual term and sued in *quantum meruit.* Cowen, *Isaac Isaacs* (Melbourne, 1967), 5. And see the unsuccessful petition before a magistrate in New South Wales, 1811, of a sailor who had quit, and Bruce Kercher's account of *Matthew v. Palmer* (1814), a case of an imperfectly built mill in New South Wales where the builder failed to win a *quantum valebant*; noted in B. Kercher, *Unruly Child*, 3, and Kercher, *Debt, Seduction and Other Disasters*, 168. See *Shea v. Smith & Barker* (NSWSC, Kercher, 1826) for a similar outcome (quarryman denied *quantum velebant* for stone used in tower); but here the matter had been essentially left to a jury that had heard the testimony of construction experts.

[43] *Smith v. Strange*, 2 Manitoba LR 101 at 110 (1885); *Sherlock v. Powell*, 26 Ont. C of A 407 at 410 (1899).

English rule in case A, allowed *quantum meruit* or *pro rata* recovery by the worker–plaintiff in case B.[44] Take the example of those from Upper Canada/Ontario: Several years before Chief Justice Sir John Beverley Robinson ruled on the case of the merchant's clerk who had succumbed to "gold fever," his court ruled *for* the worker–plaintiffs in three other cases. In the first case, the plaintiff had agreed to clear ten acres of land for £25 and board, the whole to be "fit for crop" by September 10, 1842, to be paid in the winter of 1844. He cleared several acres, but left the work unfinished. The defendant–employer paid others to finish the job. When the plaintiff sued for what his labor had been worth, the court was unanimous in deciding that he was "entitled to be paid" (some saying "*pro tanto*," others "*quantum meruit*"), though all also agreed that he must wait until the next winter, as agreed, for payment. In a second case, an action for the value of incomplete work done by a mason on a house, Robinson's court allowed the jury verdict for £39 to stand, inasmuch as their allowance of *quantum meruit* recovery was "in accordance with the justice of the case," in Robinson's words. In a third, an action for *quantum meruit* and *quantum valebant* (what a builder's materials were worth to the employer), a contractor who had agreed to provide the gearing for a grist mill sought partial payment even though he had failed to build according to the "signed and sealed" ("covenanted") terms. Robinson sanctioned plaintiff recovery off the explicit terms of the contract, noting that this practice was supported "by such a number of decisions that it is unnecessary to cite them particularly."[45] Chief Justice Macaulay of Upper Canada's other high court, Common Pleas, came to a similar conclusion in a comparable case, involving the construction of a barn in 1851. The employer had sold the partially completed barn, an act voiding the original contract. Macaulay held that a *quantum valebant* recovery by the barn builder "seems the just rule" (and he did cite precedential authorities for the rule).[46]

Jurists in the high courts of New South Wales and New Zealand also sanctioned *quantum valebant* awards in these years. In two of these

---

[44] See *Aikin v. Malcolm*, 2 UCQB 134 (1843); *Barton v. Fisher*, 3 UCQB 75 (1844); *Hamilton v. Raymond*, 2 UCCP 392 (1851); *Bilodeau v. Sylvain*, 4 LCR 26 (1853); *Rettinger v. MacDougall*, 9 UCCP 485 (1860) (affirming jury finding that foreman in printing office who quit after eight months on a weekly rather than an annual salary); *Donald v. Candler*, 4 Newf. 516 (1860); *Nadon v. Ollivon*, 15 Low. Can. J. 280 (1871); *Logg v. Ellwood*, 14 Ont. C. of A. 496 (1897); *Johnston v. Keenan*, 3 Terr. LR 239 (1894); *Taylor v. Kinsey*, 4 Terr. LR 178 (1899).

[45] *McMahon v. Coffee*, 1 UCQB 110 (1843); *Aikin v. Malcolm*, 2 UCQB 134 (1843); *Barton v. Fisher*, 3 UCQB 75 (1844).

[46] *Hamilton v. Raymond*, 2 UCCP 392 at 398 (1851).

cases they cited English cases in support of their judgements, while in two others they simply insisted, as had Chief Justice Robinson, that they were following long-standing English law. A review of the English citations offered indicates that they were, indeed, following recognized exceptions to the "all or nothing" rule in "entire" labor contracts.[47]

All but two of these cases noted in the previous paragraph involved building or construction contracts, not those of unpropertied laborers, and some students of labor contracts in nineteenth century America believe that distinctions were made between entrepreneurs who failed to complete "entire" construction contracts, on the one hand, and hired hands, servants, clerks, and artisans, on the other.[48] In my own analysis of such cases, I have not found that distinction to exist in the United States.[49] I explored the question of whether such a distinction was made by CANZ jurists.

It was not made. Domestic servants, laborers, shepherds, carpenters, fishermen, stonecutters, and hired hands, as often as not, *were* able to recover "off the contract" for what their labor had been worth to their employers when they quit "entire" contracts.[50] In Quebec, treatises by

---

47 *Ex Parte Tighe*, 2 Legge's R. 1100 (1858); *Morrison v. Grovenor*, 5 NSWLR 195 (1884); *Slowey v. Lodder*, 20 NZLR (CA) 32 (1901) (Justice Edwards offered a long summary of American case law on the subject of damages in labor contract breaches in his opinion.)

48 See Morton Horwitz, *The Transformation of American Law, 1780–1861*) (Cambridge, Mass., 1977), 186–88; Wythe Holt, "Recovery by the Worker who Quits: A Comparison of . . . Approaches to a Problem of 19th Century Contract Law," 1986 *Wisconsin Law Review* 677; Christopher Tomlins, "The Ties that Bind: Master and Servant in Massachusetts, 1800–1850," 30 *Labor History* 193 (1989).

49 See Karsten, *Heart versus Head*, ch. 5; and Steinfeld, *Invention of Free Labor*. And see A. W. B. Simpson, "The Horwitz Thesis and the History of Contracts," 46 *Univ. Of Chicago Law Review* 533 (1979), who questions whether the distinction existed in seventeenth and eighteenth century England, as do I.

50 See *Louise Perrault v. Jos. Perrault* [*no rel.*], Montreal 1818 (servent quitting after six months of 1 yr. contract asks for £2.8.4; employer insists she is entitled to nothing; arbitrator awards £2), noted in Grace Hogg. *The Legal Rights of Masters, Mistresses and Domestic Servants in Montreal, 1816–1829*, MA Essay, McGill Univ., 1989, p. 83; *Lamb v. Nettleton* (NSWSC, Kercher, 1826); *Bilodeau v. Sylvain*, 4 Low. Can. R 26 (1853) (same fact situation; court finds for servant and awards *quantum meruit*); *Donald v. Candler*, 4 Newf. 516 (1860); *Regina v. Lloyd*, enforcing *Potts v. Cobb*, 1 Austr. Jurist R 78 (1870); *Nadon v. Ollivion*, 15 Low. Can. J. 280 (1871); *Law v. Harding*, 19 New Br. 590 (1880); *Logg v. Ellwood*, 14 Ont. C. of A. 496 (1887); *Johnston v. Keenan*, 3 Terr. LR 239 (1894); *Taylor v. Kinsey*, 4 Terr. LR 178 (1899); *Gauthier v. Perraut*, 6 Quebec QB 65 (1897).

Pothier and Duranton served as authority for these actions,[51] while in the high courts for the Northwest Territories and New Zealand jurists in the late nineteenth century cited American authority,[52] but elsewhere it is harder to detect the legal rationale of those CANZ jurists who allowed *quantum meruit* recovery, that led them to distinguish the precedents applying the "all or nothing" rule from the facts in the case before them.

Generally, these cases rested on one or another of four premises: The first, which could be found in English treatises, had it that workers who quit "entire" contracts could recover a "partial benefit" via a *quantum meruit* "off the contract" if "the plaintiff has done something which the defendant has accepted and retained, dealing with it in a manner as to raise an implied contract to pay for it. . . . " This passage from a copy of Mayne's *Treatise on the Law of Damages*, received and sold in Nelson, New Zealand in the 1870s, was the only one marked (in pencil) by its owner before the volume found its way to the rare book collection of Victoria University's Law Library.[53] This premise served as the basis for some of the *quantum meruit* and *valebant* recoveries "off" of construction contracts that we noted at the beginning of the previous paragraph, but it also served as the authority for the *quantum meruit* recovery of a few less exalted laborers whose work had been "accepted" by their employers while they worked.[54]

A second premise was that some of these allegedly "entire" contracts could fairly be read to be apportionable, with payment due each month.[55] A third premise was that the very terms of certain contracts could fairly be understood by judge or jury to have allowed *quantum meruit* recovery.[56] Still another premise, involving associations of workers (unions), was that artisans unwilling to work alongside of those who had not joined their trade union were free collectively to quit, and to "entice" (persuade) others who were members of their association to join them.[57]

---

[51] See *Bilodeau v. Sylvain*, 4 Low. Can. R 26 (1853).

[52] See *Johnston v. Keenan*, 3 Terr. LR 239 at 241 (1894); *Slowey v. Lodder*, 20 NZLR (CA) 321 (1901).

[53] Mayne's *Treatise . . .*, 2nd ed. by Lumley Smith (London, 1872), 154.

[54] As in *Donald v. Candler*, 4 Newf. 516 (1860) (£8 12s to a fisherman who had quit work after being abused repeatedly by the master's son); *Potts v. Cobb*, Austr. Jurist R 78 (1870) (£7 for work repairing a house, accepted by owner).

[55] As in *Johnston v. Keenan*, 3 Terr. LR 239 (1894); and *Taylor v. Kinsey*, 4 Terr. LR 178 (1899). Or every day, as in *Logg v. Ellwood*, 14 Ont. C. of A. 496 (1887).

[56] As in *Law v. Harding*, 19 New Br. 590 (1880).

[57] *Gauthier v. Perrault*, 6 Quebec QB 65 (1897); overruling *Perrault v. Gauthier*, 10 Quebec CS 224 (1895). See also *Hynes, et al., v. Fisher, et al.*, 4 Ont. 60

Each of these legal grounds for requiring the employer to pay some wages to the employee who had quit was conformable to the general scope of English law; neither any one of them, nor their sum total, should be read to mean that, in effect, these jurists were bending English rules in the sorts of ways that many American courts of the nineteenth century had done to the benefit of hired hands and artisans who quit "entire" contracts. Just the same, it is worth nothing that CANZ jurists were willing to find (or were at least *capable* of finding) a legal basis for such workers to win appealed cases more often than they were not (twenty five to seventeen).

Wrongful Discharge

All right; there was no general rule granting workers the right to quit "entire" contracts at will and demand pay. But, as I noted earlier, neither was their any rule permitting employers to fire workers on "entire" contracts for "looking crooked at them," to borrow Justice Wetmore's phrase. Employees in Canada and the Antipodes had only moderate success seeking *quantum meruit* recovery when they quit "entire" contracts, but the rule was different when they were wrongfully fired from them. The "employment-at-will" doctrine, a late nineteenth century American innovation, was not borrowed by CANZ jurists. Workers who claimed to have been "wrongfully discharged" won thirty seven of forty four cases at the appellate[58] level (85 percent) from 1814 to 1908.[59]

(1883) (suit by Master Plasterers Association against Operative Plasterers Association for "enticing" workers to leave work rejected, since Master Plasterers (employers) had wrongfully sought to force four "operative" plasterers to sign "yellowdog" labor agreements indicating that they had not joined and would not join the Operative Plasterers Association).

[58] They also won all or some damage awards in thirty one of forty six cases (seven of which were dismissed) resolved in Montreal's *trial* courts, 1816–1829. Seven others were settled. Nine were discontinued. Grace Hogg, "Legal Rights...," M. A. McGill.

[59] They lost only when their attorney chose the wrong plea, as in *Raines v. Credit Harbour Co.*, 1 UCQB 174 (1843); and *Doherty v. Vancouver Gas Co.*, 1 West. LR 252 (1905); when the facts indicated that they were insolent or refused to obey reasonable orders (*Lakeman v. Goodridge*, 4 Newf. 181 (1857)); *McRae v. Marshall*, 19 Can. S.C. 10 (1891) (but fired employee entitled to his share of the enterprise's profits under the agreement); *Rose v. Winters*, 4 Terr. LR 353 (1900); and *Fleming v. Hill*, 10 Nova Sc. 286 (1876); or when they found themselves subject to the "old French" law of Pothier, which sanctioned both "at will" quitting and firing (*Lennan v. St. Law. & Atl. Ry*, 4 Low. Can. R 91 (1853) (Justice Day: Labor contracts were terminable "at the option of either party," citing Pothier; the plaintiff was, however, entitled to his pay for the two weeks he actually worked), or, comparably,

Schoolmasters, "theatrical" men, sailors, shopmen, storekeepers, fishermen, clerks, bailiffs, superintendents, herdsmen, agents, ploughmen, gardeners, surveyors, miners, tanners, carpenters, cooks, printers, journeymen, domestic servants, and common laborers all won at the appellate level when they charged their employers with wrongful discharge.[60] Neither in Queensland, Quebec, New Zealand, nor Newfoundland could an employer hire an employee to perform one task and then assign him to perform another, even with the claim that "he had not turned out to be a first-class workman."[61] And were he to discharge the worker who refused to accept such a reassignment or salary adjustment, the worker was free either to sue for her wages when they came due[62] or to sue immediately; and one worker fired in the middle of a term of employment was awarded pay both

when they simply demanded payment for work they had not done on a contract for a municipality that had ordered a halt to the work as in *Bartlett v. Munic. of Amherstburg*, 14 UCQB 152 (1855).

[60] See *Jarrett v. James* (NSW, 1814, noted in Kercher, *Unruly Child*, 55); *Morison v. Telegraph Co.*, 4 Newf. 328 (1859); *Colgan v. Munic. Council of Toowoomba*, 3 Queensland SCR 10 (1872); *Berney v. O'Brien & Co.*, 5 Newf. 260 (1869); *Garland v. Scott*, 6 Newf. 243 (1880); *Fox v. Carfagnini*, 6 Newf. 24 (1874); *Scott v. Govt. of Newfoundland*, 7 Newf. 230 (1887); *Cook v. Stabb & Roche*, 7 Newf. 240 (1880); *McKay v. Renouf, Clement & Co.* 7 Newf. 229 (1887); *Rabbitts v. Govt. of Newfoundland*, 7 Newf. 533 (1891); *Grove v. Domville*, 17 New Br. 48 (1877); *Stuart v. Sleeth*, 10 Low. Can. R. 278 (1860); *Oullet v. Fournier dit Préfontaine*, 6 Low. Can. J. 118 (1862); *Rice v. Boscovitz*, 23 Low. Can. J. 141 (1874); *Beauchemin v. Simon*, 23 Low. Can. J. 143 (1877); *Montreal Cotton Co. v. Parkam*, 23 Low. Can. J. 146 (1878); *Hill v. DeLias*, 1 NZLR (S.C.) 23 (1879); *Blake v. Kirkpatrick*, 6 Ont. C. of A. 212 (1881); *Ferreron v. O'Keefe*, 2 Manit. LR 40 (1884); *Montreal Watch Case Co. v. Bonneau*, 1 Quebec QB 433 (1892); *Les Commisaires des Ch. a Barrieres de Montreal v. Rielle*, 34 Low. Can. J. 107 (1890); *Jarvis v. C.P. Ry*, 13 Quebec CS 17 (1898); *Bain v. Anderson*, 27 Ont. 369 (1896); *Patterson v. Scott*, 37 UCQB 642 (1876); *Giles v. McEwan*, 11 Manit. 150 (1896); *Burgess v. St. Louis*, 6 Terr. LR 451 (1899); *Watson v. Ross*, 5 Aust. Jur. (Vict.) 69 (1874); *Mackie v. Wienholt*, 5 Queens. SCR 211 (1880); *Mulholland v. King*, 6 Queens LJ 268 (1895); *Coker v. Browne*, 7 Queens LJ 71 (1891); *Hornbrook v. Hayne*, 8 Queens LJ 17 (1897); *MacKenzie v. Union Fire & Marit. Ins. Co. of New Z.*, 1 NSWR(L) 103 (1880); *Wood v. Well. Woolen Co.*, 14 NZLR 296 (1895); *Wilson v. Kisri*, 18 NZLR (SC) 807 (1900); *NZ Fruit & Produce v. Taylor*, 11 Gaz LR (NZ) 43 (1908); *Russell v. Leviathan Gold Dredging Co.*, 3 Gaz. LR (NZ) 133 (1901); *Clouston & Co., v. Corry*, 7 Gaz. LR (NZ) 213 (1904); *Thompson v. Ross*, 1922 GLR (NZ) 343.

[61] *Mackie v. Wienbolt*, 5 Queens. SCR 211 (1880); *Beauchemin v. Simon*, 23 Low. Can. J. 143 (1877); *Giles v. McEwan*, 11 Manit. 150 (1896); *Berney v. O'Brien & Co.*, 5 Newf. 260 (1869); *NZ Fruit & Produce v. Taylor*, 11 Gaz. LR(NZ) 43 (1908).

[62] *Rice v. Boscovitz*, 23 Low. Can. J. 141 (1874); *Montreal Cotton Co. v. Parkam*, 23 Low. Can. J. 146 (1878).

for the months of work completed and the months remaining in the contract.[63] Employees discharged for drunkenness, for immoral behavior with a female employee, for suspected theft, or for failing to inform the employer that he had once been convicted of theft, were deemed by courts in Upper and Lower Canada, New Brunswick, New Zealand, and Queensland to have been wrongfully discharged.[64] The man hired to manage the Womblebank sheep station in Queensland may have behaved "immorally" with a female servant, but he was deemed to be entitled to damages because there had been no mention of how he was expected to behave in the contract, and such things were not to be read into labor contracts by implication![65] The warehouseman who had failed to tell his employer when hired that he had been convicted of theft was entitled to damages when he was thereupon "wrongfully" discharged when his sordid past was discovered. Justice Duff explained that one seeking work was not obliged to tell of all past crimes:

> It is not in accordance either with the policy of the law, or the dictates of Christianity, to force a man to such extremes. On the contrary, every man is allowed a *locus poenitentiae*.[66]

---

[63] *Beauchemin v. Simon*, 23 Low. Can. J. 141 (1874); *Montreal Watch Case Co. v. Bonneau*, 1 Quebec QB 433 (1892); *Mackie v. Wienbolt*, 5 Queens. SCR 211 (1880); *Oullet v. Fournier dit Préfontaine*, 6 Low. Can. J. 118 (1862); *Giles v. McEwan*, 11 Manit. 150 (1896);*Watson v. Ross*, 5 Austral. Jurist R (Victoria) 69 (1874); *Burgess v. St. Louis*, 6 Terr. LR 451 (1899); *NZ Fruit & Produce v. Taylor*, 11 Gaz. LR (NZ) 43 (1908); *Berney v. O'Brien & Co.*, 5 Newf. 260 (1869); *Stuart v. Sleeth*, 10 Low. Can. R 278 (1860) (Justice Badgley dissenting: "It would seem as if the intention of the servant was to get, if possible, a year's wages for 6 months work").

In *Hornbrook v. Hyne*, 8 Queens. LJ 17 (1897), Queensland's high court was confronted with a Laborers Act of 1880, an "entire" annual labor contract between a firm and "a Pacific Islander," and a set of regulations governing such contracts under the act in a case where the man had died before completing the contracts. Chief Justice Griffith and his colleagues ruled that his heirs were to receive his wages to the date of his death, despite the English rule in *Cutter v. Powell* (1795), which was that if one died before completing an "entire" contract, one's heirs were entitled to nothing from the employer. The man's wages accrued "from day to day," they said, because of the language of the statue, thus "taking his case out of the rule in *Cutter v. Powell*. . . ."

[64] *Patterson v. Scott*, 37 UCQB 642 (1876); *Corry v. Clouston & Co.*, 7 Gaz. LR (NZCA) 213 (1904) (reversed by Privy Council in NZPCC 336 (1905)); *Stuart v. Sleeth*, 10 Low. Can. J. 278 (1860); *Grove v. Domville*, 17 New Br. 48 (1877); *Mulholland v. King*, 6 Queens. LJ 268 (1895).

[65] *Mulholland v. King*, 6 Queens. LJ 268 (1895).

[66] *Grove v. Domville*, 17 New Br. 48 at 53 (1877).

Jurists explicitly rejected the idea of an "employment-at-will" privilege claimed by employers.[67] Instead they applied the "entire" contract doctrine to the worker's advantage, using the same reasoning that had been used to the employer's advantage when the worker quit such a contract. Thus, when a carpenter was fired in the Northwest Territories of Canada after working the busy summer months, Justice Wetmore found the facts "distinguishable" from the closest English case and held that his contract was "for a year" rather than by the month, as the employer claimed (and as the English precedent had it). Any other construction of the agreement would allow employers to fire mechanics after the more intense work of the summer months, turning them loose in the lean employment season (the winter), after misleading them as to their expected source of income for that season. Justice Wetmore put it somewhat awkwardly, but well:

> I am not very much impressed with the fact that $25 a month to a mechanic in the summertime, and to be cut adrift in the winter, is in this country wages which would create any amount of ecstacy.[68]

Similarly, when a farm couple in Manitoba were dismissed by their employer two days before the end of an annual oral contract, Justice Dubuc held that their suit was good since the defendant employer "had the full benefit of their joint labor." He was joined in this view by Justice Bain and the two jurists then used the evidence of the oral contract as "the estimate of their value [for services] that the parties had made," and allowed them *quantum meruit* recovery. And this opinion was praised four years later by Justice Wetmore as one that "does fair justice between man and man, and . . . is reasoned out with good legal logic." Justice Wetmore was "prepared to follow it" in the Northwest Territories, even though it had no grounding in English case law and "may be open to question."[69]

These jurists chose not to cite American case law in support of their "legal logic," as they might have, and as Chief Justice Sir Robert Stout of New Zealand's Court of Appeals *did* in a similar case.[70] But Stout was more willing to draw on American authority than most. His colleague, Sir Joshua Williams, Jr., offered the more common syllogism

---

[67] *Russell v. Leviathan Gold Dredging Co.*, 3 Gaz. LR (NZ) 133 (1901); *Wilson v. Kisri* 18 NZLR (SC) 807 (1900).

[68] *Burgess v. St. Louis*, 6 Terr. LR 451 (1899). The "distinguishable" English precedent was *Nicoll v. Greaves*, 33 LJ (CP) 289 (1864).

[69] *Giles v. McEwan*, 11 Manit. 150 at 162, 172 (1896); *Rose v. Winters*, 4 Terr. LR 353 at 354 (1900). (But Wetmore, instructing a jury here, allowed that the plaintiff in the case before them may have been negligent and thus subject to rightful discharge, and the jury so found.)

[70] In *Wilson v. Kisri*, 2 Gaz. LR (NZ 210 at 213) (1900).

that Justice Wetmore had employed when taking a step seemingly at variance with an English rule: When a produce company's employee was fired and then offered reinstatement at a lower status, the man sued, claiming that he had been wrongfully discharged (*New Zealand Fruit & Produce v. Taylor*). Justice Williams allowed that "there is no doubt, as is laid down in the text books, that where a servant has been wrongfully discharged, an offer by the master to take the servant back in his employ may be shown in reduction of damages." But he continued, in a more interpretive tone, that this was so "if there is nothing that could have prevented the servant from accepting the offer." And he then held that there was "no English case which I know of" where, under the circumstances in this case, "a plaintiff would be bound to accept an offer of reinstatement."[71] This was arguably so, but the fact is that Justice Williams could as easily have decided that there was "no English case which I know of" where, under those circumstances "a plaintiff would be free to *reject* an offer of reinstatement." *New Zealand Fruit* is thus an example of a CANZ jurist pointing to the *absence* of an English case that was on "four squares" with the circumstances of the case before him, as grounds for ruling in such a way as to *aid* a worker–plaintiff. There are simply too many examples of this (especially from the New Zealand Court of Appeals in the *fin* de *siécle*) to attribute this to mere chance. (I will return to this subject in my Conclusion.)

The Formal Law: Summary

In general, CANZ jurists were not as harsh toward workers when it came to labor contracts as their counterparts in England, though they were not so friendly toward them as the more liberal of the American courts. With the exception of a few decisions of the courts of Lower Canada/Quebec, jurists in Canada and the Antipodes did not behave as those American jurisdictions that allowed *quantum meruit* recovery to those who quit "entire" contracts. But a look at the total universe of appellate decisions involving labor contracts by CANZ jurists in these years reveals: (1) no distinctions being made between propertied and unpropertied laborers; (2) general disapproval of the use of punitive measures available to magistrates in the various Master & Servant Acts; and (3) firm support of the rights of workers who had provided evidence of their having been wrongfully discharged. Moreover, despite their not having accepted the Liberal American rule for workers who quit, jurists often found ways *within* the scope of English precedents to sanction *quantum meruit* recovery. The further away Common-Law-trained jurists were from the "Mother of

---

[71] *NZ Fruit & Produce v. Taylor*, 11 Gaz. LR 43 at 44 (1908).

All Common Law" (either literally, as in Australia and New Zealand, or figuratively, as with Lower Canada/Quebec and the American states), the less wedded they seemed to be to English rules regarding labor contracts.

I QUIT! – YOU'RE FIRED!: THE INFORMAL LAW OF LABOR CONTRACTS

Labor contracts in Britain and the lands of her Diaspora clearly were breached at times in the years considered in this book; but most such breaches did not end up in court, any more than had breaches in sales contracts. Throughout Great Britain, until 1875, workers who quit or failed to perform their duties *could* be imprisoned by a magistrate until they agreed to comply, but the typical reaction of a master to a servant's recalcitrance or insubordination there was "a measure of" cursing or cuffing, the *threat* of a visit to the magistrate, or of additional hours of work.

Cursings and cuffings became virtually unacceptable behavior in North America and the Antipodes in the nineteenth century, as the relative scarcity and consequent higher cost of "the help" generally precluded such treatment, inasmuch as "the help" were simply intolerant of it. Thus, the same Captain Ware who described the trial of gambling deadbeats on the Great Plains in the 1860s also reported the case of a wagonmaster who had "wrongfully quarreled" with one of his workers "in such a way as to justify the latter in leaving, and then refused to pay him." This wagonmaster was "stuck in the guard-house" himself until he paid the disgruntled worker in the post commander's presence.[72]

Work Agreements with Natives

No courts were available to Carolina traders who employed Cherokees to carry their fur pelts to eastern depots in the early eighteenth century. These carriers would "not carry any burthens with out being first payed," and a number of these men "often leave their burthens half way of the place they are designed to be Carried to, So that the Traders are Obliged to pay double burthenage for every Pack," or so Colonel George Chicken, Carolina's Trade Commissioner in Cherokee country complained to Cherokee headmen at the Elijay Council in 1725. In the future, Chicken insisted, "they must not Expect to be payed till their work is done and then you'l follow our English custome." But this proved to be a fruitless threat, for the Cherokee carriers remained

---

[72] Eugene Ware, *The Indian War of 1864*, 122.

unwilling to adopt this "English custome," and they had no labor competition in the back country for the task of carrying their deer and beaver pelts to market.[73]

A surveyor among the Okanagan Indians of British Columbia in 1866 recorded similar labor difficulties: Mr. J. Turnbull felt he could order his Okanagan employees around in what Peter Carstens calls "typical colonial style," sending them off to perform additional duties or "to carry extra baggage because one man had quit his job," or to manage a canoe in particularly dangerous rapids. Turnbull was surprised to find them "unreliable," perfectly prepared to quit their courier contracts, and was forced to pay them "a most exorbitant price" at times.[74]

Aborigines in Queensland, the Northern Territories, and the Torres Strait Islands had little real competition as well for the work that cattle ranchers and the pearl fishery counted on them to supply in the mid- and late-nineteenth century.[75] Aborigines from the Bass Strait Islands had been pressed into the service of whalers in the early nineteenth century and often treated brutally. Eventually the colonial assemblies in Australia sought to regulate and police such employment, ostensibly to protect native workers from exploitation (though not as effectively as Parliament had for Western Australia in the Pearl Shell Fishery Regulation Act of 1873). But, while such paternal concern surely counted for something, Aboriginal workers were not without their own capacities of "self-help": An official report on labor conditions in the pearling industry in the Torres Strait in 1880 claimed that, while the native divers' work was dangerous and could be unpleasant, they were "quite capable of taking care of themselves." The divers had things "almost entirely their own way, and will not bear superintendence from the whites." The "management of the boats," the "locality of the fishing," the "times of fishing," and "the actual gathering of the shell" were all left "entirely" to the native divers. In 1886, one leader of the Diaspora pearl industry claimed that "a kind of freemasonry exists between the men," who proved capable of such slow-downs and work-stoppages as suited themselves, for few British migrants could do what they did.[76]

---

73 John Phillip Reid, *A Better Kind of Hatchet*, 183–84. And see Michael McConnell, *A Country Between*, 156, on Delaware warriors carrying ammunition for the British military from Fort Pitt to Sandusky and Detroit in the 1760s "at the respectable wage of a dollar a day."

74 Peter Carstens, *The Queen's People: A Study of Coercion and Accomodation among the Okanagans of Canada* (Toronto, 1991), 65–65.

75 Ann McGrath, *Born in the Cattle: Aborigines in Cattle Country* (Sydney, Allen & Unwin, 1987).

76 Charles Rowley, *Destruction of Aborignal Society*, 188; Henry Reynolds, *The Other Side of the Frontier* (Ringwood, 1983), 180–81.

Similarly, on the plains of Queensland and the Northern Territory Diaspora settlers moved in and created sheep and cattle stations but often found it virtually impossible to "induce" sufficient numbers of their own countrymen "to shepherd" for them in these hot and barren sites. Aborigines, both men and women, however, could, at times, be persuaded to work at shepherding, cow punching, gardening, or housework. One stationowner's wife felt that "they all looked on working for us as a personal favour, and gave us to understand as much."[77] In any event, Aboriginal cowpunchers "always stipulated that in a certain number of days, weeks, or at the outside, moons," they be "relieved" of work by some "white-fellow" in order to give them the opportunity to "follow the Law" (by which they meant engaging in "walkabouts" of "their land," checking on sacred sites and "tidying up" kangaroo pastureland by controlled burning).[78]

In fact, throughout *all* of the Australian colonies the Squattocracy employed some Aboriginals as herdsmen, shepherds, and domestic servants almost as soon as they had established their stations. To the Squatters, the local Aborigines were an available, cheap source of labor, capable of learning what it took to watch over a mob of sheep or to ride herd, track, and recover stray cattle. Aboriginal workers required time off for their "walk-abouts" for certain gatherings of family and clan. Hence, they were "next-best" employees to some graziers, but highly prized when Diaspora labor was dear, as it often was. Graziers learned to live with Aboriginal absenteeism. As one in South Australia put it, "the Aboriginal must be free to come and go as he pleases....When the spirit moves him he will take his departure," and it mattered not "how many [employment contract] papers are signed."

The goldrush in southeastern Australia drew much Diaspora labor off the South Australia runs in the early 1850s, prompting significant increases in the number of Aboriginal herdsmen and shepherds. This worked well with the leasehold provisions of that colony as Robert Foster has shown: The Aborigines were, by Law, entitled to their traditional uses of the land leased by the crown to the pastoralists, and the colony's government also established a number of stations to distribute

---

[77] "A Lady," (pseud.), *My Experiences in Australia* (London, 1860), quoted in Henry Reynolds, *Dispossession*, 130.

[78] McGrath, *Born in the Cattle*, 157–60. And see Graeme Neate, "Looking after Country: Legal Recognition of Traditional Rights and Responsibilities for Land," 16 *Univ. of New South Wales Law Journal* 161 at 192–95 (1993); Richard Broome, "Aboriginal Workers on South-eastern Frontiers," 26 *Australian History* (1994), 217; and Robert Foster, "Rations, Co-existence and the Colonization of Aboriginal Labour in the South Australian Pastoral Industry, 1860–1911," Property Law and the Colonial Imagination & Experience Colloquium, Univ. of Victoria, Feb. 2001.

rations to Aborigines. Instead of fighting those arrangements, station owners in South Australia recognized them as serendipitous. "I have always been under the impression," one wrote, "that our blacks have a pre-emptive right to camp wherever they choose on the crown lands...." "It would be very unfair to the natives to keep them at a distance from the place where their natural instinct leads them to go and obtain food," another told a select committee, adding that the Aborigines "have a claim on the country just as we have, and if we shut them out from our waterholes we are doing wrong." These were enlightened views, but Foster is quite right to argue that their empathy was in large measure prompted by their satisfaction with this immobile supply of competent and inexpensive workers.

Work Agreements between Diaspora Newcomers

Christopher Tomlins has argued that both trial court judges and juries in early nineteenth century Massachusetts were generous toward workers who had quit "entire" contracts and sought *quantum meruit* payment from their employers, despite that state's high court rule against such recovery. The evidence supporting this view is limited; Tomlins offers no specific examples of this phenomenon, and it is worth noting that a hired hand who quit before his contract specified on Ebenezer Parkman's farm in 1780 expected no payment and offered to "Pay the Damage of Disappointment."[79] But Tomlins *has* found evidence of popular resistance to the English rule that a man or woman who quit an "entire" contract was entitled to nothing for the weeks or months he or she had already worked. And it appears that by the late eighteenth century some employers in the States were paying workers who quit their full back pay. One of them, Samuel Slater, explained to his partners in 1794 that even though "the Common Law [rule] is binding...I think the Law of Equity and Justice is not."[80] In any event, this much seems likely: The English Common-Law rules regarding employment contracts clearly favored the party extending the offer of subsistence and cash, payable in exchange for service once they be satisfactorily rendered. Any alteration of these rules beneficial

---

[79] Tomlins, "The Ties that Bind: Master and Servant in Massachusetts, 1800–1850," 30 *Labor History* 193 (1989); Ross Beales, "Ebenezer Parkman's Farm Workers, 1726–1782," 99 *Proceedings of the American Antiquarian Society*, pt. 1, 121, at 133 (1989). But see the evidence of a culture of "sociability" in Barbara Karsky, "Sociability in New England Farming Communities," in *Travail et Loisir dans les Societes pre-Industrieles*, ed. B. K. and Elise Marenstras (Nancy, 1991).

[80] Jonathan Prude, *The Coming of the Industrial Order* (1983), 45; Anthony E. C. Wallace, *Rockdale* (1980), 179; Steinfeld, *The Invention of Free Labor*, 160–63.

to the bargaining employee would alter the character of the bargaining process and could well affect the specific terms agreed upon. And in those states whose courts had not yet sanctioned *quantum meruit* recovery of "what one's labor had been worth" to the employer, both parties appear to have been quite capable of drafting labor contracts that reflected this new balance of power, detailing the terms under which the worker might quit work before the end of the term (*Britton v. Turner*, 6 N.H. 481, 1834).

I offer three examples: In November of 1838, a minor's guardian in North Carolina entered into a written contract on his behalf for him to work for twelve months "at the shoemaking business and other things, when called on, for the price of $50, $10 to be paid when the time is half out, and the balance when the year is out." This much was common enough; but the agreement continued: "If can't agree, part and pay according to what he is worth; not considered to be worth as much the first as last."[81] In the same year, Darius Pierce hired B. C. Thompson in Farmington, Michigan, to work in Pierce's sawmill "at $12 per month for six months," beginning in mid-February. The sum of twenty-five dollars was "to be paid by the first of May and the balance when said six months is performed[.] It is the understanding that if said Thompson should quit work before the time agreed-upon, that he is to be paid in the proportion to the worth of labor for the whole time...."[82] Somewhat less generous to the worker, but still a sight better than the typical eighteenth century labor contract, was an agreement entered into in February, 1846, by Thomas Larkin and William Anderson, for Anderson to work for a year in a soap factory "on the Sanches farm" in California for $400, "not to leave off" until "the expiration of one yr., under the forfeit of one half of his wages...."[83]

All three employers seemed unable to get their employees to agree to "entire" contracts that would justify the nonsuiting of a worker–plaintiff who quit and sought *quantum meruit* recovery ("what he is worth"). All three agreed to pay workers who quit substantial sums in addition to such partial payments as they may have received. In all three of these states – North Carolina, Michigan, and California – the harsh "all or nothing" English rule was still the Law when a worker breached an "entire" contract. Hence, these contracts are evidence that workers were able to "contract out" of that rule, that they were able to achieve the more equitable Law of New Hampshire's

---

[81] In *Cox v. Skeen*, 24 N.C. 220 (1842). Compare this with the rule and *dicta* in *McMillan v. Vanderlip*, 12 Johns. (N.Y.) 165 (1815).

[82] Cited in David Schob, *Hired Hands and Ploughboys: Farm Labor in the Midwest, 1815–1860* (Urbana, 1975), 160.

[83] *The Larkin Papers*, ed. George Hammond (Berkeley, Cal., 1953) IV, 204.

Britton v. Turner in the private "law" they had created themselves at the grass roots level.

Was this made possible merely by virtue of labor scarcity? Was it due to the egalitarian spirit of antebellum America? Or could *Britton v. Turner* have truly been as "celebrated" in worker circles as it was by midwestern jurists in the 1850s and 1860s?[84] Could workers have been inspired to insist on its terms because they were aware of it? We will almost certainly never have solid answers to this question (though we can at least venture the guess that few laborers knew of the "breakthrough" New Hampshire supreme court had provided them). But we can at least ask this comparative question: In Ontario, Australia, and New Zealand, where *Britton* found no voice and the harsh English rule prevailed, did some workers *also* insist, when they agreed to work, that they be paid for "what their labor was worth" their employer if they quit? Were the socioeconomic conditions for an "informal" *Britton v. Turner* in place in the lands of the British Diaspora – that is, did labor scarcity and egalitarian conditions in the Canadian and Australasian lands produce new "norms," manifested there in accommodations by "masters" of "servants"?

Quitting in the Colonies and Provinces

Ontario

Labor contracts created in Ontario's countryside in the nineteenth century displayed a number of the characteristics of those drafted south of the Great Lakes. Laborers there also bargained with employers for higher than average wage rates, better rations, and other conditions not mandated by the Common Law. A few examples: In April of 1835, Charles Butler, seeking to create a farm in Coburg, agreed to pay three men five dollars an acre to burn, clear, and fence twenty acres at his "Haldiman Farm," offering them the use of his log house there and a type of conacre ("land enough for potatoes[,] & oats for a Yoke of Oxen"). The oxen provided were to be theirs, in part payment. Two barrels of pork and flour, also provided, were "to be deducted from their pay," which was to become due after the harvest and sale of the first year's crop "Jan. next." The next month Butler signed an agreement with one Michael Donnegan for logging and clearing his fallow on his existing farm. The yoke of oxen provided to Donnegan was described as being "on loan," and Donnegan agreed to feed them

---

[84] See Peter Karsten, "'Bottomed on Justice': A Reappraisal of Critical Legal Studies Scholarship Concerning Breaches of Labor Contracts by Quitting or Firing in Britain and the U.S., 1630–1880," 34 *American Journal of Legal History* 213 (1990).

himself and to "run all risks regarding them." But he was to have them
for himself once the work was completed for fifty-six dollars, "in part
payment for the work." Elsewhere, in September, 1843, John Malloch
hired Andrew Hope "today, no wages agreed on." Only "afterwards"
did they agree that Hope was to have eight dollars a month. In another
journal entry, Malloch indicated that he offered a farm laborer (his
name illegible) ten dollars a month, but the man maintained that he
was worth eleven dollars. Malloch agreed to pay eleven if the man's
former employer vouched for him, and on that understanding, the
man began work.[85]

Most farmers in nineteenth century Ontario called upon sons, brothers, nephews, cousins, and neighbors for occasional intense labor
tasks. Since one's siblings and relations were often located at considerable distances from one's own farm, one's neighbors, and any "hired
hands" they might be employing, were the more logical choices for
intense tasks requiring assistance, work that had to be shared to be
accomplished economically. Reciprocation was the hallmark of work
on farms in nineteenth century Ontario, just as chore swapping between farm families had been common in Essex County, Massachusetts,
in the seventeenth and eighteen centuries, and communal corn shuck-
ing, wheat harvesting, barn raising, and flax scutching had been in
early nineteenth century Appalachia.[86] Diarist after diarist in Ontario's
mid-nineteenth century countryside recorded this cooperation among
neighbors.[87] Consider the entries of Thomas Thompson of Tullamore:
One month he might lend "Sid," his hired hand, to neighbors "for
shares" in barn raising; another, for threshing; "Bill Clifton" helped
Thompson "to thresh peas" one afternoon; he reported "asking hands

---

[85] Entries for April 16 and May 6, 1835, Charles Butler Diary, MSS Diaries, MU
838, Archives of Ontario; Entry for Sept. 8, 1843, John Malloch Journal,
MSS Diaries, MU 842, Archives of Ontario. See also entries for July 22 and
Aug. 1, 1848, Walter Hope Diary MS 338, Archives of Ontario.

[86] Daniel Vickers, *Farmers and Fishermen: Two Centuries of Work in Essex County,
Massachusetts, 1650–1850* (Chapel Hill, 1994), 60–61, 237–40, 299; Wilma
Dunaway, *The First American Frontier*, 115–16.

[87] See the Journal of Simeon Reesor of Markham, 1854–64, MS 64, Archives
of Ontario; John Ferguson Journal, 1869–79, MS 297 (1), A. of O.;
Diary of David Nelson of Otonabee, 1864–86, MU 842, A. of O.; James
Crawford Diary, 1865–1882, MU 757, A. of O. The records I consulted
never reported the appearance of female family members at such events.
These activities were the more physically intense ones of the labor/farm
cycle, and it is likely that women were not called upon for them, or were
generally involved in support activities such as cooking and serving, or
lighter agricultural/labor tasks. But it is also quite possible that these male
head-of-household diary writers either chose not to mention their contribution or never gave it a thought.

for Barn Raising," a major task, and two days later had enough hands to record: "Fine day. Raised the Barn." On another day he "took White['s] saw to Dick Thompson's," and was later "at Isaac Odlum's cutting feed with Bob Shaw's engine."[88]

Cooperative understandings were not limited to two parties, especially once expensive farm machinery began to be used in the second half of the century. I have already offered the judgement of John Kenneth Galbraith, raised in western Ontario in the early twentieth century, for they seem applicable to an earlier generation as well. They bear repeating:

> A man would have been excluded [from society] ... if he had shown himself to be unneighborly. ... The Common law on these matters was clear and well enforced. A man was obliged to put his neighbor's need ahead of his own and everyone did.... No one ever declined.... The social penalty would have been too severe.[89]

And, once again, we don't have to take John Kenneth Galbraith's word alone on this score; we have the diary of his ancestor, John Galbraith (b. 1768, Scotland), who settled in Colonel Talbot's domain, eventually establishing a profitable trade in apples, maple syrup, and hops in Blenheim. He reported many cooperative activities and informal understandings with neighbors in his farm diary, noting as well the rarer moments when these went awry. Thus, on July 1, 1835, Galbraith "Had a very hard scolding for Marg. S. Had forbidden her to get water because [her] boys would not help me to jink round the well cover." And the next July he had another "very great Scold," this time from "Mrs. B because I found fault that she would not let [her?] boy go with me to Mt. Pleasant."[90] But these incidents appear to have been most uncommon. Galbraith's diary, in any event, was the only one of some two dozen I read that contained as many such "Scolds" over what was, typically, a twenty or thirty year span. Unless John Galbraith was the only diarist willing to record such moments, they were rare.

---

[88] Entries for June 1, 1885, Feb. 22, 1890, Mar. 10, 1890, May 17, 1892, June 14 & 16, 1892, MU 871, A. of O.

[89] J. K. Galbraith, *The Scotch* (Boston, 1969), 47–48. Compare this to Barbara Karsky's findings regarding eighteenth century Massachusetts (*supra* note 79), and to Lucy Simler, "The Landless Worker: An Index of Economic and Social Change in Chester County, Pennsylvania, 1750–1820," 114 *Pa. Mag. of Hist. & Biog.* 163 at 179 ff (1990) (neighbor's children involved in cooperative work such as barn raising, quilting, threshing, hoeing, reaping).

[90] Entries for July 1, 1835, and July 25, 1836, John Galbraith Diary, MS 450, Archives of Ontario.

Labor agreements, many of which are mentioned in these diaries, were sometimes breached by the laborer – that is, he or she quit. But under those circumstances these Ontario employer–diarists never dragged the servant or hired hand before a magistrate, as the local Master & Servants Act theoretically allowed. (For that matter, I was able to find only seventeen cases involving men or women quitting or being fired in the entire appellate reports of nineteenth century Ontario.) Employer- or employee-use of the formal Law occurred more often in the context of work done *impersonally* – that is, for someone previously unknown to you, and not in one's neighborhood, in such labor disputes as might arise between such parties as the contractors and the Irish laborers at work in 1843 on the Lachine Canal.[91] This is not to say that *all* clerks, printers, domestic servants, and other employees were unwilling to sue for wages or to claim they had been wrongfully discharged; some clearly did. And dissatisfied employers sued as well. Some gentry, professional men, and merchants in Ontario seemed especially annoyed with "independent" domestic servants, "possessed," as Susanna Moodie recalled, with an "ultra-republican spirit." Those foolish enough to bring domestics with them from Britain find that "all subordination" is soon "at an end." They "fancy themselves not only equal to you in rank," but "demand the highest wages, and grumble at doing half the work, in return, which they cheerfully performed at home." They "demanded to eat at your table, and to sit in your company," and "tell you that 'they are free', that no contract signed in the old country is binding in 'Meriky'... and that you may get the money expended in their passage and outfit in the best manner you can." This was too much for Mrs. Moodie. It was too much for Colonel John Price of Windsor as well. His was "an old English family," he told his colleagues in the legislature of the United Canadas in 1847 as it was enacting a Canadian Master & Servant Act. The "fine buxom lassie" he had hired had quit "because she wasn't called a 'help' instead of a servant, or invited to the family table." Colonel Price could not "accustom his tongue to the word 'help,' in preference to the old and scriptural name of servant."[92]

In Ontario, a man like Price might take advantage of the Master & Servant Act of 1847 to try to create the social distance and degree of subordination he sought, or he might opt to fire a domestic servant unwilling to comply. But the labor market imposed its own restraints on the Colonel Prices of mid-nineteenth century Ontario. Servile domestics in the English mode were simply hard to find there. And

[91] H. C. Pentland, "The Lachine [Canal] Strike of 1843," 29 *Canadian Historical Review* 255 at 267 (1948). See also *O'Neill, et al. v. Leight*, 2 UCQB 204 (1846), and *Raines v. Credit H. Co.*, 1 UCQB 174 (1843).

[92] Moodie and Price, both noted in Craven, *supra* note 31, 189, 192.

things were worse on the "wild Canadian frontier." When a merchant named Hamilton fired his domestic servant in the mining community of Fortymile in the virtually Lawless Yukon in 1895, he was summoned to a "miner's meeting" to answer the "charge" of wrongful discharge. The miners were already dissatisfied with Hamilton's policy regarding the extension of credit to them; the meeting ordered him to pay her the rest of her salary, not for the month, but for the year, as well as to provide her with transportation, food, and lodging en route to Seattle, Washington. Sergeant Brown of the Royal Canadian Mounties, the only legal officer in the area, witnessed the affair and pronounced it "nothing but a farce" and "mob law," but it was no farce to Hamilton.[93]

Larger-Scale Employers

My archival sortie into the diaries of farmers and mechanics in the Archives of Ontario, searching for evidence of grassroots labor disputes, yielded only only about thirty five such moments of employer-employee labor-contract tension; hence, I can only hypothesize on this score. But I want to do that much: Laborers working for a single individual (typically a farmer) were rarely fired in Ontario even though the employer might have recorded a number of shortcomings he had seen in the individual's work or behavior. And hired hands appeared to be permitted to quit earlier than expected, which they *occasionally* did, without losing "what their labor had been worth" their employers.[94] Most of the diary writers were religious Methodists, Presbyterians, or Anglicans. They went to church with their hired hands and the rest of their family and neighbors.

But those who worked for corporations (typically a factory or railroad) might well be fired for shortcomings (and, in one case, when it was allowed that there *were* no particular shortcomings).[95] Corporate

---

93 Related by Thomas Stone in "The Mounties as Vigilantes: Perceptions of Community and the Transformation of Law in the Yukon: 1885–1897," in *Historical Perspectives on Law & Society in Canada*, ed. Tina Loo and Lorna McLean (Toronto, 1994), 131.

94 See especially entries in John Malloch Journal, Nov. 24, 1841, June 15, 1842, July 11, 1842, MU 842, Archives of Ontario; Sept. 19 & 21, & Oct. 3, 1871, Jonathan Sussons Diary, Archives of Ontario; Mar. 31, 1887, Apr. 9, 1987, Leeman Crawford Diary (Crawford was a carriage maker), MU 757, Crawford Papers, A. of O.; Aug. 2, 1882, James Crawford Diary, MU 757, A. of O.; June 1, Aug. 15 & 21, 1885, Thomas Thompson Diary, MU 871, A. of O.

95 E. W. Rathbun to Sir Alex. Campbell (a R.R. exec.), May 4, 1889, Sir Alex. Campbell Papers, MU 479, Archives of Ontario, on letting one Grier go "without giving him even a month's experience with the Company's business. If this . . . can be done without litigation, even at a little expense, I would be quite agreeable to it . . . ."

officials mindful of budgetary constraints, temporary downturns,[96] or
potential damage suits due to worker carelessness could be quite ruthless (though their two week severance clauses also allowed laborers to
quit at very short notice, a substantial move away from the constraints
of the prevailing master-servant statute).[97]

Let me offer a glimpse through one farm window on this subject,
the Mills farm in Blenheim: Most farmers in mid-nineteenth century
Ontario worked only about 100 acres of land and did not employ much
in the way of farm labor. Daniel Wakefield was an exception; he arrived
in Blenheim in June, 1845, with over 300 pounds and 4 young farm
laborers as the agent–farmer of one Arthur Mills, a reform-minded
English gentleman. Wakefield soon acquired 275 acres of "as good land
as can be found in Canedy," 75 of it already improved, and put his men
to work cultivating the 75 improved acres and clearing the rest. One
of them, John Hall, "aperd to be dessetesfide" with the sum Wakefield
offered and "ded not seme enclined to stay with me unles I gave im
more wagees than tha rest wich I ded not thenk em worthey of and
that wold have dessatesfide tha others at once so e left me," Wakefield
explained to Mills. Another, James Townley, agreed to serve for a year
for £14, 10s English money, but after working for two months he too
"bacame dessetsfide and want away in a very emproper maner," as did
William Randell. "They were both in my det wan tha laft me tha both
left my work wan I was away from home." Townley and Randell appear
to have disliked the task Wakefield had assigned them (splitting fence
rails), and felt they could do better elsewhere. And having received a
down payment of their wages, they left before they had given Wakefield
in labor what he had prepaid them. But they were unable to find
better arrangements and soon returned to Wakefield who reemployed
them in the "lean" winter months splitting rails and clearing twenty
acres.

Working for Wakefield, a kind of bailiff for Mills, may have been a
less personal relationship than the typical hired hand experienced on

---

[96] These might include poor weather. Thus, Dr. T. J. Gray sued the Grand
Trunk Ry. for wrongful discharge, after having been let go in December
of 1906 after working nine months. The company's defense was that all
physicians had been told upon hiring that they would be let go, along with
the construction workers they had been hired to care for in the Winnipeg
area, once the weather prevented further work. Further, the company indicated that it had helped Dr. Gray find new employment at Humbolt.
Dr. Gray asked for $220 in damages. He settled for $75. File 69, Vol. 3486,
R.G. 30, National Archives of Canada.

[97] The Irish laborers on the Lachine Canal in 1843 found even two week's
notice too long. See their complaint of March 22 on this score in Pentland,
supra note 91, at 265.

a farm in his neighborhood. Moreover, Wakefield had notified Mills that summer that he did "not expect it will [answer] to keep" all four men throughout the winter.[98] I am not suggesting that farmers with more modest assets retained laborers beyond their needs out of a sense of neighborliness, or that Wakefield behaved ruthlessly because of his intermediary status. He reemployed Townley and Randell, after all. No one was hiring laborers on farms or shops in nineteenth-century Ontario who did not need the help, and many of these arrangements were by the day, the week, or for one or two months, not the annual spring-to-spring contracts of a British hired hand. Both farm entrepreneurs and farm bailiffs were allocating their wage capital with great efficiency, treating it as the scarce resource that it was. But it may not be coincidence that the only farm I detected in Ontario with incidents of labor unrest was both the largest and the only one that was absentee owned.[99]

Australia

As is well known, most shepherds, shearers, domestics, and other laborers in the first two generations of the British colonization of Australia were transported convicts, assigned to work for free settlers, graziers, and merchants. These convict–laborers were subject to a more severe dose of Master-&-Servant-Act discipline than in the other British dominions and were flogged by the order of local magistrates for behavior that would not have warranted such treatment had they not been transported men and women. Thus, a settler named Hobler in New South Wales noted in his diary, February 15, 1828, that after "Jim" had

[98] Paul Knaplund, "Arthur Mills' Experiment in Colonization," 34 *Canadian Historical Review* 138 at 143 (1953).

[99] Allowing that, one must also allow that the records of the largest employer in early Canada, the Hudson's Bay Company, indicate that some employees, at least on occasion, enjoyed an "informal law" of labor contracts. The Company's chief factors rarely stood on the formalities of trials in disciplining "recalcitrant servants," as when Albany Post chief factor Anthony Beale whipped four men for theft in 1713 "without calling a trial." (A. Robert Baker, "Creating Order in the Wilderness: Transplanting English Law to Rupert's Land, 1835–1851," 17 *Law & History Review* 215 (1999)). And it required of employees that they give a year's notice, and claimed the right in the standard contract of employment to "dismiss a servant at any time, terminating his wages at that date," without "relief either in law or equity." (Cole Harris, *The Resettlement of British Columbia*, 43.) But when Finan McDonald quit the Company in New Caledonia (early British Columbia), the Company's governor, George Simpson, let him go: "No one should . . . be pressed to remain in the Columbia of a discontented turn of mind[,] as the feeling spreads like a contagion." (Tina Loo, *Making Law, Order and Authority in British Columbia, 1821–1871* (Toronto, 1994), 23.)

"abused and threatened Thomas," he had taken Jim to "the Police Officer, and Mr. Mulgrave," the magistrate, had "awarded him fifty lashes, which were laid on this morning – very smartly."[100]

This was all very well when the employer was bringing the Law down on a convict–employee who was abusing his own colleagues. The problem with this sort of disciplining was that "a single recalcitrant shepherd could do untold harm to sheep, and it was generally found that it was to the owner's interest to conciliate his men and treat them fairly."[101]

Eventually most of these men and women secured the right to chose their own employers or to set up for themselves, as "Emancipists," but until the late 1830s in New South Wales and the early 1840s in Van Dieman's Land (Tasmania), they were virtually the only source of both skilled and unskilled workers. And for many years thereafter they remained a most important pool of labor.

Colonists in Western Australia were not much more successful in the late 1820s than those in New South Wales or Queensland were to be at holding the indentured servants they had brought with them (or had sent for) to their long-term contracts. George Moore began on an optimistic note. The servants he had brought with him, he reported home in November, 1830, shortly after settling in to his 12,000-acre tract, "are all happy contented and healthy, and it must be my care to keep them so." But by winter he was reporting the "disrespectful tones" that his right-hand man, "James," was using. James "swears that he will leave me even if I should send him to Botany Bay," and this because Moore would "not allow him to hunt the dogs after some strange cows which have wandered on my land." On this occasion Moore "laughed him into good humor," but in a few days he was lamenting that "Masters here are only so in name; they are the slaves of their indentured servants." While not under direct supervision, one man "does nothing and if I speak to him – exit in a rage! I could send him to gaol,

---

[100] Cited in Stephen Roberts, *The Squatting Age in Australia* 1835–1847 (Melbourne, 1964), 325. Compare this to the Master & Servant law meted out in Newfoundland, in 1772, by "planter" Captain George Cartwright, who recorded that he had beaten his cooper for having been insolent ("a few strokes with a small stick"). The man complained "of being so bruised as not to be able to eat his dinner," and the next day he refused to work, "pretending he could not use his right arm." Cartwright gave him "nothing but water gruel and made a deduction from his wages for his neglect." But, as Gerald Sider has pointed out, Cartwright's papers indicate that he could be "benevolent" as well. Sider, *Culture and Class in Anthropology and History: A Newfoundland Illustration* (Cambridge, 1986), 53–54.
[101] *Ibid.*

but I do not like this extremity. Moreover, I cannot afford to lose the advantage of his time, & pay 30 pounds besides diet to another in his place." Next he was complaining to himself that his "Irish servants" were "beginning to be just as saucy as the English ones, who expect to live as well as their masters did at home; they talk of having meat & beer three times a day!" Soon he was groaning about the "Great visitings among the neighbouring servants" who "talk of forming a club!" As they had "much control over their masters already," the vision of a Servants' Club alarmed Moore. "Club-law would be a terrible exercise & increase of their power." A year after he and his servants had disembarked, he noted that one man "means to make battle to get another half year taken from his indentures," but Moore resolved to "kick most manfully against this." By January, 1832, he was reporting somewhat better news, but was not overjoyed with it: The servants had given him to understand "that if at the expiration of their stipulated periods of service, I give them as much as another master would do, they will do me the honour of remaining with me!"[102] Moore was having a difficult time adjusting to the free-labor marketplace.

So were the Russell brothers in Victoria; within a week of the arrival of nine indentured servants on the *Isabella Watson* in August, 1840, five were reported by their overseer to have "absconded," and three months later he was reporting that the gardener had "bolted," and he was "not able to get him apprehended, as I have not [got] his agreement and do not know his name." John Pascoe Fawkner told his diary on April 18, 1836, that "the Men who are at large without any Masters" in Port Phillip (Melbourne) had met with some of the "ticket-of-leave" servants of his neighbor, Henry Batman, and "they have come to the determination to resist" any effort to return them to Van Dieman's Land. Some "have been marking out land for themselves and have actually commenced building." Fawkner feared that "mischief will ensue before these men are got rid of," as they had "agreed to Stand by their Order to resist oppression to the Death."[103]

Some indentured servants managed to secure releases from these agreements not very long after arriving in the land of wallabys and stringybarks. The ensuing petitions of sheep-station Squatters to the Colonial Office for the dispatch of more convicts eventually proved to be unsuccessful, and proposals in the early 1840s for the importation of Chinese or Indian laborers met determined resistance from the

[102] George F. Moore, *Diary of Ten Years' Eventful Life of an Early Settler in Western Australia* (London, 1884), 27, 55, 60, 86–87, 91, 101.
[103] J. H. Patterson to George Russell, August 18, 1840, & Nov. 14, 1840, *Clyde Co. Papers*, II, 367, 395; *Melbourne's Missing Chronicle: The Journal of John Pascoe Fawkner*, ed. C. P. Billot (Melbourne, 1982), 62;

Colonial Office.[104] Free laborers had always been scarce, and efforts by the governor of New South Wales in the 1790s and thereafter to set maximum wage rates of laborers had failed. But it was clear to those in search of workers that "free men at Liberal wages" were preferable to convicts "for all agricultural purposes," for as Hannibal Macarthur, a large-scale farmer, put it in 1835, "the stoppage of wages for losses occasioned by neglect of duties operates as a better check on the free, than on the present convict discipline on the bond."[105]

Free laborers in mid-nineteenth century Australia were as capable of negotiating around some of the employer-friendly rules of the Common Law as their counterparts in the United States and New Zealand had been: In 1829 a worker named Colvin in Western Australia secured a provision in his contract preventing his employers from leasing to others his and his wife's labor. The papers of attorney James Martin (later chief justice of the New South Wales Supreme Court) include a copy of a contract that he appears to have helped a cooper named Thomas Taylor draft in April, 1850, securing a guarantee from the master of the *Gemini* that "his lay [share] on board" would "not be less than 5 pounds a month. Should the success of the voyage not amount to that sum," the master agreed "to pay him at that rate," but "should his lay realize more[,] he is entitled to the whole." H. Hurry & Son prepared similar contracts in August, 1859, renegotiated an existing one, to the advantage of James Tillit, a farm laborer. The first provided that Tillit would serve William Robinson [or Robertson] "for the remaining period between our former agreement dated the 12th Feb. 1859 to the 12th Feb. 1860 being the full Twelve months at the Weekly wages of Twenty-five shillings Sterling;" the second, that Robinson was to pay Tillit 47 pounds, "being the Balance of one year's wages." (Robinson signed both.)[106]

---

[104] Paul Knaplund, *James Stephen and the British Colonial System, 1813–1847* (Madison, Wis., 1953), 24–25; Stephen Roberts, *The Squatting Age in Australia*, 320, 322; Alexandra Hasluck, *Thomas Peel of Swan River* (Melbourne, 1965), 140–48.

[105] Philip McMichael, *Settlers and the Agrarian Question*, 96, 135, 152, 188. For wage rates of shepherds, bullock drivers, hutkeepers, overseers, boundary riders, artisans, and domestics, rates roughly twice those paid in Britain, see Anthony Trollope, *Australia and New Zealand* (2 vols., London, 1873), I, 150, 169–70, 227, 246, 302, 399; and Stephen Roberts, *Squatting Age*, 282, 308, 310. Bruce Kercher, *Debt, Seduction and Other Disasters: The Birth of Civil Law in New South Wales* (Sydney, 1996), 177, also makes the case that wage controls failed because "the demand for labour was greater than the supply" in the first several decades of settlement in New South Wales.

[106] Citation of Colvin contract is in F. K. Crowley, "Master and Servant in Western Australia, 1829–1851," 4 *Western Australia Historical Society Journal*

One solution set upon by pastoralists was to raise the size of the flocks being tended to by the remaining shepherds. This "made the undertaking a success financially," station owner Edward Curr reported, but he added that it "gave my brother and myself a great deal to do." As this doubling of the size of flocks tended to result in the loss of greater numbers of lambs and sheep, there were some who tried to charge these losses to their shepherds under the terms of their contracts. At least one magistrate, Thomas Potter Macqueen, would have none of it. He told a committee in New South Wales in 1837 that he had "refused to punish shepherds when brought before me" because "I considered the flocks they were in charge of were larger than they could properly attend to."[107]

While a "Squatter" might manage to find someone willing to agree to serve as a shepherd for a year or more, several months of virtual isolation[108] in the bush could serve to change that man's mind. Edward Curr might have been prompted to raise the size of the flocks his shepherds tended because of an incident that occurred "the second morning after my arrival on the station." One of his shepherds had demanded his wages and taken his departure, forcing his overseer to tend that flock until a replacement was found. Note that Curr paid the man his wages on short notice, and that he tells us in his *Reflections on Squatting in Victoria* that "wages were high, and labourers (almost all old gaol-birds and expiree convicts) exceeding independent and rowdy...." This meant that when his shearers demanded

Pt. 5 (1953), 96. Taylor, cooper - R. Tarn agreement, Sir James Martin Papers, Sydney, Apr. 6, 1850, ML MSS 240/2 (correspondence with clients), Mitchell Lib; Tillit-Robinson agreements, Aug. 29, 1859, H. Hurry & Son MS 13016/10/9 (16), Box 1 Item 5, MS Div., State Library of Victoria. And see agreement between Robert Chirinside and William Tookey regarding shearing, Aug. 25, 1894, where Tookey opted out of clause 8 ("work to be done outside") of a "standard" shearing contract Chirinside had offered and stipulated that he must be provided a shed sheltered from the weather because "I am subject to lumbago." Chrinside MS, 11127/2482/24/1; and John Dunn, fencemaker, to Neil Black, Sept. 20, 1854, notifying Black that he was accepting "the job of two railed fencing you showed me. My mates & I will do it for you at the offer you made of 110 pounds per mile, you are to let us have what rations we may require for payment." Neil Black MS. And see Thomas Day's "Reminiscences" of his and his mates' negotiating of fencing contract offers on the Little Bendigo in 1878, one of which they turned down (by a vote) after deciding they had earned enough and were ready to return to Melbourne, and after having tested the ground and found it "too hard." MS8432/986/5, St. Lib. Of Victoria.

[107] McMichael, *Settlers*, 151–52.
[108] The typical shepherd shared a hut with two others.

rum rations with their pay, he viewed them as "masters of the situation, and their ultimatum in this particular, immutable...." And, "as far as compelling" any of his laborers "to perform their agreements, under which they had all received money advances," as they could well have been in Britain, "it would have been simply impossible under the circumstances" on the Victorian plains.[109] William Lawson of Prospect, a major Squatter who had hired some fifty shepherds for three years of service found that "all save two... absconded." Stephen Roberts claims that "the lowest class of labourers had the whip hand, especially when the assignment of convicts ceased [in New South Wales] at the end of 1838 – and they knew it."[110]

My own visits with the letters and diaries of station managers and Squatters in New South Wales, Victoria, and elsewhere for these years bear Roberts out. George Moore wrote to his family from his estate in Western Australia in early 1834 that while he had "reckoned" that he could hire shepherds for thirty pounds a year, his most recently-hired shepherd "costs me 71 pounds 8 s." From Tasmania, Phillip Russell advised his brother at Port Phillip (Melbourne) in July, 1838, that he was finding "great difficulty in getting men" for their run in Victoria, or, in any event, finding it difficult to acquire *able* workers. He reported that he had hired two, but "they do not seem first rate hands." In February, 1839, he was complaining to George of the high costs of labor, advising him in March to "part with some of the hands before the expiration of their agreements, which would be a saving to the Co" (at least with regard to their rations), and in August telling him that a man he had engaged "who seemed to be a useful hand," had "left for Port Adelaide" and the new colony of South Australia. In February, 1840, his news was the same: "Wages are now nearly as high here [in Tasmania] as with you." Phillip had been obliged to pay 25 shillings an acre for reaping, "double the sum I ever paid before."[111]

A few months later Henry Meyrick was arriving in Melbourne on the *China* to establish a run of his own. He sent news to his family in Wiltshire on the next out-going vessel and reported that "the steerage passengers" on his ship "had not far to go, to look for situation," for "the *China* was crammed with people from all sides looking for servants,

---

[109] Curr, *Recollections*, 39, 40, 44, 97.

[110] Roberts, *supra* note 104, 319.

[111] Moore, *Diary*, 212 (Feb. 3, 1834); Phillip Russell to George Russell, July 17, 1838, Feb. 20, 1839, Mar. 20, 1839, Aug. 19, 1839, and Feb. 7, 1840, *Clyde Co. Papers*, II, 158, 204, 208, 238, 313. And see Mrs. Anne Drysdale's diary entry, July 25, 1840, *Clyde Co. Papers*, II, 362: Two "splitters, after working for a fortnight, went off without any wages."

& in two days . . . there was not one left." Next month he informed his mother that he was now planning to raise cattle instead of sheep, and asked if "George Hunter & his wife" were "still thinking of coming out." Were they to do so, he was prepared to offer them fifty pounds a year, "their house & rations" for the two of them and their three children.[112] William Archer, serving as overseer of a sheep station at Loowie, wrote his father in June, 1842, of the "scarcity of labour & consequent high rates of wages." And overseer Thomas Murphy explained to absentee-Squatter Samuel Winter from a Victorian sheep station in August, 1846, that the reason he had agreed to rehire a shepherd named Holden at a rate considerably more than he had offered anyone previously was that "at the time he came hire I was very much in want of men & one of the Ewe flocks broke out bad with the scabs & [I] could not get a man at any wages to dress [?dust?] them so that I was [of] necessity compelled to employ him" at the higher rate.[113]

As in Canada and the United States, workers in Australia showed little deference to their employers, employing the phrase "Jack's as good as his master." Anthony Trollope, a visitor to the Australian colonies in 1871, described domestic servants remarkably like those Susanna Moodie and Colonel John Price had described in Ontario. Maids in Victoria had "the pertness, the independence, the mode of asserting by her manner that though she brings you up your hot water, she is just as good as you . . . which is common to the American 'help.' "[114] Mrs. George Griffin, wife of the owner of a cattle and sheep station on Moreton Bay, had problems with her domestic servant in August, 1847, when she told her to wash her family's clothes apart from those of the Griffin's. In "the most abusive Language" the servant told her "she was Quite as Good as herself" and would not work "another stroke if made to separate the wash." Captain Griffin reported in his dairy that her husband encouraged her in this "insubordinate" conduct. Four years later Griffin recorded a run-in with another domestic servant, Mary Conoley, who "started off to go to Brisbane by herself." Sent after, she returned, "but still refused to work till about 3PM when she took into her head to wash up the Dinner things and then refused all other kind of work . . . because 'she was leaving.' " (Griffin "thought proper

---

[112] Letters of Henry Meyrick, May 12, & June 20, 1840, MS 7959/654, State Library of Victoria.

[113] Archer to his father, June 30, 1842, Archer Papers, Letters, 1833–55, p. 71, Oxley Library, Brisbane; Murphy to Winter, Aug. 13, 1846, Winter-Cooke MS 406–417/1.6.17, State Library of Victoria.

[114] Trollope, *Australia and New Zealand* (2 vols., London, 1873), I, 475. Trollope offers a very similar observation regarding maids in New Zealand in Vol. II, 377.

to mark [her] off from her service" two weeks later, which suggests that he viewed her work-refusals as a kind of "notice.")[115]

Sexual advances by the "master" toward such a domestic servant could be almost as risky as they were immoral, for in as egalitarian and labor-dear an environment as this one was, such behavior could lead to her calling for her release, her wages, and for damages from the local magistrate. While "masters" may have been only slightly deterred by the Law from seeking advantages in such gender-related relationships, the fact is that such a call could succeed, and that must have given *some* lascivious "masters" pause.[116]

Employers like G. F. Read, J. H. Patterson, Edward John Eyre, and Thomas Peel were prepared to charge their servants with improper conduct before magistrates, as they had in Britain. In fact, Edward John Eyre virtually boasted of doing this "at intervals" to "refractory men" while a young man, running a station on the Murray River from 1835–1836. He acknowledged that the process involved going "down the county to court, a distance of sixty miles and back," and "entailed the loss of men's labour for fully a week" as well as "my being absent from home for at least three or four days," and he allowed that "bad men" took advantage of this "and became insubordinate, trusting that I would overlook their offenses rather than suffer the extreme inconvenience and loss. . . . " Eyre dealt with such "bad men" by putting them in handcuffs the night before sending them to the magistrate. "They sometimes suffered extreme pain," sufficient to cause them to repent and promise to mend their ways. Eyre dealt with men who "used frequently to pretend to be ill for the purpose of shirking work" in an equally summary fashion. One shepherd, "whom I knew to be malingering and who had given me a great deal of trouble," he "determined to cure." He visited the man one morning in his hut: "I found him moaning most piteously and doubled up as if dreadfully cramped with pain in his bowels." He treated him with syrup of Ipecac "and saw him take it." At sunset he returned "taking with me a mixture of rhubarb, salts and strong decoction of camomile." The man reported that he was feeling better, "but I pointed out the necessity of completing his cure and insisted upon his taking it there and then. . . . If an emetic or a purge did not answer the purpose of curing a malingerer a good strong blister was sure to be efficacious." Being distrusted by Edward John Eyre could be almost as unfortunate for some in the 1830s as it was to be for others in Jamaica in the 1860s.[117]

---

[115] Diary of Cpt. Geo. Griffin, Aug. 30–31, 1847, & Sept. 11 & 27, 1851, OM72–42/1-2, Oxley Libr.

[116] Alexandra Hasluck, *Thomas Peel of Swan River* (Melbourne, 1965), 231–33.

[117] *Edw. Eyre's Autobiography & Narrative of Residence & Exploration in Australia, 1832–39*, ed. Jill Waterhouse (Melbourne, 1984), 82–83. See also Diary

Edward Curr's way of dealing with shepherds who tried "to bully me into paying them off" before their terms were up was more effective: He locked up all of the station's supply of firearms and reminded them of the angry Aboriginal tribesmen they might confront, defenseless, on their way back to Melbourne; they agreed to return to work. Captain George Griffin asked a recalcitrant cowpuncher named Ashcroft a second time "to go out and herd the Cattle" before starting "to Brisbane for a warrant." The man now agreed "to go to work" and Griffin relented, relieved ("saved me the trouble"). G. F. Read's handling of shepherd James Owens also revealed a tough-minded manner, but one with a velvet glove. In August of 1839, Owens used "the most abusive language" toward Read, the run's owner. Owens "refused to appear before a magistrate, & also to quit the place." When Read rode off to secure a warrant for his arrest, Owens absconded. But within a week he had returned and apologized for his behavior. Read informed him that he had sworn out a complaint and that a warrant would be served on the shepherd, but promised to see to it that the magistrate "treat his case as mildly as possible." The next day they rode off to the hearing. Owens was sentenced to forfeit one month's wages and to spend four months in gaol, "but upon my requesting it, the latter part of the sentence was remitted." Read had his shepherd back at work with a savings to him of several pounds.[118]

But the system didn't always work as smoothly in the colonies and dominions as some gentry there expected. Example: Thomas Peel, one of the founders of Western Australia and a cousin of Prime Minister Sir Robert Peel, had a disagreement with his farm servant, John Stansmore, over the conditions they had agreed to regarding Stansmore's trip to Perth during the wheat harvest. Peel summoned Stansmore before his fellow magistrate, a Captain Singleton, who found for Stansmore. Enraged, Peel refused to sit with Singleton in the hearing of a case of assault and battery and was censured by the colonial secretary, whereupon he took the only legal recourse left open to him – he resigned both his magistracy and his membership on the Governor's Council.[119]

of G. F. Read, Jr., July 24, 1839, J. H. Patterson to George Russell, Aug. 18, 1840, *Clyde Co. Papers*, II, 251, 367. And, yes, this was the same man who, as Governor of Jamaica in the 1860s, unleashed martial law when he perceived a wide-spread rebellion and was tried in England for the murder of a black physician-legislator caught up in that suppression.

[118] Hasluck, *op.cit.*, 200; Curr, 78–80; Diary of Cpt. George Griffin, May 19, 1847, OM72–42/1, Oxley Library, Brisbane; Diary of G. F. Read, Aug. 28 & Sept. 5 & 7, 1839, *Clyde Co. Papers*, II, 251–53.

[119] This was Karl Marx's "unhappy Mr. Peel ... of Swan River" in *Capital*, who epitomized for Marx the failure of efforts like proprietors like Peel to hold the laborers they brought with them to labor agreements akin to

Unreconstructed colonial gentlemen like Thomas Peel and Ontario's Colonel Price could shoot rather large holes in their feet trying to wield the Law like blunderbusses. And, in any event, by the 1860s, new police and stipendary magistrates who were not themselves Squatters were rendering decisions decidedly favorable to employee–litigants suing for back wages or charging unlawful discharge. Rob McQueen has clearly demonstrated this for the South Queensland Darling Downs, where Police Magistrate A. D. Broughton held court, accompanied by one or another of two urban Justices of the Peace. Few Squatter–employers took their shearers or shepherds to court any longer, and "legal counsel were more likely to be representing employees in Master & Servant actions than they were to be representing employers."[120] My own venture into this question for nineteenth-century Australia is less systematic than McQueen's; but what I found in the records of Helenus Scott, Jr., police magistrate in Newcastle from the mid-1850s to the 1870s, as well as in various letter and diary entries of station owners or managers who had been summoned before magistrates to face charges levied by their employees, resembled McQueen's findings.[121]

In any event, Squatters and their station hands either accommodated one another's want and interests, or they injured their own. Edward Curr put it well: "We had not much to do with the law" when it

those prevailing in the British Isles. *Capital*, Vol. I, "The Modern Theory of Colonization," ch 33, p. 933 in Ernest Mandel's 1977 edition.

[120] Rob McQueen, "Master & Servant Legislation as 'Social Control': The Role of Law in Labour Relations on the Darling Downs, 1860–1870," 10 *Law in Context* 123 at 129, 133 (1992). Adrian Merritt also found laborers making widespread use of Master & Servant provisions against employers; see Merritt, "The Development and Application of Master & Servants Legislation in New South Wales, 1845 to 1930," PhD., Australian National University, 1981, 208, 411–13.

And see Marie H. Fels, *Good Men and True*, 112 (a sampling of seven-and-a-half years of Melbourne police magistrate records for the mid-1840s revealing that workers were as successful in suing for wages ("wages decreed") as masters for servants absent, disobedient of neglectful), and F. C. Crowley, "Working Class Conditions in Australia, 1788–1851," Ph.D. thesis, University of Melbourne, 1949.

[121] Helenus Scott the Younger Personal Papers, Scott Family Papers, MS 38/11X (in re *James Orwin v. John Eales, John Lawrenson v. George Cox,* and *Chales H. B? v. William G?*), Mitchell Library; Charles Archer to Katie, Dec. 21, 1845, Archer Papers & Letters, 1833–55, Oxley Library, Brisbane; George Moore, *Diary*, 142 (Oct. 30, 1832: One must "satisfy every [servant] demand on the *instant* or off they go to a magistrate & make a complaint." And see the Markham diary, June 26–July 3, 1876 (Fiji), YA 1462, Mitchell Library, for an account of his brother James' trial and fine for assaulting "one of our boys."

came to Master & Servant issues; "men and masters took the law into their own hands, the former leaving their places when dissatisfied, the latter dismissing & sometimes firing their men for misconduct." This worked rather well, inasmuch as an unsatisfactory worker found no future employment "in the neighbourhood," and an unfair master soon "found himself without servants." The wise employer found that "straightforward dealings with his men [were] indispensable."[122] The sheep-station owners who dunned shepherds for each lost sheep over the course of a year[123] and dunned shearers for every sheep imperfectly shorn or cut, however slightly, might save a few shillings this season, but would find fewer shepherds to employ, fewer skilled shearers willing to "send in their sovereign" to reserve a place in the shed shortly before the next season. One visitor to Queensland's sheep stations during the shearing season in 1872 was impressed that the Squatter owners and their shearers ("free-selector" farmers), though bitter rivals over the use of the land, saw mutual benefits in cooperative behavior during the shearing time:

> Nor do they often quarrel over their work, though the laws laid down by the squatter for the governance of his men are somewhat peremptory.... Peace usually prevails [in the wool-shed], and the contracts made are carried out to an end.[124]

When Australian shearers finally decided that they needed to take collective action to improve their bargaining position vis a vis the pastoral entrepreneurs who gave them work, they turned from individual bargaining, and the occasional appeal to the courts, to organizing, to the trade-union movement. They formed the Amalgamated Shearers' Union in 1886, and the bargaining was thereafter collective, sometimes accompanied by violence. And while union/collective bargaining issues fall largely beyond the timeframe of this book and are consequently omitted, this much may be said of the sheep shearers and their bosses in this regard: It appears that, once again, reliance on

---

[122] Edward Curr, *Recollections of a Squatter in Victoria*, 395. And see George Moore's comment on his interest in a young man who sought work with him: "but his former master would not give him a certificate, because he had left him without previous warning; this is a wholesome check, resolved upon at an agricultural meeting [of station owners], greatly to the annoyance of some of the servants of the colony." Moore, *Diary*, 170.

[123] One shepherd who had lost a number of sheep "entrusted to his charge" over the course of a year in Queensland in 1858 sued his employer successfully for the full sum of his annual wages in magistrate's court, but found that verdict reversed by the Westminster-bound Supreme Court jurists. *Thorn v. Gray*, 3 Queens. SCR 210 (1859).

[124] Trollope, *Australia and New Zealand*, I, 36.

the Law-as-pronounced-by-the-courts in these disputes occurred only as a last resort.[125]

I have mentioned Parliament's creation of a Pearl Shell Fishery Regulation Act in 1873, designed to protect Aborigines, especially in Western Australia, from kidnaping and involuntary servitude. But reports continued to reach the press and the public throughout the 1870s and early 1880s of abuses of the statute, especially at Cossack, Nickol Bay, and Delambre Island.[126] At least as serious a problem was the process of recruiting South Sea islanders for the sugar plantations and cattle ranches of Fiji and Queensland. Visitors to Fiji and northern Queensland today can see the modern versions of the great sugarcane plantations created in the mid-nineteenth century. Before the invention of today's harvesting machinery, the industry was labor intensive, and the work debilitating in the tropical sun. By the late 1860s, unscrupulous planters, ranchers, and shipowners were following the example of Peruvian guano-harvesting companies that had combed the South Pacific islands for laborers in vessels some of which can be described as slave ships. Purchasing captives from coastal chiefs, or storming ashore to kidnap on their own hook, these captains brought the wrath of antislavery societies and the British and French navies down upon them. But Fijian, Australian, and British entrepreneurs like Ross Lewin were soon to be found in their wake. When Captain Palmer of *H. M. S. Rosario* boarded the *Daphne* in Levuka, Fiji, on April 21, 1869, he felt he had captured a virtual slaver under British registry. The *Daphne*, licensed in Queensland to carry forty South Sea Island contract–laborers back from their worksites in that colony to their island homes, had kidnaped or hoodwinked as many as 100 islanders and had carried them, naked and some in chains, to Fiji to work for Diaspora sugar planters there (at least one of which was owned by a former officer of the Confederate Army).[127]

This and other "outrages" (including the "martyrdom" of John Patteson, Anglican Bishop of Melanesia, clubbed to death on Nukapu Island in 1871 after five men from that island had been kidnaped by

---

[125] Peter Taylor, *Station Life in Australia* (Sydney, 1988), 99, 102–03.

[126] Henry Reynolds, *This Whispering in Our Hearts*, 164–65; R. Cranston, "The Aborigines and the Law," 8 *Univ. of Queensland Law Journal* 60 (1973).

[127] W.P. Morrell, *Britain in the Pacific Islands* (Oxford, 1960), 150, 176–77. See also Jane Samson, *Imperial Benevolence: Making British Authority in the Pacific Islands* (Honolulu, 1998), 117; Edward Docker, *The Blackbirds: The Recruiting of South Seas Labour for Queensland, 1863–1907* (1970); and William Wawn, *The South Sea Islands and the Queensland Labour Trade*, ed. Peter Corris (1973).

the *Emma Bell*) eventually led to Parliament's creation of the Pacific
Islanders Protection Act of 1872 (amended in 1875). This statute required the licensing of all labor-recruiting vessels of British registry,
the dispatch of government agents with interpreters aboard such vessels to supervise the trade, the banning of liquor and guns from the
items of labor trade, the empowering of British naval officers and consuls to seize suspected vessels operating in both the waters of a British
colony and "any Pacific island not within her dominions," the fund-
ing by Treasury of all proceedings taken against suspected kidnaper–
slavers, and the creation of "the office of High Commissioner" with
authority to create and regulate "a court of Justice" to administer
the Law.[128]

In concert with simultaneously created Queensland and Fijian immigration statutes and ordinances, these regulatory measures appear to
have had considerable effect. In any event, the Fijian "Planters Association" protested to Governor G. W. Des Voeux in April, 1882, that
islander workers on sugar plantations were being questioned after
dark by an immigration official who was not identifying himself to
overseers. The governor's response defended the practice: Melanesian workers were suffering "heavy mortality" from the workload and
living conditions. "Public officials who are conscientiously doing their
duty by the coloured races" had his support. And he pointed out that
these officials would show "special favour" in the allotment of such
laborers "to those plantations where the Immigration law is most faithfully observed."[129]

Most government agents accompanying labor–recruiters appear to
have made conscientious efforts to enforce the terms of the Law, but
this was sometimes quite difficult. R.H. Codrington, Minister to the
Melanesian Mission of the Church of England, advised Queensland's
governor that there were no interpreters available for Islanders north
of the lower New Hebredies, and that, consequently, of four recruits he
had interviewed, only one understood what he would receive in compensation (a gun, one of those banned trade items much sought after
by the recruits). Moreover, none of the four knew what sort of work
they were to perform, or for how long (some thought three months,

[128] Morrell, 178–79, 182–83; Samson, 124; Scarr, *Fragments of Empire*, 176, 204.
[129] Exchange between Planters Association, April 1, 1882, and Gov. Des Voeux,
late May or early June, 1882, appears in Fiji Misc. Papers, CY2848, Mitchell
Lib. For examples of contractual offers by maritime firms supplying "Poly-
nesian Labourers" to Fijian planters, see circular letter from A. M. Brodzick
& Co., Levuka, Nov. 6, 1883, and from Barrett & Buckholtz Co., Dec. 1,
1883, Fiji Misc. Papers, CY2484, Mitchell Lib.

rather than the actual term of three *years*). "In fact," he concluded, they "did not understand a word that was said to them. . . . " This report could have been confirmed by the government agent aboard the *Mavis* off Espiritu Santo in 1883, who noted in his journal: "it's a matter of form at present that no one on board understands them. I can't even find out their names." An Islander picked up at Pentecost Island (Raga) in 1884 told a Board inquiring into recruiting for the Queensland Sugar Company's plantation on the Johnstone River that "when I go ship Govt talk long me, me no savee talk belong him, no other boy tell me what Government talk."[130]

By the mid-1880s the system of policing Islander labor recruiting by British-registry vessels had checked many of the more egregious abuses that had been observed prior to the actions taken at the "Center" by the Colonial Office and Parliament, but one unintended consequence of this was a decline in the profitability and consequent activities of many such vessels, and their replacement by those under French and German registry. As the region's dissident official on this business, Henry Anson, Agent-General of Immigration, put it in 1887: "We preserve our morality and the Germans and French obtain cheap labour! A very one-sided contest for British traders – ethics v. business." Another consequence was that South Sea Islanders, many of whom genuinely did want to work in Fiji or Queensland, found it increasingly difficult to do so. In any event, a combination of trade-union protectionists and Queensland racists soon banned Melanesian workers altogether; nearly all were gone, deported, by 1907.[131]

South Africa

The Boers owned many enslaved Hottentots in the Cape of Good Hope. The emancipation of these slaves by Parliament and the accompanying local enforcing ordinance in 1834 led many Boers to trek over the Orange River with their slaves. Thereafter, in 1840, their Orange Free State's *volksraad* passed "squatters' laws" (*Plakkers' Wetten*)

[130] *W. E. Giles' Cruize in a Queenland Labour Vessel to the South Seas*, ed. Deryck Scarr (Canberra, 1968), 5, 6, 12. And see chapter on "Settlement and Inter-Island Recruiting, 1877–1906," in Scarr, *Fragments of Empire*; Peter Corris, ed., *William Wawn's The South Sea Islanders and the Queensland Labour Trade* (1973 ed.); Edward Docker, *The Blackbirders: The Recruiting of South Seas Labour for Queensland, 1863–1907* (Sydney, 1970), esp. chs. 7 and 8.

[131] Scarr, *Fragments of Empire*, 176, 196, 204; Samson, *Imperial Benevolence*, 116; Adrian Graves, "The Nature and Origins of Pacific Islander Labour Migration to Queensland, 1863–1906," in Shula Marks & Peter Richardson, eds., *International Labor Migration: Historical Perspectives* (1984), 114; Peter Corris, *Passage, Port and Plantation: A History of Solomon Island Labour Migration, 1870–1914* (Melbourne, 1973).

that allowed up to five Bantu families to settle on each Boer farm, to grow staples, and serve as farm laborers and servants. But the Boers in Griqua country and in Natal were not averse to enslaving Bantu children captured on raids, and "laughed" at Boer proclamations prohibiting such measures, "as meant to *gull the English* and never intended to apply amongst the emigrants themselves."[132]

When Lord Stanley, Colonial Secretary in 1842, agreed to annex Natal, he imposed equal treatment under the Law there, reluctantly agreed to by Boers who preferred the veld to further trekking. By the 1850s, British Diaspora settlers in coastal regions of Natal were cultivating some cotton and a good deal of sugar cane. The Cape Colony legislature passed a Kaffir Employment Act in 1858, but in Natal native labor was deemed inadequate. As one planter's wife noted in her diary, "The Caffre gets his month's wages, tells you he is going to his kraal for an indefinite period, and leaves you at a day's notice." The solution, there and in Jamaica, and (later) in Fiji: The importation of workers from British India, the first of whom arrived in Natal in 1860 (and in Fiji in 1878). By 1900, there were some 200,000 Indians working in Natal and Fiji.[133]

New Zealand

What sorts of labor contracts were generated in New Zealand in the nineteenth century? I identified over fifty written agreements in archive-held letter books and account books of sheep-station owners, farmers, and agricultural partnerships between 1850 and 1899. Most were "proemployer," with no "escape" clauses for the employee who might decide to quit in midstream.[134] Indeed, several contained clauses imposing financial penalties on employees under certain circumstances. For example, in February of 1860 Charles Miller agreed with James Vallance of the firm of Levin & Company in Wellington to serve as a shepherd "for the term of 12 months" for £45 to be paid "at the end of such term and if any damage or loss shall be caused by my

---

[132] William M. MacMillan, *Bantu, Boer and Briton: The Making of the South Africa Problem* (London, 1929), 93–94, 144, 178, 191, 245.

[133] W.P. Morrell, *British Colonial Policy in the Mid-Victorian Age* (Oxford, 1969), 101; W. Macmillan, *Bantu, Boer & Briton*, 185; Andrew Barch, "Losing faith in the civilizing mission: the Premature Decline of Human Liberalism at the Cape, 1840–1860," in *Empire and Others: British Encounters with Indigenous Peoples, 1600–1850*, ed. Martin Daunton & Rick Halpern (Phila., 1999), 368, 379–80; Edward Docker, *The Blackbirders*, 6.

[134] A typical one: Mr. C. A. Vallance of Levin & Company hired James Wallace on February 11, 1858, to be a general farm servant for six months "in consideration of receiving at end of such term the sum of £12/10s." Levin & Co. Collection Series 5/17/5, Turnbull MSS Papers, 1347, Turnbull Library.

neglect or carelessness to the sheep in my charge I agree to allow Mr. C. A. Vallance to deduct from my wages for such loss or damage."[135] These are hardly remarkable, inasmuch as here, as elsewhere, employers who troubled themselves with account books generally appreciated the ways that their agreements with workers might be worded to accomplish, on paper, what they wanted.

And yet these were years more characterized by labor scarcity than overabundance, years when workers ought to have been able to strike bargains to their liking. Until the 1880s and 1890s, New Zealand was a labor-seller's market. Complaints abound in the records of station owners of being "in great want of labourers and female servants," and one reported having heard "great complaints among Road contractors of the scarcity of men."[136] Another warned his associates not to hire men in Wellington to serve as ploughmen "at a lower rate than they can get in the [countryside]; they would soon become dissatisfied and go where they could get the current rate of wages in the district." The diary of William Orchard, an migrant agricultural-laborer from Cornwall who had found his way to New Zealand, confirms this, for in the 1860s he noted that his "idea" was "to get as far away from old settled places as possible, follow up the new places where labour is well paid." Orchard recorded that "in one place I could earn 10/- per day and in the other 30/- (a rolling stone gathers no moss they say)."[137]

The English colonial theorist Edward Gibbon Wakefield had argued throughout the second quarter of the nineteenth century for a "sufficient price" for Crown land in order to provide for successful colonies. In substance, this amounted to a call for higher land prices in order to avoid the creation of subsistence-level farms and to ensure decent wages for rural laborers. If an emigrant of modest means was rendered incapable of being able to buy a farm by such a policy, he would become available as a laborer, at least until he had saved enough to purchase sufficient land to operate independently. And, while serving as an agricultural or pastoral laborer, he would not experience an "irresistible ... temptation ... to quit the employer who had brought him to the colony," because high wages, coupled with the artificially

---

[135] Ibid.

[136] Extracts from letters of Charles G. Tripp of Orangi Gorge, Canterbury, for May 29, 1873, and May 4, 1874, MSS Div., Turnbull Library; Diary of E. R. Chudleigh, ed. E. C. Richard, for Dec. 4, 1875, p. 248.

[137] D. W. Hunter to Beltume & Hunter, Ltd., Wellington, Apr. 8, 1877, Letterbook for 1877, p. 3, Beltume-Hunter Papers, Turnbull Library; Wm. Orchard, cited in Miles Fairburn, The Ideal Society and Its Enemies (Auckland, 1989), 138; William P. Reeves, State Experiments in Australia and New Zealand (London, 1902), 203.

high price of land, would keep him from quitting.[138] Wakefield maintained a long-standing interest in Canada, Australia, and New Zealand, helped found the colony of South Australia, and actually emigrated to New Zealand in 1852. His views had a considerable impact on the Colonial Office's Crown land sale policy as early as 1833, and Wakefield's vision was probably part of the reason workers were as well off as they were in New Zealand in the 1850s, 1860s, and 1870s.

But Wakefield's ideals, even when they became official policy in New Zealand, were not panaceas; they did not prevent the lease of huge tracts of land to pastoralists in the South Island in the 1850s, nor did they preclude breaches of labor contracts by workers in the first thirty years of settlement. Laborers employed by the Crown, dissatisfied with wages and rations, went on strike in Russell (April, 1840) and Nelson (January, 1843). The first incident consisted in the desertion of the police boat's crew over pay. Treated as strikers, the crew was initially imprisoned. But the crew was needed, and, as Richard Hill has observed, "the Police Magistrates were soon forced to acknowledge that threat of gaoling was no solution to problems of retention." Consequently, soon after the founding of the colony, "term-contracts were tacitly ignored, and then abandoned." The second incident, at Nelson, involved a group of laborers, who petitioned the government: They "only" wanted "a right and Legal thing," the arrangement struck under the original Wakefield-influenced scheme, "one guinea/wk with rations." This had proven to be too high a rate for the colonial leaders to sustain in the early months, and their wages had been reduced to sixteen shillings per week for married, and eight shillings per week for single men. Attentive to the contract, the men protested against this breach of what "we consider our lawful rights." This "revolt of the working men" led to the arrest of its "ringleaders" by Nelson's chief constable. One of these men was freed by his comrades. But five others were taken before the police magistrate who warned them (but then released them, confronted by a crowd of their colleagues). The men were later offered small plots in exchange for reductions in their

---

[138] Wakefield was involved in Crown and corporate land sale planning in New South Wales and South Australia in the early 1830s and visited Canada as part of Lord Durham's inquiry that recommended Responsible Government (a wider suffrage and greater legislative powers as well as a union of Upper and Lower Canada). John Norman, *Edward Gibbon Wakefield: A Political Reappraisal* (Fairfield, Ct., 1963), 7–18; Wakefield, *A View of the Art of Colonization with Present Reference to the British Empire, in Letters between a Statesman and a Colonist* (London, 1849). Wakefield defined a "sufficient price" in 1836 for a parliamentary committee as "such a price as will keep the wages of labor and the profits of capital at a maximum" (Norman, p. 9).

government subsidies (which were eventually terminated). The Law had failed to produce compliance; compromise and accommodation had proved to be necessary.[139]

The diaries of rural New Zealand employers in the mid-nineteenth century contain a number of irate entries, comments about workers who had chosen to move on. Example one: John Shand complained to himself of the departure of John and Sarah Smyth, "general farm servants" employed at £70 per annum, but paid quarterly (thus "*pro rata*"), who had worked for eight months before quitting:[140]

> Left in a very shabby and dishonourable manner[;] were given 2 holidays and in return they were reengaged at £70/a, & the day prior to the time of return [from the second holiday?] refused to fulfill their engagement with the idea that Mrs. S.'s health was bad (all false)[.] She wanted more wages. Put us to very great inconvenience.

Example two: Charles Tripp, owner of the Mt. Peel sheep station in Canterbury, South Island, described the departure of "the Haywards" who "left" in January, 1861:

> [I] offered them their wages, from the 12 Nov; 9 weeks & 5 days & agreed to give them 10 weeks wages, they refused to take any less than a full quarter's from the 24th of Nov; offered them £8 instead of £6. 17s which is coming to them. . . . they refused to take any.[141]

Tripp's entries do not indicate whether the Haywards had been fired or had quit, but it seems unlikely that the Haywards would have expected pay for more days than they had actually worked if it had been they who had breached the agreement. His description of the negotiations suggest that they felt they had been wrongfully discharged, were thus entitled to a full quarter year's pay, and had therefore decided to sue. They thereby demonstrated a keen appreciation of their rights under the English wrongful-discharge rule that the high courts of the British provinces were enforcing, as we have seen, and were behaving just as were their counterparts on Queensland's Darling Downs, across the Tasman Sea. In fact, when I consulted the Plait & Civil Records Books for the Magistrates' Courts of Wellington and Christchurch for the 1890s, I found abundant evidence of what Rob

---

[139] R. Hill, *Policing the Colonial Frontier*, 155, 208, 211; W. B. Sutch, *The Quest for Security in New Zealand, 1840–1966* (Wellington, 1966), 20.

[140] John Shand Papers, Vol. III, ca. 1866, Mss. Div., Turnbull Library.

[141] Charles G. Tripp's Diary, 1856–1861, Mt. Peel Station, Canterbury Museum Archives, Christchurch.

McQueen had found for Queensland's Toowoomba Magistrates Court in the 1860s: "Tailoresses" were suing tailors; apprentices were suing boot makers and bakers; carters were suing carpenters; a host of servants and laborers were suing their employers. A much smaller number of employers appeared to be suing their employees (the ratio was about seven to one).[142]

Inasmuch as both rural workers and employers sensed the (modest) leverage possessed by the former in this (temporary) labor-seller's market, one might expect to find that employers behaved in accommodative ways. And we do detect some evidence of this. J. B. Acland of Mt. Peel, head of the Sheepowner's Federation on New Zealand's South Island, maintained that there was a real community of interest between farmer and farm laborer.[143] This might be dismissed as a self-serving statement, except that Ackland was not a farmer; he raised sheep and was merely commenting on his agrarian neighbors. Moreover, there exists confirmation of this view in the remarks before a Conciliation Board in 1908 of one John Day. Day had apparently served for some thirty-five years as the "hired hand" to farmer John Brown. He told the Board:[144]

We all have the one table [,] the boss and his family and the missus & I, we practically live on even terms.

Day's description of his employer might be dismissed as an uncharacteristic caricature (after all, he *was* named "Farmer Brown"!). But there is clear and plentiful evidence that he was just as real, and common a phenomenon in New Zealand as we have seen him to be in North America:[145] Rollo Arnold has shown us that agricultural and pastoral laborers in New Zealand were generally treated much better than their counterparts in Britain: Jem and Jack Smith wrote home to

[142] Wellington Magistrate's Court Plait Books and Civil Records Books, 1892–1893, 1892: 2098, 2311, 2382, 2411, 2420, 2427, 823, 687, 674; 1893: 1, 4, 6, 7, 30, 34, 163, 211, 372, 427, 653, 932, 950, 1050, 1073, 1197, 1274, 1334, 1340, 1447, 1499, Christchurch Magistrate's Court Plait Book and Civil Record Book, 1897–1898, entries 1032, 1214, 2319, 2402, 373, Justice, III, JC-W, New Zealand Archives, Wellington. And see the evidence of successful suits for wages in Te Kopuru's Magistrates Court, noted by Judith Bassett, "Abstemious Millhands and Bush Lawyers: The Te Kopuru Magistrates Court, 1875–1878," 1 *Australian Journal of Legal History* 221 at 234 (1995).
[143] Cited in the work of John E. Martin, the expert in this field, in his study *The Forgotten Worker: The Rural Wage-Earner in Nineteenth Century New Zealand* (Wellington, 1990), 4; see also 102.
[144] *Ibid.*, p. 4.
[145] See Karsten, *Heart versus Head*, 165–66.

England from Wanganui in 1875 that "of course" they had been provided ample provisions and accommodations "& live 1st class." They
"dine[d] along with our master & mistress every meal," and live[d]
the same as if we was his own." The farmers in New Zealand were "not
so proud as some of the poor people at home." Richard Wattam of
Lincolnshire worked near Hamilton on the North Island, also in 1875.
He reported home that "we do not work half as hard as we did in
England, & we always have 2 or 3 masters want us at once." Thomas
Warren, a twenty-eight year-old laborer from Kent with a wife and child,
wrote home from Marlborough (South Island) in the same year of his
pleasant surprise at having experienced no loss of pay while recovering
from an injury to his leg that occurred while harvesting. He added this
interesting observation on wage-earning potential and worker power
in negotiations:

> I put our wages, which are £55 a year, with food for the 3 of us,
> firing, & house-rent, at £120 a year at the very least, & I am told by
> the station hands that is very low, but then I am only a learner in
> station life, & shall have more if I stop after the year has expired,
> as I shall then be of some value as a station hand....[146]

You are free to doubt the scope of these reported salary differen-
tials; and you can imagine that emigrants wanted family and friends to
believe (and wanted to believe themselves) that they were much better off than they had been in Britain. But I remain impressed with
the pattern. Both employers and employees in New Zealand between
1850 and 1875 believed that rural New Zealand was a labor-seller's
market, and this appears to have caused employers to be more generous and accommodating toward laborers than were their contemporary counterparts in rural Britain. Consider this diary entry of E. R.
Chudleigh, serving as a "cadet" assistant manager of a sheep station
in Canterbury in 1865: "Two of the station men have been amusing
themselves by getting very drunk. They are good men so you pocket
your feelings & do not discharge them." Chudleigh *might* have learned
to "pocket his feelings" about drunken workers in the Britain he had
left a few years before, but he was still a very young gentleman rancher,
not very worldly or savvy in these or other matters. It seems more likely
that he had "learned" to behave this way toward workers in the frontier
culture of the South Island in the 1860s.

Not far from Chudleigh, John Shand and Sons was hiring rural
laborers in 1866 with interesting terms. James Hepburn and his wife

---

[146] Rollo Arnold, *The Farthest Promised Land: English Villagers, New Zealand
Immigrants of the 1870s* (Wellington, 1981), 80–84, 242, 244, 283, 287,

agreed "to look after cows, pigs, wife to take charge of the house, cook, wash, etc., attend to the milk, butter poultry and made herself generally useful for £60/annum; a month on trial, a month's notice on either side." Similarly, Thomas Maloney's contract with the Shands had a condition of fourteen days notice, "in case of a separation."[147] These were agreements more like those of domestics or factory operatives than hired hands, but they were drafted with these short-term escape clauses to accommodate a mobile workforce, not to serve the interests of an arbitrary propertied class.

It may be that there are further indications of accommodative employer behavior in these diaries and station letter books, but some are hard to decipher. Cryptic entries like these two could be read to mean very different things:

> Manuel had a row with his men so they squared up and left (Chudleigh diary, 1886)

> Paid off J. Hammond who has left to shear down the country[.] 100 rabbits 60 [wild] pigs & 3 keas was all I paid him for in addition to wages. (Hugh Hamilton dairy of Clayton sheep station, 1885)[148]

Did Manuel's "row with his men" result in their quitting, their being fired, or as seems more plausible, in their parting with their employer on mutually agreeable terms and their being paid *quantum meruit* (what their labor had been worth)? Did Hugh Hamilton's employee, J. Hammond, have an agreement allowing him to give short-term notice and quit, or is it more likely that he breached a longer-term agreement? If so, would that be why Hamilton noted (negatively) that the bounties for rabbits, wild pigs and keas (a parrot that preys on sheep, attacking their livers) were "all I paid him"? But then why would he have paid him wages "in addition"?

These entries are ambiguous; others are not. If some employers accommodated workers in these years of labor scarcity, others reacted to acts of worker independence (or quest for latitude) as if they had never left Britain! Thus, one diary keeper by the name of Godfrey in Blenheim indicated in 1868 and 1869 that he "paid off" men whom he had fired for cause, but also that he did *not* pay those who quit. A dairy farmer on the East Cape, North Island, in 1888 found that his share milkers "sought to abrogate their agreement" to work for him for three years. He sued *them* for damages, and spent several days

---

[147] John Shand Papers, Introduction, MSS Division, Alexander Turnbull Library.
[148] *Chudleigh Diary*, 343; Diary of Clayton Sheep Station, South Canterbury, 1885, by Hugh Hamilton, Mss. Division, Turnbull Library.

away from the enterprise presenting his case to the nearest magistrate. And our friend E. R. Chudleigh, now married and on his own farm at Wharekauri on Chatham Island in 1882, complained to his diary of two recently arrived domestic servants who "will not do." Within three weeks they had both quit in an "impudent" fashion, giving a "saucy notice" to his wife "that they were off in the morning." The next day one of them, Margaret, "defied" his wife with the announcement that she would neither work nor leave,

> that I should pay her all her wages up to date & that she would have the same food as I had in the parlour; I asked her to say it over again. I found she would not listen to reason & so I sent Paddy Murphy off to Waitangi to the R[esident] M[agistrate] to send a policeman over at once.[149]

Margaret was turned over to the authorities at four o'clock in the morning and given "forty-eight hours in jail for refusing work & getting drunk." This was the sort of punitive treatment under the Master & Servant Act that high court jurists in the Antipodes were no longer tolerant of, but Chudleigh had rediscovered his English Legal roots and was willing to use his knowledge of them (and perhaps his familiarity with the local authorities as well) to try to hold Margaret to the terms of the contract he had made with her. In the short term, his measures succeeded; but some seven months later, Margaret left for good.

Francis Hayter handled his work force with similar "proper British" firmness in 1890: After he fired a shearer for cutting some sheep, the other shearers staged a work stoppage. Hayter responded to that by "sacking" the classer and the roller "for cheek." But he then noted that the shearers who returned to work "won't come up for their grog." So he "went down with it to them." Perhaps this modest act of accommodation is evidence that Hayter had learned to be somewhat more responsive to worker demands. But the classer, the roller, and the shearer that he had "sacked," remained sacked.[150]

Employers like this who chose to treat workers with gloved fists sometimes had cause to regret their choices. When W. H. Jackson, the station manager for Douglas & Alderson Co., fired shearer Peter Naylor in 1865 for bad shearing, Naylor took Jackson before the local magistrate and recovered £6 payment for the several hundred sheep he had sheared. John Campbell, the manager of Edmund Gibson's Waitangi

---

[149] John Martin, *The Forgotten Worker, supra* note 143, 172 (for Godfrey); Miles Fairburn, *The Ideal Society and its Enemies*, 197; Thorne Seccombe, "Pioneer Days at Orete Point," 11 *Historical Review* 13 (March 1, 1963); *Diary of E. R. Chudleigh* (Christchurch, 1950), 304, 305, 311.

[150] Robert Pinney, *Early South Canterbury Runs* (Wellington, 1971), 216.

sheep station, offered to "pay off" a shepherd he was letting go, but the man, named Milne, "refused to go." When Campbell thereupon drew a pistol and ordered Milne to leave, Milne had Campbell called before the local magistrate and fined £3 and costs.[151] And consider these entries in the diary of Duncan McRae, Jr., a cadet at Wyndham Station, South Island:

> 11 Feb. '99 – Archie left this evening through me giving him a punching for some plain language he used towards me. 12 Feb. – I am milking the cows since Archie left.... 27 Mar. – Archie Livingstone is here to night and we settled his wages with him.[152]

Once hard times abated in the ensuing decades of labor scarcity, organized measures by workers were rare. But eventually the labor-seller's market disappeared, as more unpropertied laborers were allowed into New Zealand, and by the 1890s conditions had changed; "labor" was now abundant, and the work force was ripe for collective action. In the summer of 1893–1894, for example, shearers at Benmore sued the station management after a work stoppage involving wet sheep. Shearers, paid piece-rate, had always objected when station managers insisted that they shear sheep recently soaked by rain at the same rate as those that were dry, since wet sheep took longer to fleece and could more easily be cut by the shears. When they lost the *legal* case, the shearers responded by organizing the New Zealand Workers Union.[153]

In the same years, New Zealand's labor movement, emerging from incidents like this, secured a compulsory arbitration statute from the New Zealand legislature, and the Arbitration Court created by the statute soon affirmed the employer's duty to pay departing employees, be they Union members or not, on demand, all "earned" wages, regardless of the allegedly "entire" nature of the contracts.[154] Note that this right-to-quit-and-be-paid had been achieved in New Zealand not

---

[151] Pinney, *Early South Canterbury Runs* (1971), 117, 282; *Timaru Herald*, Aug. 5, 1865.

[152] 1898–1899 Diaries, Duncan McRae MSS #1391, Turnbull Library.

[153] Martin, *Forgotten Worker*, 192.

[154] *Ibid.*, 198. The Court also "levelled up" the wages of some workers to the rates of others in early decisions. See James Holt, "Compulsory Arbitration in New Zealand, 1894–1901: The Evolution of an Industrial Relations System," 14 *New Zealand Journal of History* 179 (Oct. 1980) at 186, 191. See also Mark Bray and Malcolm Rimmer, "Compulsory Arbitration & Managerial Control: Industrial Relations in Sydney Road Transport, 1888–1908," 22 *Historical Studies* 214 (1986) (workers in New South Wales benefitted from compulsory arbitration); and Jeremy Lee, "A Redivision of Labour: Victoria's Wages Boards in Action, 1896–1903," 22 *Historical Studies* 352 (1987).

by judicial innovation, as it had in many American states, nor by popular employee demand in contract negotiations, as in *other* American states, but by organizing, lobbying, and legislative fiat. In this regard, New Zealand's popular legal culture remained closer to its British antecedents with regard to labor agreements than did those of the States.

SUMMARY

Unions might use somewhat different measures to secure their objectives in New Zealand and the United States, but in other ways our story of the informal "law" of labor agreements finds more similarities in the experiences of workers in the United States, Canada, and the Antipodes in the nineteenth century than it does differences: Throughout these Diaspora lands domestic servants and farm laborers called themselves (and were called) "help." Except for the first generation of convict–workers in Australia, employees appeared to have been treated quite even-handedly everywhere by magistrates when they or their bosses brought a labor dispute before such authorities. In general, those working for large-scale enterprises (factories, canal authorities, absentee property owners, railroads) appear to have been more likely than those working for an individual to find problems with labor agreements. To some extent, labor scarcity mandated a sharing of work between farm neighbors, be it Massachusetts, Illinois, Tennessee, Ontario, or New Zealand. Moreover, workers everywhere appear to have been able to "contract out" of some of the less attractive aspects of labor law with employers, especially in times of this relative labor scarcity. The formal Law *mattered*, to be sure, but, as with sales contracts, it may have mattered less than the informal "law," the popular norms regarding how labor agreements actually worked.

PART THREE

Accidents

7

Judicial Responses to Negligence Claims by the British Diaspora, 1800–1910

A virtual revolution in both manufacturing and transport, spurred by technological breakthroughs, economic growth, and a resulting increase in personal spending power, produced substantial increases in land and seaborne travel, beginning in the late eighteenth century. With the development by Robert McAdam of a smooth, durable road surface at the turn of the century (the "macadamized road"), and the development of street and intercity rail transport in the second quarter of the nineteenth century, more vehicles poured into "the King's highways," carrying more persons, at greater speeds. Hence, there were also more and more accidents. Buggies overtaking carts or buggies produced some; carts, buggies, or streetcars with inattentive drivers caused others; negligent road authorities created still others; the "iron monster" – the railroad – and its waterborne rival, the steamboat, were charged with responsibility for most of the rest of the transport accidents. Factories, competing with one another to lower operating costs without expensive safety devices, sprang up throughout North America and the Antipodes, with fast-moving machinery capable of maiming or killing the inattentive or unwary laborer. These were the sites of still more negligent conduct resulting in injuries and deaths.

RULES IN ENGLISH AND U.S. COURTS

A number of the rules of negligence law in England were rejected by a majority of the high courts of the United States in the nineteenth century. By the 1840s, most U.S. jurisdictions outside of New England no longer required that there exist a statute explicitly authorizing damage suits against negligent road and bridge authorities before an injured plaintiff was allowed to sue. Most jurisdictions placed greater burdens than in England on common carriers to establish their lack of liability in the event of a collision, a boiler explosion, a derailment, or a broken stagecoach axle: The carrier was deemed to be negligent by virtue of the accident having occurred, and it was up to the carrier to overcome the *prima facie* case with evidence that would convince a jury.[1] Most jurisdictions required that evidence of the plaintiff's having contributed to the accident by his or her own negligence be left to the jury as a question of fact for them to decide, rather than serve as grounds for the nonsuiting of the plaintiff by the trial court judge, as was the case in England, New York, Pennsylvania, and a few other states. In the event that the plaintiff had been a passenger in a cab hit at a crossing or a small child hit in the street, most American high courts rejected the English rule that the driver's or parent's contributory negligence was to be imputed to the plaintiff.[2] Most engaged in a legal fiction ("allurement") to permit child trespassers injured on dangerous objects ("attractive nuisances") to be treated as invitees, a practice not observed in Britain until the early twentieth century.[3] Most jurisdictions offered a worker–plaintiff a number of exceptions to the assumption of risk and fellow-servant rules that protected employer defendants in England and several northeastern states against suits by workers injured on the job.[4] Most American jurists were more tolerant of larger than average damages awarded by juries than were English jurists, and they refused to follow the English lead of allowing judgement defendants to deduct from the award such monies as the plaintiff was receiving from an insurance company.[5] And in the United States, you will recall from Chapter 5, injured plaintiffs without adequate means to pursue their remedies were legally entitled to contract with an attorney on the basis of a contingency fee arrangement. Moreover, were a plaintiff in the United States to lose his or her suit, the loser was not required to pay the court costs and legal fees of the winning defendant, as was generally the case in England.[6]

NEGLIGENCE LAW AND CANZ JURISTS

Clearly the typical accident victim in America had a better chance to recover against the negligent party than one in Britain. Inasmuch as we

---

[1] *Thorogood v. Bryan*, 8 CB 115 (1849), rejected in *The Bernina*, 13 A.C. 1 (1887); *Waite v. Northeastern Ry.*, E., B. & E. 719 (Ex. 1858).

[2] See Peter Karsten, *Heart versus Head: Judge-Made Law in Nineteenth Century America* (Chapel Hill: Univ. Of North Carolina Press, 1997), pp. 95–101, 241–45.

[3] See Karsten, *Heart versus Head*, ch. 7.

[4] *Ibid.*, 108–26.

[5] *Hicks v. Newport, A. & H. Ry.* (1857), ref. to in *Pym, Adm. V Great Northern Ry.*, 4 B. & S. 396, 122 ER 508 at 510 (Ex. 1863); *Harding v. Town of Townsend*, 43 Vt. 536 (1870); *B & O RR v. Wightman's Adm.*, 70 Va. (29 Gratt.) 431 (1877); *Althorpe v. Wolfe*, 22 N.Y. 355 (1860); *Pitts. & Cinc. RR v. Thompson*, 56 Ill. 133 (1870).

[6] John Leubsdorf, "Toward a History of the American Rule of Attorney Fee Recovery," 47 *Law & Contemporary Problems* 9 (1984).

have already seen that CANZ courts rarely rejected English rules and precedents directly, you won't expect me to argue now that they were loose with such rules when it came to negligence; they weren't. But that doesn't mean that CANZ jurists were unwilling or unable to find their ways around such rules and precedents as they did not approve of. They, like their counterparts in both England and the United States, were capable of distinguishing the facts in the precedent from those of the case before them, sometimes with reference to "local conditions." Similarly, like their counterparts in England and the States, they could at times simply obfuscate, misinterpret, or misstate those facts, those rules or those precedents.[7] In this fashion CANZ jurists sometimes managed to create virtually the same sorts of exceptions and legal fictions as had jurists in the States who were not bound by Privy Council and often did not act with great deference toward the opinions of the courts at Westminster. Ultimately, they felt more loyalty to English Common Law than did their counterparts in the States and thus did not bend or break as many English rules and precedents, but my reading of over 600 negligence cases in the appellate reports of Canada, Australia, and New Zealand between 1830 and 1910 has convinced me that they were far more independent than has ever been imagined.

Negligence and Contributory Negligence: Questions of the Defendant's Liability and the Plaintiff's Eligibility

One of the first and most important tasks facing a plaintiff was to establish the liability of the defendant. It was not enough to prove that she had been injured when she fell from her sleeping berth in the night, when a railway porter slammed a door on her thumb, when a streetcar ran over her son, when she lost the use of a leg after receiving medical treatment, or when her buggy overturned after it hit a hole in the roadway. Jurists in Western Australia, Nova Scotia, and Quebec proclaimed the first three of these to be "purely an accident;"[8] jurists in Ontario dismissed the fourth as a case based on "mere conjecture;[9] New Zealand attributed the fifth to a "mere rut."[10] With no further proof of the railway, streetcar, or municipality's actual negligence, jurists were quite

---

[7] For an example of the two former (misstating facts and rules), in the California, Texas, and New Mexico Supreme Courts in the mid and late nineteenth century see Peter Reich, "Mission Revival Jurisprudence: State Courts and Hispanic Water Law since 1850," 69 *Washington Law Review* 869 (1994).

[8] *Richardson v. Comm. of Rys.*, 7 W.A.L.R. 172 (1904); *Can. Pac. Ry. v. Smith*, 31 Can. S.C. 367 (1901); *Montreal City Pass. Ry. Co. v. Bignon*, 18 Quebec 217 (1866).

[9] *Storey v. Veach, et al.*, 22 UCP 164 at 177 (1872).

[10] *Tarry v. Taranaki City Council*, 12 NZLR (CA) 467 (1893).

ready to dismiss the suit with the observation that the plaintiff had suffered *damnum absque injuria* (loss without compensable injury), or that it had been caused by *force majeure* (fate). Had the defendant behaved reasonably? Had he behaved (in Quebec) like *un bon père de famille* (that is, responsibly)? He was not expected to prevent injury to every lad in Montreal who dashed before a streetcar,[11] not expected to pay damages to every drunken farmer who tumbled from his wagonette at night when it hit a bump in the road,[12] not expected to keep every road as smooth as if it were a high-grade macadamized one, especially with the rainfall one was likely to see in New Plymouth or Taranaki on the west coast of New Zealand's North Island.[13]

But some "accidents" were not *absque injuria*. Those riding horses or vehicles on "the king's highway" were to respect the rights of pedestrians, and were held liable when they did not. A "poor old woman living in some obscure part of Sydney" was run down in George Street by a man who was demonstrating the liveliness of a horse he was trying to sell in 1831. She sued him, and Justice Dowling told the trial jury that such conduct was "highly improper in a populous town like this, and more especially, in the most populous street. . . ."[14] Similarly, some two generations later, Western Australia's Chief Justice Parker observed from his "experience of riding a bicycle about Perth, and seeing many cyclists ride," that cyclists often thought they were entitled "to merely ring a bell, and people in front" were "bound to get out of the way." The Chief Justice felt it was "quite time they were disabused of that idea."[15]

Nor was the carelessness of the plaintiff, often a contributing element to the accident, a necessary bar to his recovery of damages if that carelessness was slight and the defendant's carelessness was the "proximate cause." As Upper Canada's Chief Justice of Queen's Bench, Sir John Beverley Robinson, put it:

The principle that the accident must have happened from no fault of the plaintiff, cannot, in our opinion, be carried so far.[16]

---

11 As in *Montreal City Pass. Ry. Co. v. Bignon*, 18 Quebec 217 (1866).
12 As in *Mayor of Melbourne v. Brennan*, 8 Vict. LR (L) 113 (1882).
13 As in *Tarry v. Taranaki City Council*, 12 NZLR (CA) 467 (1893).
14 *The Australian*, July 22, 1831; *Howell v. Payne* (NSWSC, Kercher, 1831).
15 *Law v. Neil*, 8 WALR 50 (1906).
16 *Ridley v. Lamb*, 10 UCQB 354 at 356 (1853), in a case virtually four-square with the famous donkey case of "last clear chance," *Davies v. Mann*, 10 M. & W. 542 (1842). See also *Shannahan v. Ryan*, 20 Nova Sc. 142 (1887). But see *Devlin v. Bain*, 11 UCCP 523 (1862) (sleigh overtaking another; new trial ordered because of plaintiff's contributory negligence); *McWillie v. Goudron*, 30 Low. Can. J. 44 (1885) (defendant not resp. for bolting of plaintiff's horse due to jingling of sleigh overloaded with iron).

In coming to these conclusions CANZ jurists were applying established Common-Law rules. Those sitting in Quebec, to be sure, often drew upon French treatises or, after 1866, on the language of their own Civil Code, both of which differed from the English Common Law at times.[17] But while I find these differences between Quebec's and the other provincial courts most interesting, and will point them out whenever appropriate, these are not what we are primarily concerned with in this chapter. Rather it is the differences between jurists in the other Canadian provinces and the Antipodes, on the one hand, and those in England, on the other, with regard to negligence that constitute the primary foci of this chapter. Of secondary interest is the extent to which these Diaspora-land jurists made use of those moments when courts in the United States took issue with or rejected England rules and precedents.[18] We begin with accidents due to defective roads or

---

[17] See, for example, *Martineau v. Beliveau*, 15 LCJ 59 (1870) (hostler responsible under Code for injury caused by renter of horse when renter unavailable); *Vital v. Tétreault*, 33 LCJ 20 (1888) (no distinction in Code between savage or tame animals; if animals cause injury, owner liable, unlike English common law rule); *Murphy v. Labbé*, 27 Can. SC 126 (1897) (*bon pere de famille*). And see the historical sections of John Brierley and Roderick Macdonald, *Quebec Civil Law* (Toronto, 1993); and Louis Baudoin, "Delicts under the Quebec Civil Code," in *Canadian Jurisprudence*, ed. Edw. McWhinney (Toronto, 1958).

[18] There were a number of cases involving charges of medical malpractice in the United States and CANZ reports worth noting. The English rule, that a judge should instruct the jury to find a physician not guilty of medical malpractice if he had exercised a "fair, reasonable, and competent degree of skill" was clearly in evidence in the colonies and provinces, as was the rule of the Massachusetts Supreme Judicial Court that doctors and surgeons engaged in "country practice" were not to be held to the same standards as those in cities. The rule in some American jurisdictions that a plaintiff was not obliged to undergo a medical examination by a physician employed by the defendant was not followed in the one instance I detected where this issue had been addressed. But my evidence of medical malpractice claims heard on appeal in these years is modest: an "N" of only 14. Few useful conclusions can be drawn from this small a population. *Lanphier v. Philpos*, 8 C. & P. 475 at 479, 173 ER 581 (N.P. 1838). See also *Hancke v. Hooper*, 7 Car. & P. 82, 173 ER 37 (N.P. 1835). See, for example, *Storey v. Veach*; *Anderson v. Walker*, and *Thackeray v. Askin*, all reported in 22 UCCP 164 (1872); *Fields v. Rutherford*, 29 UCCP 113 (1878); *McQuay v. Eastwood*, 12 Ont. R. 402 (1886); *van Merev. Farewell*, 12 Ont. R. 285 (1886); *Zirkler v. Robertson*, 30 Nova Sc. 61 (1897); *James v. Crockett*, 34 New Br. 540 (1898). *Small v. Howard*, 128 Mass. 131 (1880); *Zirkler v. Robertson*, 30 Nova Sc. 61 at 70 (1879). *Filion v. Dawes*, 12 Quebec C.S. 494 (1897). For the American cases see Karsten, *Heart versus Head*, 264–66, 448–49. It may be worth noting, however, that the defendant-physicians won eight of the fourteen appeals

bridges, those occurring at road or rail crossings, those experienced by coach, streetcar, steamboat or railway passengers, and those of workers on the job.

Accidents due to Road and Bridge Defects: How Much Sovereign Immunity?

When the accident was said to have been caused by the negligence of the Crown or municipal commissioners of railways, roads, police, schools, fire departments, or hospitals, and the matter was adjudicated, these commissioners often pleaded a degree of immunity from liability based on their public ("sovereign") or charitable corporate character. In mid-nineteenth century England, and in a number of American states in midcentury as well, such bodies enjoyed substantial protection from virtually all claims except those charging willful misconduct or the grossest of negligence (malfeasance) – that is, unless a statute had been passed sanctioning suits for ordinary negligence.[19] The Crown was consequently not subject to negligence suits alleged against one or another of its creatures, such as the Prince Edward Island Railway, for which there existed no such enabling statute, and parties injured by the negligent acts of employees on this and other Crown corporate entities were denied their petitions of right in Exquecher and invited by the courts to make a formal request for *ex gratia* arbitrators.[20]

Municipal corporations, and sometimes charitable corporations as well, did not enjoy that sort of blanket immunity; they had to defend themselves with evidence that the accident was not due to any negligence on their part. Some legislatures passed "claims against the government" acts that sanctioned certain types of suits against municipalities and public works managed by the Crown.[21]

outright and secured *remitturs* (reductions in the awards) in two of the other six. Plaintiffs won outright in *Fawcett v. Mothersell*, 14 UCCP 104 (1864); *Kelly v. Dow*, 9 New Br. 435 (1860); *Sheridan v. Pigeon*, 10 Ont. R. 632 (1885); and *Stretton v. Holmes*, 19 Ont. R. 286 (1890). The *remitturs* were ordered in *Key v. Thompson*, 12 New Br. 295 (1868); and *Jeanotte v. Couillard*, 3 QQB 461 (1894).

19 For examples of sovereign immunity involving Crown officials sued while performing their duties negligently, see *Lane v. Cotton*, 1 Ld. Raym. 646 (1701) and *Whitfield v. Le Despencer*, 2 Cowp. 754 (1778).

20 *Queen v. McLeod*, 8 Can. Sup. Ct. 1 (1883); and *Queen v. McFarlane*, 7 Can. Sup. Ct. 216 (1883) (Chief Justice Ritchie and Justice Strong citing American cases and treatises in support of the immunity argument).

21 *Guimond v. Corp. of Montreal*, 24 Rap. Jud. Rev. Quebec (M.) 375 (1872) (runaway fire dept. horse); *Hesketh v. City of Toronto*, 25 Ont. C. of A. 449 (1898) (runaway fire engine team); *Peterkin v. School Trustees of St-Henry*,

In holding that municipalities had to defend themselves against *prima facie* cases, jurists in New Brunswick and Quebec explicitly preferred the general rule prevailing in the States that corporations were bound by the acts of their agents and servants – both those acts that were under formal corporate seal as well as those that were not – rather than the older English rule, adopted elsewhere.[22] Deciding that a cabman who had been arrested and beaten by Montreal police without due cause was entitled to sue the city, "notwithstanding anything in our Civil Code," Justice Mackay relied on American citations and added:

> We may live to see the American rule on this point adopted in England.... Cases of great hardship continue ... to occur there, through the enforcement of the old, Common-Law, rule. Corporations have been allowed in some cases to enrich themselves in the most unjust manner, because of the want of a Seal, at the expense of persons who have been led to deal with them.[23]

7 Q.C.S. 117 (1895); *Breux v. City of Montreal*, 9 Q.C.S. 503 (1896) (city hospital liable for scarlet fever infection of child living next to hospital); *Doolan v. Corp. of Montreal*, 12 LCJ 71 (1868); *Corp. of Montreal v. Doolan*, 18 LCJ 124 (1871), also in 19 Q 125 (1871) (carter wrongfully struck by police); *Donaldson v. Comms. of Gen. Pub. Hosp. in St. John*, 30 New Br. 279 (1891) (patient can sue hospital).

As a member of Queensland's legislature, the future chief justice of that colony, Lilley, took the view in 1865 that the government's sovereign immunity "has no foundation in public justice or convenience, and there ought to be a remedy at once." He and his colleagues passed such an act the next year. New South Wales followed suit in 1876. The Divisional Boards Act that became law in Queensland in 1879 specified that the duties of these boards "shall be" to "contruct and maintain" all roads and bridges. Hence, a woman awarded damages for injuries incurred on a defective bridge in Bundanba won an appeal to the colony's Supreme Court in 1883. See Paul Finn, *Law and Government in Colonial Australia* (1987), 71, 141; *Bundanba Divis. Bd. v. Ballin & Another*, 1 Queens. LJ 175 (1883).

[22] Among the more oft cited English precedents were *Hall v. Smith*, 2 Bing. 156, 267, 130 ER 265, 308 (1824); *Harris v. Baker*, 4 M. & S. 26, 105 ER 745 (1815); *Duncan v. Findlater*, 6 Cl. & F. 894, 7 ER 934 (H. L. 1839); and *Holliday v. St. Leonard*, 11 C.B.N.S. 192 (1861).

[23] *Doolan v. Corp. of Montreal*, 13 LCJ 71 at 73 (1868).

Mackay *could* have relied on the decision of the Law Lords in 1866 that rejected *Duncan v. Finlater* and allowed suits against corporate authorities for negligence that had led to injury or loss. See *Mercey Docks Trustees v. Gibbs*, LR, 1 HL 93 (1866). But these were years in which Quebec's jurists were "polyjuristic" (to use David Howes' apt term), drawing freely from a well of English, European and U.S. jurisprudence. See Howes, "From Polyjurality to Monojurality: The Transformation of Quebec Law, 1875–1929," 32 *McGill Law Journal* 523 (1987).

Montreal's city council appealed and both Chief Justice Duval and
Justice Badgley agreed that the city was not to be held liable for acts of
its police employees (citing a decision of the Massachusetts Supreme
Judicial Court, *Buttrick v. Lowell*), and insisted that the rule in that case
"be fully adopted here." But they spoke in dissent. Justices Drummond
and Carson led the majority of the Court of Appeals in relying on
their understanding of the French rule in such cases; they affirmed
the award to Mr. Doolan. Justice Drummond dismissed the dissenters'
Massachusetts citations: "In the opinion of eminent jurists," as well
as his own, "there had been more unjust opinions pronounced by
judges in the United States in favour of corporations than in any other
country." Justice Carson added that "equity also strongly sustained the
claim of the plaintiff."[24]

Similarly, in New Brunswick, Justice Fraser and his colleagues rejected the English and Massachusetts citations of the St. John Public
Hospital and his dissenting colleague, Justice Tuck, to hold that a patient was to be permitted to sue a charitable corporation, adopting the
opinion of the Rhode Island Supreme Court (in *Glavin v. R.I. Hospital*,
12 R.I. 411 (1879)), that injured plaintiffs could not go after the *assets*
of charitable hospitals, but could seek damages to be paid out of the
fees the hospital received.[25]

This lack of a sort of blanket immunity did not mean that CANZ
jurists were incapable of decisions that served to protect municipalities
(which is to say, municipal taxpayers) from a substantial number of
the most common sort of negligence suits, those involving defective
roads and bridges. But it may have served to "let the plaintiff in" in
many more of those cases than would otherwise have been the case.
Injured plaintiffs actually won 118 of the 175 appeals from lower court
decisions that appear on this issue in the published reports (or some
67 percent of them). Why? To answer this we must first ask what the
circumstances were that gave rise to the suits.

Most roads in colonial Canada, Australia, and New Zealand were
of the simplest sort, carved through woods and meadows with neither planks, nor hardwood blocks and tar, nor "macadamizing" materials (bits of crushed stone packed together firmly, often called a
"metalled" road). Edward Curr recalled that some fourteen years after Melbourne's settlement, "no attempt" had "yet been made to pave
or macadamize" its roadways, and that "very little" had been done

---

24 *Corp. of Montreal v. Doolan*, 18 LCJ 124 at 126, 127, 128 (1871); also in 19 Q
    125 at 128–9, 131, 133 (1871). (Drummond may have seen the decisions
    of the Massachusetts Supreme Judicial Court in this light.)
25 *Donaldson v. Comms. of Gen. Pub. Hosp. in St. John*, 30 New Br. 279 at 287,
    298–99 (1891).

"to separate the footpath from the roadway whilst, in the absence of drains, chasms, ... some eight feet deep and twenty feet wide, had been excavated by the rain." In 1871, Englishman Anthony Trollope found the roads in Australia to be "generally quite unlike our roads at home" in that "the constructed part of the road, that on which the vehicles absolutely travel, is narrower than with us." Moreover, "where distances are very great, the traveller soon loses all signs of a real road. ... Nothing has been done towards making these roads except the cutting away of a few trees and the placing of some small bridges over the gullies." As late as the 1890s, there were only some fifty miles of roads in New South Wales, all of them in Sydney, that were either macadamized or block and tar.[26]

Country roads in Canada were quite passable and slick in the winter when packed snow and icy tracks made for smooth sleighpaths, and farmers made good use of them in these months to deliver their less perishable commodities to market towns.[27] But at other times of the year these roads could be quite hazardous. Visitors as well as residents of Ontario, New Zealand, and Victoria alike complained of mud that "was often up to the hub of the forewheels" of stagecoaches. "You have half a mile at a time of boulders from 1/4 ft. to 3 ft. in diameter to go over," wrote E. R. Chudleigh in New Zealand in 1864, "innumerable gullies with soft bottoms. ... They are to be driven over and that is all." Jurists themselves, riding circuit, "spent [years] in coaches running over the roughest roads, in deep mire. ..."[28]

Not surprisingly, there were many breakdowns and accidents. Chudleigh's carriage in New Zealand, for example, went "over just one stone too many. The bolts that hold the springs to the axle went, and in one moment everything forward went, with a twing-twang buzz. It was only one of the regular smashes we often get." In Melbourne in the 1850s, two barristers, James Croke and C. H. Ebden, riding in a

---

[26] Michael Cannon, *Life in the Cities: Australia in the Victorian Age* (Melbourne, 1975), 50; E. Curr, *Recollections of Squatting in Victoria* (1883), 6; Trollope, *Australia and New Zealand* (London, 1873), II, 47–48.

[27] Thomas McIlwraith, "The Adequacy of Rural Roads in the Era before Railroads: An Illustration from Upper Canada," 14 *Canadian Geographer* 344 (1870), 356–57.

[28] J. S. MacDonald Diary, 1837, describing "my long tramp [from Windsor] to London ... a rough passage in the Stage ... passing the worst roads in the country," MSS MacDonald Papers, MU 1769, Archives of Ontario; *Diary of E. R. Chudleigh, 1862–1921*, ed. E. C. Richards (Christchurch, 1950), 122, 237: near Ashbarton and Rangitata Rivers, Feb. 20, 1864 (for "innumerable gulleys"); At Mercer, Aug. 26 1875, enroute Hamilton, North Island, by "Cobb & Co. Coach" (for mud up to forewheels); Justice "Wilson Gray," 2 *Colonial Law Journal*, 13 (Nov. 1875) (for ten years of coaches in deep mire).

buggy on Elizabeth Street, "ran into a rut or gutter then opposite the Post Office and the Glasgow Arms. Poor Croke was thrown in the gutter, and when he arose was a most sorry spectacle...." Back across the Tasman Sea, in April, 1879, Justice Henry Chapman of New Zealand's Court of Appeals was "thrown out violently on his hands, spraining both wrists and suffering dreadful pain," when his carriage "came to grief." And in many instances these accidents took place many miles from a local physician, let alone a hospital. Hence a bone broken in a fall from a coach or wagon could lead to the amputation of a limb or even to death.[29] (See Illustrations 23 and 24.)

Some of these mishaps appear to have been caused by the negligence of the drivers. That was young Bertha Harnden's opinion in Ontario in 1871. She told her diary of a "runaway" incident involving "Norman Hall and Miss Hoar [;] they weren't hurt [;] they must have been carelessly driving to get tip[p]ed out on a good road." Surely they were not *both* in control of the buggy, *both* holding the reins. None the less, the English Common Law held, virtually, that they had. If Norman was driving, Miss Hoar would have been viewed as being contributorily negligent for failing to cause him to drive with greater care, or for failing to insist that he stop and let her get off when he failed to do so; vice versa, had she been the driver.[30] That was what Abraham Luckenbach did. He and his wife noticed that the driver of the Brantford-New Fairfield coach they were riding in was drunk, and that darkness had fallen. They signaled for him to stop, got off, and began walking the rest of the way. Soon they came upon "our traveling companions, ... greatly shaken up, ... all having been thrown from the

---

[29] *Chudleigh Diary*, 122, for February 20, 1864; John L. Forde, *The Story of the Bar in Victoria* (Melbourne, 1913), 107–08; Peter Spiller, "Two Judges: Father and Son: Henry and Fredrick Chapman," Canterbury Law JD, 1991, 178; Peter Taylor, *Station Life in Australia: Pioneers and Pastoralists* (Sydney, 1988), 158–63.

[30] As in *Rigby v. Hewitt*, 5 Ex. 240, 155 ER 103 (Ex. 1850).

←

Illustrations 23 and 24. Roads throughout the lands of the Diaspora were terrible long after the invention of Robert McAdam's method of compacting bits of stone to create a durable surface (the "metaled" or "macadamized" roadbed). The coach on the road around the Rocks, Tolaga Bay, Gisborne, New Zealand did not enjoy such a roadbed (top); the carriage on the macadamized road somewhere on the West Coast, South Island, New Zealand, in the late nineteenth century did. (Alexander Turnbull Library, National Library of New Zealand, Post and Telegraph Collection, F19602 1/4/ Te Puna Mātauranga o Aotearoa, F-196281/4; G-705961/2.)

open wagon, one breaking his shoulder-blade and another being unconscious. . . ."[31] The stage had struck a stump at the edge of the road. The driver was clearly at fault, at least in part. But what of the passengers that had continued to travel under his direction, after the Luckenbachs had the sense to disembark? Should the driver's negligence have been imputed to them? And what about the road authority that had not removed the stump from the vicinity of the roadpath?

Counties and municipal road authorities, and even toll-charging road corporations might be able to defend themselves against the claims of the Norman Halls or Miss Hoars of the British provinces: Plaintiffs like these could be nonsuited upon the admission of evidence of their having contributed to the accident through their own negligence.[32] They could have found it harder to do so against the

[31] Bertha Harnden Diary, 10 June, 1871, MU 3062, Archives of Ontario; F. C. Hamil, *The Valley of the Lower Thames, 1640 to 1850* (Toronto, 1951), 169; Cf. *Berthiaume v. McCone*, 5 Q 492 at 498 (1894).

[32] As in *Charbonneau v. Corp of St. Martin*, 16 Low. Can. R 143 (1865); *Ward v. City of Halifax*, 9 Nov. Sc. 264 (1873); *Hutton v. Corp of Windsor*, 34 Up. Can. QB 487 (1874) (citing U. S. cases on both sides); *Hynes v. Pres. of Shire of Broadford*, 9 Vict. LR (L) 346 (1883); *Carston v. Munic. Council*, 7 Newf. 509 (1891); *Harrington v. Well. Harbour Bd.*, 14 NZLR (SC) 347 (1895); *Keachie v. City of Toronto*, 22 Ont. C. of A. 371 (1895); *Davignon v. Corp. of Stanbridge Station*, 14 Quebec C.C. 116 (1898) (Justice Lynch: To hold the corporation liable for the broken leg of one who had been drinking whiskey and had been thrown from his cart when it struck an intruding rock "would be simply offering a reward and encouragement to imprudence." Justice Lynch also quoted "The Sacred Writings (14 Prov. 15) . . . 'The prudent man looketh well to his going.'" And see *Gilmor v. City of St. John*, 28 New Br. 325 (1889)).

In *Gilmor* Justice Fraser noted (350) that "the American decisions" (he cited those of New York and Massachusetts, not realizing, perhaps, that this was *not* so of the majority of other states) place the burden of proof on the plaintiff to prove that she was not contributorily negligent, "and not, as with us," on the defendant. But what was just as important was the fact that in most American states the judge was not free to nonsuit plaintiffs for contributory negligence; the question was entirely one of fact for the jury, while in Justice Fraser's world the judge had the final say on the matter, as in *Gilmor*. And see the exchange in 33 *Canadian Law Journal* 57–63 (1897) between E. F. B. Johnston QC, who felt the question of negligence was one for the jury, and John MacGregor, Esq, who cited English cases to establish that the judge was to decide whether the evidence was sufficient to establish the negligence or the plaintiff was rather to be nonsuited. (But see the judiciary's sense that there were limits that judges ought to use in this prerogative in *Maw v. Township of King & Albion*, 8 Ont. C. of A. 248 (1883), citing English cases).

Sometimes this could benefit a plaintiff, as in *King v. Munic. of Kings*, 19 Nova Sc. 68 (1886), where a jury finding of plaintiff contributory

complaints of more "responsible" or "reasonable" drivers who "came to grief" because of the inadequacy of the maintenance of roads and bridges under the control of these legal entities. Once such a legal authority had actual or constructive ("ought to have known") knowledge of a defect that it was their duty to repair, their legal liability rose to a height as perilous as were the depths of some of the holes, gullies, and ruts in their roads.[33] This is why Alexander Campbell of Ottawa would write to the managers of the Bytown & Nepean Road Company, (he was a shareholder) in November, 1872, of the "hugh boulders and logs... along the line of road... here and there,... any one of which might cause serious accidents for which of course the co. will be responsible...." And it is why the owners of the Kew-to-Melbourne

negligence was set aside on review and a new trial ordered, in *Concher v. Corp. of Newcastle*, 8NSWSCR 309 (1869), where the heir of a drunken man who fell over an unlighted sustaining wall at night to his death recovered damages when the jurists in Sydney decided that he had not been contributorily negligent(!), or in *Hitchins v. Mayor of Pt. Melbourne*, 10 A-Law Times 277 (1889), where the trial judge inspected the scene of the accident and ruled on the contributory negligence question in the plaintiff's favor. But I have the distinct impression that while the rule generally helped defendants, juries tended to favor plaintiffs. (They certainly did in nineteenth century American courts: See Karsten, *Heart versus Head*, pp. 99–100). Thus, I regard the decision of New Zealand's Chief Justice Sir Robert Stout in *White v. Hampton*, 6 Gaz. LR 39 (1903), to be pathbreaking for that Dominion: Citing Justice John Forrest Dillon's famous opinion in the "attractive nuisance" leading case, *RR v. Stout*, 84 U.S. 657 (1873), the Chief Justice held that questions of negligence and contributory negligence were to be left to juries.

Lower Canada/Quebec's courts appeared to deal with contributory negligence differently: Here there were no juries in negligence cases and yet township claims of plaintiff contributory negligence rarely succeeded. See *Higgins v. Corp. of Richmond*, 17 Low. Can. J. 246 at 248 (1872), ("where there is contribution by the plaintiff to the accident, and the contribution is very small, plaintiff is not to lose his damages.)" Justice Sicotte cited Seymour Thompson's negligence treatise in *Biggins v. City of Montreal*, 29 Low. Can. J. 26 (1884) to turn away this city's contributory negligence claim. In *McDonald v. City of Montreal*, 8 Quebec C.S. 160 (1895), the court allowed that there had been some plaintiff contributory negligence, but it then applied the Code's *comparative* negligence standards and awarded $300 to the parents of a boy who had fallen on an icy sidewalk and broken a leg. *Davignon v. Corp. of Stanbridge Station*, 14 Quebec C.S. 116 (1898), is the exception.

[33] As in *Levy v. Mayor of Portland*, 3 Vict. LR (L) 226 (1877) (surveyor told of hole at edge of road); *Pascoe v. Inhabs. of Pt. Levy Rd. Dist.*, 4 NZLR (SC) 150 (1885) (ratepayers aware of hole in road). But see *McGregor v. Municip. of Harwick*, 29 Can. S.C. 443 (1899) (town not liable; no notice of danger. Province's "roadmaster" was making repairs and his men had left a pile of sand in road.)

stagecoach service offered the "badness of the road" in court in 1882 as a potential defense for the fact that a wheel had come off of one of their stagecoaches.[34]

But what defects *did* road authorities have duties to repair? Often the question could be resolved with reference to the appropriate language in the colony's or province's Road or Bridge Act, County Incorporation Act, or municipal charter. If a tollroad's board of directors had not yet taken over the responsibility to maintain a bridge built by the provincial authorities (as were the earliest bridges), and was charging no toll for its use, it would not be held liable to one injured (as in New Zealand in 1877) because of a defect in the bridge. Similarly, if a rider's horse bolted from the road (as one did in New Zealand in 1881, frightened by an object left there), and the lack of a railing sent horse and rider plunging to their deaths, the Wairarapa North Council was not to be held liable for its failure to provide a railing (nonfeasance), though it would have been had it done so, and the railing had been defective (malfeasance). And if a statute or municipal by-law made the clearance of ice and snow off of sidewalks the duty of those occupying the properties fronting the sidewalk, one injured by a fall on an icy sidewalk (as in Toronto in 1872) could well find himself turned away, even though the city had built the sidewalk.[35] But whenever the relevant statute imposed a duty on a municipality to maintain passable roads, and a traveller was injured when his horse slipped in an exposed street drain (in Brisbane's "Fortitude Valley"), jurists would reverse a jury verdict for the city and order a new trial for the plaintiff (as did Queesland's Supreme Court in 1893).[36]

---

[34] Nancy Bouchier, "A Broad Clear Track in Good Order: The Bytown & Nepean Road Co., Richard Toll Rd., Ottawa, 1851–75," 76 *Ontario History* 103 at 116 (1984); *Smith v. Robertson & Another, Anderson v. Same*, 8 Vict. LR (L) 256 (1882). The plaintiffs in this suit against the Kew-to-Melbourne stagecoach company had, however, offered a powerful alternative explanation for the accident: The company had overloaded the coach with no less than forty passengers.

For an example of a successful suit against a tollroad for the injury of one thrown from his wagon where the tollroad crossed a "macadamized road" and the crossing was defective, see *Bradley v. Brown & Street*, 32 UCQB 463 (1872).

[35] *Heathcote Rd. Bd. v. Manson*, 4 JR (NZSC) 112 (1878); *Wairarapa N. C. Council v. Spackman*, 10 NZLR (SC) 569 (1892); *Ringland v. Corp. of Toronto*, 23 UCCP 93 (1873). See also *Wakely v. Lockey*, 1 NSWR(L) 274 (1880) (no action allowed for nonfeasance in allowing bridge to remain unrepaired); *City of St. John v. Campbell*, 26 Can. S. C. 1 (1895) (in absence of New Brunswick statute creating liability, city not liable for injury caused by raised sidewalk or one out of repair, following *Municip. of Pictou v. Geldert* A.C. 524 (1893)).

[36] *Martin v. Municip. of Brisbane*, 5 Queens. LJ 3 (1893) (Justice Chubb: "Here was a corporation performing a statutory duty imposed upon them by

Straightforward statutory language posed no major problems. But road and bridge statutes sometimes contained ambiguous phrases or language of a broad and general nature, requiring jurists to decide exactly what was meant when a municipality "accepted" from the province the "authority" over a road or bridge, and sometimes they relied on English Common Law for guidance and direction. The English Common-Law rules on these matters had been undergoing some changes themselves. In the early eighteenth century, the rule had been that towns were expected to maintain roads as they had been, but had no duties to improve them to put them "in better condition" than they had been "time out of mind." Towns could leave roads as muddy and narrow as they had always been.[37] But that was the view in the early eighteenth century. By the 1840s, this standard would no longer do. Justice Patteson of Queen's Bench told a Suffolk assizes jury in 1846 that a "much used" road demanded "proportionately more" attention and that it was "not enough to say that it was as good as ever it was, or as it usually has been." Since it was "a public road, and the necessity of the public required it," the inhabitants could well be "bound to convert it from a green road into a hard one."[38]

His colleagues appeared to uphold his view on appeal. After all, they rode these roads on Nisi Prius assize duty as well. As Lord Chief Justice Denman put it, "it would be a very strange question to ask a jury, whether [a road] was precisely as bad as ever, and no worse." By the 1850s, the Common-Law standard for road maintenance was to ask whether the road was "in such repair so as to be reasonably passable for the ordinary traffic of the neighborhood at all seasons of the year."[39] That left to courts the question of what *was* a "reasonably passable" road, bridge, or sidewalk.

law...."). See also *Toms et ux. v. Town of Whitby*, 37 UCQB 100 (1875), where the court quoted from the relevant statute imposing liability on towns for failure to provide safe roads, and held a town liable for failing to provide a railing next to an embankment; and *Sherwood v. Corp. of Hamilton*, 37 UCQB 410 (1875), for a similar holding regarding a town's failure to fence a precipice.

[37] *R. v. Cloworth Inhabs.*, 1 Salk. 359, 91 ER 313 (1704); *R. v. Stretford Inhabs.*, 2 Ld. Raym. 1169, 92 ER 273 (1705).

This is only to say that towns were not liable for damages to one injured on a road that had not been maintained; it did not mean that the *Crown* was unable to deal with those responsible for road maintenance when they failed to do as they were expected to. Cynthia Herrup reports that some 36 percent of all East Sussex grand jury presentments in the 1620s and 1630s were for failures to maintain roads and bridges. (*The Common Peace: Participants and the Criminal Law in 17th Century England*, 1987, 115.)

[38] *R. v. Henley Inhabs.*, 2 Cox C.C. 334, ER (1847).

[39] *R. v. High Halden Inhabs.*, 1 F & F 677, 175 ER 903 (Nisi Prius, 1859).

But, alas, this municipal duty was a public one; all of the jurists I have just been quoting were deciding cases that had been initiated by Crown authorities. While it might be possible for the Crown to insist that municipal ratepayers in England transform certain "much used," "green" roads into "hard" ones, that still did not mean that private individuals injured on such roads or bridges were entitled under the Common Law to sue the ratepayers for their failure to patch holes, replace rotten planks, or repair weakened railings. Throughout most of the nineteenth century English jurists held that individual plaintiffs had *no* rights to sue either turnpike or municipal authorities for their "neglect to perform a public duty" unless a statute sanctioned such suits.[40] As Lord Justice James put it in 1879, "it appears to me the country would be buying its immunity from nuisances at a very dear rate, indeed, by the substitution of a far more formidable nuisance in the litigation and expense that would be occasioned by opening such a door to litigious persons...."[41]

This had been the rule in New England as well, but beginning in 1843, the other American state supreme courts, following the lead of their colleagues in Pennsylvania, New York, and Illinois, found that

[40] *Russell v. Men of Devon*, 2 Term R 667, 100 ER 359 (K. B., 1788).

[41] *Glossop v. Isleworth Local Board*, 40 *Law Times* (N.S.) 736, 12 Ch. D. 102 (1879). See also *Harris v. Baker*, 4 MUS 27, 105 ER 745 (K. B. 1815); *Duncan v. Findlater*, 6 U. & F. 894, 7 ER 934 (H.L. 1839) (turnpike statute authorized payments for management, interest on the debt and repairs, but not tort damages). Nor had rate payers the right to secure a writ of mandamus to compel municipal councils to repair a bridge; only the Crown's attorney-general could seek such a writ. See *Stowell & Others v. Geraldine City Council*, 8 NZLR (SC) 720 (1890).

Furthermore, if the negligent act that led to the accident had been that of an individual, road-bordering property owner, or an employee of a contractor working for the city or road authority, English law held the property owner or contractor (often virtually judgement proof), not the city, to be liable. *Overton v. Freeman*, 11 CB 867, 138 ER 717 (C.P. 1852).

Thus, in 1861, the Nova Scotia Supreme Court held the City of Halifax and its officials free of liability to one injured when his carriage struck an excavation mound left in the street by a property owner who was remodeling his house. This individual had sought the permission of the city's Superintendent of Streets, and had been allowed to leave the mound there temporarily, but warned to remove it by sunset. The accident occurred at sunset. Was the city liable because the superintendent had failed to have a subordinate check to see whether his terms had been complied with? Nova Scotia jurists were confident that only the property owner, and not the city, might be deemed liable. Citing English precedents, Justice Edmund Dodd noted that, "if the city [ratepayers] are liable... for the injury... then it is difficult to say where their liability is to end," and few would be willing to serve as city officials. *Evens v. City of Halifax*, 5 Nov. Sc. 111 at 118 (1861).

the mere statutory creation of a road authority with a source of funds "to pay all lawful debts" was sufficient to hold that authority liable in the event that its failure to repair defects in timely fashion led to injuries.[42]

CANZ jurists were aware of this trend in America; but they did not regard themselves to be capable of such an abandoning of the sovereign immunity tradition. Thus, in 1880, New South Wales' Justice Faucett held that a man injured when he and his cart plunged into Cooke's River due to the sad state of disrepair of the Undercliff Bridge was *damnum absque injuria* because the local authority had no duty to repair the bridge, despite the passage of a bill providing funds for such a purpose. To hold otherwise, he explained, would be to sanction suits by shippers annoyed when a harbor authority failed to spend appropriated funds to deepen a harbor in a timely fashion. The government had prerogatival rights of sovereign immunity. (And in any event, using a bridge in disrepair constituted contributory negligence.)[43] Similarly, in 1892, Chief Justice Predergast of New Zealand's Court of Appeals took note that American courts had held that road enabling statutes "expressly or impliedly prescribed" tort liability, but added that there was "no . . . provision of that sort in New Zealand." All that could be found in the relevant statute there was "that the roads are placed under the care and management of the local authorities." The rule in New Zealand was thus to be the same as that in England – that is, these authorities were not subject to suit without such statutory authority for a neglect to repair defects (nonfeasance) unless they had attempted such repairs and done them badly (misfeasance).[44] This rule "seems very hard on the individual," Chief Justice Stawell of Victoria's Supreme Court allowed in 1870, but, he added that "if we held that the plaintiff could maintain this action" against the Malmsbury municipal authorities for injuries due to a hole in the road, "we should be in effect directing the municipality how to mend its ways." Stawell surely paused to savor that double entendre; he continued with the observation that if the municipal authorities "allowed it to get worse, to become out of repair, and to be dangerous to pass," that was a matter for their consideration. "We do not think that the words

---

[42] See *Dean v. New Milford Township*, 5 W. & M. (Pa.) 545 (1843); *Weet v. Brockport*, 16 NY 161n (1853); *Browning v. City of Springfield*, 17 Ill. 143 (1855) (Lincoln & Herndon for plaintiff); Karsten, *Heart versus Head*, 267–69.

[43] *Wakely v. Lackey*, NSWR(L) 274 at 283 (1880).

[44] *Wairarapa N. C. Council v. Spackman*, 10 NZLR (SC) 569 at 576 (1892); *Caldwell v. Warren*, Ch., Bd. of Works, 5 Newf. 176 (1867); *Municipality of Pictou v. Geldert*, A. C. 524 (1893); *Gordon v. City of Victoria*, 5 Br. Col. 553 (1897).

of the [Municipal Corporations] Act render it obligatory on them to repair it" even after having been notified of its hazardous nature.[45]

If a municipality repaired a road defect and did it imperfectly, the Common-Law rule was that it could be held liable for an accident.[46] But the Law also held that a municipality would *not* be liable if it simply chose not to "mend its ways." This rule could produce results as strange as those in "wrongful death" actions (where a tortfeasor was better off if his negligent act killed the victim than if it simply injured him).

Example one: When immigration to Quebec's southeastern counties began to rise in the mid-nineteenth century, those living on one of the main routes south from Quebec City, the Gosford Road, refused to attend meetings of its council in order to avoid a quorum. Why? The provincial government wanted them to contribute to the costs of maintenance, repairs, and the upgrading of the road. Nonattendance was the way to avoid action, and thus to avoid liability. As the Crown's land agent, Jean-Olivier Arcand, put it, "everyone seems to be in a conspiracy to destroy the bridges and ditches."[47]

Example two: The Point Ellice Bridge in Victoria, British Columbia, was repaired in the mid-1890s. In May of 1896, a streetcar passing over it broke through several poorly secured beams, plunging eighty persons to their deaths. One jury found the failure of the original hinges and fasteners to have caused the accident. As such, on appeal, the British Columbia Supreme Court ordered a nonsuit and retrial, because the failure to replace those hinges and fasteners was mere nonfeasance. So a second jury held that it was the inadequacy of certain repairs that had just been completed that had been the immediate cause of the accident (thus misfeasance). In reviewing this verdict, the Supreme Court held that, since the City of Victoria Corporation had assumed the responsibility for the bridge and had (belatedly) responded to complaints about its adequacy and safety with repair work that proved to be imperfect, it was now liable.[48] Same bridge, same accident, different outcomes; but the same Common Law.

45 *Ryan v. Mayor of Malmsbury,* 1 Vict. Rep. (L) 23 at 24 (1870), and see *Clarkbarry v. Mayor, etc. of S. Melbourne,* 21 VLR 426 (1895) (Local Govt. Act said municipal authorities "may" improve roads; hence they're not responsible for injury due to hole in street, overruling *Scott v. Mayor of Collingwood,* 7 VLR(L) 280 (1891)). But see *Levy v. Mayor of Portland,* 3 Vict. LR (L) 226 (1877) (£55 awarded to one injured by hole in road affirmed).
46 *Scott v. Mayor, etc. of Manchester,* 1 H. & N. 59, 156 ER 1117 (Ex. 1856).
47 J. I. Little, *Nationalism, Capitalism, and Colonization in 19th Century Quebec: The Upper St. Francis District* (Kingston, 1989), 90 (translation mine).
48 *Gordon v. City of Victoria,* 5 Br. Col. 553 (1897); *Patterson v. City of Victoria,* 5 Br. Col. 628 (1897).

Nova Scotia's jurists tried to break from this Common-Law rule and follow a path they saw in the "several American cases" referred to by the trial-court judge. The plaintiff had been injured because of an unattended hole in a bridge. The court's majority read the province's County Incorporation Act of 1879 and Bridge Act of 1883 in the fashion of their counterparts in New York, Pennsylvania, Illinois, and other states to their southwest, to make the town liable for nonfeasance. (The case was *Geldert v. Municipality of Pictou.*) Justice Weatherbe dissented. The town had let a contract to make the repairs shortly before the accident occurred, but Weatherbe insisted that since the Bridge Act provided for provincial funds for repairs to bridges, the town was not liable. He added that, were it otherwise, as the majority would have it, "the liability of counties for damages is likely to become an intolerable burden in communities where, as is the case in many parts of the province the population is spare, and road and bridge making and maintaining difficult." (Moreover, he found a Massachusetts authority for his views.) On appeal, Privy Council agreed with Weatherbe: Towns were not obliged to repair defects; that was up to them, and the failure to do so did not generate liability.[49]

That did not keep neighboring New Brunswick's Supreme Court from "distinguishing" the facts in a case before them from this Privy-Council decision two years later, when they reversed a nonsuit in the case of one injured by a fall on a defective city sidewalk. Justice Landry who had ordered the nonsuit in *Nisi Prius*, stuck to his guns on review; *Geldert* governed. But Justices Barker and Tuck "deem[ed] it a proper, as well as a prudent course, to adhere to the decisions of this court, confirmed, as they have been, by the Supreme Court of Canada," which was to say, he did *not* "feel bound to accept [*Geldert*] as overruling the decisions of this court," since it referred to Nova Scotia statutes, and while the Common-Law issues remained the same, Barker treated the slight difference in statutory language (in New Brunswick) as warranting this distinction, and Justice Tuck agreed.[50] By such virtual legerdemain the authority due a "four-square" decision of Privy Council could be subverted.

These jurists were claiming that their decisions were based entirely on their understanding of English doctrine and on the language in the relevant provincial road statute or municipal charter. But in as many as a third of our other road, bridge, and sidewalk cases, jurists offered in *dicta* strong public policy rationales in addition to citing English (and American) precedents. Some alluded to "local

49 *Geldert v. Munic. of Pictou,* 23 Nova Sc. 483 (1891); *Pictou v. Geldert,* A. C. 524 (1893).
50 *Campbell v. City of St. John,* 33 New Br. 131 at 133, 138, 140 (1895).

conditions." In the Canadian provinces, that generally meant "different climatic conditions."[51] Jurists in Nova Scotia, New Brunswick, Quebec, Ontario, and Manitoba referred to the harshness of "our Canadian winter" in distinguishing the facts of the case before them from the English precedent offered to them. They usually offered as an alternative authoritative source on the Law, "more in point than any English cases," one or more American citations, typically from the adjacent Massachusetts, Maine, Vermont, New Hampshire, or New York high courts, "by reason of the similarity of our acts upon the subject and our climate with the acts and climate of several of the States of the American Union."[52]

The presence of such *dicta* in an opinion, however, proves to be an imperfect predictor of the way these CANZ courts ruled on cases where "different climatic conditions" were at issue. Thus, in one such case in Upper Canada's Court of Common Pleas in 1873, the corporation won, essentially because of the difficulty in dealing with the "different" (icy) conditions there, while in that province's Court of Queen's Bench some eleven years later, the plaintiff won after slipping on an icy sidewalk "so badly constructed that it was easily made dangerous" in wintery conditions.[53] The same use of local "climatic conditions" was made by Quebec jurists, with the same sort of conflicting results, in two cases only eight years apart in that province.[54] The city fathers in Winnipeg

---

[51] See, for example, *Ringland v. Corp. of Toronto*, 23 UCCP 93 at 99 (1873); *Rancour v. Hunt*, 1 Quebec C. S. 74 at 83 (1892); and *Grenier v. Mayor of Montreal*, 27 Quebec 489 at 491 (1876) (Justice Ramsay: "slippery walking is the normal condition of things.") (But Quebec's Queen's Bench reversed Ramsay's nonsuit and awarded a woman who slipped on a sidewalk and broke an arm $200.)

[52] Justice Gwynne in *Ringland v. Corp. of Toronto*, 23 UCCP 93 at 99 (1873). He cited *Merrill v. Inhabs. of Hampden*, 26 Me. 234 (1846).

Thus, Justice O'Connor of Ontario's Court of Queen's Bench made note in 1884 of the "different state of circumstances in the old country." English cases afforded O'Connor and his colleagues "but little assistance towards forming a judgement in a case of this kind," involving a fall on an icy sidewalk, "in this country." American cases were, "for a contrary reason, much more applicable and useful." *Bleakely v. Town of Prescott*, 7 Ont. R 261 at 264 (1884), affirming a judge's award of $200 to one injured on an icy sidewalk.

[53] *Ringland v. Toronto*, 23 UCCP 93 (1873); *Bleakely v. Town of Prescott*, 7 Ont. R 261 (1884).

[54] *Lulham v. Montreal & Christ Church Cathedral*, 29 Low. Can. Jur. 18 at 20 (1884) (no liability); *Rancour v. Hunt*, 1 Quebec Cour. Sup. 74 at 83 (1892) (liability, though here the fact that the defendant was an individual property owner, not the municipality, may have been more important than the actual "climatic" rationale offered.)

Illustration 25. Urban pedestrian hazards included uneven sidewalks, like this one in mid-nineteenth century Chicago, built with storeowner funds to storeowner specifications, difficult to navigate in poor weather or darkness. (In possession of author.)

won relief in 1898 from the suit of one who had slipped and fallen on ice near a public well. Manitoba's jurists there agreed with Justice Killam that there were "so many of these public wells in the city," and the winter so long, that it would be "well-nigh impossible" to "keep the walks near these wells completely free of ice." But in New Brunswick St. John's city fathers were less fortunate in 1890; Chief Justice Allen could not see "any good reason why the fact that a street has become unsafe for people to walk upon, in consequence of the accumulation of snow and ice, . . . should relieve the corporation from the obligation to remove the danger. . . ."[55] (See Illustrations 25, 26, and 27.)

Where courts came to disagree on the question of municipal liability, *dicta* in the opinions often reveal a difference in opinion as to where "the public good" was to be located. Some, sympathetic to the perspective generally reflected in the English precedents, and to what

---

[55] *Taylor v. City of Winnipeg,* 12 Manitoba 479 at 487 (1898); *Kinnealy v. City of St. John,* 30 New Br. 46 at 51 (1890) (Justice Tuck diss.). Cf. *Rancour v. Hunt,* 1 Quebec Cour Sup. 74 at 83 (1892) (landlord responsible for snow falling from roof and injuring men; Quebec Code not to be read the same way as French on right of proprietors to run rain and snowfall off onto street because of "different climatic conditions" and "murderous avalanches of ice" in Quebec).

they regarded as the relatively limited financial resources of the municipalities, held that they ought to enjoy a kind of sovereign immunity for their service to the public good; others, more sympathetic to plaintiffs and other users of the roads, held, as did most courts in the United States, that municipalities should be held liable, and offered "the public good" as their public policy rationale for this position.

Perhaps some jurists friendlier to municipality defendants had formerly been counsel for major provincial towns and cities; perhaps someone on courts friendlier to injured plaintiffs had recently suffered or witnessed a road or bridge accident while riding circuit. In any event, there was no clear consensus in Canada, Australia, or New Zealand on this subject. The courts of Upper Canada/Ontario and New Zealand tended to release municipalities from liability, "sometimes wholly disproportionate to their means and resources" that this would entail.[56] But these were only tendencies. These courts could also hold that a town *was* liable, "any other course" being "destructive of the efficiency of our roads . . . and . . . opposed to . . . the real intention of the Legislature, which is, to have the roads reasonably fit for travel."[57]

---

[56] See, for example, *Ray v. Corp. of Petrolia*, 24 UCCP 73 at 77 (1874) (quoted in the introduction); *Boyle v. Corp. of Dundas*, 25 UCCP 420 at 429 (1875); *Stowell & Others v. Geraldine Cty. Council*, 8 NZLR (SC) 720 at 737 (1890); *Featherston Rd. Bd. v. Tate*, 1 Gaz. LR (NZSC) 38 at 39 (1898) (Justice Pennefeather: "An extensive flood might sweep away half the bridges in a county. . . . neither their means nor their resources permit [local road boards] to light such fences [at washed-away bridges or to] keep men in charge to keep up such lights"). Cf. *Bonin v. Cité de Montreal*, 15 Quebec Cour Sup. 492 at 493 (1899).

[57] And just such an opinion might offer in support of this view U.S. citations and argue, as one did, that "we cannot do better than follow the reasoning of the American Judges." Chief Justice Harrison in *Castor v. Corp. of Upbridge*, 39 UCQB 113 at 123 (1876) (nonsuit reversed for one injured by telegraph poles lying in road). See also Justice Williams, in *Goldring v. Chairman, etc. of Wallace Cty. Council*, 1 Gaz. LR (NZSC) 286 at 287 (1899) (horse shies at lumber left by culvert where work underway: "the timber was so placed that it was obvious that . . . the commonplace and discreet

---

←———

Illustrations 26 and 27.   Among the "different conditions" colonial jurists expected the Law Lords of Privy Council to respect with regard to variation from Common-Law rules were the fierce winters North American cities experienced. Note the ice and snow overhanging the sidewalks in the engraving for *Canadian Illustrated News*, March 29, 1879 (top), with the results depicted in an illustration for the same magazine audience on April 5, 1879. (Archives of Quebec.)

This ambivalence was evident in other CANZ jurisdictions as well: One Quebec opinion favored a plaintiff who fell on a sidewalk with the observation that it "would be a great hardship" to the public if the Montreal Corporation were not held accountable; another, involving the same defendant in the same sort of accident twenty years later, favored the city, expressing a fear of "new taxes" were it otherwise.[58] In 1877, the Chief Justice of the Supreme Court of New South Wales, Sir James Martin, reasoned that a man whose leg had been broken when his horse fell in a defective street gutter was not entitled to recovery because "a municipality may have, as in this case, streets extending over about 70 miles, and the rates may not return over £1000 a year, the amount of rates that can be imposed being limited." In "a new country like this, where everything has to be done," and where "we have not the accumulated labour of centuries to assist us," towns should not be held liable for a failure to repair defects.[59] But that was not his colleagues' opinion. Justices Manning and Hargrave held the town of Bathurst liable for misfeasance in the construction of a poorly placed drainpipe; and Hargrave reasoned that if it were otherwise, towns would be free to ignore virtual "traps" that could "cripple" road users "for life" and use the road funds, instead, to put "kerb-stones opposite alderman's doors, or building grand town-halls, or giving pic-nics."[60]

In this case Privy Council agreed with Justice Hargrave and his colleagues when the case was heard on appeal, and appeared to dissolve the distinction between nonfeasance and misfeasance.[61] Queensland's Acting Chief Justice Harding cited that judgement and indicated that he and colleagues were "bound by it" some four years later in an appeal from a jury award to one injured when her horse fell through a bridge railing that had not been repaired when the Bundanba Divisional Board took over its administration under the terms of a provincial act.[62] But in 1895, Privy Council reversed itself, insisting that the original English Common-Law distinction between misfeasance

---

animal that conveys the Southland farmer to church and to market, would probably shy at it").

[58] *Grenier v. Mayor of Montreal,* 21 Low. Can. J. 296 (1876); *Bonin v. Cité de Montreal,* 15 Quebec Cour Sup. 492 at 493 (1899).

[59] He had a point: Simple wooden bridges over streams, for example, cost from $50 to $300 to construct in upper New York state in the nineteenth century. William Wyckoff, *The Developer's Frontier: The Making of the Western New York Landscape* (New Haven, 1988), 80.

[60] In *McPherson v. Borough of Bathurst,* NSWSCR (Knox) 204 at 207, 213–14, 216 (1877).

[61] *Borough of Bathurst v. Macpherson,* 4 App. Cas. 256 at 267 (1879).

[62] *Bund. Div. Bd. v. Ballin,* 1 Queensl. L J 175 at 177 (1883).

and nonfeasance be maintained.[63] Privy Council's view was immediately criticized by Victoria's Supreme Court,[64] but in 1908, the New South Wales Supreme Court held that the nonfeasance of road authorities was not proper grounds for liability. Chief Justice Darley's rationale did not *rely* on Privy Council's direction, so much as it did on the same sort of reasoning – the imposition of liability would be "so far reaching in a country such as this" as to make each municipality a virtual "insurer to each member of the public" for some fifty miles of roads.[65]

As I have pointed out, CANZ jurists often cited and discussed relevant American cases. This was especially so in Upper Canada/Ontario, a province that lay adjacent several American jurisdictions, where that province's Court of Queen's Bench used American authority to justify rulings for injured plaintiffs.[66] But almost as often that court's counterpart, Common Pleas, used such authority to turn such plaintiffs away.[67] Occasionally these divergent positions could surface in a

---

[63] In *Munic. Council of Sydney v. Bourke*, AC 433, 1895.

[64] *Clarkebarry v. South Melbourne*, 21 VLR 426, 1895.

[65] *Rohan v. St. Peters*, 8 S.R. NSW 649 at 652 (1908); Paul Finn, *Law & Govt. in Colonial Australia* (1987), 27.

[66] As in *Sherwood v. Corp. of Hamilton*, 37 UCQB 410 at 417–21 (1875), *Toms et ux. v. Town of Whitby*, 37 UCQB 100 at 112–15 (1875); *Castor v. Corp. of Town of Upbridge*, 39 UCQB 113 at 123 (1876); *Gordon v. City of Belleville*, 15 Ont. (QB) 26 at 28 (1888); *McKelvin v. City of London*, 22 Ont. R. 70 (1892) (Justice MacMahon first ruled that the liability of the town for one whose sleigh was overturned by contact with a boulder in the road and who fractured his thigh trying to right his horse was too remote, according to English precedents; on review MacMahon reversed himself, based on "a review of the authorities," all of them American, which convinced him that he had been "in error.". . . A case on all four with the one under consideration is *Page v. Bucksport*, 54 Me. 51 [1858] . . . another . . . is . . . *Stickney v. Maidstone*, 30 Vt. 738 [1858]. He and Justice Falconbridge applied these cases "to the present case" to affirm a jury finding of £250 for the plaintiff). See also *Ferguson v. Town of Southwold*, 27 Ont. R. 66 (1895) (citing *Embler v. Walkill*, 57 Hun (N.Y.S.C.) 384 (1892)).

[67] As in *Ringland v. Corp. of Toronto*, 23 UCCP 93 (1873) (Justice Gwynne rejecting proplaintiff American cases, cited by plaintiff's counsel, but finding the city not liable for injuries due to "our climate," similar as it and the Upper Canada and American statutes were "upon the subject of our climate with the Acts and climate of several of the states of the American Union," based on a reading of *Merrill v. Inhabs. of Hampden*, 26 Me. 234 (1846)); *Rounds v. Corp. of Town of Stratford*, 26 UCCP 11 (1876); *Maxwell v. Town of Clarke*, 4 Ont. C. of A. 460 at 470 (1879); *Schmidt et ux. v. Town of Berlin*, 26 Ont. R. 54 (1894); and *Town of Portland v. Griffiths*, 11 Can. SC 333 at 344 (1885) (Justice Gwynne citing the "very reasonable" American rule that a town (in New Brunswick) must have real or constructive notice

single case.[68] The opinions of jurists in the States, then, mattered at times and in some places, but on balance English precedents retained the greater weight. All other things being equal – that is, where the facts and legal principles in the case appeared to be "four-square" consistent with an English precedent – colonial, provincial, and Dominion courts generally followed the English precedent even though the trial court judge's views may have been "fortified with strong authority from the American courts."[69] Strong as that "American" authority might be, if it contradicted an English case head-on, it usually proved to be of little use to the party that cited it.[70]

Axles, Rails, and Collisions: The Common Carrier Duties of Provincial Railways to Passengers

I detected 83 cases of passenger injury or wrongful death suits ruled on by appellate jurists in nineteenth century CANZ reports; plaintiffs won 69 percent of these (55 of 83). Generally guided by rules found in English precedents, CANZ jurists held the owners of streetcars, stagecoaches, steamboats, steamships, and railroads to high standards of liability as common carriers when it came to the safety of passengers. However at times they chose to "distinguish" the facts of the case before them from an English rule; in these instances they preferred an "American" one.

Railway passengers, unlike most other tort plaintiffs, were not obliged to provide evidence of defendant negligence in a wide range of instances; many accidents "spoke for themselves." The passenger thrown off a streetcar by a sudden jolt, the omnibus passenger flung from the vehicle when the horses bolted, the steamboat passenger made to jump to the pier in the absence of a gangplank, the railway passenger injured in a collision, all were regarded as having *prima facie* cases against their carriers.[71] And well they might, for, as on Mark Twain's

---

of a defect in a road, bridge, or sidewalk before it could be held liable to one injured by it).

[68] As in *Connell v. Town of Prescott*, 20 Ont. C. of A. 49 at 52 ff. (1892). Compare *Gilbert v. Municip. of Yarmouth*, 23 Nova Sc. 93 at 113 (1890); *Turner v. Borough of Gouldburn*, 3 S.C. NSW 91 at 98–100, 102 (1903).

[69] As in *Lockhart v. City of St. John*, 30 New Br. 445 (1891).

[70] *Holmes v. McNevin*, 5 Low. Can. J. 271 at 275 (1861); *Same*, 9 Quebec 228 at 232 (1861); *Caron v. James*, 4 Quebec C.S. 63 (1893); *Heenan v. Iredale*, 19 NZLR (S.C.) 387 (1900).

[71] *Richardson v. Melbourne T. & O. Co.*, 1 Argus LR 23 (1895); *Pink v. Melbourne Tramway & Omnibus Co.*, 6 Vict. LR (L) 186 (1880); *Cameron v. Milloy*, 14 Up. Can. C.P. 340 (1864); *Linklater v. Min. for Rys.*, 2 Gaz. LR (NZSC) 202 (1900).

Mississippi, steamboat captains on the Hawkesbury (north of Sydney), the St. Lawrence, Lake Huron, Lake Erie, and Lake Ontario were fond of racing one another in the mid-nineteenth century.[72] "The public should be protected," wrote Justice Adam Wilson of Upper Canada's Common Pleas of a steamboat company's conduct, "against the wilfulness, perverseness, or neglect of those in whose power travelers are temporarily placed, and against whose power or influence they cannot successfully contend."[73]

Things were more ambiguous when the object that had caused the injury was a broken axle or rail. The English rule was that all parts of a transport company's equipment were to be free of any detectable defects; and in the event that such a defect caused an accident, the company was held to be liable.[74] This was the rule in both Upper and Lower Canada as early as the mid-1850s, and it remained the rule throughout the years we are considering. Thus, in 1856, Justice Day of Montreal's *Cour Supérieur* regarded evidence that the rear wheels of a railway car had come off as having proved "incontrovertibly that it was not fit for the safe conveyance of passengers," despite evidence that the axle had recently been inspected and that company witnesses had reported the equipment to have been "in perfect order." Justice Day and his colleagues "rode circuit" themselves as did their colleagues throughout the empire. This may have lent some weight to their finding that "such testimony" by company employees and witnesses established only that the defect was "unusual, and against it we have the fact of the accident...."[75] (See Illustrations 28, 29, and 30.)

But the empathy CANZ jurists may have had with passengers injured when defective equipment gave way was often tempered by the English *exception* to this rule, that the carrier was not to be held liable if the defect was extremely difficult to detect. As Chief Justice Cockburn, put it in *Stokes v. Eastern Counties Ry* (1860), in "the practical working of railway business" one could not "expect that a railway company shall be from time to time measuring with accurate specific

---

[72] Stephen Kenny, " 'Cahoots' and Catcalls: An Episode of Popular Resistance in Lower Canada at the Outset of the Union," in *Historical Perspectives on Law and Society in Canada*, ed. Tina Loo and Lorna McLean (Toronto, 1994), 80.

[73] *Cameron v. Milloy*, 14 Up. Can. C.P. 340 at 348 (1864) (reversing a lower court judge's nonsuit on grounds of contributory negligence). But see *Stacpoole v. Betridge*, 5 Vict. LR (L) 302 (1879) (award to ship's passenger reversed; company not liable for unauthorized acts of employees).

[74] Announced in the era of stagecoaches: *Aston v. Heaven*, 2 Esp. 533 (N.P. 1797), and *Christie v. Griggs*, 2 Camp. 79 (1809).

[75] *Thatcher v. Great Western Ry.*, 4 Up. Can. C.P. 543 (1854); *Germain v. Montreal & N.Y. Ry.*, 6 Low. Can. J. 172 (1856).

Illustration 28. Negligent railwaymen imperiled passengers when they left tracks or axles uninspected or when negligent telegraph operators or switchmen caused collisions or derailments. On May 25, 1865, Robert Bruce of the *Illustrated Melbourne Post* depicted a derailment that occurred the previous month on the first run of the Adelaide to Pt. Adelaide train in South Australia. According to the accompanying article, the manager of that railway, C. S. Hare, had hosted the governor, the Anglican bishop, and a host of other colonial officials and their wives on this first run, and directed the engineer to accelerate to "a tremendous pace." The carriages soon "began to oscillate in a fearful manner" due to the failure of Hare's subordinates to complete repairs to one stretch of track. After the derailing, axles and rails were reported to be "twisted and bent till they resembled the sinuosities of a snake." The carriage springs were broken into leaves, and the floor of the last carriage "dashed in." After an official investigation, Hare was dismissed. (La Trobe Picture Collection, State Library of Victoria, # 936670.)

instruments."[76] Just so, a plaintiff in New Zealand was turned away because the evidence indicated that the defect in the stagecoach axle was "absolutely latent," that it had "obviously occurred during the manufacture of the axle, "and was, in any event, "undiscoverable by any test or examination." Justice Denniston, not known for innovative propensities, took note of American citations offered by the plaintiff's counsel, and (correctly) allowed that most courts in the United States tended to hold carriers to a stricter standard of liability for defects

---

[76] 5 QB 692 at 693. See also *Withers v. Great Northern Ry.*, 1 F. & F. 165 (Ex. 1858); *Readhead v. Midland Ry.*, LR, 2 QB 412 (1869), and Rande Kostal, *Law and English Railway Capitalism*, 299–300.

Illustrations 29 and 30.   Bruce's engraving had shown witnesses rushing to the scene to aid victims. But for some time after such accidents, people from the neighborhood were able to view the devastating results (as were these spectators at the site of an overturned tram in Brooklyn, a suburb of Wellington, New Zealand (top), and these at the site of a Grand Trunk Railway collision in Ontario). Their recollections and reports to others surely affected the tendency of jurymen to send sharp messages to the derelict railway's "pocket nerve." (See Chapter 8.) (Alexander Turnbull Library, F-319371/2; Archives of Ontario, C302 N. 141.)

"discernable by any known tests" than did jurists in England. This American rule, Denniston quoted *Albany Law Journal* and *American Reports* editor Irving Browne as saying, made the carrier "an insurer that the manufacturer has not been negligent." Denniston rejected such American precedents (while citing a more "English" American case, *Grand Rapids Ry. v. Huntley* (Mich. 1878)), in exonerating the New Zealand stagecoach owner from liability.[77]

The contract to carry a person safely from point A to point B thus held the carrier to a high standard of care, but not to an absolute one. Furthermore, the carrier and passenger were free to enter into a waiver of that high standard of care for a reduced fee: Carriers could "contract out" of their common carrier liability,[78] and CANZ jurists, like their English mentors, proved to be unimpressed with decisions of their counterparts in the States who had found such contracts to be void as being contrary to good public policy.[79]

Passengers injured when they tried to climb aboard after the train had started, stuck their arms or heads out of the windows, climbed up to sit by the driver of their stagecoach, reentered a burning railroad car to retrieve a valise, or alighted before the streetcar or train had come to a complete stop, were often nonsuited for having contributed to the ensuing accident by their own negligence.[80] But on occasion jurists in Quebec, Victoria, and New South Wales were impressed with American opinions creating "principled exceptions" to "the general

---

[77] *Webb v. Cassidy*, 9 Gaz. LR (NZ) 317 at 323–24 (1906), citing *Grand Rapids RR v. Huntley*, 38 Mich. 537, 31 Amer. Rep. 321 (Browne). (The Law *did* hold railways like the Grand Trunk liable for defects in the locomotives, bridges, and other equipment that the Company manufactured itself in its workshops. See Paul Craven & Dom Traves, "Dimensions of Paternalism: Discipline and Culture in Canadian Railway Operations in the 1850s," in *On the Job*, ed. Craig Heron and Rob. Storey (Kingston, 1986), 48.) See also *Can. Pac. Ry. v. Chalifoux*, 22 Can. S.C. 721 (1894) (citing New York decisions); and *Dubé v. Queen*, 3 Ex. Can. R. 147 (1892).

[78] See *Kelly v. Australasian Steam Naviq. Co.*, 6 LRNSW 233 (1885); *M'Donald v. Victorian Rys. Comm.*, 13 VLR (L) 399 (1887); *Bicknell v. Grand Trunk Ry.*, 26 Ont. C.A. 431 (1899). But see *Carroll v. Howard Smith & Sons*, 14 LRNSW 281 (1893) (Such a contract inadmissible if negligence proved).

[79] *Bicknell v. Grand Trunk Ry.*, 26 Ont. C.A. 431 (1899).

[80] *Haldan v. Great Western Ry.*, 30 Up. Can. C.P. 89 (1879); *King v. Vict. Ry. Comm.*, 18 Vict. LR 250 (1892); *Cashmore v. Chief Comm. for Trans. & Rys. (NSW)*, 20 CLR 1 (1915); *Ross v. Chaplin*, Macassey's Rpt. (NZ) 828 (1870); *Hay v. Great Western Ry.*, 37 UCQB 456 (1875); *Thompson v. Grand Trunk Ry.*, 37 UCQB 40 (1875); *Central Vt. Ry. v. Lareau*, 30 Low. Can. J. 231 (1886); *Fletcher v. Comm. of Rys.*, 7 LRNSW 251 (1886); *Smith v. Vict. Ry. Comm.*, 28 Vict. LR 44 (1902); *Kenny v. Mayor of Dunedin*, 22 Gaz. LR (NZ) 244 (1920), (reversed by C. of A., 1921 GLR 28).

rule."[81] The Massachusetts bench held to the harsher English rule on this subject, and CANZ jurists sometimes had to sort out "good" Law from "bad."[82] Thus, Justice Isaac Isaacs of Australia's high court chose to rely on "the standard work of [American] Judge [Seymour] Thompson on Negligence" in deciding that the question of a passenger's contributory negligence was one of fact, for the jury, not Law, for the judge, as the English rule would generally have it. Justice Isaacs reported with obvious approval the fact that Thompson's treatise had rejected "from a humanitarian standpoint" the doctrinally harsh views of the Massachusetts Supreme Judicial Court "with extremely severe and scathing observations."[83]

RES IPSA LOQUITUR AND THE PRIMA FACIE CASE: PLAINTIFF PROOF OF NEGLIGENCE WHEN DEFENDANT WAS A NEIGHBOR, STRANGER, OR COMMON CARRIER

It was one thing to seek damages from a doctor who had negligently treated your wife, from a businessman on whose defective stairway you had broken a leg, from a township that had built or repaired a bridge poorly, or from a railway company that had sold you a ticket for a train that then flew off the track; those sorts of defendants could be said to have owed you certain duties.[84] It was quite another thing to charge a neighbor, let alone a perfect stranger, with the same sort of negligence. What *legal* duty did a neighbor or a stranger owe to you? Doctors were being paid; consequently they owed you particular care. Merchants could be said to have "invited" you onto their premises. Municipalities had often been given statutory duties along with their

---

[81] See, for example, *Smith v. Vict. Ry. Comm.*, 28 Vict. LR 44 (1902); and *Cashmore v. Chief Comm. for Rys. & Tramways* (NSW), 20 CLR 1 (1915), reversing *Same v. Same*, 14 NSWSR 61 (1914).

[82] Counsel for railway defendants were aware of American opinions favorable to their view of things as well, of course, especially those of the Westminster-guided Massachusetts Supreme Judicial Court, and they were sometimes able to persuade jurists to accept these opinions as accurate guides to the Law. See *Central Vermont Ry. v. Lareau*, 30 Low. Can. J. 231 (1886); and *King v. Vict. Ry. Comm.*, 18 Vict. LR 250 (1892).

[83] But Isaacs pointed as well to a decision authored by "that learned Judge," Oliver Wendell Holmes, Jr., which had "greatly qualified the rigidity" of his court's prior rulings. *Cashmore v. Chief Comm. for Rys. & Tramways (NSW)*, 20 CLR 1 at 11–12 (1915). This plaintiff's attorney also cited U.S. cases and treatises before the Supreme Court of New South Wales (14 NSWSR 61 (1914)).

[84] The standards were described in *Southcote v. Stanley*, 1 H. & N. 247 (1856), and *Gautret v. Egerton*, LR, 2CP 37 (1867), but earlier precedents were also cited.

rights; hence, they sometimes owed certain duties as well. Railways and streetcar companies had taken your money in exchange for safe passage. But neighbors and strangers only owed you the duty to behave with "reasonable care." What did that amount to, and how did CANZ jurists deal with these Common-Law rules?[85]

Neighborly Torts

A neighbor's duties in tort law might surface when a fire spread from one person's land to another's. Governed in some cities or regions by statute, in others by the Common Law of English[86] (or U.S.) jurists,[87] the disposition of this species of tort varied throughout the world of the British Diaspora. In mid-nineteenth century Ontario/Upper Canada the Common-Law English rule (that a negligent burning must be proved) was the Law in the Court of Queen's Bench.[88] But in early New South Wales, Richard Atkins, that colony's untrained chief law officer, held a government official who had caused a fire to be started on his land to be liable for the loss of his neighbor's wheat stack, despite his finding that "it must appear the effect of accident" (in this case, wind) "which it was not in his power to foresee or prevent."[89] Thereafter,

---

[85] The "leading case" of this "reasonable care" standard was probably *Blyth v. Birmingham Waterworks*, 11 Ex. 781 (1956), but Lord Holt's language in its antecedent, *Mason v. Keeling*, 1 Ld. Raym. 606 at 607 (1700), was also cited: Defendant in tort would be "answerable for all mischief proceeding from his neglect . . . unless they were of unavoidable necessity."

[86] Following *Turbeville v. Stamp*, B. & M. 559 (1697), that one was liable only if proved negligent for the spread of one's fire in the countryside, but strictly liable in a city for its spread to a neighbor's property due to the greater risks in such crowded places (made evident only a generation before in the Great Fire of London, 1666).

[87] Karsten, *Heart versus Head*, 83–84, 101–08.

[88] If you burned brush and stumps to clear your land, you were not liable in tort for damage to a neighbor's property when a wind swept in and spread the fire unless the neighbor was able to establish to a jury of your peers that you had conducted the burn in a negligent fashion. Such burning was a part of the necessary process of "improvement" of land and thus for "the public good," Chief Justice Robinson explained; otherwise "a great part of the business of life could not be carried on. . . . Misfortune and neglect should not be confounded." *Dean v. McCarty*, 2 UCQB 448 at 449, 450 (1844). This was *not* the rule in neighboring Quebec (Lower Canada) in the same years. There, when one's fire spread to a neighbor's land, there was no need to prove negligence; under French law, a strict liability prevailed. See *Fordyce v. Kearns*, 15 Low. Can. J. 80 (1870), citing Toullier and Domat.

[89] In *Lord v. Fitzgerald* (1804), noted in Kercher, *Debt, Seduction & Other Diasters: The Birth of Civil Law in Convict New South Wales* (Annandale, NSW, 1994), 112.

in both Australia and New Zealand, plaintiffs seeking damages were not so fortunate, as trained jurists applied the same rule as had Upper Canada's Chief Justice Robinson, that negligence must be proved.[90]

In New Zealand, as Magistrate E. R. Chudleigh's diary entry for March 7, 1884 indicates, some juries were willing to allow a great deal of carelessness before they attached liability to a defendant: One Robin Clough had been sued for a fire that appeared from the evidence to have been caused by his smoking in another's hay-strewn stable: "A few [on the jury] were good men and others fools, some knaves," Chudleigh wrote. "They decided that every man had a right to do as he likes. . . . the majority would not have a rider condemning smoking in stalls because it interfered with individual liberty."[91]

An eighteenth century English statute fixed liability in cases of fire in densely settled places *(Hunter v. Walker* (1888)). Cities, after all, were made up of masses of buildings in close proximity. An untended fireplace or stove might result in a fire that could be spread by a chance wind to a hundred other dwellings and warehouses.[92] But New Zealand's population was, and continued to be, essentially rural. And as late as 1929, its ranchers and farmers harbored "the impression," in the words of the editor of the *New Zealand Law Journal*, that "if they give notice to adjoining landowners of an intended burn, and the burn is planned for the proper time of year," they were under no legal liability for damage to any of their neighbors' property, however negligent they might be in containing it. This, the editor pointed out, was not the Law.[93] And yet it seems that it was – that is, it was the commonly perceived view of what the Law was, both in 1884 and in 1929 in New Zealand, and, as such, it *was* "the law," for afflicted neighbors who did not believe they could sue, and for juries that would not hold such defendants liable.

---

[90] But see *Bell v. Scott* (NSWSC Kercher 1828) (burning of stubble spread to and destroyed eleven acres of neighbor's wheat; evidence of considerable defendant negligence; Chief Justice Forbes tells jury of *sic utere tuo* maxim (use your property, but not to the injury of others); jury award of forty-five pounds).

Victoria's Chief Justice Irvine offered a public policy rationale for this rule in the early twentieth century similar to the one offered by Chief Justice Sir John Beverley Robinson nearly a century before in Toronto: "It would . . . be a serious bar on the natural use of grazing lands in Australia if landowners could not burn fire-breaks on their lands without becoming liable as insurers to all other owners should the fire spread, though every practicable precaution had been taken against it so spreading" (in *Pett v. Sims Paving & Road Const.*, 1928 Vict. LR 247 at 258).

[91] *Diary of E. R. Chudleigh* (Christchurch, 1950), 327.

[92] *Hunter v. Walker*, 6 NZLR 690 (1888); reaffirmed in *Kelley v. Heyes*, 22 NZLR 429 (1904).

[93] "Liability for Fire," *N.Z. Law Journal* (Oct. 1, 1929), 273.

Illustrations 31 and 32.   High courts in Quebec and Ontario followed
different legal traditions in determining railway liability for fires caused
by sparks from locomotive stacks that then spread from the company's
right-of-way to adjacent property. Note the proximity of the flammable
lumber of "Jordan & Bernard, Lumber Dealers" of Montreal to the

Railroads as Neighbors

Sparks, Fires and Railway Liability

Sparks spewed from the stacks of locomotives could ignite dry matter in the railway's right-of-way which sometimes spread to adjacent fences, fields, haystacks, barns, and other buildings. Aggrieved property owners who went uncompensated by their railway-"neighbor," often responded with a lawsuit. CANZ courts appeared to reveal no apparent judicial bias – that is, property-owner plaintiffs won eight, railways six, of some fourteen such cases. But that appearance may be deceptive; among CANZ jurists, those of Quebec proved to be particularly intolerant of railroads whose locomotive's sparks appeared to have caused fire damage to neighboring property owners. An example: Despite sound evidence that the Grand Trunk Railway had installed the "most approved appliances" for spark arresting on its locomotives' smokestacks, the Quebec Court of Appeals held the company liable in 1885. Justice Cross allowed that "by the rule of the English Law applicable to the case" the railway "probably" would not be held to be liable, but "our rule has always been different." Referring to French authority (and Quebec precedent), he explained that "the party exercising a dangerous occupation" was "responsible to his neighbors for the damage that may be caused to them by [its] hazardous nature..."[94] (See Illustrations 31 and 32.)

Outside of Quebec, however, jurists appeared to be friendlier to railway companies in suits charging them with having caused fires.[95] The courts of New South Wales, Nova Scotia, and Upper Canada, followed the English Common-Law rule regarding liability for fires (*Vaughan v. Taff Vale Ry.* (1860)). Thus, Justices Martin and Fawcett

---

[94] *Grand Trunk Ry. v. Meegar*, 29 Lower Can. J. 214 at 215 (1885). Cf. *North Shore Ry. v. McWillie*, 34 Lower Can. J. 55 (1889); *Central Vermont Ry. v. Stanstead & Sherbrooke Ins. Co.*, 5 Quebec QB 224 (1896) (U.S. opinions favorable to railroads critiqued by plaintiff); *Grand Trunk Ry. v. Rainville*, 29 Can. S.C. 201 (1898). But see *Sénésac v. Central Vermont Ry.*, 26 Can. S.C. 642 (1896) (proof of fault inadequate).

[95] But see *Dawson v. Regina*, 3 NZLR (C.A.) 1 (1884) (Otago saw-mill owner recovers where government – owned railway used spark-prone brown lignite fuel).

←

Montreal, Ottawa & Quebec Railway in this engraving for the *Canadian Illustrated News* in 1876 (top), and note the consequences of such a spreading fire in a similar setting at the Grand Trunk Railway depot at Pt. St. Charles, depicted in the same magazine, March 20, 1875. (Archives of Quebec.)

believed they had discharged their "duty...to the public" in 1885
when they held that a jury verdict for one who had lost sheep to
a fire that began after a longer-than-usual train had passed by was
against the evidence. After all, Justice Fawcett reasoned, "no invention has yet been discovered" that would "totally prevent the escape
of sparks from locomotive engines." Since "the use of engines propelled by steam" had been sanctioned by the statute, "we must take it
that the escape of sparks from such engines is also allowed."[96] Similarly, in Upper Canada, Justice Adam Wilson offered the same utilitarian defense of that rule in its new railway context that his predecessor, Sir John Beverley Robinson, had offered a generation before,
regarding the burning of stubble, brush, and stumps by those clearing land. Where Robinson had held that "a great part of the business
of life could not be carried on" without such acts,[97] Justice Wilson
observed in *dicta* that "there must be some reasonable allowance made
to enable new enterprises of this kind to get their road into order,
especially in new or wild sections of the country." He added that
"more should be extracted from an old company than from a new
one." In this case, for other reasons, he and his colleagues allowed a
jury verdict of $400 to stand against the Midland Railway for having
caused extensive damage to the plaintiff's brush fencing and other
property,[98] but in other cases they turned away the appeals of plaintiffs who sought a higher liability standard of railways than prevailed in
Upper Canada[99] or sought to escape from the contributory-negligence
rule imposed on adjoining property owners by both Queen's Bench
and Common Pleas: Such plaintiffs were free to use their barnyards as
they chose, but if they located them "near the track," they were to be regarded as having "submit[ted] to the risk." It seemed unreasonable to

---

[96] *Vaughan v. Taff Vale Ry.*, 5 H. & N. 679, 157 ER 1357 (Ex. 1860); *McKinnon
v. Comm. of Rys.* 6 NSWLR 247 at 251, 252 (1885). See also *Spence v. Windsor
& A. Ry.*, 10 Nova Sc. 106 (1875); and *Jackson v. Grand Trunk Ry.*, 32 Can.
S.C. 245 (1902).

[97] 2 Up. Can. QB 448 at 449, cited in *Gillson v. Northern Grey Ry.* 35 Up. Can.
QB 475 at 486 (1874).

[98] *Holmes v. Midland Ry.*, 35 Up. Can. QB 253 at 260 (1874). Cf. *Can. Southern
Ry. v. Phelps*, 14 Can. S.C. 132 at 146 (1884), affirming Ontario appellate
court judgement against railway. (Justice Henry, diss., citing *Ryan v. N. Y.
Central Ry.*, 35 NY 210 (1866)). *Flannigan v. Can. Pac. Ry.*, 17 Ont. (C.P.)
6 (1889) (award affirmed; Illinois opinion cited on jury's right to decide
questions of fact).

[99] *M'Callum v. Grand Trunk Ry.*, 31 Up. Can. QB 527 (1871); *Gillson v.
Northern Grey Co*, 33 Up. Can. QB 128 (1872); aff. 35 Up. Can. QB 475
(1874).

Justice John Wellington Gwynne that "railway companies must pay, right or wrong."[100]

Cattle on the Tracks

Cows, pigs, sheep, oxen, and horses sometimes found their ways onto railway tracks and, failing to sense the danger they were in, were killed or maimed by the onrushing locomotives. (See Illustration 33.) In the first few decades of railroading, when both locomotives and cars were smaller than they would become, a collision with a mature bullock could also derail the train.

In England, the liability of railroads in such cases was governed by parliamentary statute, while in the United States it was determined, state by state, and often county by county within states, either by statute (differing from jurisdiction to jurisdiction) or by Common-Law rules. As James Hunt has recently shown, some southern courts (such as those of South Carolina, Mississippi, and Georgia) held railroads to a high standard of care, while others (such as Alabama, Florida, and Arkansas) interpreted statutes favoring herdsmen very narrowly, essentially ignoring the absolute liability the statutes had appeared to impose on railroads.[101]

The issue was not inconsequential; in the first decade of railroading in Michigan, for example, guerilla warfare against the Michigan

[100] *Hill v. Ontario, S. & H. Ry.*, 13 Up. Can. QB 503 (1855); *Jaffrey v. Toronto, Grey & Bruce Ry.*, 23 Up. Can. C.P. 553 (1874) (reliance on U.S. cases); *Same v. Same*, 24 Up. Can. C.P. 271 at 290 (1874).

In another case, two successive juries had found the Toronto, Grey & Bruce Railway liable for fire damages; the second jury awarded $650 after a retrial had been ordered. When the company appealed again, Common Pleas again overturned the jury's judgement (albeit by a two to one vote). Similarly, Chief Justice Sir William Johnstone Ritchie of the Dominion of Canada's recently created Supreme Court offered the judgement of his colleagues that a plaintiff who "chose to place in his barn combustible materials, and to leave it in such a condition," some 200 feet from the New Brunswick Railway's tracks, could "understand the risk" and was guilty of "imprudence." And when Alberta's legislature sought to impose strict liability on railways for prairie fires that began in their right-of-way, the Supreme Court of Canada denied them the right to legislature for railways regulated by the Dominion. *New Brunswick Ry. v. Robinson*, 11 Can. S.C. 688 at 689 (1884) (Chief Justice Ritchie and Justice Strong both relied on New York authorities, such as *Collins v. NY Central & Hudson, Ry.*, 12 NY 502); *Can. Pac. Ry. v R.*, 39 Can SCR 476 (1907)).

[101] James Hunt, "Legislatures, Courts, and Nineteenth Century Negligence: Political and Constitutional Conflict over Standards of Liability," paper delivered at American Society for Legal History Conference, Minneapolis, Oct. 1997.

Illustration 33.   *The Australian Sketcher* portrayed this "Accident on the Tasmanian Railway" in June 1876, "The Train Running into a Mob of Horses." (La Trobe Picture Collection, State Library of Victoria.)

Central erupted because of the failure of that railroad to pay the full value for livestock killed by its trains (as noted in Chapter 4). Some thirty-eight farmer-rancher "conspirators" were prosecuted (defended by William Seward the future Republican governor of New York and secretary of state in the Lincoln Administration).[102]

Livestock in Lower Canada were just as oblivious to the dangers as those in Michigan. The first such cases were decided several years before that province's legislature and jurists had completed the "rediscovery" of their French legal roots. A cow that had entered the St. Lawrence & Atlantic's right-of-way via an unfenced crossing in 1851 was struck by a train and killed, and the collision derailed four of the cars. Montreal's Circuit Court ruled on appeal that the company was not statutorily obliged to fence crossings, nor was it obliged to slow its trains to avoid cattle. "The public interests must suffer" were that to be the rule. Instead the rule was that the public was "put on their guard" by the presence of the crossing "and when they hear the bell ring, it is for them to get out of the way." This was so because of

[102] Charles Hirschfield, "The Great Railroad Conspiracy," 36 *Michigan History* 97 (1952).

"the necessities of trade:"

> ... this railroad connects the waters of the St. Lawrence with the seaboard, and ... interests of immense magnitude may depend on the company being able to fulfill its engagements with the public in carrying passengers and goods at the time stipulated in their advertisements.

So the cow's owner remained uncompensated and was obliged to pay to the railroad the £4 10s that the company had paid its workers "in replacing the cars on the track."[103]

The first years of railroading in Upper Canada produced similar results. A legislative committee in 1854, looking into accidents on the Great Western's right-of-way, found that the company's engine drivers seemed to think it "great sport" to hit cattle on the tracks. That province's jurists spelled out the Common-Law rules and interpreted the relevant statutes in a pair of cases in 1858. Where the language of the relevant statute was sufficient, Upper Canada's Queen's Bench applied it, as when it found the Buffalo & Lake Huron liable for the death of an ox. The statute held the railroad strictly liable in the absence of a cattleguard or "cowcatcher" on the front of the locomotive.[104] But the statute did not protect the owners of horses who failed to keep their animals off the tracks; horses could not be fenced out as inexpensively as oxen, and their owners were consequently not entitled to remuneration – that is, unless the engineer had failed to slow his speed and sound his whistle to alert and alarm the horses. Since the Great Western's engineer *had* the "last clear chance" to avoid such an

---

[103] *Rocheleau v. St. L. & A. Ry*, 2 Low. Can. R. 337 at 339 (1852); *Same*, 3 Quebec 217 at 218 (1852).

Similarly, when cattle and horses, owned by one whose property was not adjacent the railway's right-of-way, found their way onto the property of one who was, and the animals then found their way through a breach in the fence and were killed, Lower Canada's jurists held that the statute treated such animals as trespassers and consistently turned the claims of their owners away. And they held that the custom of those engaged in animal husbandry in Quebec to lower fences in the winter to allow for open grazing (*vaine pâture*) did not entitle the owners of those adjacent the tracks to claim damages when such animals were killed. *Dubord v. Grand Tronc* (1858) and *Rae v. Grand Tronc* (1859), both noted in 14 Lower Can. R. 142n; *Roux v. Grand Tronc*, 14 Lower Can R. 140 (1864); *Perras v. Montreal et Champlain Ch. de Fer* 16 Lower Can. R. 443 (1866).

[104] Peter Baskerville, "Transportation, Social Change & State Formation, Upper Canada, 1841–1864," in *Colonial Leviathan*, ed. Allan Greer and Ian Radforth (1992), 238–39; *Huist v. Buffalo & Lake Erie Ry.*, 16 UCQB 299 (1858).

accident, and had failed to exercise that opportunity, Queen's Bench held the company liable.[105]

In 1886, Quebec's Queen's Bench held a railroad negligent and thus liable at Common Law when it failed to provide a cattleguard at a crossing, but the Dominion's legislature amended the Railway Act two years later to limit railway liability in such cases, and Quebec's Queen's Bench soon acknowledged the change and turned away the owner of three "trespassing" colts killed at a crossing with no cattleguard. Justice Robert Hall noted that the judgements of his peers on the New Jersey and Massachusetts courts were that the question of liability in such situations was not one of fact for the jury but was "relegated to the control of the judges." To Hall this information was useful, if only "to confirm the principle now adopted by this court."[106]

By 1903, a popular groundswell against the amended act of 1888 had led to a new statute that required that railroad defendants prove negligence on the part of the owners of animals killed at unguarded crossings. As Justice John Idlington of Canada's Supreme Court put it, jurists in a "long line of cases" based on previous statutes had been forced to the "manifest hardship" of turning such plaintiffs away. "To any one conversant with the history of the struggle that had gone on in the courts for half a century over the nature of the objections resting upon a railway company" to fence its track or guard all crossings, there was "nothing surprising to find a radical change" with regard to this obligation in the Railway Act of 1903.[107]

The prairie province of Manitoba shared a Populist tradition with several of its southern prairie-home-companion neighbors. So it is

---

[105] *Ferris v. Grand Trunk RR.*, 16 UCQB 474 (1858); *Campbell v. Great Western Ry.*, 15 UCQB 498 (1858), citing *Davies v. Mann*, 10 M. & W. 546 (1842).

Both the original statutes of the provincial legislatures making up the Confederation in 1867, and one created by the new Dominion of Canada, required of railroads that they fence their boundaries with all property owners who did not waive that privilege, and courts held railroads liable to property owners for the deaths of cattle or sheep that had passed through an opening left unrepaired in such fencing, while not protecting animal owners who merely *occupied* land adjacent a railroad right-of-way. Ontario's Justice John O'Connor argued that the statute should be read to extend such protection, believing that it was plausible to suppose that the legislature had intended to offer such protection as "an encouragement to actual settlement" to humble squatter-settlers who "require cattle to enable them to get along," but his pro-squatter view was a dissenting one. *Conway v. Canadian Pac. Ry.*, 7 Ontario LR 673 at 691 (1885); *Same v. Same*, 12 Ont. App. 708 (1885); *Daniels v. Grand Trunk Ry.*, 11 Ont. App. 471 (1885).

[106] *Pontiac & Pacific Junction Ry. v. Brady*, 4 Montr. LR (QB) 346 (1886); *Can. Pac. Ry. v. Cross*, 3 Quebec QB 170 at 176, 180 (1894).

[107] *Canadian Pac. Ry. v. Carruthers*, 39 Can. S.C. 251 at 254 (1907).

thus not terribly surprising that the Manitoba Court of Appeals offered a generous reading of one Railway Act provision that did not require that companies offer fencing to property owners along "sparsely-settled" rights-of-way: The owners of animals killed on such unfenced tracks, the court held, were not barred from suing by this statutory exemption. They were entitled to damages for losses unless the company could convince a jury of their peers that they had been legally negligent in allowing their animals to forage (in the same fashion as those peers allowed theirs). As Chief Justice Howell put it, "this view of the law will permit the western prairies to be settled and occupied near the railway lines." "Any other construction" of the statute, he argued in another such case, would "interfere seriously with one of the great industries" of the Canadian prairie provinces (that is, ranching).[108]

Stranger Torts

Suffice it to say here that it was sometimes difficult for the victim of a *stranger*'s negligence to establish that the defendant had failed to exhibit "ordinary care" than it was when the accident was caused by a neighbor, merchant, doctor, or employer. Of particular interest were the ways jurists dealt with the suits of persons injured or killed at railway crossings, and children injured or killed playing in the streets or on a dangerous object while trespassing. A statute or ordinance governing the speed or behavior of a railroad at a crossing or a streetcar on its route might be invoked, but unless there were witnesses able to testify to the misbehavior of the driver/engineer, the injured plaintiff faced a nonsuit; the same was so for highway accidents: Victims had to establish defendant liability.[109] (See Illustration 34.)

---

[108] *Clayton v. Can. Northern Ry.*, 7 Western LR 721 at 730 (1908); *Parks v. Can. Northern Ry.*, 21 Manitoba 103, 18 Western LR 118 at 120 (1911), affirming *Same v. Same*, 15 Western LR 445 (1910). But see *Can. Pac Ry. v. R.*, 39 Can SCR 476 (1907), where a similar Northwest Territories statute seeking to hold railways liable for prairie fires was declared void on constitutional grounds.

Western Australia's legislature did not require their colony's Commissioners of Railways to fence their lines. See *Com. Of Rys. v. Raftis*, 16 WALR 45 (1914). But when a car filled with wheat derailed in 1912, and horses on the adjacent property ate the wheat and died, the Supreme Court of Western Australia held the railway commissioners liable. *Davis Bros. v. Comm. of Rys*, 21 CLR (W.A.) 142 (1916).

[109] Some victims were able to accomplish this *without* witnesses of their own. Thus, when in June of 1860 a Major Holmes was struck by a beam that had fallen from a building under construction on St. Catherine St., Montreal,

Illustration 34. This poster, circulated in Philadelphia in 1839, speaks for itself. (In possession of author.)

he won an award of $600, affirmed on appeal, from the contractor. Justice Badgley of the Superior Court held that the likelihood of the accident could have been "foreseen" by the contractor, and that the principles attaching liability to the defendant could be detected in both English and French law (he was not specific, citing only an American treatise) "because they are founded on reason and justice, which are nothing but common sense legally applied to the circumstances of life." The defendants' liability appeared to have spoken for itself, although Badgley did not put it quite that way in this opinion that predated the English "leading case" of *res ipsa loquitur, Byrne v. Boadle* (1863), by some two years. *Holmes v. McNevin*, 5 Low. Can. J. 271 at 275 (1861); *Same v. Same*, 9 *Quebec* 228 at 232 (1861); *Byrne v. Boadle*, 2 H & C 722 (1863).

By 1893, the same sort of decision in Quebec's Superior Court would rely on article 1054 of the Quebec Civil Code: *Caron v. James*, 4 Quebec C.S. 63 (1893) (charcoal barrel fell from scaffolding).

For a *"res ipsy"* case from another CANZ court, see *Keir v. Wellington Electric Co.*, 10 Gaz. LR (NZSC) 401 (1907) (citing U.S. authorities).

Accidents at Crossings

By the second half of the nineteenth century railroads and, eventually, trams were claiming hundreds of lives each year at crossings in Britain, North America, and the Antipodes. At first, questions arising in litigation flowing from these accidents were answered by jurists drawing upon established English Common-Law rules: Railways were negligent if they failed to warn those approaching such crossings with proper signs at the crossing, and with the display and sounding of lights, bells, or whistles by the approaching tram or train. Moreover, this negligence had to be proved by the plaintiff. "My experience and observation," said Nova Scotia's Justice Nicholas Meager, "have satisfied me that the [tram] motormen are careful and diligent in their efforts to avoid accidents and injuries."[110] But Justice Meager's views notwithstanding, transport industry personnel were, at times, not only negligent, but reckless; the employees of one Canadian railroad, for example, were reported to have "regarded it as good clean fun when a roadway paralleled the tracks, to frighten horses out of their senses with monstrous blasts on the whistle."[111]

The English rule had it that plaintiffs were contributorily negligent and might be nonsuited if they failed to use "due care" in crossing,[112] but this was a highly subjective standard, with some jurists (and a few jurors) expecting much of pedestrians and wagon drivers, and other jurists (and most jurors) expecting much less, and refusing to allow such nonsuits.[113] "It cannot for a moment be conceived," wrote Justice Robert Hall of Quebec's Queen's Bench, one of the most generous courts for these sorts of plaintiffs, "that three men would have deliberately and unnecessarily risked their lives in attempting to cross the railway before this approaching train if they had heard the slightest sound that indicated the proximity of so fearful of a danger." But Justice Hall's views were not uniformly shared by his compeers on the

---

[110] In *Inglis v. Halifax Elec. Tram Co.*, 32 Nova Sc. 117 at 124 (1899) (but this was mere *dicta*, the court affirmed the judgement for the plaintiff).

[111] Stevens, *Canadian Railways*, 105. See *Vars v. Grand Trunk Ry.*, 23 UCCP 143 (1873); and *Victoria Ry. Comm. v. Coultas*, 12 Vict. LR (L) 895 (1886).

[112] This rule relied on the principles announced in *Butterfield v. Forrester*, 11 East 60 (1809), applied to crossing in *Hawkins v. Cooper*, 8 C. & P. 473, 173 ER 580 (N.P. 1838), and elaborated on by Tindal C. J. in *Sills v. Brown*, 9 C. & P. 601, 173 ER 974 (N.P. 1840): An injury that had been "occasioned in any degree to the incautious conduct of the plaintiff herself" was not to be adjudged the responsibility of the defendant.

[113] See *Leahy v. Comm. Of Rys.*, 7 WALR 44 (1904) (with much attention to late 19th century English decisions that limited the trial judge's discretionary nonsuit authority). See Karsten, *Heart versus Head*, 99–100, on juror reluctance to hold plaintiffs contributorily negligent.

courts of Upper and Lower Canada.[114] Legislatures added rules of
their own, of course, spelling out specific requirements that railways
and trams were to meet at crossings, and sometimes altering the duties
of those crossing the tracks as well (a subject we will revisit in the final
chapter).[115]

Government-owned railway corporations sometimes sought to protect themselves from liability for accidents by creating by-laws requiring

[114] In *La C. du Ch. de F. Can. du Pac. v. Birabin dit St. Denis*, 4 Quebec QB 516
at 522 (1894). Thus, Chief Justice Robinson of Upper Canada's Queen's
Bench affirmed a judgement against the Grand Trunk liable in 1860 for
such an accident with the observation that it was "incumbent on railway
companies for their own sakes to be most earnest with their servants" with
regard to the sounding of warnings in *Tyson v. Grand Trunk Ry.*, 20 UCQB
256 (1860), but Justice Badgley of Lower Canada's Superior Court, Quebec,
held a brewer whose sleigh had been hit by a Grand Trunk train to have
been contributorily negligent, citing the English leading case (*Butterfield
v. Forester*, 11 East 60 (1807) in *Moffatt v. Grand Trunk Ry.*, 16 Lower Can.
R 231 (1866) (See also *Marshall v. Grand Trunk Ry.*, 5 LCR 339 (1855)
(crossing victim can sue in tort despite statutory six-month limit on suits
by "creditors" of railways); *Browne v. Brockville & Ottawa Ry.*, 20 UCQB
202 (blacksmith crossing in wagon contributorily negligent); *Vars v. Grand
Trunk Ry.*, 23 UCCP 143 (1873) (hand car caused carriage horses to shy);
Grand Trunk Ry. v. Rosenberger, 9 Can. S.C. 311 (1884) (no bell sounded);
Green v. Toronto Ry. Co., 26 Ont. R 319 (1895) (no gong sounded); *Cie du
Grand Tronc v. Bourasse*, 4 Quebec, QB 235 (1894) (Ry. used Westinghouse
air brakes; pl. guilty of "gross" contributory negligence); *Curran v. Grand
Trunk Ry.*, 33 Lower Can. J. 330 (1889); and *Blake v. Can. Pac. Ry.* 17 Ont.
R (C.P.) 177 (1889)).

[115] Thus, an Ontario statute imposed bell and whistle duties on railways and
removed the burden on the plaintiff of proving she was not contributorily
negligent. See *Rosenberger v. Grand Trunk Ry.*, 32 UCCP 349 (1882) (statute
regarding failure to sound warning extends to accidents resulting from
horse having been frightened by unexpected sound of train in proximity);
and *Peart v. Grand Trunk Ry.*, 10 Ont. (C. of A.) 191 at 199–200 (1884).
The New Zealand Public Works Act of 1876 indicated "that the people
should take some risk on themselves" at crossings, and took away the right
to cross at private road crossings when a train was approaching, but this did
not suffice as a defense when the local Caversham Borough Council had
warned the railway authorities of the obscured view at the crossing and the
railway had failed to take corrective action. See *Mayo v. The Queen*, 1 NZLR
(SC) 113 at 115, 118 (1881) (pl. counsel cited American authorities).
    The rule under Quebec's Code was one of *comparative*, not contributory
negligence; damage awards were cut down by the degree of plaintiff's negligence, but if the defendant was proved negligent, the plaintiff received
something. See *C. da Navigation du Richelieu et d' Ontario v. St. Jean*, 28 Low.
Can. J. 91 (1883); *Dumouchel v. Grand Tronc*, 4 Quebec C.S. 379 (1893);
Jacquemin v. Montr. Street Ry., 11 Quebec C.S. 419 (1897); *Fleury v. Quebec
Distr. Ry.*, 13 Quebec C.S. 268 (1898).

drivers to make complete stops at crossings before proceeding. In 1912, a motorcyclist was killed in Wellington, New Zealand, "between the Queen's Wharf and a spot beyond Cuba Street extension," when he failed to come to a complete stop for a train of the government-owned Te Aro Railway that was within a half mile of the crossing, as the by-law required. None the less, his heirs sued the Crown, and won appeals both before the New Zealand Supreme Court and Court of Appeals. New Zealand's Justice Worley Edwards and his colleagues viewed the by-law as one made by the railway commissioners *ultra vires* (beyond their lawful powers). Justice Edwards knew from personal experience that it was hard to control such motorcycles as were available in Wellington in 1912, for he had lost control of one himself in the vicinity of the Supreme Court building there at the age of sixty-five, to the delight of the local bench and bar.[116] He was prepared to set aside a by-law that required all drivers to come to a full stop, and he offered an economic-efficiency rationale for this judgement:

> If every person who drives a vehicle across any one of these [designated full-stop] crossings or upon or along the line of railway were to obey this by-law, the traffic of the city would in some parts, notably at the end of Queen's Wharf, be brought to a standstill without any necessity or corresponding advantage.[117]

This judgement thus came at the expense of both real railway resources and purported railway authority. The New Zealand Railway Ministry consequently appealed to Privy Council, but the Law Lords allowed that "a plenitude of local knowledge assisted their lordships" on the New Zealand Court of Appeals. They joined a respect for "local conditions," with a further cost-benefit analysis: The New Zealand jurists "seem to have recognized the grave public inconvenience" of the by-law. "To what purpose," asked Lord Sumner, was "this waste of energy" in forcing all vehicles (many of them now propelled by hesitant internal combustion engines) to come to complete stops? Significantly, Lord Sumner cited "the very excellent judgement of the [Supreme] Court of the United States in *Grand Trunk Ry. v. Ives*," holding that railways could not "arbitrarily determine in advance what shall constitute ordinary care." Each case "must stand upon its own merits and be decided on its own facts and circumstances."[118] In this instance, "local

---

[116] Robin Cooke, *Portrait of a Profession* (Wellington, 1969), 71–72.

[117] *King v. Broad*, 33 NZLR (CA) 1275 at 1286 (1914) (Denniston, J., diss.).

[118] *The King v. Broad*, NZPCC 658 at 666 (1915); *Grand Trunk Ry., v. Ives*, 144 US 408 at 427 (1891).

conditions" (and an American citation) had convinced the Law Lords themselves.

Usually it was the CANZ jurists, not the Law Lords, who borrowed Law from American courts in "crossings" cases, as with other negligence issues. A few Canadian jurists cited the "many able judgements, very instructive and of much value," of New York and Pennsylvania and "the excellent and useful treatise on Railway Accident Law by Mr. Patterson of Philadelphia" (who also served as counsel to the Pennsylvania Railroad) in holding that a trial court judge was entitled to nonsuit a plaintiff when clear evidence of her contributory negligence had been admitted.[119] But other jurists rejected such prorailway U.S. citations. The "stop, look, and listen" rule of "the Pennsylvania State Courts" did not impress Ontario's Queen's Bench, nor did "*certaines authoritiés Américanes,*" impress Quebec's *Cour Superior* (though such opinions were ones that Quebec's jurists acknowledged they *were "obligeé d'arrêter et de regarder."*)[120] These two provinces, bordering American jurisdictions as they did, however, were aware of, and quite willing to cite the opinions of *other* state courts, those more friendly to the crossing victim's point of view.

The English standards were avoided, as they were in other situations, by reference to the "fact situation": "The circumstances of every case differ from the circumstances of every other case," Chief Justice John Douglas Armour of Ontario's Queen's Bench wrote in a crossing-accident case, "and it is impossible to frame a hard and fast rule applicable to every case." So he and his colleagues rejected the "hard and fast rule" proposed by the Canadian Pacific Railway's counsel, along with the cases counsel cited. There was "no English decision on the point," Chief Justice John Hawkins Hagarty of Ontario's Court of Appeals announced in another crossing case in the same year (1891). He then proceeded to refer to the treatise on railroad law written by Isaac Redfield, Vermont's former Chief Justice, as well as opinions from Illinois, Maine, Vermont, Wisconsin, and New York, in affirming an award of $8,000 to the victims.[121] Seven years later Ontario's Chancellor Sir John Alexander Boyd affirmed an award against the Hamilton

---

[119] Morrison, J., in *Johnston v. Northern Ry.*, 34 UCQB 432 at 438 (1874); Gwynne, J. (diss.), in *Can. Pac. Ry. v. Fleming*, 22 Can. S.C. 33 at 51 (1893). But in *Halifax Elec. Tramway v. Ingles*, 30 Can. S.C. 256 (1900), Justice Gwynne (diss.) relied solely on English authorities to establish this right of trial judges to nonsuit plaintiffs for contributory negligence.

[120] *Hollinger v. Can. Pac. Ry.*, 21 Ont. R 705 at 710 (1891); *Fleury v. Quebec Distr. Ry.*, 13 Quebec CS 268 at 269 (1898).

[121] *Hollinger v. Can. Pac. Ry.*, 21 Ont. R. 705 at 711 (1891); *Sibbald v. Grand Trunk Ry.*, 18 Ont. C of A 184 at 191 (1891) (Justice Osler also cited

Street Railway, dismissing the company's argument that the victim's age (he was ninety two) constituted a kind of contributory negligence. Pedestrians of all ages, infirmities, and characteristics had equal right of access to and use of the streets, and so it was laid down in an opinion of Massachusetts Chief Justice Lemuel Shaw, "a very eminent Judge" in "a Court perhaps of highest authority in any of the American States" in "one of the first cases growing out of the use of street cars."[122] Thus, by the 1890s, Ontario's courts had adopted the plaintiff-friendly rule of most American jurisdictions.

On two occasions CANZ jurists referred to the value of the railways to the general public in crossing-accident opinions. New Zealand's Justice C.W. Richmond made note of the immense advantages" that "rapid locomotion" brought, in reversing a jury finding for one injured at a private crossing. "Residents" on a line of travel "must to a large extent accept responsibility for their own safety" in using them, he wrote, since it was "impracticable" to impose "undue interference with the use of the line" by requiring railways to exercise the same restraints at private crossings as at public ones. The other comment was offered by Nova Scotia's Chief Justice Sir William Young in *Conlon v. Halifax City Railway* (1871), alluding to the "reminder," offered by the streetcar company's counsel, "that foreign capitalists were invited by the Government... to come into the Province to construct this work," and that it had "conferred...blessings...on the community." Chief Justice Young reminded the company's counsel in turn that the street railway concession had also "conferred large benefits on certain classes, to the signal inconvenience and loss of other classes equally entitled to the protection and care of the Legislature." Thus, when its improperly laid rails caused a carriage to overturn, the Nova Scotia chief justice and his colleagues were unimpressed by counsel's comments.[123] (No clear pattern here, but railway, streetcar, and tram companies lost 58 percent (50 of 85) cases reported in CANZ appellate reports between 1850 and 1910.)

---

several American cases in a concurring opinion (198)). See also *Desrousseau v. Boston & Me. Ry.*, 34 Low. Can. J. 252 (1889).

[122] *Haight v. Hamilton Elec. Ry.*, 29 Ont. R 279 at 281 (1898). Cf. *Gosnell v. Toronto Ry.*, 21 Ont. C. of A. 553 at 556 (1894).

[123] *N.Z.Ry. Comms. v. Trask*, 13 NZLR (CA) 139 at 149 (1894); and see *Gallogly v. Melbourne & Hobson's Bay United Ry.*, 1 VLR) (L) 58 at 65 (1875) (Justice Stephen: "the foot passenger must take care of himself" and "the fewer exceptions are made to that rule the better."); *Colon v. Halifax City Ry.*, 8 Nov. Sc. 209 at 220 (1871) (Chancellor James Johnstone cited American authorities in his opinion).

Nervous Shock: Coultas, Privy Council, and U.S. Jurists

One well-reported instance of a thwarted Common-Law innovation by a CANZ court concerned a crossing accident, the *Coultas* case. In May, 1886, a crossing guard in Victoria opened a gate for a couple in a cart on their way from Melbourne to Hawthorn. In the ensuing course of crossing the railroad tracks, the cart's wheels were scraped by an onrushing train that had failed to slow sufficiently or to sound signals. One of the cart's occupants, Mrs. Mary Coultas, sued for the "severe shock" she experienced "which brought on a miscarriage." The Victorian Railway Commissioners' counsel argued that the train had caused no actual physical injury to Mrs. Coultas, a standard requirement in all such personal injury cases, but Justice Kerferd noted one English case of a woman who had literally been frightened to death by a violent trespass. The fright she had experienced "formed an element which the jury considered in connection with the amount of damages." The case was *Huxley v. Berg* (1815), which actually differed from *Coultas* is two regards: First, the action of the defendant had been intentional and deliberate, not an act of negligence; and, second, the court in *Huxley* had admitted the evidence of the wife's fright "not as a substantive ground of damage" in itself, but only to support the proof that the defendant's *trespass* had been violent.[124] Nervous shock was not understood as late as 1888, when the *Coultas* case was reversed by Privy Council, which insisted on the English rule that the plaintiff must be physically touched for a tort to occur.[125]

Coultas was followed in Ontario decisions in 1898 and 1905, but it was "distinguished" (that is, not followed) in the high courts of New South Wales (1896), Western Australia (1906), and New Zealand (1922).[126] As Justice Herdman put it in the New Zealand opinion,

---

124 *Huxley v. Berg,* 1 Stark. 98, 171 ER 413 (1815), noted in *Coultas et Uxor v. Vict. Ry. Comm.*, 12 Vict. LR (L) 895 (1886).

125 *Victorian Ry. Comm. v. Coultas,* LR 13 App. Cas. 222 (1888).

It was not until 1889 that Professors Church and Peterson made a case for it in their *Nervous and Mental Diseases.* Hence, the action of Privy Council is not surprising, even if it was disappointing to the Coultas's. Alfred Stirling, "Liability for Nervous Shock," 2 Australian Law Journal 46 at 49–50 (June 15, 1928).

126 *Henderson v. Can. Atl. Ry.*, 25 Ont. C. of A. 437 at 444 (1898); *Geiger v. Grand Trunk RR,* 10 Ont. L.R. 511 (1905); *Rea v. Balmain New Ferry Co.*, 17 NSW LR 921 (1896); *Daly v. Comm. of Rys.*, 8 West. Austr. LR 125 at 127 (1906); *Stevenson v. Basham & Another,* 1922 NZLR (SC) 225 at 230–32. (*Coultas* was also "doubted" in an English King's Bench opinion and a Scottish appellate case; *Dulieu v. White,* 2 KB 669 (1901) (citing two U.S. decisions rejecting Privy Council's *Coultas*); *Coyle v. Watson,* 1915 A.C. 1. See also *Pugh v. London, Br. & S.C. Ry,* 2 QB Div. 248 (1896).

"we in New Zealand are no doubt bound to follow" Privy Council's judgement "unless the facts of the present case can be distinguished." They did not appear to be; a woman three months pregnant had been frightened, had become "hysterical," and had miscarried. There had been no physical touching. Yet Justice Herdman concluded that the "evidence proves that physical harm was so closely bound up with the shock which Mrs. Basham suffered that it may be said that shock was accompanied by actual physical injury."[127] CANZ jurists did not like Privy Council's decision, but, unlike the high courts of Minnesota, New York, Rhode Island, Texas, California, South Carolina, and Illinois, they could not simply reject it as bad Law.[128] So some of them "distinguished," or merely obfuscated the facts to arrive at the desired end.

Heroic Risks: Was a "Good Samaritan" Contributorily Negligent in the Provinces and Dominions?

We have now seen how CANZ courts generally dealt with defendant claims of contributory negligence, but there remains one special case to consider: Sometimes a "Good Samaritan" sprang forward to scoop up a child or a "half-blind" elderly person from the path of an onrushing train, tram, or "runaway horse,"[129] or to rescue a supine soul trapped in a burning building, and sometimes that person was injured or killed in the process. What legal rights to redress did such heroes and heroines have in the event that the negligence of the railway company or hotel could be proved? Were they subject to nonsuit for having been contributorily negligent?

This was the rule in England, and it did not matter in the least to jurists there that the heroine felled by the train was the grandmother of the child she had been trying to save.[130] But it was not the rule in the United States. There, high court after state high court followed the lead of New York's Court of Appeals in ruling that such heroes and heroines were *not* to be nonsuited. Neither New York's jurists nor those of any other court cited any English authority in support of this proposition (there being none), but more than one referred to the

---

[127] *Stevenson v. Basham & Another*, 1922 NZLR (SC) 225 at 231–32.

[128] See *Illinois Central RR v. Latmier*, 128 IU. 163, 21 NE 7 (1889); *Purcell v. St. Paul City Ry.*, 48 Minn. 34, 50 NW 1034 (1892); *Mitchell v. Rochester RR*, 151 N.Y. 107 (1896); *Simone v. The R.I. Co.*, 28 R.I. 186, 66 Atl. 202 (1907); *Hill v. Kimball*, 76 Tex. 210, 13 SW 59 (1890); *Sloane v. So. Cal. RR*, 111 Cal. 688, 44 Pac. 320 (1896); *Mack v. South Bd. RR*, 52 So. Car. 323, 29 SE 905 (1898).

[129] As did "Ned Darton" on a street in Sydney in the late nineteenth century in Edward Dyson's short story "The Conquering Bush" in *Below and On Top* (Melbourne, 1898), 1.

[130] *Waite v. N. Eastern Ry.*, El., Bl. & El. 719, 120 ER 679 (1858).

Law's "regard for human life" or to "the dictates of humanity."[131] This jurisprudence flowed straight from the heart.

Canadian courts addressed the question on four separate occasions between 1875 and 1910. The first two of these were heard before Ontario's jurists. A railway worker named Anderson at the Collingwood wharf noticed a woman in the path of a backing gravel train without a lookout; he was killed pushing her to safety. A trial court jury awarded his survivor $3,600, but he was deemed contributorily negligent at two successive appellate-level hearings. Justice Burton found him "heroic and praiseworthy" and embraced the American rule, but Justices Strong and Draper rejected it, the latter noting that the man owed a greater duty to his own family than to this stranger. Seventeen years later another jury found for a man injured trying to stop a team of horses startled by a municipality's negligent blasting of rocks and terrain. Needless to say, the case was appealed, and, once again, the American rule found an ally, in Chancellor Boyd, who pointed out that the English rule followed in *Anderson* was rejected by "a consensus of American authority." On further appeal, Justice Meredith was critical of "the unwisdom and inhumanity of such law" as the rule in *Anderson*, but he held that *Anderson* was "binding," *if* it was found to be applicable. In this case, he and a majority of his colleagues on the Court of Appeals distinguished the facts in *Anderson* from those before them: *This* plaintiff was the *owner* of the runaway team, and the court wondered whether he might not have been liable for harm that the team could have done had he not sought to control it. As such, it held that the plaintiff–owner had not been contributorily negligent. Hence, his actions were not quite the same as those of the "reckless" hero in *Anderson*.[132]

When jurists from Canada's western provinces addressed the question, however, the story was different. A man, appropriately named Love, was burned going back into a blazing hotel without a fire escape in Fairview, British Columbia to save "Miss Hunt." Nonsuited at trial, he won a new trial on appeal from the British Columbia Supreme Court. His counsel cited American authorities and the court adopted the principles of those jurisdictions. The question of whether Mr. Love

---

[131] *Eckert v. L.I.R.R.*, 43 NY 502 (1871); *Corbin v. Phila.*, 195 Pa. St. 461 (1900); *Linnehan v. Sampson*, 126 Mass. 506 (1879); *Donahoe v. Wabash, St. L. & Pac. RR*, 83 Mo. 560 (1884); *Pa. Co. v. Langendorff*, 48 Ohio St. 316, 28 NE 172 (1891); *Peyton v. Teras & P.RR*, 41 La. Ann. 861, 6 So. 690 at 691 (1889) Karsten, *Heart versus Head*, 252–54.

[132] *Anderson v. Northern Ry.*, 25 UCCP 301 at 317, 320, 323 (1875); *Connell v. Town of Prescott*, 20 Ont. C. of A. 49 at 52, 54, 62 (1892).

had been contributorily negligent should have been left to the jury, and Justice Drake did not sound as if he would have held him so: Mr. Love "would have disgraced his manhood" had he not rescued Miss Hunt.[133] Several years later, in Winnipeg, a man was knocked unconscious by a carelessly driven tram, in the act of saving the life of a two-year-old child on the tracks. Justices Richards and Perdue took slightly different paths to arrive at the same destination. Justice Richards noted that *Anderson v. Northern Ry.* and *Eckert v. Long Island Ry.* (the leading case in the United States) were in conflict. He conveniently found "no case in the English reports" dealing with the fact situation (though one *had*),[134] and announced he was free to treat *Anderson*, a mere "Canadian case," simply as bad Law. "The promptings of humanity towards the savings of life are among the noblest instincts of mankind," he observed, borrowing the phrase from an American defender of *Eckert*. Justice Perdue's more cautious path in this case was to hold that *Anderson* was still good Law, but to find that its facts were "quite distinguishable" from those before the Manitoba Supreme Court. That allowed him to embrace *Eckert* as well, and he strengthened this posture of deference-to-Westminster by pointing out that Sir Fredrick Pollock, in a recent edition of his treatise on Torts, "regards with approval the principles laid down in the *Eckert* case." That was Perdue's English authority, but he quoted the "common law" authority offered in *Eckert* as well: "To save human life is a lawful act, to put it on no higher ground. . . ."[135]

Accidents to Strangers (and Neighbors) who were Children
Children played in the streets of London, New York, Montreal, Melbourne, and Auckland as they had done in other streets for as long as the memory of man runneth (Zechariah, 8:5). But with the increase in traffic, such play became increasingly dangerous. Victorian fencemaker Thomas Day noted in his diary his own fear of being "run over" on Collins Street during a visit to Melbourne in 1885, and while riding an omnibus the next day he remarked on how its driver was compelled to swerve "every few yards to avoid a collision."[136] It was said in Auckland, no more than twenty years after the signing of the Treaty of Waitangi, that "children have their brains beaten out by horses illegally at large," and that "we behold carts left without carters" that

---

[133] *Love v. Fairview,* 10 Br. Col. 330 at 335–36 (1904).
[134] *Waite v. Ry.,* supra note 131.
[135] *Seymour v. Winnipeg Elec. Ry. Co.,* 19 Manitoba R. 412 at 414, 417 (1910).
[136] Day, "Diary, or Reminiscences," pp. 4, 6, MS 8432/986/5, St. Lib. Of Victoria

Illustration 35.   Children playing in the streets in New York City (top) could be hit by carts, buggies, and streetcars. (Lewis Hine Collection, Library of Congress.)

"run away, and run over the lieges with impunity."[137] When children were struck by a wagon or streetcar driven by an inattentive driver or when they were injured while trespassing on another's property, the accident sometimes resulted in a lawsuit that presented CANZ jurists with a choice: Follow the English rule or find a way to the newer one from the States. (See Illustrations 35 to 38.)

In mid-nineteenth century England the Common Law held young children to essentially the same standard of care as adults when the tots raced into the street, into the path of a carriage or tram.[138] Moreover, English jurists were prepared to hold that parents and guardians who let their children venture into harm's way had contributed to the accident by such negligent acts, and to impute this contributory negligence to the injured child.[139] When the youngster had been injured on or in

---

[137] Richard Hill, *Policing the Colonial Frontier,* 289, fn. 98.
[138] Lord Denman sought to establish a lower standard of care for young children in *Lynch v. Nurdin,* 1 Ad. and El. (N.S.) 29, 113 ER 1041 (QB 1841), but his views were "doubted" in *Lygo v. Newbolt,* 9 Ex. 300, 156 ER 129 (Ex. 1854). The harsher *Lygo* rule was thereafter followed, as in *Hughes v. Macfie & Another,* 2 Hurl. & Cot. 744, 159 ER 308 (Ex. 1863).
[139] *Waite v. Northeastern Ry.,* 28 LJ (QB) 258 (Ex. 1858) and El., Bl. & El. 719, 120 ER 679 (Ex. 1858); followed in *Wright v. Ry.,* 4 Allen (Mass.) 283 (1862).

Illustration 36. Trolleys and carriages contend with cyclists and pedestrians on a busy moment at the corner of Yonge and King Streets, Toronto, in 1901. (Archives of Ontario, S3779.)

some dangerous object on another's property, a suit on his[140] behalf was turned away by jurists in the Mother of All Common Law with the observation that the child had been a trespasser, and that property owners owed trespassers very little in the way of duties under the law of tort.[141]

[140] With very few exceptions, injured child trespassers, in Britain, the United States, and the CANZ jurisdictions, were male. Boys, it seems, engaged in more "daring" behavior than girls in the nineteenth century. See Karsten, *Heart versus Head*, 423 (Boys were the victims in 114 of 136 appealed accident cases involving children in the nineteenth century U.S. reports (84 percent).) See also the data collected by The Survey Committee of the Cleveland Foundation on "What 14,683 Cleveland Children were Doing on June 23, 1913," in George Johnson, *Education Through Recreation* (Cleveland, 1916), 48–51 (twice as many boys as girls were playing in the streets; more girls than boys were playing in yards.)

[141] *Blyth v. Topham*, Cro. Jac. 158, 79 ER 139 (KB 1608); *Sarch v. Blackburn*, 4 Car. & P. 299, 172 ER 712 (N.P. 1830); *Gaudret v. Egerton*, 2 LR (CP) 371 (1872). This was the English standard throughout our period, and beyond. See *Latham v. Johnson & Nephew, Ltd.*, 1 KB 398 at 416, All ER 117 (1911–1913);

Illustration 37.   Is the policeman arresting, or merely comforting the distraught trolley operator in this engraving for the cover of *Leslie's Weekly*, August 29, 1895?

Jurists in most of the United States rejected all of these rules: By the 1860s, they insisted on treating children under ten or twelve as having a substantially lower standard when it came to "due care;" such children were not yet adults and were not to be regarded as adults in

and *Comm. for Rys. v. Quinlan*, 1 All ER 897 (1964) (rejecting both the judgement of the New South Wales Supreme Court (1964 NSW 157), which had employed the American "attractive nuisance" licencee fiction, and the Australian Supreme Court (1961 ALR 16, 104 CLR 274; 1964 ALR 900), which argued that the licencee/trespasser distinction should cease to exist).

Illustration 38. One innovation designed to reduce injury to inattentive or less agile pedestrians was this "people-catcher," mounted here on a tram in Christchurch, on its way to Papanui, New Zealand. (Alexander Turnbull Library, G-84061/2.)

Law. By the 1880s, they refused to permit any imputation of parental
contributory negligence to children at all. They also held that children
"drawn" to dangerous objects on the property of others by virtue of the
"alluring" or "attractive" nature of the object were to be treated, not as
trespassers, but as "invitees," with all of the increased liability as such
status imposed on the property owner (usually a corporation).[142] It will
come as no surprise that I wanted to know how CANZ jurists reacted
to this Anglo-American distinction.

Needless to say, in Diaspora communities that were experiencing
the same sort of transportation revolution, there were many children
"run over" who were "hurt Badly" – among them the three year old
killed when an unattended horsecart started up on Lambton Quay
in Wellington, New Zealand, March 2, 1860, and the lad run over in
front of a carriage maker's shop near Kingston, Ontario, on April 27,
1887.[143] All told, I found nearly forty cases in the CANZ reports where
children or their "best friends" were the plaintiffs. Defendants lost
74 percent of these appellate cases. Why?

They lost *every one* of the cases where the child had been hit in a
street. Children were "in the habit of riding behind waggons," and
"amus[ing] themselves by coasting or tobogganing on the streets,"
wrote Ontario's Chancellor Sir John Alexander Boyd in a case of one
who had been crushed to death playing on a pile of heavy logs left un-
secured in the street. After all, he pointed out, children were free to
"play on the highways when there is no prohibitory local law." He relied
heavily on U.S. case law in support of this opinion (indeed the words of
his that I have just quoted are virtually the same as those of several U.S.
jurists). Other CANZ jurists found Lord Denman's rather unEnglish
views in *Lynch v. Nurdin* (QB 1841) to be sufficient grounds to hold defendants liable.[144] Quebec's Justice J. J. Curran, for example, faulted

---

142 See Karsten, *Heart versus Head*, chs. 7 and 8.

143 *NZ Spectator*, Mar. 3, 1860, p. 2; Leeman Crawford Diary, Apr. 28, 1887, MU
      757, Crawford Papers, Archives of Ontario.

144 *Ricketts v. Corp. of Makdale*, 31 Ont. R. 610 at 615 (1900). Cf. *Bates v. Brett*,
      18 NSWLR 267 (1897) (unattended cart moved, running over boy; jury
      verdict for defendant reversed on appeal); *M'Kinnon v. Morris*, 11 Vict. LR
      175 (1885) (stones left by road contractors injured boy; award affirmed);
      Winnepeg Elec. Ry. v. Wald, 41 Can. S.C. 431 (1909) (defective fender resp.
      for injury to young girl; award affirmed; *Pilon v. Shedden Co. & Cullen*,
      9 Quebec C.S. 83 (1896) (boy injured riding horse; award affirmed);
      Turner v. Isnor, 25 Nova Sc. 428 (1893) (award affirmed in case where horse
      ran over two children); *Levoy v. Midland Ry.*, 3 Ont. R. 623 (1883) (award
      to six-year-old who lost foot at crossing affirmed on appeal); *Merritt v.
      Hepenstal*, 25 Can. S.C. 150 (1895) (award affirmed; delivery man had
      run over child); *Beauchamp v. Cloran* 17 Quebec 178 (1866) (bread cart

the defendant in *Pilon v. Shedden Co.* for having failed the French standard of care to the young plaintiff, the "protection of a *bon pere de famille*," but he also quoted from an American treatise on negligence law and rejected the "English cases" that treated children much the same as adults with regard to contributory negligence: "These decisions have been condemned" and were, in any event, "directly opposed to the current American cases" on the question. Furthermore, Justice Curran, like Chancellor Boyd, offered *dicta* remarkably similar to that of these compeers to his south: "A boy is naturally giddy at the age of 13...."[145]

Defendants sometimes charged the parents of the injured child with contributory negligence for having allowed the youngster to play in the street unattended, arguing that this parental negligence should be imputed by the court to the child as it was in England. This English rule applied both to children and passengers in omnibuses and cabs injured when their inattentive drivers collided with a tram or train.[146] While New Zealand's Frederick Chapman criticized the English rule (in a lecture) as being "so little consonant with reason," and R. V. Rogers (a Toronto barrister turned treatise writer) compared it unfavorably to an opinion of the New Jersey Supreme Court that had rejected it, I found no instances in the CANZ appellate reports of any *court* willing to do so when the injured plaintiff was an adult passenger in a cab or wagon driven by a negligent driver that collided with a train.[147] But

---

broke seven-year-old's leg; plaintiff wins); *Sangster v. T. Eaton & Co.*, 25 Ont R 78 (1894), 21 OAR 624 (1894), 24 Can SCR 708 (1895); *Hesketh v. City of Toronto*, 25 Ont. C. of A. 449 (1898) (fire engine hit boy; award affirmed); *Toronto Ry. v. Mitchell*, Can. S.C. (Coultée) 349 (1905) (motorman responsible for injury to child at crossing); *Tobin v. Mayor of Melbourne*, 8 Vict. LR (L) 41 (1882) (spark from steamroller injures eye of girl returning from school; award affirmed); *Moffat v. Ry. Comms.*, 15 LRNSW 405 (1894) (award affirmed to family of ten-year-old girl killed by tram); *Clarke v. Borough of North Sydney*, 14 LR NSW 499 (1893) (six-year-old boy returning from school who fell in excavation in road; award affirmed). Cf. *Courtemauche v. Les Clercs Peroissiaux*, 4 Quebec QB 490 (1895) ($500 to family of child who drowned at school); *Heenan v. Iredale*, 19 NZLR (SC) 387 (1900) (horsecart ran down boy; nonsuit reversed).

145 *Pilon v. Shedden Co & Cullen*, 9 Quebec C.S. 83 at 84 (1896). For several examples of American *dicta* of this sort see Karsten, *Heart versus Head*, chs. 6 and 7.

146 The English rule in the driver-passenger cases was laid down in *Thorougood v. Bryan*, 8 C.B. 15, 137 ER 452 (1849); and *Rigby v. Hewitt*, 5 Ex. 240, 155 ER 103 (Ex. 1850).

147 For instances of its application in Upper Canada (Ontario) see *Winckler v. Great West. Ry.*, 18 UCCP 250 (1868); *Rastrick v. Great West. Ry.*, 27 UCQB 396 (1868); *Boggs v. Great West. Ry.*, 23 UCCP 573 (1874); *Nicholls v. Great*

when it came to the imputation of parental contributory negligence to a child injured in the street, Justice Townsend resolved the issue on the one occasion on which that issue was joined, *Turner v. Isnor* (Nova Scotia, 1893), by reporting that he had simply found "no decided case in England" that was "four-square" on the facts of the case before the court; he therefore turned to American treatises and cases for relevant precedents in order to turn away this defense argument.[148]

Child Trespassers and the Allurement Doctrine

While children were seen by CANZ jurists to possess the right to play in the streets, those injured while trespassing on another's property were sometimes treated quite differently. After all, the English rule was that defendants in these sorts of cases owed trespassers no standard of "due care" whatsoever; the only limit to their use of their property was that they were not to injure trespassers deliberately.[149] Most American courts rejected this rule and treated trespassing children injured on notoriously dangerous objects as invitees who had been "allured" or "attracted" by the owners of such objects due to the workings of their innocent, childish instincts,[150] but while CANZ jurists found ways to utilize the American decisions when it came to children injured on *public* land, they had more difficulty in doing so when the child was a trespasser, and gave judgements for the defendant in seven of fourteen of those sorts of cases that I could identify.

When the child was a newsboy, hawking his papers on a streetcar or tram (see Illustrations 39 and 40), CANZ courts had few difficulties in finding that he was due no special treatment by the company or its agents. Newsboys did not purchase tickets; they were not passengers. Nor had they been "allured" to the tram by their "childish instincts;" they were youthful trespassing entrepreneurs, who could be (carefully)

West. Ry., 27 UCQB 382 (1886). On Justice Chapman's views, see Peter Spiller's fine dissertation, "Two Judges: Father and Son: An Analysis of the Careers of Henry C. and Frederick Chapman," Univ. of Canterbury Law, 1991; R. V. Rogers, *The Law of the Road* (Amer. ed., S.F., 1884), 66, citing *Bennett v. NYRR*, 36 NJL 223 (1873).

148 *Turner et al. v. Isnor*, 25 Nova Sc. 428 (1893). Curiously, R. V. Rogers, the Toronto attorney who did not care for the rule imputing a driver's negligence to a passenger, had no problem with it when it came to imputing a parent's negligence to a child. (Rogers, *supra* note 148, 27).

149 *Blyth v. Topham*, Cro. Jac. 158, 79 ER 139 (K.B. 1608); *Sarch v. Blackburn*, 4 Car. & P. 299, 172 ER 712 (N.P. 1830).

150 *Stout v. S.C. & P. RR*, 2 Dillon 294, 23 Fed. Cas. 183 (1872), affm'd. in 84 U.S. 657 (1873); *Keffe v. Milw. & St. P. RR*, 21 Minn. 207 (1875). See Karsten, *Heart versus Head*, ch. 7, for a more through analysis of both English and American views on this subject.

Illustration 39. The "attractive nuisance" or "allurement" rule emerged in the courts of the United States in the 1870s as a consequence of horrendous accidents that befell young trespassing children on railroad turntables like these, designed to enable workers to reverse a locomotive's direction. When the locomotive was not present and the turntable left unattended (as it generally would have been), teenagers would crank it around, and younger children climb aboard for a ride. With its upright guys, twelve feet tall, "which could be seen from a considerable distance," it looked "not unlike a circus merry-go-round" to children, or so one jurist put it. *Nagel v. Missouri Pacific RR*, 75 Mo. 653 at 658 (1882). Note the party atmosphere, complete with small children, on this J class locomotive on a turntable in New Zealand in 1888. (Alexander Turnbull Library, National Library of New Zealand, E. R. Williams Collection, G-254821/1.)

ejected, and were not entitled to damages in the event of a collision, a derailment, or a jarring stop.[151]

Similarly, a twelve-year-old boy injured in playing with a fog signal that he had taken from a railway handcar in Toronto, another twelve-year-old in Woollahra, New South Wales, whose arm was crushed playing on a borough's crane left at a quarry near a public playground, and a ten-year-old whose foot was crushed playing on an unlocked

---

[151] *Blackmore v. Toronto Str. Ry.*, 38 UCQB 172 (1876) (Chief Justice Harrison of Queen's Bench Division, citing American cases, favored the plaintiff; but the Court of Appeals, citing only English authorities, reversed); *Coll v. Toronto Ry. Co.*, 25 Ont. C. of A. 55 at 63 (1898). And see *Mills v. Woolverton*, 9 App. Div. 82 for the same rule regarding a newsboy. But see *Martin v. The Queen*, 2 Can. Ex. 328 (1891) (child forced to jump off train by brakeman; leg crushed; $3,000 award affirmed).

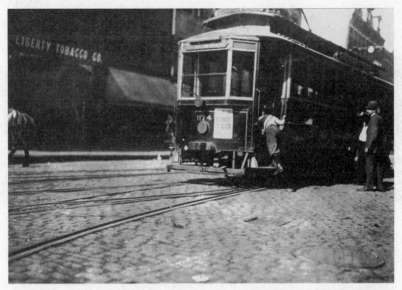

Illustration 40.   Children on streetcars and trams/trolleys could be contributorily negligent, theoretically freeing the transit firm of liability, evidenced in this Lewis Hine photo of a newsboy jumping aboard a trolley in Boston (top). (Lewis Hine Collection, National Child Labor Committee Papers, Library of Congress.)

truck shifter at the Port Melbourne railway pier in Victoria, were all turned away remediless. Ontario's Chancellor Boyd told the first that the company was "under no obligation to the stray children" of the neighborhood "to fence or lock or house these fog signals in such a way as to render access to them more difficult." Trespassers were trespassers whether they were twelve or thirty-two, and to "condone" the "alleged curiosity of youth" would "place too high a premium on the so-called irrepressible movements of the youthful body and mind," and would "impose a servitude on landowners which would prove a cruel and grievous burden."[152] When counsel for the second lad cited the leading American case for the "allurement" doctrine, *RR v. Stout*,[153] he found no takers: "I am quite unable to understand how the decision in *RR v. Stout* can be supported," Chief Justice Sir Fred Darley told him.[154] Counsel for the third lad convinced Victoria's Chief Justice

[152] *McShane v. Toronto, H. & B. Ry.*, 31 Ont. R. 185 at 188 (1899).
[153] 84 U.S. 657 (1873).
[154] *Patterson v. Borough of Woollahra*, 16 NSWLR 228 at 233 (1895). See also the criticism of the American "allurement," or "attractive nuisance" doctrine by Angus MacMurchy and Shirley Denison, editors of *Canadian Railway*

Higinbotham that he had been "invited" onto the pier and attracted to the dangerous machine, but he did not convince Higinbotham's two colleagues.[155]

But as in so many other instances, there were other CANZ jurists who saw things much the same way as had the American jurists of the Great Plains who created the attractive nuisance doctrine and those of the Corn and Bible Belt states who adhered to it. Bruce Kercher tells us of a suit in Sydney's Magistrate's Court in 1811: A child who had gone onto a neighbor's property to pet a chained dog was savaged by the animal; a familiar story. The owner's defense, that the boy was a trespasser, was rejected by the court, according to the account in the *Sydney Gazette*, as a "strange mode of reasoning," since the owner would have been responsible if the dog had injured anyone on lawful business (that is, a "licencee" or "invitee").[156] If this was reported by the *Gazette* correctly, it was clearly at variance with English Common Law,[157] and it thus anticipated by nearly two generations the creation of the Common-Law rule in the United States that might have sustained this judgement.[158] Similarly, when a twelve-year-old boy fell to his death through an open cellar door adjacent a highway in Upper Canada in 1856, Chief Justice Robinson ruled that he was no trespasser, and that, even if he had been, the jury was free to decide whether his "want of discretion" could fairly be attributed to his age and immaturity. Robinson relied on Lord Denman's views in *Lynch v. Nurdin* though these views had been "doubted" by the Court of Exchequer in 1854.[159]

Later, in the 1890s, most of Ontario's jurists embraced the American "allurement" doctrine. Thus, a child, injured in a store by a mirror that fell on him when he touched it, was nonsuited at trial as a contributorily

---

Cases, II (Toronto, 1903), 253–56, and their preference for the opinions of the northeastern U.S. jurisdictions that joined the English courts in holding to the older trespasser defense.

[155] *Slade v. Victorian Ry. Comms.*, 15 Vict. LR 190 (1889) (but it was English case law that was at issue here, especially the scope of Lord Denman's rule in *Lynch v. Nurdin*; no American cases were noted.)

See also *Farrell v. Grand Trunk Ry.*, 2 Ontario Weekly Rpts. 85 (1903) (no recovery to heirs of boy killed while trespassing on defective bridge).

[156] Bruce Kercher, *Debt, Seduction & Other Diasters*, 114, citing "John Burgess's Case," *Sydney Gazette*, 18 May 1811, 2.

[157] See *Sarch v. Blackburn*, 4 Car. & P. 299, 172 ER 712 (N.P. 1830), for a "four-square" case.

[158] See *Daley v. Norwich & W. RR*, 26 Ct. 591 (1858), and Karsten, "Explaining the Fight over the Attractive Nuisance Doctrine: A Kinder, Gentler Instrumentalism in the 'Age of Formalism,'" 10 *Law & History Review* 45 (1992).

[159] *McIntyre v. Buchanan*, 14 Up. Can. QB 581 at 583 (1857); *Lynch v. Nurdin, supra* note 139; *Lygo v. Newbolt*, 9 Ex. 300, 156 ER 129 (Ex. 1854).

negligent licensee, but his suit was restored on appeal. Chief Justice Armour spoke of the mirror as "attracting" the child and read from the leading American treatise on negligence (Shearman & Redfield) to the effect that earlier English opinions holding such children contributorily negligent were now "condemned in England" and were "directly opposed to the current of American cases." Six years later, Justice Thomas Ferguson described timbers left in the street that had rolled onto a child as "an invitation" and "an allurement to boys and children for the purposes of playing," and cited American authority for this view. Similarly, while Chief Justice William Meredith held that the grain hoist that a five-year-old boy had been injured on did not quite qualify as an "attractive nuisance," he quoted at length from *Keffe v. RR*, the Minnesota Supreme Court decision that provided the most elaborate explication of the rule, and clearly signaled that he accepted every aspect of this rule. "Had it been that young children had, to the knowledge of the defendant, been accustomed to play upon it," the Chief Justice explained, the grain hoist's owner would have been liable.[160]

The House of Lords adopted the attractive nuisance doctrine in 1909, citing the U.S. Supreme Court opinion, *RR v. Stout*,[161] but by the 1920s, the English Common Law courts had severely limited that decision, prompting legal commentators in New Zealand and Australia to describe these decisions as "Draconian and not humanitarian," "difficult to speak of" with "either respect or restraint." In 1934, the *New Zealand Law Journal*'s commentator observed of an English opinion turning away the suit of a six-year-old boy injured by the collapse of earth piled near a wall by town authorities: "Anyone who has walked

---

[160] *Sangster v. T. Eaton Co.*, 25 Ont. R. 78 at 82 (1894); *Ricketts v. Corp. of Village of Markdale*, 31 Ont. R. 610 at 619 (1900); *Smith v. Hayes*, 29 Ont. R. 283 at 288–89 and 291 (1898). See also *Makins v. Piggott & Inglis*, 29 Can. S.C. 188 (1898); *Delage v. Delisle*, 10 Quebec Banc du Roi 481 (1901); and *Prattis v. Municip. of Bexley*, 15 SRNSW 232 (1915) (thirteen-year-old boy injured on disused quarry crane adjacent highway; padlock broken by other children; defendant's council cited a Maine Supreme Court opinion that rejected the attractive nuisance rule (*Stinson v. City of Gardiner*, 42 Me. 248 (1856)), but the new South Wales Supreme Court upheld a £350 award to the plaintiff. (By this time, however, the court might have relied on an opinion of the Law Lords, *Cooke v. Midland RR of Ireland*, App. Cas. 229 (1909), wherein *Stout v. RR* had been cited approvingly.)

[161] In *Cooke v. Midland RR of Ireland*, App. Cas. 229 (1909); followed in *Prattis v. Municp. of Bexley*, 15 SRNSW 232 (1915); *Wilks v. Bexley Munic. Council*, 9 Local Govt. Rpts. (NSW) 29 (1928) (concrete mixer on road; ten-year-old boy on way to school lost hand in cogwheels; award affirmed) (apparently Bexley had learned little between 1915 and 1927).

with boys of this age would call it a direct challenge."[162] Perhaps CANZ
jurists were not as generous toward trespassing children in these years
as were their counterparts in the States, but they were more generous
than their British mentors.

HURT ON THE JOB: CANZ JURISTS AND THE ASSUMPTION
OF RISK AND COMMON EMPLOYMENT RULES

Men and women injured while at work sometimes claimed in lawsuits
that their employers were responsible.[163] Where such suits went to
trial, the workers (or their executors, in the event that the injury proved
fatal) offered evidence that the employer had negligently placed them
in harm's way by virtue of his unsafe equipment or dangerous worksite,
his failure to advise the employee adequately of the hazardous nature
of the work, or the careless instructions offered by one of his agents.
Employers generally responded by claiming one or more of the following defenses: (1) The worksite and equipment were appropriate
and safe; the employee had herself been careless, contributing to her
injury; (2) the third party responsible for her injury had *not* been the
agent of the employer (a "vice principal" or "superior servant") but
a mere "fellow-servant," working in "common employment" with the
injured employee, and it was this "fellow-servant" who should have
been sued, not the employer; (3) the risks had been understood by
the employee and were assumed within her contractual agreement, or,
more specifically, that the employer had explicitly "contracted out" of
liability with the employee, offering free or low cost medical care and
funeral expenses in exchange. In general, American courts offered

---

[162] S. A. Wiren, "Road Trespassers and Children," 10 *New Zealand Law Journal*
204 (1934), commenting on *Liddle v. North Riding of Yokshire C.C.*, 50 T LR
377 (1934); P. F. P. Higgins, *Elements of Torts in Australia* (Sydney, 1970), 341,
commenting on *Comm. for Rys. (NSW) v. Cardy*, ALR 16, 104 CLR 274 (1961)
(a trespassing fourteen-year-old boy who fell into hot ashes was entitled
to sue; trespasser/licencee distinction adjudged void by High Court of
Australia; Privy Council rejected this and insisted on this distinction in
Comm. for Rys. v. Quinlan, 1 All ER 897 (1964), NSW 157 (1964), ALR 900
(1964), App. Cas. 1054 (1964). But Victoria's Supreme Court rejected this
reversal in the eloquent opinion of Justice Deane in *Hackshaw v. Shaw*, 155
CLR (Victoria) 614 at 659 (1984).

[163] Simultaneously, employers who felt that a worker had been injured due
to his or her own carelessness might well fire that worker, as was a lad
who cut off part of his thumb operating a boot manufacturer's press in
Fitzroy, Australia, in 1882. See Michael Cannon, *Life in the Cities: Australia
in the Victorian Age* (Melbourne, 1975), citing the example of Richard
White's testimony before the *Victorian Royal Commission on Employees in Shops*
(1882–1884) p. 5057.

more exceptions to the assumption of risk and fellow servant rules than did English courts, and the question of whether the employee had been contributorily negligent was generally left in America to the juries that decided, overwhelmingly, for plaintiffs.[164] How were these matters decided by jurists in Canada, Australia, and New Zealand?

Employee Contributory Negligence

CANZ employers did manage to win a number of appeals to set verdicts aside because of the employee's contributory negligence (or, in the event that the trial judge had nonsuited the plaintiff on these grounds, to sustain that nonsuit). This was particularly so in Canadian and Australian jurisdictions,[165] and some of these jurists cited "a mass of authority in the United States which is closely in point, and in harmony with these views," which is to say that they relied on the minority point of view in the American states on the role of the jury.[166] But

---

[164] See Karsten, *Heart against Head,* 96–100, 108–25.

[165] See for example, *Miller v. Reid,* 10 Ont. R. 419 (1885); *Badgerow v. Grand Trunk Ry.,* 19 Ont. R. 191 at 195 (1889); *Headford v. McClary Mnfg. Co.,* 23 Ont. 335 (1893); *Fortier v. Lauzier,* 14 Quebec C.S. 359 (1898); *Garard v. Allan,* 15 Quebec C.S. 81 (1898); *Hunt v. Wilson,* 15 Quebec C.S. 355 (1899); *Davies v. Can.-Am. Coal & Coke Co.,* 1 West. L.R. 55 (1905); *Fonseca v. Lake of Woods Milling Co.,* 1 West. L.R. 553 (Manitoba) (1905); *Fawcett v. Can. P. Ry.,* 8 Br. Col. 393 (1901); *Warmington v. Palmer & Christie,* 8 Br. Col. 344 (1901); *Nightingale v. Union Colliery,* 9 Br. Col. 453 (1903); *Devers v. Montreal Steam Laundry Co.,* 27 Can. S.C. 537 (1897); *Montreal Rolling Mills v. Corcoran,* 26 Can. S.C. 595 (1896); *Can. Paint Co. v. Trainor,* 28 Can. S.C. 350 (1898); *Burland v. Lee,* 28 Can. S.C. 348 (1898); *Roberts v. Hawkins,* 29 Can. S.C. 218 (1898); *Fawcett v. Can. Pac. Ry.,* 32 Can. S.C. 721 (1902). For Australian examples, see *Copeland v. Wentzel,* 1 So. Aus. LR (Pelham) 30 (1865); *Davidson v. Wright,* 13 Vict. LR 351 (1887); and *Shanahan v. Taranganba Gold Min. Co.,* 3 Queensl. LJ 147 (1889). But see *Warmington v. Palmer,* 32 Can. S.C. 126 (1902) (reversing a judgement of the British Columbia Supreme Court that had set an award and judgement aside because of worker contributory negligence). See also *Jamieson v. Huddart, Parker & Co.,* 25 So. Aust. LR 110 (1892) (question of contributory negligence for the jury); and *Withell v. Lowe & Others,* 2 W.W. & A'B. (L) (Victoria) 57 (1865) (contributory negligence question had been properly left to jury).
    Once again, where the trial judge in Quebec was satisfied that both plaintiff and defendant shared responsibility for the accident, he employed a comparative negligence formula. See *Marshall v. Cowans,* 10 Quebec C.S. 316 (1896); *Bergeron v. Tooke,* 9 Quebec C.S. 506 (1896); *Abbott v. Anderson,* 15 Quebec C.S. 281 (1898).

[166] Hunter, C. J., and Martin, J., in *Nightingale v. Union Colliery,* 9 Br. Col. 453 at 462, 464, 467 (1903); Richards, J., in *Fonseca v. Lake of Woods Milling Co.,* 1 West. LR 553 at 555 (1905).

the burden of proving the injured worker contributorily negligent was essentially on the employer, and often this was not easily accomplished. Quebec's jurists seem to have been more reluctant than those elsewhere to find against injured workers on grounds that they had been contributorily negligent. This may have been due to the existence of the comparative negligence standard in Quebec, or it may have been due to the fact that the trials in Quebec were juryless, that the judges were themselves forced to make the difficult decisions of liability that were generally left to juries elsewhere. In any event, when a worker was injured moving a massive cutlery manufacturer's new grindstone into place with no foreman present, the *Cour Superieur* disregarded the fact that he had urged his comrades: "Now, boys, let us hurry up and [then] have some beer" just before the stone fell, crushing his leg. Justice DeLorimer held that this "certainly" was "no evidence against him." On the contrary, it was up to the employer "even to protect [workers] to a certain extent against their own imprudence." Similarly, Justice Hall of Quebec's *Banc de la Reine* held that an injured packinghouse worker's award at trial should not be disturbed despite evidence of his carelessness, since he was not to be defeated simply "for having forgotten for a moment a source of danger behind him."[167]

Employee Assumption of Risk

What of the claim by the employer that the worker had assumed the risk of the injury at issue as a part of his or her labor contract? Jurists in the British colonies and provinces (and, especially in the Canadian ones) were willing at times to follow the English rule and agree with employers that workers injured or killed on the job had assumed the risk of the accident that befell them.[168] The fifteen-year-old girl whose hand was injured on a hot roller at the Montreal Steam Laundry when she fainted had assumed the risks of the work, explained Justice Robert Hall:

> Otherwise an element of risk and uncertainty would be introduced into business transactions, which, in the end, would operate seriously against the interests both of capital and of labour.

The tone of Justice Hall's rationale for the assumption of risk rule was utilitarian, but its short-term result clearly favored employers. None the less, one does not want to make too much of this opinion.

---

[167] *Ibbottson v. Trevethick*, 4 Quebec C.S. 318 at 319 (1893); *Geo. Matthews Co. v. Bouchard*, 8 Quebec QB 550 at 554 (1897); affirmed in 28 Can. S.C. 580 (1898).

[168] First enunciated in *Priestley v. Fowler*, 3 M. & W. 1 (Ex. 1837), and elaborated on in *Skipp v. Eastern Counties Ry.*, 9 Ex. 223 (1853).

Montreal Steam Laundry v. Demers was one of only thirteen CANZ appellate decisions (all but two of them Canadian) decided for the employer where the central question was whether the employee had assumed the risk.[169] This English rule, favoring the employer, was much more often the minority point of view in CANZ courts. In 1865, Victoria's Justice Williams held that an employee's "knowledge" of the risk he ran in working a puddling machine for a gold-mining firm was "part of the contract," that his wages "may be . . . adequate to the risk," and that when nothing was done of the problem with the machine after he had complained to his employer, he should have quit. This was certainly the view of both the English courts of Exchequer and (until 1887) Queen's Bench.[170] But Chief Justice Stawell and the rest of the Victoria Supreme Court disagreed and affirmed a jury verdict of £350

[169] A laborer killed in the cave-in of a sewer excavation had "quite as much knowledge" of the "dangerous character" of the jobsite "as his master, and voluntarily engaged in it knowing its dangerous character," held Justice John Douglas Armour of Ontario's Queen's Bench in 1887, citing English authority. In *Murphy v. City of Ottawa & Doyle*, 13 Ont. R. 334 at 342 (1887); Hall, J., in *Montr. Steam Laundry v. Demers*, 5 Quebec QB 191 at 195 (1896). See also *Sheerman v. Toronto, G. & B. Ry.*, 34 Up. Can. QB 451 (1874); *Lavoie v. Drapeau*, 31 Low. Can. J. 331 (1887); *Shanahan v. Taranganba Gold Min. Co.*, 3 Queensl. LJ 147 (1889); *Mercier v. Morin*, 1 Quebec B. Roi 86 (1892); *Reid v. Barnes*, 25 Ont. R. 223 (1894); *Rogers v. Toronto Pub. School Bd.*, 27 Can. S.C. 448 (1897); *Noel v. Duchesneau*, 15 Quebec C.S. 352 (1899); *Fonseca v. Lake of Woods Milling Co.*, 1 West. LR (Manitoba) 553 (1905).

In St. Louis in 1785, an attorney for one who had leased a slave spoke of "the well-established custom of the place" that "the risks of accidental death are assumed by the leased Negro's owner, because in the agreements made . . . it is ordinarily stipulated that the leased Negro will not be exposed to this or that danger." This would suggest that the rule in the French province of Louisiana, then, was one of assumption of risk, but it would also suggest that parties "ordinarily" dispensed with this rule by contracting out of it. Stuart Banner, "Written and Unwritten Norms in Colonial St. Louis," 14 *Law & History Review* 62 (1996).

[170] *Dynan v. Leach*, 26 LJ Ex. 221 (1857) (no recovery when worker knew of unsafe machinery and continued); *Assop v. Yates*, 2 H. & N. 768, 157 ER 317 (Ex. 1869) (same); (but not if worker had been assured by boss that the defect would be repaired: *Clarke v. Holmes*, 7 H. & N. 937 (Ex. 1862)); *Seymour v. Maddox*, 16 LTOS 387 (QB 1851) (no liability where actor fell through known hole in stage passageway); *Brooks v. Courtney*, 20 LT 440 (Q.B. 1869); and Griffith *Griffith v. Earl of Dudley*, 8 QBD 357 at 363 (1882). But in 1887, Queen's Bench began to waver; in *Thomas v. Quartermaine*, 18 QBD 685 (1887), it recognized that genuine knowledge by the worker of the danger involved was the only fair basis for the assumption of risk rule. And in *Thrussell v. Handyside & Co.*, 20 QBD 359 at 364 (1888), Justice Hawkins in very unBenthamite language, held that, though the worker knew of the danger, he could still recover damages, because "he was obliged

to the employee (who lost an arm due to the insufficiency of a gear chain).[171] And CANZ jurists decided some thirty five other assumption-of-risk appeals for the employee – that is, employees won 73 percent of the reported assumption-of-risk appeals. (See Illustrations 41 and 42.)

Why did employees win so decisively? Was this mere chance? Mere failure on questions of Law or evidence of defendants? Were plaintiffs with less-than-solid cases more "risk-averse" than defendants in similar straits when it came to appeals? I don't think so. Modern research indicates that individual plaintiffs often decide to appeal quite oblivious to the costs or likelihood of success, out of a stubborn insistence on their "rights,"[172] and I found no evidence that such stubborn behavior was absent a century ago. Conceivably corporations were more likely to press on in order to establish a precedent favorable to their perspective on review, but the results were the contrary – published reports of decisions *unfavorable* to corporate tort defendants. In fact, these opinions suggest a general willingness on the part of CANZ jurists to see things the employee's way.

CANZ jurists were not averse to signal their disapproval of "dangerous things" on the worksite to which employees were exposed, and they sometimes offered a kind of cost-benefit analysis/public-policy rationale. Many of the dangerous objects could have been guarded with "a trifling expenditure," or by employing "means, perhaps a little more expensive and a little slower in operation" in order to avoid the risk. "Manufacturers should realize" that it was "in their interest to comply with the precautionary measures" adopted by their competitors "in similar establishments," since, "in doing so . . . they may rest assured that they will save often troublesome and expensive litigation, sometimes irreparable injury, and, in some cases, . . . valuable lives."[173] But while they called for expenditures from employers, they seemed less demanding of workers: When a worker could not be proved to have been aware of the danger, or when he became aware of it and complained, only to be told to continue working, the courts were more sympathetic than their English counterparts. Thus, in a case holding

to be there; his poverty, not his will, consented to incur the danger." See Peter Bartrip & S. B. Burman, *The Wounded Soldiers of Industry*, 12–183, and Rande Kostal, *Law and English Railway Capitalism*, 260–80, for good summaries of the English case law on worker accidents.

[171] *Withell v. Lowe & Others*, 2 W.W. & A'B. (L) (Vict.) 57 at 59, 60 (1865).

[172] Scott Barclay, *The Act of Appealing: Challenging a Cost-Benefit Analysis* (Amer. Bar Found. Working Paper, 1992).

[173] *Citizens Light & Power Co. v. Lepitre*, 29 Can. S.C. 1 at 5 (1898)l *McCloherty v. Gale Mnfg. Co.*, 19 Ont. C. of A. 117 at 120 (1892); *Scanlan v. Detroit Bridge & Iron Works*, 16 Quebec C.S. 264 at 267 (1899); *Matthews Co. v. Bouchard*, 28 Can. S.C. 580 at 589 (1898).

George Westinghouse

Courtesy of Louisville & Nash

Thousands of brakemen were killed or maimed coupling w
and pin.

Illustrations 41 and 42. Jurists in England and the United States answered somewhat differently the question of whether workers assumed all of the risks associated with their jobs, and whether their foreman or train conductor was their "fellow servant" or a "superior servant" representing their employer. Among the more hazardous jobs in the nineteenth century were those of brakemen, coupling cars before the adoption of the automatic coupler, and hand braking those cars, often in dark or slippery conditions, before the introduction of the Westinghouse Air Brake (depicted in these illustrations for Thomas Cooley's *The American Railway* (1889)) and navvies (like these men building the Raurimu Spiral in late nineteenth century New Zealand). (Archives of New Zealand, Wellington, AAVK W3493, New Zealand Railways, B & W Negatives.)

Illustrations 41 and 42 (*continued*)

that the employee had assumed the risk of the injury that had be-
fallen him, Justice F. N. Andrews of Quebec's *Cour Superieur* took issue
with "Mr. Justice Ramsay in *Corner v. Byrd*,"[174] for Ramsay's observation
that "philanthropists are never so charitable as when they are spending other people's money." Instead, Justice Andrews relied on Justice
de Loremier's views (noted earlier in this chapter) in holding that
employers were "bound to protect...employees by the best possible
means, and even, to some extent against their own imprudence."[175]

---

[174] MLR, 2 QB 262.
[175] Those of Justice de Loremier in *Ibbotson v. Trevethick*, 4 Quebec C.S. 318
(1893).

The employer in Quebec was "soin d'un bon père de famille." But Justice Andrews expected more than this standard or the Civil Code called for:

> The position of employee is a difficult one. The least exhibition of unwillingness on their part may lead to the loss of their situation; their attention, too, is taken up with the manual labour they are in the act of performing. They are by education and training far less capable of foreseeing and avoiding danger than their employers. Their case . . . is not unlike that of seamen, whom the Law of England constantly protects against their own imprudence. . . . If courts do not take this view, . . . employees will be exposed to be the victims of a callous desire on the part of employers to make the most money possible, and [employers will] spend the least on the safeguards required to protect life and limb of those who work for them.[176]

This might be dismissed as merely a further case of *Quebecoise* exceptionalism[177] except that Justice Andrews' views were shared by his counterparts on the high courts of New Zealand, Nova Scotia, Ontario, and the Dominion of Canada. A few examples: In the appeal of a worker who had been nonsuited at trial, Chief Justice Adam Wilson of Ontario's Queen's Bench rejected the rule that a worker who had warned his employer of a work-site hazard but continued to work, was unable to sue because he had assumed the risk. It was "hard to apply that maxim in many cases against a workman when the choice before him is to run the risk or give up his work, or starve." The chief justice managed to distinguish some of the facts of the case before him from a recent English case with great similarities, and found another way to downplay its importance: "No doubt it will be taken to the House of Lords."[178] Two years later Ontario's Court of Common Pleas took a similar view in the case of an ironworker injured working with some defective mechanical shears. The man had been "afraid of an accident," but in this case he had not complained "for fear of dismissal." None the less, the jury's award of damages to him was affirmed: "The facts of each particular case must be ascertained and considered," Justice

---

[176] *St. Arnaud v. Gibson,* 13 Quebec C.S. 22 at 26, 28 (1898).

[177] See *Parent v. Schloman,* 12 Quebec C.S. 283 (1897); *Price v. Roy,* 8 Quebec Q.B. 170 (1898), and *Lussier v. Anderson,* 20 Low. Can. J. 279 (1877), for other examples of the reluctance of Quebec's jurists to apply the assumption of risk rule.

[178] In *Dean v. Ontario Cotton Mills,* 14 Ont. R. 119 at 128 (1887), citing *Thomas v. Quartermanie,* 17 QB Div. 414, 18 QB Div. 685 (1887). In both cases workers had suffered because of failure to provide a safe work environment in the vicinity of scalding liquid, but in *Dean* a statutory duty to protect workers from falling into boiling dye vats existed.

Hugh MacMahon observed, and since this work had to be "done immediately," this plaintiff lacked a true "opportunity" to show his employers "why he considered the work dangerous."[179] Similarly, New Zealand's Court of Appeals affirmed a jury award to a carter who had lost his leg moving coal from a mine to a train in a tram truck with a defective brake. The company charged that he had known of the risk and had consequently assumed it. His attorney responded that his only alternative had been to quit the job, and that "faced with a loss of earnings," he had "therefore acted in a sense under compulsion." This argument, unsupported by any English authority, was still good enough for the Court of Appeals. Those with "special privileges granted to them for the conduct of traffic upon tramways," wrote Justice Worley Edwards, "can, in effect, compel the persons whose duty or necessity compels them to use the tramways to run the risk of being maimed or killed, whether they know the risk or not."[180]

[179] *Madden v. Hamilton Iron Forging Co.*, 18 Ont. R. 55 at 57, 62 (1889) (Justice MacMahon did cite Lindley, L. J., in *Yarmouth v. France*, 19 QBD 647 at 661 (1887) on the worker's "fear of dismissal" as authority, but in *Yarmouth* the worker had been assured by his superintendent that if he were injured, his employer would compensate him). See also *Thompson v. Wright*, 22 Ont. R. 127 (1892) ("a mere lad" injured at a stamping machine didn't assume risk; improper materials); *O'Connor v. Hamilton Bridge*, 25 Ont. R. 12 (1894) (unguarded set-screw on oiling drill); *Hurdman v. Can. Atl. Ry.*, 25 Ont. R. 209 (1894); *Haight v. Wortman & Ward Mnfg. Co.*, 24 Ont. R. 618 (1894); *McCullough v. Anderson*, 27 Ont. C. of A. 73n (1895) (farm hand did not assume risk of kick from horse). And see *Connolly v. Shives*, 18 New Br. 606 (1879); *Tobin v. New Glasgow Iron, Coal & Ry.*, 29 Nova Sc. 70 (1896); *Hamilton Bridge v. O'Connor*, 24 Can. S.C. 598 (1895) (affirming Ontario opinion); *Toronto Ry. v. Bond*, 24 Can. S.C. 715 (1895); *Webster & Edmonds v. Foley*, 21 Can. S.C. 580 (1892).

[180] *Harris v. Ford & Others*, 28 NZLR (CA) 426 at 431, 437 (1909) (statute made tram owners answerable for accidents due to their negligence). This was the same Justice Edwards who affirmed a magistrate's award to one injured by the failure to employ lock chains on the rear wheels of a threshing machine. Using the "difference in conditions" tack, he distinguished the "very different" standards in New Zealand, with its (regionally) "soft or sandy soil," from "conditions... which prevail in England," where the machine had been manufactured. See *McIntosh v. Stewart*, 2 Gaz. LR (NZSC) 285 (1900). See also *Namby v. Joseph & Seegar*, 9 NZLR (SC) 227 (1890); *Andrews v. The Queen*, 15 NZLR (CA) 562 (1897); *Rudy v. The King*, 3 Gaz. LR (NZ) 287 (1901); *Wellington & M. Ry v. Macleod*, 19 NZLR (CA) 257 (1900); *Doyle v. NZ Candle Co.*, 20 NZLR (SC) 686 (1901); *Baillie v. Wellington Harbour Bd.*, 14 Gaz. LR (SC) (NZ) 91 (1911).

But if workers did not assume risks when they were "forced" to "work or starve," what about workers injured or killed when they assumed dangers voluntarily, in an emergency or crisis? Employers were clearly not liable to such employees in nineteenth-century England, and were protected from

In short, the assumption of risk rule lost some of its bite in its interpretation and application, especially in Quebec and New Zealand, but in other CANZ courts as well.

The Fellow-Servant or Common-Employment Rule

The same can be said of the fellow-servant or "common-employment" rule, especially in Quebec and Australia. In the earliest reported cases in Upper and Lower Canada, Nova Scotia, New Brunswick, and New Zealand jurists applied the harsh English doctrine[181] that a worker injured due to the negligence of one not acting as agent for the owner or corporation was not entitled to sue either of them, but was forced back upon the often judgement-proof negligent fellow worker.[182] Jurists in

suits in the same fashion in the province of Victoria as well. But this was not the case in Quebec, where a lumber mill worker, trying to help save the company's pier during a flood, was drowned *Degg v. Midland Ry.*, 1 H. & N. 773, 156 ER 1413 (Ex. 1857). A miller's shop assistant lost an arm after agreeing to help his employer work on the screws of a moving mill, a fact situation consistent with those in the English precedents stating the rule. The man was held to be "purely a volunteer, actuated by zeal for his master's service," with a "moral" claim to compensation, perhaps, but no legal one. *Knox v. Stephens & Another*, 1 Victorian R. (L) 102(1870). Nor was it to remain the case in England where a miner was overcome trying to help a rescue operation in another district mine, without having been asked to do so. Justice Day "would have thought" that the company miners "had an implied order in case of danger to life to assist as much as possible, and do anything by which they might think their assistance would be of real use in saving the lives of their fellow men." *Roebuck v. The Norwegian T. Co.*, 1 Times L.R. 117 (1885). *Price v. Roy*, 8 Quebec QB 170 (1898); affirmed, but reduced by half for comparative negligence, in *Price v. Roy*, 29 Can. S.C. 494 (1899) (where Justice Taschereau characteristically felt the full award should be allowed and that the deceased had been "ordered" to help, and Justice Gwynne characteristically felt he was a mere volunteer and should be nonsuited).

181   See *Priestley v. Fowler*, 3 M. & W. 1 (Ex. 1837); *Hutchison v. York, N. & B. Ry.*, 5 Ex. 343 (1850); *Wigmore v. Jay*, 5 Ex. 354 (1850); *Skipp v. Eastern Counties Ry.*, 23 LJ(Ex.) 23 (1853); *Bartonshill Coal Co. v. Reid*, 3 Macq. 265 (H. Of L. 1858), overruling *Dixon v. Rankin*, 14 D. 420 (Scot.) (1852), and, in a rare action by an English high court, citing as authority an American opinion, that of Chief Justice Lemuel Shaw in *Farwell v. Boston & Worcester RR*, 45 Mass. 49 (1842). See also *Morgan v. Vale of Heath*, 5 B. & S. 570, 13 LT(NS) 565 (Ex. Ch. 1865), and *Tunney v. Midland Ry.*, 1 LR 291 (CP) (1866).

182   These jurists cited both English and Massachusetts cases as authority for this rule *Deverill v. Grand Trunk Ry.*, 25 Up. Can. QB 517 at 525 (1866) (citing C. S. Lemuel Shaw's opinion in *Farwell v. Boston & Worcester RR*, 45 Mass. 49 (1842)) and second-guessing the trail court jury regarding the competence (a defendant duty) of the negligent fellow servant); *Fuller v. Grand Trunk Ry.*, 18 Quebec 147 (1865) (citing both English & U.S. cases); *Bourdeau v. Grand Trunk Ry.*, 18 Quebec 374 (1866); *Campbell v. Gen. Mining*

New South Wales and Victoria, however, took the path many midwestern American courts were simultaneously taking – that of creating principled exceptions to the rule.

The Vice-Principal Exception

In English and Scottish courts, virtually every employee of a company qualified as a fellow-servant of an employee injured due to that person's negligence. Chief engineers, clerks of works, building site foremen, and mine managers were held to be mere fellow-servants of third engineers, laborers, and miners.[183] But many jurisdictions in the United States disagreed, counting train conductors and engineers, indeed some counted foremen and section bosses, to be superior servants. And a number of CANZ jurists agreed with their American compeers. One man who lost his arm due to the insufficiency of a gear chain on a mining company's puddling machine succeeded in 1865 when the New South Wales Court found the negligent mine manager to be a "vice-principal" – that is, an agent for the company, not a fellow servant. Another, in Ballarat, injured mounting a mining firm's insecurely fastened ladder, recovered when Victoria's Supreme Court came to the same conclusion in 1871. Heirs of a "repairer," killed when a careless engine driver let a cage fall on him at the Koh-i-norr Mine in 1871, won a damage award and survived the company's appeal to the same Victoria Supreme Court. The careless engine driver had caused accidents before, for which he had been fired. But he had been rehired. Chief Justice Stawell drew this distinction:

> For the acts of an incompetent servant the Defendant would not be responsible to [an injured] fellow-servant; but we think it is different in the case of carelessness.

Justice Barry put it this way:

> [One] works with an incompetent fellow-servant at his peril, . . . but from carelessness he cannot guard so well and I think the employer should be held answerable.[184]

Assoc., 7 Nova Sc. 415 at 423 (1868) (citing the harsh British opinion on who was and was not a vice-principle, *Wilson v. Merry*, LR, 1 SC & Div. App. 326 (1868); *McBride v. Brogden*, 2 JR (NZCA) 14 (1876) (citing *Wilson v. Merry*); *Carney v. The Caraquet Ry.*, 29 New Br. 425 (1890). See also *Drew v. Corp. of Town of East Whitby*, 46 Up. Can. QB 107 (1881); *McFarlane v. Gilmour*, 5 Ont. R. 302 (1884); *Montreal Rolling Mills v. Corcoran*, 26 Can. S.C. 595 (1896) (*Wilson v. Merry* cited).

[183] *Seale v. Lindsay*, 11 CB(NS) 429 (1861); *Brown v. Accrington Cotton Spring Co.*, 3 H. & C. 511 (1865); *Lynch v. Marchmont*, 29 JP 375 (1865); *Wilson v. Merry*, 1 HL (Scot.) 326 (1868) (the leading case).

[184] *Withell v. Lowe*, 2 W.W. & á B. (L) 57 (1865); *Band of Hope & Albion Consuls v. Mackay*, 2 Vict. R. (L) 158 (1871); *Chambers v. Willey*, 3 Vict. R. (L) 17 at 19 (1872).

More striking is the way that this court avoided the effect of the fellow-servant rule in *Chandler v. Melbourne & Hobson's Bay Railway* (1871). Here a railroad's shipwright was injured when a shunting locomotive proved to be defective and a second company train struck the train the employee was riding, in part because the train's guard had placed no taillight on the last carriage. When the railway's counsel argued that the fellow-servant rule should be applied, he was interrupted by Justice Williams:

> But should there not be someone to see that the guard does his duty? Ought there not to be a superior officer to see that the rules are obeyed?

Counsel responded:

> The station-master's duty was to see that the trains were dispatched properly.

Justice Williams:

> Is not the Company responsible for that?

The court then held the company responsible, explicitly refusing to shift the liability to any of the negligent fellow-servants. Chief Justice Stawell allowed that his decision was "without precedent," but he reasoned that, while the employee "might possibly be entitled to a verdict" against one or more of them, "he would not recover damages as against his fellow-servants" because of their lack of assets, "and the Defendants in the action" would thereby not be "answerable for the enhanced injuries fairly attributable" to their employee's negligence. "As, then, the Plaintiff could not recover damages for [his injuries] from the employed, he would be without redress unless he could do so from the employer." Hence, the supreme court approved the jury's award of £1000.[185] That is, Victoria's jurists in *Chandler* refused to apply the fellow-servant rule essentially because to do so would have been to say that a man injured by the act of railroad employees would go uncompensated, while the railroad was there, with plenty of assets available to the court!

When the rule finally *was* observed in Victoria two years later, it drew the dissents of Justice Higinbotham over the next decade and clearly was applied by his colleagues Stawell and Williams only because they felt "compelled to adhere to the law as expounded" in England.[186]

---

[185] *Chandler v. Melbourne & Hobson's Bay Ry.*, 2 Victorian R. (L) 71 at 73, 76–77 (1871).

[186] *North Shenandoah Co. v. Fallover*, 4 AJR 109 (1873); *Brown v. Bd. of Land & Works*, 8 Vict. LR (L) 414 at 427–28 (1882) (where Higinbotham read the definition of a superior servant in the British Employer's Liability Act of

This seems to have been the case in Victoria's trans-Tasman neighbor, New Zealand, as well. Three years after Victoria's Supreme Court fell in line with the harsh English common employment decisions, New Zealand's Court of Appeals handed down its case of first impression on the subject, *McBride v. Brogden* (1876). A day laborer, subcontracted by a gaffer for railroad work near Dunedin was thrown from a truck due to debris on the track and to the truck's excessive speed. The company's construction superintendent had been aware that the men were being transported to work in that fashion, and the man's counsel argued that the construction chief was "a sort of vice-principal" or agent of the company, not a mere fellow servant, as the British leading case, *Wilson v. Merry*, would have it. Justice Joshua Williams allowed that "opinions may differ as to the reasonableness or expediency" of the common-employment rule, but he and his colleagues were resigned to their lot as administrators of the Common Law as "found" by jurists in the Mother of all Common Law, and "since the case of *Wilson v. Merry*," there could be "little doubt" that the construction chief "must be considered as a fellow servant...."[187]

Wherever and whenever the rule made its appearance in the 1870s and 1880s, in Victoria, in New South Wales, in New Zealand, in Nova Scotia, and in Ontario, it drew resistance and protest as "one of the worst specimens of 'Judge-made law' in existence," as G. R. Barton, editor of the *New Zealand Jurist* put it. It was "just as repugnant to a sense of justice on the one hand" as it was "illogical on the other." Barton, a barrister product of Westminster's own Inner Temple, was not averse to calling the "English authorities" for the rule "manifestly illogical." "A case is clearly made out for the interference of the Legislature," he concluded, anticipating by only a few years the British Employer's Liability Act.

Aware of the rule's rejection in Scottish courts before the Law Lords imposed it on them in 1858, Chief Justice William Young of Nova Scotia's high court spoke of the rule as "another of the numerous instances in which the Scottish laws and institutions are superior to the English." He bowed to authority on the subject in 1868, but in 1877, in the case of a mine worker injured in an explosion due to the actions of the mine's manager, he entered in dissent his "strong opinion that companies in such cases should be liable" (while his colleagues cited

1880, "one who has any superintendence entrusted to him," and argued that, despite the leading case of *Wilson v. Merry*, he was "at liberty ... to adopt this definition" and treat a foreman as a superior servant in Victoria. Chief Justice Stawell and a colleague disagreed, feeling bound to follow the rule in *Wilson v. Merry*, though they did invite the province's parliament to attend to the matter). Cf. *Hele v. McIlwraith, McEacharn & Co.*, 2 ALR (Vict.) 56 (1896) (citing *Wilson v. Merry* in a "four-square" case).
[187] *McBride v. Brogden*, 2 JR (NZCA) 14 at 32 (1876).

the English leading case, *Wilson v Merry*).[188] And in 1894, Nova Scotia's high court held the City of Halifax liable for the death of a worker killed in a cave-in caused by the man's foreman.

Where Young properly compared the common-employment doctrine invidiously to its Scottish predecessor, jurists in Ontario, a northern neighbor of the United States, tended to invite invidious comparison between the doctrine's most outrageous component, the "vice-principal" or "superior servant" rule, and American decisions that held an intermediate-level supervisor like a conductor or foreman (let alone a ship's master, the negligent party in *Wilson v. Merry*) to be a "vice-principal" or agent of the company. Noting the "marked difference between English and American law on the 'fellow workman' question," Chief Justice Hagarty of the Court of Appeals explained "with some regret," that "we have to follow the former." Several years later, Justice James Garrow was still unable to adopt the American version, "which I would willingly follow if I could," as it "seems to me a very reasonable and sensible [one]."[189]

Lower Canada/Quebec's British-bred judicial majority initially held that, since railways were "of recent introduction, and had no existence at the time we derived our [legal rules] from France," railway worker injuries caused by fellow workers were subject to the common-employment rule prevailing in both the British Isles and the United States, and Justice Badgley specifically denied that Lower Canada was "to be governed" by the very different "French law" in cases of this kind. But soon after the Union of Upper and Lower Canada had been ended and Quebec had reemerged with its own executive, legislative, and judicial voices (1867), its *Banc de la Reine* rejected the English common employment, assumption of risk, and contributory negligence rules *en banc* for the French codified Civil Law doctrines of *respondeat superior* and comparative negligence. In the words of Justice Mousseau:

J'aime mieux, sur ces questions de responsabilité, les termes plus clairs, et plus précis du Droit Francais, de notre droit.[190]

---

188 *2 New Zealand Jurist* (NS) 174 (1877); *Sanderson v. Smith*, 3 LRNSW 31 (1882) (especially the opinion of Sir George Innes, J.); *Campbell v. Gen. Min. Assoc.*, 7 Nova Sc. 415 at 422 (1868); *Smith v. Intercolon. Coal Min. Co.*, 11 Nova Sc. 556 at 561 (1877); *McInnis v. Mataga Min. Co.*, 25 Nova Sc. 345 (1893); *Taylor v. City of Halifax*, 26 Nova Sc. 490 (1894).

189 Hagarty, C. J. O., in *Matthews v. Hamilton Powder Co.*, 14 Ont. C.of A. 261 at 265 (1887); Garrow, J., in *Woods v. Toronto Bott Co.*, 11 Ont. LR 216 (1905). Cf. *Rudd v. Bell*, 13 Ont. R. (Ch.) 47 at 52 (1887). But see *Murphy v. City of Ottawa & Doyle*, 13 Ont. R 334 (1887).

190 *Fuller v. Grand Trunk Ry.*, 18 Quebec 147 (1865); *Canadian Pac. Ry. v. Goyette*, 30 Low. Can. J. 207 at 210 (1886).

Thereafter, employers were held responsible, as *bons pères des familles*, for the injuries of workers caused by fellow workers,[191] as well as by unsafe machinery or places. In 1898, for example, Justice F. W. Andrews of Quebec's *Cour Superieur* held an employer liable under the *res ipsa loquitur* rule for injury to a worker when a large piece of coal fell on him in the hold of a ship, and added that it was "just and expedient that the risk and consequences of such so-called accidents should be borne rather by the employers who can protect themselves [with insurance] than by their employees...."[192]

This *bon père de famille* rule set the law of work accidents in Quebec apart from that elsewhere in Britain, the Antipodes, and North America. Arthur McEvoy has drawn our attention to the proemployer bias of the Anglo-American common law as late as 1911 in his analysis of New York's Triangle Shirtwaist Factory Fire, and he is certainly right. But a virtually identical sweatshop fire produced an entirely different legal aftermath in Quebec City some sixteen years earlier. A four-story "*fabrique à tabac*" began to fill with smoke on April 25, 1895. As in the New York fire, workers on the upper stories first rushed to the exits but were told by their foreman (*contremaitre*), "*retournez à vos places; il n'y a pas de danger.*" Most did so, but the smoke failed to subside, and eventually all sought refuge and escape. The windows had been barred, as were the doors in the Triangle. The survivors of one victim, Alphonsine Thibeaudeau, who had leaped to her death, were among those who sued the owners. They were awarded $2000, affirmed on appeal in Quebec's Queen's Bench.[193] Under the *Code Civil*, Quebec's workers enjoyed a status in court by 1890 that their counterparts in the rest of the Anglo-American world would not enjoy for another generation.

The other CANZ jurists were not free to follow Quebec's path, but they could, and often did, follow two of the narrow paths away from the fellow-servant rule left to them under the English decisions, two

[191] *Morin v. Nadeau*, 7 Quebec C.S. 219 (1895); *Queen v. Filion*, 24 Can. S.C. 482 (1895); *Dupont v. Quebec S.S. Co.*, 11 Quebec C.S. 188 (1896); *The Asbestos & Asbestic Co. v. Durand*, 30 Can. S.C. 285 (1900) (affirming an award of $2000 for one killed in a dynamite explosion).

[192] In *Joint v. Webster*, 15 Quebec C.S. 220 at 223–24 (1898). Justice Andrews did allow, however, that this rule was "a very hard one," for employers "employ the only men available. They give them proper tackle – and still the law will hold them responsible for these accidents...." He was clearly "of two minds." And see *Daragon v. City of Montreal*, 8 Quebec C.S. 169 (1895) (city resp. for cave-in caused by firemen passing too closely by excavation).

[193] *Macdonald v. Thibeaudeau*, 8 Quebec QB 449 (1899); Arthur McEvoy, *The Triangle Shirtwaist Factory Fire of 1911: Social Change, Industrial Accidents, and the Evolution of Common-Sense Causality* (Amer. Bar Found. Work. Paper #9315, Chicago, 1994).

of the several paths being widened over the years by the courts of several American state jurisdictions: the subcontractor and incompetent servant exceptions.[194]

The Subcontractor Exception

A worker who worked for one employer and was injured by the negligent act of the employee of someone else employed at the same site by the same employer was barred in England from suing the negligent man's employer[195]; but CANZ jurists held otherwise, reasoning that he was not in common employment with the negligent employee of the separate subcontractor, and therefore the rule that a master was responsible to third persons for the acts of his servants should apply. Thus, a miller's carrier, injured by a wheat bag thrown by a farmer's hired hand in Victoria in 1869, was held to be out from under the constraints of the common employment rule. So were stevedores in New Zealand and Quebec, and lumbermen, ironmongers, and general laborers in New Brunswick, Ontario, and New Zealand.[196] While most of these decisions relied on English authority, both counsel and court sometimes made use of American decisions, as in *Nystrom v. Cameron* (NZ, 1891). There a charter party vessel had been offloaded by stevedores, one of whom was injured when ordered by the first mate to work a winch; a sling full of cargo fell on him due to a crewman's negligence. After concluding that the subcontractor exception applied and the man was entitled to the jury's award of £750, Justice Joshua Williams explained the rationale behind the exception in taking exception to the views of his English counterpart, Lord Bramwell. Bramwell had put this hypothetical to a parliamentary committee:

> Suppose there are two tradesmen that have got jobs at one house; the one is a plasterer, the other is a plumber. If the plasterer's servant does an injury to the plumber's, the plasterer's servant may maintain an action against the master plasterer; and if the plumber's does an injury to the plasterer's the plasterer's servant may maintain an action against the master plumber.

[194] See Karsten, *Heart against Head*, 108–25.
[195] *Wiggiett v. Fox*, 11 Ex. 832, 156 ER 1069 (1856); *Waller v. S. E. Ry*, 2 H. & C. 102, 159 ER 43 (1863). This rule was eventually overturned, in *Johnson v. Lindsay & Co.*, AC 371 (1891).
[196] *Delong v. Burrell-Johnson Iron Co.*, 25 New Br. 140 (1885); *Nystrom v. Cameron*, 9 NZLR (CA) 413 (1891); *Brown v. LeClerc*, 22 Can. S.C. 53 (1893); *Hatfield v. St. John Gas Light Co.*, 32 New Br. 100 (1893); *Can. Atl. Ry. v. Hurdman*, 25 Can. S.C. 205 (1895); *Earl v. The King*, 5 Gaz. LR (NZ) (CA) 361 (1903); and *Gerard v. Keith*, 15 Gaz. LR (NZSC) 74 (1912). But see *Claridge v. Union Steamship Co.*, 11 NZLR (CA) 294 (1892) (no liability decided).

Bramwell then offered this advice to these tradesmen:

It would be a prudent thing for these two persons, if engaged in a difficult and dangerous job, to say, let us go into partnership and have our servants in common, and then the plasterer might injure the plumber and the plumber might injure the plasterer and nobody be liable.

Justice Williams had no sympathy for this view, as the irony in this artful comment on Bramwell indicates:

Lord Bramwell has been well called a master of the Common Law.... He certainly could not be suspected of wishing to take what might be called the popular view of the case.[197]

The Incompetent Servant Exception

Somewhat more daring were the appellate decisions allowing juries to find, contrary to English practice, that the negligent worker who had caused the accident was identifiably incompetent in a position requiring care and judgement.[198] In such an event, the employer was held liable for having failed in his duty to provide a competent fellow servant. This standard was applied to a boiler engineer in Lancaster, New Brunswick (in 1885), a pile driver in St. John's Harbour, Newfoundland, and a foreman in Hamilton, Ontario (in 1886), a saw-mill manager in Vancouver, British Columbia, another mill manager in Melbourne, Victoria, a conductor in Toronto (all in 1892), a loom fixer in Ontario (in 1897), and an engine driver in Ontario (in 1901).[199] And, most strikingly, it was creatively employed by Victoria's Supreme Court in 1895 in an opinion that sanctioned a jury finding that an employer was liable for the act of "an unknown party" of "unknown competency" who had caused a miner to fall into a hole filled with scalding water drained from a boiler at midnight.[200]

The common employment rule took a heavy toll on worker suits in the provinces, but CANZ jurists managed to find for these plaintiffs

---

[197] 9 NZLR (CA) 413 at 434–35 (1891).

[198] Such an attack on the fellow-servant rule had failed in England in *Tarrant v. Webb*, 18 CB 797 (1856).

[199] *Matthews v. Hamilton Powder Co.*, 12 Ont. R. 58 (1886), overruled in 14 Ont. C. of A. 261 (1887); *Bulger v. Simpson*, 7 Newf. 130 (1886); *Foley v. Webster, et al.*, 2 Br. Col. 137 (1892); *Behm v. McDougall*, 14 Austr. Law Times 47 (1892); *Weegar v. Grand Tr. Ry.*, 23 Ont. R. 436 (1893), affirmed in *Gr. Trunk Ry. v. Weegar*, 23 Can. S.C. 422 (1894); *Baird v. Dunn & Gregory*, 33 New Br. 156 (1895); *Can. Coloured Cotton Mills v. Talbot*, 27 Can. S.C. 198 (1897); *Lake Erie & Detroit River Ry. v. Scott*, Can. S.C. cases (Coultée) 211 (1901).

[200] *O'Driscoll v. North Duke Cold Min. Co.*, 17 Argus L.T. 64 (1895).

Table 7.1. *CANZ Appellate Court Outcomes in Personal Injury/Wrongful Death Cases*

Defendant	Plaintiffs Won	Defendants Won
Doctors	6 (43%)	8
Road and bridge authorities	118 (67%)	59
Vehicle owner (plaintiff a child)	30 (74%)	11
Ry/tram/stagecoach (plaintiff a passenger)	55 (69%)	28
Ry/tram (plaintiff crossing)	50 (58%)	35
Corporation/employer (plaintiff a worker)	122 (69%)	58

	Overall*	
	Plaintiffs Won	Defendants Won
	393 (65.7%)	205
Workman's Comp.	78 (64%)	44
Court, New Zealand,	1901–1912**	

* These figures include other issues with small numbers of cases ("heroes," nervous shock, *res ipsa loquitur*, etc.).

** J. W. MacDonald, solicitor to the Public Trust Office, described some 122 decisions handed down by New Zealand's Workman's Compensation Court under the terms of the Workman's Compensation Acts of 1900 and 1908 between 1901 and 1912 (dealing with questions of whether the injury occurred under employment conditions, whether the plaintiff was an employee or an independent contractor, whether the employee had been "skylarking" (gross negligence, etc.). Workers won 64 percent of these. See J. W. MacDonald, *The Workman's Compensation Act* (Wellington, 1913).

in twenty six of the fifty decisions on the issue that I could identify between 1865 and 1905 – stretching, "distinguishing," or avoiding the English rule at least as often as not.

Employee-Accident Summary

CANZ jurists sometimes evaded the harsher edges of the English Common-Law rules of contributory negligence, the assumption of risk, and common employment. Worker–plaintiffs won some 122 (69 percent) of the 180 reported cases I detected that yielded clear outcomes. (See Table 7.1.) If we exclude from this population those from the jurisdiction of Quebec, where, by the 1880s, the English Common-Law rules no longer prevailed, the percentage drops to about 59 percent (of a total of about 150), including 58 of 105 (55 percent) of all Canadian cases. This is not as successful a rate as that of nonworker accident victims (who won about 70 percent of nearly 350 reported cases), but it is far more successful a rate than has been represented in the work of the two best analyses of tort law in late nineteenth century Ontario, those of Rande Kostal and Eric Tucker.[201]

[201] Rande Kostal's essay on "work-related accident law in Ontario, 1860–1886," to be sure, is not based on an aggregate analysis. He offers instead a more focused "incursion into the social history" of this subject by means of a thick description of the explosion at the Hamilton Powder Company in Cumminsville, Halton County, in 1884, and the ensuing litigation. One day in September, 1884, the company's owner arrived to inform his foreman–manager of a rush order by the Canadian Pacific Railway. Increase production without increasing risks, the owner said, and then he left. Several days later, in midday, something or someone created a spark in a "shaker" machine and the ensuing explosion at the factory killed several men. Their survivors sued, winning both at trial and at the first appellate level (the Court of Queen's Bench), before losing before the Ontario Court of Appeals. There, they were told by Chief Justice Hagarty with "some regret," that one of their deceased spouses (the operator of the "shaker" machine) had been contributorily negligent, that the fellow–servant and assumption of risk rules were applicable, and that, in any event, the defendant had offered proper instructions to his plant superintendent. (*Matthews v. Hamilton Powder Co.*, 12 Ont. 58 (1886); reversed in *Same v. Same*, 14 Ont. C of A 261 (1887)).

The law of work-related accidents in Ontario in the mid-1880s, Kostal observes, offered such survivors "little more than a symbolic gesture" in such lower court victories, themselves "a matter of court theatrics" where the community "validated their perceptions of the accident in legal ritual and categorization." The "hegemony of the law" rendered working people quiescent while it protected capital. It was a law of "rulers and the ruled." (R. W. Kostal, "Legal Justice, Social Justice: An Incursion into the Social History of Work-Related Accident Law in Ontario, 1860–1886," 6 *Law & History Review* 1 at 15, 18 (1988).)

In 1886, labor advocates secured the passage of Ontario's Employer's Liability Act, and once that statute was in place, Ontario's high courts applied it in cases where workers were injured in explosions. Thus, corporate fellow–servant defenses were terminated whenever the company's liability rested on one or another of the conditions required of it under the Act. (See, for example, *Fairweather v. Owen Sound Stone Quarry*, 26 Ont. 604 (1895) (improper appliances).) It is perfectly true, as Kostal says, that the Common Law with regard to work-related accidents was not very friendly to workers injured in explosions. But neither was it particularly unfriendly in CANZ courts. Workers won six of eleven such explosion-accident cases on appeal between 1877 and 1905. And, after all, it would be difficult to identify a more hazardous job than one at a factory manufacturing gunpowder or dynamite, unless it would be a mine or quarry where such explosives were in constant use. Such occupations seem the epitome of the term "assumption of risk." Workers lost in *Matthews, Smith v. Intercol. Coal Mining*

**Judicial Reactions to Statutory Alterations
of Work-Related Accident Liability**

Parliament and the legislatures of the various United States slowly
responded to the plight of "the wounded soldiers of industry" with
legislation designed either to reduce accident frequency (such as the

Co. 11 Nova Sc. 345 (1893); *Dominion Cartridge Co v. Cains,* 28 Can. SC 361
(1898); *Davies v. Can.-Am.* Coal & Coke Co., 1 Western LR 55 (1905).
Workers won in *St. John Gas Light Co. v. Hatfield,* 23 Can. S.C. 164 (1894);
Cowans v. Marshall, 6 Quebec QB 534 (1897); *Doyle v. New Zealand Candle
Co.,* 20 NZLR (S.C.) 686 (1901); *The Asbestos & Asbestic Co. v. Durand,* 30
Can. S.C. 285 (1900) (a dynamite manufacturer; Quebec had no fellow-
servant rule); and *McArthur v. Dominion Cartridge Co.,* A. C. 72 (1905) (won
at Privy Council no less, on appeal from the Supreme Court of Canada).
Cf. *Fairweather v. Owen Sound Stone Quarry Co.,* 26 Ont. R 604 (1895).

Eric Tucker's study of the law of workplace accidents in Ontario from
1850 to 1914 also faults that province's jurists for failing to ameliorate
the effects of the assumption-of-risk and common-employment doctrines.
He notes that some American courts had done so and supposes that
Ontario's courts were free, "in part," to follow the American, rather than
the English authorities. They failed to do so, he tells us, because of their
lack of understanding of the relative powerlessness of workers in the new
industrial environment and lack of sympathy for working class people.
"The courts endorsed the legal positions advocated by employers and
rejected the rules workers believed would serve them best." Thus, "there
were no reported cases in Ontario in which an employee succeeded"
on the grounds that the party that had caused his or her injury was an
incompetent servant. (Tucker, *Administering Danger in the Workplace: The
Law and Politics of Occupational Health and Safety Regulation in Ontario,
1850–1914* (Toronto, 1990), 45, 47–91.)

My reading of the reports of Upper Canada/Ontario in these years
causes me to be considerably less critical of Ontario's judiciary. While
there were a number of times (I detected nineteen) in these years that
Ontario's appellate courts reported cases in which injured workers lost at
that level, there was a greater number of times (29) when they won (60
percent), including two instances when the incompetence of negligent
fellow workers proved to be elements in the victories. (*Interim Rpt. on
Laws Rel. to the Liab. of Employers to Make Compensation to their Employees for
Injuries Rec. in the Course of their Employment*... (Toronto, 1912), minutes of
Evidence, 187–88, reported in R.C.B. Risk, "'This Nuisance of Litigation:'
The Origins of Worker's Compensation in Ontario," in *Essays in the History
of Canadian Law,* ed. David Flaherty (Toronto, 1983), 456.

Tucker might be said to hold the views of the labor leader who told the
Ontario Commission on Employer Liability in 1912: "When we get into
law, we always know who comes out best. We know the man with money
and the man who has influence comes out on top, and we know the
District judge ... is not a member of the working class, but a member of
the wealthy class himself." Having the financial resources to enable you to
press your suit, in the absence of the contingency fee contract, was, indeed,

Factories Act of 1844) or to abrogate one or another of the harsh Common-Law rules (as in the Employers Liability Acts of 1875 and 1880). In mid century, English jurists read such statutes liberally, favoring employees, as in *Couch v. Steel* (1854), where Lord Chief Justice Campbell of Queen's Bench held that a statute requiring ships to maintain a proper supply of medicines warranted a Common-Law remedy to one who had suffered from a breach of that statute.[202]

By the 1880s and 1890s, CANZ legislatures, following the lead of Parliament and responding to pressure from the friends of Labor, passed various statutes requiring a safer workplace. These measures were clearly necessary; Law & Economics theory would have it that railway companies would respond to legal rules holding them liable for accidents they could have prevented by purchasing safety devices up to the value of the probable damages to be generated. But as one railway expert (solicited by the Ontario legislature's Select Committee on Railway Accidents in 1880) indicated, his experience had taught him "that Railroad companies will not soon make any change to save lives of men unless compelled to do so," and his views were not unique.[203]

a problem, unless one was supported by a trade union. And it was clear that most magistrates and trial judges were not of the working class. But, like R.C.B. Risk, I find myself persuaded by the response that the Commission's Chair, Chief Justice Sir William Meredith of Common Pleas (about to become Chief Justice of the Court of Appeals), gave to this labor leader:

As a whole, the sympathies, as far as a judge is permitted to have sympathies, have been with the working man, and where they have had to determine against him in hard cases it is because they have been compelled by the law to do so.... You think a court is entitled to do natural justice; but the court has no such power. The court is confined to administering justice according to the law.... The fault is not in the administration of justice; you must change the law. (*Interim Rpt. on Laws Rel. to the Liab. of Employers to Make Compensation to their Employees for Injuries Rec. in the Course of their Employment*... (Toronto, 1912), minutes of Evidence, 187–88, reported in R.C.B. Risk, "'This Nuisance of Litigation': The Origins of Worker's Compensation in Ontario," in *Essays in the History of Canadian Law*, ed. David Flaherty (Toronto, 1983), 456.)

[202] Followed in *Doel v. Sheppard*, 5 E. & B. (1856); This opinion was rejected as bad Law by Exchequer in 1877, but revived by Queen's Bench in 1898 (*Atkinson v. Newcastle Waterworks*, 2 Ex. Div. 441 (1877); *Groves v. Lord Wimborne*, 2 QB 402 (1898).)

See Cornish and Clark, 518–19; Bartrip & Burman, 172, and R. L. Howells, "Priestley v. Fowler and the Factory Acts," 26 *Modern Law Review* 367 (1963), for good accounts of judicial interpretation of such statutes.

[203] Hugh Sells to Select Comm., Feb. 2, 1880, MSS Rpt. of Select Comm. on Ry. Accidents, ont. Leg., 1880, MU RG 49–95, No. 1, Archives of Ontario. See also the views of G. E. Dalby, Yard Master of the Northern Railway,

Some of these statutes concerned specific unsafe objects (such as unblocked frogs at railway switches), others with specific industries (especially those affecting miners and seamen). Some stipulated that the failure of the employer to provide safe equipment, or a "seaworthy" vessel, would act as a bar to the application of the assumption-of-risk or fellow-servant rules. These statutes were subject, within limits, to judicial interpretation, and when CANZ jurists were called upon to perform this function, they tended to produce readings of the statutory language favorable to worker–plaintiffs (in nine of thirteen detected instances (70 percent)).

A few examples: When a seaman fell from a peak halyard he knew to be defective while furling the foresail on a steamship, a Wellington, New Zealand magistrate nonsuited him; but Justice Worley Edwards read Section 154 of the Shipping and Seaman's Act of 1877 to apply to steamships equipped with such auxiliary sails as well as the schooners and other sailing ships the statute addressed. The "seaworthiness" language was intended "for the benefit of the seamen," Edwards held, and the man's suit was restored.[204] Ontario's Parliament passed a statute in 1881 making Ontario railroads liable to "any person" injured due to a road's failure to block or "pack" any "frog" (part of the switching apparatus that could trap and hold a man's foot in the path of an on-rushing train). When counsel for the Canadian Pacific Railway claimed that "the American decisions" were "uniform" in holding that workers were not the "persons" mentioned in their statutes imposing liability, Chancellor Boyd of Ontario disregarded the argument: "To leave these men out of the benefit of the act, would be to minimize its scope. . . ." When the company appealed this judgement, and cited a decision of the U.S. Supreme Court in a case with a similar statute and fact situation, the Court of Appeals politely distinguished the two statutes. In the words of Justice Burton, the U.S. Supreme Court opinion (*Randall v. B. & O. RR*, 109 U.S. 478 (1883)) "would be entitled to our gravest consideration" and "I should hesitate a good deal before setting up my own opinion against the unanimous decision of that tribunal," but in the American case the statute had not addressed the accident at issue as squarely as had Ontario's. Affirming a verdict for the survivors of a worker killed because of an inadequately blocked frog in another such case, Justice William Meredith responded to the Michigan Central Railway's insistence that it was impossible to block these devices in such

in the same report. This committee later recommended that companies be required to block all frogs, acquire automatic couplers, install better handrails and running boards, and maintain a distance of seven feet over the tops of all boxcars.

[204] *Namby v. Joseph & Seegar*, 9 NZLR (SC) 227 at 231–32 (1890).

a way as to guarantee that no one would lose life or limb, by directing the company to look elsewhere: "Relief should be sought from those who make, and not from those who merely administer the laws."[205]

The ultimate statutory change regarding work-related accidents was workman's compensation, passed in one form or another throughout Britain, North America, and the Antipodes in the *fin de siècle*. Early versions, like the Worker's Compensation Act passed by Ontario's legislature in 1886, required of workers that they bring any equipment defects they became aware of to the attention of a supervisor if they hoped to overcome the presumption that they had assumed those risks, and it continued in force the employer's defenses that the worker had been contributorily negligent or had been injured due to the carelessness of a fellow worker. But this version did attack the harsh English vice-principal rule by defining "superintendence" personnel, workers "to whose orders and direction the workman... was bound to conform," such as foremen, and other key figures, like signalmen and engineers, to be agents of the employer, *and* it established that a *prima facie* case of employer negligence had been made if the plaintiff could establish that the accident had been due to defective machinery or nonobservance of shop safety rules.[206] Final versions, like the British Workers Compensation Act of 1897 (or its counterpart, New Zealand's Worker's Compensation Act of 1900, amended in 1908), abrogated

[205] *LeMay v. Can. Pac. Ry.*, 18 Ont. R. 314 at 319 (1889); *LeMay v. Can. Pac. Ry.*, 17 Ont. C. of A. 293 at 300 (1890); *Misener v. Mich. Cent. Ry.*, 24 Ont. R. 411 at 415 (1894). See also *Rodgers v. Hamilton Cotton Co.*, 23 Ont. R. 425 (1893); *Brown v. Great Western Ry.*, 2 Ont. C. of A. 64 (1877) (statutory duty to stop train at crossing of another railway); *Behn v. McDougall*, 14 Austr. Law Times (Vict.) 47 (1892) (incompetent servants assigned by supervisor responsible for injury to pl.; superintendence defined by local Employer's Act of 1890, perhaps a response to Chief Justice Stawell's call for such a law in 1882 (*Brown v. Bd.*, 8 Vict. LR(L) 414) *Kervin v. Can. Coloured Cotton Mills*, 28 Ont. R. 73 (1896); *Goldsworthy v. The Brilliant Extended Gold Min. Co.*, 9 Queensl. LJ 254 (1899); *Laurenson v. Count Bismark Gold Min. Co.*, 4 Vict. LR (L) 83 (1878); *Holland v. Stockton Coal Co.*, 19 NSWLR 100 (1898); *Rice v. Ottawa & Gatineau Ry.*, 6 Quebec C.S. 33 (1894); *Fairweather v. Owen Sound Stone Quarry Co.*, 26 Ont. R. 604 (1895); *Eaton v. Caledonian, United & N.Z. Gold Min. Co.*, 8 Queensl. LJ 3 (1897). But see *Pilmer v. No. 1 South Oriental & Glanmire Gold Min. Co.*, 10 Queensl. LJ 87 (1900) (equipment failure beyond company's control); *Monkhouse v. Grand Trunk Ry.*, 8 Ont. C. of A. 637 (1883) (Dominion railway not subject to terms of Ontario statute *re* blocking of frogs); *Clegg v. Grand Trunk Ry.*, 10 Ont. R. 708 (1886) (same); and *Hamilton v. Grossbeck*, 18 Ont. C. of A. 437 (1891) (unguarded circular saw not a "defect" subject to Factories Act).

[206] Described in R.C.B Risk, "'This Nuisance of Litigation': The Origins of Worker's Compensation in Ontario," in *Essays in the History of Canadian Law*, ed. David Flaherty (Toronto, 1983), 436.

both the fellow-servant and assumption-of-risk rules *and* the requirement that the negligence of the employer be proved. Injured workers
were free to chose either the statutory route (easier to establish, unless
they had been "skylarking" (grossly negligent) but with a compensation limit of £500 when the accident was caused by a fellow-servant),
or the older Common-Law route (encumbered with no compensation
cap, but leaving intact the old employer defense obstacles and the duty
to prove employer negligence).[207]

[207] See *Brown v. Heenan & Founde, Ltd.*, 10 Gaz. LR (NZSC) 692 (1908), and
J. W. MacDonald, *The Worker's Compensation Act, 1908* (Wellington, 1915),
1, 7, 18. Similarly, there was no contracting out of liability for ship owners
under the Shipping & Seaman's Act of 1877. See *Namby v. Joseph & Seegar*,
9 NZLR (SC) 227 at 230 (1890). For the Canadian version's evolution see
Canada Southern Ry. v. Jackson, 17 Can. S.C. 316 (1890); *Rodgers v. Hamilton
Cotton Co.*, 23 Ont. R. 425 (1893); *Toronto Ry. Co. v. Snell*, 31 Can. S.C. 241
(1901); *Washington v. Grand Trunk Ry.*, 24 Ont. C. of A. 183 (1897) (Act lim-
its recovery to three years pay or $1500); and Dianne Pothier, "Workers'
Compensation: The Historical Compromise Revisited," 7 *Dalhousie Law
Journal* 309 (1982–83); and R.C.B. Risk, "Sir William Meredith, C. J. O.:
The Search for Authority," 7 *Dalhousie Law Journal* 713 (1983).
  The English Court of Queen's Bench had held in *Griffiths v. Earl of Dudley*
QB Div. 357 (1882) that employers might lawfully *require* of employees that
they contract out of this protection for a company's insurance policy. New
Zealand's statute did not permit employers to bargain with employees in
this fashion. To a considerable extent this provision was necessary because
of the propensity of employers in previous decades to coax or force workers to waive such protections as had been provided by earlier Employer
Liability Acts. While there is certainly clear evidence that some workers did
contract out, the fact is that some of these workers were more interested in
contracting out than their employers were in having them do so. Some, especially skilled workers, sought to avoid the medical insurance payments
that the Government required of workers under some of these statutes.
Thus, some 153 locomotive department railroad workers in Christchurch,
New Zealand, petitioned the Ministry for Public Works in July, 1881, to
avoid being made to join the Railway Sick Benefit Society. Membership for
these engine drivers and firemen was "altogether unnecessary," they explained, "because we already have a Society.... Further, the great Majority
of us are members of other Friendly Sick Benefit Societies [sanctioned by
the Friendly Society Act of 1875] which offer us considerably more advantages than the Railway Society could possibly do." Nevertheless, the fact
remains that many less skilled workers who lacked access to such Friendly
Benefit Societies, were encouraged and were willing to contract out of the
earlier versions of statutory employer liability in exchange for higher wages
or employment itself. And there existed a period of a decade or two during
which workers were held by CANZ jurists (following English precedent)
to be ineligible to claim the benefits of the first generation of employer
liability statutes because they had waived these statutory rights. Bartrip and

SUMMARY

We have now seen how CANZ jurists dealt with issues of tort law in appeals involving fires, accidents on roads and bridges, children injured in streets or while trespassing, train and tram passengers, those crossing the tracks of such trains and trams, and work sites.

The frequency with which these CANZ jurists[208] drew upon American cases for rules, generally to help those suing corporations, surprised me. Children injured on roads or private property, injured passengers, strangers at crossings said by carriers to have been contributorily negligent, and injured workers claiming that the negligence of a "superior servant" rendered their employer liable, often benefitted from the use of American citations in CANZ appellate reports. But this use of American judge-made Law almost invariably came in the side door. That is, if a CANZ jurist could "find" no English precedent that was exactly "on the point," and could point to one from the States where the fact situation, as well as the Law, appeared to be, he could justify its use. But only then.

In the absence of both clear English and American precedents, CANZ jurists provided "the rule" based on "the principles" of the Common Law. But this *rarely* amounted to the declaring of *new* Law. Even in the "nervous shock" case (*Coultas v. Victorian Railway Commissioners*), the decision to dispense with a "physical touching" requirement in personal injury Law drew on a reading (however imperfect) of an English appellate case. But that is the point: While they were not willing to innovate overtly, CANZ jurists were, at times, remarkably skilled

---

Burman report (*Wounded Soldiers of Industry*, 172) that, as a consequence of this decision, some companies forced their employees to contract out of protection, but most did not. Locomotive Dept. petition, July 9, 1881, NZ Archives, R/3/Acc R 2476; Ry. Sick Benefit Society Files, 1878–1922. The English precedent was *Griffiths v. Earl of Dudley*, 9 QB Div. 357 (1882). The cases I detected that barred suits by workers in the provinces who had contracted out of Employer Liability Act abrogations of the assumption of risk doctrine were *Kelly v. Reid Newf. Co.*, 8 Newf. 584 (1903), and *The Queen v. Grenier*, 30 Can. S.C. 42 (1899) (distinguishing *Grand Trunk Ry. v. Vogel*, 11 Can. S.C. 612 (1885). But see *Roach v Comp. du Grand Tronc*, 4 Quebec C.S. 392 (1893) (Company's insurance policy for worker required waiver of liability; deemed void because company had exceeded its authority (action *ultra vires*)).

[208] Attorney-contributors to CANZ law journals offered citations from U.S. courts as well. See, for example, N.W. Hoyle citations regarding collateral or casual negligence in 43 *Canadian Law Journal* 305 at 324–25 (1907), and those of C.B. Labatt in 38 *Canadian Law Journal* 273 at 313 (1902). And see *Seed v. Somerville*, 3 NZ WCC 39 (1904), where Chapman, J, cited *Milw. RR v. Kellogg*, 94 US 469.

at "distinguishing," obfuscating, and selectively citing. With the exception of Quebec's courts (which broke with English Common-Law rules of contributory negligence and of work-related accident law after the legislature's adoption of the *Code Civil* and the conscious decision of that province's jurists to return to certain French rules of Law), CANZ jurists followed English rules, sometimes quite slavishly, with regard to fires, contributory negligence, child trespasses, road-authority immunity from suit, latent defects in common-carrier vehicles, and certain of the employer's defenses in work-related accident Law.

Overall, plaintiffs won two of every three of these appeals (393 of 598 or 65.7 percent). Why? Individual plaintiffs must have been both less willing and less able to hazard appeals than corporate defendants. Given the loser-pays-fees rule, and the (formal) illegality of contingency fees outside of the United States, ordinary passenger, "stranger", and worker–plaintiffs were financially at a disadvantage in suing corporations, and, consequently, they tended to settle whenever they felt the likelihood of winning was not decisively evident. But corporate defendants also learned the wisdom of settling suits they might not win, and injured plaintiffs could find skilled counsel. We will see this story of negotiation and settlement unfold in the next chapter.

In any event, we are speaking here of a success rate at the *appellate* level – that is, at the point where all of the parties had already persevered to judgement at trial; hence, the additional risks of an appeal were not faced as an entirely unfamiliar hurdle. Moreover, Scott Barclay's recent analysis of the decision that individuals make to press ahead with an appeal offers no support for the cost-benefit explanation of that decision.[209] So we ought not simply dismiss the high plaintiff success rate as a function of what economists call risk-averse behavior. Risk aversion may account for *some* of the unexpected variance from a hypothetically expected fifty/fifty outcome, but if my reading of these cases has been at all accurate, it has revealed a proplaintiff bias among many CANZ jurists, especially when the plaintiff was a worker injured on the job or a child injured in the street.

[209] Scott Barclay, *The Act of Appealing: Challenging a Cost-Benefit Analysis* (Amer. Bar Foundation Working Paper, 1992).

8

Beneath the Iceberg's Tip: Personal Injury Suits, Out-of-Court Settlements, and Trial Court Awards: The Real Law of Accidents

So much for the "Law of Accidents" as pronounced by jurists on appellate courts. This Law mattered, to be sure, beyond the pages of the published reports: Solicitors, barristers, trial court judges, and magistrates, as well as some outside of the legal profession, paid attention to these rules, advised their clients, or their jury, of them, and were to that extent governed by them. But the appellate cases in which the rules of tort law are to be found were still only the very tip of an iceberg of accident law – that is, once one defines "law" broadly to encompass the entire process wherein accident victims are either "made whole" or given little or no redress, the instances where a victim's rights and compensation were determined in a formal courtroom trial consist of a tiny percentage of the sum total of the cases. A victim first had to decide to seek redress; she then had to know how to proceed in order to obtain that redress, and that generally meant that she needed to consult an attorney. That attorney had to know what he was doing, and had to be able to discover enough of the facts of the accident to force the defendant's attorney to settle for an adequate figure, or to win in court. Each of these contingencies can be thought of as barriers that had to be overcome before the accident victim was likely to receive compensation. Or, to employ a different metaphor, each represent levels, or layers, in the iceberg of accident-victim instances that lay beneath the visible tip of litigated ("formal Law") cases. So, to understand the "informal law" of accidents in Britain and her Diaspora's lands in the nineteenth century we begin at the point where the victim approached the cause of her injury.

THE SETTLEMENT PROCESS

Some accident victims in England and the British provinces living under the Common Law in the eighteenth and early nineteenth centuries simply did not seek legal counsel and demand redress. There were a number of potential reasons for this: First: They may have felt resigned to their misfortune as their "fate." Thus, an oil drill worker who lost a thumb in Canada West/Ontario in 1866 when his boss dropped the ram on it was quoted as saying that "he was thankful it was no worse, and nobody was to blame." Similarly, Anthony Trollope, visiting New Zealand in 1872, witnessed an example of my sainted Irish grandmother (who was often reported to have said of her threadbare winter coat, "Not a problem; my pride will keep me warm"): Trollope wrote that "a poor girl whom I had injured [he had accidentally ruined several hours of her work efforts] refused the money that I offered her, saying that though she was only a poor Irish girl without a friend in the world, she was not so mean [low] as that."[1]

Second reason for not seeking legal redress: They may simply not have believed they had "much of a case." Some may have relied on the advice of friends, or on their own judgement, to come to that conclusion.[2] Or, just as likely, they may have been persuaded by the company-paid doctor, investigator, or lawyer. Third reason: The victim may well have lacked the resources (or the willingness to commit those she possessed) to hire an attorney in a legal environment where contingency fee arrangements were void in Law and the loss of one's suit meant that one was ordered to pay the winner's costs (true everywhere except the United States). When this was the case, and the victim sought to deal with the corporation's attorney herself, settlements took less time and were for considerably smaller sums than those where the signed release or correspondence file indicated that the victim had been represented by an attorney.[3]

Needless to say, this was what corporate officials wanted to hear, and when they suspected that they might be held liable in the event of a suit, they did what they could to take advantage of that fatalism, especially before it was overcome by a "touter" for a local attorney. And "touters" there were, especially in the United States, but almost certainly elsewhere as well, by the second half of the nineteenth

---

[1] Anthony Trollope, *Australia and New Zealand* (2 vols., London, 1873), II, 351; *Anderson v Stiver*, 26 UCQB 526 at 527 (1867).

[2] Example: Dr. James Wright to J. Blythe, Chicago, Burlington & Quincy Railroad solicitor, September 20, 1883, describing his conversation with "a son-in-law and the old lady herself," in securing an agreement from Mrs. Lera Davis ("the old lady") to settle a claim for her injuries at a railroad crossing for $100. 33 1880 4.62/ Legal/ C B & Q Archives, Newberry Library.

[3] For evidence of this, see the settlements in the Out-letter Report Books of T. J. Potter, Burlington Divisional Superintendent of the Chicago, Burlington & Quincy RR, 3 P6.17/C, B & Q Archives, Newberry Library, and a few in other railroad corporate records that I examined. The pattern, however, was for victims to communicate with the railway, at least eventually, through an attorney.

century. Attorneys specializing in personal injury litigation made use of ambulance drivers, police, and hospital staff (sometimes referred to as "lead men") as well as their own "runners" and "touters" to identify and capture clients. By the 1890s, this process was known by its now-familiar term, *ambulance chasing*. It was countered by those employed by railway and streetcar companies – "claims adjusters" who descended just as quickly on victims to hold the "touters" at bay while seeking their signature on a form that released the company from liability.[4] (Thus, the New South Wales Government Railway Commissioners were probably not unique in instructing their ambulance squad leaders to "assist the senior local [railway] officer to obtain the names, addresses, nature of injuries of sufferers," as well as to "see that they are not subjected to any annoyance from unauthorized or irresponsible persons asking questions.")[5]

Corporate legal staff (investigators, doctors-on-retainer, local attorneys-on-retainer, claims agents, solicitors) sought to act swiftly in order to forestall the victim's retaining an attorney who might gather facts and file a suit. This propensity was especially pronounced in the United States, where the contingency fee contract was explicitly sanctioned. But if the responsibilities of corporate claims agents were stretched over too great an expanse to deal effectively with potential suits flowing from the relatively constant incidences of accidents, the company's interests could suffer. This explains the response of James Fentress, General Solicitor for the Illinois Central, to an inquiry from that company's board of directors in 1890 about the increase in the previous year in the number of personal injury suits within "the southern division" (Louisiana, Mississippi, Tennessee, and Kentucky). Mr. Head, the company's "Personal Injury Agent," continued to be based in Chicago, Fentress explained (apparently against an earlier recommendation of his). This was simply too far from the southern division "to get facts at first hand, or to settle damage cases before the parties injured had enlarged their demands or have been stimulated by some pestiferous lawyer."[6]

Consider the case of Leo Hughes, a railroad man who lost an eye in Nokomis, Saskatchewan, when dynamite being used by his foreman

4 For examples of this in the case reports and law journal literature of the time, see my "Enabling the Poor to Have Their Day in Court: The Sanctioning of Contingency Fee Contract, A History to 1940," 47 *DePaul Law Review* 231 at 256–58 (1998).

5 P. 22, "Instructions... [regarding] Accidents... (Sydney, 1911), Rec. Gr. 82, New South Wales Govt. Railway Archives, Transport House, York St., Sydney.

6 Fentress to A. G. Hackenstaff, Secretary to the Bd. Of Dirs., Jan. 28, 1890, Annual Report Minutes, 1888–1890, +3.4/ Illinois Central Archives, Newberry Library.

exploded prematurely. His manager wrote to the company's vice president: "I am caring for this man, with a view to preventing, if possible, a claim for compensation. . . . He frankly admits the loss of his eye to be purely accidental." Someone may have persuaded young Hughes that the foreman had been at fault and that his employer, the Grand Trunk Railway, therefore had a statutory duty to compensate him. Or he may simply have responded to a new cultural expectation of care and compensation that is said to have emerged by the second half of the nineteenth century. (I will have more to say of this later in this chapter). In any event, Leo Hughes eventually did retain a lawyer in Winnipeg, who wrote the office of the general counsel to the railway, claiming the foreman was "guilty of the most gross negligence," and asking for $3000. After investigating, Assistant Solicitor H. J. Symington advised his superior that there was "no doubt in my mind that this is a case where the best settlement possible should be made, rather than have the company go before a jury. . . ." Hughes settled for $1100, $100 of which appears to have been earmarked for his attorney.[7]

The (English) Great Western's solicitor used the same reasoning in the case of a Mr. Ware's claim for an injury he had incurred at the Cardiff station in late 1883. Ware had asked for £250. Since a "verdict against the company for some amount" was deemed likely, and Ware was "in the hands of rather unscrupulous Solicitors," the company's solicitor told the directors that "the costs alone of both sides if the action had proceeded would have amounted at least to this sum and the commission day was imminent." He persuaded the company's and the plaintiff's physicians to agree on the medical costs and offered Ware 200 pounds, which Ware accepted. "The costs of [trial] would have been heavy and would have fallen upon the company."[8]

I detected three similar instances when legal beagles of the Chicago, Burlington & Quincy recommended to their superiors the settlement

---

[7] E. B. Smith to Frank Morse, 18 June, 1908, Thornburn to Grand Trunk, no date; Symington to ?, July 23, 1908, RG 30, Vol. 3493, file 233, *Grand Trunk v. Hughes*, Grand Trunk Legal Counsel Files, Archives of Canada, Ottawa. For examples of such settlements (that is, where the facts were against the company) in the earliest stages of railroad development in the United States see James Dilts, *The Great Road: The Building of the Baltimore & Ohio, the Nation's First Railroad, 1828–1853* (Stanford, 1993), 392–95.

In the United States, where the contingency fee contract was lawful, and the losing party generally did not have to pay the winner's costs, a good accident specialist like St. Paul's Humphrey Barton could build the facts of the case with modest expense and then credibly threaten to proceed to trial, often forcing a good second offer out of the company.

[8] #2929 (Ware), Reports of Solicitors upon Legal Business, 1884, Great Western, PRO/RAIL/250/490, Public Records Office, and see the chief solicitor's similar observations on the claim of a Mr Hart, file #3149, in the same report for 1884.

of cases in order to avoid costs of gathering evidence and "trying the case," costs that would double or triple the company's expenses "whether [the] verdict was for or against us."[9] A further example: H. H. Ostler, the Crown's solicitor for the New Zealand Ministry of Railways, advised the general manager that he had settled a claim arising from an accident at Whangamarua for the substantial sum of £1408, "as I thought this less than Mr. Fox would probably recover from a jury...." All told Mr. Ostler settled with seven victims of this accident, three of them for £2000 each, but the general manager had no complaints for he had already advised the ministry that the railways were clearly liable for the maximum figure allowed by statute to the families of passengers killed in such accidents as this one (£2000), "and the department will no doubt have to pay the full amount in each case."[10] Thus, by settling, the ministry at least eliminated its own legal fees, the "costs of court," and the costs of the plaintiffs' counsel "according to the scale."[11]

The same New Zealand Railways Ministry was advised to settle with a Mr. Hartley, one of the many passengers injured in the accident at Rakaia, South Island, in 1899. The company hired the services of two physicians, V. Diamond and J. H. Townsend, to treat and assess the injuries of Rakaia victims. They reported to W. H. Gaw, the Railway's Traffic Manager at Christchurch, that Mr. Hartley was "not improving." His right leg was "wasting very considerably; and he now complains of weakness in his right arm." But there was more:

This patient is employing a great deal of introspection and is more than ever convinced that he is seriously hurt, the result being that his ailment progresses at a rapid rate. The sooner his claim is settled, the better.[12]

9 J. Besler to H. Stone, Esq. (Gen. Mngr., Chicago), 22 Oct. 1885 ($200 in death of worker); T. J. Potter to Charles Perkins, V. P., March 22, 1879 (Durfee case); Gottard In-letters, 3G5.3/ C B & Q Archives; J. Blythe to T. J. Potter, V. P., Feb. 7, 1884 (Travis case), Legal/33 1880 4.62/C B & Q Archives, Newberry Lib.

10 Crown Solicitor to Gen. Manager, Sept. 7, 1914, Gen. Man. to Min. of Rys., June 26, 1914, R/3/14/2525 (1), Claims for 1914 Whang. Accident (5 killed, 14 inj.), New Zealand Archives. Ostler was serving as the assistant to John Salmond, New Zealand's Crown Solicitor, in these years.

11 These costs of counsel were fifteen guineas per day in New Zealand in 1899 (see *McJenna v. Craig,* 18NZLR(SC) 529 (1899)). And see the postaccident preventive orders issued by the Canadian Northern's Superintendent that workmen "must not ride on cars passing over" a particular scale located too close to a building "nor passing between upright timbers and cars while on the scale." J. R. Cameron to M. H. MacLeod, 24 March, 1908, File 26–39, Vol. 8693, R.G. 30, Archives of Canada.

12 Diamond and Townsend to Gaw, June 8, 1899, p.5, 99/1009, Pt.1, Series 4, Ry. Ministry, NZ Archives, Wellington.

Across the Tasman Sea, officials of Queensland's Railway Commission also called upon medical advice. Example: In 1908, Ms. Jinee U. Laugher suffered a sprained neck when the train she had alighted started with a jolt, throwing the door to her carriage against her. After reviewing the facts, the general traffic manager recommended "a small sum in settlement," but Ms. Laugher reported that she had suffered much pain; indeed, so much that she could "not ask the railway commissioners to pay" for it all, as "that would ruin the Railway." Dissatisfied with the railway's response, she acquired the services of McGrath & Hunter, Solicitors, who obtained the statement of a fellow-passenger in support of her version of what had happened and filed a claim for "traumatic neurasthema." The railway's medical expert, Dr. John Thompson, summarized for the general traffic manager the published professional views of railway medical experts throughout the world on "traumatic neurasthema" and concluded that the claim (for 2000 pounds) was most excessive and the illness itself, dubious. But Dr. Thompson warned his employers of the known influence of "witness box" testimony from victims like Ms. Laugher upon juries (he called it "the hysterical claptrap"). The railway commissioners' solicitors then offered her 100 pounds. She told her solicitors the offer was "ridiculous"; six months later (one year after her injury) she agreed to a settlement of 550 pounds, 50 of it presumably meant for her solicitors.[13]

Several of the railway archives I examined contained evidence like the passage just cited, evidence of the real injuries suffered by the victim seeking compensation. Sometimes that evidence can be found in the record of the trial, as it is in the Illinois Appellate Court's description of the four surgical amputation procedures that had left a train conductor in "great pain" for long duration," a "perfect wreck."[14] On other occasions there is no such evidence of the victim's suffering. It is sometimes possible to deduce such information. Example: On July 14, 1890, Robert and Ellen Webber of Paddington, New South Wales, signed a bond releasing the New South Wales Railway Commissioners from future claims for Mrs. Webber's injuries incurred as a passenger en route Sydney when an accident occurred at Goulburn. Mrs. Webber was clearly injured badly, for the commissioners paid her 2500 pounds (plus 64 pounds for medical and legal expenses), a huge sum, about 30 times the median income of heads of households at the time. But

Anthony Trollope had written in 1872 of the new railway bridge at Rakaia: "The whole thing looked like sudden death." (*Australia and New Zealand*, II, 368.)

[13] Laugher file, A/12383/1909.2203, Queensland PRO, Runcon.
[14] *Velie v. J., A., & N. RR* 36 Ill. App. 450, at 458 (1889).

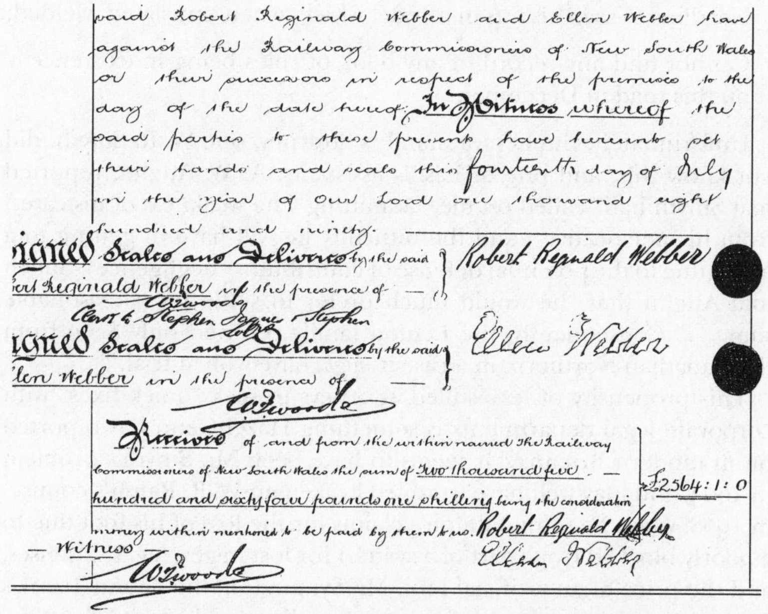

said Robert Reginald Webber and Ellen Webber have against the Railway Commissioners of New South Wales or their successors in respect of the premises to the day of the date hereof. In Witness whereof the said parties to these presents have hereunto set their hands and seals this fourteenth day of July in the year of Our Lord one thousand eight hundred and ninety.

Signed Sealed and Delivered by the said Robert Reginald Webber in the presence of — C A Woods Clerk to Stephen Jaques & Stephen Solrs } Robert Reginald Webber

Signed Sealed and Delivered by the said Ellen Webber in the presence of — C A Woods } Ellen Webber

Received of and from the within named The Railway Commissioners of New South Wales the sum of Two thousand five hundred and sixty four pounds one shilling being the consideration money within mentioned to be paid by them to us. — £2564:1:0

Robert Reginald Webber
Ellen Webber

— Witness — C A Woods

Illustration 43. The final section of the form signed by Ellen Webber and her husband Robert, releasing the New South Wales Railway Commissioners from further liability in exchange for their payment to the webbers of 2,564 pounds. Note her signature. (Archives of NSW Ry. Commissioners, 161/Box 4/ 1889/ 37–1897/#40, Transport House, Pitt Street, Sydney.)

a glance at the signatures of husband and wife on the release suggests that she was the victim of a crippling accident, for while her husband's signature is bold and clear, hers is not (see Illustration 43).[15]

In Canada, the Canadian Northern Railway's general counsel, Z. A. Lash, became convinced that the company should settle with the heirs of engineer H. H. Lemon, killed in a collision in December, 1902, after learning from the newly appointed general superintendent, E. A. James, that he had "not been able to find an employee of this road who has a book of rules, nor have I found a man who has passed an examination in train rules." Later James telegrammed Lash:

> Capable numerator flail appended redound oozing appended boulevard oozing sabre beningnity incision explain optimal ticket rooted incision december.

[15] R. Gr. 161/ Box 4/ 1889/ 37–1897/ 15/ #40, Archives of New South Wales Railway Auth., Transport House, York St., Sydney.

Needless to say, this was in a code, which, when translated, yielded:

Cannot find any record of any book of rules being in existence on this road in December.

Unfortunately, the Lemon family's attorney, one W. R. Smyth, did not know this, and one of Lash's assistants, A. W. Anglin, reported that Smyth had "called on me," admitting "the weakness of his case," from his perspective, "and the difficulty he will have in getting to a jury" (due to the potential defense of contributory negligence). Smyth told Anglin that "he would much prefer to settle for a reasonable sum...." Consequently, the Lemon family received only $200 from the Canadian Northern, in a case it *might* have won at trial.[16]

This propensity of less skilled attorneys to seek "quick fixes" with corporate legal departments is something Hazel Genn has reported on in modern Britain.[17] It seems to have been Mr. Smyth's problem in 1903, and may well have troubled brakeman W. R. Ralph's counsel in 1908, when he settled Ralph's claims for the loss of his foot due to a poorly blocked frog (part of a switch) for lost wages, legal expenses, and the price of an artificial foot. Mr. Symington, the Grand Trunk's assistant solicitor, aptly called this "an excellent settlement."[18]

This "quick fix" outlook clearly afflicted attorney H. J. Sissons in 1902. Sissons was representing James McPherson who had broken a collar bone in a fall from a load of lumber during the construction of a bridge for the Canadian Northern Railway. Sissons advised the company's counsel that he had witnesses of the negligence of the company's doctor, who had treated McPherson, and would "not be wholly in want of the kind of evidence which a jury is apt to be largely led by." But he then let down his guard (or rather, McPherson's guard). He was, he told the company's legal beagles, "a young lawyer" who could not "as well afford to take up pauper cases" here in the provinces as he might in Toronto, and "at any rate," Sissons did "not care much" for the case. He "would much like to have a settlement offered." He asked for his costs, "a small fee," and $100 for Mr. McPherson. Obligingly, the company settled with Mr. McPherson for $110.[19]

[16] James to William Mackenzie, President, undated; James to Lash (telegram), June 11, 1903 (James *did* find one copy of the rulebook, on June 30); Anglin to Lash, undated, file 82–4, Canadian Northern Ry. Legal dept., Vol. 9066, R.G. 30, Archives of Canada.

[17] Hazel Genn, *Hard Bargaining: Out of Court Settlement in Personal Injury Actions* (Oxford, 1987).

[18] File 171, Grand Trunk legal counsel records, Vol. 3491, R.G. 30, Archives of Canada.

[19] Sissons to Office of Gen. Counsel, Nov. 10, 1902, Can. Northern Ry. legal dept. files, 82–1, Vol. 9066, R.G. 30, Archives of Canada.

Sometimes the railway's lawyer simply called the bluff of an attorney who seemed to present a weak case. Most companies employed accident investigators whose probe into the claim could provide the company with the incentive to resist. Thus, a Mr. Bond, an investigator employed by England's Great Western Railway, reported to the company's solicitor on a Mrs. Chadwick, injured in an accident at Dudley in 1883: "while she has sustained a general nervous shock," she was "making the most of her injuries," claiming "that the shock had caused injury to the womb, and brought on piles." Later she "looked quite well and fat." The solicitor's report recommended rejecting as "most excessive" here claim for sixty pounds in damages. Similarly, Inspector J. Gray advised W. H. Gaw, the Christchurch Traffic Manager for the New Zealand Railways of the condition in which he found one of the Rakaia accident claimants:

> Personally I do not believe anything is wrong with Mrs. Brown except excessive stoutness and strong power to imagine herself ailing and aching, and an itching to handle some Railway cash.[20]

A similar fate was in store for the claim of James Murphy, who injured his legs while unloading the Grand Trunk's rails in 1907. The company's doctor reported to the railway's law office that the injury was not serious and that the victim suffered from "acute alcoholism." When Murphy's attorney, H. Vivian, Esq., of Winnipeg, claimed $4000 in damages, but later offered to settle for $500, Assistant Solicitor Symington responded by doubting the veracity of Mr. Vivian's report of medical costs ($84.20) as well as Mr. Vivian's own costs, which he had placed at $75. "I fail to see how the mere issue of a Statement of Claim could give rise to so great an amount," Symington wrote. But he offered to "help you out in this matter." The company would "pay you your actual disbursements, or, say, $100, conditional, of course, upon a discontinuance of the action being filed." Mr. Vivian entered into a settlement on behalf of his client for $125.[21]

[20] File #2978, Report of Solicitors upon Legal Business, Jan.–Dec. 1884, Great Western Railway, PRO/RAIL/250/490, Public Records Office, Kew Gardens; Rakaia Accident, 99/1009, Pt.2, Nov. 18, 1899, Railway Ministry Series 4, New Zealand Archives, Wellington. For another example, see the investigation of the claim of Mrs. Mary Ann Shaw (wife of contractor Thomas Shaw) for 500 pounds for injuries and nervous shock due to the Pugarry Junction derailment in 1911; the files of her case indicate that she was spied upon by an investigator who prepared two reports (6 & 11 August, 1911). Mrs. Shaw settled for 250 pounds, indicating that the investigator had uncovered little that could be turned to the Railway's advantage.

[21] *Grand Trunk v. James Murphy*, file 163, Vol. 3491, R.G. 30, Archives of Canada.

An attorney's claim letter alone thus accomplished very little for his client. But once he had gathered evidence, interviewed relevant witnesses, and commenced an action with a court, he was more capable of effective negotiations with the railway's counsel. "I fancy that until action has been commenced and proceeded with to a certain extent it is not likely that any settlement can be effected," the Canadian Northern's general counsel wrote to the general superintendent in 1904 concerning the case of an engineer killed by an engine being backed without a rear light or the sounding of a bell. A coroner's inquest had blamed the railway, and once the family's attorney put the case on the docket in Quebec, a province with a *bon père de familie* rule in work-related accidents, the company settled for $1000.[22] This was considerably less than might have been awarded at trial, but the man's family would have been told that, while their case was a good one, they would also have been aware that there were no such things as certainties, and that, in any event, most of the fees in preparing and arguing the case would have to be borne by them. Moreover, going to trial would mean that the final outcome might be set many months into the future. When the plaintiff moved the case to trial, the filing of formal actions, taking of depositions, and costs of court could cost the defendant company as much as £350 for legal fees alone (in addition to whatever might be awarded the plaintiff, or eventually given to her in a belated settlement). In short, the expenses for both the plaintiff's and the company's attorneys were modest before the case was fully developed; they could be considerable thereafter.[23]

Plaintiffs faced specific problems when railway attorneys won retrials. Throughout the British Commonwealth corporations that had won such retrials sought to make the plaintiff's next step expensive. And this could be accomplished at times in the relatively plaintiff-friendly courts of the United States. Thus, the Illinois Central's solicitor reported with satisfaction to the board of directors in December, 1889, that, after winning a retrial of Emma Harrison's case, his office had also "obtained [a] rule" from the appellate court requiring "the plaintiff to give security for costs." She had won a $1000 jury award in Grenada County, Mississippi, at the first trial but, he reported, she and her attorney were not going to pay such a sum into court, and as such, "the suit will be dismissed."[24]

---

[22] Z. A. Lash to E. A. James, 29 Oct., 1904, *Adm. of Boon v. Can. Northern*, file 82–10, Vol. 9066, R.G. 30, Archives of Canada.

[23] See *Caldwell v. Union Steamship Co.*, 17 Gaz. LR(NZSC) 700 (1915).

[24] Annual Rpt. Of General Solicitor, Dec. 1889, 1890 Board Minutes, +3.4, Illinois Central Archives, Newberry Lib.

Consider also the case of Clara Woolsey, executrix of John Woolsey, a Canadian Northern man killed in an accident at Edmonton in May, 1906. Woolsey, an engine driver, had taken his wife and her friend into the cab of his engine for a look when a defective union joint gave way and he was scalded to death. A critical piece of evidence, a repair book, could not be located by local company officials, and the assistant solicitor, George Macdonnell, told D. J. McDougal, an Ottawa barrister whose firm sometimes argued cases for the Canadian Northern, that "this is one of those rare cases of velvet where I might as well take the agency charges." The company lost at trial and the jury awarded Mrs. Woolsey $8000, but the company appealed. The appellate court found sufficient error to order a new trial, and when Mrs. Woolsey's attorney pressed on and filed an appeal of this judgement with the Supreme Court of Canada, Macdonnell told General Superintendent Hanna that "we think we can do better if we show fight than if we look too anxious to settle." Inasmuch as both sides were unsure of what the outcome of this new appeal might be, they did reach a settlement. Mrs. Woolsey's attorney was the first to blink; he asked for $2500. The company's legal beagles got him to cut that figure in half and paid out $1200; less than $1000 of that would go to Mrs. Woolsey.[25]

A memo that constituted the last entry in this file indicated that the company had paid over $2000 in additional funds for legal services and court costs in fighting this case. And this was evidence of a widespread phenomenon:[26] As much as 5 percent of all passenger train revenues went out again as expenditures of various kinds related to personal injury/wrongful death suits.[27] And the *relative* costs of actual payments to victims (whether as a settlement or a trial award) to the rest of the legal office's expenses (court costs, witnesses, attorney's fee, office expenses) was 27 percent to 73 percent, if the London & Northwestern's figures for 1869–1871 can serve as any standard.[28] This appears to have been similar to the legal expenses per settlement of the Illinois Central for the year 1889[29] and the London & Northwest Railway in the mid-1860s.

[25] Woolsey file, #82–19, Vol. 9066, R.G. 30, Archives of Canada.

[26] Rande Kostal has calculated the trial costs to British railways in the 1860s for such personal injury/wrongful death suits to be £300. (Kostal, *infra* note, 61, 381.)

[27] This, in any event, is the figure I come up with from my U.S., Canadian, and New Zealand evidence, and it can also be derived from the data offered by Rande Kostal, *Ibid.*, 305.

[28] London & Northwestern Law Committee Records, Euston Station, 1869–1872, PRO/RAIL/410/411.

[29] Treasurer's Report, 1889, Board Minutes, Jan.–Mar. 1890, +3.4, Ill. Cent. Arch., Newberry Lib.

Once in a while railway officials tried to avoid the costs involved in preparing to litigate by simply sidestepping the plaintiff's attorney and dealing directly with the plaintiff herself. In the one instance that I detected where a court became aware that this had happened, the practice was condemned and the company's success undone. One Jeremiah Johnson had been killed at a Grand Trunk crossing in Ontario. His widow, Mary Johnson, had been approached by a company official after her solicitor had filed an action, and without that solicitor being present, she had accepted $500 and signed a general release. On advice of counsel, she soon formally repudiated the settlement and returned the $500. A trial court jury awarded her $1000, and the company appealed, arguing that her original settlement should have been binding upon her. But Ontario's Court of Queen's Bench turned them away and affirmed the trial judgement. Chief Justice John Douglas Armour cited a Wisconsin Supreme Court case in holding that the company had acted unfairly in dealing with Mrs. Johnson behind her solicitor's back, and that such dealing rendered her release voidable at her will. The Johnsons were black, and Justice William P. Street noted that Mary Johnson was illiterate. Street derived from this that the parties to this agreement to settle were "not on equal terms" and he scolded the "clever men of business" who had orchestrated it.[30]

I can't say how widespread this practice may have been. I found little evidence of this sort of side stepping of plaintiff's attorney in the files of the legal counsels of nine of my ten railway archives, but I did notice it once in my sampling of the records of the Chicago, Burlington & Quincy. Lera Travis's attorney had sought $2500 for injuries she suffered at a defective railway crossing in 1883, and "did not want to settle for less than $1000." The company's local attorney advised the main office that he was sending "Doctor [James] Wright" to speak to the plaintiff. That worthy soon reported that he had ascertained that the victim's son had contacted the attorney, and that he had spoken to her son-in-law, gaining access to "the old lady" herself. The upshot was that he had secured a settlement and release for $100. Doctor Wright

---

[30] *Johnson v. Grand Trunk Ry.*, 25 Ont. R. 64 at 66, 69 (1894). For further evidence of judicial solicitude for the plight of black plaintiffs in Canada see *Brasell v. Grand Tronc*, 11 Quebec C.S. 150 at 167 (1897) (Justice Pagnuelo: "C'est un homme de couleur qui trouvera plus difficilement de l'emploi qu'un blanc.... Il reste boiteux, et ne pourra plus exercer l'emploi de porter."); *Calhoun v. Windsor Hotel Co.*, 4 Quebec C.S. 471 (1893); *Johnson v. Sparrow*, 15 Quebec C.S. 104 at 106–08 (1899); affirmed 8 Quebec Q.B. 379 (1899); declaring discrimination in theatres "entirely uncompatible with our free democratic institutions"); *In re Hutchison & Bd. of School Trustees of St. Catharines*, 31 UCQB 274 (1872) (declaring school segregation illegal). But see *Dunn v. Bd. of Ed. Town of Windsor*, 6 Ont. R. 455 (1885).

already had a free railway pass; he asked that his services in this case be rewarded by the company's sending him one for his wife.[31]

Carl Gersuny offers an example of just such a case of corporate chicanery with regard to Isabella Salmon, a worker at the Dwight Manufacturing Company in turn of the century New England. Her injury suit was settled for her medical costs, a month's wages, and $100 for pain and suffering after the company's insurer told its agent to "please employ Mr Luther White or some reputable attorney in Chicopee to bring friendly suit against you for the purpose of making a binding settlement. . . . Mr White will understand this."[32] Isabella Salmon was not to know that the attorney who represented here in such a "friendly suit" was actually the agent of the company (or its insurers). And this may have been quite common. William Thomas has found that interstate railroads in the American South regularly keep many of the more competent attorneys in communities their lines served "on retainer, " prohibiting their taking any case against their line or any other railway's, and generally the cost of these retainers was little more than a free pass. Moreover, both he and James Dilts, writing of the B. & O. Railroad, report that physicians were "retained" in the same fashion, and at least some of these doctors were prepared "to extort" from the injured party "a promise . . . that no lawyer would be employed," or so the Central of Georgia's attorney reported of the successful efforts of his "personal friend," one Dr. Peebles.[33]

Another variable effecting the company's decision as to whether to offer a settlement was its assessment of the abilities of the foe it faced. A relative novice like Smyth, Sissons, or Vivian did not command the respect of one who specialized in personal injury litigation. There were a few such men in every provincial capital, and for the Canadian railways with branches that extended into Vermont, Michigan, or Minnesota, there were others, offering contingency fee arrangements, prepared to sue in either state or federal court. Thus, when Mrs. A. C. Bainbridge was injured in a passenger car derailment en route Winnipeg to St. Francis, in January, 1903, she retained the services of F. D. Larrabee of Minneapolis. Larrabee's letter to the Canadian Northern's counsel in Minnesota, Hector Baxter, seemed harmless enough. He wanted to negotiate a settlement "on a fair basis and not try to extort money for fancied injuries," and if her injuries

---

[31] Wright to J. Blythe, Sept. 20, 1883, Legal/ 33 1880 4.62/ C B & Q Archives, Newberry Lib.

[32] Gersuny, *Work Hazards and Industrial Conflict* (Hanover, N. H., 1981), 85.

[33] Dilts, *The Great Road*, 311; William Thomas, "How the Interstate Railroad Changed the South," paper delivered at American Society for Legal History Conference, Minneapolis, 1997.

proved not to be serious, "we will not ask for large damages." Nevertheless, Baxter advised the company's Chief Solicitor, Z. A. Lash, that Larrabee was "an expert damage suit lawyer of this city" who "makes a specialty of litigation of this kind." Lash responded that he doubted that the American courts would have jurisdiction over the case, and suspected (correctly, as we have seen) that Larrabee would have greater difficulty with the rules of law on the matter in a Manitoba court. But he had Baxter arrange for two physicians to examine Mrs. Bainbridge, and he soon settled with her for $625, an arrangement that Baxter pronounced "very satisfactory."[34]

In the Bainbridge suit, the plaintiff's application to an American court was disputable; in other cases it was not, and in these instances the Canadian Northern's chief solicitor had to factor any differences in the rules of Law between the two legal systems that might affect the outcome. Thus, when a drover named Eggertson on a free pass was injured in a collision that occurred in Minnesota, the company's man in Minneapolis, Hector Baxter, advised Lash in a lengthy legal memo that "whatever the rule may be in Canada, it would not be wise to go to trial in either the State or Federal Courts of this country under the facts given."[35] Here, in the Bainbridge and Eggertson cases, were clear statements from the corporate trenches of the effects that a "jurisprudence of the heart" had produced in the American courts in the nineteenth century.

Consider, however, the plight of Samuel Walker, a Canadian Northern switchman, who lost both his legs in an accident in Winnipeg. Walker chose to sue in his contractual home, Minnesota, and Baxter advised Lash that Walker's attorney, Humphrey Barton of St. Paul, was "a damage suit lawyer" who "has had great success in getting large verdicts against railroads for personal injury cases." Consequently, Baxter got the case removed to the federal district court. Offering further evidence of the point Edward Purcell made recently about this phenomenon,[36] Baxter told Lash:

> The Federal Court does not respond as the State Court does to the popular clamor against corporations and especially railroads. We will also have the advantage of a jury selected from the rural parts of the state, instead of simply from St. Paul. . . .

Baxter recommended the retention of Pierce Butler, a "first class trial lawyer," despite his fee of $100 per day. Butler, who would soon

---

[34] File 82–3, Vol. 9066, R.G. 30, Archives of Canada.

[35] File 82–18, Vol. 9066, R.G. 30, Archives of Canada.

[36] Purcell, *Litigation and Inequality: Federal Diversity Jurisdiction in Industrial America, 1870–1958* (New York, Oxford Univ. Press, 1992), 92–94.

rise to serve on the U.S. Supreme Court and be remembered as one of the ultraconservative "Four Horsemen" of the 1930s, proved at first to be "very strongly of the opinion that we have no defense." After conferring with a Canadian Northern attorney named Clark on "this matter in relation to the application of Canadian laws," however, he seems to have changed his mind; there was no settlement. The federal trial jury, despite any rural roots it may have had, delivered a verdict for switchman Walker of $15,000, but Butler appealed successfully to the federal circuit court where he won a new trial. (And one of the circuit court jurists supporting his view of the case was none other than Willis Van Devanter, another future member of the notorious "Four Horsemen.") In this case, at least, the plaintiff's resource to American jurisprudence does not appear to have worked, at least not at first,[37] though it seems clear that he had been provided a better chance of success in that legal venue rather than the one on the northern side of the border.

When, as was usually the case, the injured party had no recourse to American Law, his suit might still prompt an offer from the Grand Trunk, Canadian Northern, New South Wales, Victoria, London & Northwest, or New Zealand Railway Ministries if the facts of the case clearly indicated that both the Law and a jury would favor the victim at trial. David Cockerill, a laborer employed by the Canadian Northern at Beaver Mills to help drive piles for a new bridge, had both legs fractured in May, 1901 when a heavy hook slipped. His attorney sought a jury trial at Winnipeg, and counsel for the railway reported that they had learned that Cockerill's foreman had been told that the hook's guard was "too much worn and dangerous" to continue to be used. "He says he asked Mr. Balfour, who was superintending the work, to allow him to have it repaired, and that Mr. Balfour refused." Cockerill's counsel was probably aware of this and would consequently prevail; counsel employed by the Canadian Northern recommended that Mr. Lash approve an offer to settle.[38]

Occasionally I detected something of a conscience at work in the bowels of these railway solicitors' offices. The (English) Great Western's chief legal counsel seemed particularly to possess a respectable one. On April 2, 1884, for example, he reported to the company's directors on the trial of the suit of a Mrs. Brooker before Baron Huddlestone and a jury. This lady had been injured in an accident at Westbourne Park station six months before, and her attorney may

---

[37] Walker file, 82–23, Vol. 9067, R.G. 30, Archives of Canada. The issue on appeal was Walker's contributory negligence. I could find no further indication of the final outcome of this case.

[38] Cockerill file 82–5, Vol. 9066, R.G. 30, Archieve of Canada.

not have been especially skillful. Her claim, Mr. Adam reported, "was practically abandoned at trial, but we were aware Mrs. Brooker's injuries had proved to be more serious than had first been anticipated and that it is doubtful when she will recover." As such, he had not pressed the company's case as vigorously as he might have, and she had secured an award of 400 pounds. "The verdict is not unreasonable," Mr. Adam observed somewhat chivalrously.[39]

The general solicitor of the Illinois Central displayed similar humanity in his annual report for 1887. A man named Lewis had suffered compensable loss when put off the train at the wrong stop by the conductor. The solicitor told the conductor that the Illinois Central "would attach everything he had & follow him up so as to recover all we lost by his negligence." The conductor acknowledged his fault and offered Mr. Lewis $200, which offer was accepted. Now the general solicitor recommended to the board that the company "pay the $200 and keep the honest fellow."[40]

And these instances prompt me to offer another observation: The ten railways whose records I have examined were not alike in the ways in which they treated claims. Some appeared to have been considerably less willing to accommodate claimants "fairly." (I know; the word is a subjective one, but I hope by now I have earned enough of the reader's confidence in my judgement to use it.) While Charles Perkins headed the C. B. & Q. (1881–1901), that company paid a number of "gratuities" to "deserving" employees or their "destitute" survivors, some of which covered only lost income or funeral expenses, but many quite substantial.[41] And in virtually every case the records included an assessment by someone in the solicitor's office that the company would not be held liable were the case to go to court. In one instance, President Perkins approved a payment of $500 to a "destitute" Mrs. Workman and her daughter. Their main provider, a young trainman, had been killed in an accident caused by a fellow-worker (a signalman). Because

[39] April 2, 1884 (Brooker), Reports of Solicitors... 1884, PRO/RAIL/250/490.

[40] J. D. Lewis case, October 1887, Ann. Rept. Of Gen. Sol., Dec. 1887, Bd. Minutes, Ann. Rept. 1887, Box 4/ +3.4/ Illinois Central Archives, Newberry Lib.

[41] I detected twenty-three such payments in sampling records between 1885 and 1888. The median figure was $200 (high of $1200, low of $24.50). T. Goddard In-letters, 3G5.3/ C B & Q Archives, Newberry Libr. For evidence of such "gratuities" (*ex gratia* in the language of equity) elsewhere in the lands of the Diaspora see the payment of fifty pounds plus fifty-two pounds per year(pay as a gatekeeper) for the widow of a railway laborer named Brazil, Brazil file, A/12299/5994/2 (1899), Queensland PRO, Runcon.

the young man was twenty-one-years old, and the accident had occurred in Missouri, the rights-of-survivorship were limited to his wife
and children; he had neither. "Had the accident occurred in Iowa or
Illinois," Perkins (a former Illinois Central solicitor himself) wrote, his
dependent mother and sister would have acquired such rights. Perkins
would not have them denied this substantial *solatia* on a "purely technical ground."[42]

In ways like this England's Great Western and London & Northwestern railways, the Chicago, Burlington & Quincy, and New Zealand's
Ministry of Railways seemed considerably more willing to accommodate either employees, passengers, or both than (for example) the
London, Brighton & South Coast. And this latter company was also
the most aggressive in pressing police court prosecutions against those
traveling without a ticket or in a state of intoxication. Perhaps the
holiday-bound character of some of that company's clientele serves to
explain their policies. In any event, the policies and practices of one
company were not mirror images of those of every other one.

How did injured passengers who settled fare? The London & Northwest, Rande Kostal tells us, spent an average of 219 pounds per personal
injury claim in 1868–1869, the equivalent of over $1300 Canadian.
My reading of some seventy such settlements paid by the London &
Northwest between 1869 and 1872 produced a median payment of
326 pounds. The median for some 129 settlements paid out by the
(English) Great Western in 1884, 1897, 1898, and 1899 was only thirty
pounds, but a number of these involved claims limited to damaged
clothes (including one to a C. Morrell of Steveaton of 12s 6p for damage to his hat). The median settlement paid by the Great Western in the
massive Slough accident of June 16, 1900, on the other hand, was 268
pounds (N = 281), for most of the claimants were badly injured passengers. My median settlement figure, then, for some 483 settlements
by three English railways between 1869 and 1900 was 205 pounds, very
close to the average calculated by Kostal for a slightly earlier period.[43]
To these I can add some twenty-four settlements made by officers of
the Illinois Central and the C. B & Q. between 1874[44] and 1889, thirty-
three Canadian suits of passenger–plaintiffs settled between 1897 and

[42] Perkins to Wirt Dexter, Gen. Supt., Jan. 26, 1885, Gottard In-letters, 3G5.3/
C B & Q Archives, Newberry Libr.

[43] Kostal, *Law & English Railway Capitalism*, 377; Great Western Railway
Accident & Compensation Case Book, 1897–1900, PRO/RAIL/270/22,
Reports of Solicitors..., 1884, PRO/RAIL/250/490, and Accident &
Compensation Case Book, 1897–1900, Great Western Railway, PRO/
RAIL/270/22, Public Records Office.

[44] One of the Illinois Central settlements I detected occurred much earlier, in 1858, but it involved the wrongful death of an employee, not a

1917, nineteen settlements reached by representatives of the State Railway Authorities of New South Wales (1860–1890) and Queensland (1898–1911), some thirteen settlements made by New Zealand's Railway Ministry in the 1890s, and another one hundred eight made to persons injured or killed in the Rakaia accident in New Zealand's South Island in 1899 – a total of 185.[45] The median settlement was the equivalent of $330 US. And recall that when one separates out the settlements made with those Canadian passengers threatening to sue in American courts from the rest of the Canadian settlements, American-law passengers received more than those targeting Canadian courts.[46]

THE ALTERNATIVE ROUTE FOR INJURED WORKERS: WORKER'S COMPENSATION

The railways *would* offer "deserving" employees or unfortunate passengers or bystanders modest sums to compensate them for actual medical expenses and lost earnings, under the right circumstances, but it took a good attorney to get anything further, for past and future pain and suffering or future loss of expectation. Consider the case of Michael McLaughlin, who lost a thumb in an accident laying track near Portage la Prairie in 1906. His supervisor reported to the division engineer at Winnipeg that a nut had become frozen in the tumblings shaft that McLaughlin was holding, "out of which he could not get his hand." He was "a very careful worker in every respect," and this accident had in no regard been "owing to carelessness on his part." In turn, the engineer, L. B. Merriam, told the Grand Trunk's Assistant Solicitor Symington that it would be "not only humane but good policy to make a reasonable settlement with him." With no one representing McLaughlin, however, Symington was under no pressure to be generous. He paid the man's hospital and doctor's bills and gave him $60 for two months of wages he had lost; nothing more.[47]

---

passenger. Emma Leffingwell release, Nov. 13, 1858/ Personnel/ 3.92/ Ill. Cent. Arch., Newberry Libr.

[45] These are to be found in Series 4, Railway Ministry Records, files 91 through 99 (subnumbered), especially 99/1009, parts 1–3, Archives of New Zealand. In addition, to these, I found files of several settlements, and several jury awards at trial, for a derailment in 1882 and a collision in 1914, in Series 4, files 82/621, 83/1625, 83/2926, 83/3380, 84/2972, 84/3533, 88/1569, 89/260, 91/1738, and other such files.

[46] The New Zealand figure is virtually identical to the £60 median settlement offered by the London & Northwestern Railway for an accident in the late 1860s. (Derived from figures in Rande Kostal, *infra* note 61, 381–82.)

[47] McLaughlin file #65, Vol. 3486, R.G. 30, Archives of Canada.

McLaughlin's settlement was, in effect, made outside of the Common Law's domain. And that was exactly what Worker's Compensation did; it bypassed the Common-Law remedies and offered a no-fault, bare-bones alternative. We can compare the awards offered under each system by aggregating data available in the records of the legal counsel for the (English) Great Western, the Canadian Northern, the (Canadian-U.S.) Grand Trunk, and the New Zealand Railway Ministry for settlements, the figures reported in these records and in appellate reports for trial court awards, and the figures of payments made to employees by the Canadian Northern, on the one hand, and the provincial worker's compensation boards, on the other, in the early twentieth century after this latter alternative was in place.

Injured workers who simply turned to their employers for compensation received little more than Michael McLaughlin, and this was so as late as 1919. In the three months I sampled from that year, some 118 payments were made by the Canadian Northern, in March, May, and October. The median payment was $56 dollars, plus $11.50 for medical expenses. Simultaneously, those Canadian Northern workers who sought recovery from the new alternative vehicle, the provincial worker's compensation boards, received even less. Of the 91 workers in May and October who received compensation from the Manitoba and Alberta boards, the median award was $30.50 plus $10 in medical expenses.[48]

Workers who initiated lawsuits in England, Canada, and New Zealand and then settled received considerably more than those who opted for worker's compensation when available. Between 1897 and 1900 some seventy five claims under the terms of the Workman's Compensation Act of 1897 were settled by the Great Western; the median settlement payout was 150 pounds (though a third were under 100 pounds). The files of two important Dominion railways for the first decade of this century contain the reports of some forty-four settlements with workers; the median settlement was $1100. Because of the business of the Grand Trunk in northern New England and the Canadian Northern in Minnesota, some twenty-six of these settlements went to men whose attorneys threatened to sue in U.S. courts. And here the figures are most revealing, confirming the fear these companies had of U.S. law and U.S. juries. While these men or their heirs were offered a median settlement of $1700, those threatening to sue in Canada (N = 18) were given a median settlement of only $930.[49]

---

[48] Sampled from File 82–84, Vol. 9071, R.G. 30, Archives of Canada. (1919 was the first year for which I could find such data.)

[49] The former figures, for the Great Western, are found in Accident & Compensation Case Book, 1897–1900, PRO/RAIL/270/22; the latter are drawn

AWARDS FOR PERSONAL INJURY OR WRONGFUL DEATH

Bartrip and Burman calculated the typical award at trial in certain county courts in England in the early 1880s to be about eighty pounds, with the sums paid over in settlements being considerably less than that. But the median jury award out of some fifty-two awards recorded in the Solicitor's reports of the English Great Western Railway for 1884, 1897, 1898, and 1899 (N = 52) was 250 pounds, and ten of these (nearly 20 percent) were over 1000 pounds. English juries may not have been as generous as those in the United States, as we will soon see, but they appear to have become increasingly generous throughout the nineteenth century, especially toward railway accident victims.[50]

While 197 of my litigating Canadian, American, Australian, and New Zealand passengers were accepting settlements in the *fin de siècle*, another 53 pressed ahead to a trial verdict. Five of the 17 litigants from the United States and seven of the 36 from the other Diaspora lands, lost at that stage, but the other 41 either won awards (or were provided "conditional" awards by CANZ juries that had "found" for the defendant corporation on other grounds); their median in the United States was $2800; in Canada, $3500; in New Zealand and Australia,[51] £700 ($3500 approx.); quite comparable, but larger than those awarded by English juries.

I can supplement this spare evidence of trial court awards from railway counsel records with evidence of several hundred awards to passengers, "strangers," and employees detected in the CANZ appellate reports from the 1840s to 1910. Theoretically, those cases that were appealed and reported could have been the ones with more substantial

from the Canadian Northern's legal dept. files from 1897 to 1916 in Volumes 9066, 9067 and 9071 of R.G. 30, and the Grand Trunk's Suit Reports, in Vols. 3486, 3491, 3493, and 13,336 of R.G. 30, Archives of Canada.

    Prior to the passage of Workmen's Compensation legislation, it was possible in New Zealand for workers unsuccessful in securing compensation for injuries from the railway ministry or the courts to petition the legislature with success for hospital expenses and disability pay. See 83/2926, Series 4, Railway Ministry, New Zealand Archives.

50 Great Western Railway Accident & Compensation Case Book, 1897–1900, PRO/RAIL/270/22, Reports of Solicitors . . . , 1884, PRO/RAIL/250/490, and Accident & Compensation Case Book, 1897–1900, Great Western Railway, PRO/RAIL/270/22, Public Records Office; Bartrip & Burnam, *Wounded Soldiers of Industry*, 173, 175.

51 I detected only one Australian jury award figure: 167 pounds to William Clark, a "teacher of Dancing," injured on a Great Southern train in New South Wales in 1868. Record Group 169, Items 1–12, NSW Ry. Solicitor's Sundry Agreements, Contracts & Bonds, State Ry. Auth. Of NSW Archives, Transport House, York St., Sydney.

awards at stake. If this were so, the figures available in the appellate reports would have only one function – that of enabling us to distinguish awards where the defendant was a private corporation from those where the defendant was a municipality or an individual. That we will do, but I have come to doubt that the awards that appear in the reported appellate cases differ substantially from those I detected in the records of U.S., English, Canadian, and New Zealand railway counsel files. All told, I detected some 555 award figures for personal injury or wrongful death in the CANZ reports between the 1840s and 1910.[52] Of these, sixty-seven were jury awards to passengers injured on stagecoaches, trams, streetcars, vessels, or railways; the median award to these individuals in New Zealand and Australia was £500; in the Canadian provinces outside of juryless Quebec, it was $1250. Another seventy-two were jury awards to workers; the median of these awards in Australia and New Zealand was £520; in the Canadian provinces other than Quebec, it was $1800. In short, the figures recorded in the appellate reports (median year: 1888) were somewhat *smaller* than those I detected in the railway counsel files for the years from 1897–1917.

I suspect that the differences may be due to two facts: First, many of the appellate report awards mulcted much smaller defendants than those whose files I reviewed, and, as we shall see, the larger the defendant's coffers were, the larger was the jury's award. Second, the awards in the years *before* the 1890s (and half of the appellate awards fall into that timeframe) were made by juries to plaintiffs when incomes, medical costs, and standards of living were all slightly *lower* than they would be by the time the Canadian and New Zealand railways lost their twenty-four trial cases.

In any event, from this point on, I will be referring to figures that are derived from the 555 awards I detected in the CANZ appellate reports, the 38 awards I detected in English reports (as well as some 52 detected in the files of the Great Western), and from some 178 others detected in an earlier study of American appellate reports from the 1830s to 1899, and I will be treating these figures as a satisfactory general proxy for the total population of unreported awards at trial.

---

[52] This figure (555) was substantially higher than the number of awards I detected in the larger corpus of nineteenth-century American reports largely because, under the English (and CANZ) rule, the trial jury was generally asked to provide a "conditional" award figure even when it separately decided for the defendant. (See *Wood v. Pittfield*, 26 New Br. 210 (1887) and *Rajotte v. Can. Pac. Ry*, 5 Manitoba 365 at 369 (1889)). This reporting of "conditional" jury awards in cases where the jury had found for the defendant led to the larger data base.

Let me begin by summarizing what I had found in a similar study of American jury awards for personal injury.[53] The deeper the defendant's pockets, the larger the jury's award. Thus, the median award in medical malpractice cases was $2000, while it was $2250 when the defendant was a municipal corporation (road and bridge accidents), and $6000 when the defendant was a streetcar, stagecoach, steamboat, or, more commonly, a railroad company. This propensity could even be detected when the defendant had intentionally caused an injury, and was thus subject to punitive damages ("smart money") in addition to compensatory damages. The median award in assault and battery cases was only $1000; the juries quite consciously took the defendant's ability to pay into account. Thus, in the twenty-four cases where an *individual* was the defendant, the average award was $891, while in the nine assault cases where a *corporation* was the codefendant (typically because the aggressive party had been, and remained, in its employ, his behavior unrepudiated), the average award was $3965.

I wondered whether this pattern would appear in a disaggregation of the 555 CANZ awards. It did. Let me begin with assaults.

I found forty-six reported jury awards for assault and battery. The median figure for the thirty-seven of these in which the defendant was an individual was $300;[54] it was $1200 for the ten cases in which there

53 Karsten, *Heart versus Head,* ch. 8. These did not include wrongful death awards, one difference between the two sets of figures.
54 These were *Aird v. Raine* (NSWSC, Kercher, 1825) (10 pounds); *Fuller v. Drake* (NSWSC Kercher, 1827) (15 pounds); *Girard v. Rapey,* (NSWSC, Kercher, 1827) (1 farthing); *Nowlan v. Whitfield* (NSWSC, Kercher, 1827) (25 pounds); *Nowlan v. Young* (NSWSC, Kercher, 1828) (25 pounds); *Rex v. Leighton* (NSWSC, Kercher, 1829) (20 pound fine); *Rex v. Litch* (NSWSC, Kercher, 1826) (50 pound fine); *Johnson v. Rushford,* 2 Austr.L.T.(Vict.) 58 (1880); *Bruce v. Rutherford,* 1 W.N. (NSW) 102 (1885); *Kohan v. Stanbridge,* 16 SRNSW 579 (1916); *Dame v. Faddy & Connell,* 1 Newf. R.120 (1818); *Gillier v. Brookman,* 22 Nova Sc.10 (1889); *Bulmer v. O'Sullivan,* 28 Nova Sc 406 (1896); *Inglefield v. Markel,* 9 Nova Sc. 188 (1873); *Henderson v. Scott,* 24 Nova Sc. 232 (1892); *Holmes v. McLeod,* 25 Nova Sc. 67 (1892); *Driscoll v. Collins,* 31 New Br. 604 (1892); *Schokl v. Kay,* 10 New Br. 244 (1862); *McDonald v. Cameron,* 4 UCQB1 (1847) (Chief Justice Robinson affirming an award of £62 10s to an 11-year-old girl held in a root cellar overnight by a landowner for picking one gooseberry on his property); *Glass v. O'Grady,* 17 UCCP 233 (1866); *Hickey v. Fitzgerald,* 41 UCQB 303 (1877); *Curtiss v. Townsend,* 6 UCCP 255 (1856); *St. John v. Parr,et al.,* 7 UCCP 142 (1857); *Belcher v. Arnott, et al.,* 9 UCCP 68 (1859); *Macdonald v. Cameron,* 4 UCQB1 (1847); *Short v. Lewis,* 3 UCQB (O.S.) 385 (Wm.IV); *Percy v. Glasco,* 22 UCCP 521 (1872); *Soules v. Doan,* 39 UCQB 337 (1876); *Davis v. Luman,* 8 UCQB 599 (1851); *Dunham v. Powell,* 5 UCQB (O.S.) 675 (1839); *Devaltamier v. McCready,* 18 Quebec 107 (1865); *Piché v. Guilmette,* 3 Quebec C.S. 358

were multiple defendants or the defendant was a corporation.[55] This led Upper Canada's Chief Justice of Common Pleas, William Henry Draper, to complain in 1862 "that large corporations should be heavily mulcted in damages upon the assumption of their greater ability to pay," led Justice Lewis Drummond of Lower Canada's Queen's Bench to observe similarly three years later of "the strange prejudice which some people have against companies. . . ," and led the New Brunswick Supreme Court to remit nearly 70 percent of the $5200 awarded by a jury to three fly-fishermen in 1884. (A fisheries officer had pointed a pistol at them in enforcing the game laws, and Chief Justice John Allen suspected that the jury was as generous as this because they were confident that "the government would pay the damages.")[56]

Some of these assault victims had suffered serious, life-threatening, and deliberate, beatings. Hence, it is not surprising that the median award for these sorts of acts when committed by individuals ($300) was slightly higher than the median awards ($250 (N = 52)) made to those injured (some "severely") by the *negligent* acts of ordinary mortals riding horses, driving sleighs, carelessly firing weapons, permitting barrels to roll off scaffolds, or failing to prevent bricks, loose cornices, ice, or snow from falling on passers-by,[57] and virtually the same as that handed down when the negligent party was a physician or surgeon

(1893); *Neill v. Taylor*, 15 Low. Can. R 102 (1865); *Courtant v. Sert*, 1 Quebec 19 (1740); *Pettier v. Martin*, 14 Quebec C.S. 223 (1898); and *Grantillo v. Coporici*, 16 Quebec C. S. 44 (1899).

55 These were *Merritt v. Keim, Macleod & Butterworth* (NSWSC, Kercher, 1826) (200 pounds to ship's passenger); *Wilson v. Saunders*, 1 New Br. 347 (1831); *Williamson v. Grand Trunk Ry.*, 17 UCCP 615 (1867); *Dancey v. Grand Trunk Ry.*, 19 Ont. C. of A. 664 (1892); *Can.Pac.Ry. v. Blain*, A. C. 453 (1904); *Grinsted v. Toronto (Street) Ry.*, 24 Ont. R. 683 (1894); *Davis v. Ottawa Elec. Ry.*, 28 Ont. R. 654 (1897); *Steadman v. Venning*, 22 New Br. 639 (1883); *Cunningham v. Grand Trunk Ry.*, 9 Low. Can. J. 57 (1864); *Curtis v. Grand Trunk Ry.*, 12 UCCP 82 (1862).

56 *Curtis v. Grand Trunk Ry.*, 12 UCCP 89 at 95 (1862); *Cunningham v. Grand Trunk Ry.*, Low. Can. J. 57 (1864); overturned in 11 Low. Can. J. 107 at 112 (Drummond) (1865); *Steadman v. Venning*, 22 New Br. 639 at 643 (1883).

57 *Wardell v. Francis* (NSWSC, Kercher, 1829) (thirty pounds for kick from horse); *Hovell v. Payne* (NSWSC, Kercher, 1831) (fifty pounds for woman run down by horseman); *O'Neil v. Emerson*, 6 Quebec C.S. 307 (1894) ("much pain and inconvenience"); *Robinson v. Bletcher*, 15 UCQB 159 (1856) ("injured severely" by sleigh); *McLeod v. Meek*, 6 Terr. LR 431 (1898) (weapon); *Caron v. James*, 4 Quebec C.S. 63 (1893) (barrel from scaffold); *Dugal v. Peoples Bank*, 34 New Br. 581 (1899) (ice & snow falling from roof); *Roberts v. Mitchell*, 21 Ont. C of A 433 (1894) (cornice fell on passerby); *Howard v. Oliver*, 19 Ont. R.719 (1890) (bricks falling); *Crane v. Murray*, 8 Newf. 549 (1902); *Martin v. Taylor*, 9 Nova Sc. 94 (1872); *Lownds v. Robinson*, 11 Nova Sc. 364 (1877); *Cheeseman v. Hatheway*, 23 New Br. 415 (1883);

(median = \$356 (N = 9)).[58] The larger awards did not go to those injured by individuals, no matter who those individuals were or what they had done; they went to those injured (or killed) by corporate defendants, and, even here, as in the United States, it mattered greatly whether these were small, local municipal corporations or large, national entities. The median award to those injured or killed on defective roads, sidewalks, or bridges was \$600 (N = 148),[59] whereas half of the passenger victims of common carriers received \$1000 or more (N = 87), half of all crossings victims were awarded \$1600 or more (N = 75), and the median award to employees negligently injured or killed was \$1650 (N = 139). Table 8.1 says it all: Juries were nearly twice as generous when the defendant was a municipal corporation than they were when he was an individual, and they were over twice as generous still when the corporation was large than when it was small (a town corporation or a small stagecoach partnership). Yet it appears that they were less generous than American juries by a factor of about three (see Tables 8.1 and 8.2).

What do we make of the first of these findings – that CANZ juries appeared to discriminate against corporations? Could the numbers

Keenan v. Yeats, 28 New Br. 148 (1889); *Phillips v. Byrne*, 3 Vict. LR(L) 179 (1877); *Geirk v. Connolly*, 13 Vict. LR(L) 446 (1887); *Ackroyd v. Campbell*, 11 LRNSW 470 (1890); *Spencer v. Murdock*, 2 Tasmania LR (N & S) 193 (1904); *White v. Hampton*, 6 Gaz LR (NZSC) 39 (1903); *Fleming v. Paterson*, 6 Gaz LR (NZCA 381 (1904); *Turner v. August*, 11 Gaz LR (NZSC) 715 (1909); *Lysnar v. Binnie*, 6 Gaz LR(NZSC) 498 (1904); *Devlin v. Bain*, 11 UCCP 523 (1862); *Shanahan v. Ryan*, 20 Nova Sc. 142 (1887); *Stilliway v. Ogden*, 20 Ont. R. 98 (1890); *Hasson v. Wood*, 22 Ont. R.66 (1892); *Carroll v. Freeman*, 23 Ont. R. 283 (1893); *Reid v. Barnes*, 25 Ont. R. 223 (1894); *Hopkins v. Owen Sound*, 27 Ont. R. 43 (1895); *McCullogh v. Anderson*, 27 Ont.C of A 73n (1895); *Dandurand v. Pinsonnault*, 12 Quebec 100 (1854); *Falardeau v. Couture*, 2 Low. Can. J. 96 (1857); *Beauchamp v. Cloran*, 17 Quebec 178 (1866); *Beliveau v. Martineau*, 21 Quebec 155 (1872); *McRobie v. Shuter*, 25 Low. Can. J. 103 (1880); *Lyons v. Laskey*, 33 Low. Can. J. 80 (1889); *Trudel v. Hossack*, 4 Quebec QB 370 (1894); *Vital v. Tetreault*, 34 Low. Can. J. 26 (1889); *Berthiame v. McCone*, 5 Quebec C.S. 492 (1894); *Pilon v. Shedden Co.*, 9 Quebec C.S. 83 (1896); *Brousseau v. Bourdon*, 13 Quebec C.S. 46 (1897); *Langlois v. Drouin*, 13 Quebec C.S. 49 (1898); *Pacquette v. Bessette*, 7 Quebec C.S. 441 (1895); *Rioux v. Heelan*, 8 Quebec C.S. 520 (1895); *Forget v. Baxter*, 7 Quebec Q.B. 530 (1898); *Lavoie v. Drapeau*, 31 Low. Can. J. 331 (1887); *Noel v. Duchesneau*, 15 Quebec C.S. 352 (1899); *White v. Gualdinger*, 7 Quebec Q.B. 156 (1898); *Lamouredex v. Fournier*, 33 Can. S.C. 675 (1903); *Murphy v. Labbé*, 27 Can. S.C. 126 (1897); *Hawley v. Wright*, 32 Can. S.C. 40 (1902).

[58] These cases are listed in Chapter 7, note 18.

[59] At this point the numbers of cases become too great for full citations. Many have already been referred to; others will be. I ask the reader simply to take my word for the numbers of these and other categories of accidents (railways).

Table 8.1. *Personal Injury and Wrongful Death Damage Awards – England, United States, Canada, Australia, and New Zealand, 1808–1910**

Median Awards in English Appellate Reports, 1771–1873 (N = 38)
£100
(£250 where def. a ry. Corp., 1884–1900 (N = 52))**

Median Awards in American Appellate Reports, 1808–1896 (N = 178)

Assaults (N = 33)
Def. an individual (N = 24)

  (*average*) $891
Def. a corporation (N = 9)
  (*average*) $3,965

Personal Injury (Negligence) (N = 145)
Median = $5,000
Def. a doctor (N = 20)
  $2,000
Def. a municipal corp. (N = 38)
  $2,250

Def. a private corp. or streetcar, and pl. a
Passenger/invitee (N = 83)
  $6,000

Median Awards in CANZ Appellate Reports, 1840–1910 (N = 555)

Assaults (N = 46)

Def. an individual (N = 37)
  $300
Def. or co.-def. a corporation
  (N = 10)
    $1,200

Personal Injury/Wrongful Death
  (N = 510)

Def. an individual (N = 52)
  (nonphysician)
    $250
Def. a physician (N = 9)
    $356

Def. a municipality (N = 148)
    $600

Def. a private corp, plaintiff a
passenger (N = 87)
    $1,000
Def. a corporation, plaintiff an
employee (N = 139)
    $1,650
Def. a railway or streetcar, and
plaintiff was crossing (N = 75)
    $1,600

---

* New Zealand, Australian, and until 1853, Canadian provinces used the British pound. Canada then adopted decimal currency. (See below for currency conversion.) The U.S. dollar was worth 10–20 percent less then the Canadian in these years.

** Rande Kostal, *Law and English Railways, 1825–1875* (Oxford, 1994), 375–76. Bartrip and Burnam, *Wounded Soldiers of Industry*, report (173, 175) that the average damage award at some ninety-five trials under the terms of the Employers Liability Act of 1880 (involving employee injuries or deaths) in English county courts in 1881 and 1882 was about £91. (The median award would have been lower; perhaps £80.) This was, and is, the case: The trial award was smaller than those appealed.

(*continued*)

Table 8.1 (*continued*)

British Pound, Canadian Dollar, and U.S. Dollar Currency Conversions,
*1850–1900**

1 British £ worth from 5 to 7 U.S. $, 1855–1900
1 British £ worth from $4.86 to $5 in Canadian/Nova Scotian currency,
    1853–1890
1 British £ worth 5 U.S. dollars in 1873
1 Canadian £ = 4 U.S. $, 1851
1 Canadian $ = 2 U.S. $, 1864 (Civil War Greenbacks)
10 Canadian $ = 11.5 U.S. $, 1888

---

* B. R. Mitchell, *British Historical Statistics* (Cambridge, 1988), 702; D. C. Masters, "The Establishment of Decimal Currency in Canada," 33 *Canadian Historical Review* 129 (1952); *Clarke v. Fullerton*, 8 Nova sc. 348 at 358 (1871); *Souther v. Wallance*, 20 Nova Sc. 509 at 513 (1988); Anthony Trollope, *Australia & New Zealand* (2 Vols., London, 1873), II, 440n.

be lying? Could the nature of the accidents, or the behavior of corporate counsel account for these discrepancies? I think not. Victims who pressed their suits to trial resolution tended to be those who had suffered greatly, whether it be at the hands of a negligent neighbor[60] or a careless corporation. And while railways' lawyers were sometimes eager to persuade their corporate bosses that a particular case should be litigated or appealed, they appeared to have had in mind the legal issues at stake, not simply the size of a particular jury's award. After all, the railways tended to view settlements as their primary cost containment measure. Thus, there was clearly no point in contesting a case one was likely to lose, and little point in contesting one that one stood a respectable chance of losing, given the costs of litigation.[61] In fact, then, as now, most cases went to trial only when both sides were convinced that they could win. And the result, at least with the London & Northwestern's suits tried between 1869 and 1871, was that the company lost ninety-seven and won eighty-seven of these, close enough to the predictable fifty-fifty split.[62] Settlements were cost effective, as the general manager of New Zealand's Railways explained, in defending the

---

[60] Thus, the reporter for Quebec's Cour Superior described the plaintiff in *Berthiaume v. McCone* (1894), a pedestrian run down on a "macadamized road" by a fifteen-year-old boy in a wagon, as having had injuries to his head "as if a rasp had passed over them.... His life was for some days in danger." *Berthiaume v. McCone*, 5 Quebec C.S. 492 at 498 (1894).

[61] Rande Kostal has come to the same conclusion regarding railway company attorneys in England in the 1860s and 1870s. See Kostal, *Law and English Railway Capitalism, 1825–1875* (Oxford, 1994), 298.

[62] Calculated by using the quarterly returns reported in PRO/RAIL/ 410/411.

Table 8.2. *Median Awards by Juries/Judges in England, the United States, Canada, Australia, and New Zealand, 1840–1910*[*]

Jury (N = 543)

In Australia and New Zealand (N = 85)
£400

In Canada (N = 233)
$1,320
  Def. an Individual (N = 34)
  $300

  Def. a Municipality (N = 88)
  $700
  Def. a Railway, Factory, Streetcar, etc.
  (N = 195)
  $1,925

In the United States (N = 145)
$5,000
In England, 1773–1873 (N = 38)
£100
In England, railway accidents, 1884,
  1897–1900 (N = 52)
  £250

Judge (N = 145)

In Australia and New Zealand
(N = 23)
£100

In Canada (N = 122)
$370
  In Quebec (N = 95)
  $300[**]
  Elsewhere in Canada (N = 27)
  $650
  Def. a Ry., Factory, Tram, etc.
  (N = 58)
  $750
  Def. an Individual (N = 25)
  $150
  Def. a Municipality (N = 44)
  $365

---

[*] Numbers in Tables 8.1 and 8.3 differ because there were a number of awards reported without a corresponding indication as to whether or not a jury had heard the case.

[**] One reason for the smaller median award figure offered by Quebec's jurists might be that a number of these awards had been made using a *comparative* negligence standard not available to jurists outside of this province – that is, some plaintiffs received only a fraction (typically half) of what they might have had had they not contributed to their accident through some negligence of their own, but elsewhere such plaintiffs might receive nothing if either judge or jury saw them as having been contributorily negligent.

expenditure of some £776 pounds per year over a five-year period to the minister for railways in 1909. These expenses were necessary to settle "amicably" the many "extortionate claims" made "in connection with almost every railway accident that occurs," in order "to avoid the expenses of litigation and the risk of excessive damages being awarded owning to the natural generosity of Juries...."[63]

---

[63] Gen. Man. to Min. for Rys., Oct. 1, 1909, "Performance of legal work for N.Z. Rys., 1882–1932," R/3/AccR2381/14/1538/1, N.Z. Archives.

The chief solicitor to England's Great Western Railway often expressed this same fear of juries. Example: A man named Houghton had waited too long to reboard. His train began to pull out of the station and in jumping aboard he was dragged down the length of the platform and seriously injured. His contributory negligence seemed clear, but that question, the chief solicitor advised the directors, "cannot, I fear, be kept from the Jury, and if it is left to them, we know by experience what the result will probably be, and in this case no doubt the verdict would be a substantial one." [64] The Illinois Central's general manager complained in 1875 to its president of the "aid and comfort" given accident victims by the people of Water Valley. Among the offenses these railroad townsfolk had committed were advising "Mrs. Dowd to sue us" and "stand[ing] security for her," and "urging Mrs. Montgomery" (whose husband had been killed in an accident in the car shop) "to sue us" and "not to accept any compromise." The assistant solicitor to that company complained later in the century of the generosity of jurors in Mississippi in recommending that the settlement of a wrongful death action for $11,000 be approved. He described the railroad's local attorney, who had secured this settlement, as "one of our best fighters in that State, yet he does not hesitate to recommend the payment of this enormous sum" due to his experience with juries in that area. The company's claims agent advised its general superintendent in the same year of "the prejudice against railroads fostered in many places by the [local] bar and judiciary."[65] And what was evident in England, the American midwest and south, and New Zealand was just as clear in Canada. In 1905, a Canadian Northern official bemoaned the company's prospects in a suit filed by a female passenger hit by a mailbag thrown from a car. She had suffered a miscarriage, and "the matter is unfortunately one which will be very much in the hands of the jury."[66] When the Canadian Northern

---

[64] #3216 (Houghton), Reports of Solicitors..., 1884, and see similar comments in #2980 (Barker), #2984 (Mrs. Marshfield), #2891 (Wheeler), PRO/RAIL/250/490, Public Records Office.

[65] E. D. Frost to Pres. McComb, June 2 29, 1875, Frost Out-letters, 1875–76/ 6/ N6.1–11/ Illinois Central Archives, Newberry Libr.; David Lightner, "Labor on the Illinois Central, 1852–1900," Cornell Univ. PhD, 1969, 372, 373. See also the comment of Henry Stone, Gen. Mngr. Of the C B & Q, of an "unfriendly Coroner's jury, surrounded by influences hostile to us." Stone to Stillman Allen, Esq., Nov. 2, 1888, Goddard In-letters, 1882–1896, 3G5.3/ C B & Q Archives, Newberry Libr.

[66] J. H. Munson to Z. Lash, May 25, 1905, June 2, 1905, Everett file, 82–6, Vol. 9066, R.G. 30, Archives of Canada.

After the jury's anticipated award was announced, this official assured the company's general counsel that "instructions have been given to

turned unsuccessfully to the Manitoba court of appeals in objection to a jury award of $2500 to the family of a brakeman killed in 1906, its on-the-spot counsel advised its chief solicitor against a further appeal to the Supreme Court of Canada:[67]

> My impression is that the [Supreme] Court will go against me as this Court is an anti Corporation Court.

What explains the large jury awards against railways? The evidence is overwhelming: If the Canadian Supreme Court could be characterized as "an anti-Corporation Court" in 1909, the juries of England, the United States, Canada, Australia, and New Zealand could well have been characterized in that way as soon as the railways and their fellow corporate tortfeasors appeared on the landscape. Thus, a jury in Delaware in 1857 awarded a sheep drover seriously injured in a collision some $13,000, at a time when the median annual income for heads of households was about $400. Another, in New York State, a watchmaker whose hip was dislocated when an axle broke on a Western Railroad car in September, 1850, received $9900 from an equally generous jury, while another a year later gave a passenger whose shin bone had been broken in a collision near Croton, New York, some $6000. On appeal, Justice Ira Harris commented on this latter award that "everyone who has had much experience in the trial of causes has had occasion to observe the fact that in actions against railroad corporations to recover damages for personal injury, jurors are apt to be far more Liberal in awarding damages than in other cases of a kindred character."[68]

To Justice Harris' north, a jury in Upper Canada awarded a passenger who lost a leg in 1852 the princely sum of £6178. Three years later Lower Canada's Chief Justice Mondelet felt called upon to complain of "the most monstrous fines" levied against railroad companies due to "the mere caprice of juries excited by public clamour." The family of a miner killed in Alberta was awarded $3153 by a jury, of which $2500

---

prevent this [practice, which] prevailed at Ft. Francis," from "occuring again." This was not an uncommon consequence of the fact-finding process of this and several of the other railway legal counsels whose records I reviewed.

[67] O. H. Clark to Gerald Ruel, Feb. 17, 1909, file 82–28, Vol. 9067, R.G. 30, Archives of Canada. On the general attitude of the Supreme Court of Canada toward railroad corporations in the first decade of the twentieth century, see Bernard Hibbitts, "A Change of Mind: The Supreme Court of Canada and the Board of Railway Commissioners," *University of Toronto Law Journal* 60 at 68–76 (1991).

[68] *Flinn v. P., W. & B.RR*, 1 Houst. (Del.) 467 (1857); *Hegeman v. Western RR*, 16 Barb. (N.Y. S.C.) 353 (1853); *Clapp v. Hudson River RR*, 19 Barb. (N.Y.S.C.) 461 at 464 (1854).

was for loss of future earning capacity and pain and suffering, despite clear evidence that the man had been killed instantly, had cancer, and had been given less than two years to live.[69]

And the phenomenon was not confined to eastern North America. In New South Wales in 1862, a woman who got off a train that had not come to a complete stop, at the invitation of its conductor, and consequently broke a leg was awarded £238 for her medical care and another £1000 in consolation for her pain and suffering, by a sympathetic jury. A worker in Victoria who lost an arm when a pipe fell from a crane received £1750 12s, including £500 for pain and suffering, from another generous jury.[70] The injured plaintiff and her counsel who persevered in the action to the stage of a jury verdict often did so because of their conviction that the juries would, indeed, reach deeply into the pockets of corporate tortfeasors. The "deep pockets" phenomenon is neither an American, nor a modern creation, but can clearly be found in the behavior of plaintiffs and juries throughout the British Empire in the nineteenth century.[71] Thus, the counsel for a father and daughter injured at a Canadian Pacific Railway crossing in February, 1896 told the jury in his opening statement that the sums the two sought as compensation were "triffling" ones "which the defendant, a wealthy corporation, whose system extended from the Atlantic to the Pacific" were "well able to pay." He also pointed out to them that the company's president received "a salary of $50,000 a year"[72] a figure comparable today to $2,500,000). A woman, injured boarding a government-owned train in New Brunswick in 1881, sued the conductor who had caused her injury, and was awarded $2000 by the jury. Chief Justice Allen, who had presided over the trial, was prompted to say in his appellate opinion, "very probably the jury were influenced

[69] McGarry, Adm. v. Can. West Coal Co., 2 Alb. LR 270 (1908).

[70] Batchelor v. Buffalo & Br. Ry., 5 UCCP 127 (1854); Ravary v. Grand Trunk Ry., 6 Quebec 66, 1 Low. Can. J. 280 at 283 (1857); Thompson v. Comm. for Rys., 2 NSWSCR 292 (1863); McDade v. Hoskins & Another, 18 Vict. LR 417 (1892); Hall v. McFadden, 21 New Br. 586 at 628 (1882). Cf. Can. Atl. Ry. v. Henderson, 29 Can. S.C. 632 (1899).

[71] This was so in England as well, as Rande Kostal has shown (Law & English Railways, 308). Thus, the Railway Record complained on November 19, 1870, that juries seemed to "organize themselves into a sworn brotherhood of warfare against the pockets of railway shareholders," while one railway manager told a parliamentary committee in the same year that omnibus proprietors had never been ordered by juries to pay damages to passengers or pedestrians as large as those of railway companies (P P Commons (1870) X, Allport, Q. 806, cited in Kostal, 308n). This was my impression as well. See Karsten, Heart Against Head, ch. 10

[72] Sornberger v. Can. Pac. Ry., 24 Ont. C. of A. 263 at 266 (1897).

by the idea that the government would pay the damages." (He had "pointed out to the jury that they ought not to be influenced by any such consideration," but believed that they had clearly ignored this admonition.) That was the view of an observant jurist. But listen as well to the view of an observant plaintiff: W. Harding, the head of a family injured in the Rakaia accident in New Zealand, wrote this note to his solicitor:

> Were I claiming from a private individual who may be poor and consequently greatly inconvenienced or perhaps unable to pay the sums required, the matter would be different, but as these demands will have to be satisfied from the public funds, there can be not the slightest inconvenience to anyone and, of course, no question of ability to pay the whole of the loss to the Colony arising from the disaster will be as a drop to the ocean, and I feel convinced these facts would be taken into consideration by any jury or assessor giving damages in these cases.[73]

Mr. Harding was correct. While the railway's counsel sought to settle with him at figures substantially higher than those offered to those less serious in their purpose, he chose to reject these offers and press on to trial. He and three members of his family won jury awards ranging from £750 to £1,500 (but two others for only £75 and £100 each in actions tried *without* a jury).

Were victims less willing to demand compensation in the earliest stages of railway development than they were by the end of the century? Did the public develop a sense of causality enabling its injured members to charge others with fault more readily in 1899 than they had in 1869, as Randolph Bergstrom has concluded in his analysis of New York City accident litigation from 1870 to 1910?[74] Railway, streetcar, and tram development in Canada closely parallels that in the United States, whereas in Australia and New Zealand streetcars and railways appeared on the scene several decades later in the century. If we compare the number of such accident suits appearing in the appellate reports of the Canadian provinces from 1850 to 1900, we see a progression, to be sure (see Table 8.3), but one that can be accounted for entirely by such variables as population increase, increase in railway and street-car mileage, increases in trips per year, and increases in vehicle speed

---

[73] Harding to his solicitors, Acton, Adams & Kippenberger, July 24, 1899, sagely passed by the solicitors on to the New Zealand Railways legal counsel, Series 4, 99/1009, Pt. 1, p.4, Railway Ministry MSS, Archives of New Zealand.

[74] Randolph Bergstrom, *Courting Danger: Injury and Law in New York City, 1870–1910* (Ithaca, 1992). But see my reservations about Bergstrom's findings in *Heart versus Head*, 443–45.

Table 8.3. *Railway/Streetcar/Tram Cases in Canadian Reports,** *1850–1899*

1850–59	1860–69	1870–79	1880–89	1890–99
12	17	45	77	109

* Numbers in Tables 8.1 and 8.2 differ because one of three reported torts did not indicate the amount of the award, or were verdicts for the defendant.

(offset in part by increases in safety features and measures). In short, while Bergstrom's detected change in popular willingness to sue in the late nineteenth century in New York City may well have occured elsewhere, it cannot be detected in the Canadian appellate reports. Perhaps one would only detect it in lower court time-series analysis; perhaps it appeared on the scene later in Canada, in the twentieth century. Or perhaps Table 8.2 indicates that it was there in Canada from the beginning.

T. J. Potter, the Burlington Divisional Superintendent for the C B & Q Railroad, certainly expected victims to sue in 1874 and 1875. His reports to the road's general superintendent clearly anticipated suits after each derailment or collision. He wrote more than once, of known victims who had died, "Don't think we are liable, but the estate will bring suit." After an accident at Woodburn on September 27, 1875, he listed all of those injured, told his superior that he didn't think there was "any question about our liability," reported that his claims agent, a man named Hepburn, "is trying now to settle" with the victims before they could bring suit, and added that he had "not been able to find" one victim, Charles Raspe, "to settle since ten days after the accident."[75]

The willingness of accident victims to sue may have appeared in England just as quickly as it did elsewhere. No one has accused the English of the 1860s of being ready to sue at the drop of an ambulance-chasing solicitor's hat. Weren't they expected to take their share of the ills of the world, to keep a stiff upper lip? But Rande Kostal has pointed out that the London & Brighton Railway received some 400 personal injury claims "within forty-eight hours of the New Cross disaster" in 1868, and while most of these were settled, "more than 100 of them went to trial as full-fledged lawsuits."[76] Kostal, you will recall

75 Potter Out-letters, 33 1880 8.21/ C B & Q Archives, Newberry Libr.
76 Rande Kostal, *Law and English Railway Capitalism, 1825–1875* (Oxford, 1994), 379, citing testimony before a parliamentary committee in 1870.

from Chapter 5, has established that there were plenty of attorneys in England prepared to take accident cases on something approaching a contingency fee basis by the 1860s, and I confess to the same impression; the "unscrupulous solicitors" the Great Western's chief legal counsel complained of in 1884 were finding clients without much difficulty, and so were those representing the parties suing the London & Northwestern some fifteen years earlier. In one accident at Slough some 318 persons filed claims against the Great Western; only four of these were later marked "withdrawn" or "not pressed." Of the rest, 28 went to trial, 4 were not marked as being resolved in any particular fashion, and some 278 were settled (one, that of a Mr. J. Talyarkham of Bombay, for 5756 pounds, another, that of a Mr. C. Hohler of Ovington Square, for 5000 pounds).[77]

On rare occasions a juryman's bias surfaced. Consider the four jurors in Illinois in 1870 who indicated in voir dire that they were inclined to "lean against" the Chicago & Alton Railroad in a case before them, and particularly the one of them who allowed that he would do so "because the company is able to stand it," whereas a private individual should "have a little mite the advantage." (All four were challenged for cause; the trial judge refused to grant the challenge.) And consider juryman White in Barrie, Ontario, who managed to tell a witness he knew in a medical malpractice suit in 1896 to "remember" as she gave her evidence that the plaintiffs "were poor boys and that I was to consider their poor old mother anyways," since "if they lost the case they would be ruined," whereas the negligent physician "was a rich man" and "would not feel it" if he "lost $4000 or $5000."[78]

Appellate judges in Mr. White's Ontario complained that juries "generally have a strong sympathy for, or leaning in favour of, plaintiff's cases . . . ," and that their awards were "so many premiums held out to unfortunate or careless people," making railway and municipal corporations "pay most unjustly." This may have been the view of the Supreme Court of New South Wales in 1826 when it granted a new

---

The New Zealand Railway Commissioners clearly expected all the victims of the Rakaia disaster to make claims, as did the Queensland Railway Commissioners after the derailment at Pugarry Junction (and eight out of nine injured passengers did file claims in that case). But the former accident occurred in 1899; the later in 1911. They were the first major accidents in each jurisdiction for which I found records. All we can say is that there does not *appear* to have been a victims' cultural learning-curve in the Antipodes.

[77] Accident & Compensation Cases Book . . . , entries for June 16, 1900, PRO/RAIL/270/22.

[78] 51-*Chicago & Alton v. Adler*, 56 Ill. 344 (1870); *Laughlin v. Harvey*, 24 Ont. C. of A. 438 (1897).

trial to a stagecoach company, judging as "excessive" a jury award of 200 pounds to a passenger injured when the coach overturned. It was clearly the view of Upper Canada's Chief Justice James Macaulay in 1855, when he and his colleagues on Common Pleas remanded as excessive the jury award of £6,178 to the man who had lost a leg in an accident. With the observation that "certain hazards attend such mode of travelling," Macaulay sanctioned the Buffalo & Brantford Railway's call for a new trial on the understanding that the railway would pay into court £500 at that time – that is, Macaulay regarded £500 as minimal, but adequate compensation, a figure that was one-twelfth the size of the jury's award.[79]

So much for our first finding: CANZ juries did indeed view corporations as having deep pockets that should be picked now and then to send them a message regarding the negligence of their employees and to "make whole" those whom those employees had injured. But what of our second finding – that CANZ and English juries, especially those in Canada, were considerably less generous than those in the United States in these years (see Table 8.1). What explains this? One possibility is that American jurors were simply much better off and thus had much greater expectations. The typical American worker throughout the *fin de siecle was* about 30 percent financially better off than the typical Canadian worker, and slightly better off than the typical Australian or New Zealand worker,[80] and this may well account for a part of the difference in jury awards. But it can only explain a small part.

[79] Morrison, J. in *Lucas v. Town of Moore,* 3 Ont. C. of A. 602 at 614 (1879) (reversing a jury award of $2,500 to heirs of a man killed when his sleigh went into a ditch); Wilson, C. J., diss., in *Goldsmith v. City of London,* 11 Ont. R. 26 at 37 (1886) ($500 to widow who had stumbled over a curb); *Stedman v. Rose & Co.* (NSWSC, Kercher, 1826); Macaulay, C. J., in *Batchelor v. Buf. & Br. Ry.,* 5 UCCP 470 (1855) (Macaulay had also recommended £500 after the first trial had been remanded, 5 UCCP 127 (1854)). But see *Robinson v. Can. Pac. Ry.,* 33 Low. Can. J. 145 (1889), where Quebec's court of Review left untouched a jury award of $6,500 to the heirs of Patrick Flynn, a bankrupt fishmonger "working at the rate of about a dollar a day as an assistant journeyman in defendant's boiler shops," who had been killed unloading a machine from a vehicle; and *White v. Grand Trunk Pac. Ry.,* 2 Alberta 522 (1910), where the supreme court of this Prairie province affirmed a jury award of $5,000 to a permanently injured "common laborer."

[80] The median income of heads of household in the United States in 1890 was about $450, while in New Zealand in the same year it was about £90, and in Canada about $270, but the Canadian dollar was worth 10 to 20 percent more than the U.S. dollar. "Inquiry into the Cost of Living in New Zealand," 20 *Dept. of Labour (NZ) Journal* 274 (April 1912); M. N. Arnold, "Wage Rates, 1873–1911," Discussion Paper, Econ. Dept., Victoria Univ. of Wellington, Apr. 1982; *Annual Statistics of New Zealand,* 1873; conversations

Another possibility is that Canada was populated, disproportionately, with parsimonious people. It certainly did have more than its share of cany Scots. But I am not inclined to give much weight to this sort of a "chary Celt" explanation. (After all, many of the plaintiffs were Scots as well.)

A third possibility is that Canadian trains, streetcars, and road defects simply did not cause as serious damages as did those south of the border. But that sort of jingoistic view of accident law is no longer politically correct, and I consequently reject it, out of hand (or, perhaps, tongue in cheek). We will say no more of it.

A fourth possibility is that those who sat in the jury boxes of Canada and the United States were simply not the same sorts of people. This hypothesis presumes that men (and they were all men in these years) of different "stations in life" might behave differently, in that they would be more likely to have been major ratepayers to municipalities being sued, and may have been stockholders of railway and manufacturing firms, or may at least have been more sympathetic to such enterprises. In any event, it was clearly the case that for most of the nineteenth century jurors in Ontario were chosen from a list of men of property by county selection committees comprised largely of officers of the courts. This meant that, from the perspective of at least one attorney representing the elite and the corporate entities that they created, "the greatest confidence existed on the part of the clients" in "the impartiality" of the "decisions" of juries made up, as they were, from "the names of Gentlemen."[81]

In 1836, a Reform-dominated assembly proposed that elected town officers chose jurors by lot from a list of all adult males in the township: This was rejected by the governor's council as being a scheme "without precedent in the British Dominions," but in 1850 Robert Baldwin, the Reform attorney-general secured the passage of just such an arrangement, and for the next eight years jury boxes truly reflected the social structure of their communities.[82] These juries of the 1850s have

with Dr. Jock Phillips of the New Zealand Historical Branch Commission; *Labor in Canadian-American Relations*, ed. H. A. Innis (Toronto, 1937), 86, 178, 179. See also income figures in Stephen Roberts, *The Squatting Age in Australia, 1835–1847* (Melbourne, 1937), 282, 308, 310; and Anthony Trollope, *Australia and New Zealand* (2 Vols., London, 1837),I, 150, 169–70, 227, 246, 302, 399.

[81] J. S. MacDonald Diary, 1837, describing Petty Jurors in Hamilton, MSS, MacDonald Papers, MU1769, Archives of Ontario.

[82] Paul Romney, "From Constitutionalism to Legalism: Trial by Jury, Responsible Government, and the Rule of Law in Canadian Political Culture," 7 *Law & History Review* 121 at 137–38 (1989).

been found to have acquitted foremen accused of manslaughter or homicide by misadventure in the wrongful deaths of their men,[83] and the evidence presented in this chapter found them to have been as generous as American juries toward injured plaintiffs whose suits were against railway corporations, not foremen. This is what prompted the Chief Justice of Upper Canada's Queen's Bench, Sir John Beverley Robinson, to tell his counterpart, J. B. Macaulay, Chief Justice of Common Pleas, that since the passage of the new jury selection act, juries tended "to favour any available weakness" in the defendant's case and were "dispose[d]" to "believe that the poor are always in the right – at least when they find themselves engaged in a contest with the rich."[84]

But that was before 1858. In that year, a Conservative government secured a new statute reestablishing a hefty property qualification for jurors and setting up county-wide jury selection committees dominated by court officers.[85] Substantial property qualifications for jurors were the law in the maritime provinces as well throughout the nineteenth century.[86] This may well explain the less generous awards offered by Canadian juries in these years.

By contrast, juries throughout most of the United States by the 1830s were drawn from all social strata, and were disproportionately comprised of men from the middle and lower levels of these strata.[87] In the 1820s, New South Wales jurors in civil matters had to be "substantial property owners" with a 300 pound freehold, but by 1836 most householders there qualified as jurors though many had arrived as convicts. The colony's attorney-general declined to press the prosecution of a cattle-thief because he believed the jury's "respectable citizens" had "chose[n] to pay fines for non-attendance rather than associate with

---

83 Paul Craven and Dom. Traves, "Dimensions ofPaternalism: Discipline and Culture in Canadian Railway Operations in the 1850s," in *On the Job*, ed. Craig Heron and Rob. Storey (Kingston, Ont. 1986), 51.

84 Robinson to Macaulay, 1852, cited in Paul Romney, *Mr. Attorney: The Attorney-General for Ontario, 1791–1899* (Toronto, 1986), 291–97; P. Brode, *Sir John Beverley Robinson* (Toronto, 1984), 257.

85 Romney in 7 *Law & History Review* 121 at 138 (1989).

86 Thus, in *Christie v. City of Portland*, 29 New Br. 311 (1890), the high court ordered a new trial because a juror had been challenged successfully because he was a ratepayer in Portland. The high court pointed to the New Brunswick Jury Act, requiring that jurors possess at least $400 in real estate, in ruling that ratepayers were not to be disqualified simply because they might be disinclined to find against plaintiffs or award small damage awards.

87 See David Bodenhamer, *The Pursuit of Justice: Crime and Law in Antebellum Indiana* (N.Y., 1986); and Tony Freyer, *Producers and Capitalists: Constitutional Conflict in Antebellum America* (Charlotteville, Va., 1994), 22, 144.

jurors who had been convicts...."[88] At first New Zealand's jurymen were to be freeholders,[89] but this rule was, in short order, set aside. Throughout the years that we are concerned with, New Zealand's courts not only sanctioned juries of "ordinary" folk, but also refused to sanction "special" juries in cases where English rules would have called for them, for such juries, "composed almost wholly of employers" in cases where employees were suing their employers, "would therefore be in a sense a class tribunal."[90]

In short, my "read" is that the relatively lower awards offered by juries in England and Canada in the nineteenth century were at least in part due to their social composition and attendant "stiff-upper-lip" culture.

THE GENEROSITY OF JURIES AND TRIAL-COURT JUDGES COMPARED

Wherever one looks in these years, be it to the provinces, the United States, or England itself, one finds juries to have been substantially more generous than judges. Most personal injury cases, outside of Quebec, were tried before juries. When the jury's award was appealed as either excessive (by the defendant) or inadequate (by the plaintiff), and the figure was altered by the appellate court, it tended to be reduced (24 times, by an average of 50 percent) far more often than it was increased (5 times, by an average of 80 percent). This might well be a function of the specific facts brought before these particular courts, but it does not explain a more significant phenomenon: When I determined that an award had been made by a jury (N=318), it tended to be over three times as large as those where that duty was the purview of a judge (N=145). (See Table 8.3.) This was so whether the defendant was an individual, a municipality, or a railway, and it was as true in the United States as it was in the British colonies and Dominions.[91]

---

[88] Bruce Kercher, *Unruly Child*, 72–73; J. M. Bennett & Alex Castles, *A Source Book of Australian Legal History* (1979), 46; Stephen Roberts, *The Squatting Age in Australia, 1835–1847* (Melbourne, 1935), 26. In South Australia, the Wakefieldian colony, the qualification for jury duty was set at £100 of realty or personal property in 1837.

[89] *New Zealand Gazette & Wellington Spectator*, #214, Mar. 8, 1843, p.2.

[90] Richmond, J., in *Scott v. Kirkcaldie*, 6 NZLR(SC) 272 (1888); Williams, J., in *Hutton v. Mill*, 14 NZLR(SC) 518 (1896).

[91] This is still the case in the United Kingdom. The median auto liability award there in 1974 was £1819, which in San Francisco the same year it was $26,000. Most of the difference is due to the fact that in the United Kingdom if only one party prefers the case be heard without a jury, there is no jury, and as one British personal injury specialist put it in the early 1980s:

HIGH-COURT JURISTS AND JURY AWARDS: A CASE
OF HIGH AND LOW LEGAL CULTURES IN DIRECT
CONTACT WITH ONE ANOTHER

When jurists served as trial court judges few were as bold in their instructions to juries regarding the quantum of damages as was Pennsylvania's Chief Justice John Bannister Gibson, who, serving as a trial judge at *nisi prius* in 1852, told his jurors that there was "no measure or standard of damages for a broken limb; and you therefore ought to be Liberal against the author of it. You ought certainly to give enough, for it is safer to err, if at all, against the party who was the cause of the injury, than against an innocent man who suffered it."[92] But many CANZ jurists *were* prepared to instruct juries to award damages "fairly," "but not with a niggardly hand." When jury awards were appealed, some appellate jurists complained that they were inadequate;[93] others, that

> "The judges are ex-rugby playing public school boys – quite tough. . . . Some judges are terribly mean. In America you've got juries and [an attorney] can play on the jury's heartstrings . . . whereas in this country we have much more spartan sorts of judges. . . . They are not so keen on pain and suffering and loss of amenity." Hazel Genn, *Hard Bargaining: Out of Court Settlement in Personal Injury Actions* (Oxford, 1987), 78.
>
> An analysis of awards by juries and judges in some twenty-four urban courts over a one month period in the United States in 1988 revealed a similar, sharp difference: The median jury award was $26,000, while the median award by a judge alone was $8,500. But Marc Galanter has argued that the type of cases brought to the forums were different, reminding us of Harry Kalven's Chicago Jury Project finding in the early 1960s: When the same *type* of case was presented to a judge, on the one hand, a jury on the other, the jury awards averaged only 20 percent higher than those of judges. Harry Kalven, "The Dignity of the Civil Jury," 50 *Virginia Law Review* 1065 (1964); Marc Galanter, "The Regulatory Function of the Civil Jury," in *Verdict*, ed. Robert Litan (1993), 72. While I attempted to control for some of this sort of selection bias by comparing cases with similar defendants, I readily allow that some of the difference I have reported could well have been a function of mere selection. *Some*, but not much: Consider the low award median for Quebec, where virtually all cases were decided by judges. Selection played no role there.

92 In *New Jersey RR v Kinnard*, 21 Pa. St. 203 (1853).

93 Stephen C. J. in *Thompson v. Comms. for Rys.*, 2 NSWSCR 292 at 296 (1863); Smith, J., diss., in *Germain v. Montr. & N.Y. Ry.*, 6 Low. Can. R. 172 at 174 (1856) ("too small"); Smith, J., diss., in *Marshall v. Grand Trunk Ry.*, 4 Quebec (Superior Ct.) 369 (1856) (would have given £180, not the £80 that Day and Badgley, JJ, had given a worker with a fractured finger); *Keith v. Intercolonial Coal Min. Co.*, 18 Nova Sc. 226 at 232 (1885) (jury award of $1000 to boy who lost legs at crossing bringing lunch to father in mine "extremely moderate"); *Church v. City of Ottawa*, 25 Ont. R. 298 (1895) (new trial; inadequate sum); *Snowden v. Waitomo City Council*, 16 Gaz. LR(NZSC)

they "might be ruinous to the defendant" or that the plaintiffs claims had, after all, been "exorbitant."[94] Sometimes the jurists regarded the plaintiff as the villain, for behaving "[un]reasonably in bringing this action,"[95] more often they blamed the jury.[96] Occasionally they worried about the defendant's ability to pay (as when Chief Justice Robinson of Upper Canada's Queen's Bench observed that the award of £200 to a passenger who lost a leg due to the negligence of a horse car conductor might be too great for the company's "profits to bear").[97] Or they faithfully offered variations of the "stiff-upper-lip" view of life expressed by Baron Pollock in 1853:

> A jury most certainly have a right to give compensation for bodily suffering unintentionally inflicted, and I never fail to tell them so. But when I was at the bar [the 1830s and 1840s] I never made a claim in respect of it, for I look on it not so much as a means of compensating the injured person as of damaging the opposite party. In my personal judgement it is an unmanly thing to make such a claim. Such injuries are part of the ills of life, of which every man ought to take his share.[98]

542 (1914) (Justice Cooper: "Some juries might have awarded a larger amount" than £300 to a boy who lost a hand playing with gelignite detonator caps negligently left out); Wurtele, J., diss., in *Vital v. Tetreault*, 34 Low. Can. J. 26 (1889) ("Two or three thousand dollars will hardly compensate the plaintiff for the injury he has sustained in losing his thumbs." ($500 had been affirmed.))

[94] Jette, J., in *Vital v. Tetreault*, 34 Low. Can. J. 26 at 27 (1889); *Hepenstal v. Merritt*, 33 New. Br. 91 at 92 (1895) (Justice Harrington.: "If there is any cause for complaint, it is that the damages are too small"); *Gracie v. Canada Shipping Co.*, 8 Quebec C.S. 472 at 481 (1895); *Welscam v. Montreal Str. Ry.*, 32 Low. Can. J. 246 (1888) ($400 to injured passenger; $216 of this for loss of income, $184 for "his sufferings and his impared condition" and "reasonable exemplary damages"); Curran, J., in *Graham v. Smith*, 12 Quebec C.S. 240 at 243 (1896); Jette, J., in *Jeanotte v. Couillard*, 3 Quebec Q.B. 461 at 474 (1894): "*Dois-je le condamer à une somme considerable? Avidement non, ce serait une mavaise doctrine, que de donner judgement pour une somme trop considerable*" (reducing from $300 to $50 an award to parents of a child who died because her physician had written an incorrect prescription).

[95] *Torpy v. Grand Trunk Ry.*, 20 UCQB 446 at 451 (1861) (but the award of £75 to a worker whose ankle had been "strained" in a collision was affirmed).

[96] As in *Pink v. Melbourne Tramway & Omnibus Co.*, 6 Vict. LR(L) 186 at 189 (1880); *Jackson v. Hyde*, 28 UCQB 294 at 296 (1869); *Baker v. Pa Co.*, 142 Pa. St. 503 at 510, 21 Atl. 979 (1891); and *Torpy, supra* note 95.

[97] *Thompson v. Macklem et al.*, 2 UCQB 300 at 303 (1846) (Robinson, C. J., *affirming* the award.)

[98] In *Theobold v. Ry. Pass. Ass. Co.*, 18 Jurist 583 at 585–86 (Ex. 1854).

Compare the views of Victoria's Chief Justice Madden in his opinion on the appeal of a case brought on behalf of a nine-year-old boy who had lost two fingers of each hand at a negligently managed railway crossing. The jury had awarded him £1000; the Victoria Supreme Court viewed this as excessive and ordered a new trial. In the words of the chief justice:

> It is never to be assumed that any one man will be so far blessed that he will go through life without illness and without any checks to his occupation, always having the work he desires to have, . . . that he will not be subject to those constant interferences which befall all of us.[99]

Chief Justice Robert Harrison of Ontario's Queen's Bench put it this way in 1877 in an appeal from a juryless award of $1000 to a conductor injured in a collision: "It is often said that juries lean against corporations. This has never been said of Judges."[100]

In the case of the passenger who had lost a leg in an 1854 accident on a Buffalo and Bradford Railway train, the difference between what the jury had awarded and what the appellate court thought adequate was in a ratio of twelve to one. But, more commonly, the difference in perception between "high" and "low" legal culture as to what was "just," while substantial, was such that the jurists yielded, in part because of the tradition of respect for such a jury prerogative as this, in part because of their perception that were they to send the case back to be tried again, the second jury would be quite likely to find for the plaintiff "in the same way, and perhaps even increase the amount of damages," as Justice Richards of Upper Canada's Common Pleas put it in 1854. (Simultaneously Justice Richards signaled to the Ontario & St. Lawrence Steamboat Company that it would be wiser to reach an out-of-court agreement with a passenger who had lost the use of an arm in an accident on a pier, than to try this case a second time, for if, as he predicted, the second jury were to offer more than this already "considerable" award, he and his colleagues would not "interpose" a second time.)[101]

Justice Richards appears to have been correct: Juries hearing a case remanded for a second trial appear to have awarded substantially more than the first jury, both in England, the United States, and the other Diaspora lands.[102] I am not sure, however, what weight to give the

99 Madden, C. J., in *Ritchie v. Vict. Ry. Comm.*, 25 Vict. LR 272 at 276 (1899).
100 Harrison, C. J., in *Brown v. Gr. West. Ry.*, 40 UCQB 333 at 341 (1871).
101 *Grieve v. Ontario & St. L. Steamboat Co.*, 4 UCCP 387 at 398 (1854).
102 See, for example, *Shaw v. Boston & Worcester RR*, 74 Mass. 45 (1857); Kostal, *Law & English Railways*, 298n; *R. B. Jordan v. Ill. Centr. RR*, Miss. Dist. Ct.,

observation of Justice George King of the New Brunswick Supreme Court who, while remitting to $1000 a jury award of $1500 to an injured passenger, complained of "the bad habit of St. John jurors on second trials *against a corporation*" to *treble* the award.[103]

DIASPORA JURISTS, ENGLISH JURISTS, AND RULES REGARDING DAMAGE AWARDS

Diaspora jurists, then, preferred a considerably smaller quantum of damages in personal injury and wrongful death actions than did juries. But they were sometimes more generous than their English compeers in deciding which rules trial courts might use in arriving at those award figures. Example one: The jury in England (and, for that matter, in the United States) was not to take into consideration the number of dependents a plaintiff had in calculating a damage award. They learned of the extent of his injuries, his medical expenses, his income and any loss of income he had suffered and was likely to suffer in the future. But they were not free to decide that an injured laborer with six dependents should receive more than one with none at all.[104] This was not the case in New South Wales. A jury there was told in 1881 that a laborer, who had been struck and injured by a buggy, supported a family that included five small children. When they awarded the man £200, the defendant appealed the admission of that evidence regarding the size of the man's family, but without success. It was "high time that a court should declare such evidence admissible," Justice Windeyer opined, while his colleague, Chief Justice Sir James Martin, justified the admission of these facts with this creative expansion of the concept of mental suffering:

> His anxiety of mind may have been greatly increased by the consciousness that he is now unable to maintain his family, and this anxiety may, I think, be taken into account in estimating the damages to which he is entitled.

"If there is no authority in favour of this view," he added, "it is high time that a precedent should be made."[105]

1899 ($5500 awarded at first trial, remanded, $6500 awarded at second trial), 1890 Bd. Mins., Ann. Rpt. Of Gen. Solicitor, Dec. 1899, +3.4/ Ill. Cent. Archives, Newberry Libr.; and other cases I detected and recollect, but cannot presently retrieve from my files.

[103] *Rainnie v. St. John City Ry.*, 31 New Br. 582 at 589 (1892) (Italics mine. This case had been retried, and the second jury had trebled the first jury's award).

[104] See, for example, *Donaldson v. Miss. & Mo. RR.*, 18 Iowa 280 at 280 (1865).

[105] *Devir v. Curley*, 3 NSWLR 322 at 334 (1882).

Example two: When a Mr. McAskill's horse stumbled over an obstruction on the road, and Mr. McAskill tumbled off and was injured, he sued the District Council of Spalding, South Australia. The Council's counsel questioned him at the trial about his habits and previous occupations. On appeal, Justice Bunde criticized this probing.

> Defendants as a public body are not justified in raking up matters relating to the plaintiff's character and instructing their counsel to put questions to him as to things which happened long ago, and to refer to and treat him as if he were a loafer. Whatever may be plaintiff's station in life, he has a right to be protected from having such annoyances inflicted upon him when seeking to establish his claims in the Courts of the Colony.[106]

Example three: As early as 1860, jurists in Quebec, in interpreting United Canada's wrongful death statute, were allowing a *solatium* or bereavement sum in addition to the sum calculated to replace the income lost to the family of one wrongfully killed. Justice Alywin specifically rejected the rule of Baron Pollock of the Court of Exchequer that "only pecuniary damages" be ordered. He thought it was "necessary to consider the peculiarity" of Pollock's views. Alwyin reminded his audience that Baron Pollock "had decided that in an ordinary action for injuries done by negligence there could be no damages given to compensate for the bodily sufferings of the plaintiff, because, as he said, suffering is the common lot of humanity." He was certainly citing Pollock correctly here, as one can see by looking back to page 485. But Alywin insisted that " it must be admitted that his views were peculiar indeed. . . ." Justice Alywin preferred French law, "as old as the hills" and "settled by the wisdom of ages" on bereavement *solatia*, and referred as well to "decisions of the United States" and Scotland (especially a Scottish assizement in 1542 to pay a substantial *solatium* to the children of David Forest "because David Forest was a good, honest substantial man, and the other party a rich man"). "Scotch law," Justice Alywin concluded, was "the proper quarter to look to for elucidation" on this subject. And, inasmuch as the courts of Lower Canada in the midnineteenth century were practicing "polyjural jurisprudence," borrowing legal principles from several quarters, this reliance on "Scotch law" is not surprising.[107]

This practice was ended by the Canadian Supreme Court in 1887 when it insisted that the wrongful death statute be interpreted the

---

[106] *McAskill v. Dist. Council of Spalding,* 24 S. A. L.R. 140 at 142–43 (1891).

[107] *Ravary v. Grand Trunk Ry.,* 6 Low. Can. J. 49 at 50–51 (1860). See David Howes, "From Polyjurality to Monojurality: The Transformation of Quebec Law, 1875–1929," 32 *McGill Law Journal* 523 (1987).

same way in Quebec as it was elsewhere in Canada.[108] And in 1899, Ontario's Court of Appeals held that while an award to the younger brother of a young man killed in a packing plant accident was entitled to the trial court award on his behalf, a similar award to the dead lad's mother was not within the law "whatever may be the case in some of the States of the country to the south of us."[109] Nevertheless, jurists on both the Ontario Court of Appeals and the Supreme Court of Canada held that one whose wife had been negligently killed at a railway crossing by the acts of agents of the company was entitled to a substantial loss-of-consortium *solatium*. The $5800 awarded by the jury included sums for the usual loss of her services to the family *and* a more questionable sum for the loss of "moral training" that she would have provided their children. The majority opinion of Chief Justice Sir William J. Ritchie quoted at length from American decisions in support of this award. (As usual, Justice John Wellington Gwynne dissented.)[110]

Example four: An excellent example of both of the trends that I have been describing (of CANZ jurists awarding lower sums themselves, but being more willing than their English compeers to hold defendants liable): *McGarry, Adm. v. Canada West Coal Co.* (Alberta, 1908). The family of a badly injured miner who had died of cancer before the final vetting of his appeal was awarded $3153 by a jury. Inasmuch as his cancer had been the primary cause of his death, the Alberta Supreme Court ordered a second trial, which, by agreement of the parties, was without a jury. Justice Stuart awarded the family only $1070 at this venue, responsive to the argument that it had been the man's cancer, and not his injuries, that had been the primary cause of his death. None the less, Justice Stuart did serve future plaintiffs well with his critique of the views of Baron Bramwell (in *Kramer v. Waymark*, 1866): Inasmuch as the young plaintiff had died of complications shortly after incurring the injury, Bramwell had reasoned, there had been little loss to compensate and no one entitled to receive it. Justice Stuart was "unable to appreciate the justice of the view there taken." The boy had "died of the very injuries complained of," and it seemed to Justice Stuart that Baron Bramwell's rule meant that "the more severely a defendant injured a plaintiff, if he only hurt him badly enough so that he would be sure to die anyway in a very short time, the damages recovered should

---

[108] *Can. Pac. Ry. v. Robinson*, 14 Can.S.C. 105 at 124 (1887).

[109] Osler, J., in *Wilson v. Boulter*, 26 Ont. C. of A., 184 (1899). See also *Cox v. McKenzie*, 22 Nova Sc. 226 (1890) (father can't recover costs of medical care for injuries to small children hit by carriage, as he could have in Massachusetts, because English rule required that he establish loss of income due to their injuries, and the children were too young).

[110] *St. Lawrence & Ottawa Ry. v. Lett*, 11 Can.S.C. 422 at 440–44 (1885).

be proportionately, not greater, but less."[111] Bramwell's rule had been "doubted" before in England, but since we are concerned here with knowing what CANZ jurists felt about English rules they did not like, Justice Stuart's *dicta* are a proper part of our story.

So are the views of Justice Edwards of New Zealand in example five, a case involving another miner, one of several killed in a disaster at one of the pits of the Greymouth-Point Elizabeth Railway & Coal Company in 1896: A newspaper subscription had raised a relief fund of £32,657, entitling each of the children of the victims to the sum of 12s 4p per week. When the company's counsel argued that it should be allowed a set-off of this figure from the jury's award, consistent with the principle enunciated by Lord Ellenborough of the English Court of King's Bench,[112] Justice Edwards responded for the Court of Appeals:[113]

> This company is actually claiming the benefit of this £32th which the charitable public have subscribed. It was subscribed, however, not for them, but for the benefit of the widows and children of these unfortunate men.... It is some satisfaction... to think that this company... will not be able to claim the benefit.

A sum raised by a newspaper was not quite what Lord Ellenborough had been referring to, but the legal question was essentially the same. In *Goodsell*, the deceased had named his family the beneficiary of a life insurance policy. Inasmuch as the object of compensation, Ellenborough told the jury, was to make the aggrieved party whole but no more than whole, the jury should take into account other resources available upon the victim's death, such as an insurance policy, in awarding damages. This rule was rejected by American courts: One who paid an insurance premium should not have his foresight and financial sacrifice serve to offset the culpability of one who had negligently caused his death.[114] This was also the view taken in examples six and seven; the two cases I detected on the issue of life insurance and damage awards in CANZ courts: *Beckett v. Grand Trunk Ry.* and *Jennings v. Grand Trunk Ry.*, both decided in Ontario in the 1880s. When the trial court judge in *Beckett* deducted some $3,000 of insurance money from a jury's award of $6,000 to the survivors of a victim of a crossing accident, Ontario's Queen's Bench rejected Lord Ellenborough's view of the law

---

[111] *Kramer v. Waymark*, 35 LJ, Ex 148 (1866); *McGarry, Adm. v. Canada West Coal Co.*, 2 Alb. LR 270 at 299, 302 (1908).

[112] In *Goodsell v. Boldero*, 9 East 72, 103 ER 500 (K.B. 1807).

[113] *G.-P.E. Ry & Coal Co. v. McIvor*, 16 NZLR (CA) 258 (1897).

[114] See Karsten, *Heart versus Head*, 287–88, for a brief account of this issue in nineteenth-century America.

and restored the $3,000. This judgement was upheld on appeal, both by Ontario's Court of Appeals and the Supreme Court of Canada, and in both venues American cases were cited in support of these decisions (albeit dissenting jurists on each bench were also to be heard to point out that such American decisions could, however regrettably, not be followed when they were in conflict with "our own legal sages.").[115]

Examples eight and nine: A railway executive purchased life insurance, the company specifying that he was not insured for an accident due to his stepping on or off a moving train. He was killed in just such a fashion, and the company refused to pay. Quebec's Queen's Bench ruled in 1891 that such behavior was part of his job, and that the company's agent knew, or ought to have known this. Similarly, the estate of a man killed while coupling railway cars and screening coal was told by his insurance company that his policy had specified that he do no more dangerous work than shoemaking. The judge charged the jury: "We know, if we go into a shoe factory . . . there are steam engines and belts and pulleys and machinery. . . . We will have to bring in your own knowledge of life. . . ." The jury ordered the company to pay $2,100 to the estate, and the company appealed to the New Brunswick Supreme Court. Justice Barker for the court, upheld the lower court's actions with these observations: The deceased was not bound to "debar himself, at the risk of forfeiting his policy, from ever utilizing for the purposes of his business any of the improvements of modern science because he might thereby incur some new danger to life." He was not "obliged, literally, to 'stick to his last' forever."[116]

SUMMARY

Beneath the high-court tip of the English, U.S., and CANZ accident law iceberg, beneath the story of high court jurists wrestling with harsh English rules, distinguishing facts, selecting among sometimes ambiguous English precedents, reaching occasionally for a "kinder, gentler" American precedent, is our story of how accident victims actually fared. It is hard to say how many Cockneys, Kansans, Canuks, Kiwis, and Cockatoos chose not to seek compensation from those who appeared

---

[115] *Beckett v. Grand Trunk Ry.*, 8 Ont. R. 601 at 618–19 (1885); *Grand Trunk Ry. v. Beckett*, 13 Ont. C. of A. 174 at 181, 187 (Hagarty, C. J.: "our own legal sages") and 205 (1886); *Same v. Same*, 16 Can. S.C. 713 (1887); *Same v. Same*, Can. S.C. Cas. (Cameron) 228 at 233 (1887); *Jennings v. Grand Trunk Ry.*, 15 Ont. R. 477 (1887).

[116] *Accid. Ins. Co. of N. A. v. McFee*, 35 Low. Can. J. 146 (1891); *Day, Adm. v. Dominion Safety Fund Life Assoc.*, 32 New Br. 533 at 541–42 (1894). A "last" was, of course, a piece of equipment used by artisan shoemakers in these years.

to have been responsible for their injuries. But if the figures provided
by railway companies, or reported in newspapers, on the occasion of
a railway accident were at all reliable, *most* victims of railway accidents
were prepared to turn to the railways for redress about as soon as the
railways began mangling people.

Not all of these victims acted through the agency of a lawyer, and
some of those who did selected lawyers unskilled in this emerging
field of tort. After facing one another down, most of these victims'
claims ended with the victim (or survivor) signing a general release
and receiving a settlement, be it from a delicting doctor, a careless
corporate road authority, an inattentive industrialist, a slack streetcar
company, or a reckless railway. Worker–victims using this Common
Law legal process generally fared better than those who simply filed
a claim with a provincial workman's compensation board after these
were created in the *fin de siecle.*

Settlements of suits against Canadian railways pending in American
courts were twice as large as those of cases pending in Canadian courts.
Canadian railway counsels viewed the rules of Law in American courts
as being decidedly less favorable to them than those in Canadian
courts. This substantial difference in U.S. and Canadian settlement
medians is consistent with the evidence of notable differences in trial
court jury awards meted out by these little groups of North American
neighbors. Both of these differences may, in part, be due to a slightly
higher standard of living in the "Republic to the south," but it may also
be due to the fact that, after 1858, Canadian jurors were carefully chosen by officials from a more propertied class than were their grass-roots
counterparts in the United States, Australia, and New Zealand.

Jurors everywhere were more generous when the defendant was
corporate. They were twice as generous to those injured on municipal
roads than they were to those injured by the acts of individuals, and
they were twice as generous again to those injured by large public or
private corporations than they were to those injured by smaller ones
(road authorities). The unnamed juror from Illinois who would "lean
against the railroad "because the company is able to stand it," Juryman
White of Ontario who would remind a witness that the plaintiffs were
"poor boys" and the defendant "a rich man," and Plaintiff Harding
of New Zealand who "felt convinced" that "any jury" would consider
there could be "not the slightest inconvenience to anyone" in tapping
into the vast "public funds" available to compensate victims of a railway "disaster" had simultaneously discovered the "deep pockets" rule
of "informal" law, and the desirability of sending signals to those "sensitive" pockets to persuade such defendants to take measures that would
reduce the frequency of negligent acts, and the ensuing accidents.

For some reason, juries were also more generous to workers than they were to passengers.[117] This finding is counterintuitive, and I do not have a ready explanation for it. Jurors, after all, were not disproportionately working class and were more likely to see railway accidents from the perspective of passengers. Were jurors simply reaching out empathetically to injured workers? Or were worker injuries simply more serious ones? I don't know.

Finally, we noted the decidedly less-generous character of judges when it came to awarding (or to approving jury) damage awards. But we also noticed that appellate jurists were reluctant to send cases back for retrial, because they had cause to fear that the second jury would increase the award. And we found these same high court jurists to be willing to tinker with some harsh English rules regarding evidence, bereavement *solatia*, or insurance monies when it came to damage awards, to the advantage of plaintiff–victims. At these moments, once more, they cited U.S. cases in support of their un-English judgements.

In short, "high" and "low" Diaspora legal cultures treated accident victims with somewhat greater compassion than their English counterparts (though CANZ juries displayed less of this compassion than that displayed by their American counterparts). The "low" legal culture of the jurors, being, as it were, as one with the typical victim–plaintiff, created an informal legal rule of its own – the rule of "deep pockets." And this rule did not await a late twentieth century "liability crisis" to make its appearance; it sprang full blown from the very first juries to deal with reckless railroads in the 1850s.

---

[117] Once again, the CANZ medians for worker settlements was $1,100; for passenger settlements, $725; for worker awards, $1,650; for passenger awards, $1,000.

9

Further Sorties into the High, Middle, and Low Legal Cultures of the British Diaspora, with Some Conclusions

Throughout the lands of the British Diaspora in the seventeenth, eighteenth, and nineteenth centuries, jurists offered up their versions of English Common Law, which varied somewhat from jurisdiction to jurisdiction, but (until altered by statute) everywhere constituted the Law. Simultaneously, ordinary folk developed their own "common-law" norms and rules of behavior, some of which stood in contrast to one or another of these Common-Law or statutory rules. The resulting "high" and "low" legal cultures often coexisted without grave consequences, but they sometimes produced out-and-out confrontations over issues involving land and agreements. The Common Law won some of these contests; the "common law" of popular norms won others.

The final section of this conclusion addresses these dichotomies and these contests. But we begin with an answer to one of our questions about the Law – namely, what we have learned in comparative perspective of how jurists in the different corners of the Common-Law world introduced or adjusted English Common-Law rules to the circumstances and values of their region and times. A middle section offers such observations as seem warranted by my modest forays into the world of the first tier of other judicial officials (lawyers, resident and stipendiary magistrates, and legislators).

THE COMMON LAW: HIGH LEGAL CULTURE

Disposing of Our First Query: CANZ Jurists and American Judicial Authority

Jurists in both the Canadian provinces and those of the Antipodes clearly made significant use of American judicial authorities, at least until the *fin de siècle*.[1] (By my count, at best 30 percent of the instances

---

[1] Among those who also point to a decline in the use of American citations in Canadian courts by the end of the century are H. Patrick Glenn, "Persuasive

of CANZ jurists making substantial use of American authorities occurred after 1875.) S. I. Bushnell has calculated that one in every eight opinions of the Supreme Court of Canada cited American cases or treatises, and the vast majority of these citations were used to support the court's decision. (These jurists rarely bothered to cite American decisions simply to "differ" from them.[2]) This sounds about right for Nova Scotia, New Brunswick, and Ontario, and a bit high for the rest of the CANZ courts. But my selective look at issues in property, contract, and tort does not warrant my reporting precise figures, especially inasmuch as Bushnell and others have indicated that the most widespread uses of American citations were in the fields of mining, copyright, patent, and insurance law,[3] fields of formal law left largely unexplored in this book. Let's be content with the conclusion that many CANZ jurists were willing to draw on examples of American jurisprudence for "guidance."

This use of American authorities was generally defended for one of two reasons: Either there was said to exist "no exact precedent" in the English reports (which warranted a search for "light" in "the powerful reasoning of the great [American] judges"[4]), or "our local

---

Authority," 32 *McGill Law Journal* 261 (1987); S. I. Bushnell, "Comment: The Use of American Cases," 35 *University of New Brunswick Law Journal* 157 (1986); Blaine Baker, "The Reconstruction of Upper Canadian Legal Thought in the Late-Victorian Empire," 3 *Law and History Review* 219 at 274 (1985); and, most systematically, Bernard Hibbitts, "Her Majesty's Yankees: The use of American authorities in the Courts of Victorian Nova Scotia," Paper presented at American Society for Legal History Conference, Richmond, Va., 1996.

[2] S. I. Bushnell, "Comment: The Use of American Cases," 35 *University of New Brunswick Law Journal* 157 at 163 (1986).

[3] Bushnell, *loc. cit.*; Bora Taskin, *The British Tradition in Canadian Law* (London, 1969).

[4] Bliss, J., in *Ralston v. Barss,* 1 Nova Sc. 75 at 83 (1837); Reporter David Kerr in preface to 3 New Br. R. x (1842); Appellants' attorney and Strong, J., in *Queddy River Driving Boom Co. v. Davidson,* 10 Can. S.C. 222 at 228, 235 (1883), noted in J. N. MacIntyre, "Use of American Cases in Canadian Courts," 2 *University of British Columbia Law Review* 478 (1966); Strong, J., in *Cosgrave v. Boyle,* 6 Can. S.C. 165 at 173, 175 (1881) (relying on "the rule of the American courts" to achieve "mercantile convenience" in the absence of English or Canadian precedent regarding sufficiency of notice of death of endorser of note at maturity); Spragge, Ch., in *Deedes v. Graham,* 20 Grant's Ch. (Ont.) 258 at 270 (1873) (opinions of "American Judges" of "high legal reputation" are "entitled to respectful consideration"); Henry, J., in *Church v. Fenton,* 5 Can. S.C. 239 at 257 (1880); Ardah, J, in *Parry Sound of Lumbering Co. v. Ferris,* 18 Can. L.J. (Ont.) 413 at 416 (1882); *Pullman Palace Car Co. v. Sise,* 3 Quebec Q.B. 258 (1894); *Dupont v. Quebec S.S. Co.,* 11 Quebec C.S. 188 (1896); Prendergast, C.J., in *Hansen v. Cole,*

circumstances" were said to warrant a "relaxation of the English rule" and a reliance on the "common sense" (to be found in American opinions that were "precisely in point," given "the circumstances of what is commonly called a new country"[5]). These "local circumstances" might have consisted of undeveloped land with stands of timber held by lease or a life estate, the right to the use of a riparian estate being used as well by a miller or logger, or simply an icy sidewalk. In any event, some CANZ jurists were drawn to American case reports and treatises "so as to make my judgement as instructive as I am capable of doing" (as New Zealand's Justice Henry Chapman put it in 1849).[6]

How did they learn what this American jurisprudence was? Auctioneer Augustin Cuvillier told a parliamentary committee in 1825 that the British Diaspora settlers in Quebec's so-called Eastern Townships bordering New York, Vermont, and New Hampshire were unfamiliar with both English and French-Quebec law; rather they "understand best" the laws "that are now prevalent in the United States of America." And recall that Judge McCord, sitting in Bedford, one of these townships, drew upon the contracts treatise of Vermont's Nathaniel Chipman in his deliberations.[7] This borrowing is understandable where the ordinary business transactions of farmers and merchants in those townships would have been with their closest neighbors, those just across the border. But how was a judge or attorney (let alone a lay person) in Otago

9 NZLR (SC) 272 (1890); Williams, J., in *Brown v. Bennett*, 9 NZLR (C.A.) 487 at 506 (1891) ("great weight of authority" regarding promissory notes given to "American text-writers" in "the absence of decisive English authority"); Richmond, J., in *In re Aldridge*, 15 NZLR (CA) 361 at 368 (1893); Stout, J., in *Com. for Land & Income Tax v. Dilworth*, 15 NZLR (CA) 133 at 136 (1893) (regarding relevance of American opinions on charitable bequests: "The American cases are of importance, because there, as here, there is no established church").

5 Oliver Mowat, Esq. "Observations on the Use and Value of American Reports in Reference to Canadian Jurisprudence," ed. W. Ardagh, Esq., 3 *Upper Canada Law Journal* (O.S.) 3, at 7 (1857); Ferguson, J., in *Ratté v. Booth*, 11 Ont. R. 491 at 514 (1886); Chipman, C.J., in Rector of *Hampton v. Titus*, 6 New Br. 278 at 324 (1849); Young, C.J., in *Titus v. Haines*, 11 Nova Sc. 542 at 546 (1877); Reporter David Kerr in preface to 3 New Br. x (1842); Justice Henry Chapman of New Zealand, Mar. 17, 1849, noted in Peter Spiller, "Two Judges, Father and Son: An Analysis of the Careers of Henry Chapman and Frederick Chapman," University of Canterbury (N.Z.), unpub. J.D., 1991, pp. 39, 56; Isaacs, J., in *Amalg. Soc. of Engineers v. Adelaide S.S. Co.*, 28 Comm. L.R. (Austr.) 129, at 145, 156 (1920).

6 Spiller, *loc. cit.*, 39, This was the sort of "dialogical" jurisprudence that David Howes identified in Quebec-bred jurists like Tachereau in the late nineteenth century (in his essay on "Dialogical Jurisprudence" in *Canadian Perspectives on Law & Society* ed. W. W. Pue & B. Wright (Ottawa, 1988)).

7 Brian Young, *The Politics of Codification*, 24, 30.

or Melbourne to know what a jurist in Massachusetts or New York had said of a legal issue?

When we pose the question of American citations in CANZ opinions this way, their appearance becomes even more remarkable, for one thing is clear: American reports and treatises were simply not as available to most CANZ jurists as were English reports and treatises. Thus, a number of references to American cases were limited to what had been reported of the case in a treatise[8]; in these instances, jurists sometimes complained of the fact that the full text of the apparently relevant American case was not "within reach."[9]

Rarely did a CANZ court signal that it had delayed its deliberations and gone out of its way to obtain such an opinion, but I detected one such moment,[10] and that leads me to wonder how often such measures took place. My hunch is that they were uncommon, as there were few jurists truly drawn to American authorities for guidance who would have been the natural candidates for such a step. (One was Isaacs in New South Wales; another, Stout in New Zealand; others, Strong and Burton in Ontario.)

In the early and mid-nineteenth century – that is, in the years before the *American Reports* and *American Decisions* series, the West Publishing Company's regional reporters, and the *Albany Law Journal* and *Central Law Journal* appeared (the 1870s and 1880s) – the primary carriers of American jurisprudence overseas were the reports of the U.S. Supreme Court and the treatises of Story, Kent, Sedgwick, Angell, and Greenleaf.[11] These made their way to the shelves of CANZ barristers and jurists via interesting routes. In Nova Scotia no American volumes were to be seen before 1840. But when Prince Edward Islands' Samuel Cunard began in that year to offer trans-Atlantic service via Halifax,

---

[8] See, for example, *Ralston v. Barss*, 1 Nova Sc. 75 at 82 (1837); *Laforce v. Ville de Sorel*, 34 Lower Can. J. 66 (1890); *Slowey v. Lodder*, 20 NZLR (CA) 321 at 347 (1901).

[9] Bliss, J., regarding an Admiralty opinion of Justice Joseph Story, noted in *Ralston v. Barss*, 1 Nova Sc. 75 at 82 (1837).

[10] Burton, J., in *Anderson v. Northern Ry*, 25 UCCP 301 at 323 (1875) confessing that he was "responsible for the delay" in "the delivery of this judgement" since he had persuaded his colleagues to obtain and read *Eckert v. Long Is. RR*, 43 NY 502 (1871), the leading case on the waiver of contributory negligence where plaintiff had engaged in a heroic rescue attempt.

[11] See, for example, Mowat lecture, 1857, Osgoode Hall, *supra* note 5, p. 5; McIntyre, *supra* note 4, p. 488; G. Blaine Baker, "The Reconstruction of Upper Canadian Legal Thought in the Late Victorian Empire," 3 *Law & History Review* 219 at 254 (1985); Young, *Politics of Codification*, 136 (Quebec's codifiers cited Story on Contracts, Story on Partnerships, Kent's Commentaries, Sedgwick on Damages, Greenleaf on Evidence, and the New York Civil Code in their draft code on commercial law).

the publishers of American jurisprudence entered that market and competed effectively with all competition.

Similarly, by the 1870s American publishers were shipping copies of American editions of English legal treatises to Canada, Australia, and New Zealand under the terms of British copyright law. These were less than half the price of the English versions and had the additional virtue of offering elaborate notes on the ways that American courts had dealt with similar issues and fact situations, notes "of considerable value in practice," as the editor of the *New Zealand Jurist* put it in 1878.[12] The same New Zealand editor also recommended to his readers an annual subscription to Irving Browne's *Albany Law Journal* with this cost-benefit observation:

> £1 per annum is certainly not much to pay for the means of making oneself familiar with the current law and legislation of the States.[13]

By the late 1890s, American reports were clearly available in Ontario, where they were cited in 20 percent of all the appellate report cases dealing with the law of property between 1895 and 1897. Later, two Americans created the legal *Cyclopedia of Procedure and Practice* (40 volumes, 1901–1912) (forerunner to *Corpus Juris*), which drew upon English and Canadian authorities in addition to American ones, and was widely used abroad. "It was the only thing of its kind at hand," as R. St. John MacDonald has put it, "and if reference was made to a relevant American case, how better to garnish a judgement or argument than by citing it?" The appearances of *Halsbury's Laws of England* (31 volumes, 1907–1914) and the *Canadian Cyclopedic Digest* (7 volumes, 1919–1925), neither of which drew attention to American authorities, cut sharply into the propensity of Ontario's barristers and jurists to draw upon their encyclopedic knowledge of American cases.[14]

---

[12] Philip Girard, "Themes and Variations in Early Canadian Legal Culture: Beamish Murdock and his 'Epitome of the Laws of Nova Scotia,'" 11 *Law & Society Rev.* 101 at 134 (1993); 3 *New Zealand Jurist* (NS), Pt. 8, p. 107 (1878). See also *Ibid.*, Pt. 4, p. 53 (1878).

[13] 3 *New Zealand Jurist* (NS), Pt. 4, p. 62 (1878). See also reference to the Dillon-Thompson *Central Law Journal, Ibid.*, Pt. 8, p. 116.

[14] R. St. John MacDonald, "Observations on the Land Law in the Common Law Provinces of Canada," in *Canadian Jurisprudence*, ed. Edward McWhinney (Toronto, 1958), 201; Louis Knafla, ed., *Law and Justice in a New Land: Essays in Western Legal History* (Toronto, 1986), 67. Of course some English, and several CANZ treatise writers reported American cases, constituting another source of enlightenment for the CANZ bench and bar. See, for example, Luther Broad, *The Law of Innkeepers in New Zealand and the Licencing Commission Guide* (Nelson, South Island, 1887) (citing California and Minnesota decisions, pp. 13 and 15).

A few resourceful CANZ jurists and members of the bar gained their initial insights into the appeal of American appellate reports from their residence in the States as students, law apprentices, sojourners, or later in their professional careers or retirement. This was especially true of the many practitioners and judges in New Brunswick and Nova Scotia who had attended Harvard Law in the second half of the nineteenth century,[15] but there were other Commonwealth visitors to the States who brought back legal ideas.

Among the examples of this that I might offer, I have selected the views of a New Zealand barrister about whom I know very little. In 1876, the Otago Law Society published a lecture by one of its leaders, William Downie Stewart, who had compared English and American jurisprudence for the Society's membership. In the early twentieth century, American reformers were to draw upon New Zealand's remarkable legislative experience in creating a basic social welfare state in the *fin de siècle*,[16] but in the 1870s, New Zealanders like Stewart, of Liberal persuasion, were much impressed by the judicial and legislative innovations they detected in the States.

Many of the judge-made alterations in Common-Law rules that Stewart noted dealt with the law of crime; most of the innovations in the civil law that he described (especially family and property law) had been initiated by state legislatures. In any event, for our purposes, Stewart's general thesis was that New Zealand's legal community ought to give these innovations "attentive and impartial consideration." But he was particularly attentive to "Positive" Law: Homestead exemption acts, married womens' property acts, the extension of mechanic lien law to laborers, the election of judges, the protections and rights extended to indigent, criminally accused defendants, the waiver of oath taking for abjuring witnesses, these were among the legislative-made alterations in Common-Law rules that had impressed both Stewart and Sir Robert Stout, the future Liberal minister and chief justice (Stout marked the margins of a copy of Stewart's speech frequently).[17]

---

[15] See Philip Girard, "The Roots of a Professional Renaissance: Lawyers in Nova Scotia, 1850–1900," 20 *Manitoba Law Journal* 148 at 165 (1991).

[16] The classic account of this is Peter Coleman, *Progressivism and the World of Reform: New Zealand and the Origins of the American Welfare State* (Lawrence, Kansas, 1987).

[17] W. D. Stewart, *English and American Law: A Lecture to Otago Law Students Society, 24 June 1876* (Dunedin, 1876), #26 of Vol. 32, Stout Pamphlets, Beaglehole Library, Victoria University Library, Wellington, New Zealand. Stout also owned copies of American legal pamphlets, such as John Lawson's *The Civil Remedy for Injuries Arising from the Sale or Gift of Intoxicating Liquors* (St. Louis, Central Law Journal, 1877) #3, Vol. 43, Stout Pamphlets.

Westminister's Magnetic Appeal: Explaining the Supremacy of English Precedent in the Canadas and the Antipodes

All right: American legal authorities were sometimes cited as authority or "guidance" by CANZ jurists. But while this is interesting, we can easily make too much of this. Yes, there were individual jurists who tended to cite Americans, and, yes, there were specific legal problems that tended to have American judicial opinions proposed as part of their solutions. But these were relatively uncommon. The typical CANZ jurist was wedded to English solutions, and even on those occasions when one did offer an American solution to a particular dilemma, he generally trumped it in the same opinion by offering English citations that came to the same, or a similar, conclusion.[18]

Several of those who have read the opinions of Canadian and Australian jurists of the nineteenth century have noted this "absence of a creative approach." H. E. Read, for example, called them the views "of English judges applying English law in Canada, rather than those of Canadian judges developing Canadian law to meet Canadian needs with guidance of English precedent."[19] And two of these analysts have explained this propensity by claiming that the first generation of colonial jurists, before the eras of Responsible Government, were "undistinguished English barristers who had obtained their appointments through political patronage and had no great commitment to an outpost of empire in which they had no inclination to settle." This first generation or two of jurists were "conservative in both law and politics," and, "lacking independence or tenure," they "felt the need to please their colonial and Whitehall masters."[20]

---

[18] See, for example, *Gooderham v. Hutchison*, 5 UCCP 241 at 256 (1855) (where Macaulay, C.J., cited "*Swift v. Tyson* and the doctrine of Story" on the question of promissory notes and preexisting debts, but then dwelt at length on a number of comparable English decisions); and *Lomax v. Jarvis*, 6 NSWLR 237 at 241–42 (1885) (where Chief Justice Sir James Martin noted in a riparian rights case that there were relevant cases offered by "courts in America, whose decisions on such points are referred to in England as of very high authority," but then actually cited and discussed *English* opinions).

[19] Read, "The Judicial Process in Common Law Canada," 37 *Canadian Bar Review* 265 at 268 (1959). See also Risk, "The Golden Age: The Law about the Market in Nineteenth Century Ontario," 26 *University of Toronto Law Journal* 307 at 341 (1976); Ross Parsons, "English Precedents in Australian Courts," 1 *University of Western Australian Law Review* 211 (1948); Harold Luntz, "Throwing Off the Chains: English Precedent and the Laws of Tort in Australia," in *The Emergence of Australian Law*, ed. M. P. Ellinghaus, *et al.* (Sydney, 1989), 70–88.

[20] Graham Parker, "Canadian Legal Culture," in *Law and Justice in a New Land: Essays in Western Canadian Legal History*, ed. Louis Knafla (Toronto, 1986),

These remarks do describe *some* of the first generation of CANZ jurists. After all, Upper Canada's jurists held office only at the pleasure of the Crown until 1834. And several of Newfoundland's early chief justices (in the 1790s and early nineteenth century) were without formal legal training; others were characterized as mere "place seekers," or criticized for their venality. But this view implies a sycophancy that is utterly lacking in several of those whom I encountered. Thus, other of Newfoundland's chief justices in these same years, John Reeves and Francis Forbes in particular, appear to have been skilled, impartial jurists willing to act independently of the will of the colony's governor.[21] And, when Forbes was reassigned to New South Wales as the chief justice of that convict colony, he wrote to the Colonial Office of what he had learned in Newfoundland: Colonial jurists should not be held strictly to English legal rules but should be allowed to express opinions reflecting their "local knowledge and experience." "Pray do not fetter us too much, for be assured that we can do the thing [the production of justice?] better here than it can be done at home." As chief justice of the New South Wales Supreme Court, Forbes simplified a number of procedural rules. "The forms of the law," he warned, "may be sedulously resorted to as a covering for chicanery and fraud." The colony's inhabitants "might be excused for believing" that such formal rules as had been introduced by his predecessor (Barron Field) were intended to "fil[l] the pockets of the practitioners" rather than to "facilitat[e] the ends of justice."[22]

15. See also K. Mack, "The Development of an Australian Legal System," in *The Emergence of Australian Law*, ed. Ellinghaus, *loc. cit.*, 326.

Hazel King's essay, "Pulling Strings at the Colonial Office," 61 *J of the Royal Australian Hist. Soc.* 145 at 147 (1975), demonstrates that political connections certainly mattered to those seeking colonial appointments, but she writes that "the professional qualifications of candidates for judicial appointments were more carefully examined" than those seeking merely to be governors. She also concludes of the one jurist whose career she describes, W. W. Burton, that his appointments were not due to "mere nepotism," and that "he was well qualified by experience and ability to be a Chief Justice [of New South Wales], and was to prove himself [deserving] of the office." (156) J. H. Bennett has thoroughly revised (downward) the reputation of J. F. Hargrave, another justice of that court, in "Patronage and the Law," 66 *J of the Royal Austr. Hist. Soc.* 97 (1980), but it is worth noting that Hargrave owed his elevation to local connections, and that his shortcomings were matters of specific competence, not integrity or servility.

21. See Christopher English, "Newfoundland's Early Laws," 23 *Manitoba Law Journal* 55–75 (1996); Bruce Kercher, "Law Reports . . . of Sir Francis Forbes as Chief Justice of Newfoundland," 19 *Dalhousie Law Journal* 417 (1996).

22. Forbes to Wilmot, 14 Aug. 1824, Letters in Catton Papers, noted in B. Kercher, "Practice Note" (1824), note 2, Kercher NSW Sup. Ct. website.

Of a different, but equally independent bent, were the brothers Bent (Jeffrey and Ellis), one the chief law officer, the other a member of the first supreme court of New South Wales. By the 1820s, they had ruled that both pardoned convicts and ticket-of-leave holding "Emancipists" were no longer to be eligible to own property, to sue, to represent others in court, or to testify. This led some unprincipled free debtors of such creditors to engage in a "monstrous attempt at fraud," in the words of Judge Roger Therry, by refusing to pay their debts and challenging the legality of the proceedings in the event that their exconvict creditor tried to force them to pay through the ordinary forms of the law. Justice Jeffrey Bent's refusal in 1814 to listen to the arguments of Emancipist attorneys led to a virtual cessation of civil actions (there being so few other litigators in the colony). In 1817, Justice Bent was replaced, and the Supreme Court thereupon got around the formal problem he had brought to the fore by using a legal fiction: The court pretended not to know if the Emancipist attorney or the Emancipist suitor before them had truly been a felon in the absence of the formal documentation establishing that this was so. Parliament eventually rectified the problems that the independent-minded Bents had created.[23]

John Walpole Willis was no sycophant either. Willis, an English equity expert, was appointed to the Court of King's Bench of Upper Canada in 1827 and removed the next year after allying himself openly with "Reformer" opposition leaders to secure legal reforms. Willis was later appointed, in 1841, to the Supreme Court of New South Wales, but he again called for more sensible bankruptcy and insolvency laws, necessary in a colony "whose rapid progress in commercial property has never been ... equaled in the history of the world." The absence of these reforms "had driven debtors and creditors to expedients and compromises ... which have not always been lawful, or even just. ..."[24] Willis clashed again with Crown officers there over legal "principles" and was again removed from office.

Benjamin Boothby of the South Australian Supreme Court was no law reformer, but, like Willis, he was also no sycophant. Boothby stubbornly refused to see things the way many colonial leaders would have liked. Believing that "rules formulated by the finest English minds

---

[23] Bruce Kercher, *Unruly Child*, 32, 36–37, citing C. H. Currey, *The Brothers Bent* (Sydney, 1968); *Bullock v. Dodds*, 2 B. & Ald. 258, 106 ER 361 (1819); Roger Therry, *Reminiscences of Thirty Years in New South Wales and Victoria* (1863, reprinted 1974), 319, 330–31; Hilary Golder, *High and Responsible Office* (Sydney, 1991), 17.

[24] *Ex Parte Lyons, in re Wilson*, 1 Legge (NSW) 140 at 146 (1839), noted in Bruce Kercher, "An Indigenous Jurisprudence: Debt Recovery and Insolvency in the New South Wales Court of Civil Jurisdiction, 1788 to 1814," 6 *Australian Journal of Law & Society* 15 at 40–41 (1990).

and buttressed by centuries of tradition should [not] be set aside for Antipodean convenience," he declared the first Torrens land registration statute as well as a number of other products of South Australia's legislature invalid on the grounds that they were "repugnant" to language in parliamentary statutes. Boothby was eventually recalled, and Parliament rectified the problem he had created by passing a Colonial Laws Validity Act in 1865, narrowing the test for repugnancy.

Justice Algernon Sydney Montagu was removed from office (like his namesake) by Governor W. T. Denison of Van Dieman's Land in 1847 after Montagu disallowed local legislation, and his colleague, Chief Justice Sir J. L. Pedder, almost suffered the same fate. Both were given opportunities by Denison to change their views; neither was willing to do so.[25]

Most CANZ jurists in the nineteenth century acted with very unsycophant independence because they genuinely believed that the Law of Westminister (not Whitehall or its local representative) was supreme. But this meant that they could also act like legal pedants. In 1828, the Bench in New South Wales required a division of the Bar into barristers and solicitors "in like manner as the same is divided in England," fragmenting the colony's existing legal resources despite a real scarcity of qualified lawyers. This decision was "influenced by the judges' adherence to tradition and . . . their belief that the colonial administration should be modeled on British customs and institutions," in Kenneth Mack's words. The jurists of New South Wales also required "wigs and gowns, totally unsuitable to the Australian climate," as well as new English rules of court "as soon as they became known in the colonies."[26] It was neither sycophancy nor class consciousness that led Justice William a'Beckett to hold in 1848 that the overseers of sheep runs be treated, as the Common-Law rule had it, as the agents of the owners of these runs. Justice a'Beckett allowed that "strictly" following the English Law of Agency might well produce "difficulties," but he

---

[25] A. J. Hannan, "Mr Justice Boothby," *Proc. of the Royal Geographical Society of Australasia: South Australian Branch*, 1957; David Swinfen, *Imperial Control of Colonial Legislation* (1970), 171–82; J. M. Bennett and J. R. Forbes, "Tradition and Experimentation: Some Australian Legal Attitudes of the Nineteenth Century," 7 *Univ. of Queensland Law Journal* 181 (1971); B. Kercher, *Unruly Child*, 93–98; B. A. Keon-Cohen, "J. W. Willis," 8 *Melbourne Univ. Law Review* 703 (1972); P. A. Howell, "The Van Dieman's Land Judge Storm," 2 *Univ. of Tasmania Law Review* 253 (1966). And consider the principled debate between Justices Willam Burton (conservative) and Francis Forbes (liberal) regarding usury in New South Wales in 1833. Kercher, *Unruly Child*, 89–90; *MacDonald v. Levy*, 1 Legge (NSW) 39 (1833).

[26] Kenneth Mack, supra note 20, p. 327. See also Alex Castles, *An Introduction to Australian Legal History* (Sydney, 1971), 139–40.

pointed out that this had been so when he had represented clients as a New South Wales barrister, and referred those upset by his decision (the owners of these stations) to "the legislature" for "alteration."[27] Chief Justice Alfred Stephen reported to the Colonial Office in 1846 the "earnest desire" of "myself and my colleagues to uphold in this distant portion of the Empire, the high and honorable character of British Judges," but this was no mere sycophancy. The chief justice and his colleagues *were* British judges, and, what is more, they were proud of it. Thus, before his elevation to the Supreme Court of New South Wales John Fletcher Hargrave had served as the twenty-first editor of Volume I of Blackstone's Commentaries. And thus, Justice William Burton would write to the editor of *The Australian* in 1841:

> The more English customs were introduced into this Colony in the administration of justice, the better it would be for its inhabitants.[28]

This propensity was just as evident in Canadian appellate courts, as I hope I have demonstrated. In 1884, Wallace Graham, a barrister from Nova Scotia, reported to a colleague that the Supreme Court of Canada "took back-water in an instant" from an opinion of a Canadian court "when an English case was thrown at them,"[29] and this certainly describes how their colleagues in Ontario and the Maritimes sometimes behaved. Only the jurists of Lower Canada/Quebec [at least by 1870], armed with the sanctions of the Act of 14 George III, c. 83, the Quebec Civil Code, and the support of Privy Council,[30] were prepared to say, with Justice Drummond that they were "not going to be bound by any judgement in England or France to submit, without protecting against this attempt to break through our [codified] Law," to rely on "our Code" when "considering the various modes in which verdicts can be dealt with."[31]

Similarly, in Australia and New Zealand, most high court jurists were both comfortable with and prepared to cite the latest English authorities on a point of Law, and this is hardly surprising, inasmuch as it was not until the appointment of Robert Stout in the 1890s that the New Zealand Court of Appeals was graced with a member who had been

---

[27] *Taylor v. Sutherland*, a'Beckett (NSW) 43 (1848).

[28] Grizel Gray, "Biographical Notes" (on Hargrave), ML DOC 1908, Mitchell Library, Sydney; J. M. Bennett, *A History of the Supreme Court of New South Wales* (Sydney, 1974) xvi, 35.

[29] Cited in James Snell, "Relations between the Maritimes and the Supreme Court of Canada: The Patterns of the Early Years," in *Law in a Colonial Society: The Nova Scotia Experience*, ed. P. Waite, S. Oxner and T. Barnes (Toronto, 1984), 154.

[30] *Trigge & Trigge v. Lavallee*, 7 Lower Can. J. 85 at 93 (1862).

[31] *Gugy v. Brown*, 16 Lower Can. J. 225 at 241 (1872).

born and trained in New Zealand.[32] This would account for the fact that Justice C. W. Richmond was outraged in 1891 by a proposal being floated by New Zealand's Liberals "to do away" with appeals to the Judicial Committee of the Privy Council; Justice Richmond regarded "British influence as the most potent in the world for civilization and Christianity," and believed it to be "treason to weaken it, cowardice to abandon it."[33]

Law Lords and Antipodean Jurists: Poles Apart

There were, however, moments Down Under when even the most dedicated followers of the Mother of All Common Law would waiver. From the early 1840s on, the Supreme Court of New South Wales refused to adapt Privy Council's view of that colony's bankruptcy statute. Later, in 1886, that court's chief justice allowed that the colony's Customs Act might be "very peculiar, but not more peculiar than the judgement of the Privy Council" on the Law. Similarly, in *Tooth v. Power* (1890) his colleague, Justice Windeyer angrily scolded Privy Council for its recent misunderstanding (in *Barton v. Muir*) of the reason for the differences between the New South Wales and Queensland land laws regarding dummy selectors, differences the Law Lords had attributed to "circumstances of climate, of soil and produce" distinguishing these adjacent provinces. The New South Wales statute had said nothing to prohibit dummy selection by the Squattocracy itself; by the time the Queensland statute had been drafted this shortcoming had become clear. Justice Windeyer and his colleagues were quite peeved with "their Lordships, unacquainted" as they were "with the history of land legislation in Australia." They failed "to have contemplated the possibility of attempted evasions of the Law in the older colony, making the later legislation of the other colony more sternly clear in its terms of prohibition. . . . " The justice consequently called upon the New South Wales legislature "to take steps" necessary to "secure the presence on the Judicial Committee of the Privy Council" of an Australian jurist.[34]

---

[32] This pattern was, of course, to be expected, and was characteristic of Canada and Australia as well. In 1861, for example, over 53 percent of all those living in Australia had been born in the United Kingdom; by 1891 that figure had fallen to 26 percent. Oz-bred and trained jurists were available by the 1870s. Justice J. G. L. Innes appears to have been the first Australian-born jurist, appointed in New South Wales in 1881. C. M. H. Clark, *A History of Australia, IV,* 383 (Melbourne, 1978); Kercher, *Unruly Child,* 93.

[33] Richmond-Atkins, II, 576 (11 and 18 March, 1891).

[34] Paul Finn, *Law and Government in Colonial Australia* Melbourne, 1987, 44; *Peacock v. Powell,* 7 NSWLR 139 at 145 (1886); *Tooth v. Power,* 10 NSWLR 143

Windeyer and his colleagues were bettered several years later by their peers across the Tasman: In 1903, the Privy Council reversed a decision of the New Zealand Court of Appeals regarding the efforts of certain trustees of property for the use of Maori children to apply the *cy pres* principle in order to create government scholarships, and the reaction of the New Zealand Bench and Bar was one of outrage. In the course of their opinions, the Law Lords had criticized the propriety and sense of justice displayed by the New Zealand high court. Soon after these views reached New Zealand, the Court of Appeals held an extraordinary session, attended by most of the islands' leading attorneys. Sir Robert Stout, the chief justice, spoke first, protesting the language used by the Law Lords as well as the decision itself, and criticizing other Privy Council decisions regarding questions of title and conveyancing. He was followed by the former chief justice, Worley Edwards, and by Justice Joshua Williams, who complained of the "ignorance" of these "four strangers sitting 14,000 miles away," who "displayed every characteristic of an alien tribunal." "We are responsible for our judicial conduct," Justice Williams concluded, not to these "four strangers," but "to our fellow-citizens in this Colony. . . . " These remarks from the bench were then echoed by similar ones offered by W. L. Travers, Esq., seconded by the "large numbers of solicitors in Court," all of whom rose with Travers when he delivered his defense of the Court of Appeals.[35]

This well-staged protest was, nevertheless, just that – a protest, not a rebellion. Appeals to Privy Council from New Zealand decisions continued throughout the twentieth century, albeit even the more doctrinal of New Zealand's jurists remained uncomfortable at times with the arrangement: In April, 1904, shortly after the formal protest had been staged, Justice John Edward Denniston noted in his diary the difficulty he was having in finding his "way through the conflicting English decisions on [the] Workmen's Compensation Act." They seemed "illogical and unsatisfactory," and Justice Denniston wanted to follow "my own construction of the section in question. But to do this I would have had to go against authorities I have no right to dissent from, however much I may disagree." A month later Denniston complained again to his diary, this time of Privy Council's reversal of a New Zealand Court of Appeals decision. The Law Lords "have a way of 'reading words into' a Statute when in a difficulty." Such a step was "not open to a Court

---

at 158–59 (1890). The best account of the issue is David Swinfen, *Imperial Appeal: The Debate on the Appeal to the Privy Council, 1833–1986* (Manchester, 1987).

35 "New Zealand Bench and Bar Protest to Privy Council decision in *Wallis v. Solic. Gen.*, NZPCC 23 (1903)," Appendix to NZPCC 730 at 745, 756, 759 (1903).

of less dignity," and it was not "open to appeal" when done by Privy Council.[36] Isaac Isaacs, M.P., soon-to-be justice on the High Court of Australia, offered a similar view in 1902: Privy Council was "as unable to interpret the meaning of our statutes as if they were living in the planet Mars."[37]

Once the proposed constitution for the Federal Commonwealth of Australia had been approved by Parliament, in 1900, the new High Court of Australia acquired the final say in all matters involving the balance of power within the federation (state-federal questions). By 1906, it had exercised this power, twice upsetting both the Supreme Court and the Government of Victoria. That state appealed directly to Privy Council, and the Law Lords announced that the High Court had been in error. The High Court lost no time in making clear (in *Baxter v. Comm. of Taxation*, 1907) that it would not defer to Privy Council on questions of federal-state power.[38]

Privy Council *could* override "local knowledge" at times. But how meaningful were the Law Lords' decisions in restraining CANZ jurists? After all, fewer than one in 20,000 cases decided by CANZ courts in the nineteenth century reached the Law Lords. There was no ordinary appeal to Privy Council granted in cases where the issue concerned interlocutory orders, or where the issue had not yet been finally resolved at the appellate level, or in cases involving insolvency, or where the judgement was for a sum less than $4,000 (in Lower Canada/Quebec; £500 in New South Wales).[39] And Privy Council was unwilling to grant

---

[36] John G. Denniston, *A New Zealand Judge: Sir John Edward Denniston*, (Wellington, 1939), 127. (The latter case was *Smith v. McArthur*, NZPCC 323 (1904) 124.)

[37] Zelman Cowen, *Isaac Isaacs* (Melbourne, 1967), 87. See also Johnston, J., in *Highett v. McDonald*, 3 JR(N.S.) (S.C. of Northern Dist., NZ) 102 at 104 (1878) (finding a forty-year-old English statute regarding the sale of liquor to be "applicable to the circumstances of the Colony" and hence "to have been solemnly adopted" when the Colony was created).

The Supreme Court of Australia declared itself free of review by the Law Lords in *Parker v. Rex*, 37 Aus. L.J.R. 3 at 11 (1963), and *Skelton v. Collins*, 39 Aus. L.J.R. 480 (1966).

[38] See *D'Embden v. Pedder*, 1 CLR 91 (1904); *Deakin v. Webb*, 1 CLR 585 (1904); *Webb v. Outrim*, AC 81 (1907); *Railway Servants* 3 CLR 807 (1906); *Baxter v. Comm. of Taxation*, 4 CLR 1087 (1907). And see Bruce Kercher, *An Unruly Child*, 159–60, 171–73, for a review of these issues.

[39] Waldo Dunn and Ivor Richardson, *Sir Robert Stout: A Biography* (Wellington, 1961), 176; *Great Western Ry. v. Fawcett v. Braid*, 7 Lower Can. J. 141 (1863); *Lacrois v. Moreau*, 16 Lower Can. R. 180 (1865); *Darling v. Templeton*, 19 Lower Can. J. 125 (1875); *S.E. Ry. v. Lambkin*, 22 Lower Can. J. 21 (1877); *Renny v. Moat*, 23 Lower Can. J. 262 (1879); *Jones v. Municipal Council of Sydney*, 1 NSWR (L) 315 at 320 (1880) (where the Supreme Court turned away Sydney's "leave to appeal" to Privy Council its grant to the plaintiff of a

appeals "by special leave" (appeals of grace) when the central matter at issue was a factual one, or where the issue was not of a serious public character.[40] CANZ jurists did not defer to the authority of Westminister jurists because of any threat of appeal to Privy Council; they were well aware that Privy Council posed no significant threat per se to their judgements. They deferred because they regarded themselves, essentially, as peers of Westminister jurists, as proud bearers of the Common-Law tradition.

Authority Distinguished: Explaining the Propensity of CANZ Jurists to Avoid Fanciful, Illogical, and Unsatisfactory English Precedents

As proud bearers of the Common-Law tradition, many CANZ jurists found some English precedents to be "fanciful," "illogical," or "unsatisfactory."[41] Few, to be sure, were willing to "make new Law"; few took John Salmond's admonition to heart. ("In deciding questions on principle, Salmond wrote in 1900, jurists were "in reality searching out the rules and requirements of natural justice and public policy." So long as they "affect to be looking for and declaring old laws, they cannot adequately express the principles in which they are in reality making new.")[42] But some CANZ jurists rebelled at the application of specific rules or precedents.

Sometimes they merely grumbled a protest in *dicta* as they deferred to the offensive precedent; but, just as frequently, they held that the

---

new trial in a case where the jury appeared to have awarded an insufficient sum as damages in a nuisance suit, though a larger award at such a retrial would probably have risen to the required £500 minimum to warrant such an appeal).

[40] *Canada Central Ry. v. Murray*, 27 Lower Can. J. 163 (1883); *Johnston v. Minister of St. Andrews*, 3 AC 159 (1877); *Ex Part Clergue*, AC 521 (1903); *Can. Pac. Ry. v. Blain*, AC 453 (1904).

[41] Justice Adam Wilson in *Gardiner v. Ford*, 13 UCCP 446 at 449 (1863); Justice John Denniston, diary entry, April, 1904, *A New Zealand Judge, supra*, note 36, 124.

[42] Salmond, "The Theory of Judicial Precedents," 16 *Law Quarterly Review* 376 at 389, 390 (1900). Salmond, to be sure, was no "legal realist" himself. He favored the following of imperfect precedents if they were hoary enough to have been relied on by solicitors and their clients (382). Neither he nor his contemporary in Massachusetts, Oliver Wendell Holmes, Jr., whose essay "The Path of the Law" (1897) was more pointed than Salmond's in establishing the capacity of jurists to make new law, put such views to the test in their own legal practices, as they persistently treated English rules and precedents with essentially the same respect as their unabashedly doctrinal colleagues. See Alex Frame, *Salmond: Southern Jurist* (Wellington, 1995), 220; and Peter Karsten, *Heart versus Head*, 229–30.

cases cited were not "exactly in point," leaving them free "to decide this question apart altogether from authority, and entirely on principle."[43] Or they held that "the authorities leave us free to draw our own inference from the facts," and then distinguished "the facts" before them from those in the offending citations.[44] Alternatively, they held that there was "a conflict of opinion in England," leaving them free to chose between these conflicting authorities.[45] Another view offered was that the "local circumstances" provision of the parliamentary act creating the Colony's legal institutions allowed them to alter certain Common-Law rules or ignore certain parliamentary statutes.[46] Still another view was that they need not be controlled "unthinkingly" by a recent decision of an English appellate court other than Privy Council, "the only tribunal whose decisions are binding upon us."[47]

We have seen numerous examples of these means of avoiding unappealing English precedents in Chapters 1, 2, 5, 6, and 7. I add here that while a *few* jurists seemed to have acquired reputations for one or another of these propensities,[48] they were not at all confined to the opinions of "liberals." Doctrinaire "conservatives" like Sir John Beverley Robinson, Christopher Richmond, William Foster Stawell, John Gwynne, and John Denniston seemed at times to be just as prepared to find their way around English authorities they didn't like.

---

[43] *McPherson v. Borough of Bathurst*, NSWSCR (Knox) 204 at 207–13 (1877) (Sir James Martin, C.J., in dissent).

[44] Richmond, J., in *Claridge v. Union Steamship Co.*, 11 NZLR (CA) 294 at 306 (1892); distinguishing facts from those in *Rourke v. White Moss Colliery Co.*, 2 CPD 205 (1877).

[45] Robinson, C.J., in *Bartlett v. Municip. of Amherstburg*, 14 UCQB 152 at 156 (1855).

[46] See *In Re Swinden* 16 South Austr. L.R. 7 (1882); David Williams, "The Foundation of Colonial Rule in New Zealand," 13 *New Zealand Univ. Law Review* 54 (1988) (on the English Laws Act of 1858); David Neal, *The Rule of Law in a Penal Colony: Law & Power in Early New South Wales* (Cambridge, 1991), 223; "The Foundation of Colonial Rule in New Zealand," 13 *New Zealand University Law Review* 54 (1988).

Upper Canada/Ontario jurists may have utilized the "local circumstances" provision when they decided to set as the procedural rule of court costs that the losing and winning parties pay only their own costs (contrary to the English practice of having losers pay the costs of winners). See *Eddy v. Ottawa City Pass. Ry.*, 31 UCQB 569 at 576 (1871); *Drake v. Wigle*, 24 UCCP 405 at 409 (1874); *Church v. Fuller*, 3 Ont. (QB) R. 417 at 420 (1883).

[47] Justice Adam Wilson in *Gardiner v. Ford*, 13 UCCP 446 at 449 (1863); Chief Justice Sir James Martin (dissenting), in *McPherson v. B. of Bathurst*, NSWSCR (Knox) 204 at 213 (1877).

[48] Thus, J. L. M. Richardson writes of New Zealand's Chief Justice Sir Robert Stout: "This desire for reform led to some of his decisions running ahead of precedent."

Consider the case of New Zealand's Justice Denniston. Born and educated in Scotland, John Denniston migrated in his twenties to the South Island. He received further legal training at the new University of Otago at Dunedin, where he was a classmate of Robert Stout. As a barrister, Denniston enjoyed the works of Utilitarian theorists: Jeremy Bentham, John Austin, and John Stuart Mill. He was named to the Court of Appeals in 1889, and while I found him to be more inclined to follow the leads provided by the courts of Westminister than his colleagues, I also found that he sometimes did so quite ambivalently. He confided to his diary from time to time a certain discomfort in this deference to those "English decisions that were, in his judgement, "illogical and unsatisfactory." Thus, he confessed, in February, 1894, to a "growing" tendency to "see distinctions, always a defect of mine," between the English authorities and the facts of the New Zealand case before the court. (I have already noted Justice Denniston's criticism of Privy Council decisions.)

In another passage Denniston recorded that he had just "finished a judgement on a case in a charitable bequest which ought to be law, if it isn't. I have endeavored to distinguish the case from some decisions of the House of Lords which have carried the law a long way in disregarding the obvious intention of the Testator." In this instance, Denniston allowed the rather vague bequest to distribute Charles Abels' assets "amongst local charitable or benevolent institutions" to "go to such, to use a Christchurch instance, as the McLean Institute for Indigent Gentlewomen," instead of Mr. Abels' heirs, who had been led to believe they had solid English precedents on their side.[49]

There is, of course, nothing terribly revolutionary in such an act of "distinguishing," but it seems to me that Bruce Kercher's delicious description of Justice Lionel Murphy (fl. 1975–86) could apply to some of Murphy's nineteenth century predecessors – that is, some were "adoptor[s]" of the inherited legal tradition of England, not ... empty vessel[s] through which it passed unchanged."[50]

Moreover, when CANZ jurists appeared to be deliberately choosing to "distinguish" an English precedent like this from the facts in the

49 J. G. Denniston, *A New Zealand Judge: Sir John Edward Denniston* (Wellington, 1939), 32, 33, 84, 124. (The Christchurch bequest case was *Clarke v. Attorney-General*, 33 NZLR 963 (1914)).

For a similar, more public revelation of this down under distress with English common law testamentary rules, see Lilley C.J. in *Re the Will of Adams*, 5 Queens. LJ 1 at 2 (1893): "I have always felt rather rebellious towards the English decisions." This was the same Lilley who, as a legislator, had objected to the English doctrine of sovereign immunity (noted in Chapter 7).

50 Kercher, *An Unruly Child*, 184.

case before them, the winners *tended* to be the poor or weak, like these "Indigent Gentlewomen" of Christchurch, *not* the rich or powerful, like Mr. Abels' heirs or the many corporate defendants we have met in these pages. Generally, CANZ jurists, like their British (and, for that matter, most American) counterparts, declined to address the implications for "growth," "development" or "economic efficiency" in applying a rule or precedent. One final example of this: When the New Brunswick Supreme Court was asked to sanction the debentures created by that province's legislature to finance a railroad linking the province to Maine and American markets beyond, Justice Allen held that the British Parliament's North American Act of 1867 vested these kinds of powers solely in the Parliament of the Dominion of Canada. He allowed that the opinion would result in "much disappointment and very serious inconvenience and loss," but he explained that he and his colleagues "dare not shrink from the discharge of our duty, which in this, as in every other case that comes before us, is plain, simple and imperative, that is, to declare the law as we honestly believe it to be, wholly regardless of consequences."[51]

Generally speaking, in ambiguous situations CANZ jurists were simply not given to handing down decisions that rendered the Law in ways that benefitted entrepreneurs or others of their own social class. Richard Atkins, the Judge-Advocate for New South Wales in the first decade of the nineteenth century noted in his journal that his aim (in ignoring the Common-Law rule regarding immediate enforcement of judgement debts in debtor – creditor suits) was "to shelter the weak & innocent from the detestable attacks of fraud & calumny; to protect the poor & defenseless from the fatal influences of the rich & great."[52] One of Atkins' successors, Judge Advocate Wylde,

---

[51] *Queen v. Dow*, 14 New Br. 300 at 310 (1873). Cf. *Regina v. Ross*, 2 Legge's R (NSW) 857 (1854); *Stevens v. M'Clung*, 2 Legge's R (NSW) 1226 (1859); *Hood v. Corp. of Sydney*, 2 LR (NSW) 1294 (1860); *Gardiner v. Chapman*, 6 Ont. (Ch.) 272 (1884).

[52] There being no Court of Chancery, Atkins granted extensions of time and issued installment payment orders to debtors as a Court of Chancery or Court of Request might have done. See Bruce Kercher, "An Indigenous Jurisprudence: Debt Recovery and Insolvency Law in the New South Wales Courts of Civil Jurisdiction, 1788–1814," 6 *Australian Journal of Law and Society* 15 at 28–31 (1990).

The early governors of New South Wales exercised both executive and judicial powers in a sense; hence, it is worth noting that at least two of them exhibited this same prounderdog mentality: Governor Bligh, of HMS *Bounty* fame, wrote in 1806 that he intended to "do justice and relieve the oppressed poor settlers who . . . are honester than those who wish to keep them under." He was overthrown by his second mutinous crew, the officers

called a meeting of New South Wales magistrates in 1822 to invalidate former-Governor Macquarie's Proclamation that British Master & Servant legislation was operant in that colony, and his colleague, Chief Justice Francis Forbes, reversed a number of anti-Emancipist judgements made by Exclusivist magistrates in the 1820s.[53] Similarly, in Victoria, Judge Robert Molesworth was said to be impartial: All suitors before him were "absolutely equal." Once, when a suit was "brought by some comparatively poor miners" against a "very wealthy mine owner" for encroachment and removing gold from their mine, "counsel for the rich man attempted to smooth over and make light of his acts." Judge Molesworth rejected his sophistry: "I don't make any distinctions between underground robbers and over-ground robbers."[54] George Higinbotham, a reform-minded member of Victoria's supreme court, referred to the Squatter elite as "the wealthy Lower Orders" and subscribed 200 pounds to the maritime workers' strike fund in 1890. While Chief Justice Stawell and other of Stawell's more doctrinal colleagues found some statutes generated by Victoria's legislature "repugnant to the Law," Higinbotham never seems to have met a statute he didn't like. And it is no coincidence that these "repugnant" statutes were generally reforms of the Common Law, changes to the Law of Torts and Property that Higinbotham welcomed (or could at least live with), but that

of the New South Wales Corps, when he objected to their abuse of their control of customs and imports. The man sent out to replace him, Lachlan Macquarie, similarly wrote in 1817 that it had "been a uniform measure of my government, and one alike approved by my head and by my heart, to rule [humanely]." Brian Fletcher, *Landed Enterprise and Penal Society: A History of Farming and Grazing in New South Wales before 1821* (Sydney, 1976), 101; J. M. Bennett and Alex Castles, *A Source Book on Australian History* (1979), 6.

53 David Neal, *The Rule of Law in a Penal Colony: Law and Power in Early New South Wales* (New York, 1991), 108, 110.

54 John L. Forde, *The Story of the Bar in Victoria* (Melbourne, 1913), 292.
New Zealand's Justice Christopher Richmond, one of the leaders of the Conservative Party, revealed a concern that he at least appear impartial to a relative in March, 1880: "I must not stay on at the Club [in Auckland] much longer. It is scarcely the place for a judge. . . . It is prudent to keep oneself more apart than is possible in a Club." To Emily Richmond, 15 March, 1880, *The Richmond-Atkinson Papers*, ed. Guy Scholefield (2 vols., Wellington, 1960), II, 476. Later Justice Richmond became incensed at the Liberal land reforms of 1891 which forced graziers like him to sell their leaseholds back to the State for homesteads. He wrote his daughter in August of that year with sarcasm that it had been his "folly to have invested in land" that the legislature now declared "belongs to 'the people' and not to me." But he and his colleagues upheld and enforced the land laws. *Ibid.*, II, 584.

Stawell and others could not.[55] In the late nineteenth century, Justice Joshua Williams of the New Zealand Court of Appeals evinced a "deep personal interest" in the plight of working men," and was seen as "too sympathetic a man to forget Equity." Justice Williams was named to the first New Zealand Court of Arbitration in 1897, and his contemporary, William P. Reeves, said of this New Zealand institutional innovation in labor-management relations that, while there were "jurists to whom it would [have been] a joy to wreck such a Law; [Justice Williams] tried to make it succeed."[56] In the early twentieth century, Justice Henry Bournes Higgins, President of the Australian Court of Conciliation and Arbitration, insisted that "the value of human life" was "too valuable to be a shuttlecock in the game of moneymaking and competition." Similarly, his countryman, Justice Isaac Isaacs (while serving on Privy Council) maintained (with regard to industrial accidents and safety legislation) that courts of Law were "living organism[s]," that they were "fully seized of the corporate sense of the community," and that "life" was "the supreme consideration." The "old balancing of the Common Law of reasonable care for employees' safety, on the one side, and on the other, such reasonable conduct for self preservation as is expected in ordinary life where men meet on an equal footing," was a "fallacious standard."[57]

In short, CANZ jurists were willing to obfuscate, distinguish away, or ignore English precedents that appeared to stand in the way of social

---

[55] W. P. Reeves, *State Experiments in Australia and New Zealand* (1902), II, 89; Paul Finn also identifies Higinbotham as an advocate of judicial restraint.

  In this regard Higinbotham resembles Pennsylvania's Chief Justice John Bannister Gibson, a Jacksonian Democrat, the chief voice of judicial restraint in his day, who offered a blistering critique of the voices of "repugnancy" on the U.S. Supreme Court, Chief Justice John Marshall, and Justice Joseph Story. On Gibson see Stanley Kutler, "John Bannister Gibson: Judicial Restraint and the 'Positive State,'" 1965 *Journal of Public Law* 181.

[56] Reeves, *State Experiment*, II, 118; W. D. Stewart, Jr., *Portrait of a Judge: Sir Joshua Strange Williams* (Wellington, 1945), 39, 74–75; *Hulton v. Mills*, 14 NZLR 518 (1897). See also G. A. Wood, "Contruction & Reform: The Establishment of the New Zealand Supreme Court," 5 Victoria Univ. Wellington Law Rev. 1 at 2 (1968), on the work of Chief Justice William Martin and Justice Chapman in producing procedural changes "freeing the new courts from the heavy weight of English legal tradition." And see *In re Nash*, 2 NZLR (S.C.) 286 (1884) (on the rejection of the English need for property to be involved in the decision to appoint a Guardian for an orphan).

[57] Higgins in 32 *The Survey* 455 (1914), noted in Peter Coleman, *Progressivism and the World of Reform: New Zealand and the Origins of the American Welfare State* (Lawrence, Kansas, 1987), 139; *Bourke v Butterfield & Lewis Ltd.*, 38 Com. L.R. 354 at 369 (1926).

justice, and when they did reveal biases regarding the litigants, they rarely favored entrepreneurs or a landed elite.

STATUTORY INNOVATIONS

We have seen that some CANZ jurists were inclined at times to bend or ignore particularly obnoxious English Common-Law rules. But they generally held their noses and toed the line. How was it, then, that James E. Fitzgerald could write from Wellington in 1882 that New Zealand was free of "tradition,... precedent,... and old-world prejudices"?[58] The answer: Because Fitzgerald was not referring to jurists; he had in mind the institution that jurists sometimes referred to themselves as the only proper forum to alter the Common-Law rules – the legislature.

Until 1865, the British Parliament extended only limited authority to colonial assemblies to make laws for themselves.The Colonial Office sometimes denied "royal assent" to such changes as these assemblies might make. CANZ legislatures of the nineteenth century were free to adopt such statutes amending the Common Law as were warranted by purely "local circumstances," *or* as were being adopted by *Parliament.* But until 1865, their capacity to go beyond such alterations was somewhat limited. (Thus, when Victoria's legislature permitted four years of desertion to serve as grounds for divorce in 1860, assent was denied inasmuch as this had not been permitted under Parliament's Divorce Act of 1857.) Prior to 1842 the Colonial Office confirmed some 245 colonial statutes, but disallowed 280 others. Between 1842 and 1865, as Britain ushered in the Era of Responsible Government, it confirmed 345 such statutes and disallowed only 58.[59]

None the less, the Colonial Office did sanction a substantial number of pre-1865 legislative alterations of rules affecting land, commercial transactions, and judicial procedure. Victoria's Judicature Act gave Equity priority over Common-Law rules in cases of conflict between the two.[60] South Australia removed sovereign immunity in 1853; New South Wales followed suit in 1857. New South Wales abolished

---

58 Fitzgerald, *The Possible Future Development of Government in Free States,* p. 8, cited in Peter Coleman, supra note, p. 20; David Swinfen, *Imperial Control of Colonial Legislation, 1813–1865: British Policy toward Colonial Legislative Powers* (Oxford, 1970), 151–55, *passim.*

59 Harrison Moor, "A Century of Victorian Law," 16 *Journal of Comparative Leg. and Int. Law* 175 (3rd s.) 175 at 199 (1934); Alex Castles, *An Introduction to Austrialian Legal History* (Sydney, 1971), 156.

60 Bruce Kercher, "An Indigenous Jurisprudence? Debt Recovery and Insolvency Law in the New South Wales Court of Civil Jurisdiction, 1788 to 1814," 6 *Australian Journal of Law & Society* 15 at 48 (1990); Alex Castles, supra note 59, p. 109.

debt imprisonment in 1843 long before it was abolished in Britain (1869), and created bankruptcy, land execution, and land registration reforms that predated English ones by several decades. When the Privy Council's Law Lords disapproved of the amoral nature of the New South Wales Bankruptcy Act of 1841, that colony's Supreme Court ignored them, holding that Privy Council had not rendered an "express decision" on the subject. And when the Law Lords addressed the matter a second time, the New South Wales jurists ignored them again.[61]

Once given more of their own reins in 1865, CANZ legislatures took a number of significant initiatives of their own, adopting compulsory labor-management arbitration laws in New Zealand and New South Wales, recalling the leases of huge sheep stations to generate home-steads, forcing employers to pay wages within twenty four hours of due dates in New Zealand, regulating corporations more vigorously than elsewhere in the Empire in Victoria, where the legislature also protected wages from debt attachment proceedings and gave workers creditor priority in bankruptcies. And several of these products of Oz and Kiwi legislatures (such as the Torrens system of land registration and certain irrigation and gold mining statutes) found their way into Canada's federal and provincial statute books. Indeed, as Jeremy Finn has shown, in a few instances British legislative lobbyists (e.g., the Marriage Law Reform Association) successfully persuaded colonial legislatures in South Australia and Victoria to create desired statues there in order to help them persuade the British Parliament to do the same.[62]

Legal change in the British colonies, dominions, and provinces then came at the hands of legislators, as in the United Kingdom, not at the hands of jurists. In the United States jurists were reluctant to change legal rules as well, though they *sometimes* did so. And they *sometimes* struck

---

[61] Bruce Kercher, *Unruly Child*, 100, 116; Paul Finn, *Law and Government*, 41; John Gava, "The Revolution in Bankruptcy in Colonial New South Wales," in *The Emergence of Australian Law*, ed. M. P. Ellinghaus, et al. (Sydney, 1989).

[62] J. L. Robson, ed., *New Zealand: The Development of its Law and Constitution* (2nd ed., London, 1967), 417; Kercher, *Unruly Child*, 135; Tom Brooking, "Superficial Similarities: Why Did Farmer Protest Assume Such Different Forms in Late 19th Century New Zealand and the United States?" in *New Worlds? The Comparative History of New Zealand and the United States*, ed. Jock Phillips (Wellington, 1989), 135–36; H. Moore, *supra* note, p. 197; Jeremy Finn, "Reverses in the Flow: A Preliminary Inquiry...," 17 Annual Austr.-New Z. Legal History Society meeting, Melbourne, July 1998; Finn, "'It Might be Worth Trying it in Our Dominion': Adoption of Australasian Legislation by Canadian Legislatures in the Nineteenth Century," Legal History Conference, Australian National University, Canberra, Feb. 2000.

Note that the Colonial Laws Validating Act of 1865 left Parliament free to legislate for the colonies on some matters, such as shipping.

down statutes that appeared to them to violate the terms of written constitutions, something beyond the powers and prerogatives of CANZ jurists (at least until after the adoption in Australia and Canada of written constitutions).[63]

Two Australian legal scholars (Clark and Renard) have aptly described the "deep, almost hysterical fear of the possible effects" of Common-Law rules regarding riparian rights in nineteenth century Victoria, rules based on "the rigorous methodology of precedent." The problem concerned "agricultural development," which would be impeded if "the rights of downstream riparian owners" were to be "cumulatively built up in Common Law." This "fear" led to legislative intervention, because there was no likelihood that Victoria's jurists would respond to arguments of practicality or economic considerations that flew in the face of good English precedent.[64]

Nowhere was this need for "Positive Law" more evident than in the Law regarding roads and railways. Once avenues of transit had been opened and traffic appeared, some governors, councils, and legislatures felt called upon to impose "rules of the road," above and beyond those that the popular wisdom had itself generated. Simple questions of the right-of-way, and of overtaking situations, could be answered by jurists using Common-Law principles. But provincial and municipal councils stepped in to regulate more specific conduct, and to impose fines on those failing to observe these ordinances. In the early eighteenth century, a Quebec ordinance imposed a fine of ten livres upon one mounted who knocked a pedestrian down, and ordered churchgoers to walk their horses once they were within ten arpents of the church; a century later officials in Lower Canada were imposing regulations on sleighs.[65] Such mundane decrees as these over the next century regulated the conduct of those who made use of "the Queen's highways." In 1828, a court in New South Wales sentenced a man

---

[63] This is not to say that CANZ jurists were unwilling to void provincial statutes or municipal ordinances drafted *ultra vires* or in conflict with a dominion or parliamentary statute; they clearly were.

　　When it came to a change such as compulsory arbitration, some American Union leaders were just as leary of this statutory abrogation of "freedom of contract" as both their employer counterparts and a substantial number of American jurists. See Peter Coleman, *supra* note 57, pp. 142–43.

[64] S. D. Clark and I. A. Renard, "The Riparian Doctrine & Australian Legislation," 7 *Melbourne Univ. Law Rev.* 450 at 479 (1970).

[65] Richard Cole Harris, *The Seigneurial System in Early Canada* (Madison, Wis., 1966), 157; Stephen Kenny, "'Cahots' and Catcalls: An Episode of Popular Resistance in Lower Canada at the Outset of the Union," in *Historical Perspectives on Law and Society in Canada*, ed. Tina Loo and Lorna McLean (Toronto, 1991), 78, 81.

to three month's imprisonment for running over and killing a child while driving his carriage at a trot in the community of Currick. In the next year, the Sydney Police Act declared wrongful the breaking-in of horses in public places (a centuries-old problem) and the "driving [of] barrows and carriages on pavements." Other cities adopted similar measures. Thus, in Wellington, New Zealand in early 1896 James Doyle was fined for "being the owner of a horse found in Hospital Rd. without any person having charge thereof." John Stewart was fined for "having caused a hole to be made in Wilson St" and for failing "to cause a light to be fixed upon or near the same from sunset to sunrise." Frank Withers and six others were fined for riding a bicycle on a footpath. Henry Clark was fined for failing "to be constantly attendant" on his cab "when on a stand in Jervis Quay." And James Malley was fined for driving after dark on Lambton Quay "without having 2 proper & sufficient lights."[66] The Wellington Magistrate's Court also fined a number of individuals for getting "upon a train at the Te Aro Ry Station while the said train was in motion," for permitting "cattle to wander in the [right-of-way] of the New Zealand Greater Railway Line," and for "trespass on the Wellington & Manuwatu Railway by driving a horse & buggy along the same." It was just as willing to award £10 to a passenger injured alighting from a train that was without a proper step.[67] With such misdemeanor ordinances, the government in New Zealand and its counterparts in Australia and Canada sought to reduce the number of injuries to passengers and strangers on streetcars and railways.

Many CANZ streetcars and railways were government-owned and operated, with directors empowered to make by-laws binding on employees and the public alike.[68] Most American streetcars and railways were privately owned chartered companies, and while they might fire or demote a careless engineer or switchman, most had not been given the public power to impose misdemeanor fines on errant employees, nor were such workers liable to suffer criminal penalties except for the most gross negligence in the event of an accident.[69] But whether

---

[66] *Rex v. Pigott* (Kercher NSWSC 1828); Richard Hill, *Policing the Colonial Frontier* (Wellington, 1986), Pt. 1, I, 119; Record of Proceedings in Criminal Causes & Miscellaneous Matters in Magistrate's Court, Wellington, New Zealand, 1896 Justice, JC - WI, 1, New Zealand National Archives, files 52, 246, 306, 698, 739, 741, 742, 743, 849, 886–90, 900, 1029.

[67] *Ibid.*, files 53, 203, 514, 602, & 701. *The Dominion (Wellington)*, Feb. 27, 1918, p. 9.

[68] But recall that some of these by-laws were deemed *ultra vires*, as in *King v. Broad*, 33 NZLR (CA) 1275 (1914).

[69] Tony Freyer, *Producers versus Capitalists: Constitutional Conflict in Antebellum America* (Charlottesville, Va., 1994), 186; Walter Licht, *Working for the Railroad: The Organization of Work in the Nineteenth Century* (Princeton, 1983).

publicly or privately managed, streetcar and railway corporations were subject to legislative oversight. And in the event of a major accident, or an untoward series of smaller ones, CANZ railways appear to have been subjected to investigations by legislative committees more frequently than American ones.

The reports of these investigative committees in Canada recommended measures to prevent such accidents in the future: fencing rights-of-way to prevent derailments when cattle were struck; filling in unblocked frogs at switches to protect the feet and lives of switchmen; providing better handrails and running boards, automatic couplers, and more standing room between the tops of boxcars and bridges or tunnel overpasses for brakemen; "prescrib[ing] rules and regulations for the government of railroads" to discipline employees; making carelessness and intoxication-on-the-job punishable by magistrates; and eventually creating the office of "Inspector of Accidents," whose assistants investigated injuries to determine whether modifications to equipment or procedures were in order. Paul Craven has pointed out that Canada West/Ontario's legislative investigation of the Baptiste Creek Railway disaster of 1854 led to the exoneration of the Great Western Railway's managers and the future criminalization of employee negligence that might lead to accidents.[70] This is so, and the incident may well have been a case of class-conscious (or unconscious) regulating of the public's welfare. But if the immediate result did not properly hold accountable those managers who may have been at fault, it is still possible that the long-term consequence may be said to have been that brakemen, switchmen, and other railway workers, to say nothing of passengers, experienced safer conditions than they had enjoyed before the appearance of some of the language in that statute.

Similar steps were taken in Australia and New Zealand. Thus, when an unattended engine resulted in the death of two New Zealand Railway employees in 1883, one man was fired, another reduced in rank

---

[70] See, for example, *Reports of Commissioners [Matthew Cameron & William Coffin] on Accidents and Detentions of the Great Western Railway, Canada West* (Quebec, 1855) (copy in Archives of Ontario); Report of Select Committee on Railway Accidents, Ontario Legislature, 1880, Record Group MU, 49–95, No. 1, Archives of Ontario; Paul Craven, "The Meaning of Misadventure: The Baptiste Creek Railway Disaster of 1854 and its Aftermath," in *Patterns of the Past*, ed. Roger Hall et al. (Toronto, 1988), 108ff; Craven and Tom Traves, "Dimensions of Paternalism: Discipline and Culture in Canadian Railway Operations in the 1850s," in *On the Job*, ed. Craig Heron and Rob. Storey (Kingston, 1986), 49, 51; Correspondence of J. Clarke, Asst. Inspector of Accidents, British Columbia, throughout 1908, regarding role of operating lever and defective buffer in accident to foreman H. E. Shumway of the Canadian Northern Railway at Winnepeg, April 16, 1908, file 26–52, Vol. 8693, R.G. 30, Archives of Canada, Ottawa.

and suspended, and a third fined two days pay, and the descriptions of these actions, accompanied by accounts of what each man had done or failed to do, was printed and circulated throughout the yards.[71] The "stop-look-and-listen," assumption of risk, and common employment rules were supposed to cause those crossing tracks and those employed to operate the trains to be more careful, more watchful of one another; they were expected to reduce the likelihood of accidents.[72] But railway companies did not rely on such judge-made rules to do the job; they held their employees accountable to elaborate safety regulations of their own, to be found in handbooks regularly updated that employees were expected to read and remember.[73]

While new "Heart"-inspired judge-made rules surely helped, "the people" chose, through their elected representatives, to add to these Common-Law doctrines other rules: requirements for platforms and crossings, guard rails, night lights, bells and whistles, as well as speed limits and worksite rulebooks with the force of Law. Ultimately, these "Positive" Laws may have made a greater difference than those introduced through the ponderous, if sometimes inspiring workings of the Common Law's ways.

ATTORNEYS AND MAGISTRATES: MIDDLE LEGAL CULTURE

A Word about Attorneys and Settlements

The Common-Law courts of Great Britain and her Diaspora offspring pronounced the Law and decided the fate of litigant claims, to be sure. But, then, as now, most litigation was "settled out of court" between the solicitors employed by the contending parties. By the nineteenth century this was the case with regard to both "plea bargaining" in criminal cases and the "settling" of civil litigation. C. W. Brooks has shown that by the late eighteenth century, English solicitors realized that they earned as much from settlements as they would from paying barristers to

---

[71] *Notices* (Circular #2/104/83, #2/105/83), Locomotive Superintendent, Addington, regarding Adams, Engineer, Christchurch, Lennie, A., Guard, and Blackmore, W., Vol. 83/3380, Railway, 4, New Zealand National Archives.

[72] This had been the public policy rationale in the "leading case" of both the "assumption of risk" and "fellow-servant" rules, *Farwell v. Boston & Worcester RR*, 45 Mass. 49 (1842).

[73] See, for example, Karsten, *Heart versus Head*, 116–17; New South Wales Railways, R82/1 (Rules & Regs. of the NSW Govt. Rys., 1907–1915), Transport House, Sydney; Victoria Public Recs. Off. (Laverton), VPRS, Discipline of Employees. And see VPRS 3619 (Accident Reports, 1871–1912, and Railway Inquiry Board, *Report of the Bd. . . . into the Working and Management of the Victorian Railways* (Melbourne, 1895)).

conduct full courtroom presentation. Arbitration and solicitor-to-solicitor settlements increased in frequency as a consequence; formal in-court litigation declined, despite both population and economic growth.[74] We have seen that merchants, commodity brokers, and tradesmen had learned to avoid the expense, uncertainties, delays, and unpopularity of litigation as well (in Chapter 5), and we have seen the widespread use of the settlement process in accident cases (in Chapter 8). There are more stories to tell of this process, but these are largely dependent upon one's locating the kinds of records or recollections of the process that enable one to reconstruct it, and this takes considerable "ferreting out."

Moral Considerations, Equity, and Good Conscience: The Role of Magistrates' Courts

For most inhabitants of Britain, North America, and the Antipodes in the eighteenth and early nineteenth centuries, the local resident magistrate was the most important legal dignitary they were likely to confront. The colonial, provincial, and American magistracy was modeled, depending on the jurisdiction, after either the English justice of the peace (JP) or the Court of Requests commissioner, or, more commonly, after both. Of the former of these officers of the law various judgements have been passed. JPs were often chosen from the elite tip of their local society, and this surely predisposed them to see the world through the lenses of the propertied. But at least one effort to assess the extent to which they displayed bias in mid-nineteenth century England has found that they tended to follow the rules of Law and to have behaved fairly.[75] Their model, however imperfectly followed, would have been Sir Richard Grosvenor, JP in Cheshire in 1603, who held that he and his compeers should strive to "Be a chancellor rather than a justice among your neighbors," and to "persuade & move them to a reconciliation." "When poor men shall be brought before you to examine," he advised, "labour to discover the truth, but entrap not poor & simple men in their own words.... "[76]

In 1846, there were some 400 Courts of Requests throughout England, available to the lower and middle classes for dispute

---

74 Brooks, "Interpersonal Conflict and Social Tension: Civil Litigation in England, 1640–1830," in *The First Modern Society*, ed. A. L. Beier, et al. (Cambridge, 1989), 357 at 381.

75 See David Phillips, "The Black County Magistrates, 1835–1860," 3 *Midland History* 161 (1975–76). Cf. Gerry Rubin, "The County Courts & the Talley Trade, 1846–1914," in *Law, Economy and Society, 1750–1914*, ed David Sugarman and G. R. Rubin (1984), 321–48.

76 Noted in Cynthia Herrup, *The Common Peace: Participation and the Criminal Law in Seventeeth Century England* (Cambridge, 1987), 88.

resolution. Thereafter their functions were assigned to county courts. H. W. Arthurs has found the Courts of Requests to have been useful forums of "communal justice," and believes that they were only abolished because of the opposition of lawyers who resented their wide-ranging (and thus extra-legal) discretionary powers, as well as their exclusion of lawyers from the process.[77] But it is worth noting that in 1831 in Wales they were seen at Methyr Tydfil as mere instruments of creditors seizing furniture for unpaid debts (work undone by mobs who restored those goods).[78] Separate Courts of Requests were established in Upper Canada in 1792, but were abolished in 1841, their duties assumed by division court judges. They were created in New South Wales in 1823 and abolished there, in stages, in 1847 and 1858. Victoria also created and then soon abolished these ancient courts, in 1852.[79] Thus, in North America and the Antipodes most local justice was dispensed by magistrates.

I have examined the nineteenth century records of a number of New Zealand magistrates' courts and have read what some of my colleagues (who have made more systematic use of such records than I) have had to say about them. But I confess that, while this enables me to offer a few generalizations regarding these institutions and their contemporary reputations, I know less of this "middle kingdom" of the law than I do of either its high or low counterparts.

None the less, this much can be said: Some of the earliest resident magistrates, especially in Australia, meted out a justice that was sometimes especially hard on lower class individuals (we know something of this from the work of Hilary Golder, David Neal, and Bruce Kercher, as well as from the successful appeals of these individuals to the New South Wales Supreme Court).[80] Some of these men had been captains of convict vessels; others had been military officers or

---

[77] H. W. Arthurs, *'Without the Law': Administrative Justice and Legal Pluralism in Nineteenth Century England* (1985), 26–27, 29, 40–45.

[78] David Jones, *Before Rebecca: Popular Protests in Wales, 1793–1835* (London, 1973), 139–42.

[79] J. T. Aitchison, "The Courts of Requests in Upper Canada," 41 *Ontario History* 125 (1949); Larry Bakken, *Justice in the Wilderness: A Study of Frontier Courts in Canada and the United States, 1670–1870* (1986), 38; J. M. Bennett, "Early Days of the Law in County Districts," 46 *Australian Law Journal* 570 (1972); W. H. Winder, "The Courts of Requests," 52 *Law Quarterly Review* 369 (1936); James Martin, Esq., to Editor, *The Australian* (Pt. Macquarie), Apr. 1, 1839, calling for more Courts of Requests for debt recovery, Sir James Martin Papers, CY1770, (ML MSS 240/1), Mitchell Library; Bruce Kercher, *An Unruly Child* (1996), 73, 151–52.

[80] Thus, in 1826, a New South Wales jury awarded a plaintiff fifty pounds for his having been prosecuted maliciously by a magistrate/stockman who had threatened to "see him transported" for his alleged theft of a bullock (*Klensendorffe v. Oakes* (Kercher, NSWSC, 1826); and in 1827 the Supreme

petty officers.[81] Charges were levied against some in early Newfoundland, New Brunswick, Nova Scotia, Vancouver Island, and New South Wales for their "notorious culpable practices," and several were removed from the lists as a consequence. In early nineteenth century Ontario, many magistrates were American Loyalists-in-exile or their offspring, and many of these were notoriously intolerant of Ontario's "Reformers," perfectly willing to look the other way when these figures were assaulted or their printing presses destroyed. Eventually these gave way to men less familiar with the lash, and a few, like Benjamin Crawford of early nineteenth century New Brunswick, and Roger Therry, an Emancipist Commissioner of the New South Wales Court of Requests in the 1830s, distinguished themselves for their humanity and for their willingness to take extraordinary measures to reconcile feuding neighbors before they became parties to a lawsuit.[82]

Court of New South Wales found that the magistrates of Parametta had unfairly sided with one of their own against a couple who had quit work at the local Orphan's School when their employee, the school's master, resigned. Cf. J. K. McLaughlin, "The Magistracy and the Supreme Court of New South Wales, 1824–1850," 62 *Journal of the Royal Australian Historical Society* 91 at 96 (1976); and Hilary Golder, *High and Responsible Office: A History of the New South Wales Magistracy* (Sydney, 1991), 24–32. See also Steven Roberts, *The Squatting Age in Australia* (Melbourne, 1964), 285–88 (on the finding of a NSW Committee in 1844 that "there is no functionary in Her Majesty's Dominions to whom is entrusted more absolute power of the property of his fellow subjects").

[81] Governor Macquarie had appointed some Emancipist JPs. In 1819 the Bigge Commission called for him to remove them. In 1829, the New South Wales Supreme Court replaced them with Exclusivists. It was some time before there were significant numbers of former convicts named to sit in judgement. David Neal, "Law and Authority: The Magistracy in New South Wales, 1788–1840, " 3 Law in Context 45, at 55, 63 (1985). See also Bruce Kercher, *An Unruly Child*, 151; St. Roberts, *Squatting Age*, 25.

[82] W. S. MacNutt, *The Atlantic Provinces*, 186; Christopher English, "Newfoundland's Early Laws," 23 *Manitoba Law Journal* 14 (1996); D. G. Bell, "Maritime Law under L'Ancien Regime," 23 *Manitoba Law Journal* 16(n. 45) (1996); Bruce Kercher, *An Unruly Child*, 151; Carol Witton, "Lawless Law: Conservative Political Violence in Upper Canada, 1818–1841," 13 *Law & History Review* 111 (1995) (magistrates didn't interfere when they had witnessed assaults on Reformers and destruction of their presses); Paul Romney, "From the Types Riot to the Rebellion: Elite Ideology, Anti-legal Sentiment, Political Violence and the Rule of Law in Upper Canada," 79 *Ontario History* 113 (1987) (on illegal measures taken by Conservative lawyers and their clerks against Reformers); Greg Maquis, "A Machine of Oppression under the Guise of Law: The St. John Police Establishment," 16 *Acadiensis* 63 (1986); Philip Girard, "The Rise and Fall of Urban Justice in Halifax,1815–1886," 8 *Nova Scotia Hist. Rev.* (1988);

Resident magistrates appeared at times to have acquired the tendency to rule against those litigants who could pay the costs of court when the other party was clearly penniless.[83] Consequently, in the second half of the nineteenth century such magistrates, who were paid largely from costs collected from litigants, were replaced by stipendiary magistrates (styled police magistrates in some cities), men paid regular salaries (stipends). By the 1860s, these newly appointed police/stipendiary magistrates began to take over most of the day-to-day court duties in Australia from the Squatter resident magistrates. These men also appear to have been more responsive to suits brought by employees, and the numbers of such suits waxed, while those of employers waned.[84]

These lower court figures were empowered to hear many lesser civil and criminal cases, and the political struggle over the scope of their jurisdiction was often intense, inasmuch as they represented local "debtor" power against distant "creditor" higher courts.[85] But at the core of their powers was the statutory language calling upon

Gene H. Homel, "Denison's Law: Criminal Justice & the Police Court in Toronto, 1877–1921," 73 *Ontario History* 176 (1981); Judith Fingard, *Jack in Port: Sailortowns in the Maritimes* (Toronto, 1982); Hamar Foster, "British Columbia: Legal Institutions in the Far West, from Contact to 1871," 23 *Manitoba Law Journal* 293 at 312, 326 (1996); and Allen Steinberg, *The Transformation of Criminal Justice, Philadelphia, 1800–1880* (Chapel Hill, N.C.,1989). And see Christopher English, "From Fishing Schooner to Colony: The Legal Development of Newfoundland, 1791–1832," in *Law, Society & the State*, ed. Louis Knafla & Susan Binnie (1995), 73 at 90, on unpopular judgements of the naval Surrogate Court in 1819 and 1820 that led to that court's termination.

[83] See Judith Fingard, *Jack in Port*; Allen Steinberg, *The Transformation of Criminal Justice: Philadelphia, 1800–1880.*

[84] See Foster, British Columbia," 330; Rob McQueen, "Master and Servant Legislation as 'Social Control': The Role of Law in Labour Relations on the Darling Downs, 1860–1870," 10 *Law in Context* 123 (1992); Marie H. Fels, *Good Men and True,* 112 (on Melbourne Police Office records sampled over a seven-and-a-half-year period from the mid-1840s, demonstrating that masters were just as likely to be sued with success ("wages decreed") by servants as they were to sue servants for neglect of duty, disobedience of orders, or absence without leave). Cf. A. Merritt, "The Development and Application of Master and Servant Legislation in New South Wales – 1845 to 1930," unpub. PhD. Diss., Australian National Univ., 1981.

[85] See, for example, Lars Golumbic, "Who Shall Dictate the Law? Political Wrangling between 'Whig' Lawyers and Backcountry Farmers in Revolutionary Era North Carolina," 73 *North Carolina Historical Review* 56 (1996). (A similar political struggle in New Hampshire resulted in a court test (The Ten Pound Note case) of the constitutionality of a similar local-friendly statute.)

both resident magistrates and court of requests commissioners to use "moral considerations" and to apply "equity and good conscience" in coming to judgements. Those trained in the law often found these powers outrageous invitations to "disregar[d] the law, doing violence to Blackstone & to Burn [author of a manual for JPs], as well as to many of the lesser lights of that great science," as "Vindex" put it, objecting to some recent magisterial decisions in a classic exchange on the subject in the *Nelson Examiner* [New Zealand] in 1851.[86] This critique drew a response from Magistrate George White, who defended the practice of "excluding all special pleadings & legal technicalities" from his court, and reminded readers of the truism: "The glorious uncertainty of the law." White also observed of precedent that it was either "a policy to keep the great body of the people in a state of ignorance, or it is a practical confession that wisdom degenerates, and can only hobble along on stilts & crutches of precedents."[87]

Similar defenses of the uncomplicated nature of magistrate's courts were offered in New Brunswick in 1850, and, at the opposite pole, in South Australia in 1880. The admission of lawyers and Law-ways "could in no way" help litigants who now were able to argue their own cases, unencumbered "by the introduction of those legal technicalities which puzzle the heads of more assuming practitioners," and, in any event, the savings at the level of magistrate's court to the litigants in both court costs and time were significant. "The lawyers might suffer," wrote J. B. Sheridan in Adelaide, but ordinary folk were the beneficiaries.[88]

South Australia's Local Courts Act (1861), which empowered that colony's magistrate's courts, was declared unconstitutional by Justices Boothby and Gwynne in 1865, but Parliament immediately resuscitated the civil side of the "equity and good conscience" powers in the Colonial Laws Validity Act (28 & 29 Vic. c 63, 1865), while

---

[86] "Vindex" was elaborating on an earlier theme struck in the pages of this paper by one Henry Adams, who had noted that actions for more than £20 were heard before a judge who followed English precedent and from whom there was available an appeal, whereas action for less than £20 were heard by untrained magistrates from whom there was no effective appeal, "so there is one law for the rich & another for the poor." *Nelson Examiner*, X, Sept. 13, 1851, p. 114; *Ibid.*, Sept. 27, p. 122, available in microfilm, Alexander Turnbull Library, Wellington.

[87] *Ibid.*, Oct. 4, pp. 126–27.

[88] D. G. Bell, "A Perspective on Legal Pluralism in 19th century New Brunswick," 37 *Univ. of New Brunswick Law J* 86 at 92–93 (1988); J. B. Sheridan, *First Impressions of a Law Reformer* (Adelaide, 1880), 6–7. And see H. Robert Baker, "Creating Order in the Wilderness: Transplanting English Law to Ruperts' Land, 1835–1851," 17 *Law and History Review* 217, 243 (1999), on the effective extra-legal qualities of the Hudson's Bay Company's dispute-resolution methods in the Red River region, described as "the smoothing system, or rather no system at all," by Alexander Ross.

New Zealand's Supreme Court upheld that colony's grant of such powers to its magistrates and refused to overturn their decisions for any
inconsistencies with Common-Law rules in a series of cases beginning
in 1864.[89]

THE COMMON LAW VERSUS "COMMON LAW": THE COLLISION OF HIGH AND LOW LEGAL CULTURES

In her study of crime in early New South Wales, Paula Byrne observed
that "ordinary people had their own notions of morality, marriage,
and the workings of the convict system," and that both "convict and
free," they "made their own law" and "mapped their own boundaries of
legality and illegality." Bruce Kercher recently offered a similar verdict
regarding that colony, as did E. P. Thompson and Jane Neeson for eighteenth and early nineteenth century England, Susan Lewthwaite and
Paul Romney for early nineteenth century Upper and Lower Canada,
and Brendan McConville and Alan Taylor for the eighteenth and early
nineteenth century United States. In these pages I have made the
same claim regarding nineteenth century New Zealand, Australia, the
United States, and Ontario: Ordinary folks often ignored the "high"
Law of courts and legislatures and made their own "common law," created their own norms and rules. This is probably the most important,
and the least commonly appreciated truth that social and cultural historians have uncovered in the past generation (albeit anthropologists
have know about and reported on it for a century).

We seem perfectly prepared to accept the importance of Constitutions, statutes, and Common-Law rules in the lives of people, and that
is, to a point, perfectly understandable and reasonable. We need to
know what the formal Law was, for the formal Law often had considerable import. But we must continue to acquire a greater understanding
of the breadth and depth of that importance in all of its particulars.
Some Laws were scrupulously observed, others quietly ignored, still
others, vigorously resisted. That vigorous resistance was sometimes sufficient to disable, or compel an alteration in a statute or Common-Law
rule. But at other times resistance proved to be insufficient, even futile.
In either case, it often involved real *costs* (both to those resisting and
those being resisted). These costs were not always calculated rationally;

---

[89] *Davies v. Quarrel*, Pelham's R. 1 (1865); *Pearson v. Clark*, Macassey's R. 136
(1864); *Mete Kingi v. Davis*, 1 NZ Jurist (NS) 117 (1875) (award by magistrate of £10 for false imprisonment of Maori plantiff by defendant's servant
affirmed "on grounds of equity & good conscience" citing sec. 111 of Resident Magistrates Act of 1867, despite the decision's being at odds with the
common law rule); *Hill v. DeLias*, 1 NZLR (S.C.) 23 at 25 (1879) (Justice
Gilles: Court "cannot review" findings legitimately based on "equity & good
conscience").

people can behave quite stubbornly when their sense of fairness, or their dignity, or both, are offended. Moral outrage is a familiar theme in "high"-"low" legal-culture wars. Today one thinks of the Freemen, the Pro-Life/Pro-Choice battlegrounds, Doctor Kevorkian and the euthanasia skirmishes. In the past, the battles raged over encroachments on Aboriginal lands, squatter's rights, slavery, alcohol, the Bible in public schools, cattle killed on railroad tracks, railroad bonds, and taxes.

The stories of these struggles over "law" and "rights" are the stuff of legal, cultural, and sometimes "political" history. Recent studies by political scientists, interested in the "impact" of U.S. Supreme Court decisions on the rights of the criminally accused, prayer in public schools, and abortion, for example, indicate that the key court decisions regarding these matters did not alter norms as much as had been assumed.[90] We will never have too many of these sorts of "impact" studies of past court decisions and statutes, for we all too often simply assume that high court judgements produce the results that can be inferred from a "rational-actor" model – that is, one that presumes that the language of the opinions had all of their intended consequences; and this is often untrue.

In this book we have distinguished between "public" and "private" matters: Some differences that rose in the British Diaspora lands were ones that neighbors could resolve – disputes over boundary lines, fencing, animal trespasses, locally negotiated agreements for goods or services, local obligations with regard to road maintenance, the burning of stubble, the sharing of a stream, and the like. These were, formally, issues of "private" Law, and they remained "private" precisely because they rarely erupted into irreconcilable public controversies that municipal councils or provincial legislatures were called upon to resolve. But some of these disputes proved *not* to be resolvable by neighborly norms. The rule announced by the Court of King's Bench in 1788 regarding the practice of gleaning, for example, proved to be impotent, for the practice continued for a century.[91]

Other disputes tend to be more "public" in nature: Tenants and landlords, with many common interests (sometimes written into the

[90] See, for example, R. Birkby, "The Supreme Court and the Bible Belt: Reaction to the *Schempp* decision," 10 *Midwest Journal of Politics* 265 (1974); Susan Hansen, "State Implementation of *Roe v. Wade*," 42 *Journal of Politics* 372 (1980); "*Gault* and its Implementation," 3 *Law & Society Review* 509 (1969); D. Manwaring, "The Impact of *Mapp v Ohio*," in David H. Everson, ed., *Supreme Court as Policymaker* (Carbondale, Illinois, 1968), 1–43

[91] Described in Chapter 1. See Peter King, "Gleaners, Farmers & the Failure of Legal Sanctions in England, 1750–1850," 125 *Past & Present* 116 (1989); Neeson, *Commoners* (1993).

covenants drawn up between them, sometimes simply agreed to "off the covenant") also have had more intractable differences that resulted in the crafting of prolandlord statutes (and often bloody attempts to enforce them), and in protenant statutes (weakening the capacity of landlords to raise or collect rents). Similarly, many issues involving title to land were simply too central to settler interests to be resolved by private arbitration or neighborly norms.[92] Thus, the need for public registration laws, for statutory rules regarding inheritances and conveyances, and thus the tendency for some such disputes to be litigated.

The State in Britain, North America, and the Antipodes often interfered with the property and personal rights of its subjects in other ways in these years in order to accomplish some perceived public end. Sometimes this interference was tolerated as a necessary means to a desired end; one thinks of most criminal statutes, as well as those concerning public health.[93] But other of these statutes (and their local counterparts, municipal ordinances) led to protests and resistance. One thinks of the efforts of government to check the smuggling of taxed or prohibited goods and of the efforts of municipalities and counties to prevent the sale of liquor without a license. Both of these sorts of laws were violated openly in the valley of the lower Thames in Upper Canada in the 1830s and 1840s,[94] as elsewhere (one thinks of the resistance in the 1760s and 1770s to the enforcement in the American colonies of the Navigation Acts, and the resistance in Vermont and the seaports to Jefferson's embargo of American shipping in 1807).

The State's need for revenue often led to defiance when the taxes imposed on people's property were regarded as inequitable (as they often are). One thinks of the resistance in England to excise taxes in 1757, and of that in the American colonies in the 1760s and 1770s to

---

[92] See, for example, the evidence of a breakdown in the capacity of both Congregationalist churches and town meetings to resolve property and mercantile disputes in colonial New England, noted in David Konig, *Law and Society in Puritan Massachusetts: Essex County, 1629–1692* (Chapel Hill, 1979); and William E. Nelson, *Dispute and Conflict Resolution in Plymouth County, Massachusetts, 1725–1825* (1981).

[93] For example, on the measures taken in New York City in the mid-nineteenth century to end cholera epidemics see Michael Les Benedict, "Contagion and the Constitution: Quarantine Agitation, 1859–1866," 25 *Journal of the Hist. of Medicine* 177 (1970).

[94] Fred C. Hamil, *The Valley of the Lower Thames* (1951), 156, 175. In 1831, sixteen men were indicted in Sandwich for tarring and feathering a man who had testified against another for selling liquor without a licensce. Only four were tried; only one was found guilty by the jury (175).

the several measures adopted by Parliament to raise funds to pay for the military establishment in North America, of the political and extralegal resistance to property taxes in western Massachusetts in 1786 (Shay's Rebellion), in western Pennsylvania in 1794 (the Whiskey Rebellion), in eastern Pennsylvania in 1795 (Fries Rebellion), of South Carolina's "nullification" of the federal import tariff in the early 1830s, of the resistance in Missouri to the raising of funds to be loaned to railroad companies, and of the resistance in the mountain South to the federal liquor revenue tax imposed after the Civil War.[95]

This last mentioned confrontation, between federal revenue officials and southern resistors to the statute, has been analyzed recently by Wilbur Miller. A federal excise tax on distilleries, imposed shortly after the Civil War, fell hardest on small distilleries in Appalachia. Their persistent resistence to the Law ("moonshining") led to the deployment of army units to assist the treasury and justice department agents charged with its enforcement. One Virginian called the law "oppressive and unjust" in 1873; another southerner argued that "tradition was more binding the Law," and that he was "only exercising" his "natural rights" when he resisted. In 1877, an Alabama newspaper advised its readers, "in accordance with nature's law of self-preservation, to take care of ourselves," and in 1890 another Alabaman referred to "a man's right to make a little licker." Some federal deputy collectors, district attorneys, and judges in West Virginia, Georgia, and North Carolina were clearly partial to "moonshiners," and while other officials scrupulously sought to enforce the Law, resistance to it and sympathy with those resisting was widespread.[96]

Taxes were only the most common public laws to draw fire. Stephen Kenny has described the utter rejection by the *habitants* of Quebec of the ill-conceived sleigh law imposed on them by the new British Administrator of Canada East, Sir John Colbourn, in 1839. Dirk Hartog

---

95 See, for example, Helen and Edmund Morgan, *The Stamp Act Crisis* (1953); Oliver Dickerson, *The Navigation Acts and the American Revolution* (1952); Jesse Lemisch, "The American Revolution seen from the Bottom Up, "in *Towards a New Past*, ed. Barton Bernstein (1968), 3–45; Van Beck Hall, *Politics without Parties: Massachusetts, 1780–1791* (1972); Thomas Slaughter, *The Whiskey Rebellion: Epilogue to the American Revolution* (1986); Walter Jennings, *The American Embargo, 1807–1809* (1921); Douglas Jones, "The Caprice of Juries: Enforcement of the Embargo in Massachusetts," 24 *American Journal of Legal Hist.* 307 (1980); William Freehling, *Prelude to Civil War: The Nullification Controversy in South Carolina, 1816–1836* (1966); David Thelen, *Paths of Resistance: Tradition and Dignity in Missouri*; Wilbur Miller, *Revenuers and Moonshiners: Enforcing the Federal Liquor Law in the Mountain South, 1865–1900* (1991).

96 Miller, *Revenuers & Moonshiners*, 40, 68, 114, 144, 153, 178.

has documented the failure of ordinances designed to keep pigs off the streets of New York in the first half of the nineteenth century,[97] and I have pointed in these pages to the failure in New Zealand of Laws obliging Diaspora settlers to keep their animals off the streets of towns and cities. Other examples might be offered, but perhaps the point has been made: Public laws designed, after all, to resolve conflicting felt-needs by legislative fiat sometimes failed to achieve their objectives. Some still do.

My dichotomy of "public" and "private" Law, however, is not a sufficient explanation of all the tensions we found between high and low legal cultures, because some "private" disputes could not be (or in any event, were not) resolved by the popular application of norms. The decidedly *un*neighborly behavior detected by John Demos and David Konig in seventeenth century New England, by Douglas Greenberg in eighteenth century New York, by Susan Lewthwaite, John Weaver, W. Thomas Matthews, and Paul Romney in early nineteenth century Upper Canada, by Sean Cadigan in nineteenth century Newfoundland, by Paula Byrne in early nineteenth century New South Wales, and by Miles Fairburn in nineteenth century New Zealand are clearly consistent with my own evidence (from New Zealand, Australian, and Canadian diaries) that popular norms are no more than that: "norms," capable of being ignored or violated. And this was especially so in "frontier" settings, where the "norms" were either ill-defined or weak, or both.[98] It was reported, for example, of the young Kable brothers

---

[97] Kenny, "Cahots and Catcalls: Popular Resistance in Lower Canada," in *Historical Perspectives on Law & Society in Canada*, ed. Tina Loo; H. Hartog, "Pigs and Positivism," 1985 *Wisconsin Law Rev.* 899.

[98] See John Demos, *Entertaining Satan:* (New York, 1982); David Konig, *Law and Society in Putitan Massachusetts*; Douglas Greenberg, *Crime and Law Enforcement in the Colony of New York*; Susan Lewthwaite, "Violence, Law & Community in Rural Upper Canada"; John Weaver, "Crime, Public Order and Repression: The Gore District in Upheaval, 1832–1851," 78 *Ontario History* 177 (1986); W. T. Matthews, "The Myth of the Peaceable Kingdom: Upper Canada Society during the Early Victorian Period," 94 *Queen's Quarterly* 383 (1987); Paul Romney, "From the Types Riot to the Rebellion: Elite Ideology, Anti-legal Sentiment, Political Violence and the Rule of Law in Upper Canada," 79 *Ontario History* 113 (1987); Sean Cadigan, *Hope and Deception on Conception Bay*; Paula Byrne, *Criminal Law and Colonial Subject*; Miles Fairburn, *The Ideal Society and its Enemies* (Auckland, 1989). Michael Sturma is not comfortable with a depiction of mid-nineteenth century New South Wales as one of violent convicts and social disorder, but, while he corrects the overstating of that view, his evidence still indicates a much higher rate of violent crimes and public drunkenness in 1830 than in 1860. *Vice in a Vicious Society: Crime and Convicts in mid-nineteenth Century New South Wales* (St. Lucia, 1983).

of Windsor, New South Wales, in 1822 that they were "a terror to the peaceable inhabitants," being "under the erroneous notion" that since they were "born free," they were "subject to no control or legal obligation."[99]

Why might this have been so? Why were certain Laws so lightly regarded on these frontiers? In the first place, the process of settling North America and the Antipodes for fishing, farming, grazing, and mining in these years flowed from an Imperial vision. While somewhat less authoritarian and brutal than its Spanish, Portugese, Dutch, and French counterparts, this British Imperial vision still invited its people to settle "discovered" lands belonging to others – the Aboriginal people of North America and the Antipodes, people treated by the Crown as "subjects." And, for all the quite genuine concern for these Aboriginal people the Colonial Office and its provincial agents displayed, the flood of Diaspora settlers invariably overwhelmed the treaties, protectors, and Law provided to shield the natives. The "informal law" practiced by the British Diaspora under the banner of "natural rights" or other such aphorisms operated at times as masks for racist, outright dispossession of natives from land sought for farms, pastures, or mines. My Irish-American mother had a rather low opinion of British Imperialism, and I can appreciate why, from her perspective. But I think I have come to appreciate the perspective of those Colonial Office officials, colonial governors, protectors, and jurists when they sought to restrain the British Diaspora "periphery" in its headlong assault upon the legal rights of those who were "in possession" of the domains they craved in North America and the Antipodes.[100]

In the second place, some Laws were lightly regarded on the "periphery" and the "hinterland" because the British Diaspora were not made up of ordinary Britons. Some were genuine felons, pushed

---

99 Byrne, *Criminal Law & Colonial Subject*, 195.

100 Thus, I think Peter Sack's "simple but distinct fact" that "justice . . . has never been and never will be the goal of any form of government – colonial or metropolitan, German or Briton," to be hyperbole, or overkill. The Glenelgs, Stevens, Philips, Gipps, Gordons, Martins, Marshalls, and Greys deserve more than that. (Sack, "Colonial Government, 'Justice,' and the Rule of Law," in *European Impact and Pacific Influence*, ed. Hermann Hiery and John Mackenzie (London, 1997), 190.

Whether German imperial treatment of South Pacific Islanders was as even-handed as British or not, it seems clear that French imperial treatment in the region was, from its inception to as recently as 1973, decidedly less generous. See Robert Aldrich, *The French Presence in the South Pacific, 1840–1940* (Honolulu, 1990), 178–80; and Howard Van Trease, "The History of Land Alienation," in *Land Tenure in Vanuatu*, ed. Peter Larmour (Suva, 1984), 18, 20.

from the Mother Country, while others were merely more adventurous than those who remained in Britain – that is, some were drawn *to* the colonies by the opportunities they perceived there. Of these latter, Geoffrey Best has sagely observed that emigrants represented Britain's "uneasy classes" – that is, those prepared to "do violence to all those traditional affections, loyalties, and attachments upon which the mid-Victorian . . . set peculiar binding value."[101] And this would have been so whether they were Irish peasants, Scottish crofters, English artisans, Welsh miners, or Men-of-Prope'ty.

Appreciating this helps us to understand why Squatters in Australia and "settlers" in the Ohio Valley had little tolerance for the indigenous people's "inefficient" use of the land, why educated barristers like George Moore in Western Australia could chafe against "the due course of English Law." But to say that we can appreciate or understand men like Moore or their more brutal contemporaries is not to say that we have to accept their reasoning uncritically. There were pressures from the Colonial Office, from local missionaries, from the appeals of indigenous people themselves, for compassion, even-handedness, and compensation. We can listen to those squatters and "settlers," but when I do, I am reminded of the stage directions that F. Scott Fitzgerald provided in his play, *The Vegetable*. Describing a particularly obnoxious character, he said "you can understand how she got this way, but you don't have to like her for it."

In the third place, Law on the frontier/periphery sometimes "failed" because Diaspora emigrants were often socially isolated from one another during the first decade or more of settlement (which is why Lois Carr found so few parents naming guardians for their children in their wills in the first decade of settlement of the colony of Maryland). Miles Fairburn feels that the relatively high volume of civil litigation he and his graduate students detected in the records of early colonial New Zealand was due to the "inadequacy of . . . informal social mechanisms of control."[102] These mechanism eventually developed in New Zealand, as elsewhere, but in the first generation of settlement of that colony, as well as that of New South Wales, Victoria, Virginia, New York, and Ontario,[103] the "informal social mechanisms of control," which I have been calling neighborly ways, were often missing.[104]

---

[101] Best, *Mid-Victorian Britain, 1851–1875* (1991), 127, noted in David Gagan, *Hopeful Travelers: Families, Land and Social Change in Mid-Victorian Peel County, Canada West* (Toronto, 1981), 98.

[102] Fairburn, *The Ideal Society and its Enemies*, 307.

[103] (But probably not New England or South Australia, where the settlers were more homogeneous in their backgrounds and predispositions.)

[104] See, for examples, Gwenda Morgan, *The Hegemony of the Law: Richmond County, Virginia, 1692–1776* (1989); Lois Carr, "The Development of the

In the fourth place: Some "neighbors" in the Diaspora settlements of North America and the Antipodes simply found it harder than others to get along. The Scottish crofters who settled among French Canadiens in southern Quebec during the nineteenth century, the Mormons who created communities in antebellum Illinois and Missouri, and especially those British emigrants who carved homesteads out of Micmac, Cherokee, Shawnee, Australian Aborigine, or Maori domains cannot, or should not, be equated with those who settled in communities comprised of their own kirk and kin. Those who formed Orange lodges in Upper and Lower Canada or in the cities of the northeastern United States when Irish Catholics began to settle would see some of their numbers engage in "whitecapping" before long; and, similarly, those who feared and despised "savages" found it hard to be neighborly to "savage" neighbors.[105] Many frontier communities of the British Diaspora proved to be remarkably able to develop neighborly ways and strong communities. One thinks of certain early New England and Lower Canada/Eastern township settlements, and of the Wakefieldian settlements of South Australia and the Wellington region of New Zealand. But for most of the Diaspora settlements, neighborly norms did not develop quickly unless the settler populations were of homogeneous cultural backgrounds.

And even when communities matured and lines of communication opened across ethnic and religious divides, two barriers remained: Firstly, workers in the increasingly complex industrial-commercial economy of the late nineteenth century found that the terms of the various Master & Servant Acts that had provided the formal basis of much employment law were not negotiated away as easily in this new, impersonal work environment as they had been in the earlier one, where farmer and hired hand, master and journeyman, dealt face to face with one another day-in, day-out. The corporate contract of employment had become standardized, crafted to provide the

Maryland Orphan's Court, 1654–1715," in Aubrey Land & Lois Carr, eds., *Law, Society and Politics in Early Maryland* (Baltimore, 1977), 41; Douglas Greenberg, *Crime and Law Enforcement in the Colony of New York, 1691–1776* (Ithaca, 1974); Paula Byrne, *Criminal Law and Colonial Subject: New South Wales, 1810–1830* (Cambridge, 1993); Marie Fels, *Good Men and True,* 112 (on the high incidence of assaults and drunkenness in Melbourne's earliest police records); Susan Lewthwaite, "Violence, Law and Community in Rural Upper Canada," in Jim Phillips, et al., *Essays in the History of Canadian Law: Vol. V* (Toronto, 1994), 353.

[105] See B. Palmer, "Discordant Music: Charivaris and Whitecapping in Nineteenth Century North America," 3 *Labour/Le Travailleur* 5 (1978); Daniel Rolph, *"To Shoot, Burn and Hang": Folk-History from a Kentucky Mountain Family and Community* (1994).

employer with all the legal nuances available to control the worksite.[106] And thus began the struggle to transform the old guild, apprentice, and journeymen institutions into the modern craft and company-wide union movements, and to secure the right to organize, boycott, strike, and bargain. The collective action taken, in the process, produced some violent confrontations and (ultimately) resulted in labor legislation.[107]

Secondly, while damages incurred in an accident involving neighbors could be "forgiven and forgotten" (if minor) or "compensated" (in local exchanges of goods, labor and other services), those caused by a negligent railway engineer, switchman or dispatcher to a passenger, employee or crossing victim could not be handled in the same fashion. The railways quickly developed a quite formal process of settling such claims, involving investigations, the gathering of evidence, and an assessment of the relevant rules of Law. They often rejected damage claims in ways that would have struck ordinary folk as unfair (had they been privy to the process, which, of course, they were not). This forced some accident victims either to go uncompensated (which many simply endured), to be greatly undercompensated, or to employ an attorney and "go to law." When no settlement was reached this adversarial process tended to result in damage awards, provided by peers of the victim–plaintiff, that were larger by a factor of three than those that such juries levied against individual defendants, a phenomenon that has come to be called "deep pockets," but which might more accurately be styled "sending a message to the heartless corporation." This process of settling accident claims and awarding damages a century ago would be quite familiar to accident victims and litigants in the present. Indeed, it appears that the process we are familiar with today was essentially *set* 150 years ago.

While disputes between neighbors in "mature" communities over boundary lines, fencing, or animal trespasses could generally be settled amicably without recourse to the Law, those between Diaspora settlers and their *Aboriginal* neighbors often could not. Similarly, while one who was the creditor of a local customer (or a neighbor) generally dealt "out of court" with his or her debtor, rewriting the terms of repayment, or refinancing the debt, those indebted to a creditor quite *distant* from the community (as in post-Independence Plymouth County and Virginia, or the late nineteenth century midwest (railroad bonds))

---

[106] See Christopher Tomlins, *Law, Labor, and Ideology in the Early American Republic* (1993), Pts. 3 & 4.

[107] See, for example, Louis Adamic, *Dynamite!* (New York, 1968); Jeremy Brecher, *Strike!* (1972); and Karen Orren, *Belated Feudalism* (New York, 1991).

might reject negotiation and rely instead on a friendly jury (as we saw in Chapters 4 and 5). When the decisions of local courts friendly to such debtors were overturned by higher courts, those debtors were sometimes prepared to pressure local officials called upon to enforce such judgements into refusing to cooperate.

Local juries were powerful curbs on certain legal constraints when it came to game law prosecutions, federal efforts to halt the liquor trade with Indians, and other such "center" – "periphery" points of tension and disagreement. And when the issue was title to one's land, a "stupid jury" might well be persuaded to favor the cause of a neighbor whose evidence did not rise to the level required under English Common-Law standards (as Colonel Talbot had put it in early nineteenth century Ontario, and as other "proprietors" would have put it in early New South Wales or colonial North America). In fact, only in cases of those who had stripped the land of its timber in violation of the terms of their leases did I find juries tending to favor landowners over leaseholders, possibly because these jurors were more likely to be landowners themselves (or tenant farmers who were honoring their leases) than they were to be "cut-and-run" timber thieves. Juries intervened in the Law as well when negligent railroads, steamboat companies, and trams caused injuries. They were disinclined to see plaintiffs turned away without compensation for slight acts of contributory negligence, and they were inclined to send wake-up calls to "the pocket nerve" of negligence corporations to prompt them to lower the risks.

These exceptions noted, the fact remains that most of what was "private" law in 1750 was still "private" law in 1900, and, more importantly, most disputes involving neighbors were still being resolved informally by those neighbors. In fact, as John Phillip Reid has shown (in his classic study of informally arranged property and contractual relationships among "partners" on the Overland Trail to Oregon and California in the mid-nineteenth century), those who began the trip as perfect strangers in St. Louis none the less felt bound by such terms they had entered into when pooled property had later to be divided. Despite the absence of courts or police, there was virtually no theft or violence, and disputes were resolved amicably.[108]

The British Diaspora may have been more litigious than were their contemporaries in China or Japan. Perhaps they did not possess as much of a socially mandated communal ethos as did those societies, did not generate as much public pressure to resolve disputes privately. Perhaps they still don't.[109] But that does not mean that we should think

---

[108] John Phillip Reid, *Law for the Elephant: Property and Social Behavior on the Overland Trail* (1980).

[109] This comparative question is a complex one. For good analyses see John O. Haley, *Authority without Power: Law and the Japanese Paradox* (N.Y.,1991);

of the Diaspora as going to Law willy-nilly. Most disputes were settled "informally" by rules that were set by popular norms. These norms changed, from time to time. And that change is the stuff of historical inquiry. I repeat Bronislav Malinowski observation: "the true problem is not to study how human life submits to rules – it simply does not; the real problem is how the rules become adapted to life."[110]

Rules adopted by ordinary people "work"; those they don't accept, those forced upon them by "pig-headed" legislators, often don't work. And, in any event, the Law can fail to achieve its objective, even where it has considerable support, if it is not crafted with great care. Perhaps the most thoroughly documented study of such a failure, James Willard Hurst's massive account of the legislative and judicial efforts to address the serious and growing problem of the depletion of Wisconsin's timber resource, illustrates this truth.[111]

That is not to say that all such efforts at forcing change in popular norms are wrong headed or bound to fail. One has only to think of Civil Rights legislation; there the "wrong headed" view was that of Justice Henry Brown in *Plessy v. Ferguson* (1896), who concluded the court's judgement with this observation: "Legislation is powerless to eradicate racial instincts or to abolish distinctions based on physical differences, and the attempt to do so can only result in accentuating the difficulties of the present situation." This view has surely been disproved in the past generation in the United States. The antilynching bill that won approval in the House of Representatives in 1922 did die of filibuster in the Senate, but it may have sent a signal to local southern law-enforcement officials, for the number of lynchings in the United States declined thereafter. And, in any event, it bears noting that both the antilynching proposal and the Civil Rights legislation of the 1960s were prompted by Civil Rights activists supported by an upwelling of popular revulsion with the norm prevalent in Justice Brown's age. Norms, like Common Law, *can* change.

In any case, we can agree that the Law, as pronounced by both legislatures and courts, is not the whole story of legal history. It is

---

Jerome Cohen, "Chinese Mediation on the Eve of Modernization," 54 *Calif. Law Rev.* 26 (1966); D. F. Henderson, *Conciliation and Japanese Law: Tokagawa and Modern* (Seattle, 1965); Takeo Tanase, "The Management of Disputes: Auto Accident Compensation in Japan," 24 *Law & Society Rev.* 651 (1990); Alan Macfarlane, "Law & Custom in Japan," 10 *Continuity & Change* No. 3 (1995).

[110] Malinowski, *Crime & Custom in Savage Society* (1926), 127.

[111] Hurst, *Law and Economic Growth: The Legal History of the Lumber Industry in Wisconsin, 1836–1915* (Madison, Wis.,1964). See also Arthur McEvoy, *The Fisherman's Problem: Ecology and Law in the California Fisheries, 1850–1980* (Cambridge Press, 1986); and Hendrik Hartog, "Pigs and Positivism," 1985 Wisconsin Law Review 899.

certainly a central arm of the State. But John Kenneth Galbraith's "common law," the "law" of ordinary people's norms, sometimes defies the Law's reach. Some English legal rules were unacceptable in North America and the Antipodes. Some of them were altered by governors, innovative jurists, or (eventually) by Diaspora legislatures. But just as often, they were simply "amended" or "rendered null and void" by ordinary people exercising popular norms. This latter process deserves a central place in future stories of contests between "the Law's Majesty" and "the People's Will."

Cases Discussed

Cast of Characters

544

Reid, Chief Justice (Low. Can. K. B.), 155

Richards, Justice (Manitoba), 413

Richards, Justice (Up. Can. C. P.), 490

Richmond Justice C. W. (N. Z. C. of A./Min. of Lands), 45, 85, 204, 252–3, 409, 509, 513, 516n54

Riel, Louis (Meti leader), 109–10

Ritchie, Chief Justice William J. (Can. S. C.), 493

Robinson, George (protector), 62–3, 65

Robinson, Chief Justice John Beverley (U. C. Q. B.), 59, 108, 127, 153, 195, 218–9, 313, 316, 318, 366, 398, 423, 486, 489, 513

Rogers, Justice Molton (Pa.), 208

Rogers, R. V. (attny./treatise writer, Ont.), 419

Royal, Joseph (Meti leader), (no page number)

Russell, Geo and Rbt. (partners in Clyde Co., Vic.), 144, 339, 341

Russell, Lord John (Col. Sec.), 159

Saggamore, John (Mass. Bay native farmer), 247–8

Salmond, Sir John (N.Z. Solic.-Gen./ treatise writer), 88n138, 82–3, 101, 512

Saltonstall, Sir Richard (Mass. Bay grazier), 247–8

Sanborn, Justice (Low. Can.), 190

Scott, Helenus, Jr. (police magistrate, NSW), 288, 346

Scully, William (Anglo-Irish Diaspora landlord, Ill.), 136

Seddon, Richard (Prime Min. N.Z.), 91–2

Sedgwick, Theodore (U.S. treatise writer), 154, 501

Sequin (sachem of Springfield area natives), 54

Seward, William H. (N.Y. attorney/ politician/land agent), 173, 221, 400

Shand, John (Diaspora settler, N.Z.), 353, 356

Shaw, Chief Justice Lemuel (Mass.), 409

Sherk, Andrew (milldam owner, Ont.), 219

Sherwood, Justice Henry (Up. Can. Q. B.), 312

Short, Justice (Low. Can./Quebec Superior Ct.), 157

Sifton, Clifford (Can. Supt. Gen. of Ind. Affairs), 77

Singleton, Cpt. (magistrate, West. Aus.), 345

Sissons, H. J. (attorney Can.), 458

Slater, Samuel (New Engl. industrialist), 329

Smith, Sir Harry (Gov. Cape Colony), 94, 95, 124n14

Smith, Jem and Jack (farm servants, N.Z.), 355

Smith, W. M. (garden-owner, N.Z.), 246

Smyth, Robert Brough (amateur ethnographer, Vic.), 117

Smyth, W. R. (attorney, Can.), 458

Spencer, Chief Justice Ambrose (N. Y. S. C.), 125

Sproat, Gilbert (Can. Ind. Aff. Comm.), 110

Staines, Robert (chaplain, Hudson's Bay Co.), 242

Stambaugh, S. C. (Indian agent, Green Bay), 279

Stanley, Lord (Col. Sec.), 68, 350

Stansmore, John (servant, West. Aus.), 345

Stawell, Chief Justice William F. (Vic.), 379, 428, 435, 436, 513

Stephen, Chief Justice Alfred (NSW), 508

Stephen, James (Perm. Under Sec. Colonial Office), 62, 69–70, 74, 84, 141, 147n1, 218n79

Steward, William Downie (attorney, N.Z.), 503

General Index